The Dimensions of
PHYSICAL EDUCATION

Edited by

Lori E. Ciccomascolo, EdD
Associate Professor
Department of Kinesiology
University of Rhode Island

Eileen Crowley Sullivan, EdD
Assistant Dean
Office of Partnerships and Placements
Feinstein School of Education and
 Human Development
Rhode Island College

JONES & BARTLETT
LEARNING

World Headquarters
Jones & Bartlett Learning
5 Wall Street
Burlington, MA 01803
978-443-5000
info@jblearning.com
www.jblearning.com

Jones & Bartlett Learning books and products are available through most bookstores and online booksellers. To contact Jones & Bartlett Learning directly, call 800-832-0034, fax 978-443-8000, or visit our website, www.jblearning.com.

Substantial discounts on bulk quantities of Jones & Bartlett Learning publications are available to corporations, professional associations, and other qualified organizations. For details and specific discount information, contact the special sales department at Jones & Bartlett Learning via the above contact information or send an email to specialsales@jblearning.com.

Production Credits
Publisher, Higher Education: Cathleen Sether
Senior Acquisitions Editor: Shoshanna Goldberg
Editorial Assistant: Prima Bartlett
Production Manager: Julie Champagne Bolduc
Production Editor: Jessica Steele Newfell
Associate Marketing Manager: Jody Sullivan
VP, Manufacturing and Inventory Control: Therese Connell
Composition: Cenveo Publisher Services
Cover Design: Kristin E. Parker
Cover Image: © Transfuchsian/ShutterStock, Inc.
Printing and Binding: Malloy, Inc.
Cover Printing: Malloy, Inc.

To order this product, use ISBN: 978-1-4496-5190-9

Library of Congress Cataloging-in-Publication Data
The dimensions of physical education / edited by Lori E. Ciccomascolo, Eileen Crowley Sullivan.
     p. cm.
  Includes bibliographical references and index.
  ISBN 978-0-7637-8076-0 (pbk. : alk. paper)
  1. Physical education and training. I. Ciccomascolo, Lori E. II. Sullivan, Eileen Crowley.
  GV341.D54 2011
  613.71—dc23

                              2011027801

6048
Printed in the United States of America
15 14 13 12 11   10 9 8 7 6 5 4 3 2 1

Brief Contents

Contents

Preface

The idea to write *The Dimensions in Physical Education* came about after more than 20 years of employing textbooks that focused on general issues of education and translating how they relate to physical education and health education, for a number of our methods and foundations courses. In addition to using a general education textbook, we also would collect various articles about physical and health education and create a reading packet for students. Even now with the current technology and the Internet, we have to search for appropriate articles, and we are still unable to find suitable readings. We finally thought it best for our students and instructors that we write an all-in-one, accurate reader text that represents the most important issues in our discipline.

This book covers diverse, educational, and current yet essentially ageless topics, including the meaning of physical education, information about the teacher, content about the needs of students, curriculum issues, assessment, technology, diversity, and other dimensions such as professional development and service-learning. The last chapter of the book presents letters to the reader from physical educators and administrators with relevant topics not usually addressed in a textbook. All the chapters provide content for beginning and veteran students and teachers to read, reflect on, and discuss while addressing the real-life issues that confront undergraduate and entry-level graduate students and professionals. The themes and concepts addressed in this book are timely and central to the core of the meaning and dimensions of physical and health education. *The Dimensions in Physical Education* not only will help students learn but also will encourage reflection on the most essential components in the field of physical education, health education, sport education, and teaching practices in these disciplines. We believe the articles provide a solid foundation for beginning students and professionals new to the discipline.

As veteran teachers of introductory and elementary and/or secondary methods courses, we have a clear vision as to what instructors will find most helpful in teaching these topics to prospective teachers. The format of this text allows instructors to select and teach the content of the chapters in any order that meets the needs of their own students and courses. Bolded key terms in each article are defined at the end of the article. The discussion questions were written by each specific author and will guide a lively and productive class discussion of content. The instructor might choose to use one or two of the discussion questions for assessment measures or for a reflective essay assignment. The underlying premise that theory into practice is the best approach for presenting and discussing the topics in the book allows professionals to realize the importance of the material. All of the chapters include a Research Review that provides the readers with a lens into the world of research in our discipline. The Research Reviews provide the most up-to-date, innovative, and cutting-edge research results of a topic relevant to the corresponding chapter. This allows instructors to teach and communicate the need to research and collect data with their students so that new methods, strategies, and information can be used to improve our discipline. In addition to the text, we offer a companion website (**go.jblearning.com/ciccomascolo**) with two supplementary articles.

Each author has written with passion and persuasion about his or her area of expertise, and we hope the readers will enjoy the tone and heartfelt enthusiasm in his or her words. We cannot thank the authors enough for their time and expertise and the care they took in writing about their expertise. Their enthusiasm for this book was contagious, and we certainly couldn't have done this without them. They have been our inspiration throughout this entire process.

We are student-centered individuals who are constantly thinking of innovative ways to help our students to enter into dialogue with experts in their field. We are dedicated to promoting the importance and necessity of physical and health education and are excited that, with the help of the amazing editors and staff at Jones & Bartlett Learning, especially Shoshanna Goldberg, Prima Bartlett, and Jess Newfell, we can effectively meet that goal with this text. For the instructors adopting this text, we hope you enjoy using the articles to challenge students to think about the "big picture" of how all of the dimensions of physical and health education connect to each other. For the students reading this text, we are honored to be a part of your educational journey and we wish you success in learning and teaching in our discipline.

Acknowledgments

This book is dedicated to my parents, Catherine and Joseph, who taught me to be a lifelong learner in every dimension of life.

I would also like to thank Shoshanna Goldberg, Prima Bartlett, Jess Newfell, and the editorial team at Jones & Bartlett Learning for all of their guidance, support, and professionalism throughout the entire process of this book.

Special thanks to the intelligent and talented authors who were very giving of their time, expertise, research, and experience in order to teach future physical and health educators about realistic issues and situations they will encounter in their own classrooms.

Thanks and love to Ann, Lisa, Olivia, Robert, Judith, Karen, and Suzanne.

—*Lori E. Ciccomascolo*

My family means the world to me, and their support through this process has been invaluable. My husband, Billy, is always there for me; he understood all of the weekends when we missed our time together and our special movie dates. Thank you, Billy, for encouraging me throughout this journey. My son, Brendan, has listened to me talk about everything I had to accomplish for the book, and he is a good listener. Our Skype times often consisted of me merely rattling off my "to do" list. Now you are writing and editing your own book, Brendan, and completion of your doctoral degree in Applied Math from Carnegie Mellon is right around the corner! To my daughter, Cassie, thank you for being more than a daughter to me; we have talked as friends and teacher colleagues throughout this entire process. And, thank you for being an extra eye for my reflective teaching article. There aren't many moms who send their daughters a plethora of research articles on teaching! I am excited as you move forward into your second year of teaching after earning your MAT from Boston University; your Latin students in Bronxville, New York, are lucky to have you as their teacher. You are a fourth generation educator in the family! My Mom's aunt was a teacher, Mom was a teacher, I taught at BU for 28 years, and now you and Brendan are carrying on the family tradition.

Thank you to my colleagues who are experts in their field and agreed to write articles for this book. I appreciate your time in sharing your thoughts that will benefit our future educators and leaders in our field. This text could not have happened without your input; I value our work together. The team at Jones & Bartlett Learning has been invaluable, too. Thank you to Shoshanna Goldberg, Prima Bartlett, and Jess Newfell for guiding and supporting our work.

And last but not least, I am dedicating this book to my Mom, Patricia Louise Crowley. She has always inspired me to do my very best; she has been there every step of the way, from being the class mother each year in school, teaching me to play tennis, supporting everything I do, and sharing her love of teaching and working with children. She was a classroom teacher and I inherited her passion for teaching. Thank you for all you have done for me, Mom. You have always been and continue to be my inspiration.

Love and thanks to my family (my sisters and brother plus my mom and mother–in–law), dear friends, and colleagues who made this book a reality.

—*Eileen Crowley Sullivan*

About the Authors

■ EDITORS

Dr. Lori Ciccomascolo attended Southern Connecticut State University (BS in Communication and MS in Exercise Science) and Boston University (EdD in Curriculum and Teaching) and is an Associate Professor of Kinesiology at the University of Rhode Island (URI). She is currently the interim Associate Dean of the College of Human Science and Services and is the co-chair of URI's Graduate Student Learning Outcomes and Assessment Committee. Her research interests focus on developing and implementing curricular interventions (e.g., girl-serving, outdoor education, leadership) that promote the adoption and maintenance of physical activity among urban K–12 students. Her publications have appeared in the *Journal of Physical Education, Recreation, and Dance* and the *Women in Sport and Physical Activity Journal*, and she has presented at regional and national conferences in the fields of communication, physical education, and physical activity.

Dr. Eileen Crowley Sullivan attended Skidmore College (BS in Physical Education), University of Maryland (MA in Physical Education Administration and Curriculum), and Boston University (EdD from Curriculum and Teaching Department in the School of Education) and taught at Boston University for 28 years. She served as the Program Coordinator of Physical Education, Health Education, and Coaching Specialization at Boston University's School of Education and launched a 16-credit all-online Graduate Certificate in Physical Education, Health Education, and Coaching. Her teaching responsibilities at Boston University included the professional preparation of teachers for licensure in Physical Education and Health Education. She was the coordinator and supervisor of student teachers for prepracticums and final practicums in the local schools. In addition to teaching theory and methods classes for physical education majors, Dr. Sullivan taught the required movement education class for all elementary education majors. She taught undergraduate as well as graduate courses and particularly enjoyed mentoring doctoral students.

She recently accepted a new position with Rhode Island College's Feinstein School of Education and Human Development and serves as the Assistant Dean for Partnerships and Placements. She formalizes all placements for practicums and student teaching, plans professional development for the cooperating teachers and college supervisors, and cultivates district partnerships. Her research interests include teacher education, teacher effectiveness, parameters of student teaching, use of movement for cognitive reinforcement, the level of student involvement, and cooperative play. She consults and conducts numerous workshops for the professional development of cooperating teachers, as well as elementary education classroom teachers to learn about the benefits of movement, and is well known for her presentations on the "New PE." She serves as a movement specialist, working with local and national organizations to promote effective physical education programs. Some of her most recently published research focuses on the teaching behaviors of majors and non-majors, triangulation assessment with the use of a systematic observation instrument in the gymnasium, and assessment of student teachers using two different teaching approaches. Other recent publications focus on games and game analysis: *50 Best Games and Group Challenge Activities, Linking the Body and Brain: A Manual for Physical Education Game Modification, Unique Games, and Sports Around the World* (Ed.), "Character Education in the Gymnasium: Teaching More Than the Physical," and "Critical Game Analysis and the Multi-Dimensional Nature of Games for Young Children." Many know Eileen as the "Games Queen," and she even carries her passion for games into her family life. Eileen has two adult children, Cassie and Brendan, and lives in Shrewsbury, Massachusetts, with her husband Bill. She enjoys golf, tennis, outdoor activities, her dear friends, book club nights, and beach time at the Cape.

■ CONTRIBUTORS

Holly L. Alperin, EdM, CHES, designs, implements and evaluates professional learning opportunities for states and local education agencies funded by the Centers for Disease Control and Prevention's Division of Adolescent and School Health in the areas of Asthma Management, Coordinated School Health, and HIV Prevention. Additionally, Holly has a background in health education and has provided professional development to teachers and administrators at the local, state, and national levels.

Kate Balestracci, MS, RD, is a Program Coordinator for the Rhode Island Supplemental Nutrition Assistance Education Program (SNAP-Ed), who works with low-income children, adults, and seniors as well as mentors undergraduate and graduate nutrition students. In addition, she is an adjunct lecturer for the University of Rhode Island.

Amy L. Baltzell, EdD, is the Director of the Sport Psychology Program at Boston University, taught the first Sport Psychology course offered at Harvard University, teaches courses in Positive Psychology, and is the author of *Living in the Sweet Spot: Preparing for Performance in Sport and Life*. She is a licensed counseling psychologist and consults in the area of performance enhancement and mindfulness with athletes, musicians, teachers, coaches, and sport teams.

Avital Pato Benari, EdD, has implemented, developed, and enjoys teaching nutrition and health education courses for undergraduate and graduate students at Boston University. She has worked for 18 years as a private practitioner and nutrition consultant for HMOs and hospitals, has taught numerous nutrition and wellness seminars for special interest groups, and has developed programs, courses, and professional development workshops for diverse healthcare professionals.

Erik W. Black, PhD, holds a joint appointment as an Assistant Professor in the University of Florida Colleges of Medicine and Education. His research focuses on distance learning, medical education, and health outcomes.

Justine Boisvert, a University of Rhode Island graduate, is teaching physical education and health for grades 6–12 in Barrington, Rhode Island, after teaching for Los Angeles Unified at the Mark Twain Middle School in Venice Beach, California. She also is working on a masters in PETE at West Virginia University.

Emily Clapham, EdD, is an Assistant Professor at the University of Rhode Island. She teaches classes in pedagogy and adapted physical education and enjoys supervision of practicum students. Her research interests include the New PE, motivation in PE, and using technology in PE settings.

Aimee Doherty, EdM, is an elementary physical education teacher and field hockey coach in Belmont, Massachusetts. She teaches students in grades K–4 a variety of manipulative, locomotor, and nonlocomotor skills in order to prepare them to make lifelong decisions regarding their health and fitness.

Pat Degon, EdM, is the Director of Health/Physical Education/Family and Consumer Sciences for the Shrewsbury Public Schools in Shrewsbury, Massachusetts. She has served as a Board member for Massachusetts Association for Health, Physical Education, Recreation, and Dance (MAHPERD), Action for Health Kids, and Interdisciplinary Health Education and Human Services Advisory Council.

Donna Marie Duffy, PhD, is a faculty member in the Department of Kinesiology at the University of North Carolina, Greensboro (UNCG). Dr. Duffy also is the Director for the Program for the Advancement for Girls and Women in Sport and Physical Activity in the Center for Women's Health and Wellness at UNCG.

Kevin E. Finn, MA, ATC, CSCS, is an Assistant Professor of Health Sciences and Sports Medicine at Merrimack College in North Andover, Massachusetts. His area of expertise is curriculum and teaching in the health professions with a focus around increasing school-based physical activity in children.

Matt Freeman, EdM, is entering his twelfth year as a physical education teacher at South Middle School in Braintree, Massachusetts. He enjoys his job as a middle school physical education teacher because he has the ability to be a positive role model for his students.

Ann Marie Gallo, EdD, is an Associate Professor and the Physical Education Teacher Education Coordinator at Salem State College. Her research areas include practical assessment and innovative curriculum in physical education.

Laura Galopim, MEd, is a middle school physical education teacher and health educator for grades 6–8 for Weston Public Schools in Massachusetts; she has served as the Weston High School Varsity Field Hockey Coach for the past 14 years. She also has directed an overnight field hockey camp for ages 10 through 17 each summer for the past 10 years.

Susan Metzger Gracia, PhD, is Director of Assessment at Feinstein School of Education and Human Development at Rhode Island College and Associate Professor in Educational Leadership and PhD Education programs at the same institution. Her research interests include educational assessment, psychometrics, program evaluation, and school/teacher change.

Linda M. Grossi, MEd, is a Health and Physical Education Teacher at Gilbert Stuart Middle School in the Providence, Rhode Island Public Schools District. As an educator, her favorite part is being involved with her students both in the classroom and after school, but as important is being an integral part of the school community, district, and state levels.

Disa Hatfield, PhD, MA, is currently an Assistant Professor at the University of Rhode Island in the Department of Kinesiology. Dr. Hatfield's research interests include the hormonal responses to resistance exercise, nutritional supplementation, children and exercise, and athletic performance.

Teddi Jacobs, MEd, is the Coordinator of Physical Education grades K–8, Health Education grades 7–8, and Health and Fitness grades 9–12 for the Public Schools of Brookline, Massachusetts. She is responsible for curriculum development and implementation, supervision and evaluation of teachers, and collaboration with students, parents/guardians, teachers, administrators, and other school staff.

David Kaufman is a high school technology teacher working in an urban district in Massachusetts. He also is a doctoral candidate at Boston University in Educational Media and Technology and the proud father to a beautiful girl, Sarah.

Swapna Kumar, EdD, is a Clinical Assistant Professor of Educational Technology at the School of Teaching and Learning, University of Florida. Her teaching and research focus on blended and online education, teaching with new technologies, and online communities.

Donna Lehr, PhD, is an Associate Professor and Coordinator in the Special Education Program, Department of Curriculum and Teaching at Boston University. Her primary areas of research are the education and alternate assessment of students.

Bernice Lerner, EdD, is director of adult learning at Hebrew College. She has taught Ethical Decision Making for Education Leaders at Northeastern University, and Character and Ethics Education at Boston University, where she served as Director of the Center for the Advancement of Ethics and Character.

Jessica Licata, MS, is presently a doctoral student in the Special Education Program at Boston University and is working as a consultant for the School of One Program for the New York City Department of Education. Her primary interest is employment outcomes for students with severe disabilities.

Wenhao Liu, PhD, is a faculty member with the Physical Education Department at Slippery Rock University of Pennsylvania. He has been interested in research regarding children's and adolescents' physical activity participation.

John McCarthy, EdD, is involved with various projects and grants in the area of coach education and training in sport leadership. His work at Boston University and the Institute for Athletic Coach Education focuses on developing programs to help youth sport participants in schools, especially those from underserved neighborhoods.

Kyle McInnis, ScD, is Professor of Exercise Science at the University of Massachusetts and a Fellow of the American College of Sports Medicine. His scholarly work in the area of physical activity and health includes being author and editor of several leading textbooks and related publications.

Jeff McNamee, PhD, is an Associate Professor at Linfield College. Dr. McNamee teaches courses in the areas of teaching methodology, outdoor pursuits, and assessment.

Marybeth P. Miller, PhD, is an Assistant Professor in the Physical Education Department at Slippery Rock University. Dr. Miller's experiences include teaching professional theory, elementary methods, and professional activity courses and student teaching supervision at the undergraduate and graduate levels; her research focuses on service-learning.

Catherine Moffitt, PhD, earned her doctorate in Educational Leadership while teaching elementary physical education. Throughout her 20-plus years of teaching she has been on many committees at the district and state level, which have enhanced her teaching. She is currently a physical and health educator in Charlestown, Rhode Island.

Tony Monahan, PhD, taught courses in the areas of health and wellness, individual activities and games, and adapted physical education at the University of Rhode Island and Eastern Connecticut State University.

Kelly Nelson is a graduate of the University of Rhode Island. She is a K–8 physical education teacher in Brookline, Massachusetts, and is working on her masters in PETE at West Virginia University.

David Nichols, EdM, was the Health Education Director of Andover Public Schools in Massachusetts from 1997 to 2008. He is enjoying teaching graduate-level courses, including Development of the Health Education Curriculum, Community Health, and Problems in Health Education, in Boston University's School of Education.

Christopher Nightingale, EdD, is a Clinical Assistant Professor of Athletic Training at the University of Maine and oversees the clinical education experience of the athletic training education majors. His areas of interest and research include the professional preparation and induction of allied healthcare professionals.

Gary Nihan, MEd, recently retired as the K–12 Director of Health and Physical Education for the Danvers Public Schools in Massachusetts. He is currently serving as an adjunct instructor in the PETE program at Salem State University. Over the past 36 years, Gary has taught physical education from preschool through higher education.

Kathy Peno, PhD, is on faculty in the School of Education at the University of Rhode Island. She teaches Educational Psychology to preservice teachers and trains inservice teachers on topics such as Effective Instruction and Assessment in the Block and Problem-Based Instruction.

Lauren Percoco earned a bachelors in exercise and health science and conducted independent research study with Dr. Kyle McInnis at the University of Massachusetts, Boston.

Heather Perkins has been teaching elementary physical education for the North Kingstown School Department in Rhode Island for the past 20 years. Her passion for outdoor adventures does not just involve her school family; she enjoys seasonal outdoor adventures with her own family.

Christopher Roland, EdD, is Managing Principal of the Organization Development firm Roland/Diamond Associates, Inc., with offices in Hancock, New Hampshire, and West Hartford, Connecticut. As a consultant, facilitator, and coach, Dr. Roland helps create safe and comfortable learning environments in order for his clients to respond to change/transition, to develop or reinforce teamwork, and to strengthen leader effectiveness.

Shawna J. Southern is an elementary health and physical education teacher in Providence, Rhode Island. She also is a former RI Teacher and Technology Initiative Trainer and uses technology to motivate her students.

Sarah Sparrow Benes, EdD, is the Program Coordinator of the Physical Education and Health Education Program in the School of Education at Boston University. She teaches a variety of courses in both physical education and health education and recently completed a dissertation on skills-based health education, which is her research interest.

Pamela A. Storme is a physical education, health, and adapted physical educator at Melville Elementary School in Portsmouth, Rhode Island. She is past-president of the Rhode Island chapter of the American Alliance for Health, Physical Education, Recreation, and Dance (RIAHPERD) and has presented at many state, district, and national conferences.

Deborah Tannehill, PhD, is a Senior Lecturer in the Physical Education and Sport Sciences Department and is the Course Director for the Graduate Diploma in Physical Education. Dr. Tannehill's teaching, research, and professional service are focused on teaching and teacher education in physical education and sport, curricular initiatives, assessment, instructional strategies, supervision, and mentoring.

Philip M. Tate, PhD, was educated at Wake Forest University, Duke University, and the University of Chicago and studies award-winning teachers. He taught in the public schools of North Carolina and at the University of Virginia, and since 1991 he has taught courses in the foundations of education, curriculum, and teaching at Boston University.

Gay L. Timken, PhD, is Associate Professor of Physical Education Teacher Education at Western Oregon University. Dr. Timken works with preservice and in-service teachers to ensure that children and youth experience the best physical education possible.

Kerri Tunnicliff, PhD, has been teaching for 15 years at the high school and college level and is currently an Associate Professor and the Coordinator of Adapted Physical Education at Rhode Island College. Dr. Tunnicliffe's greatest joy in teaching is the look on a teacher candidate's face when they influence a student's life.

Melissa C. Wiser, MA, is currently pursuing her PhD in Sport Humanities at The Ohio State University. She teaches courses on race and gender in sport and her research focuses on the rules, governance, and officiating of women's lacrosse.

Steven Wright, EdD, is the Coordinator of the University of New Hampshire Kinesiology Pedagogy (Physical Education Teacher Education) Program. Although he is a teacher, administrator, and researcher, his greatest joy by far is teaching young people how to teach.

Furong Xu, PhD, is an Assistant Professor in the Kinesiology Department at University of Rhode Island. Dr. Xu is particularly interested in research on physical activity promotion in children.

CHAPTER 1

An Introduction to Physical Education and Health Education: The Meaning of Our Discipline

■ CHAPTER OVERVIEW

It is exciting to share this first chapter overview because the articles in this chapter help to clearly define the role that physical education and health education play in children's lives, schools, and society in general. This chapter sets the foundation for the rest of the book; as a reader you need to have a sound understanding about these disciplines before further investigation and analysis of some of the parameters of these fields.

The first article provides a historical overview of the meaning of physical education in the schools. It discusses the meaning of physical education, with a specific focus on exploring the differences between what is called the "old" or "traditional" physical education (PE) versus the New PE, and includes an examination of the curriculum or content. Two teacher scripts provide the reader with a hands-on activity to act out two scenarios, one of a physical education teacher teaching a fourth grade soccer class as a traditional PE class and the second as a New PE class. At the end of the article, two sections—"The 13 Traditional (Old) PE Components" and the "The 13 New PE Components"—summarize the key points. By becoming more knowledgeable about the

New PE, parents, administrators, teachers, and higher education professionals can work together to meet the needs of our high-tech yet physically inactive youth of today. The article confirms the benefits of and need to teach to the whole person for him or her to become a physically active individual.

Similar to the New PE, there is a new and improved method of health education, and the author of the second article in this chapter explores the meaning of health and health education. She also defines skills-based health education, clarifies the role of skills, defends why a skills-based health education is effective, and outlines what an effective skills-based health education classroom looks like. The inclusion of knowledge, attitudes, and skills with Bandura's (2004) Social Cognitive Theory (SCT) is linked to skills-based health education. Each component of the SCT is discussed with specific skills-based health education examples.

The need to develop and use a comprehensive health education approach in schools is the theme for the third article. The methods of developing and implementing a planned and varied program that contains goals, objectives, and a content sequence and that addresses learning styles and individual needs are discussed. Exemplary/promising health education programs are presented, and specific elementary and secondary programs are cited that address various health topics. The discussion of these health programs, models, or curricula provides the reader with numerous references. Social norming and teaching to the needs of students at all points on the risk behavior spectrum is an important concept throughout the article.

An additional article—available online at **go.jblearning.com/ciccomascolo**—is a comprehensive overview about physical education curricula, the need for standards-based curricula, and the current status of educational reform in our field. Factors that influence curriculum development in physical education, such as societal interests, mobility, accessibility, choice, accountability, and time, are defined and discussed. Curriculum planning, the role of assessment in a standards-based curriculum, and how to select activities are explained. The reader will be well informed about standards-based curriculum development in physical education after reading and studying the sections of this article.

The Meaning of Physical Education: Definition, Clarification, and an Overview of the Old and New PE

Eileen Crowley Sullivan

Scholars, school personnel, parents, students, and health and physical education professionals feel there is a mixed awareness and lack of agreement on the meaning of **physical education**. The implications and growth of the discipline must be examined to better understand the meaning of physical education as it relates to the development of the physical education curriculum in meeting the needs of students. The intent of this article is to define, explore, and clarify definitions of physical education throughout the years in order to distinguish between what is known as the **traditional (or old) Physical Education (PE)** and the **New Physical Education (PE)**. This is quite a difficult task because the physical education program or curriculum involves three intertwined variables: (1) the teacher, (2) content, and (3) students. These variables are difficult to isolate because in an effective physical education curriculum they work in harmony. For the purposes of this exploration into the meaning of physical education, focus will be directed toward the content.

■ WHAT IS PHYSICAL EDUCATION? DEFINITIONS THROUGH THE YEARS

The word *physical education* has different meanings to each of us, thus we need to investigate some definitions, from the 1950s to the present, in order to appreciate and understand the differences between what is now known as the old PE and what we call the New PE. Changing times have influenced these definitions, and exploring the differences reveals significant themes.

Scott and Westkaemper (1958) tell us that the field, which was then just over a hundred years old, "developed from an unappreciated, unwanted appendage of the curriculum into an indispensable phase of the general curriculum of all students" (p. xii). The authors define PE as "planned instructional experiences in the fundamental skills, games, sports, dancing, gymnastics, and aquatics" (p. 245). Miller and Whitcomb's (1963) definition of PE informs us that physical education had a place in the school in order to meet the needs of the whole child or person. The fundamental objectives included teaching to the physical objectives of physical fitness, growth and development, and physical skills. Physical education also developed the social-emotional objective; the intellectual objective is the final one included in the discussion of the meaning of physical education. "In the field of physical education, children's intellectual growth has probably been overlooked and ignored in favor of physical, social and emotional growth. This intellectual objective includes 'knowledges and appreciations' about the history, background, terminology, rules, strategies, and understanding about the sports, dancing, and other physical activities" (Miller and Whitcomb, 1963, p. 5).

During the 1970s the definition changed to: "Physical Education must provide an environment of varied social and psychomotor experiences for all children. Traditional programs involving a few games and dances along with spontaneous play activity no longer meet the developmental needs of our children in our changing sociological culture" (Arnheim & Pestolesi, 1978, p. 4). Physical development addressing physical efficiency, physical fitness, motor control, and skill development were placed at the very top of an "elementary hierarchy objectives chart." Value, attitude, and appreciation of learning about the physical domain were included in the objectives, but they were secondary objectives located at the bottom of the chart. The common theme that emerges from these definitions during the early years, from the 1950s to the late 1980s, pertains to the physical or the psychomotor domain in isolation of the other domains. Students learned about fitness, skill development, and how to play selected sports, but the content did not incorporate teaching students how to apply this content outside the physical education classroom.

In 1988, Kirchner said, "the primary purpose of physical education is to help each child develop to his or her full potential" (p. 4). More specifically, he further defined physical education as a program that enhances physical growth and development; develops and maintains maximum physical fitness, useful physical skills, social skills, wholesome recreational skills, intellectual competencies, and creative talents; and enhances a child's self-esteem. Although the focus was still on the physical domain, and physical fitness was listed as the first objective, this definition begins to address the need to plan and teach to the physical and social side of PE. The definition also makes us aware of planning to be sure the program is a positive one that assists with improving social skills so children feel good about themselves. Perhaps this was the start of moving away from only teaching physical fitness and sport activities to planning games and activities that are physically active yet recreational and enjoyed by all.

A definition that establishes the movement of what would become known as the New PE states that programs "help students develop the knowledge, attitudes, motor skills, behavioral skills, and confidence needed to adopt and maintain physically active lifestyles" (National Center for Chronic Disease Prevention and Health Promotion, 1997, p. 205). Note that the first part of the definition does not attend to the physical, but rather the affective domain of emotions and attitudes. This definition shows the progression of attending to the individual needs of our children, from the physical to the social, emotional, and intellectual components. In years past more attention was directed solely to the physical side of our programs.

Pangrazi (2006) defines physical education as education through movement that encompasses all three domains: **psychomotor**, **cognitive**, and **affective**. He also emphasizes that an effective program needs to meet the needs of *all* children and students, not just the elite athletes who are physically skilled. This is another common theme that arises when exploring the meaning of physical education over the years. In the past, programs were planned without all students' needs in mind, but rather were geared toward the skilled student who could play and do well in all physical sports and activities. Graham, Holt/Hale, and Parker (2009) remind us that physical education relates to school programs that guide children and teach them how to be physically active, not just during the school day but also during their lifetimes. They also clearly state that physical activity is a *behavior* and physical education is the *program* that teaches our youngsters how to achieve those behaviors.

Perhaps the best and most appropriate definition of physical education, and the one we should all use, is presented by the National Association for Sport and Physical Education (NASPE), the governing body for the PE profession. It states, "Physical activity is critical to the development and maintenance of good health. The goal of physical education is to develop physically educated individuals who have the knowledge, skills, and confidence to enjoy a lifetime of healthful physical activity" (NASPE, 2004). It further defines what constitutes a physically educated person with six national content standards that serve as a guideline for the New PE curriculum:

- *Standard 1:* Demonstrates competency in motor skills and movement patterns needed to perform a variety of physical activities
- *Standard 2:* Demonstrates understanding of movement concepts, principals, strategies, and tactics as they apply to the learning and performance of physical activities
- *Standard 3:* Participates regularly in physical activity
- *Standard 4:* Achieves and maintains a health-enhancing level of physical fitness
- *Standard 5:* Exhibits responsible personal and social behavior that respects self and others in physical activity settings
- *Standard 6:* Values physical activity for health, enjoyment, challenge, self-expression, and/or social interaction

Based on NASPE's criteria, PE programs need to teach students to be able to perform a variety of motor skills and physical activities, including how to become and stay physically fit, so that they know and want to be active outside of PE class time. NASPE developed the first content standards in 1955, but these standards, similar to the early definitions of PE, did not link performance to content as they do today. The shift from physical fitness and competitive team-based sports to a program that highlights the cognitive and affective domains with appropriate performance outcomes clearly helps to define what we call the New PE in the twenty-first century.

■ THE TRADITIONAL PHYSICAL EDUCATION

A good means of discovering what constitutes the traditional versus the New PE is to ask your family, friends, and colleagues about their past experiences in physical education. For the past 25 years the list of comments from different people have ranged, such as "I hated everything about gym class," "Dodgeball wasn't too bad because we picked off the kids we didn't like," and "Gym was OK because I was an athlete so I did well." About two-thirds of all comments, in my unofficial long-term survey, revealed that individuals enjoyed elementary PE but by middle school and high school years they were turned off. Those that liked PE in the later school years appeared to have a stronger curriculum with objectives directed toward lifetime fitness and sports, as compared to the old PE, which consisted of team sports and activities that could not be played after high school. It's hard to distinguish the content from the teaching here, but many students stated that with the old PE their teacher didn't seem to care, but with the New PE, teachers were involved and helped students challenge themselves on the rock wall or with a variety of physical activities that they could enjoy outside school. Yoga, tennis, golf, Ultimate Frisbee, volleyball, speed walking, and the use of the weights or time in the fitness room were components of the New PE as told to me by my college-age students. Those that disliked and even hated PE said they were always selected last for teams, played team sports, and never learned anything about how to be active outside of PE class.

In the traditional PE, content included playing elimination tag games where not everyone had a turn to play all roles of the game; those that were tagged out first were usually the ones who needed to get the most exercise. Sports, and mostly team sports like basketball, field hockey, soccer, and even football, were played during class time with the old PE. There were monotonous and boring sport drills where students were graded on how quickly they could perform a physical skill. Scores and results were recorded and this data were often used as a measure for grading. It's no surprise that many grew to detest physical activity because they were not being taught skills they could use outside of class. It shouldn't matter how quickly you can dribble a soccer ball around cones for a skill test, but rather it should matter that you know how to control the soccer ball to be able to dodge an opponent or pass to a teammate when you play a recreational game.

Recall that physical fitness was a primary goal of the old PE curricula, and about one out of three adults relayed their account of how they were humiliated during the fitness-testing unit, which usually occurred during the winter months (Sullivan, 2009). In fact, one 19-year-old student told me he worked with his parents to finally have the school use a code number instead of real names when the PE teacher posted the fitness scores on the bulletin board for all to view. The purpose of these fitness tests was usually never revealed to the students; they often did not even have the opportunity to see their results and use them to improve their fitness levels. These and other improper administrative issues, use of the fitness data, and lack of making connections to the students' real lives were imperfections of the old PE. Most importantly, the fitness testing and humiliation of not performing well in front of others solidified the students' dislike for physical activity. The way the fitness tests were administered in the old PE had a detrimental impact on the students who did not perform well; they were not motivated to become active outside of PE class time, and this may even have negatively impacted their attitude about exercise in their later years.

I perform another informal data collection about the traditional and New PE at the start of every semester (1990–2009). On the first day of teaching a movement education course for elementary education and early childhood majors, when asked about PE experiences, more than half of the students still state they had negative experiences. Most of their elementary experiences were acceptable, but many still played elimination games where they sat out and did not participate. Yet, for the most part, the elementary experiences were fairly positive. This is in agreement with my previous unofficial survey with family, friends, and colleagues. For all groups, it was during the middle school and secondary school years that most of the people had trouble with the physical education content and teaching methods. They complained about being ridiculed in front of their peers when they couldn't do a sport and they didn't care for the physical fitness testing. Many said the sport activities were boring and teachers still favored the athletes.

My sister Kathy, now 59 years old, detested physical education during all her years in school. She remembers gym class as a time when she didn't have any fun learning new movement skills because the emphasis was placed on sport drills and sports, not lifetime fitness activities. My sister also remembers the athletes always shining in class, and they were the ones who demonstrated the skills for the teacher. She continues to ask me, "Why did we have to play field hockey? When am I ever going to play field hockey again?" To this day I am still trying hard to tell her

to keep an open mind about physical activity and exercise, but she can't get those images of gym class out of her mind. She told me she "hated every minute of gym class." These strong negative memories illustrate some of the concepts that represent the old PE.

Let's try to summarize the traditional PE: a whistle around the neck of a gym teacher and students being singled out with limited playing time and exclusion games where only the athletes excelled. All the athletes excelled in the activities, and they may have even been the elite ones to be nominated as captains; these captains selected teams, and individuals were embarrassed when they naturally chose friends and athletes first. Class was called "gym," and there may have been long lines with one student active at a time. Competition was prevalent during each class and there was little social interaction. The structured classes of sports and sport drills had students playing full-size sport games only at the end of a unit. Grades may have been based on skill level, attendance, or even dressing for class, and students did not know how hard they were working or the level and amount of their physical activity. Although physical fitness was important, it was usually presented as a separate unit during the winter months. Motivational devices were not used, and perhaps the only form of technology was a stopwatch to time how quickly students moved through sport skill drills. Finally, most PE programs did not define and use district, state, and national standards for content.

■ THE NEW PHYSICAL EDUCATION

Melograno and Kelly, in their text *Developing the Physical Education Curriculum: An Achievement-Based Approach* (2004), remind us that the purpose of physical education has been influenced and affected by popular culture, as shown in the changing definitions over time. Health and hygiene were stressed during the early twentieth century, and then social recreational goals were most important. Most of our physical fitness tests were developed during the war years and the physical requirements for military training. The 1950s are connected to total fitness, and then the 1970s, with that era's social justice issues, had physical education programs teaching more to the individual and social needs. "More recently, the concept of wellness focuses on disease prevention rather than the treatment of sickness. Disease prevention measures include personal health regimens and lifestyles that emphasize fitness" (Melograno & Kelly, 2004).

The 1990s were the start of what we could call the obesity, health, and fitness crisis; these years may have contributed to some of the reasons for the shift from an old PE to a New PE. New statistics come to the forefront every day about obese and unfit children and adults. The Centers for Disease Control and Prevention (CDC) statistics on the prevalence of obesity and lack of physical activity highlight the need for effective New PE programs that teach students how to become physically fit and maintain a healthy lifestyle. Teaching students how and why they should move will assist them in decreasing the risk of many diseases and health conditions such as coronary heart disease, type 2 diabetes, some cancers, hypertension, dyslipidemia, stroke, and even sleep apnea and sleep problems. The shift back to individualized fitness and physical activity, coupled with teaching about healthy eating habits and nutrition, are the goals of the New PE.

Many, including John Ratey (2008), the lead author of the text, *Spark: The Revolutionary New Science of Exercise and the Brain*, credit Phil Lawler as the pioneer for the New PE revolution in the early 1990s.

Lawler, now the director of the PE4Life Academy in Naperville, Illinois, was a physical educator who reflected on the PE profession and the health of our children. With the reports of obesity and unfit children, as well as inactivity and competitive sports in many PE classes, he revised his PE content and teaching. He decided to focus on participation, cardiovascular activities, and the use of effort and not skill for PE grades. Students were required to challenge themselves and run a mile once a week during PE class. They worked to meet their personal bests and could raise their grade each time they improved. They would move up a letter grade with each personal best. This type of personal and what could be called **authentic or "real" assessment** "led to the founding principle of the approach he dubbed the New PE. Students would be assessed on effort rather than skill. You didn't have to be an athlete to do well in gym" (Ratey, 2008, p. 16). This introduction to the New PE set the foundation for Ratey's book, which defines the mind–body connection and the need to exercise not only for our health, but also to help improve learning.

Neil F. William's "Physical Education Hall of Shame" article in 1994 helped provide the impetus to begin calling physical education "the New PE" in the late 1990s and the start of the twenty-first century. In his article, Williams, a professor at Eastern Connecticut State College, identified games and physical activities that were considered inappropriate to teach during PE class because of one or more of the following elements (Williams, 1994, p. 17):

- Absence of the purported objectives of the activity or game
- Potential to embarrass students in front of the rest of the class
- Focus on eliminating students from participation

- Overemphasis on and concern about the students having "fun"
- Lack of emphasis on teaching motor skills and lifetime physical fitness
- Extremely low participation time factors
- Extremely high likelihood for danger, injury, and harm

Seven games were inducted into the Hall of Shame in 1992:

- Dodgeball
- Duck duck goose
- Giants, wizards, elves
- Kickball
- Musical chairs
- Relay races
- Steal the bacon

Then in 1994, six more games were added to the list:

- Line soccer
- Red rover
- Simon says
- Messy back yard
- SPUD
- Tag

Williams (1994) clearly explains why each game was nominated based on the listed elements, but a physical educator could modify and then teach one of the listed games with the specific modifications so that it would not be considered a "Hall of Shame" game.

Limited research can be found on what constitutes the New PE. Emily Clapham's (2008) dissertation, "An Analysis of Physical Activity and Elementary Physical Education Curricula Using Heart Rate Monitors and Pedometers," may be the most up-to-date review of literature concerning the New PE. She reviews the meaning of physical education, components of a traditional PE program, the

development of our national standards, the use of skill themes (Graham, Holt/Hale, & Parker, 2009) to teach elementary physical education, the meaning of the New PE, the state of assessment in physical education, and the use of motivational devices, such as pedometers and heart rate monitors as well as supportive curricula for these technological devices.

The lack of hard data, scholarly articles, and research-based articles defining and analyzing the New PE forces us to examine the literature that has been written through the lenses of different people. Articles that describe the trend of moving from hard core fitness classes and team-based competitive sport PE programs to a more personalized, individualized, and challenging fitness and activity curriculum are titled, "Gym Class Renaissance," "The Death of Dodgeball," "Leveling the Playing Field," and "New PE Trend Stresses Fitness and Fun." The *Edutopia* electronic journal presented a special report on the New PE with articles with titles including "All the Right Moves," "Fresh Methods to Keep Kids Active," "Active Bodies, Active Minds: Students Move to Learn," and "The New PE Curriculum: An Innovative Approach to Teaching Physical Fitness," and a video about the New PE called "Smart Moves: The New PE." These titles demonstrate the shift to the New PE content and teaching methods, which teach to the needs of the individual to become a physically educated person for a lifetime.

■ CONTENT RECOMMENDATIONS FOR THE NEW PE

Upon review of the limited literature about the New PE, we are continually reminded that the physical activities taught need to be developmentally appropriate, challenging, unique, and simple activities that meet the needs of everyone. Each individual needs to be exposed to a variety of activities and then be comfortable with those physical skills to be able to know how to participate and enjoy physical activity long after PE class ends. The New PE articles often stress the need to teach lifetime fitness and wellness concepts and physical activities. Even the terminology associated with the New PE highlights the individual at the core of the objectives, curriculum, and teaching methods. Perhaps this individual approach to teach to the needs of everyone was the missing ingredient from the earlier days of the traditional PE.

Sullivan and Clapham (2008) created teacher scripts (included at the end of this section) that review the essential differences between the New and the old PE. The teacher dialogues illustrate a fourth-grade soccer PE class from the past and then a New PE class with similar soccer content. Read the scripts, and then the bulleted components of the old and the New PE. The scripts help to compare how the traditional PE used competition, skill tests, fitness, and teacher-directed lessons and how the New PE addresses the individual's needs, authentic assessment, and the use of data-driven technological devices. With the New PE, physical educators prefer, and rightly so, to call their class physical education instead of **gym class**. Remember that the gym or gymnasium is the place to teach, and not the name of the class. Everyone should be involved all the time with the New PE, and students should be working at their own levels. Heart rate monitors and pedometers are used to help students monitor their levels and learn about the level and amount of physical activity. With the focus on cooperative activities and limited competition against others, enjoyment levels are higher with the New PE. Physical fitness should be blended with most lessons and not taught solely as a separate subject

(Sullivan, 2003). School, district, state, and national standards are implemented and used to plan lessons with the New PE.

Finally, exemplary New PE content and programs should follow the NASPE elements from the report "What Constitutes a Quality Physical Education Program?" The criteria categories from this report are:

Opportunity to Learn

- Instructional periods totaling 150 minutes per week (elementary) and 225 minutes per week (middle and secondary school)
- Qualified physical education specialist providing a developmentally appropriate program
- Adequate equipment and facilities

Meaningful Content

- Instruction in a variety of motor skills that are designed to enhance the physical, mental, and social/emotional development of every child
- Fitness education and assessment to help children understand, improve, and/or maintain their physical well-being
- Development of cognitive concepts about motor skill and fitness
- Opportunities to improve their emerging social and cooperative skills and gain a multicultural perspective
- Promotion of regular amounts of appropriate physical activity now and throughout life

Appropriate Instruction

- Full inclusion of all students
- Maximum practice opportunities for class activities
- Well-designed lessons that facilitate student learning
- Out of school assignments that support learning and practice

- No physical activity for punishment
- Uses regular assessment to monitor and reinforce student learning

■ TECHNOLOGY AND THE NEW PE

The use of technology is at the forefront of the New PE; physical educators are using computer programs, the Internet, iPods, iPads, tablets, flip cameras, smartphones, and digital cameras. Schools may have fitness centers with video games like Dance Dance Revolution, Xbox, and Wii systems that allow students to "exergame," or exercise by playing a video game. Perhaps the use of pedometers could be included here too; even though they are not quite a technology item, they are a motivational device (and not used with the old PE), so do consider them with this technology discussion. The use of pedometers and now heart rate monitors, which calculate and track a student's heartbeat and target heart rate zone, are perhaps the most preeminent and significant uses of technology that have started to revolutionize the New PE. In an article titled "Technology Brings the 'New PE' to Schools," Carter (2008) reported that more than 10,000 schools across the United States are using heart rate monitors during PE class. Every school should be using pedometers and heart rate monitors to teach students how to track the amount and level of their physical activity sessions with the New PE curriculum.

■ CONCLUSION

Inquiry into past definitions of physical education help establish the differences between what can now be called the traditional (or old) PE and the New PE. The adjustments in program content are evident. The old PE content consisted of competitive team sports, elimination games, regimented fitness units, sport skill drills, grades based on skill levels, and a lack of standards-based curriculum development. The old PE was more focused on the physical domain without recognition of the whole person. Then there was a shift to program content that addressed the needs of all students and not just the athletically inclined, and cooperative lifetime fitness activities were stressed. The New PE also has a wellness approach, with students working toward personal physical fitness and wellness goals with motivational technological devices like pedometers and heart rate monitors that can be used for authentic assessment. School, district, state, and national standards have become essential components for planning the New PE curricula. Although there is not an explicit reference to who coined the term *New PE* or when it was coined, there can be agreement that the New PE in the twenty-first century is drastically different than traditional PE.

In conclusion, we all need to work together to meet the needs of our students and continue to define, clarify, and implement the New PE content to teach about physical activity, personal fitness, and a healthy lifestyle, including being active. Although this deliberation has focused on PE content, the human variables of the teacher and the student need to be considered in partnership with the content in order to have effective and successful New PE programs.

■ TEACHER SCRIPTS ABOUT THE OLD AND NEW PE (SULLIVAN & CLAPHAM, 2008)

Script 1: Grade 4 Soccer Lesson During "Gym" Class: Traditional PE

"Good morning. Get in your squads for gym class. Straight lines please. Captains, take attendance."

"Start your warm-ups." (Lead a few exercises.)

"Sit in your self space. Today we are going to continue our soccer unit. We will be practicing controlling the ball and passing."

(A fourth grader raises her hand.) "Yes, Cassie?"

"When will we play a game?"

"You know we always play a game at the end of the unit."

(Another student raises his hand.) Josh asks, "When are we doing push-ups, sit-ups, and running?"

"As always, we do our fitness unit in the winter months."

"OK, class, let's move to the fields. Nice lines and no talking. We'll be selecting new captains for the drills outside. We'll do some drills and practice what we need to play a game. There will be a skills test next week. I will be timing how fast you dribble a soccer ball around cones with a stopwatch. We're off!"

(On the field after selecting new captains) "Straight lines and let's have you dribble the soccer ball around the cones. Do remember the proper way to control the ball. "Remember, part of your grade in PE will be skills, combined with your attendance, appropriate dress, and fitness level."

Script 2: Grade 4 Soccer Lesson (As Part of an Invasion and Team Sport Unit) During Physical Education Class: The New PE

"Good morning class. Please put on your heart rate monitor and pedometer for Physical Education."

"We are going to warm up today with Bean-Bag Sneaker Tag. Everyone is 'it.' If your sneaker gets tagged with a beanbag then you need to freeze, raise your hand, and practice one of the stretches or exercises we have learned in class. When you tag your classmate's sneaker with a beanbag, you need to move into a straddle position. In order to become unfrozen, one of your classmates will toss or slide the beanbag in between your feet or legs. Ready, go!"

(Note that 6 minutes pass and the entire class is physically active at a moderate to high level 100% of the time.)

"OK! Great work everyone. I liked how you moved safely and you used good dodging, chasing, and fleeing skills we have been practicing with tag games. Take a look at your heart rate and number of steps. Remember to try to raise your heart rate into your personal target-training zone. Also, look at how many steps you have taken so far. What is your step goal today?"

"How many have the beep turned on with their heart rate monitor to show their activity level above the target zone? Remember we learned how to do this last week. Ask a classmate or come see me if you need help."

"We are going to continue with our soccer unit. We will be practicing controlling the ball and passing."

(Fourth grader raises her hand.) "Yes, Cassie?"

"When will we play a game?"

"We're going to play a mini game today when we work on our soccer skills, cardiovascular endurance, and agility."

"OK, class, let's move to the fields. Enjoy talking to someone you have not walked with in the past few weeks as we move outside. Try to talk about what healthy foods you enjoy and what physical activities you do outside of school time."

(On the field) "Let's move into cooperative groups to work on passing. Everyone with a fall birthday please come over here and pick up a ball. Everyone should have his or her own ball. Everyone with a winter birthday come over here please, and summer, over here."

(Teacher provides skill cues and reminds students how to pass.) As students practice their passing skills, the teacher says, "Continue to look at your heart rate and note it may be a little lower during this skill practice time. You will be working with less intensity as you pass the ball back and forth without the cardiovascular exertion of running like you were doing with the tag game earlier. It should be higher when you are all playing and running during the soccer game at the end of class."

"Have fun as you practice."

(A fourth grader raises his hand.) "Yes, Josh?"

"Will we be downloading our data together from the heart rate monitors?'

"By next class, I will print individual heart rate sheets for you and you will analyze and write about the data in your journal. We will also learn how to write good objectives for fitness plans."

■ THE 13 TRADITIONAL PE COMPONENTS

- Class called *gym*
- Teacher-directed lessons
- Long lines and squads for exercises
- Structured classes
- Intimidating procedures
- Competition stressed
- Skills taught but games usually played at end of units
- Fitness often presented as a separate unit and not integrated into the other units
- Students often do not have fun as they practice skills
- Students do not know how hard they are working or their level of physical activity
- Grades often based on skill level
- Lack of standards-based curriculum development and assessment
- No technology (perhaps a stopwatch)

■ THE 13 NEW PE COMPONENTS

- Class called *physical education* because we educate about the physical (and more than the physical, too)
- Everyone active, all-inclusive, small groups
- No humiliation and intimidation
- Cooperative focus with enjoyment
- Fitness is blended (Sullivan, 2003) with other PE content
- Motivational devices used to personalize and monitor physical activity
- Enjoyment levels raised
- Individuals work at own physical level and challenge themselves by setting personal goals
- Wellness or health-related focus
- Each child uses own piece of equipment (most of time or all active in some way)
- Each child working towards their own personal fitness goals throughout the lesson
- Standards-based curriculum and assessment; more authentic assessment
- Technology supports the pedagogy (pedometers, heart rate monitors, iPads, iPods, computers, and other fitness devices such as smartphones)

■ KEY WORDS AND DEFINITIONS

affective domain   The emotions, temperaments, and even the values of the learner.

authentic or "real" assessment   Evaluating the learner in a real or true to life environment; in physical education this would mean using evaluation criteria during a game or sport setting.

cognitive domain   Learning the rules of a game or sport, concepts about proper body mechanics, knowledge about content, or processing any factual information.

New Physical Education (PE) This school class or program addresses the needs of all students with content that teaches how and why to be physically active through cooperative, all-inclusive physical activities and lifetime fitness skills using motivational devices like pedometers and heart rate monitors.

physical education The proper title for the New PE class that is taught in the schools and aligned with district, state, and national standards.

psychomotor domain Teaching the physical content, such as how to run, jump, throw, or leap; the physical skills needed to play a sport; physical fitness activities; and any skill that involves "doing" or an action.

traditional (or old) Physical Education (PE) The class or program in schools that taught elimination games, competitive team-based sports, and isolated fitness activities through teacher-directed lessons that often humiliated the non-athlete. It turned off most of the students from exercising and being active outside the school day.

■ DISCUSSION QUESTIONS

1. What are your reactions to the definitions of the traditional PE versus the New PE? Did your PE experiences match either of these paradigms? How so?
2. How have the definitions of physical education changed over the years, and why? To what extent does the culture and climate of the educational world affect these definitions?
3. What are the central issues associated with the old and the New PE?

4. Should the New PE be used in elementary and secondary schools, or should it just be directed to the students in the upper grades? Why?
5. If pedometers and heart rate monitors are an essential part of the New PE, how can all schools afford to purchase these technological devices?

■ EXTENSION ACTIVITIES

1. Form cooperative groups and talk about each student's past physical education experiences. Each student talks for a minute with an overview of elementary, middle, and high school PE experiences. Then, each participant shares their thoughts about the positive and negative aspects of their time in PE. Elect a recorder, and have that person fold a piece of paper in half to create two vertical columns; a "+" is posted at the top of one column and a "−" is posted at the top of the second column. After groups complete the chart, have them compare their experiences with some of the definitions in this article. Was the New or traditional PE prevalent? Why? Regroup the entire class and compile a mini data sheet about the experiences. Talk about how past experiences may influence current thoughts about exercise and physical activity.
2. Read Neil Williams's Hall of Shame article and then add to the list of games that should not be played during PE class. Be sure to reflect on Williams's criteria, NASPE standards, and pedagogical issues when selecting games or physical activities. Try to organize your own PE Hall of Shame games by grade, skill theme, or some other organized manner.
3. Work as individuals or in small groups to write your own teacher script that shows

the difference between the traditional and the New PE for a particular grade or PE content theme. Each group can peer edit the scripts. Then, the scripts can be read or acted out and students can record and post them on the course website for review. An alternative technology component could be recording a podcast of the scripts.

■ REFERENCES

Arnheim, D., & Pestolesi, R. (1978). *Elementary physical education: A developmental approach.* St. Louis, MO: Mosby.

Boss, S. (2000). Gym class renaissance: In the new PE every kid can succeed, not just the jocks. *Northwest Education Magazine, 6*(1).

Carter, D. (2008). Technology brings the "New PE" to schools. *eSchool News.* Retrieved June 15, 2011, from http://www.eschoolnews .com/2008/06/10/technology-brings-new-p-e-to-schools

Clapham, E. (2008). An analysis of physical activity and elementary physical education curricula using heart rate monitors and pedometers. Unpublished dissertation. Boston: Boston University.

Graham, G., Holt/Hale, S., & Parker, M. (2009). *Children moving: A reflective approach to teaching physical education* (8th ed.). Boston: McGraw Hill.

Kirchner, G. (1988). *Physical education for elementary school children* (2nd ed.). Boston: McGraw Hill.

Melograno, V., & Kelly, L. (2004). *Developing the physical education curriculum: An achievement-based approach.* Champaign, IL: Human Kinetics.

Miller, A., & Whitcomb, V. (1963). *Physical education in the elementary school.* Englewood Cliffs, NJ: Prentice-Hall.

National Association for Sport and Physical Education (NASPE). (2003). What constitutes a quality physical education program? Position paper. Reston, VA: Author.

National Association for Sport and Physical Education (NASPE). (2004). *Moving into the future: National standards for physical education* (2nd ed.). Reston, VA: Author.

National Center for Chronic Disease Prevention and Health Promotion, Centers for Disease Control and Prevention. Guidelines for school and community programs to promote lifelong physical activity among young people. *Journal of School Health, 76*(6), 202–219.

Pangrazi, R. (2006). *Dynamic physical education for elementary school children* (15th ed.). San Francisco: Benjamin Cummings.

Rapaport, R. (2008). Schools exercise fresh methods to keep kids active. *Edutopia.* Retrieved April 23, 2009, from http://www.edutopia.org/ new-physical-education-movement

Ratey, J., & Hagerman, E. (2008). *Spark: The revolutionary new science of exercise and the brain.* New York: Little Brown.

Scott, H., & Westkaemper, R. (1958). *From program to facilities in physical education.* New York: Harper and Row.

Sullivan, E. (2003). The ABCs of interdisciplinary physical activities: What physical educators need to know. Presentation at the Massachusetts Association for Health, Physical Education, Recreation, and Dance (MAHPERD). Worcester, MA: MAPHRED.

Sullivan, E. (2009). Survey in SED PE 511: Movement Education. Fall 2008, Spring 2009, and Summer 2009. Boston: Boston University.

Sullivan, E., & Clapham, E. (2008). Teaching an old dog new tricks: Traditional or the old PE versus the new PE. A teacher script about the old and the new PE.

Williams, N. F. (1994). The physical education hall of shame. *Journal of Physical Education, 65*(2), 17–20.

■ ADDITIONAL RESOURCES

American Council on Exercise. Forget new math, this is new P.E. Retrieved May 11, 2009, fromhttp://www.acefitness.org/healthand-fitnesstips/healthandfitnesstips_display .aspx?itemid=135

Clapham, E. (2011). "Catch the wave of the new PE." PowerPoint Presentation at AAHPERD National Convention (March 31, 2011). San Diego: AAHPERD.

Cummiskey, M. "The new PE: Resources for quality physical education." Retrieved June 15, 2011, from http://www.thenewpe.com

Education World. New PE stresses fitness and fun. *Education World / Curriculum Article.* Retrieved May 12, 2009, from http://www.educationworld.com/a_curr/curr346.shtml

Edutopia. (2010). The new PE runs on fitness not competition [Video]. Retrieved June 1, 2011, from http://www.edutopia.org/new-physical-education-movement-video

Ober, A. (2008). Students learn that active bodies lead to active minds. *Edutopia.* Retrieved April 23, 2009, from http://www.edutopia.org/active-bodies-active-minds-students-move-to-learn

Rapaport, R. (2008). Schools exercise fresh methods to keep kids active. *Edutopia.* Retrieved April 23, 2009, from http://www.edutopia.org/new-physical-education-movement

Sullivan, E. (2007). Character education in the gymnasium: Teaching more than the physical. *Journal of Education, 187*(3), 85–102.

Sherman, L. (2000). The death of dodgeball: A generation of high-tech couch potatoes meets a new kind of PE. *Northwest Education Magazine, 6*(1).

The Need for Skills-Based Health Education

Sarah Sparrow Benes

■ WHAT IS SKILLS-BASED HEALTH EDUCATION?

What do you think about when someone mentions health education? Some might think about "sex" education or listening to lectures about various health topics; others might not have experienced health education at all. As with physical education, health education is typically something that people have many different ideas about and have had many different experiences with. Therefore, it is imperative to start by establishing a good definition of **health education**. According to the Centers for Disease Control and Prevention (CDC), health education is "a planned, sequential, K–12 curriculum that addresses the physical, mental, emotional, and social dimensions of health. . . . It allows students to develop and demonstrate increasingly sophisticated health-related knowledge, attitudes, skills, and practices" (CDC, 2008). The goal of health education should be to help students develop into individuals who can maintain healthy lifestyles by adopting and promoting healthy behaviors, while avoiding risky health behaviors. This goal has been defined as **health literacy**, which is "the capacity of an individual to obtain, interpret, and understand basic health information and services, and the competence to use such information and services in ways which are health enhancing" (Gold & Miner, 2002, p. 6).

Based on these definitions, it is clear that health education needs to be a comprehensive curriculum that includes a variety of health topics, addresses various dimensions of wellness, and provides opportunities for students to gain knowledge, develop competence in skills, and develop attitudes that will allow them to become health literate. It is this core idea of combining skills, attitudes, and knowledge in a health education curriculum that is the basis of the skills-based approach to health education. **Skills-based health education** is a curriculum designed around teaching students skills in the context of health and the dimensions of wellness. This includes teaching specific sets of skills (which are discussed in this article), establishing beliefs and attitudes towards health that are health enhancing, and providing students with the knowledge they need to apply the skills and be healthy.

■ WHAT DO SKILLS HAVE TO DO WITH HEALTH EDUCATION?

In order to answer this question, let us first begin with two scenarios. Have a piece of scrap paper nearby to write down some ideas as you read through these situations.

Scenario A

Becky is a high school student at a party at a classmate's (Rick's) house. Rick decided to throw a party because his parents were away and he wanted to celebrate before the start of the senior year. Becky wasn't sure she wanted to go in the first place, but her friends convinced her it would be fun so she decided to go. When they got to the party, almost everyone there was either drinking or doing drugs, just "having a good time." Becky had never had a drink or tried drugs before and wasn't sure she wanted to, but her friends were drinking and people kept telling

her just to try it, just have a drink—it's not a big deal. In addition, everyone else was doing it and did seem to be having fun.

1. What influences does Becky have to deal with in this situation?
2. What does she have to *know* to be able to make a healthy decision here?
3. What does Becky have to be able to *do* to make a healthy decision?
4. How can Becky get herself out of this situation?

Scenario B

Billy is a senior in high school who realizes he should be healthier, especially because he will be going to college next year and he wants to be in better shape so he can try out for the football team. He doesn't exercise regularly and he doesn't have the best eating habits. He has seen a lot of information on television and in the media about how to lose weight and gain muscle. Many of his friends use supplements to help them gain muscle and get in shape. Billy is confused because he has heard that some of these supplements and diets can be harmful to one's health. In addition, he really doesn't know much about how to exercise for weight loss while building muscle.

1. What does Billy need to *know* to help him develop a weight loss/muscle building plan?
2. What does he need to be able to *do* to get started and maintain a program?

This section will give some suggestions for possible answers to the questions listed in the preceding scenarios. In the first situation, Becky is addressing her own feelings about drinking as well as her friends' feelings about drinking, and has to deal with the context of being at a party with many other students and classmates. Becky needs to know the risks of drinking alcohol and doing drugs, and she needs to understand that her peers and the situation are influencing her to make a decision to drink. If Becky wants to make a healthy decision not to drink or do drugs, she needs to know the steps in making a sound decision, have refusal skills to say no, be able to analyze the situation, and be able to weigh consequences. She needs to have communication skills to tell her friends why she doesn't want to participate, and she needs to be able to advocate for herself and confront her friends.

There are many ways that Becky can get herself out of this situation, some of which include refusing to drink or do drugs but staying at the party, calling a cab to bring her home, or calling another friend or her parents to come and get her so she can remove herself from a potentially bad situation. However, all of these options require her knowing and being able to access different resources as well as feeling comfortable enough to use them. Becky needs more than just knowledge to help her in this situation—a situation that is becoming more common in today's high schools and even middle schools.

In the second situation, Billy needs to know how to create a healthy eating plan and how to safely lose weight while gaining muscle. Billy needs to know how to access correct, appropriate information, which means he needs not only to be aware of proper resources, but also to be able to analyze the influences of the media, advertising, and his friends. The Internet has allowed more information to circulate, but it also contains a lot of incorrect, harmful information. It is essential that students know how to find and use appropriate resources. Billy also needs a basic understanding of his body to know how he can use better

nutrition and exercise to help him achieve his goals. Billy needs to be able to access information, and be able to set and achieve goals in order to change his lifestyle and practice the health-enhancing behaviors of eating right and exercising and to develop a healthy, safe weight loss/muscle building program and a healthier lifestyle.

These scenarios attempted to demonstrate the importance of **skills** in leading healthy lifestyles. As the scenarios demonstrate, it isn't enough just to have knowledge or a healthy attitude; you also need to be able to *do* something to help keep (or get) yourself healthy. The ability to do something requires a certain set of skills that one feels comfortable using in a variety of situations. Being and staying healthy is an active, lifelong process during which we constantly need to apply knowledge and skills to a multitude of different situations. This is why learning and developing competence in skills is essential to maintaining a healthy lifestyle, and should be an integral part of any health education curriculum. Think of skills-based health education as being similar to the goal of physical education, which is to teach students fundamental motor skills and patterns that they can use to be physically active now and in the future. Essentially, skills-based health education is doing the same thing— teaching students the fundamental skills they need to be able to be healthy now and in the future.

Now that a definition of skills-based health education has been discussed and scenarios have shown how skills are important in health, the next question is: What skills should we be teaching our students? In 2007, the Joint Committee on National Health Education Standards came out with an updated set of health education standards that reflects the shift towards skills-based health. These standards are in place to provide a framework for developing and implementing an effective health education curriculum. The eight standards are:

1. Students will comprehend concepts related to health promotion and disease prevention to enhance health.
2. Students will analyze the influence of family, peers, culture, media, technology, and other factors on health behaviors.
3. Students will demonstrate the ability to access valid information, products, and services to enhance health.
4. Students will demonstrate the ability to use interpersonal skills to enhance health and avoid or reduce health risks.
5. Students will demonstrate the ability to use decision-making skills to enhance health.
6. Students will demonstrate the ability to use goal-setting skills to enhance health.
7. Students will demonstrate the ability to practice health-enhancing behaviors and avoid or reduce health risks.
8. Students will demonstrate the ability to advocate for personal, family, and community health. (Joint Committee, 2007, p. 8)

These standards also provide performance indicators for each grade level that explain what students should achieve, related to each standard. These indicators, or what we might call benchmarks, help with the development and implementation of curricula, as well as assessment and evaluation of students and the health education program. It is important to note that many states also have their own frameworks or standards, which must be considered, included, and aligned with the designated curriculum. These frameworks are not always aligned with the National Health Education Standards, but health educators should work to integrate both sets of guidelines into curricula to best meet the needs of the students.

■ A SKILLS-BASED HEALTH EDUCATION CLASSROOM

This section will discuss how Bandura's (2004) **Social Cognitive Theory (SCT)** supports the use of skills-based health education, and how it can be used as a theoretical framework. This section will provide some examples of what skills-based health education might "look like" in the classroom. The research review later in this chapter will provide evidence from studies that support the use of skills-based health education; as a result, this will not be discussed here.

SCT offers a framework that supports the use of skills-based health education in the classroom, specifically the inclusion of knowledge, attitudes, and skills. SCT suggests that health behavior is determined by knowledge, perceived self-efficacy that one has control over his or her health habits, outcome expectations, health goals, and perceived facilitators and impediments to action (Bandura, 2004). This section will discuss each piece of the SCT and then will suggest ways to implement this in health education classrooms.

The first determinant of health behavior is *knowledge* (Bandura, 2004). A student must have knowledge about behaviors, both risky and health-enhancing, as a stimulus for change. In the context of skills-based health education, knowledge refers to both content knowledge *and* knowledge of skills, because content alone is not enough to stimulate behavior change. The knowledge component only lays the foundation for the other influences on health behavior and health behavior changes.

In the classroom, the knowledge component can be implemented in a variety of ways. The content can be presented through direct instruction, videos, scenarios, research projects, and reading materials, to name a few methods. The actual method used should be determined by deciding how to best meet the needs of the students. Skills-based health education does support the need for content knowledge but also suggests the content should set the context for the teaching of skills and developing healthy attitudes.

The second part of knowledge as a health determinant in skills-based health education is skill knowledge. Teaching health education skills is very similar to teaching skills in physical education. Skills are modeled for the students, students are provided with skill cues to help them understand the step-by-step process of performing the skill, and feedback is provided to help them perform the skill correctly. The same steps should be used in skills-based health education. Students should be provided with time to observe the skill being modeled by the teacher, a classmate, or another individual, and then time should be spent allowing students to practice the skill. Feedback should be provided about the skill performance to help students achieve success.

Goal setting will be used to demonstrate how this might be implemented in the classroom. First, students are taught the SMART acronym for goal setting, which states that goals should be specific, measurable, attainable/adjustable, realistic, and time-based. Next, students are presented with examples of SMART goals and are asked to identify each component of the SMART acronym in the goals. Examples of goals that are not SMART could also be provided, and students could be asked to identify why the goals don't represent SMART goals. Then students are given opportunities to write

their own goals using the SMART acronym, allowing them to practice goal setting. These goals then are evaluated and students are provided with feedback to help them learn to set SMART goals. This could be followed up with an assignment asking students to try and fulfill their goals by keeping a journal and recording their thoughts and reflections about the journey. This is just one example of how modeling, observation, practice, and feedback can be used in the classroom to teach a health skill. To best serve students, health educators should think about health knowledge as both content and skills and create methods to teach these that will best enable students to learn and transfer the knowledge into the real-world setting.

Once a student knows and understands the content and skills necessary for health behavior change, the next step is to assist the student in developing **self-efficacy**, which is the belief that their actions will produce the desired results (Bandura, 2004, p. 144). In the skills-based health education classroom this can be done by allowing students to practice health skills such as decision making and refusal skills in a safe environment, but also through assessment and evaluation (feedback) of the skills. Ideally, this practice, assessment, and evaluation should be performed in a lifelike or authentic setting, which will allow for application and transfer of skills.

To develop self-efficacy, it is helpful to use scenarios and/or role play so the students are able to perform the skills and witness the positive outcomes. Include student input here because they know the types of situations they are dealing with in their lives and can help create more realistic situations. Relevant and applicable scenarios used in class will result in better transfer of skills and learning when students need to use the skills outside of the classroom. Keep in mind that allowing them to practice skills is not enough; feedback must be given to help students attain levels of competence in these skills, which will subsequently increase their self-efficacy. Helping students develop high levels of self-efficacy in applying the health skills learned in the classroom will have a significant impact on the other health behavior determinants, including goals and outcomes.

Outcome expectations refer to the expectations students have about the outcomes of their health-related actions (Bandura, 2004). One reason this is particularly important for health education is that health education typically occurs in the adolescent years when peer pressure and peer acceptance are extremely important (as shown in the preceding scenarios and by research, but this is beyond the scope of this article). Students can be taught the necessary skills in the classroom and can practice and master the skills to build self-efficacy, but what happens after that?

To facilitate positive outcome expectations, the skills-based approach includes educating students about attitudes and beliefs surrounding health behaviors and actions. For example, in the role play situation discussed earlier, the students were taught the skills through modeling, observation, practice, and feedback and the students feel high levels of self-efficacy in using the skill in the classroom. However, the ultimate goal is for students to feel the same levels of self-efficacy when applying the skill outside of the classroom. Outside of the classroom, their friends are pressuring them to use drugs, perhaps making the student feel guilty, ashamed, or "uncool" (as in Becky's case). Despite their self-efficacy developed in the classroom, they might *expect* a negative outcome in the real world as a result of these pressures that weren't present in the class-

room. In order to best prepare students for the realities of these actions, the health educator also needs to address outcome expectations by discussing these outside factors, bringing them into scenarios and allowing students to talk about and reflect on how the outcomes expectations will influence their ability and confidence in using the skill. It is important for the teacher to help students realize that not as many people are engaging in these behaviors as they believe and show them that not "everyone is doing it." Teachers could also help students understand the potential consequences to their actions and the actions of others. This is another piece of skills-based health education that will be determined by the needs of the students because every group and every student faces different struggles, different situations, and different pressures.

SCT suggests that another key determinant in health behavior is having goals as well as plans for accomplishing those goals (Bandura, 2004). Students must be able to make appropriate, realistic goals and must be able to formulate plans to accomplish these goals. This can help keep students motivated in the face of setbacks and negative experiences and can help them make long-term changes in their lifestyles. This directly relates to the previous discussion about SMART, but highlights the importance of the skill of goal setting in health education. Without the ability to set goals, students will struggle to make the changes necessary to support a healthy lifestyle. Skills-based health education will not only teach students goal-setting skills but also allow them opportunities to apply these skills and develop goals that can help them live healthier lives.

Lastly, SCT suggests that students must understand *perceived facilitators and impediments* (Bandura, 2004). The National

Health Education Standards include standards regarding analyzing influences, accessing valid information, and the ability to advocate for themselves and others. These are processes that can help students realize and understand the potential facilitators and impediments to their health behaviors and their health-related actions. Skills-based health education will provide students with the knowledge and skills necessary to identify and, hopefully, overcome obstacles and take advantage of facilitating factors and influences in their lives.

There is no "right way" to teach about facilitators and impediments in the classroom. Knowledge of pedagogy and creativity will assist you in determining the best ways to help students learn about the facilitators and impediments to being healthy and making health-enhancing decisions. It is important to recognize that identifying facilitators and impediments is very personal, so health educators should allow time for students to reflect on their own situations and perhaps have group discussions in which students (if comfortable) share their own situations or situations they have been in and discuss the facilitators and impediments. Guide students to develop strategies to enhance the facilitators and decrease and overcome any impediments.

Knowledge, self-efficacy, outcome expectations, goals, and perceived facilitators and impediments influence a student's ability and desire to change health behaviors (Bandura, 2004). In a skills-based classroom, students are presented with content and skill *knowledge*, are allowed time to practice and master skills (which can increase *self-efficacy* as well as *outcome expectations*), and are encouraged to work together, but also are encouraged to reflect on their own, which can influence *outcome expectations* and *perceived facilitators and impediments*.

The SCT provides support for the use and effectiveness of implementing skills-based health education in your classroom.

There is no one way to implement skills-based health education. The health educator should determine the needs of the students, establish the objectives to achieve, and build a curriculum that integrates knowledge, skills, and attitudes to help students to be healthy, health-literate individuals. Many of the ideas for implementation presented in this article can be classified as **participatory learning**. Participatory learning uses processes similar to those that naturally assist children in learning behaviors (modeling, observation, and practice), with the added benefit of allowing students to practice these behaviors in a safe environment and, in the case of a classroom, receive feedback to help them achieve competence (World Health Organization, 2003). Skills-based health education teaching methods should focus on interactive, participatory learning and instruction through which students learn knowledge, skills, and attitudes regarding health that will assist them in creating and maintaining a healthy lifestyle.

■ WHY SKILLS-BASED HEALTH EDUCATION?

The CDC reports that each day 4,000 adolescents ages 12–17 try a cigarette; of the 19 million new cases of sexually transmitted diseases each year, almost half are in people ages 15–24; and alcohol is used by adolescents more than illicit drugs or tobacco and accounts for 41% of motor vehicle deaths (CDC, 2009). These statistics suggest that there is a need for health education that works, in which teachers can teach students what they need to be healthy and avoid risky health behaviors. This is especially important at the secondary level (middle and high school) because students are in a critical stage in their lives when they are developing the behaviors and lifestyles that they will embrace and carry into adulthood. Skills-based health education is one approach that has the potential to help schools improve health education and provide students with an education that helps them become health-literate individuals who will live healthy, productive lives.

CONCLUSION

There is a need for quality, effective health education in our schools. One method for providing students with this education is to use a skills-based health curriculum that teaches them the knowledge, skills, and attitudes that will enable them to adopt health-enhancing behaviors and avoid risky health behaviors. This article has defined skills-based health education, provided support for the need for skills in health education, and discussed Social Cognitive Theory (SCT), which provides a framework for understanding and supporting the efficacy of using a skills-based approach. Lastly, this article has briefly discussed some ideas for methods of implementing the components of skills-based health education in the classroom. Reflect on what has been presented here and decide how to best integrate skills-based health education into current or future practice. Educators have the unique opportunity to teach students what they need to know: the knowledge, skills, and attitudes they need to live healthy, productive lives. Using skills-based health education will help health educators make the best of this opportunity. Some parting words of inspiration: "No knowledge is more crucial than knowledge about health. Without it, no other life goal can be successfully achieved" (Allensworth, 1993, p. 1).

KEY WORDS AND DEFINITIONS

health education   A comprehensive curriculum that includes a variety of health topics, that addresses various dimensions of wellness, and that provides opportunities for students to gain knowledge, develop competence in skills, and develop attitudes that will allow them to become healthy individuals.

health literacy   The goal of a comprehensive health education curriculum, defined as the ability of an individual to become healthy and maintain health through their lifetime by using a variety of health-enhancing skills.

participatory learning   A style or method of learning/instruction that uses modeling, observation, and practice to teach skills and that encourages and facilitates student involvement in the learning and teaching process.

self-efficacy   A person's belief that they can do something.

skills   Something students need to be able to *do* and have competence in to lead healthy lifestyles by avoiding risky behaviors and engaging in health-enhancing behaviors (e.g., goal-setting).

skills-based health education   A curriculum designed around teaching students skills in the context of health. This includes teaching specific sets of skills, establishing beliefs and attitudes towards health that are health enhancing, and providing students with the knowledge they need to apply the skills and be healthy. This is similar to the definition of health education, but the key point to remember is *the focus is on skills*. The planning should start with expected behavioral outcomes based on health-related skills and then specific content should be included.

Social Cognitive Theory (SCT) A theory that proposes that health behavior is determined by knowledge, perceived self-efficacy that one has control over their health habits, outcome expectations, health goals, and perceived facilitators and impediments to action (Bandura, 2004).

■ DISCUSSION QUESTIONS

1. Based on the information presented in this article, do you think skills-based health education is an effective way of teaching health? Why or why not?
2. How would you plan a skills-based health curriculum? How is it different from/similar to planning a non-skills-based health curriculum?
3. How do you think students would react to a skills-based health education? Why?
4. How would teachers react? Why?
5. What are the key points to take away from this article? How will you use this information?

■ REFERENCES

Allensworth, D. D. (1993). Health education: State of the art. *Journal of School Health Education, 63*(1), 14.

Bandura, A. (2004). Health promotion by social cognitive means. *Health Education & Behavior, 31*(2), 143–164.

Centers for Disease Control and Prevention. (2007). Coordinated school health. Retrieved August 8, 2009, from http://www.cdc.gov/HealthyYouth/CSHP/#1

Centers for Disease Control and Prevention. (2009). Health topics. Retrieved September 6, 2009, from http://www.cdc.gov/HealthyYouth/healthtopics/index.htm

Gold, R. S., & Miner, K. R. (2002). Report of the 2000 Joint Committee on Health Education and Promotion Terminology. *Journal of School Health, 71*(2), 3–7.

Joint Committee on Nation Health Education Standards. (2007). *National health education standards: Achieving excellence* (2nd ed.). Atlanta, GA: American Cancer Society.

World Health Organization. (2003). Skills-based health education including life skills: An important component of a Child-Friendly/Health-Promoting School. Retrieved May 31, 2011, from http://whqlibdoc.who.int/publications/2003/924159103X.pdf

The State of Health Curricula Today

David Nichols

In their quest to improve the lives of others, health educators are continuously in search of exciting ways to positively influence the behavior of their students. This commitment to making a difference in the health of others steers the curricula as students are encouraged to make good decisions. Vital health information is passed along by educators in diverse ways in an attempt to promote safety and enrich the lives of those under their tutelage. Methods of instruction constantly evolve as teachers combat the abuse of drugs, mental illness, sexually transmitted diseases, teen pregnancy, and the influences that impact premature disease. A **comprehensive health education** approach is necessary in this pursuit because learning styles and individual uniqueness necessitate varied instruction.

No student is exactly like another, and it has become apparent to the majority of health educators that there is a need to attack instruction from different perspectives. Historically, curriculum initiatives with a narrow focus that plead with students to "Just Say No" have proven to be unsuccessful at reducing risky behaviors. Programs that stress abstinence only in sexuality education have not achieved the lofty goal of significantly curtailing promiscuous behavior. Health instruction simply has to do better. A comprehensive approach that assists in the prevention of the onset of disease and increases life span and quality of life is essential. Students need to become proficient in interacting with others in order to function at optimal levels. Fortunately, in the past decade we have gotten a handle on what works for many students in the prevention of risky behaviors. Health educators armed with established curricula can now improve student well-being because proven health resources and guidance are well within reach.

The federal government's release of *Healthy People 2020* (http://www.healthypeople.gov) sets goals for health promotion and disease prevention. The ambitious promotion highlights a 10-year strategy committed to promoting health and preventing illness, disability, and premature death. *Healthy People 2020* is committed to the vision of a society in which all people live long, healthy lives. This includes several new features to help make this vision a reality:

- Emphasizing ideas of health equity that address social determinants of health and promote health across all stages of life
- Replacing the traditional print publication with an interactive website as the main vehicle for dissemination
- Maintaining a website that allows users to tailor information to their needs and explore evidence-based resources for implementation

There is also a new application (http://www.challenge.gov) called, "myHealthyPeople" that will assist communities and work places in tracking progress with the objectives through special apps. This valuable resource maps out the nation's needs and the path we should take to combat destructive influences.

The National Health Education Standards developed in 2007 by the Joint Committee on National Health Standards recognizes the critical role of schools in combating our nation's health problems while simultaneously acknowledging research-based advances related to effective practices in the field. Teachers and administrators can use these standards as a framework for designing or selecting curricula and for providing a basis for assessment of student achievement. Individual states, under the guidance of their departments of education, also have published frameworks that coincide with the National Health Standards and serve as local guides to provide students with the benchmarks needed to lead healthy lives. These statewide frameworks synthesize current research and set learning standards for elementary, middle, and high school students. National and state health education guidelines assist in the determination of what should be taught, but local needs must be examined to truly tailor the curriculum to a specific community. An extremely valuable source of information that can help teachers and administrators ascertain the risk status of their students is the Centers for Disease Control and Prevention's (2007) Youth Risk Behavior Surveillance System. This national survey provides information on risk behaviors and patterns of negative or positive change. After health standards are researched and surveys scrutinized, a comprehensive health education plan can be enacted. The need for a total approach to maximize the health literacy of our children is paramount in guiding the direction of health initiatives.

For many years health education teachers introduced **home-grown health programs** full of ideas that they guessed would be successful in educating students and provide positive learning experiences. Often a trial and error system dictated what lessons would be taught. Word of mouth and suggested favorite lessons governed the selection of instruction, rather than instruction designed around long-term outcomes to meet the needs of the targeted audience. Health education programs were not consistent in their approach or comprehensive in their overall service. Well-meaning teachers struggled to keep pace with the times and attend to teaching trends. In 1994, Congress directed the U.S. Department of Education's Office of Educational Research and Improvement to establish panels of experts and practitioners to evaluate health programs and to recognize those that were considered to be exemplary or promising. Suddenly, it was not necessary for school systems to reinvent the wheel. After establishing local needs, teachers could instruct their students in prevention programming judged against rigorous criteria that were proven to be effective. These **exemplary/promising programs** completed with fidelity are now able to change behavior positively and instill risk-protective factors for intended populations and settings. Home-grown initiatives are still needed to provide a variety of approaches within comprehensive programming, but only when coupled with tried and true exemplary programs that have documented success. The selection and implementation of such programs has changed the landscape of health education because results can be measured statistically over time.

Effective health curricula are comprehensive in scope and are designed to provide a myriad of learning experiences for students during their school years. Health education is a process that teaches students to develop knowledge about healthful decision making, and this process continues by facilitating learning experiences that influence better life choices. This article is primarily concerned with early childhood through secondary school; however, health instruction should continue after secondary school in higher education settings and in personal growth initiatives. A comprehensive prevention program should begin in early childhood; plans must promote responsible decision making and develop resilience from the outset. Young children must be encouraged to take initiatives toward positive health and believe that their actions will benefit themselves and others. It is necessary to start at the very beginning of the educational continuum with a process, not an event. In order for children to internalize a sense of self-confidence and to appropriately handle external pressure in later years, confidence must be built upon daily. Speakers or special programs can pique interest, but are not likely to change behavior over time. Carefully chosen programs will achieve desired results.

One such program that builds resiliency is the U.S. Department of Education–recommended Reach Out to Schools: Social Competency Program, *Open Circle Curriculum*. Based at the Stone Center at Wellesley College and first piloted in 1986, the program targets elementary students in kindergarten through fifth grade by focusing on social competency skills such as communication, self-control, and problem solving. This program encourages teachers to set up twice weekly class meetings that last for 15 to 30 minutes so children can practice and learn social skills. Students role play, discuss, and learn to identify and squelch conflicts. A **common health language** carries from grade to grade, fostering communication among the classroom teacher, specialists, and students. The exemplary program Life Skills Training (National Health Promotion Associates [NHPA], 1998), created by Gilbert Botvin, also addresses a wide variety of risk factors and social skills in conjunction with drug prevention. The 3-year elementary program begins in the third grade. Lessons are geared toward decision making, communication, social skills, advertising, stress, tobacco information, and assertiveness. Sequential instruction is provisioned in student guides that encourage students to write in a problem-solving manner. Writing prompts encourage students to take ownership of a variety of topics and blend nicely with school literacy goals. This program continues in the adolescent years with another 3-year prevention curriculum intended to prevent tobacco, alcohol, and drug abuse. It is well documented by reviewers selected by the U.S. Department of Education that students who participate in this program demonstrate a statistically significant decrease in levels of tobacco, alcohol, and marijuana use compared with control groups.

There is no recommended national curriculum currently available that all schools can follow; however, state models, such as the Michigan Model (Educational Materials Center, 2003), by the Michigan Department of Community Health, have been adopted by several communities because of their strong parental involvement. This curriculum reinforces prevention messages from a variety of sources and provides lessons incorporating skills-based instruction for students in grades K–12. Growing Healthy (National Center for Health Education, 2005) teaches children in kindergarten through sixth grade about their bodies and the principles of health and wellness. The curriculum is based on the premise that children are more likely to establish good habits early if they truly understand the workings of their body. Second Step, by the Committee for Children (2009), is a school-based violence prevention program for students in pre-K through ninth grade that can change children's attitudes and beliefs about violence. The program instructs children about the warning signs of aggressive behavior and bullying. NetSmartz, from the National Center for Missing and Exploited Children (2009), is an interactive safety resource that uses online training to teach children in elementary and secondary schools how to be safer when using the Internet. This program is free of charge and is continually modified to meet ever-changing communication demands.

Kindergarten through second grade curricula can initiate learning components that engage children using current literature of interest. Messages of personal safety, body awareness, and nutrition should begin at this early stage of development. Then, the upper elementary years are an opportune time to introduce science-based curricula where a knowledge of body systems such as the respiratory, digestive, cardiovascular, nervous, and endocrine systems are explored. It is of the utmost importance that children at an early age have a basic and age-appropriate knowledge about the functions of their bodies. The impact of teaching these systems at this age can peak the excitement of self-awareness, and can also aid in decision making. For example, it can be dangerous to provide a list of detrimental inhalant acts to children because providing information about these acts might arouse risky behavior in some. It is hoped that students with a knowledgeable background gained at the appropriate time will understand the impact of impairing vital systems and therefore not attempt risky behavior. It is also appropriate to discuss students' changing bodies and puberty within science-based systems units because the very nature of the subject takes on a more mature educational meaning after reviewing other major body physiology.

A number of different strategies are used in the design of exemplary curricula; however, similarities exist in all of them. All quality programs establish evidence of effectiveness and have explicit goals with respect to changing behavior. Promising programs consider the stage of the intended population and the setting where the curriculum will be taught. Role playing often is used as an effective strategy in which students act out scenarios that assist them in resisting negative external pressure. Positive decision-making skills are encouraged as students convert real life circumstances into action.

Curricula designed to change behavior use different tactics in their pursuit of instilling protective factors in students. Life Skills Training (NHPA, 1998) in the adolescent years stresses reflective student writing. Toward No Tobacco Use (Project TNT) uses novel games designed for fifth through eighth graders to teach the short- and long-term consequences of cigarettes and smokeless tobacco use (Substance Abuse and Mental Health Services Administration, 2009). TNT instructs students in how to replace negative impressions of resisting peer pressure with proactive positive thoughts. Project Alert (Best Foundation, 2009), a drug prevention program for middle school students that focuses on tobacco, alcohol, marijuana, and inhalants, uses a series of video portrayals to dispel the student belief that drug use is widespread. This program motivates students to identify pressures to use drugs and teaches them to rebut messages encouraging them to use. Finally, Project Northland (Hazelden Information and Educational Services, 2009), a multiyear alcohol use prevention program for students in grades six through eight, incorporates audiotape vignettes that lead discussions that help to delay the use of alcohol. Although it is beyond the scope of this article, leading research indicates that limiting early onset assists in reducing alcohol-related problems among students.

Parent–student discussion of peer relationships, rules in the home, and the influence of media are included in comprehensive programs that are successful in curtailing negative behavior. Recognizing that students often resist conversation with parents about health concerns and risky behaviors, teachers can initiate necessary discussion in homework assignments. Students can complete assignments that promote parent interviews, garnering their opinions on health topics. Conducting interviews within the community at large is another effective strategy. An interview assignment that asks the question of a local citizen that uses tobacco, "Are you happy that you smoke?" is sure to promote an enlightening and memorable response. Problem-solving questions that lead to making an actual commitment can serve as catalysts for meaningful discussion. Students asked to respond to the question, "If you were at a party and an acquaintance appeared to pass out due to alcohol consumption would you let them sleep it off, walk them around, or get help?" must come to terms with their decision. Ideally, should the situation occur in real life they would have the insight to react in an appropriate way, learning that in a medical emergency help is needed.

Project Northland's eighth-grade curriculum (Hazelden Information and Educational Services, 2009) takes the party scenario one step further by teaching students about community influences on alcohol use. Recommendations for community action are discussed as various players involved in a party, including parents and the police, dramatize roles and actions. Northland's high school curriculum, Class Action, developed from research funding by the National Institute on Alcohol Abuse and Alcoholism, examines the social and legal consequences of underage drinking through six court cases. Students are provisioned with casebooks, information on existing laws, alcohol information, affidavits, and depositions. Students serve as jurors and act out relevant roles in cases that probe drinking and driving, fetal alcohol syndrome, date rape, violence, vandalism, and school alcohol policies.

Guest speakers can spark interest in the health curriculum, but caution must be taken. For many years educational institutions featured their favorite speakers, hoping to impact students favorably. **One hit wonders** should not take the place of a comprehensive program and often can be detrimental. The former substance abuse addict who provides testimony to past indiscretions and later recovery often takes on a heroic persona. Students can feel they could beat the abusive cycles as well, instead of not using in the first place. Time and time again speakers address students in a language that is difficult for them to understand or insultingly demeaning. Resource speakers must be carefully chosen for their expertise and willingness to guide instructional objectives. Physicians, nutritionists, safety personnel, and health agency representatives can be valuable additions to a program, but they must be able to relate to their target audience.

Fellow students can provide empathy for causes that emphasize understanding. It can be quite helpful for high school students to speak as peer educators to those in the middle school because their influence can be extremely positive. One school system in the Boston area actively reverses this process as elementary students write letters and speak to high school students, telling them that they look up to them as their babysitters, coaches, referees, and counselors. They then ask the older students not to drink alcohol and especially not to drink and drive because they do not want them to get hurt. Although this tactic would not work in every community, it has proven to be an effective deterrent to the abuse of alcohol.

For many years, teachers, parents, and even religious organizations have tried in vain to scare youth straight so students won't participate in high-risk behavior. Despite decades of antidrug programs that stressed the negative results of participating in at-risk behaviors, a significant impact on student behavior has been unattainable. Educators, realizing this, have recently turned to a "social norms" approach to combat substance abuse. Rather than frightening students out of misbehaving, **social norming** uses the results from detailed survey data to convince students that most young people are already refraining from risky behavior and they should too. If students believe an outcome will be positive and viewed by others as positive they are more apt to do it. Knowing that peer pressure can be based on perception, focus groups organize campaigns to spread the message of positive behavior. Exhibiting posters and flyers along with public service announcements and media portrayals can positively alter the impression that large numbers of students engage in risky behaviors.

Social norming operates under the principle that most students are "good kids," who do not participate in outrageous and dangerous behaviors. There has been criticism of social norming approaches, especially on college campuses, because a young person's environment can have as powerful an effect on behavior as expectation. However, high school students and middle school students clearly feel that more students engage in risky behaviors than actually do, and by providing accurate data in a positive way, negative misperceptions can be thwarted. By reframing data that usually highlights the negative actions of a few students, a comprehensive program can feature the majority who are not.

Health educators are cognizant of the effect they have on their students and often are eager to convince those students of ways to protect their health. It is important to be honest in this quest because misinformation can hamper the intended response. Years ago, trusted health personnel, knowing the dangers of steroid misuse, implied that steroids do not enhance muscular strength. Instead of focusing on the danger of side effects, well-meaning educators twisted the truth in an attempt to encourage students not to engage in this risky behavior. The net result was that steroid use increased and students wondered what other falsehoods they had been told.

A teacher's integrity is of the utmost importance in all health instruction. It is advantageous to use accurate, scientific information and strategies that involve research-based practices. It is also necessary to recognize the link between the objective and the best method to reach that objective. An example of this link between objective and activity comes in the observation of a savvy teacher stressing the consequences of partaking in sexual activity. The instructor passes around a jar filled entirely with white beans and requests that each student close their eyes, reach in, and select a bean. All students receive a white bean and the class is told, "This is your chance of getting a sexually transmitted infection or becoming pregnant if you refrain from sexual contact. No chance at all." The instructor then searches the Internet for the latest up-to-date

information that gives statistical data on percentages of obtaining a variety of infections from participating in sexual activity. She or he estimates the number of colored beans that represent the percentage of a variety of infections and drops them in the jar. The teacher then repeats the process with the chance of pregnancy and puts more beans in the jar. Finally, he or she asks each student to once again, close their eyes and select a bean. The students visibly see "who got what" and identify immediately with the meaning of the statistical information provided. Matching methods to content so that students have a clear idea of the information being given is central to the development of the curriculum.

Health education can be very personal, and methods that may be successful in reaching one student may not be effective or meet the needs of another. It is vital to try a variety of instructional approaches to reach preset educational objectives, but it must be realized that the teacher will not be able to prevent risky behaviors in all. It is, therefore, necessary to teach students at both ends of the **risk behavior spectrum**. A lesson on the necessity of designated drivers may not be appropriate for high school students because they are not of legal drinking age; however, those students who do engage in risky behavior must be reminded, "Although I don't believe it is a good idea for you to drink alcohol, if you make a different choice never get behind the wheel."

Curriculum design needs to assess the intended population, discover why a lesson may falter, and outline lessons in meaningful ways. For example, a teacher in a comprehensive health education program constantly stresses to students the reasons why they should abstain from promiscuous sexual behavior. However, after surveying classes he or she discovers that several students are participating in dangerous experimental behavior. The teacher then teaches methods of birth control and what he or she deems "safer" sexual practices. Not satisfied that he or she is doing the best for the students, the teacher then interviews several of them, only to discover that there is a disturbing lack of verbal communication between the girls and boys in the class in regards to sex. Students are simply afraid to discuss sexual intimacy, much less safe sex practices, with the opposite sex. The teacher then designs activities that encourage more and clearer conversations between boys and girls. In mock scenarios the teacher pairs off students to practice discussing safer sex and birth control methods. The learning atmosphere created is one where students feel supported and are able to express their innermost fears with partners. It is not surprising that schools that use instruction that meets the direct needs of their students are able to decrease sexual intercourse and activity rates over time.

CONCLUSION

The successful selection of methods and resources to implement in a health education curriculum answers the charge, "Let us put our minds together and see what we can do for our students." An effective comprehensive curriculum combines a variety of approaches with both exemplary practices and homegrown ingenuity. Teachers who know that there is nothing more important than their interaction with students and who wake up each morning thinking of ways to make students become more resilient need to be at the center of the selection of activities. Attention must be paid to those who tirelessly prepare exercises that help increase student comprehension and who understand that there are multiple ways of nurturing decision making. Administrators must realize that the education of the child and ultimate happiness of students has so much more to do with feeling good about yourself and connectedness than with pencil and paper. The impact of health on the student clearly impacts academic success. It is unreasonable to expect students engaged in substance abuse, disordered eating, risky sexual behavior, and depression to fully achieve their maximum academic potential. Health affects students in so many ways. Leaders who are instrumental in creating the necessary environment and curriculum guidance that provide students with an atmosphere filled with belonging truly can make a difference.

KEY WORDS AND DEFINITIONS

common health language Terminology and similar experiences introduced in health programs in order to foster increased communication among students and teachers. Social competency skills are reinforced that build a sense of community and promote positive relationships.

comprehensive health education Coordinated school programs designed to deliver and evaluate planned and varied curricula with goals, objectives, and a content sequence. Comprehensive health education takes into consideration different learning styles and individual uniqueness.

exemplary/promising health programs The identification and designation of health programs that promote safe, disciplined, and drug-free schools. Programs that are proven effective when judged against rigorous criteria.

home-grown health programs Health education programs and activities devised by local teachers and administrators that are designed to provide positive learning experiences. Favorite lessons often govern the selection of instruction.

one hit wonders Resource speakers, plays, and demonstrations designed to have a positive impact on a student audience so as to change behavior and enrich health instruction.

risk behavior spectrum Behavioral, environmental, and inherited influences that provoke action toward behavior that promotes ill health.

social norming Rather than scaring students out of participating in risky behaviors, this strategy uses survey data of actual student behavior to accentuate the fact that many students do the right thing. The intent of the approach is that if students knew the truth they would feel less pressure to engage in dangerous activities.

■ DISCUSSION QUESTIONS

1. A number of steps are suggested before planning a curriculum. What data should be analyzed, and why is a comprehensive approach necessary?

2. Total reliance on home-grown initiatives has historically led curriculum planning astray. Is there a place for these activities in a comprehensive health program?

3. Why are different strategies necessary in prevention?

4. One technique available to combat risky behavior in middle school students is social norming. Explore ways to use a statistically positive approach to promote healthy behavior.

5. What are other examples of exemplary/ promising health education programs? Research one program presented—or not—in this article. Be prepared to present a 5-minute, data-based review to the class.

■ REFERENCES

BEST Foundation for a Drug-Free Tomorrow. (2009). *Project alert*. Santa Monica, CA: RAND.

Centers for Disease Control and Prevention. (2007). *Youth risk behavior surveillance system*. Atlanta, GA: Author.

Committee for Children. (2009). *Second step: A violence prevention curriculum*. Seattle, WA: Author.

Educational Materials Center. (2003). *Michigan model for comprehensive school health education curriculum*. Mt. Pleasant, MI: Central Michigan University.

Hazelden Information and Educational Services. (2009). *Project Northland*. Center City, MN: Author.

Healthy People 2020. *The mission, vision, and goals of Healthy People 2020*. Retrieved June 15, 2011, from http://www.healthypeople.gov/2020/TopicsObjectives2020/pdfs/HP2020_brochure.pdf

Joint Committee on Health Education Standards. (2007). *National health education standards: Achieving excellence*. Athens, GA: American Cancer Society.

National Center for Health Education. (2005). *Growing healthy*. New York: Author.

National Center for Missing and Exploited Children. (2009). NetSmartz. Retrieved May 31, 2011, from http://www.netsmartz.org

National Health Promotion Associates. (1998). *Life skills training*. Hartsdale, NY: Author.

Office of Disease Prevention and Health Promotion. (2002). *Healthy People 2010: National health promotion and disease prevention objectives*. Washington, DC: U.S. Department of Health and Human Services.

Reach Out to Schools: Social Competency Program. (2009). *Open circle curriculum*. Wellesley, MA: Wellesley College, The Stone Center.

Substance Abuse and Mental Health Services Administration. (2009). *Project towards no tobacco*. Washington, DC: U.S. Department of Health and Human Services.

Research Review

Physical Activity and Physical Education Curricula Using Technology

Emily Clapham

A single subject research design (ABAB) was used to examine the amount and level of participation in physical activity among 106 suburban fourth and fifth graders during physical education class and whether the use of a **technological device** and/or teacher instruction contributed to increased participation in physical activity. Although the research focus was on the **amount and level of activity** in the gymnasium, the use of the technological devices, either a **heart rate monitor (HRM)** or a **pedometer (PED)**, was studied. A curriculum, which was **interdisciplinary** (lessons) and based on the **skill theme curriculum** pedagogically centered on the use of the technological devices and written specifically for the study, was also developed and studied.

A pilot study (Clapham, 2007) was conducted a semester prior to implementation. Fourth- and fifth-grade subjects from an urban school were asked to participate in the research project. Six preservice physical education teachers were asked to teach in the study. The researcher held 8 hours of teacher training for the preservice teachers. There were six participant groups:

> Group 1: HRM-instruction (HRM-I)
> Group 2: HRM (HRM)
> Group 3: HRM-control (HRM-Control)
> Group 4: PED-instruction (PED-I)
> Group 5: PED (PED)
> Group 6: PED-Control (PED-Control)

Major revisions were made to the design of the research project upon the completion of this pilot study.

There also were six participant groups employed for this research. There were three fourth-grade PED groups and three fifth-grade HRM groups. The HRM and PED groups wore HRMs and PEDs, respectively, while participating in typical or traditional physical education classes. The activities alternated between locomotor activities, like tag games, and manipulative activities, like striking, kicking, and dribbling. The HRM SC and PED SC groups wore the technological devices and received **supportive curricula (SC)**/instruction with the devices representative of the New Physical Education (PE). The supportive curricula lessons included the same activities as the traditional PE classes; however, these lessons offered rationale and background information on using the HRMs and PEDs. The students were taught how to read and interpret their step count and heart rate information from the devices. The students were also asked to look at their step counts and heart rate information periodically throughout the lessons. The traditional PE classes wore the devices and participated in their PE class without receiving this supportive information from the teacher. The No HRM group wore a pedometer and received the same supportive curricula as the HRM SC group.

This group served as the HRM control group because it would determine whether the supportive curricula encouraged students to produce more physical activity or whether it was actually the HRM device. One experienced physical education teacher taught all of the groups to ensure credibility and reliability.

Steps/minute data were collected from the PED groups. Averages of steps/minute were calculated and a one-way analysis of variance (ANOVA) was conducted to compare the groups to one another. Steps/minute and heart rate data also were collected from the HRM groups. Averages of steps/minute and heart rate in beats per minute (bpm) were calculated and a one-way ANOVA was conducted for both measurements. The results pointed towards a correlation between supportive curricula for HRMs and PEDs and an increased level and amount of physical activity.

The average steps/minute for the PED groups were:

- *PED SC A:* 69.9 steps/minute
- *PED SC B:* 89.52 steps/minute
- *PED:* 72.64 steps/minute

Table 1-1 displays the results and significance of the PED groups. The PED SC A and B groups wore PEDs and received the supportive curriculum (New PE) from the physical education teacher. The PED group wore the PEDs and received a traditional PE curriculum. The table outlines the results from the PED groups indicating which groups were significant at the 0.05 level. The study alternated between 2 weeks of baseline data in which all of the groups received the same lessons and 2 weeks of treatment data in which the PED SC A and B groups received the New PE curriculum and the PED group received the traditional PE curriculum.

The first two baseline weeks indicated that the two PED SC groups are significantly different at the 0.05 level. The first two treatments indicated that PED SC A is significantly different from PED SC B in treatment two. This means that PED SC A was naturally more active than PED SC B according to the baseline data collected. Baseline three and treatment three indicated that the PED SC B group was more affected by the treatment conditions than PED SC A in that there was a carryover effect in baseline three and a significantly higher

TABLE 1-1 Fourth-Grade Pedometer Groups Results	
Treatment Condition	**Significance at the 0.05 Level**
Baseline one	PED SC A < PED SC B
Baseline two	PED SC A > PED SC B
Treatment one	No significance
Treatment two	PED SC A > PED SC B
Baseline three	PED SC A < PED SC B PED SC B > PED
Baseline four	No significance
Treatment three	PED SC A < PED SC B PED SC B > PED
Treatment four	No significance

number of steps taken in treatment three. Although it is difficult to draw conclusions from this data, the PED SC A and B groups were consistently the most active after the treatment sessions.

The average steps/minute and average bpm for the HRM groups were:

- *HRM:* 98 steps/minute and 143.36 bpm
- *HRM SC:* 116 steps/minute and 153 bpm
- *No HRM SC:* 89 steps/minute

Table 1-2 displays the results and significance of the HRM groups. Similar to the PED groups, the study alternated between 2 weeks of baseline data in which all of the groups received the same lessons and 2 weeks of treatment data in which the HRM SC group received the New PE curriculum and the HRM group received the traditional PE curriculum. In addition, there was a No HRM SC group. This group did not wear the HRMs but received the same supportive curriculum that the HRM SC received.

The results indicated that the HRM was more active than the HRM SC group and the No HRM group. In treatments one and two the HRM SC group had significantly more steps and a higher heart rate than the other groups. This indicated that the treatments were effective. Baselines three and four showed no significance. In treatment three, the HRM and the HRM SC groups were more active than the No HRM SC group. Finally, in treatment four, the HRM SC group was more active than the HRM and the No HRM SC groups. This indicated that the treatment was effective and the technological device aided with a supportive curriculum was the most effective in promoting the most physical activity among fifth graders.

To summarize, the steps/minute and average heart rate data collected from the PED and HRM groups was analyzed and interpreted by the researcher. The researcher found that higher numbers during the first two baseline lessons indicated some groups were naturally more active than others. Higher numbers during treatment lessons

TABLE 1-2 Fifth-Grade Heart Rate Monitor Groups Results		
Treatment Condition	**Steps/Minute Significant at the 0.05 Level**	**Average Heart Rate Significant at the 0.05 Level**
Baseline one	HRM > HRM SC HRM > No HRM	No significance
Baseline two	No significance	HRM SC > HRM
Treatment one	HRM SC > HRM HRM SC > No HRM SC	HRM SC > HRM
Treatment two	HRM SC > HRM	HRM SC > HRM
Baseline three	No significance	No significance
Baseline four	No significance	No significance
Treatment three	HRM > No HRM SC HRM SC > No HRM SC	No significance
Treatment four	HRM SC > HRM HRM SC > No HRM SC	No significance

indicated whether the treatment groups were effective or not. In addition, higher numbers during the second two baseline lessons indicated a carryover effect from the SC as a result of treatments 1 and 2. Finally, higher numbers during treatment lessons in SC groups indicated that the technology and SC groups were more effective.

Six students were randomly selected from each group (36 students total) to participate in a mini interview group at the completion of the research project. There were three students per group, and two interview groups per participant group. This study employed a casual, unstructured interview. The results of the student interviews revealed some interesting information regarding the effect of HRMs on the level and amount of participation in PE. When asked what they enjoyed about using the HRMs, student one responded, "Just seeing my heart rate because I never really thought of it before." Student four added, "How fast your heart rate goes was very helpful" and "It is very hard to find your pulse with your fingers." Student two responded, "It's pretty cool to just see how hard you are breathing" and "I thought it was interesting to see a device that can actually show your heart rate, pretty interesting" (Clapham, 2008). When asked if the HRMs helped them to participate in PE, student one responded, "No, could still participate in activities without it." When asked if the students would like to wear the HRMs for every PE class, many of the students reported having issues with it working and taking a long time to put on the HRM. For example, student five responded, "It takes a lot of time to put on the equipment." Student six added, "I had constant issues with it working" (Clapham, 2008).

The students in the HRM SC group enjoyed wearing the HRMs, and, when asked why they enjoyed using the HRMs, student one responded, "To find out how hard we were working by looking at the heart rate." Student two responded, "To find out how hard we were working by looking at the heart rate, learning something new." Student five added, "It was something we had never done before." Student six added that the "watch—how you could see heart rate, it showed me if my heart rate was low then it showed me that I wasn't trying very hard." The students in the HRM SC group found the HRMs "Interesting, fun and educational. Could use it for different things to see your limit" (Clapham, 2008).

The students also learned new vocabulary words from the HRM and PED supportive curricula. The students in the HRM SC group learned the following words:

- *Pump:* Your heart is a pump. It pumps blood throughout your body and goes faster once you exercise.
- *Lungs:* Hold oxygen that you need to breathe.
- *Heart:* Pumps blood and keeps you alive.
- *Arteries:* Carry blood through the body away from the heart.
- *Blood vessels:* Tubes.
- *Red blood cells:* Blood cells that carry oxygen in the blood.
- *Vein:* Carries blood that travels in the body and towards the heart.

The students in the HRM group learned eight vocabulary words. They said they learned about different systems and that the pulse can be taken at the neck. The differences between these two sets of vocabulary words demonstrate a deeper level of understanding of the use of HRM in PE with the HRM SC group. Some examples of the HRM and PED words are heart rate, pulse, carotid artery, radial artery, and beats per minute. These words are regularly used in a traditional PE class. The No HRM SC group used the same words as the HRM SC group. Some examples of the PED SC words include pedometer, average gait, steps, stride, and calories.

The PE teacher was also interviewed by the researcher to gain more insight into the research project. The results of the teacher interview provided data regarding the effect of HRMs on the level and amount of participation in PE. According to the PE teacher, "Some of the students were frustrated with the time spent attaching the HRMs and getting them working." When asked if she thought the HRMs motivated the students to participate in PE, the teacher expressed a sincere interest in their value to a PE program. Overall the PE teacher felt that the benefits probably outweighed the negative issues with the students putting the HRMs on in a timely manner. The PE teacher stated "the pedometers provided motivation for self-improvement in PE class for each individual" (Clapham, 2008). Throughout the interview and implementation of the SC, the PE teacher viewed the PEDs as a better motivation tool because they were easier for the students to use. Based on the teacher interview and information from the students in the PED group, it appears as though the HRMs and PEDs did affect their participation in PE.

When asked if she thought the SC was effective, the PE teacher responded, "Yes, the students saw a correlation of rest, active, and **moderate-intensity physical activity**, and the effects on number of steps and heart rate." She also noted, "I think the curricula will influence their effort for activity level. Many students have asked to purchase HRMs and PEDs." To further demonstrate her support of the motivational tools used, the PE teacher shared a story. "One student whose parents 'opted out' would sneak a

pedometer from the rack and monitor himself—adults can't stifle a kid who wants to learn." The PE teacher added that the curriculum "Kept students focused and raised self-esteem." She also added, "My students loved the challenge of the pedometers, heart rate monitors and the intellectual challenge of the SC" (Clapham, 2008).

Several conclusions were drawn from this research project. First, for the PED groups, PEDs combined with supportive curricula may increase the amount of physical activity in fourth graders over using PEDs alone. For the HRM groups, HRMs, combined with supportive curricula, may increase the level of physical activity in fifth graders more than HRMs alone.

This research ultimately indicated that the use of technological devices accompanied with supportive curricula provided by a competent physical education teacher results in increased amounts and levels of physical activity among fourth and fifth graders. Ultimately, physical educators not only need to use technology in physical education class, but also need to provide meaningful lessons on how to interpret feedback provided by HRMs and PEDs in physical education.

In conclusion, the research provided several important recommendations for practitioners:

- HRMs and PEDs should be considered a critical tool and motivational device to combat the lack of physical activity.
- HRMs and PEDs support the New PE.
- The HRM and PED content with the supportive curricula may increase steps/minute (for HRMs and PEDs) and average heart rate (for HRMs).
- All HRM and PED vocabulary words used in the research and activities proved to be valuable in the supportive curricula.

- HRMs and PEDs helped to keep children on task and focused during PE class time.
- The HRM and PED supportive curricula may have aided in comprehension of how to use the devices in PE.
- The HRM and PED supportive curricula may have aided the PE teacher with how to incorporate these devices into PE classes.
- The supportive curricula supported the New PE.

■ KEY WORDS AND DEFINITIONS

amount of physical activity Measured by the number of steps each subject has taken. Steps are measured by the use of a pedometer. The average range of steps for fourth and fifth graders during a 45-minute physical education class was 1200–1600, 47.5 steps per minute (Clapham, 2007).

heart rate monitor (HRM) A device a person can wear that measures and displays heart rate information while participating in exercise. The device has a monitor strap held in place around the chest by an elastic band. The heart rate is displayed on a watch.

interdisciplinary lessons Academic subjects (classroom curricula) are included in the physical education curriculum. Research suggests that students learn best when movement is involved. Using activities and games collaboratively supports learning in the classroom and movement setting (Kovar et al., 2007).

level of physical activity Measured by each subject's heart rate information. Heart rate is measured in beats per minute by a heart rate monitor.

moderate-intensity physical activity A level of effort in which a person should experience: some increase in breathing or heart rate, a "perceived exertion" of 11 to 14 on the Borg scale (the effort a healthy individual might expend while walking briskly, mowing the lawn, dancing, swimming, or bicycling on level terrain), a level of 6 metabolic equivalents (METs), or any activity that burns 3.5 to 7 calories per minute (kcal/min) (Centers for Disease Control and Prevention [CDC], 2007).

pedometer (PED) A noninvasive tool that allows for instant feedback regarding a person's activity level. It measures vertical accelerations of the body (steps) and captures a variety of activities that enhance the concept of "lifestyle activity" (Rooney, Smalley, Larson, & Havens, 2003).

skill theme curriculum "Skill themes are fundamental movements that are later modified into the more specialized patterns on which activities of increasing complexity are built" (Graham, Holt/Hale, & Parker, 2004, p. 12). Once the basic skill themes are learned to a certain degree of proficiency, they can be combined with other skills and used in more complex settings, such as those found in dance, games, and gymnastics. The intent is to help children learn a variety of locomotor, nonmanipulative, and manipulative skills that they can use to enjoyably and confidently play a sport or perform a dance consisting of an intricate set of movements. The intention of this model is to help physical educators think about and design curricula that will "guide youngsters in the process of becoming physically active for a lifetime" (Graham, Holt/Hale, & Parker, 2004, p. 12).

supportive curricula The instruction provided by the teacher in the participant groups receiving special pedagogy designed to provide the student a conceptual framework for using the technological devices. The instruction aims to get the student excited and motivated about using the HRMs and PEDs and also supplies the student with background information on using the HRMs and PEDs during PE class. The teacher will use interdisciplinary lessons for this purpose.

technological device A device that assists with measuring the level and amount of physical activity; for example, PEDs and HRMs.

■ DISCUSSION QUESTIONS

1. What was the purpose of this research study?
2. How does the purpose of this study contribute to and support the New PE?
3. How were the technological devices implemented in the research to collect data?
4. What type of data were collected in the research?

5. What were the major findings and conclusions from the research, and how can you apply the findings to the real world of teaching?

■ REFERENCES

Centers for Disease Control and Prevention. Physical activity for everyone. Glossary of terms. Retrieved January 4, 2007, from http://www.cdc.gov/nccdphp/dnpa/physical/terms/index.htm

Clapham, E. D. (2007). *Pilot study.* Unpublished manuscript. Available from author.

Clapham, E. D. (2008). *An analysis of physical activity and elementary physical education curricula using heart rate monitors and pedometers.* Doctoral dissertation. Boston: Boston University.

Graham, G., Holt/Hale, S. A., & Parker, M. (2004). *Children moving: A reflective approach to teaching physical education* (4th ed.). Mountain View, CA: Mayfield.

Kovar, S., Combs, C., Campbell, K., Napper-Owen, G., & Worrell, V. (2007). *Elementary classroom teachers as movement educators.* New York: McGraw-Hill.

Rooney, B., Smalley, K., Larson, J., & Havens, S. (2003). Is knowing enough? Increasing physical activity by wearing a PED. *Wisconsin Medical Journal, 102,* 31–36.

CHAPTER 2

The *Teacher* in the Triad of Teaching and Learning (Teacher-Student-Content)

■ CHAPTER OVERVIEW

Take 10 seconds and write down the top 10 lectures you have ever experienced. Now write down the top 10 teachers who have enhanced your life either personally or academically. The assumption is that remembering the top 10 teachers in your life is easier than the lectures. What is it about some teachers that make them so memorable and effective? The first article in this chapter discusses the excellence of teaching in every subject, particularly physical and health education.

Getting to know one's students is a characteristic of an effective teacher, but it also helps in managing a classroom. Classroom management is an area of teaching that has been often debated and discussed among teachers and administrators. Some beginning teachers try to *control* their students instead of *managing* them, which can leave teachers frustrated when the students don't behave exactly as they'd wish. It is important that beginning teachers learn best practices of classroom management, both at the elementary and secondary level so that learning can take place with little to no distraction. The second article in this chapter provides readers with some good advice on how to manage a classroom and manage students' behavior.

The third article provides insight on student behavior in a different way, as it takes on the topic of character education in schools. The author provides a sound framework for understanding the meaning of character, character education, and teaching character education while discussing two strategies that have helped young people to internalize good habits of heart and mind. The author suggests that students develop good character from imitation and that character education is not optional, that it happens in schools everyday even if it is not included in the school's formal curriculum. Physical and health educators can be role models to their students, so it is important to reflect upon their own behavior inside and outside of the classroom.

The fourth article in this chapter explains the need for teachers to be reflective in order to improve instruction. Definitions of reflection and reflective teaching provide a background for examination into a research-based teacher evaluation model, the Danielson Framework for Teaching (Danielson, 1996). Then a specific assessment tool for teacher reflection, the Teacher Performance Criteria Questionnaire (TPCQ), is presented. Each reader will be well informed about how to use the TPCQ to assess their own or others' teaching behaviors.

Excellent Teachers: Implications for Physical Education and Health Education

Philip M. Tate

Most teachers begin their career with only a vague idea about what it means to be an excellent teacher. Their image of a great teacher is based on their own encounters with excellent teachers and on their visions of themselves as charismatic teachers. Examining the four traditions of research on teaching (Shulman, 1986) can help refine that image by correcting, clarifying, and expanding conceptions of excellent teaching and by providing inspiration so novices can reach high and persevere. But, a danger lurks in thinking about exceptional teachers during teacher education. It is similar to learning basketball by studying Michael Jordan and trying to "be like Mike"—beginners can be daunted by what they perceive to be the overwhelming contribution of raw talent and by realizing how far they will have to go to get to excellence. However, if teacher candidates are willing to assume the long-term view of teacher development, they should find that thinking about pedagogical exemplars can be useful and encouraging.

■ GOOD TEACHERS

Four kinds of research studies provide the background for understanding excellence in teaching. In the middle of the twentieth century, researchers were interested in the characteristics of teachers, leading to many investigations about what makes someone a good teacher. Ryans's (1960) project was the climax of this movement. He summarized the findings of many research studies and then argued that most of them were neither very scientific nor particularly helpful. Just knowing that teachers should have a good sense of humor or be kind to their students does not explain how good teaching leads to good learning. Ryans concluded that researchers should focus on teacher behaviors rather than on teacher characteristics.

Ryans (1960) presented his summary of the findings of the research on personal attributes as three clusters of the characteristics of good teachers (see **Table 2-1**). Most good teachers seemed to fit fairly well in one category or the other. Beginning teachers often envision themselves as a Pattern X_0 teacher, the understanding, friendly, and sympathetic

TABLE 2-1 Three Typical Patterns of the Characteristics of Good Teachers	
Pattern X_0	Understanding, friendly, sympathetic
Pattern Y_0	Responsible, businesslike, systematic
Pattern Z_0	Stimulating, imaginative, enthusiastic

Source: Adapted from Ryans, D. G. (1960). *Characteristics of teachers: Their description, comparison, and appraisal.* Washington, DC: American Council on Education.

one. However, they quickly learn that simply being a pal to their students will not help them learn, nor will they gain the respect they need to manage classroom activities. Beginners rarely aspire to be responsible, businesslike, and systematic (Pattern Y_o), but they will not be able to survive their first few years of teaching, especially in a physical education setting, unless they develop these characteristics. More recent research has confirmed the importance of stimulating, imaginative, and enthusiastic teaching (Pattern Z_o), and novice teachers like to see themselves as exemplifying those qualities. However, even though beginners are usually appreciated for their willingness to make learning more engaging, the management of stimulating learning experiences in any field requires management skills that tax new teachers' abilities.

■ EFFECTIVE TEACHERS

Researchers in the 1960s, 1970s, and early 1980s took up the challenge of discovering the behaviors typical of an **effective teacher**. They developed protocols such as checklists for observing the actions of teachers and then used these new methods in **process–product** (more accurately, pretest–intervention–posttest) **research** (Brophy, 2001). Critics pointed out that most of these behavioral projects were seriously flawed. The interventions were often trivial; standardized tests, which were the most commonly used assessments, were not designed to measure the kinds of learning studied; and the time frames of many of the projects were so short that measurements of changes in students' knowledge were suspect. Worse, most of the projects concerned pedagogical actions that the poorly funded researchers were already

sure were going to prove effective in raising test scores. In fact, the results of almost all of the studies proved to be statistically significant, making it very difficult to distinguish sloppy research from serious scholarship.

Even though behaviorist research was of limited value, several findings have proven beneficial (see **Table 2-2**). Many of these findings describe the classroom management skills that would be indispensable in accomplishing the kinds of engaging lessons that beginning teachers hope to teach.

TABLE 2-2   Behaviors of an Effective Teacher
Creates a supportive classroom or gym environment
Enforces clear and consistent rules
Treats students equitably
Takes an active role
Sets and communicates high expectations
Holds students responsible for progress
Teaches students how to regulate their own learning
Keeps a brisk pace
Provides time for practice
Uses praise judiciously
Individualizes and provides assistance
Structures discussion questions around powerful ideas
Allows for wait time after asking a question
Organizes group work appropriately
Monitors student progress
Gives immediate individual feedback
Provides explicit structure for curriculum
States specific learning objectives
Aligns curriculum to broader goals of learning

For example, effective teachers create powerful learning environments by developing a few clear rules for student behavior; enforcing those rules fairly; communicating clear, high expectations; keeping activities moving at a reasonable pace; and providing immediate and useful feedback. Note that these behaviors could match well with any of the patterns revealed by the earlier research on the characteristics of good teachers.

■ EXPERT TEACHERS

From the 1980s to the early 2000s, researchers turned from studying teacher behaviors to studying teacher thinking. The research on how teachers learn and use different kinds of knowledge was based on prior psychological studies of experts and novices in fields such as chess and architecture and led to a conception of the **expert teacher** (Berliner, 1986; Schön, 1990; Shulman, 1987).

A list of the kinds of knowledge found in expert teaching is in **Table 2-3**. Beginning teachers should realize that it normally takes many years of dedicated work and reflection to gain these types of knowledge. For example, novices usually study developmental theory and how to handle groups of children or adolescents in their teacher education programs, but their learning curves in such areas rise sharply as they gain valuable experience during their first two or three years of teaching. Please note that experience alone cannot result in the development of the forms of knowledge and processes of thinking that are the distinguishing marks of expert teachers. Teachers must reflect objectively and productively about their practice, often with the assistance of a mentor, before experience can become expertise. Even though the path to expertise is long and difficult, it is better for rookies to aspire to

TABLE 2-3 Types of Knowledge of Expert Teachers
Sound understanding of content
Grasp of developmental theory
Understanding of group processes
Perception of particular classroom context
General frames for setting and understanding learning/teaching problems
Repertoire of possible solutions to common teaching problems
Repertoire of effective methods for specific instructional context and content
Experience base for making decisions
Ability to recognize and handle routine tasks without thinking (automaticity)
Understanding of how to provide feedback
Capacity for reflection about student learning and teaching practice

think like an expert teacher than to blindly imitate an admired teacher or "wing it" on their own. A good place to start would be to develop purposefully and refine reflectively routines for normal and repeated behaviors, such as beginning class or putting away learning materials. This growth in expertise can lead to **automaticity** in everyday tasks, freeing the teacher to concentrate her or his immediate attention on more crucial instructional issues.

■ TRANSFORMATIVE TEACHERS

Recently, educational researchers have been challenged to focus on what teachers do to enhance student achievement. Willing to accept the challenge but unwilling to slide back into the unfruitful behaviorist paradigm, they have been forced to invent new ways to study the effects of accomplished teachers. One such method has resulted in **value-added research** (American Educational Research Association, 2004). These projects use modern computers to keep track of the records of thousands of students and teachers over long periods of time. By accounting for the gains individual students make from year to year, researchers can distinguish which districts, schools, and teachers have been adding the most educational value to students' achievement scores. One intriguing discovery has been that students of certain teachers consistently learn much more, as measured by standardized tests, than students of other teachers in the same school. Another is that students who are taught by two or three of these effective teachers consecutively are much more successful in school in the future, and students who have two or three poor teachers in a row are much less likely to bloom. A notable aspect of this finding is that these results cut across lines of ethnicity, class, and gender—even well-to-do students are helped or harmed by exceptionally strong or weak teachers. For example, Pedersen, Faucher, and Eaton (1978) were able to trace the powerfully positive and harmful influences of first grade teachers in the same urban school. Students from Teacher A's class received better grades and teacher comments in school and were likely to have better jobs than the students from the other teachers' classes, regardless of who their subsequent teachers were.

An advantage of the value-added model is that teachers can be compared to other teachers who work with very similar students, solving the problem of evaluating unfairly teachers who face very difficult challenges. One problem of value-added research is that dependence on test scores and large sample sizes does not yield much information about

the nature of the individual **transformative teacher**. At present, research is underway to discover what is so special about teachers identified as being more productive than their colleagues.

■ EXCELLENT TEACHERS

Some of the recent research on teaching has been conducted by combining all four of the research traditions just discussed. In an attempt to distinguish excellence from mere competence in teaching, award-winning teachers have been interviewed and observed, and the letters and notes nominating them for teaching honors have been analyzed. Nomination forms contain information about the characteristics and transformative effects of exceptional teachers, classroom observations provide evidence of teacher behaviors, and interviews expose the thinking of these experts. There are problems with using teacher awards as a criterion for sifting out excellent teachers: awards programs can have political agendas, and some teachers' stories, such as tutoring in a prison or teaching homeless children, are much more captivating than others'. However, teacher award and teacher recognition programs have proven to be accurate at identifying excellent teachers, and by including runners-up in the samples, the effects of politics and public relations in the selections processes can be mitigated (Tate, 2001).

The preliminary results are presented in **Table 2-4**, which is framed in terms of the four research traditions. The results reveal important propositions about the core meaning of teaching and uncover possibilities for masterful practice that might inspire teachers at every stage of their careers. Several of these findings deserve further emphasis and explanation.

TABLE 2-4 Distinguishing Marks of Excellence in Award-Winning Teachers	
Personal Characteristics	**Knowledge**

Personal Characteristics

Humble
Optimistic
Curious (lifelong learner)
Enthusiastic
Energetic
Empathetic
Other-oriented, dedicated
Caring
Well-integrated (mature, sane)

Transforming Effects on Students

More interest in subject and in learning
High academic achievement in later
  schooling
Recognition for achievement in scholastic
  and extracurricular endeavors
Improved self-confidence
Better attitude and conduct
Community leadership
Occupational and financial success

Knowledge

Deep and broad knowledge of the structure
  and methods of the subject
Knowledge of best ways, and next
  best ways, to help students learn
  specific lessons
Understanding of children in the
  community
Understanding of the individual children
  in his or her classroom or gym

Knowledge

Ability to perceive the learning
  environment quickly and accurately
Imagination to practice-teach lessons in the
  "virtual classroom" in his or her mind
Expertise in choosing appropriate solutions
  from his or her teaching repertoire
Capacity for critical and objective
  reflection about his or her own teaching

Behaviors

Interpersonal
Gives self unselfishly and unreservedly
Serves as advisor (listens)
Provides model of moral adult
Pedagogical
Develops and states overall aims clearly
Motivates every student to learn
Reaches each and every student
Teaches thinking skills along with
  content
Awakens appreciation for subject and for
  learning in general
Ecological
Sets productive classroom environment
  (physical, emotional, moral, intellectual)
Balanced in terms of challenge, risk,
  and safety
Collaborative
Self-motivating
Busy
Positive, enjoyable, fun

■ QUALITIES OF EXCELLENT TEACHERS

Have you ever wondered what is the difference between a good teacher and an excellent teacher? The following qualities are what excellent teachers possess to make a difference in a student's academic and personal life.

Caring

Teachers should never be ashamed to say that they love children or adolescents. Excellent teachers might very well care, and act lovingly, more than mediocre teachers do. But, caring is not enough for any teacher. Caring teachers demonstrate their affection by doing what they were hired to do, which is to help the students learn something worthwhile.

Empathy

It should be obvious that possessing and using emotional empathy is an advantage for someone who wants to be a good teacher. However, it is the use of **intellectual empathy** that sets excellent teachers apart from the rest. To be able to perceive and understand how someone else thinks and learns well enough to design a generative learning experience just for her or him is a remarkable and powerful capacity, one that is at the heart of the practice of teaching.

Motivation

Every teacher's task is to challenge, inspire, and stimulate students' learning, yet few are able to do this consistently. The most-mentioned verbs in the nomination forms for teacher awards are acts of motivation, such as *stimulate* or *inspire*.

Ecological

Even though teachers' main task is to motivate, psychologists and learning theorists have concluded that in the final analysis teachers cannot really cause anyone to learn anything beyond basic skills. Meaningful and long-term learning results from the intrinsic motivation of each student. So, how do excellent teachers solve this dilemma? They relinquish their role as dispenser of information and instead attempt to design environments where most students are likely to be learning something worthwhile most of the time. A proper environment allows students to learn best.

Using a Virtual Classroom

Award-winning teachers report that they spend most of their waking moments, and even some of their dreaming time, trying out their ideas for lessons in extremely authentic copies of their classrooms that they carry in their minds. They can "see" how each of their students will react when they try this or that teaching "move" in their **virtual classrooms**. Then, when they teach the lessons for real, they have already tried out most of the possible permutations that might occur, so their instruction seems natural and spontaneous. All teachers do this to some extent, but excellent teachers' descriptions of this aspect of their pedagogical imagination are exceptionally detailed and realistic.

Beginning teachers can find thinking about the distinctive features of excellence to be a little daunting. The dispositions, skills, and behaviors of master teachers seem to be related to personality traits that many novices feel they will never possess. However, it is helpful to remember that it takes years of reflective practice to become an expert. And, it is very likely that simply being aware of the sort of person a beginning teacher must become in order to be considered an excellent teacher can provide a reasonable template for self-development. For example, beginners can channel their natural love for children or adolescents into a strong commitment to their students' education. They can intentionally ask individual students to tell them what they are thinking as they are attempting a learning task, a behavior that can help build intellectual empathy. Neophytes can work hard to set classroom environments that are designed for students' learning rather than for the teacher's instruction. They can realize that their preoccupation with planning and teaching lessons over and over again in their minds is a sign of growing expertise rather than ineffectiveness. They can rest assured that because becoming a great teacher is almost the same thing as becoming a great human being, their efforts at self-improvement in teaching will have a powerfully ennobling effect on their development as persons.

■ **THINKING ABOUT EXCELLENCE IN TEACHING PHYSICAL EDUCATION AND HEALTH**

Teaching physical education and, to a certain extent, health education is different from teaching other school subjects in several key ways. First, the curriculum is different. In physical education, the focus is on learning skills and attitudes more than learning content. In particular, the opportunity to teach important lessons about character, teamwork, courage, self-respect, perseverance, and so forth, is available in every lesson, an advantage that classroom teachers envy. In health, the curriculum concerns issues that are more fundamental to the well-being of students—fitness, diet, self-concept, disease prevention, sexuality—than most topics in other classroom subjects. Second, students' intrinsic motivation for participating may be either much stronger or much weaker than in core academic courses. Some children and adolescents look forward eagerly to the physical activity in "gym" whereas others dread the thought of demonstrating their lack of coordination to the whole class. Third, physical education presents some tricky management issues. The physical movements of a large number of children or adolescents must be monitored and guided. Students in poorly managed classes have heightened opportunities for goofing off and for becoming injured. The teacher may be in physical contact

with students more than in other instructional situations, a circumstance that could improve possibilities both for teaching the whole child and for courting trouble.

These distinctions might seem to divert the search for excellence in teaching physical education and health into an examination of exceptional coaches rather than exceptional classroom teachers. However, there are several reasons why novices should focus on teaching instead of coaching. First, researchers agree that the most distinctive characteristics, actions, and thinking of excellent coaches are related to their role as teachers (Jones, 2006; Nater & Gallimore, 2006). Second, in the new physical education, which emphasizes lifelong fitness and health rather than sports and needless competition, the instructor functions more as a teacher than as a coach (Sullivan, 2013).

Excellent teachers in physical education and health certainly exemplify the findings of research on excellence in teaching, especially in the ways that they design and manage fertile and engaging learning environments. Novice teachers in any field could learn a great deal about the nature and possibilities of teaching by observing and thinking about the work of these masters. Beginning teachers who observe and discuss teaching with outstanding physical education and health teachers have an advantage in their quest to become excellent teachers.

■ **KEY WORDS AND DEFINITIONS**

automaticity   The ability of an expert to be able to avoid unnecessary thinking while performing a routine task by depending on deep-rooted memory gained from repeated practice.

effective teacher   A teacher whose behaviors result in measurable gains in student achievement, usually gauged by standardized tests.

expert teacher   A teacher whose knowledge, thinking, decision making, and reflection demonstrate a high level of expertise.

intellectual empathy   The capacity to understand quickly and thoroughly what others know and how they think and to imagine how to help them learn better.

process–product research   Research on effective teaching that follows a pattern of pretest–intervention–posttest to change teaching behaviors and measure student outcomes.

transformative teacher   A teacher who has earned a reputation for teaching in a way that produces dramatic and long-lasting improvements in students' lives.

value-added research   Educational research that measures, usually by comparing test scores, the value that individual teachers, schools, and/or districts add to the achievement of students.

virtual classroom   The mental image of a teacher's learning setting, including the physical, emotional, moral, and intellectual environments, where she or he practices teaching moves in preparation for instruction in the real setting.

■ DISCUSSION QUESTIONS

1. Think about an excellent teacher you know well. His or her teaching may take place in almost any sort of educative situation. Which three or four of the characteristics, behaviors, knowledge, and transformative effects listed in this article are obvious hallmarks of her or his teaching?

2. Which of the characteristics, behaviors, knowledge, and transformative effects listed in this article do you already

possess? Which will be more difficult for you to acquire?

3. Which of the items in your responses to the first two questions would be the most difficult to measure? Can you think of better ways to measure excellence in teaching?

4. How is it that excellent teachers can reach almost all of their students?

5. What might you do to shift your view of teaching physical education and health from a coaching perspective to a teaching perspective?

■ REFERENCES

American Educational Research Association. (2004). Teachers matter: Evidence from value-added assessments. *Research Points, 2*(2). Retrieved January 22, 2010, from http://www.aera.net/publications/?id=314

Berliner, D. C. (1986). In pursuit of the expert pedagogue. *Educational Researcher, 15*(7), 5–13.

Brophy, J. (2001). Generic aspects of effective teaching. In M. C. Wang & H. J. Walberg (Eds.), *Tomorrow's teachers* (pp. 3–45). Richmond, CA: McCutchan.

Jones, R. L. (Ed.). (2006). *The sports coach as educator: Re-conceptualizing sports coaching.* London: Routledge.

Nater, S., & Gallimore, R. (2006). *You haven't taught until they have learned: John Wooden's teaching principles and practices.* Morgantown, WV: Fitness Information Technology.

Pedersen, E., Faucher, T. A., & Eaton, W. W. (1978). A new perspective on the effects of first-grade teachers on children's subsequent adult status. *Harvard Educational Review, 48*, 1–31.

Ryans, D. G. (1960). *Characteristics of teachers: Their description, comparison, and appraisal.* Washington, DC: American Council on Education.

Schön, D. A. (1990). *The reflective practitioner: How professionals think in action.* New York: Basic Books.

Shulman, L. S. (1986). Paradigms and research programs for the study of teaching. In M. C. Wittrock (Ed.), *Handbook of research on teaching* (3rd ed., pp. 3–36). New York: Macmillan.

Shulman, L. S. (1987). Knowledge and teaching: Foundations of the new reform. *Harvard Educational Review, 57,* 1–22.

Sullivan, E. C. (2013). The meaning of physical education: Definition, clarification and an overview of the old and New PE. In L. E. Ciccomascolo & E. C. Sullivan (Eds.), *Dimensions of physical education*. Burlington, MA: Jones & Bartlett Learning.

Tate, P. M. (2001). Excellence in teaching: Myths and legends. In T. Arnold (Ed.), *Facing change: Proceedings of the AIESEP World Sport Science Congress* (pp. 1.45–1.51). Rockhampton, Queensland, Australia: Association Internationale des Escoles Superieures d'Education Physique and School of Health and Human Performance, Central Queensland University.

Classroom Management: Strategies for the Beginning Teacher

Pamela A. Storme

As a physical education (PE) teacher, specificity, rituals, and routines are key to a manageable and effective class inside the gymnasium or outside on the field or court. In fact, class management is a delicate navigation of classroom advance planning. Further, there needs to be rule setting, establishment and implementation of daily protocols, routines, and interventions (Baker, Lang, & Lawson 2002; Clark, 2007; Freiberg, 2002).

As physical education teachers, we are continually looking to challenge our students with new and innovative ideas. However, we need to make sure that we are delivering our lessons in a way that is clear, concise, and consistent. We should view ourselves as managers of a teaching environment. There are appropriate and inappropriate ways to deliver lessons in a classroom setting, and this article will review some best practices of classroom management.

■ BACKGROUND INFORMATION ABOUT PHYSICAL EDUCATION CLASSROOM MANAGEMENT

As an example of best practices of classroom management, the **National Association of Sport and Physical Education (NASPE)** has created *Appropriate Instructional Practice Guidelines* for K–12, a side-by-side comparison grid that "includes developmentally appropriate and inappropriate practices in elementary, middle and high school physical education classes" (NASPE, 2009, p. 1). The NASPE grid organizes the practices into five separate sections: (1) Learning Environments, (2) Instructional Strategies, (3) Curriculum, (4) Assessment, and (5) Professionalism.

The Learning Environments section includes the topic of "Establishing the Learning Environment." The following are some characteristics that NASPE states should be present within your classroom learning environment:

- A positive learning environment.
- Maximized learning focused on participation.
- An atmosphere of respect and support from the teacher and the child's peers.
- Fair and consistent classroom-management practices that encourage student responsibility for positive behavior.
- Students are included in the process of developing class rules/agreements.
- Bullying, taunting, and inappropriate student remarks and behaviors are dealt with immediately and firmly.

Setting a positive and appropriate class learning environment is imperative during the first few classes of the year. Then, as teachers, we need to ensure that we follow those expectations the rest of the school year. This sets the standard and expectations for all classes; also be sure to include reminders of the guidelines throughout the year so as to review the expectations and consequences.

As a practicum or student teacher, you are walking into another teacher's classroom, which can often be intimidating. However, the classroom learning environment is already preset with expectations and rules. It is up to you to know and follow these expectations and rules that are present and to ensure you are creating the proper teaching environment as per your cooperating teacher's expectations.

■ THE BASICS OF CLASSROOM MANAGEMENT IN A PHYSICAL EDUCATION SETTING

Consider this scenario: When Mrs. White arrived at school this morning, she had her lesson plans that she had preset the day before on her desk. She reviewed the student outcomes and equipment lists for the morning classes. Mrs. White will be using station work as a culminating lesson on the throwing unit for the first-grade classes. Targets on the wall were placed in station locations at the end of the previous day. Mrs. White has all of the equipment she needs and set up her stations around the perimeter of the gymnasium. The gymnasium is the size of a small elementary gymnasium with no bleacher room. The stations would not be officially set up because the students would be doing an instant activity, or one they participated in right when they entered the gymnasium, before the station work.

When the first class enters the gymnasium, the students walk around the red perimeter line to where they pick up their assigned numbered pedometers. Once their pedometers are on, the students report and sit in the discussion area. The line leader from the classroom places the class behavior chart on the floor. Mrs. White explains to the students the tag game they will be playing that enforces overhand and underhand throwing technique. She cooperatively chooses a male and female to be the first two taggers. (Note that there is a system in place so everyone has an equal turn to play the special roles in games and sports.) Every 2 minutes the taggers will choose another tagger of the opposite gender. At the conclusion of the tag game (7–10 minutes), Mrs. White gives her transition words of "Stop, look, and listen." The students then transition back to a designated area, as given in the directions.

It is now time to start the directions of the station work. As Mrs. White starts at station number one, she is giving the students the main objective of that station. As she is clearly explaining the directions at each station, she makes minor adjustments to the stations. Mrs. White also shows an example of what each task should look like. When it is time to go to the stations, Mrs. White disperses the students as quickly as possible by assigning two males and two females at each station, where possible. She is careful to make sure that the groupings are ones that will "work," or groupings that are fair. She has had the opportunity to get to know her students well and this assists with the groupings.

Appropriate and fun music is turned on and the students participate at the stations for the next 25 minutes in class. When beginning their last station, Mrs. White lets them know the proper start and stop signals and reminds the students how to work well together.

The music is turned off, and "Stop, look, and listen" is stated. The students make their way back to the discussion area for the closure of the lesson. Mrs. White asks the students a variety of questions and makes sure each individual has the opportunity to answer a question. She also calls her students by their names. Questions included:

- What station did you enjoy the most?
- What station was the most difficult? Why?
- What station was the easiest?
- What did you have to remember to do with your arms and legs when doing any of the stations today?
- How can you use what you learned here in class with sports you play or for activities outside of class time?

After closure questions are completed, students are handed their pedometer log sheets for the day, to log their steps. Once completed, students put the log back in their class folders and then class folders back in the designated box for the class. Students then line up by the exit door. This is a procedure that the students have learned and there is not any wasted time here. They know how to write in their logs, where the folders must be placed, and how to line up.

■ AN OVERVIEW OF THE STRUCTURE OF THE LESSON

The Planning

In order to deliver a clear lesson, you need to have the knowledge to present that lesson, goals and objectives set for the students, and the equipment set up and ready for them. What did Mrs. White do to successfully execute the planning phase?

The Lesson

If the students are ready to enter your gymnasium door, do they know what is expected of them? This is the start of the classroom-management practice. **Rituals and routines** should be set well before students enter the gymnasium for class. In the beginning of Mrs. White's lesson, what would be easier to handle: students who walk into the gymnasium, put their pedometers on, and are ready to learn in a safe environment or students who run through the gymnasium, cluster at the pedometers, and run on high energy all over the gymnasium? When transitions happen in a fast and organized fashion, more movement and skills can get accomplished. What were some of the rituals and routines in Mrs. White's PE class?

Appropriate Practice During the Lesson

In the setting, there were examples of appropriate practice for expectations for student learning, class organization, and class design (NASPE, 2009). Upon entering the gymnasium, Mrs. White explained the objectives for the tag game to the students, followed by objectives for the **stations**. Groupings for the stations were made based on students who would work well together as well as work towards their goal at each station. The lesson design included an instant activity, focus of instruction, and closure summarizing the objectives of the lessons (NASPE, 2009).

When expectations and objectives are clearly set before the students start to work, more learning will take place for the students. As you develop and teach more lessons you will improve strategies in your teaching. Lavay and French (2007) suggest that having strategies in one's teaching can include proactive methods to help prevent problems before they occur.

■ BEHAVIOR MANAGEMENT IN CLASSROOM MANAGEMENT

In recent years, effectively managing behavior has become even more challenging with the increased numbers of children and youths who are identified as at-risk or with disabilities. In reality, an unmanageable class is unteachable (Lavay & French, 2007). As years progress, it seems that there are more inclusion or co-teaching model classrooms. When co-teaching or teaching in an inclusion classroom, there is a possibility that there are behavior issues with identified students in the classroom. When you have set the expectations and objectives, make sure as a teacher you stick to them. When you let things "slide" the behavior of the class will start to shift. Often, it will be harder to manage.

In any classroom, there will be students who may be off task for many different reasons. Knowing a child's background will help you in redirecting the student, if necessary. Having an open line of communication with the general classroom teacher will also help you in your behavior management techniques with certain students. There also are classes in which you might have support from a classroom aide. This classroom aide might be assigned to one or multiple students to monitor in certain capacities. Have an open line of communication with this person.

He or she will be able to provide valuable information about the student. The aide should know what works for the student or students and what strategies help meet the needs of the student(s). Recognize that the aide is an assistant to the student, but helping the student stay on task will also assist in dealing with a positive class management plan.

If not all students are acting positively, there are many different ways to help redirect a student who is exhibiting behavior that is not appropriate.

- There can be the subtle walk up to the student approach. This shows the student you notice what she is doing. As a teacher, eye contact is also a strong way to tell the student you notice. This is an effective nonverbal way to indicate your intent.
- If you are giving directions and a student is talking continuously, this behavior needs to be addressed. Perhaps you could ask the student to move to a better learning spot to listen. A good learning spot is an area where he will focus on the expectations.
- If the student performed a skill correctly in the past, ask her to show it to you again. Once the skill is completed, give positive reinforcement to encourage the good skill behavior.
- If the student's general classroom has a behavior chart, explain to the student that you will be reporting her behavior back to the classroom teacher.
- If doing an activity with pedometers and the student is not being safe (running vs. jogging), ask him to pause for 1 minute. He will lose 1 minute of steps toward his class totals.
- At the end of class, have a brief discussion with the student. What went right and what went wrong? What can the student work on for next class?

According to Marzano et al. (2003), the guiding principle for disciplinary interventions is that they should include a healthy balance between negative consequences for inappropriate behavior and positive consequences for appropriate behavior.

■ CLASSROOM MANAGEMENT STRATEGIES FOR THE BEGINNING TEACHER

As a beginning teacher it is important to understand some proactive approaches to dealing with student behavior. Here are a few suggestions:

- *Be prepared with your lesson.* Have what you need for your lesson ready to set up if not already set up in the gymnasium. You will probably have to go in to school early or stay later than your contractual time in order to get lessons planned or set up.
- *Communicate with your students.* A simple "hello" and a greeting to each student as they enter your gymnasium will show that you care. Talk to the students about their likes and dislikes. When asking questions to the class, call on a wide variety of students to get a wide range of answers. They will always surprise you.
- *Move around.* Move around to see everyone. Do not station yourself in one spot during a game or lesson. Move to a different part of the gymnasium to get a different view every few minutes. Students will notice. When a student is exhibiting an off task behavior, moving towards them will also show them that you notice their behavior and do not like it.
- *Revise your lesson and activities* (even on the spot). If something doesn't work,

change it! Do not set yourself up for failure. If you can't figure out how to change it, poll the students. It works! If there is a safety issue, then stop the activity immediately.
- *Use positive—not negative—words.* "I love how Sarah is staying on her scooter the proper way." This will send a message to others who might not be sitting properly to fix their position. When appropriate, take the student to the side; tell them you notice what is going on and your thoughts.
- *Have structure.* Rituals and routines will be your best friend. The students will know what is expected of them.
- *Do not sit down in a chair and teach physical education class!* If you are teaching your students to be active, you cannot do this while sitting in a chair being inactive.

■ CONCLUSION

Classroom management is a topic that many beginning teachers find intimidating. Setting up a class routine, preparing well ahead of when a class first begins, sharing rules and consequences with students on the first day of school, and planning a creative curriculum are all proactive ways to manage a classroom, and for physical education teachers, the gymnasium is our classroom. In addition, getting to know one's students and what makes each one of them tick is an important part of classroom management because it allows the teacher to better understand how to manage the students' behavior. Finally, it is important that a teacher "catches" students doing things right and rewards positive behavior in addition to, when appropriate, calling out misbehavior.

KEY WORDS AND DEFINITIONS

National Association of Sport and Physical Education (NASPE) Part of the American Alliance for Health, Physical Education, Recreation, and Dance; a professional membership association that sets the standards for best practices in quality physical education and sport.

rituals and routines Used by teachers to create structure and/or a pattern that students understand they will follow before, during, and after a lesson.

stations Structure the participation of students in a lesson where they will go from one activity to another, in separate groups, usually for a specific amount of time (e.g., stations in a basketball lesson could include passing, shooting, 3v3 game, and free throws).

DISCUSSION QUESTIONS

1. In your elementary or secondary PE classes, did your physical education teachers have a class routine set up for your class to follow? If so, what was it? If not, what was the structure?
2. Give examples of what the characteristics of Establishing the Learning Environment would look like in the PE classroom.
3. Would you agree or disagree that the planning phase sets the stage for a successful lesson? Why or why not?

4. A middle school student comes up to you before PE class and states that she does not agree with the school's PE curriculum. How do you handle this situation?
5. During a third-grade focus lesson, three students are talking in the back. You have acknowledged their talking. They stopped but continued talking again. They are impeding others' ability to hear the directions for the lesson. How would you handle this in the least disruptive way?

REFERENCES

Baker, W. P., Lang, M., & Lawson, A. E. (2002). Classroom management for successful inquiry. *The Clearing House, 75*(5), 1–5.

Clark, D. (2007). Classroom managment challenges in the dance class. *Journal of Physical Education, Recreation and Dance, 13*, 21.

Freiberg, H. J. (2002, March). Essential skills for new teachers. *Educational Leadership,* 56–60.

Lavay, B., & French, R. (2007). Do PERD professionals get enough training in behavior managment and supervision in physical activity settings? *Journal of Physical Education, Recreation and Dance, 17*, 11–13.

Marzano, R. J., Marzano, J. S., & Pikering, D. (2003). *Classroom management that works: Research-based strategies for every teacher.* Alexandria, VA: Association for Supervision and Curriculum Development.

National Association of Sport and Physical Education. (2009). Appropriate instructional practice guidelines. Retrieved June 1, 2010, from http://www.aahperd.org/naspe/standards/nationalGuidelines/Apppracticedoc.cfm

Educating for Character: Mandatory, Optional, or Inevitable?

Bernice Lerner

Sarah is a gifted middle-school athlete. She runs down the basketball court with grace, dodging opponents, her ponytail flying behind her. Valuing teamwork, she passes the ball to strategically positioned teammates, regardless of a given individual's ability to keep it in play. For Sarah, including others trumps scoring points.

Greg, also in middle school, has been playing basketball for less than one year. Tall and confident, he is disinclined to pass the ball to anyone else. Enjoying shouts of "Go Greg!" from the sidelines, he dribbles until he eventually takes a reckless shot, invariably missing the basket.

Were Sarah to "hog the ball," we would think her action "out of character." Were Greg to suddenly exercise restraint, we would likewise note the inconsistency. In how they behave on the basketball court, in the classroom, or at a party, Sarah and Greg are practicing ways of being and relating to others. They are developing their characters.

What *is* **character**? The word comes from the Greek *charrassein*, meaning to engrave. The more we repeat certain behaviors, the more they become part of who we are. Think of individuals you know well. Can you say who among them would never divulge a secret, who is likely to share it with another person, and who might be tempted to broadcast it? Can you predict who will run to assist someone who has fallen, who is likely to work hard, who will feign sickness when asked to do a chore? Though we are all composed of a mix of traits, and situations are often complex, we can generally predict how people we know will respond to events and in conversation: in accordance with their characters.

What is *character education*? It is those innumerable character-shaping experiences that occur where young people spend time. In school, character education occurs in the gymnasium, in the cafeteria, in hallways, and in classrooms. In these various milieus, young people learn what is permissible and what is unacceptable; what is frowned upon or praiseworthy. Aspects of their characters are being shaped by what is explicit (their school's climate and distinctive character) and what is invisible (their school's culture and **ethos**). And we can be sure that they are attuned to what they may seem oblivious to: nuances of adult behavior. In the words of psychiatrist Robert Coles,

> . . . the child is an ever-attentive witness of grown-up morality—or lack thereof; the child looks and looks for cues as to how one ought to behave, and finds them galore as we parents and teachers go about our lives, making choices, addressing people, showing in action our rock-bottom assumptions, desires and values, and thereby telling those young observers much more than we realize. (Coles, 1998, p. 5)

Young observers not only discern adults' behaviors, attitudes, and values, but also imitate what they see. And not all adults display qualities worthy of emulation. I am reminded of children I know who have a parent who is envious, greedy, or self-absorbed. These children fortunately have other adults in their lives who are fair, even-tempered, and respectful. Among such positive role models are teachers who care to know them, and other adults at school who exemplify a maturity they do not always see at home. Schools of education would do well to impress upon future teachers that they might be that adult exemplar for children. Teacher training should include courses on character education, which ought to begin by emphasizing the importance of a teacher's striving to be honest and hard-working, a person of laudable character whose ways young people will discern.

Ideally, teachers and other adults in schools will be more than good role models. They will be able to meaningfully guide students, helping them to sort out—and consider moral responses to—difficult questions. Rick Weissbourd (2003) explains that, "The moral development of students does not depend primarily on explicit character education efforts but on the maturity and ethical capacities of the adults with whom they interact—especially parents, but also teachers, coaches, and other community adults" (p. 5).

Schools of education and professional development programs can help teachers to reflect on and further develop their ethical capacities. They can help educators to realize that they can influence students' moral development by virtue of their own "moral energy and idealism, their generosity, and their ability to help students develop moral thinking without shying away from their own moral authority" (Weissbourd, 2003, p. 6). In an age of **moral relativism**, teachers need moral compasses in order to call things what they are: good, evil, right, wrong. In taking clear stands, they provide students with reliable anchors with which to ground their own choices.

Beyond the inevitable shaping of character that takes place in school, are there deliberate strategies that effectively spur students' moral development? For millennia, and in schools the world over, educators have endeavored to foster good citizenship in the young. The purpose of this article is not to delve into the political, historical, and social trends that have given rise to various incarnations of "character education," but rather to provide a sound framework for understanding what this activity entails. We have discussed the development of character through imitation. Let us now examine two universal and timeless strategies that have helped young people to internalize good habits of heart and mind:

1. *Strategy 1:* Putting before them inspirational stories
2. *Strategy 2:* Providing for them opportunities to practice **virtue**

Before outlining the aforementioned strategies, we must understand what we mean by virtue. The root of the word *virtue* is *vir*, meaning strength. A virtue is a particular moral excellence or commendable quality. It is that which decent people consider to be good for an individual and community. Whereas one might one day *value* watching football games, and the next change one's preferred leisure time activity to playing golf, *virtue* is unchanging. It informs one's choices and responses in all situations. Virtue is requisite for leading a good life; vice has the opposite effect. Virtue is what well-conceived character education aims to help students practice.

- *Strategy 1:* Putting before students inspirational stories. When Coach Bill Belichick wanted to instill courage and perseverance in the New England Patriots, he took team members to see the IMAX film about Ernest Shackleton, the Antarctic explorer and intrepid leader of the Endurance Expedition of 1914–1916. Raoul Wallenberg, the Swedish diplomat who issued visas to Budapest's Jews whom the Nazis slated for death, was inspired to undertake dangerous activities by the protagonist in the movie *The Scarlet Pimpernel.* British public school students called to serve in the First World War were steeped in stories of their heroic forebears. Narratives in film, literature, history, and current events provide young people with a store of memorable cases they can refer to when faced with challenges in their own lives. Teachers of all subjects should strive to build students' repertoire of stories, prompting them to analyze the character of characters, to discern the presence or absence of virtue in imagined and real (albeit removed from their immediate orbit) lives.
- *Strategy 2:* Providing for students opportunities to practice virtue. Aristotle argued that "we become just by doing just acts, temperate by doing temperate acts, brave by doing brave acts" (Aristotle, Book II: 1103 a33). The physical education class provides excellent opportunities for practicing teamwork, fairness, and healthful behaviors. For example, in a unit on wellness students can be encouraged to keep track of the time they spend walking, or how many steps they

take in a given day. Are there ways they can build walking into their routines? If they adopt the habit of walking more or further than they ordinarily would, this will gradually feel natural to them. They will experience discomfort if days go by and they are unable to "get their walking in." Barring extenuating circumstances, this virtue of caring for self, manifested in a wholesome habit, can be sustained for the whole of their lives.

In trying to help students make wise choices, the physical education teacher must bear in mind the risks of students going too far with a given practice. Aristotle explains that

> *it is the nature of . . . things to be destroyed by defect and excess, as we see in the case of strength and of health; exercise either excessive or defective destroys the strength, and similarly drink or food which is above or below a certain amount destroys the health, while that which is proportionate both produces and increases and preserves it. (Aristotle, Book II: 1104 a16)*

Aristotle's examples are apt. There is no "one size fits all" with regard to the right amount of food and physical activity. There are, however, "right" amounts for each individual, at particular times.

When students see athletes using steroids to enhance their performance, or models who starve themselves to maintain their appearance, they register extreme behaviors. How can today's physical education teachers help young people "hit the mark" in their own lives, developing habits that will serve them well in the present and future? They ought to encourage students to exercise their powers of discernment, to question—and note the consequences of—public figures' choices. Judging others from a safe vantage point can help young people sharpen their convictions and map their own way. The pursuit and practice of what is healthful and best requires will, and is indicative of strong character.

Aristotle's **Doctrine of the Mean** (4th century BC) is a useful construct. Students of almost any age can brainstorm examples of vice (extremes of excess and defect) and identify an intermediary course of action (i.e., virtue). In almost every situation in which they find themselves, young people will have a choice of action. In addition to aiming for a moderate response, they can learn to ask, "What would the wisest person I know do?" And, they can develop the habit of reflecting on their own biases or proclivities, consciously leaning away from their usual ways and toward a more just and wise course of action. Finally, on the playing field, in physical education class, in life, if they are unable to choose what is best for themselves and others, those of good character will choose what is or will be least harmful.

Let us now revisit the characters of Sarah and Greg. In the words of an eighth grader who attends a Boston area school, "It is hard for me to think of people in my school who are really that different in life than they are in a sports game." Sarah's generosity and Greg's spiritedness may need proper channeling. The factors that shaped (and are shaping) their respective characters—with regard to sport and other domains—are consequential. Consider English journalist William Makepeace Thackeray's (1811–1863) dictum:

> *Sow a thought. Reap an action.*
> *Sow an action. Reap a habit.*
> *Sow a habit. Reap a character.*
> *Sow a character. Reap a destiny.*

These words indicate that even seemingly minor thoughts and actions are of consequence. Mindful character education, concerned with young people developing good habits, keeps in view the **telos** or ultimate purpose of human life. Its large question: How can we help young people "reap" a worthy "destiny"? Behavior on the basketball court, at home, or in class is not as fleeting or immaterial as it may seem. According to Aristotle, "It makes no small difference . . . whether we form habits of one kind or another from our very youth; it makes a very great difference, or rather all the difference" (Aristotle, Book II: 1103 b25).

The existential philosopher Viktor Frankl (1959) concurred with Aristotle on the importance of developing good habits. In illustrating how virtue is a **disposition** of choice, he identified three forms of destiny. The first of these, one's biological endowment, involves inheritance, and concerns matters about which one has no say. The second, one's external environment, is—especially in the early years of one's life—also not chosen. The third form of destiny, one's attitude, is determinative. People who choose to "look on the bright side," who see "the glass as half full," shape their destiny in powerful ways. Negativity is likewise revealed in a person's habits, character, and destiny. What follows further elucidates Frankl's three forms of destiny:

1. *Biological endowment:* Individuals possess—to greater or lesser degrees—innate temperaments and talents. Sarah's athletic skill and generous disposition are apparent on the basketball court. Greg may have inborn enthusiasm or spiritedness that can be properly channeled in sport, and that may serve him well in other spheres. One's biological endowment can limit or expand one's

possibilities for achievement in numerous areas.

2. *External environment:* Our destinies are partly shaped by the milieus we are born into and those situations we navigate throughout the course of our lives. Young people may flourish or suffer on account of their home environments, their neighborhoods, and the schools they attend. Some schools are academically rigorous; some have strong traditions; some lack a sense of decorum and order. Sarah and Greg may each thrive in certain classes, and do less well in others. Schools that have a strong ethos, that purposefully educate for character, are excellent environments.

3. *Attitude:* Given our capacities and the situations in which we find ourselves, we are faced with choices: What should we think, say, or do? What attitude should we adopt? There exists a range of responses to nearly every situation, and our outlook will determine how we fare. Our attitude *is* our destiny. From our limited snapshot of Sarah and Greg, we are afforded a glimpse of their attitudes toward self and others.

A teacher I met at a statewide conference told me of her work with several hundred homeless children in western Massachusetts. She explained how many of them did not have notebooks, let alone computers. Despite their disadvantages, some of these children worked extremely hard. "They will," she told me, "break out of their circumstances and improve their lives." I wondered aloud, "Were these ambitious kids academically gifted?" "No," she answered. "It's all about attitude."

In visiting an inner city high school, I had a conversation with a teacher who works with students from foreign countries. She expressed to me her concern that they will pick up certain American teenage habits, such as shoving others in the hallways. At the risk of stereotyping, she shared an observation: "Immigrants who know that they cannot return to the countries from which they came have a strong work ethic—they appreciate opportunities given them and try to achieve goals." After a moment's reflection, she added, "They have such a positive attitude" (Lerner, 2007).

Most every teacher can relay a story about a student whose diligence and fortitude have helped him or her to overcome difficulties. All of the adults in a school—administrators, teachers, secretaries, and librarians—can encourage students, no matter their temperaments and abilities, no matter the circumstances of their lives, to adopt positive attitudes.

Again, the physical education class is rich with opportunities for practicing "attitudinal values" or virtue. As an 8th-grade athlete explains,

> *With its rules and regulations sports can teach a child to become a better person by giving them opportunities to succeed while helping a team. If they can learn that helping others and being part of a team is [a] more successful [approach] than doing everything by themselves, an important life lesson is learned. (email exchange with Seamus Matlack, 2009)*

This student aptly connects good habits with faring well, echoing Aristotle, Viktor Frankl, and William Makepeace Thackeray.

Character education is not mandatory in schools, nor is it an option. It goes on all the time, for better and for worse. School leaders have choices to make. They can *choose* to deliberately educate for good character. They can make their institutions places where virtue is underscored and consistently practiced. Teachers can provide instruction that inspires students, motivating them to practice good habits and lead good lives. They must be mindful—any character education strategy will miss the mark if the adults with whom students interact are not themselves exemplars.

■ KEY WORDS AND DEFINITIONS

character   Moral or ethical quality/ strength; instinctive qualities that make a person recognizable.

disposition   An inclination or tendency; natural mental and emotional outlook or mood; characteristic attitude.

Doctrine of the Mean   Aristotle's (384–322 BC) doctrine that moral virtue is a disposition of choice lying in a mean between two extremes relative to our natural tendencies. The mean is the point we ought to pursue, and is determined by the moral insight of one with practical wisdom.

ethos   The underlying sentiments that inform the beliefs, customs, or practices of a group or society; the dominant assumptions of a people.

moral relativism   The view that ethical standards, morality, and positions of right or wrong are culturally based and, therefore, "we can all decide what is right for ourselves." The concept that there are no moral absolutes, that "anything goes," and that life is ultimately without meaning.

telos   The end of a goal-oriented process; ultimate end.

virtue   Moral excellence, goodness, uprightness; force, potency.

■ DISCUSSION QUESTIONS

1. Choose one person who influenced the development of your character. Describe his or her attitudes and dispositions.
2. What stories might you put before students to inspire them to strive for personal excellence?
3. What concrete opportunity might you provide in teaching physical education that will help students practice good habits?
4. Which of your own dispositions are sure to be noticed by your students? Which are worthy of emulation? In what ways might your character be strengthened?
5. Do you think it is the role of the physical educator to discuss morals and character? Is so, why, or, if not, why not?

■ REFERENCES

Aristotle. (1925). *The Nicomachean ethics*. David Ross (Trans.). Oxford, United Kingdom: Oxford University Press.

Coles, R. (1998). *The moral intelligence of children*. New York: Penguin.

Frankl, V. (1984). *Man's search for meaning*. New York: Simon & Schuster.

Lerner, B. (2007). How do we care? Locating the heart of a noble profession. *Education Week, 26*, 36.

Weissbourd, R. (2003). Moral teachers, moral students. *Educational Leadership, 60*, 6–11.

Using Reflective Practices with the Teacher Performance Criteria Questionnaire

Eileen Crowley Sullivan

How do educators improve their teaching? Educational philosophers, researchers, administrators, and practitioners have pondered the answer to this question for years. Although we all may not agree on the answer to this question, we might be able to agree that teaching is a complex process. The three variables of the teacher, the content, and the students all play significant roles in teaching and the examination of how teachers can improve their teaching.

The focus of this article is on the first variable, the teacher, and more specifically teacher evaluation, reflection of teaching behaviors, or the practice of **reflective teaching**; however, the other two variables need to be considered partners in the process. In addition, the need to be a reflective teacher is discussed, as is the research-based teacher evaluation framework, the Danielson Framework (1996). Finally, there is a complete description of a teacher reflection assessment instrument, the Teacher Performance Criteria Questionnaire (TPCQ). Background information about the TPCQ, the 11 variables of effective teaching, and the 3 methods of implementing the TPCQ are explained.

■ REFLECTIVE TEACHING AND THE NEED TO BE A REFLECTIVE PRACTITIONER

It is likely that the term *reflection* or *reflective teaching* can be found in every teaching methods book or article about teaching, whether it be research based, anecdotal, or even a newspaper article about education. These two terms have been widely used in the literature to indicate a teacher's use of examining teaching practices and the success and/or failure of a lesson.

Review the following definitions of the word *reflection*:

- Boud, Keogh, and Walker (1985) defined reflection as "an active process of exploration and discovery."
- "Reflection deepens insights and promotes thinking about ways to improve practice" (Gimbel, 2008).
- "Reflection is careful and analytical thought by teachers about what they are doing and the effects of their behavior on their instruction and student learning" (Arends, 2009).
- Reflection is the "[m]ental process of the teacher candidate in which he/she considers relevant instructional and contextual factors (i.e., student diversity, developmental differences, type of motor skills), the achievement of student learning outcomes and the use of assessment data to modify instruction and enhance future student learning" (NASPE, 2008).

All four of the definitions inform us that reflection is a process, a means of thinking about something. As related to teaching, it is a way of analyzing what teachers do in order to improve instruction. The fourth definition is specifically for physical education, but the meaning of the definition, without the specific reference to the physical skills, can easily be applied to any discipline.

Reflective teaching means not only thinking about our teaching, but also using what we discovered to then improve the next lesson, teaching practices, and future lessons. In order to develop as a teacher, it is important to learn how to become a reflective practitioner. Teachers must do more than just teach a lesson; they must teach, reflect, and then use the information from the reflection to improve their lesson after critical analysis and the use of feedback. Stronge (2002) clearly reviews the role of reflective practice and makes the connection of reflection to effective teachers. He tells us effective teachers "continuously practice self-evaluation and self-critique as learning tools" (p. 20). He calls **reflective teachers** "students of learning" who are curious about the art and science of teaching and how theory is connected to practice. Finally, he reminds us that effective teachers do not shy away from feedback and they use thoughtful questions in reflecting.

Rink (2006) informs us that the reflective practitioner not only takes time to think about what he or she is doing and why, but also asks the right questions about his or her teaching. "Reflective practitioners are willing to ask good questions about the goals and practices of their teaching and to keep an open mind about their experiences. Reflective practitioners are willing to tie the big ideas about teaching (e.g., fostering in each child a positive sense of self) with a routine teaching act (e.g., choosing teams) and see the connection" (Rink, 2006, p. 338).

Reflective teachers use a variety of formal and informal assessments to critique their lessons and to examine their teaching behaviors. It is beyond the scope of this article to review assessments for reflective teaching, but because teaching is a skill that can be improved, a systematic and data-driven approach will assist with identifying areas of strengths and weaknesses. In the physical education discipline, Darst and Pangrazi (2006) dedicate an entire chapter on "Improving Instruction Systematically," and methods for systematically observing instruction are described. Darst and Pangrazi (2006) also outline the Arizona State University Observation Instrument (ASUOI) and its 14 categories of teacher behaviors. An assessor tallies the number of times a particular teaching behavior is displayed and calculates a percentage for each behavior. For example, the teacher could have used praise 6.5% of the class time or he or she could have used questioning only 2.0% of the time. This feedback could then be used to set specific goals for teaching improvement. Reflective teachers would seek out opportunities to collect and then apply the feedback from instruments like the ASUOI. If you are a beginning teacher, you also need to be more cognizant of the reflective process because "new and beginning teachers actually have two jobs when they start to teach; they have to teach and they have to learn to teach" (Feiman-Nemser, 1982).

■ THE COMPLEXITY OF TEACHING AND DANIELSON'S FRAMEWORK

Charlotte Danielson (1996) informs us of the complexity of teaching; teachers typically make over 3000 nontrivial decisions daily, from what to teach, to how to teach, how to assess, and class management issues. She reminds us that the teaching profession combines the skills of many professions, from business and human relations to theater arts. Her research-based Framework for Teaching divides the complex activities of teacher responsibilities into four areas:

- *Domain 1:* Planning and Preparation
- *Domain 2:* Classroom Environment
- *Domain 3:* Instruction
- *Domain 4:* Professional Responsibilities

These descriptions define what teachers should know and be able to do as effective teachers. The most updated information about this framework can be found on the Danielson Group website (http://www.danielsongroup .org/theframeteach.htm). Currently there are 22 components and 76 smaller elements of teaching that are arranged into the four listed domains.

Reflective practice is outlined in Danielson's Framework in Domain 4 (a), Reflecting on Teaching, with descriptions for unsatisfactory, basic, proficient, and distinguished reflection. The description in the Distinguished Category for reflective practice states: "Teacher makes a thoughtful and accurate assessment of a lesson's effectiveness and the extent to which it achieved its goals, citing many specific examples from the lesson and weighing the relative strength of each" (Danielson, 1996, p. 107). The rubric from the Use in Future Teaching element, Distinguished Category, states: "Drawing on extensive repertoire of skills, the teacher offers specific alternative actions, complete with probable successes of different approaches" (Danielson, 1996, p. 107). These descriptors define the actions of a successful reflective practitioner; a teacher must not only reflect on his or her teaching, but also use feedback from previous lessons and modify instruction.

The Danielson Framework is used and modified by many school districts as an evaluation and professional development tool for teachers to analyze their teaching. Teacher preparation programs have also taught their teacher candidates Danielson's Framework as part of their teacher candidate preparation program, and learning the framework early in a teaching career is beneficial. Individual teachers use the framework to self-assess by using the reflective questions and rubric not only to assess their teaching, but also to develop professional plans to improve. The Reflection Sheet (Danielson, 1996) for teachers guides the reflective process and allows the individual to self-reflect on a lesson. Questions asked here include:

1. As I reflect on the lesson, to what extent were students productively engaged?
2. Did the students learn what I intended? Were my instructional goals met? How do I know, or how and when will I know?
3. Did I alter my goals or instructional plan as I taught the lesson? Why?
4. If I had the opportunity to teach this lesson again to this same group of students, what would I do differently? Why?

The purpose of presenting the Danielson Framework is to validate that reflective teaching is an intricate process; in order to improve, a teacher must make a determined effort to effectively critique his or her teaching. An assessment instrument to achieve this goal of reflecting on a teacher's behavior is presented in the following section.

■ THE TEACHER PERFORMANCE CRITERIA QUESTIONNAIRE

Background Information

Rosenshine and Furst (1971) investigated teacher effectiveness through accumulated process–product studies, attempting to relate teaching variables to student achievement.

Eleven variables were identified and defined that measured teacher performance across the disciplines. Using the 11 variables from Rosenshine and Furst's work, Cheffers and Keilty (1980) created the Teacher Performance Criteria Questionnaire (TPCQ), a valid and reliable 16-question instrument with a four-point Likert scale. Of the 11 variables in the TPCQ, the first 6 received strong support, so 2 questions each were developed to measure these variables. The remaining 5 variables received less support, so 1 question per variable was generated to reflect the content of each variable. It was concluded, through an 86.7% content validity, 83.0% internal consistency, 96.0% reliability of ratings, and a rater agreement of 89.95% (Cheffers & Keilty, 1988), that the TPCQ was a valid and reliable measure of teacher effectiveness based on its 11 variables.

Since the origin of the instrument in the early 1980s, the TPCQ has been used successfully for data collection. Cardoza and Cheffers (1990), Butler (1993), Sullivan (1997, 1999, 2001), and other researchers have used the instrument to collect data on teacher effectiveness and teacher behaviors. Prior to 1999, no formal revisions had been performed since the first validation. In 1997, Sullivan conducted a formal investigation and revisited the instrument through critical examination of the description of the variables, word choice of the questions, and how each question accurately measured the content of the teaching variables. Slight changes were made to update and improve the instrument so it could be used well into the twenty-first century (Sullivan, 2001).

The TPCQ is presently a three-page instrument with one page for the definition of the variables and two pages for the 16 questions. Below each recorded question, a space is provided to circle a 4 (Always), 3 (Mostly), 2 (Occasionally), or 1 (Never) on

the Likert scale. The 11 variables for the revised TPCQ are:

1. Clarity
2. Variability
3. Enthusiasm
4. Personal efficiency
5. Opportunity to learn
6. Accepting and encouraging
7. Use of criticism
8. Use of structure and summary comments
9. Question technique
10. Probing
11. Difficulty level of instructions

A complete copy of the variables with descriptions and the Teacher Performance Criteria Questionnaire is included in **Box 2-1**.

Implementation of the TPCQ

The TPCQ is an effective assessment instrument for teaching behaviors (Sullivan, 1999). The three assessment methods—**self-assessment**, **supervisor assessment**, and **triangulation assessment**—are outlined in this section, but the use of the instrument is not limited to these three methods. It is important to note that there is subjectivity with this assessment instrument, and in the future exemplars may be developed for each rating scale score. These exemplars could be discipline specific to signify exemplary (4, which is an "Always" rating) versus unsatisfactory (1, which is a "Never" rating). Finally, it is recommended that the TPCQ not be used for grading purposes for preservice teacher candidates. Instead, the TPCQ should be used for exploration into the examination of reflecting on teaching behaviors and then planning to improve upon defined variables of effective teaching. District and school teaching evaluations could include the TPCQ, but

Box 2-1   The Teacher Performance Criteria Questionnaire

The Teacher Performance Criteria Questionnaire (TPCQ) is composed of 16 questions relating to teaching effectiveness that reflect the content of the 11 variables identified by Rosenshine and Furst in Smith's *Research in Teacher Education* (1971). The variables were identified through a careful review of process–product (teaching behavior/student achievement) studies. This instrument is a revision of Cheffers and Keilty's validation of the questionnaire (1981) and a revisit to the instrument to update wording and content validity (Sullivan, 1999).

The 11 variables to which the questions are addressed are as follows.

1. *Clarity (Questions 1 and 2):* The clear presentation of information and direction as reflected by the appropriateness and delivery of the content of the lesson.
2. *Variability (Questions 3 and 4):* Reflects flexibility in procedural organization, teacher modification, and adaptability.
3. *Enthusiasm (Questions 5 and 6):* Apparent through teacher interest, excitement, and involvement during class, as evidenced by tone of voice, facial expression, bodily involvement, and creativity.
4. *Personal Efficiency (Questions 7 and 8):* The teacher is crisp, efficient, task-oriented, and well organized.
5. *Opportunity to Learn (Questions 9 and 10):* Influenced by the amount of time allotted for learning material presented in the lesson.
6. *Accepting and Encouraging (Question 11):* The teacher is accepting, encouraging, and a listener to the students.
7. *Use of Criticism (Question 12):* Refers to the method of controlling the class with disapproval methods.
8. *Use of Structure and Summary Comments (Question 13):* Use of adjectives, metaphors, and analogies, which refine and enlighten interest in learning. Teacher use of intelligent, helpful summary of factors.
9. *Question Technique (Question 14):* The use of questions by the teacher.
10. *Probing (Question 15):* The teacher's ability to elicit in-depth answers from students in a manner that encourages further elaboration by the student or another student. Teacher also initiates questions of this sort to encourage student elaboration on various content levels.
11. *Difficulty Level of Instructions (Question 16):* Refers to whether the students were appropriately challenged by the level of difficulty of the material presented; whether it was too difficult or too simple.

Before using the questionnaire, please read each question carefully. After observing the lesson, circle the rating scale score that best describes the teacher or student behaviors considered in each question.

4	3	2	1
Always	Mostly	Occasionally	Never

1. Was the material presented in a clear and concise manner?

4	3	2	1
Always	Mostly	Occasionally	Never

2. Did the teacher demonstrate expert knowledge and understanding of the material for the level of students in the class?

4	3	2	1
Always	Mostly	Occasionally	Never

3. Did the teacher present a variety of skills and techniques to assist in instruction?

4	3	2	1
Always	Mostly	Occasionally	Never

4. Did the teacher vary teaching methods and organizational procedures?

4	3	2	1
Always	Mostly	Occasionally	Never

5. Was the teacher's behavior characterized by consistent enthusiasm and interest in the lesson?

4	3	2	1
Always	Mostly	Occasionally	Never

6. Did the students appear interested and involved in the lesson?

4	3	2	1
Always	Mostly	Occasionally	Never

7. Did the teacher go about his/her task in a crisp, organized manner?

4	3	2	1
Always	Mostly	Occasionally	Never

8. Was the class managed in a planned sequential way?

4	3	2	1
Always	Mostly	Occasionally	Never

9. Were the students provided with the opportunity to become engaged in the learning experiences?

4	3	2	1
Always	Mostly	Occasionally	Never

10. Did the students take the opportunity to learn the content of the lesson?

4	3	2	1
Always	Mostly	Occasionally	Never

11. Did the students provide input that the teacher acknowledged, accepted, and, where possible, applied it to the lesson?

4	3	2	1
Always	Mostly	Occasionally	Never

12. Did the teacher avoid the use of harsh criticism (verbal and nonverbal) in maintaining lesson control and evaluating student performance?

4	3	2	1
Always	Mostly	Occasionally	Never

13. Did the teacher use inspirational and helpful analogies at appropriate times?

4	3	2	1
Always	Mostly	Occasionally	Never

14. Did the teacher use a variety of questioning techniques of the material presented?

4	3	2	1
Always	Mostly	Occasionally	Never

15. Did the teacher use probing questions to elicit in-depth answers?

4	3	2	1
Always	Mostly	Occasionally	Never

16. Were most of the students appropriately challenged by the level of difficulty of the material presented?

Notes about the teacher's behaviors using TPCQ variables

_____

_____

_____

_____

_____

_____

_____

_____

_____

_____

as with any sound evaluation, there should be multiple assessment measures.

Coding forms for the TPCQ were developed to assist with recording and reflection. The TPCQ Coding Sheet allows one person to record numbers (see **Box 2-2**), and the TPCQ Coding Sheet for Triangulation Assessment allows three coders to score (see **Box 2-3**).

■ **METHOD 1: SELF-ASSESSMENT**

Following the completion of a lesson, whether the lesson runs for 10 minutes, 45 minutes, or 3 hours, the teacher reflects on his or her lesson. The teacher would review the definitions of the 11 TPCQ variables, and then either circle the appropriate number (1–4) on the TPCQ Instruction Sheet or use the TPCQ Coding Sheet to place a number next to each question. This self-reflection upon teaching behaviors provides what could be considered a score for each variable of effective teaching. The teacher/assessor must be honest with her- or himself, and notes could be recorded beside each score indicating the reason for the score. It would be best to complete the TPCQ Coding Sheet immediately following a lesson. If a video camera or recording device is used, the designated lesson, or part of a lesson, could be recorded and the teacher could complete a TPCQ Coding Sheet after reviewing the recorded lesson. After finishing the TPCQ Coding Sheet, the teacher should review and analyze the scores and select one or two of the variables (TPCQ questions) to improve upon. An action plan of how to improve the selected teaching behaviors should be developed.

Box 2-2 Teacher Performance Criteria Questionnaire Coding Sheet

4	3	2	1
Always	Mostly	Occasionally	Never

Name: _____

Date: _____

Class: _____

Question	Variable	Code
1. Was the material presented in a clear and concise manner?	Clarity	_____
2. Did the teacher demonstrate expert knowledge and understanding of the material for the level of students in the class?	Clarity	_____
3. Did the teacher present a variety of skills and techniques to assist in instruction?	Variability	_____
4. Did the teacher vary teaching methods and organizational procedures?	Variability	_____
5. Was the teacher's behavior characterized by consistent enthusiasm and interest in the lesson?	Enthusiasm	_____
6. Did the students appear interested and involved in the lesson?	Enthusiasm	_____
7. Did the teacher go about his or her task in a crisp, organized manner?	Personal Efficiency	_____
8. Was the class managed in a planned sequential way?	Personal Efficiency	_____
9. Were the students provided with the opportunity to become engaged in the learning experiences?	Opportunity to Learn	_____
10. Did the students take the opportunity to learn the content of the lesson?	Opportunity to Learn	_____
11. Did the students provide input that the teacher acknowledged, accepted, and, where possible, applied it to the lesson?	Accepting and Encouraging	_____
12. Did the teacher avoid the use of harsh criticism (verbal and nonverbal) in maintaining lesson control and evaluating student performance?	Use of Criticism	_____
13. Did the teacher use inspirational and helpful analogies at appropriate times?	Use of Structure and Summary Comments	_____
14. Did the teacher use a variety of questioning techniques of the material presented?	Question Technique	_____
15. Did the teacher use probing questions to elicit in-depth answers?	Probing	_____
16. Were most of the students appropriately challenged by the level of difficulty of the material presented?	Difficulty Level of Instructions	_____

Notes

_____

_____

_____

_____

_____

Box 2-3   Teacher Performance Criteria Questionnaire Coding Sheet for Triangulation Assessment (Three Coders)

4	3	2	1
Always	Mostly	Occasionally	Never

Name: _____

Date: _____

Class: _____

Question	Variable	Coder 1	Coder 2	Coder 3
1. Was the material presented in a clear and concise manner?	Clarity	____	____	____
2. Did the teacher demonstrate expert knowledge and understanding of the material for the level of students in the class?	Clarity	____	____	____
3. Did the teacher present a variety of skills and techniques to assist in instruction?	Variability	____	____	____
4. Did the teacher vary teaching methods and organizational procedures?	Variability	____	____	____
5. Was the teacher's behavior characterized by consistent enthusiasm and interest in the lesson?	Enthusiasm	____	____	____
6. Did the students appear interested and involved in the lesson?	Enthusiasm	____	____	____
7. Did the teacher go about his/her task in a crisp, organized manner?	Personal Efficiency	____	____	____
8. Was the class managed in a planned sequential way?	Personal Efficiency	____	____	____
9. Were the students provided with the opportunity to become engaged in the learning experiences?	Opportunity to Learn	____	____	____
10. Did the students take the opportunity to learn the content of the lesson?	Opportunity to Learn	____	____	____
11. Did the students provide input that the teacher acknowledged, accepted, and, where possible, applied it to the lesson?	Accepting and Encouraging	____	____	____
12. Did the teacher avoid the use of harsh criticism (verbal and nonverbal) in maintaining lesson control and evaluating student performance?	Use of Criticism	____	____	____
13. Did the teacher use inspirational and helpful analogies at appropriate times?	Use of Structure and Summary Comments	____	____	____

14. Did the teacher use a variety of questioning techniques of the material presented?   Question Technique   ____ ____ ____

15. Did the teacher use probing questions to elicit in-depth answers?   Probing   ____ ____ ____

16. Were most of the students appropriately challenged by the level of difficulty of the material presented?   Difficulty Level of Instructions   ____ ____ ____

Notes

_____

_____

_____

_____

_____

■ METHOD 2: SUPERVISOR ASSESSMENT

College faculty members have used the TPCQ to evaluate the teaching behaviors of students teaching mini or peer lessons during their practicum experiences in college. As previously mentioned, it is not suggested that this instrument be used to determine a grade, but rather to assist the preservice students in critically examining their teaching. College supervisors have used the TPCQ during their work with teacher candidates (student teachers). A supervisor could observe a lesson by a teacher candidate and then complete a TPCQ Coding Sheet immediately following the lesson. The supervisor could record notes on the form throughout the observation. The results could be used to lead a valuable discussion on the teaching behaviors of the teacher candidate. The supervisor and teacher candidate would be able to work together to target areas for improvement and growth as well as documenting those behaviors that were well established. For an enhanced discussion in this student teaching situation, the teacher candidate could complete a TPCQ after teaching the lesson the supervisor observed. The two scales, those of the teacher candidate and the supervisor, could be used for a discussion about the teaching behaviors. As with the self-assessment, simply recording the scores is not sufficient to complete the reflective teaching cycle. Reasons for the scores and the means of improving the ratings must be outlined. It is best to select one or two variables with specific and detailed plans for improvement. Note that a cooperating teacher could also complete the TPCQ supervisor assessment. Furthermore, the supervisor and cooperating teacher could each complete a TPCQ on the lesson by the teacher candidate.

■ METHOD 3: TRIANGULATION ASSESSMENT

As the word *triangulation* indicates, there are three coders involved with this third method of implementing the TPCQ. The three coders could be the teacher candidate, cooperating teacher, and college supervisor or the beginning teacher, colleague, and principal. Research with TPCQ triangulation has been conducted with the three coders of college student (self), peer college student, and professor. The investigator implemented the TPCQ with a movement education class of physical education majors and non-physical education majors. Ten of the 17 subjects/teachers in the class were randomly selected to participate in the TPCQ triangulation assessment. Each teacher taught an integrated game lesson using movement to reinforce content. Immediately following the teaching of the lesson, a triad completed the TPCQ with respect to the same lesson and teacher. The student teacher used TPCQ for a self-assessment, a peer from the class used TPCQ to assess the student teacher's performance, and the investigator served as the professor who assessed each teacher's effectiveness with TPCQ. Thus, three independent individuals were using the same instrument, the TPCQ, to measure teacher effectiveness through the 11 variables defined in the questionnaire. Each evaluator rated the teacher and the lesson, incognizant of each other's TPCQ scores (Sullivan, 2001).

TPCQ triangulation can be completed with any three coders scoring the same teacher, and one coder could be the teacher him- or herself as the self-assessment coder. All three coders can use the TPCQ Coding Sheet for Triangulation Assessment; each coder can record his or her scores and then the paper can be folded back so each coder cannot view scores from the other coders. There also is the option of each coder completing the TPCQ Coding Sheet, which was designed for one coder.

■ CONCLUSION

There is no question that teaching is complicated, but teachers must take the initiative to analyze their teaching in order to improve. Self-assessment is a critical tool in teaching, and the term *reflective practitioner* should only be applied to a teacher who actively engages in the ongoing process of examining how he or she teaches. The use of assessment instruments, like the one presented here, the Teacher Performance Criteria Questionnaire, can assist teachers in examining their teaching and targeting areas of strengths and those that need to be enhanced. Teachers need to be honest with themselves as they look in the teaching mirror. All teachers, beginning and experienced, need not only to reflect, but also to use the feedback from the reflective process and take action to improve. "Skillful teachers are made, not born" (Saphier & Gower 1979).

■ KEY WORDS AND DEFINITIONS

reflective teachers   Teachers who use a variety of formal and informal assessments to critique their lessons and examine their teaching behaviors.

reflective teaching   The process of a teacher critically examining his or her instruction through a formal or informal means of thoughtful questions and assessment in order to improve instruction based on the feedback and to enhance student learning.

self-assessment   A teacher who dissects his or her teaching and lesson, and thinks about what happened during the teaching process; one who analyzes student performance is using self assessment. Self-assessment should also include the step of asking good questions about the teaching and making plans to improve practices.

supervisor assessment   Teacher evaluation when a principal, administrator, colleague, or a person of higher authority evaluates the teaching.

triangulation assessment Three evaluators or coders record a teacher's behaviors.

■ DISCUSSION QUESTIONS

1. Why is it important to become a reflective practitioner?
2. Learn more about the Charlotte Danielson Framework for Teaching and present what you learned to the class. Have different people learn about the domains. What are some discipline-specific examples in physical education and health education for each domain?
3. Review the 11 TPCQ variables of effective teaching behaviors in a small cooperative group. Discuss each variable and record at least one example that would show exemplary performance in your field (physical education, health education, or another discipline). Can you think of other variables that make a good teacher?
4. Use the TPCQ to code someone teaching a class. Write a short narrative analyzing the teaching behaviors using the results and data. Be sure to cite examples and to discuss the reasons for recording a given score, from 1–4.
5. Interview a practitioner who is teaching in the schools and have him or her share the evaluation process the district uses for teacher evaluation. Who conducts the evaluation? How often are they evaluated and what instrument is used? Does a specialist in physical education or health education evaluate the physical or health education teacher or is it the building principal? Why or why not?

■ REFERENCES

Arends, R. (2009). *Learning to teach*. Boston: McGraw-Hill Higher Education.

Boud, D., Keogh, R., & Walker, D. (1985). What is reflection in teaching? In D. Boud, R. Keogh, & D. Walker (Eds.), *Reflection: Turning experience into learning* (pp. 18–40). New York: Nicholas.

Butler, J. (1993). *Teacher change in sport education*. Unpublished dissertation. Boston: Boston University.

Cardoza, P., & Cheffers, J. (1990). Describing a student, beginning teacher and experienced teacher behaviors. Proceedings from the AIESEP: Foundation for Promotion of Physical Activity. Jyvaskyla, Finland.

Cheffers, J., Gilfillan, R., & Sullivan, E. (2000). *Instruction sheet for the teacher performance criteria questionnaire (TPCQ)*, Version IX. Available from the authors.

Cheffers, J., & Keilty, G. (1981). Developing valid instrumentation for measuring teacher performance. *International Journal of Physical Education, 17*(2).

Danielson, C. (1996). *Enhancing professional practice: A framework for teaching*. Alexandria, VA: Association for Supervision and Curriculum Development.

Darst, P., Zakrajsek, D., & Mancini, V. (Eds.). (1989). *Analyzing physical education and sport instruction*. Champaign, IL: Human Kinetics.

Feiman-Nemser, S. (1982). Learning to teach. In L. Schulman & G. Sykes (Eds.), *Handbook of teaching and policy* (pp. 150–171). New York: Longman.

Gimbel, P. (2008, January). Helping new teachers reflect. *Principal Leadership*, 6–8.

National Association for Sport and Physical Education. (2008). National initial physical education teacher education standards. Retrieved May 31, 2011, from http://www.aahperd .org/naspe/standards/nationalStandards/ PETEstandards.cfm

Rink, J. (2006). *Teaching physical education for learning*. Boston: McGraw-Hill.

Rosenshine, B., & Furst, N. (1971). Research on teacher performance criteria. In B. Smith

(Ed.), *Research in teacher education: A symposium* (pp. 37–72). Englewood Cliffs, NJ: Prentice Hall.

Saphier, J., & Gower, R. (1979). *The skillful teacher: Building your teaching skills.* Carlisle, MA: Research for Better Teaching.

Stronge, J. (2002). *Qualities of effective teachers.* Alexandra, VA: Association for Supervision and Curriculum Development.

Sullivan, E. (1997, December). Self-evaluation of nonmajor student teachers in a university laboratory physical education program. Proceedings from the International Association for Physical Education and Sport in Higher Education (AIESEP) (pp. 181–190). Singapore: AIESEP.

Sullivan, E. (1999, April 7). Evaluating teachers and coaches: The teacher performance criteria questionnaire (TPCQ) revisited. Proceedings from the International Association for Physical Education and Sport in Higher Education (AIESEP). Besancon, France: AIESEP.

Sullivan, E. (2001). Variation with the implementation of the teacher performance criteria questionnaire (TPCQ): Triangulation assessment with self, peer, and professor. In *Facing Change: Proceedings of the International Association for Physical Education and Sport in Higher Education (AIESEP) World Sport Science Congress* at Rockhampton, Australia, 2000. Central Queensland: University Press, School of Health & Human Performance, (pp. 2.78–2.85).

Tate, P. M. (2001). Excellence in teaching: Myths and legends. In T. Arnold (Ed.), *Facing change: Proceedings of the International Association for Physical Education and Sport in Higher Education (AIESEP) World Sport Science Congress* (pp. 1.45–1.51). Rockhampton, Queensland, Australia: Association Internationale des Escoles Superieures d'Education Physique and School of Health and Human Performance, Central Queensland University.

Research Review

Details for a Physical Education–Specific Mentoring Program

Christopher Nightingale

Mentoring is a process in which new professionals are assisted at the beginning of their career by more experienced peers. The concept of mentoring has been used in many fields, including health care, business, and education (Kram, 1985). Within education, many locations require some form of mentoring for new teachers, but few design entire programs to address the specific needs of new physical educators. Although all new teachers have certain needs at the start of their career, regardless of content area, physical education teachers tend to have a very different experience in their day-to-day teaching than the more traditional classroom-based teacher. Physical education teachers are often itinerant and may spend only 1 or 2 days each week in a given school. Whereas a classroom teacher might see the same 20 children in her or his classroom for an entire school year, a physical educator might encounter several hundred different students at multiple schools in the course of a school week (Graber et al., 2008).

Physical educators use equipment that can pose a safety risk if misused by their students. The physical educator that lets his or her attention wane, even momentarily, may find him- or herself dealing with an injured student. Research indicates one in three injuries to school children occur in physical education class, whereas less than 17% of total schoolchildren injuries occur in the classroom (Sosnowska & Kostka, 2003).

Traditional classroom teachers tend to be members of larger academic departments and may have peers in their content area that can help them with issues. Physical educators may be the only individual in a school teaching PE content. This can create feelings of isolation that need to be addressed by new physical educators. It might be easier to identify an experienced teacher to serve as a **mentor** for an English or science teacher than for a physical educator.

The purpose of this research review is to present some of the current available information regarding mentoring that is tailored specifically for the needs of new physical education teachers. Two specific styles of research are conducted within this field, and attention will be given to both. The review will conclude with a presentation of a framework for implementing a **physical education–specific mentoring** program. This model is the result of research conducted for a doctoral dissertation (Nightingale, 2009) where the investigator completed a case study analysis

of such a program. The case study was conducted during the 2005–2006 and 2006–2007 calendar years. The research considered the mentoring of new physical educators at the elementary and secondary levels and encompassed interviews, document review, and direct observation sessions of mentors, mentees, and program nonparticipants in a school district.

■ CASE STUDY APPROACH

The first type of article is the **case study approach** of presenting one particular mentoring program and the benefits it offers for its participants. An example of the case study approach is the work of Jordan, Phillips, and Brown (2004). These authors presented a review of the Tennessee Technical University's program for training elementary- and secondary-level physical education teachers and physical education teacher supervisors. The researchers note that "knowledgeable supervision and mentoring are key elements in developing good teachers" (Jordan et al., 2004, p. 219). The particular program that these professors describe includes instruction in the use of planning formats and evaluation tools used by the Tennessee Department of Education. The planning formats that are considered in this course are the Tennessee Instructional Model (TIM), which addresses specific ways that lesson plans are to be written and conducted within the state, and the Tennessee Value-Added Assessment System (TVAAS), which uses standardized testing of students to evaluate whether students are making adequate progress in school (Jordan et al., 2004). Students in the course are indoctrinated into the utilization of these state-specific instruments. Participation in this course also requires a 30-hour practicum in public school instruction, assessment, and lesson planning. Coordinating faculty members from the university guide and assess the development of skills in teaching and in supervision, and graduates receive supervision experience that normally would not be encountered.

Gaskin, Lumpkin, and Tennant (2003) note that new faculty in higher education physical education programs also benefit from mentoring. These authors propose that **induction physical educators** do not exist simply at the elementary or secondary level and that collegiate physical educators face challenges in their early days. These authors note that mentors can help new faculty members with teaching behaviors, conducting research, service expectations, and adapting to the institutional culture (Gaskin, Lumpkin, & Tennant, 2003).

The need for mentoring for induction physical educators also was promoted by Gagen and Bowie (2005). These investigators inform us that mentoring helps improve teacher retention as well as improve the practices of new physical educators. These authors note that mentors offer support that can "make the difference between being overwhelmed and being motivated to find a way to succeed" (Gagen & Bowie, 2005, p. 41). Mentors provide support in developing a wide array of instructional strategies, including classroom management, discipline, developing effective classroom routines, organizing lesson plans, and fulfilling the requirements and expectations of the school for its teachers. Mentors can target ineffective teaching practices used by novice teachers and inform the new teachers that something might not be working as well as they believe. Gagen and Bowie assert that it is important for mentors to have training before taking on the responsibility of helping a new teacher adapt. Training improves mentor–**protégé**

communication, helps mentors better understand novice teacher needs, and shows mentors different strategies for helping their protégés. For example, some **mentees** learn how to handle disciplinary issues by discussing scenarios with their mentors. Other new teachers need to observe real-time disciplinary encounters administered by experienced teachers to develop their own skills. Training can help prospective mentors understand the best ways to help their mentees grasp new concepts and improve their teaching. Gagen and Bowie are strong proponents for formalized mentoring. They assert that novice teachers might be able to find an informal mentor that serves a beneficial role, but by providing training to mentors and teaching them about the specific needs of mentees, the process is more likely to be successful and effective for more new educators.

■ MENTORING FOR SPECIAL POPULATIONS

The second variety of physical education mentoring research consists of studies that examine the impact that mentoring has on a specific subpopulation of physical education teachers. Examples include the effects of mentoring on ethnic minorities or specific genders. A good example of this style of research is the work of Brown and Evans (2004), who hypothesized that some male physical education teachers perpetuate gender bias by taking on male students as protégés in their classes. They note that teachers often serve a powerful role in the "social construction of gender relations" for students, and a male hegemony can be perpetuated if care is not taken (Brown & Evans, 2004, p. 48). These authors gathered "life history data" through qualitative interviews with eight male students before, during, and after their graduate school experience studying physical education. These students all identified a male physical education teacher during their formative experiences who assumed the role of mentor for them and had a "powerful bearing on his outlook and educational career" (Brown & Evans, 2004, p. 55). Gender roles were observed by the researchers, and they found that each of the subjects they interviewed served the role of being one of the more gifted athletes in their school experience. The subjects also believed that their gender facilitated the mentoring relationship with their instructors.

The work of Brown and Evans is similar to that of Schempp and Graber (1992), who noted that new physical education teachers must face various contradictions as they move through the process of becoming an educator. At various stages in their lives (from youth when they are physical education students, through the educational experiences, to the induction phase), individuals must scrutinize the practices they observe and the knowledge they have been given. Each individual needs to understand the process and structure of the system of physical education and how they fit within the system (Schempp & Graber, 1992). A mentor at any or all of these stages can provide insight and help an individual gain perspective. According to the authors, those individuals who find their place within the field of physical education are able to understand the system and are therefore best able to make the transition into the role of physical educator.

Schempp also has indicated that mentors can be useful to induction teachers by serving as role models. New teachers often benefit by observing experienced teachers and integrating what they observe into their own teaching. Schempp (2003) states, "To adapt to their environments and establish social order in their classes, beginning teachers

most often mimic the routines of their senior colleagues" (p. 16).

Research by Hodge (1997) examined the impact of mentoring on physical education students from diverse cultural and socioeconomic backgrounds and how mentoring has helped minority students fit into the field of physical education. Hodge found that pairing students of color with similar mentors provided them support and guidance. This research was conducted through both quantitative surveys and qualitative questionnaires, and considered the experiences of African American, Asian, Pacific Islander, Israeli, and African students who were either enrolled in or had graduated from graduate physical education programs in the United States. Seventy-three percent of respondents indicated that they sought out a mentor, even if one was not assigned to them in their program. Fifty-eight percent of the subjects indicated that access to an ethnic minority mentor was a critical component of their success (Hodge, 1997).

■ SAMPLE PROGRAM

An example of a mentoring program that integrates essential components for teachers is presented in **Table 2-5**. This program requires that all new physical educators complete several specific activities during summertime orientation sessions in their district. These activities include completing surveys about their comfort level with teaching specific units and interviewing with departmental administrators. This information is then used by the administration to gain insight into the new teachers' personalities and individual needs, thus facilitating the process of connecting them with the most appropriate mentors. These orientation activities are used to adjust the ways in which the two

TABLE 2-5   Components of a Physical Education Mentoring Program

Summertime Orientation Sessions

Acclimation to district and specific schools

Surveys to learn what new teachers are and are not comfortable teaching

Interviews with departmental administrators to facilitate pairing with mentors

Monthly New Teachers' Meetings

Social opportunity to interact with peers and share experiences with others

Information dissemination from district administrators about coming events

Guest speakers about how to teach specific content

Opportunities to practice teaching specific content

One-on-One Mentoring Sessions

Release time for mentors and mentees to meet

Opportunities to observe each other teaching classes

No set agenda; freedom to explore what mentor/mentee want

Two years required participation for all new physical educators

other main program components, a series of monthly new teachers' meetings and one-on-one mentoring sessions, are implemented for individual new physical education teachers. The table indicates the three major devices used to help new physical educators adjust to their positions. These data represent the results of a case study design of a physical education–specific mentoring program.

All new physical education teachers participate in a programmatic orientation in late summer before the beginning of their first year of teaching. This orientation serves as an opportunity to provide the new physical education teachers with time to acclimate to the culture of the specific school district, school, and department in which the new teachers are employed. The specific curriculum for the year is presented and areas in which new physical educators traditionally struggle are addressed during this orientation period. Concurrently, the departmental administrators informally interview the new teachers in an attempt to learn more about their personalities with the hope of selecting an appropriate match to serve as their mentor.

Prospective mentors receive training about how they may best be able to serve their mentees. Upon completion of this training, mentors are carefully teamed up with the new teachers. The process of pairing mentors with new teachers is a subjective one, so there should be latitude in allowing either a mentor or mentee to request a change in pairing if either believes that the chemistry of the partnership is not conducive to assisting the new physical educator in their professional development. With careful consideration given to the matching process this should, however, be a rare occurrence. Prospective mentors should be identified by the departmental administrators and approached about serving in this role, rather than simply waiting for experienced teachers to volunteer. Not every experienced teacher has the temperament or attitude to be an effective mentor, and it is vital that program administration feel confident that the mentors are benefiting the new teachers.

Another element of the orientation period should be a questionnaire that all new teachers are required to complete. This questionnaire should gather information about the aspects of the curriculum that the new teachers feel comfortable with and those they might need help with. The results of these surveys should be used later to generate meeting topics for the follow-up monthly new teacher meetings held by the physical education department.

The final important aspect of the summertime orientation period is to provide time for new teachers to meet their mentors. This allows the partners time to begin developing their relationship. By giving time for the mentor and mentee to interact with each other during a summertime orientation period, the new physical educator has begun to develop a support system, which should be firmly in place before the first day of school. If such a relationship is developed later, time constraints and the demands of the school day can interfere with the process of gaining needed assistance.

■ MONTHLY NEW TEACHERS' MEETINGS

New teachers should be awarded continuing education credits or another incentive for attending monthly new teachers' meetings. Meetings should typically begin with new teachers being given ample time to connect with each other and to share their experiences with other teachers who are also new to the field. It is advisable that two meetings be held each month, one for teachers at the elementary school level, the other for secondary school teachers. This grouping recognizes the difference between teaching at these two educationally and developmentally different levels. The opportunity to interact with each other is an important priority, particularly for elementary-level teachers, because many of these teachers work in different buildings and can often develop a sense of isolation as the only new physical educator within a particular school.

The next phase of these meetings involves an information-sharing period in which departmental-level administrators share important day-to-day information with the new teachers. Often this information is time sensitive and deals with events that are due to occur within the upcoming weeks. Examples of this information include sharing the way that grades need to be submitted electronically at the end of the term, and the procedures for inventorying and ordering new equipment.

Finally, a workshop-type presentation should occur, in which a different mentor each month presents specific content regarding teaching the district's curriculum. These presentations consider specific activities and proficiencies, and occur in the weeks leading up to the teaching of the particular unit during the school year. For example, if the elementary educators were going to be undertaking a unit on teaching the skills associated with floor hockey in the month of February, the January new teachers' meeting should feature a presentation on the teaching of striking with an implement for young children and instructing older children in floor hockey game rules and strategies. Presentations should feature role playing and opportunities for the new teachers to practice using the skills they learned to reinforce the best ways to teach the specific content.

■ ONE-ON-ONE MENTORING SESSIONS

The third element of a successful physical education mentoring program is the one-on-one mentoring that occurs between the new teachers and their assigned mentors. Release time should be arranged for the pair to work together and openly discuss the new teacher's performance. No formal schedule for meeting times needs to be pre-arranged; mentors and mentees should be given the latitude to meet at their own convenience. The program objectives, however, should encourage mentors to seek out meetings with mentees at least weekly in the early part of the school year and at least every other week thereafter.

More or fewer meetings can be scheduled as the participants deem necessary. Mentors should be required to verify with the program directors that meetings are occurring. This documentation or tracking of the hours could be completed electronically.

There does not need to be a written agenda for one-on-one mentoring meetings. Mentors and mentees need to be free to explore topics and address particular issues as they see fit. One may consider this arrangement to be one in which malfeasance may occur. This system could be manipulated by mentors or mentees that elect to skip meetings or to use release time in unproductive ways. It is possible to minimize the likelihood of this happening by the careful selection of mentors and the specific training that the mentors receive. If appropriate mentors are trained early on to value the process and treat it respectfully, then potential for problems can be minimized. By requiring no formal reporting on the specific topics addressed in mentoring meetings, mentees tend to be more open and free with the topics they discuss. There is no fear of reprisal for asking questions and no concern that questions about how to improve poor performance will lead to censure from the departmental administration. The program is created to put new teachers at ease with qualified mentors and to help them improve in their day-to-day performance in teaching physical education. It is not a way to check up on a new teacher's performance.

Although formal meetings are encouraged throughout the mentoring process, informal meetings are encouraged as well. The informality works well with some mentor/mentee pairs and helps them bond as professionals and as friends. Mentors and mentees who develop camaraderie outside of the professional relationship tend to work well together. Mentors and mentees who share lunch periods or discuss current events develop deeper bonds, which facilitate sharing of information.

Mentors and mentees should be granted release time not only for meetings, but also to observe each other in their teaching roles. New teachers should have the opportunity to observe their mentors role modeling successful teaching behaviors in real-time physical education activities. Mentors can use release time to observe their mentees teaching and to formulate strategies that might help the mentees improve their performance.

This three-tiered approach (summertime orientation sessions, monthly new teachers' meetings, and one-on-one mentoring sessions) for the development and implementation of a mentoring program for new physical educators is not an easy process to implement. It takes a careful coordination of effort on the part of many people, from school administrators to the new teachers themselves, to make a mentoring program work effectively. Such a plan benefits from financial support and can potentially strain resources for a district. A mentoring program of this design is not something that can be implemented without a full commitment from the teachers and administration of a physical education department. Fortunately, the research indicates that this effort is rewarded by both improved job performance and improved job retention of the new physical educators.

■ KEY WORDS AND DEFINITIONS

case study approach   This style of research focuses on presenting a single institution or phenomenon for in-depth review.

induction physical educators Educators who are at the beginning of their career.

mentee   A less experienced professional who participates in a mentoring relationship (synonymous with protégé).

mentor   A person who is a more experienced professional who participates in a mentoring relationship.

mentoring   A process in which a more experienced professional offers support and guidance to a less experienced professional.

physical education–specific mentoring program   A specific curriculum designed to address the professional needs of new teachers in the field of physical education.

protégé   A less experienced professional who participates in a mentoring relationship (synonymous with mentee).

■ DISCUSSION QUESTIONS

1. Which concepts of physical education–specific mentoring research require further investigation?

2. In what ways can working with a mentor assist an induction physical educator?

3. Which specific elements of the sample program presented are the most beneficial for helping a new teacher acclimate to a new setting? Which are beneficial for helping a new teacher become comfortable with didactic content?

4. There are advantages and disadvantages to formalizing the mentoring process. Which style of mentoring (formal or informal) would work best for you? Why?

5. Should a school district implement a district-wide mentoring program in addition to specific mentoring for new physical education teachers, as described in this article?

■ REFERENCES

Brown, D., & Evans, J. (2004). Reproducing gender? Intergenerational links and the male PE teacher as a cultural conduit in teaching physical education. *Journal of Teaching in Physical Education, 23*, 48–70.

Gagen, L., & Bowie, S. (2005). Effective mentoring: A case for training mentors for novice teachers. *Journal of Physical Education, Recreation, and Dance, 76*(7), 40–45.

Gaskin, L. P., Lumpkin, A., & Tennant, L. K. (2003). Mentoring new faculty in higher education. *Journal of Physical Education, Recreation, and Dance, 74*(8), 49–53.

Graber, K. C., Locke, L. F., Lambdin, D., & Solmon, M. A. (2008). The landscape of elementary school physical education. *Elementary School Journal, 35*(3), 21–24.

Hodge, S. (1997). Mentoring perspectives of physical education graduate students from diverse backgrounds. *Physical Educator, 54*, 181–195.

Jordan, P., Phillips, M., & Brown, E. (2004). We train teachers: Why not supervisors and mentors? *Physical Educator, 61*, 219–221.

Kram, K. E. (1985). *Mentoring at work: Developmental relationships in organizational life.* Lanham, MD: University Press of America.

Nightingale, C. J. (2009). *A physical education teacher mentoring program: A case study.* Doctoral dissertation. Boston, MA: Boston University.

Schempp, P. G. (2003). *Teaching sport and physical activity: Insights on the road to excellence.* Champaign, IL: Human Kinetics.

Schempp, P. G., & Graber, K. C. (1992). Teacher socialization for a dialectical perspective: Pretraining through induction. *Journal of Teaching in Physical Education, 11*, 329–348.

Sosnowska, S., & Kostka, T. (2003). Epidemiology of school accidents during a six school-year period in one region in Poland. *European Journal of Epidemiology, 18*, 977–982.

CHAPTER 3

The *Student* in the Triad of Teaching and Learning (Teacher-Student-Content)

■ CHAPTER OVERVIEW

Apollo 13 and its unsuccessful attempt to land on the moon sets the stage for the first article's theme on teamwork and team-building activities. The author cleverly defines teamwork and leadership with a lively discussion about stimulating leadership and team development, descriptions of experiential learning, and the need to design a relevant activity to teach teamwork and leadership. The requirement to process or debrief team-building activities reminds us that the method might be more important than the product. Kolb's experiential learning cycle is reviewed with this section of the article. Finally, indoor and outdoor experiential activities with a space theme are presented. The explicit descriptions, instructions/rules, and debriefing questions provide a valuable resource for physical educators and other teachers.

The second article provides an introduction with clear definitions, a short history of the education of children with disabilities, and a discussion about the legal rights of students with disabilities and their families. This background information allows the reader to understand some essential basic information before reading about the rationale for inclusive education. A description of practices and strategies that are designed to ensure that appropriate and individualized programs are provided to students includes presentation of the Universal Design for Learning, differentiated instruction, and peer support. The authors successfully remind us that with the increase in the number of students with disabilities in both general and physical education classes, educators need to be cognizant of how to best plan and teach to the needs of these students.

The parameters of, need for, and contribution of positive psychology to physical education and health education teachers are described in the third article. The central question of what contributes to our happiness is explored; this question is the foundation of positive psychology or what is right and not wrong with people. The relationship of character strengths and virtue is explored. Specifically, Peterson and Seligman's (2004) Virtues in Action (VIA) classifications are presented. The last section of the article talks about the challenges and the benefits of using positive psychology when motivating students in the classroom and on the sport field.

The fourth article in this chapter provides specific and detailed scientific evidence about our inactive youth of today and the rising epidemic of obesity. The topics of inactive youth, health issues associated with obesity, and environmental factors during childhood that have contributed to obesity are presented. Then obesity prevention and treatment, as well as the association between physical activity and academic performance are reviewed. "How Teachers Can Help Make a Difference" at the end of the article is a valuable checklist for any educator to assist in preventing childhood obesity and lack of physical activity.

Using Team-Building Activities to Form a Community of Leaders

Christopher Roland

The year 2009 marked the 40th anniversary of the landing of Apollo 11 on the moon. Mission Commander Neil Armstrong and Lunar Modular Pilot Edwin Aldrin Jr. touched down on the Sea of Tranquility on July 20, 1969, at 3:17 PM while Command Modular Pilot Michael Collins orbited overhead. The incredible level of **teamwork** that was required to make this all possible was truly remarkable. But why was teamwork needed in the first place? Here was a group of intellectually gifted leaders in their respective fields: aeronautics, electronics, computers, systems, and meteorologists. But, left alone, this "team" would have simply been a collection of individuals who would be unlikely to respond efficiently and effectively to a challenge. Kotter (1999) shares the first two key steps for what leaders and teams need to do to respond to demands, changes, and challenges: *establish a sense of urgency and create a vision.* This is exactly what John F. Kennedy did on May 25, 1961, on his "Man on the Moon" special address to Congress:

First, I believe that this nation should commit itself to achieving the goal, before this decade is out, of landing a man on the moon and returning him safely to the earth. No single space project in this period will be more impressive to mankind, or more important for the long-range exploration of space; and none will be so difficult or expensive to accomplish. (Kennedy, 1961)

The event was mesmerizing—schoolchildren, their teachers, and parents witnessed, and later discussed, an event that people are still talking about today, and certainly will be well into the future.

The landing on the moon received huge press—before, during, and after. But what also received a fair amount of press 9 months later was a critical failure that required an even greater level of teamwork than ever before. This was the remarkable journey of Apollo 13 with Mission Commander Jim Lovell, Command Module Pilot Jack Swigert, and Lunar Module Pilot Fred Haise—one more real life **team-building** "exercise" that can be analyzed and dissected, pointing out the critical elements required for simulated team-building activities that are intended to help form any team, community, or group. Clips from the movie *Apollo 13* are often used in team development workshops and programs, frequently prompting lively discussion and debate about the elements of developing a team.

■ TEAM AND LEADERSHIP LESSONS

Apollo 13 was beautifully and seamlessly launched from Cape Kennedy (now Cape Canaveral) on April 11, 1970. Two days later, on April 13, the Command Module *Odyssey* was rocked with an explosion followed by the infamous communication to Mission Control: "Houston, we've had a problem." Upon analysis, a series of problems—not just one problem (or the hoped-for instrument error)—reared their ugly heads:

- The onboard computer was signaling a major glitch.
- The craft had mysteriously switched antennas.
- Two of three fuel cells were generating no electricity.
- Two panels supplying power were losing voltage.
- One oxygen tank had ruptured and emptied (apparently the cause of the explosion).

One of the key criteria for effective leaders and teams is the ability to solve problems and make timely decisions. Thirty-six-year-old Mission Control Director Eugen Krantz moved into action by calmly stating, "Let's solve the problem . . . and let's not make it any worse by guessing" (Usteem, 1998,

pp. 68–69). His co-director Glenn Lumney followed with "We've got a lot of long-range problems to deal with" (p. 71).

Teamwork was needed here—on the ground and in space. A few key characteristics of effective teams, so dramatically played out in 1970, include:

- A determination to meet conflict head-on, a capacity of commitment, a focus on accountability, and a focus on results (Lencioni, 2002)
- The need to build and sustain trust (Covey, 2007; Reina & Reina, 2006)
- Asking for help, the ability for self-disclosure, learning to listen, asking for support, and dealing with adversity (Snow, 1992)
- The ability to respond to adversity, change, and transition (Stoltz, 1997; Stoltz & Weihenmayer, 2006)

■ SIMULATING LEADERSHIP AND TEAM DEVELOPMENT

For decades, teachers have sought stimulating, engaging leadership and team development activities—ones that will provide simulated problems, decision-making points, and a need for collaboration. One of the best examples is an aircraft simulator, in which the instructor can program the computers to simulate a wide range of malfunctions. Today the simulators, in addition to helping pilots refine their individual piloting skills, help with *cockpit resource management*, in which the pilot and co-pilot need to work cooperatively and collaboratively to prevent errors and, in the event of an error, diagnose and deal with it promptly. This concept was illustrated when US Airways Flight #1549 landed on the Hudson River on January 15, 2009. Pilot Chesley "Sully" Sullenberger, first officer

Jeffrey Skiles, and flight attendants Sheila Dell, Doreen Welsh, and Donna Dent worked exquisitely together to get everyone out of the aircraft without any major injuries.

EXPERIENTIAL LEARNING: ENGAGING STUDENTS IN LEARNING

Experiential learning has its roots in various sources including John Dewey, Carl Rogers, and Albert Bandura. Rogers highlighted the need for congruence, empathic understanding, and unconditional positive regard, as well as active listening and valuing self-worth. These ideals are incorporated into virtually every successful experiential learning process (Weigand, 1995). The **experiential learning cycle** was introduced by Kolb and Fry in 1975 and is a "guiding star" to help teachers learn how to translate an experiential activity into a valued learning tool. Kolb's experiential learning cycle incorporates four elements:

- *Concrete experience:* An activity, simulation, or event that aims at stimulating and motivating the student
- *Observation and reflection:* The "what" we did—how it impacted team members and lessons learned
- *Forming abstract concepts:* The "so what"— how this activity, simulation, or event will help students apply lessons learned to real-life problem solving, decision making, conflict management, and so on
- *Testing implications of concepts in new situations:* The "now what"—leveraging lessons learned into future situations and challenges

This cycle provides the teacher with a road map for the design and facilitation of engaging team-building experiences. And, design is the key!

DESIGN: THE KEY TO STIMULATING, EFFECTIVE, RELEVANT TEAM-BUILDING ACTIVITIES

Too often, time is focused on the actual teaching or facilitation of the activity, versus creating a relevant **design**. Yet without thoughtful design, team activities can become simply diversionary and recreational. Design can be defined as "... a blending of personalities, goals, expectations and past experiences with the realities of the environment, time restrictions and the available resources to create an event of meaning and perhaps beauty that can stand alone" (Napier & Luckner, 1983).

One key aspect of design is sometimes referred to as **frontloading**. Frontloading an activity allows the students to understand *why* they are being asked to participate in the activity. Team-building activities encompass a wide-range of competencies, skills, and knowledge, including verbal communication, nonverbal communication, delegation, problem solving, decision making, collaboration, and conflict management. The teacher needs to determine what component of team building he or she wants to focus on and then frontload it to the students (e.g., "OK everyone, this next activity will give you an opportunity to experience decision making under stress. Please observe how you respond to the challenge as well as how your teammates respond.") When the occasion is appropriate, it is a perfectly acceptable frontload to simply say, "This next activity will offer you a litany of team-building skills. Let's see which skills bubble to the surface." A final type of frontloading is to give students a scenario—a story—that creates a fictitious framework for why the activity is being facilitated.

■ PROCESSING THE EXPERIENCE

A critical aspect of any design is the **processing** of an activity. Also commonly referred to as *debriefing*, it is the meaning, and perhaps beauty, that allows an experiential team-building activity to become a powerful learning medium for the student. Processing is best viewed as part of an experiential activity that is structured to encourage individuals to plan, reflect, describe, analyze, and communicate about experiences (Luckner & Nadler, 1997). Processing activities can be used to help students think about the meaning of the activity and potential application to real world living prior to, during, and after the facilitation of the actual activity.

One can use the aforementioned Kolb's experiential learning cycle as a guide to help students maximize their potential learning:

- *Concrete experience: What* did you experience? How were you able to make critical decisions under stress?
- *Observation and reflection: So what* does this mean? Can anyone think of a time in real life when you were under stress and needed to make a decision?
- *Forming abstract concepts: Now what* might you do in another real-life scenario? How might you handle the situation differently?

■ TEAM-BUILDING ACTIVITIES FOR SCHOOLS AND COMMUNITIES

Now that some critical foundation tools/concepts of an experiential learning model, design, and processing have been covered, what are some examples of team-building activities? There are literally hundreds of resources available that will give new as well as highly seasoned teachers countless ideas. Examples follow that illustrate (1) a professional resource (in line with the space theme) and (2) activities that can be quickly set up indoors or outdoors.

Professional Resource: Challenger Learning Centers

From the space program and aircraft simulators has come an innovative approach to simulate the need for team and leadership development by way of **Challenger Learning Centers**. There are 47 Centers located throughout the United States, Canada, the United Kingdom, and South Korea (http://www.challenger.org/clc/index.cfm). Challenger Learning Centers are often partnered with science centers, museums, universities, and schools that endeavor to carry on the educational mission of the Challenger 51-L crew and the first teacher in space, Christa McAuliffe.

Challenger Learning Centers partner with the learning community to provide interactive learning experiences, merging science, technology, engineering, and math curricula with the modern life skills of communication, teamwork, responsible decision making, and critical thinking. The Centers offer realistic mock-ups of Mission Control and an orbiting space station. Students can create teams at computer consoles or on-board the space lab, and they must work together to meet the mission's goal, such as launching a probe or intercepting a comet. This learning experience engages students by transforming them into scientists, engineers, or researchers and placing them in a simulated space mission where they solve real-life challenges.

Regardless of a student's cultural background, economic situation, gender, learning style, or academic level, every Challenger Learning Center simulation provides students with an opportunity to succeed. Students often gain a renewed spirit of camaraderie, boosted self-esteem, and a heightened sense of the characteristics of effective teams.

The Challenger Learning Center of Northwest Indiana has recently incorporated an e-Mission program, allowing students in grades 3–10 to participate in an innovative simulation experience without leaving their classrooms. Using video conferencing equipment the students connect with a flight director at the Challenger Center to solve problems and practice teamwork.

■ CASE STUDY

For older students who may be interested in exploring the whats, whys, and hows of the actual Challenger explosion, a review of the case study, *Group Process in the Challenger Launch Decision* (Edmonson, 2002) can be facilitated as part of a Challenge Learning Center experience or in conjunction with other team activities. It is a fascinating as well as troubling example of the critical need for exemplary communication, problem solving, and decision making among a community of leaders (see **Box 3-1**).

Outdoor and Indoor Experiential Activities

The 1970s and 1980s brought a wave of growth in outdoor team development activities. Outward Bound, Project Adventure, and Boston University's Executive Challenge all used the outdoors for people to learn about various leadership and team competencies. Ropes/challenge courses were introduced first in schools and then proliferated in a wide range of venues—camps, colleges, universities, parks, and corporations—as the popularity of **indoor/outdoor experiential activities** grew. Some venues have impressive multi-level low and high elements that give students hours of learning opportunities. The main disadvantage of these structures involve cost:

1. Initial construction
2. Periodic inspections
3. Maintenance
4. Staff training/certification
5. Recurrent training

If a school district can develop a budget for program start-up as well as sustaining the program, the design and installation of a challenge course should be seriously

---

Box 3-1   Group Process in the Challenger Launch Decision

At 8:45 PM on January 27, 1986, 32 individuals from three locations—Huntsville, Alabama; Brigham City, Utah; and Merritt Island, Florida—joined in a teleconference 12 hours and 53 minutes prior to the scheduled launch of the Challenger Shuttle, known inside NASA as 51-L. The three sites joined two organizations, NASA and Morton Thiokol, that were intimately involved with the space program. Roger Boisjoly, an engineer with Morton Thiokol, had instigated the teleconference meeting upon hearing an Air Force weather forecast of 19 degrees Fahrenheit for the next morning at Kennedy Space Center on Merritt Island. Boisjoly had been increasingly vocal over the last few months about the performance of a component of the Shuttle design, the O-rings, at low temperatures. What were the implications of this new weather forecast for the launch of the Challenger?

Source: Edmondson, A. (2002). *Group process in the Challenger launch decision* (p. 1). Boston: Harvard Business School.

considered. But when cost is an issue, there are now numerous resources for portable experiential equipment that can be home-made or purchased. One of the advantages of portable equipment is just that: activities are portable—they can be quickly set up in the gym, in a classroom, or outdoors. Two activities are described here.

Activity Name: Pipeline
Number of Participants: 8–20
Activity Equipment / Materials:

- 18–20-inch pieces of 1/2-inch PVC pipe cut in half (1 per person)
- Marbles (1 per person)
- Small receptacle (e.g., plastic pitcher)

Frontload: You are beginning to form a "community of leaders," which requires a relevant team-building activity. This is it! Each leader is represented by one marble. It is the team's challenge to try to move all of the leaders through a series of "roads" that will take everyone to their destination. The objective is to try not to drop any leaders along the way.

Task: Your group must devise a method for moving all of the marbles (i.e., the leaders) along a series of handheld pieces of PVC pipe (i.e., the roads) without drop-ping the marbles/leaders, and deposit as many marbles/leaders as possible into the receptacle/destination. You have 5 minutes to plan. Please agree on your team's goal: how many marbles/leaders will *not* be dropped?

Rules:

- Each person must participate and have their own piece of PVC pipe.
- One person must be designated as the timekeeper and recorder for the Time Chart.
- The marble can only travel on the PVC pipe.

- The marble can be on only one PVC pipe at a time.
- The PVC pipe cannot touch the ground.
- When the marble is on your pipe, you cannot move your feet.
- Only the first person can touch the marble.
- If the marble drops, it cannot be moved—it is a "leader left behind."
- The receptacle cannot be moved.
- PVC pieces cannot touch each other.

Debriefing:

- *What:* What was your task? Your goal? Did you meet your goal? Why or why not? What were the key team charac-teristics that allowed you to meet your goal? What were the characteristics that need developing—which would help you meet your goal?
- *So What:* So let's take these character-istics and put them into context: which ones will be critical to help you develop your own community of leaders?

Activity Name: Lightning Construction
Number of Participants: 6–8 per team
Activity Equipment:

- Puzzle consisting of 15 wooden slats with notches ranging in size from 2 feet to 4 feet
- One set of instructions/rules
- Schematic
- One stopwatch
- One time chart (see **Table 3-1**)

Frontload: Your company, Puzzle Pleas-ers, has created an exciting new 15-piece wooden puzzle. Initial reaction to this puzzle has been phenomenal—sales numbers are skyrocketing. But produc-tion time is way, way too slow. Thus, Puzzle Pleasers is under strict time

TABLE 3-1 Time Chart for Pipeline			
Benchmark Assembly Time	Assembly Time 1	Assembly Time 2	Assembly Time 3
Min/Sec			

deadlines to create a manufacturing process that will allow each puzzle to be built in the fastest time possible.

Goal: Your four teams have been created to come up with a "knock-your-socks-off" manufacturing process that exudes high quality and efficiency.

Team Tasks: First figure out how to assemble the puzzle according to the schematic, and then reduce puzzle assembly time. You will have a maximum of three assembly attempts. Given the urgency of the situation (so many orders, so little time, customers are waiting, waiting, waiting…), the number of attempts may need to be reduced.

Instructions/Rules:

- Each team must appoint and give the stopwatch to a timekeeper/time chart recorder.
- Once you figure out how the puzzle goes together (*all* notches must be used) and record how long it took (Benchmark Assembly Time), you'll have a maximum of three attempts to develop an assembly process that allows for the fastest assembly time possible. The facilitator (the person overseeing the implementation of this activity) will determine how many attempts you will be given.
- Puzzles *must* be disassembled and pieces stacked (longest to shortest) prior to any attempt to put the puzzle together.
- Puzzles may *not* be marked or written upon.

Debriefing:

- *What:* What was your goal? Your task? What was the difference between the Benchmark Assembly Time and your Final Assembly Time? Are you pleased with the results? Why or why not? What were the key team characteristics that allowed you to meet your goal? What were the characteristics that need developing—which would help you meet your goal?
- *So what:* So let's take these characteristics and put them into context: which ones will be critical to help you develop your own community of leaders?

■ CONCLUSION

The Apollo 13 experience so clearly demonstrated that the outcome of a crisis can be determined by how well a team of leaders responds. Currently, the need for team building to form a community of leaders is critical. Unfortunately, we face a wide variety of societal adversity—the economy, violence in our schools and streets, and so on—so we must encourage those communities of leaders to become strong and highly capable teams.

Teams do not automatically form—they need instruction and practice. A wide range of engaging, experiential team-building activities are available for leaders, teachers, facilitators, and parents. By giving teams a safe and comfortable learning laboratory in which to practice, they will become more aware of their strengths and weaknesses.

And by strengthening the strengths and addressing the weaknesses, every member of the team will be able to function at a significantly higher level. Individuals then have the potential of becoming members of a truly high performing team.

■ KEY WORDS AND DEFINITIONS

Challenger Learning Centers   Offer realistic mock-ups of Mission Control and an orbiting space station for students to learn about teamwork. They often partner with science centers, museums, universities, and schools.

design   "The essence of design is helping to create an emotional connection to an intellectual problem or idea. It is the creation of an experience that engages us, moves us into action or new ideas, provokes a response, or helps to internalize ideas or methods in a way that we don't easily forget." (Napier, 1995, p. 69)

experiential learning   Involves the student in his or her learning to a much greater degree than in traditional learning environments. Related terms/concepts include experience-based learning, active learning, hands-on learning, deep level processing, and higher order thinking.

experiential learning cycle   There are four steps in the experiential learning cycle: (1) concrete experience, (2) observation and reflection, (3), forming abstract concepts, and (4) testing the implication of concepts in new situations.

frontloading   A statement by the facilitator in advance of an activity to help students understand the intent of an activity. Frontloading can include the use of a story or scenario that sets the stage for the rationale of an activity.

indoor/outdoor experiential activities   Engaging activities and simulations that allow students to "get out of their seats and on their feet," creating a link between the actual activity and real-world behaviors and practices. Many activities can be facilitated indoors or outdoors, depending on time, equipment needed, and weather conditions.

processing   Also referred to as *debriefing*; encourages individuals to plan, reflect, describe, analyze, and communicate about experiences before, during, or after an activity.

team building   A process that builds and develops shared goals, interdependence, trust, commitment, and accountability among team members and that seeks to improve team members' problem-solving skills.

team building activities for schools and communities   Engaging activities and simulations that allow students to "get out of their seats and on their feet," creating a link between the actual activity and real-world behaviors and practices. Many activities can be facilitated indoors or outdoors depending on time, equipment needed, and weather conditions.

teamwork   Two or more people organized to work together interdependently, collaboratively, and cooperatively to reach a common goal.

■ DISCUSSION QUESTIONS

1. Think about a time that you were a member of a highly effective team. The team can be one from school, sports, church, or the like. What was one key characteristic that made your team click? Why?
2. Why do you think team building is necessary in bringing together a community of leaders?

3. What is the difference between a recreational team-building activity and a team-building activity that is designed to form a community of leaders?
4. What are the advantages and disadvantages of outdoor ropes/challenge courses as a team-building tool?
5. How do you process or debrief a team-building activity?

■ REFERENCES

Covey, S. R. (2006). *The speed of change.* New York: Free Press.

Edmondson, A. (2002). *Group process in the Challenger launch decision.* Boston: Harvard Business School.

Kennedy, J. F. (1961). Special message to the Congress on urgent national needs. Retrieved June 21, 2011, from http://www.space.com/11772-president-kennedy-historic-speech-moon-space.html

Kolb, D. A., & Fry, R. (1975). Toward an applied theory of experiential learning. In C. Cooper (Ed.), *Theories of group process.* London: John Wiley.

Kotter, J. *On what leaders really do.* Boston: Harvard Press.

Lencioni, P. (2002). *The five dysfunctions of a team.* San Francisco: Jossey-Bass.

Luckner, J. L., & Nadler, R. R. (1997). *Processing the experience.* Dubuque, IA: Kendall/Hunt.

Napier, R. (1995). The art of design: The key to memory and learning. In C. Roland, R. Wagner, & R. Weigand (Eds.), *Do it and understand: The bottom line on corporate experiential learning.* Dubuque, Iowa: Kendall/Hunt Publishing Company.

Napier, R., & Luckner, J. (1983). *Making groups work.* Boston: Houghton Mifflin.

Reina, D., & Reina, M. (2006). *Trust and betrayal in the workplace.* San Francisco: Berrett-Koehler.

Snow, H. (1992). *The power of team building.* Toronto: Pfeiffer & Company.

Stoltz, P. (1997). *The adversity quotient: Turning obstacles into opportunities.* New York: John Wiley & Sons.

Stoltz, P., & Weihenmayer, E. (2006). *The adversity advantage: Turning everyday struggles into everyday greatness.* New York: Simon & Schuster.

Usteem, M. (1998). *The leadership moment.* New York: Random House.

Weigand, R. (1995). Experiential learning: A brief history. In C. Roland, R. Wagner, & R. Weigand (Eds.), *Do it and understand: The bottom line on corporate experiential learning* (pp. 2–4). Dubuque, IA: Kendall/Hunt.

Inclusive Education of Students with Disabilities in Physical Education

Donna Lehr and Jessica Licata

Any discussion about physical education in today's schools would not be complete without the inclusion of educational policies and practices related to students with **disabilities**. The number of students with disabilities who are educated in general classes, including physical education classes, continues to increase (Lee, Burgeson, Fulton, & Spain, 2007), and their presence calls for an understanding of who they are, why there are there, and how best to educate them (Hardin, 2005). It is recognized, however, that physical educators "take few adapted [physical education] courses and have little practical experience working with students with disabilities. This can result in physical educators who have negative attitudes toward including students with disabilities in their programs. In some instances, students with disabilities have been excluded altogether from physical education classes" (Hardin, 2005, p. 44).

Students with disabilities, after a long history of discrimination and exclusion from school, now have federal protections based on two laws: Section 504 of the Americans with Disabilities Act, which broadly prohibits discrimination on the basis of a disability, and the **Individuals with Disabilities Education Act (IDEA)**, which guarantees a free, appropriate, public education (FAPE) for all children with disabilities. More specifically, relevant to this article, IDEA specifies that:

Each child with a disability must be afforded the opportunity to participate in the regular physical education program available to nondisabled children unless—(1) The child is enrolled full time in a separate facility; or (2) The child needs specially designed physical education, as prescribed in the child's IEP. (Regulations: Part 300 / B / 300.108 / b.)

This article includes (1) a brief introduction to the population of students with disabilities and a review of the history of the education of students with disabilities; (2) a description of the legal rights of students with disabilities and their families; (3) a presentation of the rationale for the education of students with disabilities in general education classes, and specifically, physical education classes; and (4) a description of

practices that are designed to ensure that appropriate and individualized programs are provided to students.

■ STUDENTS WITH DISABILITIES

A student with a disability is defined in IDEA as,

a child evaluated… as having mental retardation, a hearing impairment (including deafness), a speech or language impairment, a visual impairment (including blindness), a serious emotional disturbance (referred to in this part as "emotional disturbance"), an orthopedic impairment, autism, traumatic brain injury, another health impairment, a specific learning disability, deaf-blindness, or multiple disabilities, and who, by reason thereof, needs special education and related services. (20 U.S.C. 1401(3); 1401(30) Sec. 300.8)

The labels of categories such as those used in the formal definition above are often misleading, because individual children assigned these labels demonstrate a range of knowledge, skills, abilities, and learning challenges. Some demonstrate significant motor impairments, such that physical education classes alone are insufficient to meet their needs. Those students may require adaptive physical education and/or physical therapy in addition to, or instead of, physical education. But most students with disabilities have no motor impairments and most are physically indistinguishable from their peers without disabilities. They may, however, have learning needs that require their teachers have a clear understanding of the way in which they learn, and that their teachers work closely with the students' special education teachers to enable their participation in the classes.

■ HISTORY OF THE EDUCATION OF STUDENTS WITH DISABILITIES

Children with disabilities have a history of denial of educational opportunities. Although there are records of education for this population of children in the United States from the 1700s, it is only since 1975 that comprehensive services have been mandated and that states have been required to educate *all* their children with disabilities, with no exception for level of severity or cost. Although most states have long histories of schools for students who were blind or deaf, students with learning disabilities often went unidentified, and individuals with intellectual impairments and severe disabilities were denied access to an education altogether. Students who did receive school services, did so due to the state (but not federal) laws, or local policies, often as a result of effective parent advocacy.

Propelled by momentum from the Civil Rights movement of the 1960s, advocates for children with disabilities established access to education for all students with disabilities, first through what is known as Section 504 of the Rehabilitation Act of 1973 and second by the passage of the Education for all Handicapped Children Act (EHCA) of 1975. Section 504 stated, simply, that no individual with a disability could be discriminated against in programs receiving federal funding. Because public schools receive federal funds, this law established access to school for children with disabilities. Two years later, the Education for All Handicapped Children Act was passed, which more comprehensively and more specifically addressed the education of students with disabilities in public schools and required that all receive free appropriate public education. This law has since been amended several times and renamed the Individuals with Disabilities Education Act (IDEA). IDEA's basic principles include the following:

- *Zero rejection:* All children with disabilities must be provided with special education and related services at no cost to parents, regardless of level of severity.
- *Nondiscriminatory assessment:* Assessment for the purpose of eligibility and program planning must be nonbiased in terms of cultural and linguistic differences and disability, and must be administered by qualified personnel.
- *Appropriate education:* To ensure that their special educational needs are met, **individualized education programs (IEPs)** are designed for each student. IEPs specify the priority goals and objectives related to domains of learning including academic, social and behavioral, language and communication, and physical development.
- *Due process protections:* To counter past experience in which school district personnel were the sole decision makers in regards to program placement, program design, and implementation, provisions were included in IDEA that ensured parents had the right to participate in decision making regarding their children's programs. Additionally, parents are provided the right to disagree with decisions and appeal those decisions through administrative processes.
- *Education in the **least restrictive environment**:* The education of students with disabilities, to the extent appropriate, with their nondisabled peers in general education classes is also required. For some, however, this does not occur in the general education class (Zigmond, 1995). Consequently, the decision regarding educational placement rests

with the IEP team. Among the possible options are placement in a (1) general education class with services and supports, (2) special education classroom, (3) specialized school, (4) residential school, or (5) various combination of the options listed. The law requires first considering placement in the general education setting, and then placement in other settings only when necessary. This preference for inclusive education must be understood, because it is the reason students with a range of disabilities are increasingly assigned to general physical education classes.

■ RATIONALE FOR THE INCLUSIVE EDUCATION OF STUDENTS WITH DISABILITIES

Prior to passage of IDEA, the most frequent educational placement of those students with disabilities who were provided with an education was in segregated schools and classes. Students with disabilities were found to be receiving unequal educational opportunities based on segregation, as was the case in *Brown v. Board of Education* (1954) in which separate education based on race was considered unequal education. Additionally, the writings of Nirje and Wolfensberger (Wolfensberger, 1972) fueled the position regarding the importance of integration by pointing out the undesirable creation of a devaluated social class associated with segregation and institutionalization of individuals with disabilities. They argued the need for normalization of methods in education and care to prevent this, and to improve supports and services for these individuals.

The importance of the presence of typically developing peers is also pointed to as a rationale for inclusive education. If the goal is the development of communication skills, where in a class with all other students who lack communication skills would students have models of typical peer communication? Where in a program with students who have behavioral and conduct disorders, would a student see models of pro-social behaviors? How can we teach students to function in an integrated, diverse world, if the only students they interact with are students with similar disabilities? How can we develop a future generation of doctors, lawyers, and teachers who understand diversity related to disability so all are better served, if as elementary and secondary students, they do not have longitudinal opportunities to learn alongside students with disabilities (Brown et al., 1983)? Inclusive education is often the only option to address these critical questions.

■ INCLUSION OF STUDENTS WITH DISABILITIES IN GENERAL PHYSICAL EDUCATION

Mere placement of and high expectations for students with disabilities in general education physical education classes is insufficient to ensure acceptance and achievement for students with disabilities. Some have hidden disabilities that interfere with their participation in physical education classes. Some may have difficulty understanding directions and rules, staying on task, regulating emotions, or even tolerating noise levels in gymnasiums. Although the needs across the entire group of students might vary, what many have in common is the need for adaptations to traditional approaches used for "typical" students.

Experts in special education and related services, including occupational, physical, and speech therapists, who are knowledgeable about the unique needs of such students, along with parents, guide the planning, implementation, and evaluation process and are critical resources to teachers responsible for implementing the programs.

Roles and Responsibilities

It may be particularly challenging for physical education teachers to effectively include students with physical, cognitive, and social disabilities in their classes if they had little exposure to or experience teaching these students. Mumford and Chandler (2009) pointed out that it is often the case that insufficient attention is paid to this need in physical education preparation programs. Yet the responsibilities of physical education teachers are not unlike those of any general education teacher working with students with disabilities: they must work collaboratively with parents and other school professionals to meet the needs of all students in the schools. They must observe to identify students in need of special education for referral and for eligibility, participate in assessment of student needs, and design and implement individualized educational programs in the least restrictive environment appropriate to meet the students' needs.

LaMaster, Gall, Kinchin, and Siedentop (1998) reported, however, that physical educators typically are not active participants in the IEP process. They may be unaware of the existence of an IEP for specific children in their classes. Or, as LaMaster et al. (1998) pointed out, they may be aware of the existence of an IEP for some students, but are not encouraged to review it or have any input in developing the individualized program for physical education. These situations are of particular concern because IEPs include not only information about specific

educational goals and objectives, but also important information about medical conditions and physical limitations. Because IEPs include academic, social, and physical goals to be addressed within the context of physical education classes, physical education teachers (not to mention the students) would benefit from being familiar with the goals included in IEPs (Mumford & Chandler, 2009, p. 12).

Physical education teachers are often the first to notice abnormalities in motor performance and behavior in students with mild impairments (Etzel-Wise & Mears, 2004) in the course of their instruction. Their input regarding a student's present performance in natural settings (Houston-Wilson & Lieberman, 1999) can be invaluable. If a student is determined to be eligible for special education, the physical education teacher's input is important in designing goals and objectives, and defining adaptations (Etzel-Wise & Mears, 2004; Houston-Wilson & Lieberman, 1999).

Strategies for Inclusion

Successful inclusion of students with disabilities into any class requires careful planning focused on the goals and objectives targeted for instruction for not just the class, but also the individual students in it, as well as on the methods of instruction appropriate for the individuals. Many approaches are used to guide the design and implementation of inclusive education for students in physical education classes. Several principles described in this section focus on **Universal Design for Learning (UDL)**, **differentiated instruction**, and peer support.

Based on the principles used in designing buildings accessible for all individuals, including those with disabilities, Universal Design for Learning is "a framework for designing curricula that enable all individuals to gain knowledge, skills, and enthusiasm for learning" (CAST, n.d.). When designing curricula and methods for teaching using this conceptual framework, the attributes of all students and the class and individual objectives must be considered (Lieberman, Lytle, & Clareq, 2008). The Center for Applied Special Technology (CAST) describes this approach as including three components:

1. Multiple means of representation, to give learners various ways of acquiring information and knowledge
2. Multiple means of action and expression, to provide learners alternatives for demonstrating what they know
3. Multiple means of engagement, to tap into learners' interests, offer appropriate challenges, and increase motivation

Lieberman, Lytle, and Clareq (2008) provided an example of the use of this approach in a physical education program. They described the creation of separate stations, each with a "hierarchy of goals" (p. 2), thus differentiating the curriculum for students. Students, she suggests, should be heterogeneously grouped, so students with disabilities are working alongside their peers to complete a task, even if the individual goals vary. Consider, for example, students with and without disabilities paired in a hockey drill, where they are meant to pass the puck back and forth. In that station, rules and instructions would be given in multiple representations (orally and in picture format) and a variety of equipment would be available (Frisbees, big and nonrolling, and balls, smaller and rolling) to serve as the pucks (p. 4). In this example, all students are working on the same standards-based task at the same time, but the presentation of instructions and materials are adapted in

order to accommodate those with differing communication and motor and coordination skills.

Lieberman, Lytle, and Clareq (2008) described the Functional Approach to Modifying Movement Experiences (FAMME), based on the principles of UDL, which are designed to help physical education instructors determine appropriate curriculum modifications. In planning instruction using this model, the physical education teacher does not consider the disability type of students in the group, but instead focuses on lessons and adaptations to instruction to accommodate the needs and abilities of all students. The four steps of the FAMME model are:

1. Determining the underlying components of an activity
2. Determining the students' capabilities
3. Matching modifications to the students' needs
4. Evaluating the effectiveness of the modifications used (p. 7)

Application of the FAMME approach leads to consideration of three areas in need of modification: equipment, rules, and instruction. It is expected that some modification in each of these areas will be necessary in each lesson so that all learners are accommodated. Equipment modifications may involve adapting traditional equipment or substituting other materials for the equipment while the underlying goals of the task remain constant. Examples include "longer rackets, beeping balls, guide wires, Velcro mitts, or softer balls" (Lieberman, Lytle, & Clareq, 2008, p. 8). Students can use these adapted materials and still participate in tennis, catching, and team activities.

Schumm, Vaugh, and Leavell (1994) conceptualized a three-tiered pyramid model for differentiating instruction for learners.

They suggest that planning be guided by considering what (1) all students will learn (at the base of the pyramid, with the widest area, representing all of these students), (2) what most will learn, and (3) what some will learn (the smallest area, representing the smallest group of students). In this model, all students would learn the most fundamental concepts, knowledge, and skills. The information in this bottom tier is the least complex. The second tier represents the concepts that most students will learn, and are the more complex knowledge, skills, and concepts that are extensions of the foundations. The top of the pyramid includes the knowledge, skills, and concepts that some students will learn. These are the most complex, and can be considered appropriate only for the most able students in the group. The concept of "degrees of learning" (Schumm et al., 1994, p. 611) is based on the belief that all students are capable of learning, but not all students have to share the same lesson-learning objectives. Using this model, it is possible to imagine a physical education lesson as determining that all students should learn basic throwing skills, but the level of skill can be differentiated, based, for example, on the students' distance from the target, the sizes of the targets, and the types of items to be thrown.

With these conceptual models in mind, it becomes clearer how rules, expectations, and lesson directions can be adapted to meet the needs of all students. This may require presenting information in multiple forms such as pictures or large print, or repeating the information orally (Lieberman, Lytle, & Clareq, 2008; Mumford & Chandler, 2009). The establishment of routines may be important, because they serve to provide structure and consistency (Mumford & Chandler, 2009). Expectations are made clearer, which may be critical for some students with disabilities and will likely result in time being used more efficiently, benefitting all students. Mumford and Chandler (2009), for example, suggested that breaking a period into routine segments and representing these segments in multiple forms (orally, pictorially, and graphically) will also help students move through the routines "with a sense of achievement" (p. 14).

Approaches focused on peer interaction are also recommended in physical education classes. Encouraging social interactions among peers benefits those students with disabilities who may have social problems, and those students without disabilities to be more accepting of their peers (Mumford & Chandler, 2009, p. 14). Promoting "social acceptance is one of the most important aspects of making a classroom inclusive" and gives all students opportunities to be "positive with each other" (p. 14). **Cooperative learning** groups may be appropriate for some lessons. In these groups, each participant plays an active role in the group and the task cannot be completed without the contributions of each student. Peer tutoring serves the dual purposes of providing one-on-one instruction and promoting social interaction among peers.

■ CONCLUSION

As Lieberman, Lytle, and Columna (2008) noted, "it is important to keep in mind that it is the teacher's job to fit the activity to the child, not the child to the activity" (p. 7). Lieberman and her colleagues also pointed out:

The fear, lack of experience, or preference of the GPE [general physical education] teacher should be addressed, but they should not factor into the placement decision. It is normal for a teacher to be fearful of working with a child with a disability in their class. This fear is common, as most GPE teachers have only one APE class in their undergraduate training program. This can be addressed by increasing time with the APE consultant until the teacher is comfortable, by participating in workshops or inservices, or by taking classes at a local college or university. (p. 8)

It is expected that there will continue to be an increasing number of students with disabilities in general education school and classes, including physical education classes. Mere placement, however, is insufficient to ensure successful education. Physical education teachers are charged with the responsibility of understanding the educational needs of each student, which comes through collaboration with special education and related service specialists. The product of this collaboration should be the design and implementation of lessons that are accessible for all learners based on the notions of universal design for learning and differentiated instruction.

◼ KEY WORDS AND DEFINITIONS

cooperative learning A strategy for teaching and learning designed to foster cooperation based on the creation of small heterogeneous groups of students assigned learning tasks, that requires interdependence to enable completion, and that incorporates individual and group accountability.

differentiated instruction The outcome of a planning process that results in the identification of instructional objectives, instructional approaches, and assessment methods that are appropriate to meet the needs of individual learners.

disability An impairment that affects daily functioning, and in children, affects growth and development.

individualized education programs (IEPs) The written articulation (which serves as a legal contract) of individualized designed plans that specify annual goals and objectives, along with a description of services and supports, that will be used to meet the unique needs of students with disabilities receiving special education services and supports as required by IDEA.

Individuals with Disabilities Education Act (IDEA) The comprehensive federal law that requires states provide free appropriate public education to students with disabilities ages 3 through 21.

least restrictive environment A provision in IDEA that requires students with disabilities be educated, to the extent appropriate, with their nondisabled peers and with the use of necessary services and supports.

Universal Design for Learning (UDL) A conceptual model used to guide instructional planning in a manner that recognizes the learning differences among students by universally incorporating multiple means of presentation, responding, and assessment.

■ DISCUSSION QUESTIONS

1. What is the rationale for differentiation of instruction within physical education classes?
2. What are some ways that instruction can be differentiated?
3. What are some potential benefits of inclusion for students with disabilities?
4. What is meant by Universal Design for Learning?
5. What are some steps that physical education teachers and health education teachers can take to ensure that students with disabilities are meaningfully participating in inclusive physical education classes?

■ REFERENCES

Brown, L., Ford, A., Nisbet, J., Sweet, M., Donnellan, A., & Gruenewald, L. (1983). Opportunities available when severely handicapped students attend chronological age appropriate regular schools. *Journal of the Association for Persons with Severe Handicaps, 8*, 16–24.

CAST. (n.d.). About UDL. Retrieved September 5, 2009, from http://www.cast.org/research/udl/index.html

Etzel-Wise, D., & Mears, B. (2004). Adapted physical education and therapeutic recreation in schools. *Intervention in School and Clinic, 39*(4), 223–232.

Hardin, B. (2005). Physical education teachers' reflection on preparation for inclusion. *The Physical Educator, 62*(1), 44–56.

Houston-Wilson, C., & Lieberman, L. (1999). The individualized education program in physical education: A guide for regular physical educators. *Journal of Physical Education, Recreation & Dance, 70*(3), 60–65.

LaMaster, K., Gall, K., Kinchin, G., & Siedentop, D. (1998). Inclusion practice of effective elementary physical education specialists. *Adapted Physical Activity Quarterly, 15*, 64–81.

Lee, S. M., Burgeson, C. R., Fulton, J. E., & Spain, C. G. (2007). Physical education and physical activity: Results from the School Health Policies and Programs Study 2006. *Journal of School Health, 77*, 435–463.

Lieberman, L. J., Lytle, R. K., & Clareq, J. A. (2008). Getting it right from the start: Employing universal design for learning means planning ahead for the inclusion of all students. *Journal of Physical Education, Recreation, and Dance, 79* (2), 32–39.

Lieberman, L., Lytle, R., & Columna, L. (2008). Guidelines for placement of children with disabilities. *Journal of Physical Education, Recreation, and Dance, 79*(9), p. 7–8.

Mumford, V. E., & Chandler, J. P. (2009). Strategies for supporting inclusive education for students with disabilities. *Strategies: A Journal for Physical and Sport Educators, 22*(5), 10–15.

Schumm, J. S., Vaugh, S., & Leavell, A. G. (1994). Planning pyramid: A framework for planning for diverse student needs during content area instruction. *The Reading Teacher, 47*, 608–615.

Wolfensberger, W. (1972). *The principle of normalization in human services.* Toronto: Toronto National Institute on Mental Retardation.

Zigmond, N. (1995). An exploration of the meaning and practice of special education in the context of full inclusion of students with learning disabilities: Introduction. *Journal of Special Education, 29*(2), 109–115.

■ ADDITIONAL RESOURCES

Hitchcock, C. (2001). Balanced instructional support and challenge in universally designed learning environments. *Journal of Special Education Technology, 16*(4), 23–30.

Lambert, L. (1999) A differentiated goal structure framework for high school physical education. *Journal of Physical Education, Recreation & Dance, 70*(2), 20–25.

Positive Psychology and Motivation on the Field and in the Classroom

Amy L. Baltzell

The ultimate purpose of **positive psychology** and that of teaching are in concert: there is a commitment to help others aspire toward good, healthy lives and thrive. We will consider how the ideas from positive psychology can ultimately support the physical education and health teacher in creating educational environments that help the students thrive within the classroom and during field experiences.

In the effort to help others, psychology has historically focused on what is wrong. For the past century in the United States the primary role of the field of psychology was to understand and treat clinical (mental) disorders and to help people regain homeostasis, to regain basic mental health. Psychology has been focused on clinical issues like depression, anxiety, and addictions. There has been little research on understanding and helping people live meaningful, fulfilling lives.

How is positive psychology different? Positive psychology is a new subfield of general psychology, which has started to be of interest to psychologists as well as educators and coaches around the world. The focus of positive psychology is on what is *right* with people. Within the field of positive psychology there is an ongoing empirical exploration of the factors that will contribute to helping us live good lives. There is an interest in and commitment to understanding the psychological factors that can contribute to the lives of normal, healthy people in the pursuit of happiness and living a meaningful, good life.

How, specifically, can the study of positive psychology contribute to the on-the-ground teaching of physical education and health? It can be a prompt to focus on what is right with your future students. Instead of looking at what is wrong, what needs to be improved, and what needs to be fixed we can look at what is already right with our students and strengthen what already is good. Some of the tenets of positive psychology are insightful and useful in our effort to contribute to the health and well-being of our physical education and health students. In this segment we will consider *happiness*, the value of identifying personal *strengths*, and what is needed to create learning environments to *positively motivate* students (self-determination theory).

■ HAPPINESS

Before we discuss specific concepts from positive psychology that will directly contribute to teaching physical education and health, we must consider the essence of the interest in the field of positive psychology. The central ongoing question in the field of positive psychology is: What contributes to our happiness?

Lyubomirsky, Sheldon, and Schkade, leading researchers in positive psychology, have come up with a simple metric that helps us understand the controllable and uncontrollable aspects of happiness (Lyubomirsky,

Sheldon, & Schkade, 2005). They posit that a person's chronic happiness is governed by three major factors: (1) genetic set point, (2) circumstances, and (3) **intentional activities**. They sifted through all the relevant research and have determined, as have other researchers, that about 50% of our happiness is genetically predetermined. This means that no matter what we do, about half of our happiness is attributable to genetics—our *happiness set point*. This means that there is nothing we can do to impact half of our experience of happiness (or unhappiness)—we are the way that we are due to biological predispositions.

Circumstances represent the next 10% of impact on our happiness levels. Our circumstances range based on our gender, age, where we live, where we work or go to school, and our socioeconomic status. Though clearly some of these factors can change, they tend to remain relatively stable and they tend to have only a slight impact on our happiness levels. For example, those who are physically healthy report being slightly happier than their unhealthy counterparts, and those who are married or have religious affiliations report being slightly happier than their non-married and nonreligiously affiliated counterparts. For many of us, our circumstances are relatively fixed; even when we have a significant change in circumstance, we only tend to enjoy a minor boost in happiness.

The last 40% of our happiness, our intentional activities, we can directly impact. Intentional activities are behaviors or thinking that we *choose to engage* with and we have to put *effort* toward. With intentional activities you must initiate the effort, it cannot happen to you. Here is where the hope lies and the possibility for us as educators. We set up our classroom and teaching environments to provide our students with a sense of choice and autonomy and a place where they want

to participate and put forth effort, so we are contributing to their well-being and happiness. The question for educators is, "How can we set up our teaching environment while creating tasks students want to put effort in to learn and engage?" They will go toward what they authentically enjoy, are interested in, and personally value. This helps put a framework on our work with students; we can aspire to create environments and activities that the students are genuinely interested in, ones that they can sometimes enjoy (as we know this is not always possible), and ones in which the learning or activities align with their personal values.

It is important to note that from its inception, positive psychology looked to great philosophical thinkers for insight and wisdom regarding the true source of happiness. Greek philosopher Aristotle's work serves as the philosophical underpinnings for positive psychology. In *Nichomachean Ethics*, Aristotle (1962) is quite interested in what contributes to a good life and what contributes to our happiness. Aristotle points to three factors that he assumes contribute to our happiness: (1) having good character, (2) doing what you love, and (3) having your (good) health. The second two factors may seem quite obvious. It is important that we go toward what we love doing and it is essential to take good care of our physical health.

The idea of having good character may not be as intuitive. Good character is about doing what is "right." Positive psychology has adopted a value-based perspective of happiness, which has been inspired by Aristotle. Happiness cannot just be about the hedonic indulgence of oneself moment to moment. Though intermittent experiences of pleasure are good to have, they are not enough to experience a full sense of happiness. According to Aristotelean philosophy, happiness ultimately requires creating habits of doing what is good and right, whether you feel like it (in the moment) or not. Good character habits require that you concurrently contribute to the well-being of both yourself and others. Doing what is right includes doing what is good for others and oneself and taking into consideration the benefit (or harm) of one's behavior in both the present moment and into the future.

■ CHARACTER STRENGTHS

Do we really need to talk about character and virtues when we consider happiness? According to the leaders of positive psychology, we do. One of the first efforts by the leaders in positive psychology was to learn what was right with people. Chris Peterson and Martin Seligman (2004) spent 3 years conducting research around the world to better understand what was considered the universally valued good in people's behaviors. They tried to name the factors that are generally accepted around the world as the *good* characteristics or habits of behavior in human beings when they are at their best. They were identifying habits of interacting with others that are generally respected and valued. They considered the essential ingredients of this universal good in people, their strengths. They have done a fantastic job compiling a universal list of good that can emerge in all of us. They started with a short list of overarching themes of good in which they identified a list of *virtues*. They also provided a list of the 24 dimensions of the virtues that they entitled *character strengths*. These character strengths are intended to represent human behavior when we are at our best. This list helps provide a language to conceptualize and notice the good in your future students.

We all have a unique blend of the character strengths, with some being strong and practiced (considered our "signature strengths" by Peterson and Seligman) and others lying dormant within us. Some of the factors on the list might be surprising to you. For example, the character strengths of kindness and forgiveness often aren't viewed as strengths—in fact, we might think of them as a weakness at first blush. However, upon consideration, it becomes clear how these character strengths can contribute to the happiness in ourselves—and in others—as well as contributing to our ability to thrive and achieve.

Often we take our own strengths, which are universally supported, for granted. We can easily slip into the myth that if it is easy for me than it must not be very important or highly valued. "Of course I try hard," or, "Of course I am willing to help someone who is struggling." We often think that what we do that is good, kind, right, or courageous is just what anyone else would do. Each semester students in my classes complete the signature strengths inventory (http://www.authentichappiness.sas.upenn.edu/Default.aspx), which assesses each student's personal strengths. After filling out the inventory they often report feeling surprised that a test can identify their strengths; and for many, things that they usually take for granted about themselves are highlighted and valued. This exercise tends to have a profound impact on the students. They have been given language to identify their good.

It can be invaluable to pay attention to and value the personal strengths of your students. The more they are aware of their strengths, the more likely they will be able to lean on themselves in times of difficulty or challenge. The following section provides a brief description of the 24 character strengths (Peterson & Seligman, 2004). (Please refer to the complete text or the aforementioned website for further information.)

Six Virtues and Twenty-Four Character Strengths

Peterson and Seligman (2004) created a classification of human strengths. This classification is conceptualized as *virtues in action (VIA)*. With each virtue, there are three to six *character strengths*; each character strength represents some aspect of the given virtue. A list of the six virtues follows (with the character strengths of each virtue in parentheses following each of the six virtues):

1. Wisdom and knowledge (creativity, curiosity, love of learning, open-mindedness, and perspective)
2. Courage (authenticity, bravery, persistence, and zest)
3. Temperance (forgiveness/mercy, modesty/humility, and prudence)
4. Strengths of humanity (kindness, love, and social intelligence)
5. Justice (fairness, leadership, and teamwork)
6. Transcendence (appreciation of beauty, gratitude, hope, humor, and religiousness/spirituality)

■ MOTIVATING STUDENTS IN THE CLASSROOM AND ON THE FIELD

Self-determination theory (Ryan & Deci, 2000) is one of the most influential theories of motivation within positive psychology. Ryan and Deci contend that the social conditions have a significant impact on the motivation of the individual. This means that the learning environment of the classroom has a powerful influence on students' interest and desire to learn. They state that, "Human beings can be proactive and engaged or passive and alienated largely to *social conditions* in which they develop and function" (p. 68). We of course want our students engaged. When the social

conditions are at their best our students are intrinsically motivated; they want to be in class and they want to learn. When they are intrinsically motivated they feel inspired, they strive to learn, they extend themselves, and they are interested in and committed to mastering new skills (p. 68). In contrast, when the social conditions are at their worst our students are at risk of having their spirits diminished or crushed, rejecting growth and responsibility, and becoming apathetic and irresponsible.

One of the biggest practical challenges in any classroom is to help inspire and motivate as many students as possible. What is it that our students need to be positively motivated? What will motivate them to want to participate and to enjoy what they are learning? According to self-determination theory our students have three innate psychological needs that need to be met: (1) **competence**, (2) **autonomy**, and (3) a sense of **relatedness**. These three psychological needs are interdependent; therefore, students require that all three needs be met for the psychological experiences to contribute positively to their motivation.

When our students feel *competent*, they believe in their abilities. This doesn't mean that they are good compared to others, but that they believe in their ability to successfully accomplish a task. For example, a student may not be the best runner in his or her class, but may feel competent in his or her ability to run the mile as prescribed by their teacher. Butcher, Lindner, and Johns (2002) explored the factors that contributed to tenth graders withdrawing from competitive youth sports. For the athletes involved in sport for one year or less, feeling incompetent was the number one reason they gave for dropping out of their given sport. When we don't feel competent we don't want to participate.

The second innate psychological need is autonomy. Autonomy means that one feels like they have personal control over their behaviors; behaviors are self-chosen, self-authored. When the student feels self-authored and when they feel like they want to participate in the classroom activities for their own reasons (executing an internal locus of control), their actions are aligned with their own values. Sometimes the activity can be fun and other times it may be unenjoyable—but the activity can still be aligned with the student's values. For example, the student may enjoy an in-class engaging activity designed by the teacher. In contrast, in other instances he or she may dislike the physical stretches (required in a physical education class) or the studying (required by the health class), but do them because they align with his or her personal values of being fit or doing well in school, respectively. He or she can still feel autonomy in all instances—though some may be enjoyable in the moment and others not—when the activities align with the interests/values of the student. This idea of autonomy is directly aligned with Sheldon and Kasser's (1998) concept of intentional activity—the main significant self-generated source of one's happiness. When we become involved in activities that we choose and activities that we intentionally put our effort into, we have the greatest opportunity of enhancing our well-being and happiness.

The third innate psychological need that we have is a sense of relatedness; we need to feel in harmony with and connected with others. We need to feel socially supported. This can come in the form of knowing the names of the students, taking a few minutes of class time to check in with how students are feeling, or noticing and publicly acknowledging a strength or skill of a student. In our effort to ensure that our students learn the content of our classes, we must make sure to concurrently maintain the human element in our classes. Our students are human beings first

who are in need of feeling like they belong and matter as a human being, regardless of what they have learned or of the skills they have developed.

When students experience concurrent feelings of competence, autonomy, and relatedness, they also tend to experience **intrinsic motivation**. They tend to have the desire to engage in a task for the sheer enjoyment of the activity itself. What about when the student is not enjoying what they are doing? It is not always possible to set up classroom or field activities that all students will enjoy all of the time. How can we help the students learn to value activities that in the moment are not fun or valued? The relationship, a sense of *relatedness*, with the teacher is essential. Students will perform extrinsically motivated behavior (activities that are not inherently enjoyable) when they have a teacher whom they respect, feel attached to, or experience a sense of belonging with. The positive relationship with the teacher is central to creating positive social conditions for the student to be willing to take in new values, such as trying and failing or learning a new skill. Because "extrinsically motivated behaviors are not typically interesting, the primary reason people initially perform such actions is because the behaviors are prompted, modeled, or valued by significant others to whom they feel (or want to feel) attached or related" (Ryan & Deci, 2000, p. 73). Feeling cared for is an essential contribution that a physical education or health teacher can give to each of their students.

■ CONCLUSION

The focus on what is wrong with or what is lacking in our students can be as present in the world of physical education and health education as it can be in psychology. When we grade our students' papers we look to what was not done well; when we grade tests we look to see what answers were wrong. We consider how a student could improve, from considering the gaps in their knowledge to issues with their eye–hand coordination and flexibility. There is a practical aspect to the focus on what is wrong in our effort to help our students improve and learn. The core ideas from positive psychology inspire us to look at what is already good about our students.

The contribution of the ideas from positive psychology to the teaching of physical education and health resides in helping the educator to look to what is right in our effort to help create a *want-to-engage-in* learning environment. When students experience their strengths being acknowledged, when they feel competent, feel like they belong, and feel like they are involved in activities that they value for their own reasons at choice—a place where they want to be and come back the next day—they will progressively be more self-determined and engaged with their learning. We can contribute concurrently to our students' learning and happiness through acknowledging their strengths, and creating a classroom environment that gives them feelings of competence, autonomy, and relatedness. When we can help our students willingly participate in intentional activities of learning in our classrooms, we give them their best chance to learn the most and to enjoy their engaged experiences.

■ KEY WORDS AND DEFINITIONS

autonomy Feeling and having one's behaviors driven by self-authored motivations.

competence Being able and believing in one's abilities within a particular realm to be successful.

intentional activities Behaviors, thinking, or goals that we choose to engage with and that we purposefully put effort toward.

intrinsic motivation The incentive to engage in a task for the sheer enjoyment of the activity itself rather than the external benefits one might gain.

positive psychology A new branch of psychology that is concerned with happiness and thriving of individuals and communities.

relatedness Feeling in harmony and connected with valued others.

■ DISCUSSION QUESTIONS

1. In your elementary or secondary (middle and/or high school) physical education classes, did your physical education teachers highlight your strengths? Specifically, did your teachers positively acknowledge any of your strengths such as your effort, attitude, or kindness toward others? If so, how and when did your teacher take notice of your individual strengths? If not, how might you do so with future students?

2. Aristotle suggests that happiness is a product of having good character, doing what you love, and having your (good) health. How does this understanding of happiness align with your sense of purpose as a future educator?

3. Develop three specific teaching strategies that you could use to help students move from feeling unmotivated (refusing to participate in class) to autonomously driven extrinsic motivation (they may not enjoy what they are doing but the behavior is consistent with their interests and values).

4. In your elementary or secondary (middle and/or high school) physical education classes, did your physical education teachers help create positive emotions on the part of the students in the class? If so, what do you think were some of the strategies to do so? If not, how could you help generate positive emotions on the part of your future students?

5. What are the three psychological needs that we all need to thrive and to enhance intrinsic motivation? What is one specific way to enhance each factor for future students?

■ EXTENSION ACTIVITIES

1. Work in small groups (three to five students per group). Reflect back on your physical education experiences in elementary, middle, and high school and then consider the *least competent* student in a previous class. Consider how you could help that student feel more competent. Next, consider the *least motivated* student (one that felt coerced) in a previous class. Consider how you could help that student feel more autonomous in their behavior. Finally, think of a student in a past class who felt most like an outsider. If you were that student's teacher, how could you help that student experience a sense of belonging (relatedness) in that classroom? Each student must provide at least one example in the discussion.

2. Visit the website http://www.authentic happiness.sas.upenn.edu/Default.aspx, and fill out the VIA Survey of Character Strengths inventory prior to class. Discuss how you used three of your top strengths in the past week. Next, talk about how your top three strengths could

contribute to your ability to thrive as a physical education teacher or health education teacher.

■ REFERENCES

Aristotle. (1962). *Nicomachean ethics*. Martin Ostwald (Trans.) New York: MacMillan Publishing.

Butcher, J., Lindner, K., & Johns, D. (2002). Withdrawal from competitive youth sport: A retrospective ten-year study. *Journal of Sport Behavior, 25*(2), 145–163.

Lyubomirsky, S., Sheldon, K., & Schkade, D. (2005). Pursuing happiness: The architecture of sustainable change. *Review of General Psychology, 9*(2), 111–131.

Peterson, C., & Seligman, M. (2004). *Character strengths and virtues: A handbook and classification*. New York: Oxford University Press.

Ryan, R., & Deci, E. (2000). Self-determination theory and the facilitation of intrinsic motivation, social development, and well-being. *American Psychologist, 55*(1), 68–78.

Sheldon, K., & Elliot, A. (1999). Goal striving, need satisfaction, and longitudinal well-being: The self-concordance model. *Journal of Personality and Social Psychology, 76*(3), 482–497.

Sheldon, K. M., & Kasser, T. (1998). Pursuing personal goals: Skills enable progress, but not all progress is beneficial. *Personality and Social Psychology Bulletin, 24*, 1319–1331.

Sheldon, K. M., & Kasser, T. (2008). Psychological threat and extrinsic goal striving. *Motivation and Emotion, 32*, 37–45.

Sheldon, K. M., & Lyubomirsky, S. (2006). Achieving sustainable gains in happiness: Change your actions, not your circumstances. *Journal of Happiness Studies, 7*, 55–86.

■ ADDITIONAL RESOURCES

Baumeister, R., Bratslavsky, E., Muraven, M., & Tice, D. (1998). Ego depletion: Is the active self a limited resource? *Journal of Personality and Social Psychology, 74*(5), 1252–1265.

Curzer, H. (2007). Aristotle: Founder of the ethics of care. *Journal of Value Inquiry, 41*, 221–243.

Gable, S., & Haidt, J. (2005). What (and why) is positive psychology? *Review of General Psychology, 9*(2), 103–110

Peterson, C. (2006). *A primer in positive psychology.* New York: Oxford Press.

Seligman, M. (2001). Positive prevention and positive therapy. In R. Snyder & S. Lopez (Eds.), *The handbook of positive psychology* (pp. 3–9). New York: Oxford Press.

Seligman, M., Rashid, T., & Parks, A. (2006). Positive psychotherapy. *American Psychologist, 61*(8), 774–788.

Role of Physical Activity to Reduce Obesity and Improve Academic Performance in School-Age Children and Adolescents

Kyle McInnis and Lauren Percoco

Obesity among children and adolescents has reached epidemic proportions. Data from the National Health and Nutrition Examination Surveys (NHANES) collected from 1976–1980 and 2007–2008 show the prevalence of obesity has more than tripled for those ages 2–19 years (from 5.0% to 17%; Ogden et al., 2010). According to NHANES data, nearly one in every three children (31.7%) ages 2–19 is overweight (greater than eighty-fifth body mass index [BMI] percentile using standard sex- and age-specific growth charts) or obese (greater than ninety-fifth BMI percentile). These alarming and unprecedented statistics mean that we are in the midst of one of the greatest challenges to childhood health and well-being in the recent era. Moreover, for the first time ever, children may have a shorter life expectancy than their parents (Olshansky et al., 2005).

According to the Centers for Disease Control and Prevention (CDC), approximately 17% of children and adolescents ages 2–19, or 12.5 million, are obese. The obesity epidemic has almost tripled over the past twenty years. Furthermore, there are considerable ethnic and racial differences in the United States obesity prevalence. Hispanic boys, ages 2–19 years, were significantly more likely to be obese than non-Hispanic white boys, and non-Hispanic black girls were significantly more likely to be obese than non-Hispanic white girls in 2007–2008 (CDC, 2011).

■ INACTIVE YOUTH

Physical activity has been declining in youth nationwide. Results from the Youth Risk Behavior Survey (Eaton et al., 2006) indicate that only 36% of students have been physically active at a moderate-to-vigorous intensity for at least 60 minutes/day on at least 5 of the 7 days prior to the survey. More males (48%) than females (28%) met this physical activity recommendation, but marked differences were observed in racial/ethnic minorities, with whites (39%) being more active than African American (30%) and Hispanic (33%) students (Eaton et al., 2006).

■ HEALTH IN THE BALANCE

Childhood obesity is a serious health risk; it exposes children to a variety of chronic health problems including type 2 diabetes, high blood pressure, asthma, orthopedic complications, sleep apnea, skin disorders, and other medically related complications (Dietz, 1998). Type 2 diabetes was once called adult onset diabetes because it occurred almost exclusively in adults—until childhood obesity started to rise substantially. Children and adults with type 2 diabetes have elevated blood glucose, and insulin produced by the body is often not very effective at keeping glucose levels within a healthy range. This often causes insulin levels to stay elevated in the blood, a condition known as *insulin resistance*. A high fat diet and being inactive are the primary culprits leading to obesity-related metabolic disorders such as type 2 diabetes and insulin resistance (Dietz, 1998). One study found that more than 75% of children age 10 or over with type 2 diabetes were obese (Mayer-Davis et al., 2009). Eating a healthier diet and exercising regularly can help lower the risk of type 2 diabetes in both children and adults and further reduce its serious consequences such as cardiovascular disease, blindness, and renal disease (Epstein, Myers, Raynor, & Saelens, 1998).

Overweight or obese children are more likely than normal weight children to develop high blood pressure (Freedman et al., 2007). An unhealthy lifestyle consisting of low physical activity, excess calories, and high levels of sodium intake leading to high blood pressure in children significantly raises their risk of heart disease and stroke later in life. In addition to cardiovascular risks, obese children may experience a variety of orthopedic complications (Pi-Sunyer, 1993). Children do not stop growing until they are in their late teenage years. When a child is obese the cartilage in their legs can become damaged because of the excessive weight. Over time, arthritis sets in, which occurs prematurely when obesity is present at an early age. Other health issues such as sleep apnea, defined as the intermittent absence of breathing during sleep, occur more commonly in children with obesity; skin disorders such as acanthosis nigricans (darkening and thickening of the skin) and intertrigo (inflammation of body folds in the armpits, belly, buttocks, and groin) are common in children and adolescents who are obese. Additionally, there are many psychosocial consequences of childhood obesity (Rofey et al., 2009; Strauss, 2000). Bullying has been reported to occur more frequently at every level of school for obese children and adolescents. The teasing, harassment, and rejection can lead to low self-esteem, depression, feelings of isolation, and body dissatisfaction. When a child is depressed and not satisfied with their body, it can hold them back from playing sports, socializing with their peers, and overall doing what an average child would do on a daily basis. When a child is constantly teased about their weight, it may progress to a point where they may not want to go to school or participate in normal school activities. As a consequence, there is a higher risk that obese youth may turn to drug and alcohol use to cope with their pain.

Considering the multitude of health consequences associated with adult and childhood obesity, it is not surprising that healthcare expenditures related to treating this condition are astronomical. Medical spending on adults that was attributed to obesity topped approximately $40 billion in 1998, and by 2008, increased to an estimated $147 billion (Finkelstein, Trogdon, Cohen, & Dietz, 2009). Excess weight is also costly during childhood, estimated at $3 billion per year in direct medical costs (Trasande & Chatterjee, 2009).

ENVIRONMENTAL FACTORS DURING CHILDHOOD

There have been major changes in Americans' lifestyles over the last 30 years, as childhood obesity rates have been rising. Americans now consume more fast food and sugar-sweetened beverages and eat outside the home more frequently. According to Guthrie, Lin, and Frazao (2002), this exacerbates poor eating habits and excess caloric consumption, leading to obesity. Meanwhile, **screen time** has increased, including television viewing, video games, and computers, which is directly associated with childhood obesity (Kaiser Family Foundation, 2010).

LIFELONG OBESITY

According to Singh, Mulder, and Twisk (2008), childhood obesity tracks with fidelity into adulthood. Studies indicated the risk of adult obesity was at least twice as high for obese children as for nonobese children. The risk of adult obesity was greater for children who were at higher levels of obesity and for children who were obese at older ages. These data indicate that many of the **lifestyle chronic health conditions** and psychosocial burdens of obesity that start in childhood are likely to persist throughout life.

PARENTAL INFLUENCES

Children of obese parents are more likely to also be overweight. If one parent is obese, the child is approximately twice as likely to also be overweight, and this increases to four times more likely when both parents are obese. For many children, the family environment establishes the expectations and behaviors regarding nutrition, availability of food, and integration of organized and recreational physical activity into family life (Golan & Crow, 2004).

OBESITY PREVENTION AND TREATMENT

According to a recent report to the President entitled "Solving Childhood Obesity Within a Generation" (White House Task Force on Childhood Obesity, 2010), comprehensive, multisectoral approaches are needed to address the many behavioral risk factors associated with obesity. Improving eating habits and increasing physical activity are two critical strategies. Although many of the recommendations in the presidential report will require additional public resources, creative strategies can also be used to redirect resources or make more effective use of existing investments. In total, the report presents a series of 70 specific recommendations. A summary of these broad recommendations is provided in **Table 3-2**.

TABLE 3-2 Summary of Broad Recommendations from the Presidential Report: Solving Childhood Obesity Within a Generation

Getting children a healthy start on life, with good prenatal care for their parents, support for breastfeeding, adherence to limits on screen time, and quality child care settings with nutritious food and ample opportunity for young children to be physically active

Empowering parents and caregivers with simpler, more actionable messages about nutritional choices based on the latest Dietary Guidelines for Americans; improved labels on food and menus that provide clear information to help make healthy choices for children; reduced marketing of unhealthy products to children; and improved healthcare services, including BMI measurement for all children

Providing healthy food in schools, through improvements in federally supported school lunches and breakfasts; upgrading the nutritional quality of other foods sold in schools; and improving nutrition education and the overall school environment

Improving access to healthy, affordable food by eliminating "food deserts" in urban and rural America; lowering the relative prices of healthier foods; developing or reformulating food products to be healthier; and reducing the incidence of hunger, which has been linked to obesity

Getting children more physically active, through quality physical education, recess, and other opportunities in and after school; addressing aspects of the "built environment" that make it difficult for children to walk or bike safely in their communities; and improving access to safe parks, playgrounds, and indoor and outdoor recreational facilities

Source: White House Task Force on Childhood Obesity. (2010). Solving the problem of childhood obesity within a generation. Report to the President. Retrieved June 6, 2010, from http://www.letsmove.gov/tfco_fullreport_may2010.pdf

■ ROLE OF SCHOOLS

According to the Centers for Disease Control and Prevention (CDC) (2010b), schools have been identified as an ideal setting to help young people improve and maintain physical activity and healthy eating behaviors to prevent or reverse obesity. There are many possible areas within the school system that can be targeted for effective interventions designed to reduce obesity. These include the content of school curricula, teaching methodologies, staff education, physical education programs, school food service programs, food service worker education, content and availability of vending machine snacks in school, and education efforts for parents. Resources to help schools improve the school nutrition and physical activity environment that can significantly influence children's behaviors and health are widely available, such as through the CDC website (http://www.cdc.gov/HealthyYouth).

■ PHYSICAL ACTIVITY AND ACADEMIC PERFORMANCE

There is a growing body of research focused on the association between school-based physical activity, including physical education, and academic performance among school-aged youth. A recent report from the CDC evaluated published studies from a range of physical activity contexts, including school-based physical education, recess, classroom-based physical activity (outside of physical education and recess), and extracurricular physical activity (CDC, 2010b). Based on this extensive review, time in physical education appears to have a positive relationship or no relationship with academic achievement. Importantly, increased time in physical education does not appear to have a negative relationship with academic achievement, which contradicts the practice by some schools to decrease or eliminate physical education with the hopes that the additional classroom instruction time would foster better performance in other academic disciplines.

Other studies summarized in the report explored the relationship between academic performance and recess during the school day in elementary schools. Time spent in recess appears to have a positive relationship with children's attention, concentration, and/or on-task classroom behavior. All studies found one or more positive associations between recess and indicators of cognitive skills, attitudes, and academic behavior; none of the studies found negative associations. Studies that explored physical activity that occurred in classrooms apart from physical education classes and recess also have demonstrated a positive relationship to academic performance. An example is introducing physical activity into learning activities that were either designed to promote learning through physical activity or provide students with a pure physical activity break. These studies examined how the introduction of brief physical activities in a classroom setting affected cognitive skills (aptitude, attention, memory) and attitudes (mood), academic behaviors (on-task behavior, concentration), and academic achievement (standardized test scores, reading literacy scores, or math fluency scores). Other studies summarized in the report examining the relationships between participation in extracurricular physical activities and academic performance found one or more positive associations. A number of policy implications stemming from this report are shown in **Table 3-3**.

TABLE 3-3   Policy Implications Regarding the Association Between Physical Activity, Including Physical Education, and Academic Performance

Physical activity can help improve academic achievement (including grades and standardized test scores).

Physical activity can have an impact on cognitive skills and attitudes and academic behavior, all of which are important components of improved academic performance. These include enhanced concentration and attention as well as improved classroom behavior.

Increasing or maintaining time dedicated to physical education may help, and does not appear to adversely impact, academic performance.

School boards, superintendents, principals, and teachers can feel confident that providing recess to students on a regular basis may benefit academic behaviors, while also facilitating social development and contributing to overall physical activity and its associated health benefits.

Schools can help students meet national physical activity recommendations without detracting from academic performance. Classroom teachers can incorporate movement activities and physical activity breaks into the classroom setting that may improve student performance and the classroom environment. Most interventions reviewed here used short breaks (5–20 minutes) that required little or no teacher preparation, special equipment, or resources.

School administrators, athletic directors, and teachers can develop or continue school-based sports programs without concern that these activities have a detrimental impact on students' academic performance, and also can encourage after-school organizations, clubs, student groups, and parent groups to incorporate physical activities into their programs and events.

Source: Centers for Disease Control and Prevention. (2010). The association between school-based physical activity, including physical education, and academic performance. Retrieved June 6, 2010, from http://www .cdc.gov/HealthyYouth/health_and_academics/index.htm

■ CONCLUSION

As summarized in the Presidential report "Solving Childhood Obesity Within This Generation" (White House Task Force, 2010), it is widely acknowledged that reversing this obesity epidemic will not be easy, and it will take action on all of our parts—parents and teachers, leaders in government and industry, and communities large and small. Schools will play a pivotal role in this endeavor. The simple concept we must strive to embrace is that good, nutritious food and participating in appropriate amounts of physical activity every day are essential to help children and adolescents grow healthy. Accumulating research further supports the conclusion that an active body promotes an active mind. By keeping children and youth physically active before, during, and after school, we will not only contribute to promoting a healthier student, but also better prepare them for academic success.

■ KEY WORDS AND DEFINITIONS

lifestyle chronic health conditions
Chronic diseases lasting at least several months or more; typically related to lifestyle behaviors such as lack of regular physical activity, poor nutrition, cigarette smoking, or other personal health habits. Chronic diseases generally cannot be prevented by vaccines or cured by medication, nor do they just disappear.

obesity   A condition of excess body fat; because methods to determine body fat directly are difficult, the diagnosis of obesity is often based on body mass index (BMI), a measure of the ratio of weight and height. Obesity at any age negatively affects health and well-being.

physical activity   Bodily movement produced by skeletal muscles; requires expenditure of energy and produces progressive health benefits.

screen time   Includes time spent watching television, playing video games, using computers, and surfing the Internet. Screen time is positively associated with obesity and inversely related to time spent being physically active among children and adolescents.

■ DISCUSSION QUESTIONS

1. Given the strong relationship between parents and children's health habits, what role can schools play to involve parents in reducing the burdens of obesity among students?
2. What are some barriers schools face in supporting children to achieve recommended daily physical activity? How might these barriers be successfully addressed?
3. Not all children have a positive environment in their neighborhood or community that allows them to be regularly active. In what ways can schools help improve this situation?
4. It is very important that children know the consequences of chronic health conditions associated with lack of regular exercise, poor nutrition, and obesity. How can this be effectively taught to children at a young age so they are able to comprehend these consequences?
5. What are the greatest opportunities to address healthy lifestyles of regular physical activity and nutrition at schools?

■ EXTENSION ACTIVITIES

Teachers can help prevent childhood obesity in many ways. Here are 10 strategies adapted from the Centers for Disease Control and Prevention that can help teachers make a difference (CDC, 2010b).

1. *Develop physical activity and nutrition through school health policies.* Establish local school wellness policies through a process that involves parents, students, school representatives, and the public. Examples of different components of the school wellness policy include physical education, school nutrition services, health services, counseling resources, parent/community involvement, and staff wellness.

2. *Designate a school health coordinator and maintain an active school health council.* School health councils have helped create long-lasting changes in school environments, such as the adoption of nutrition standards, establishment of student and staff walking programs, provision of adequate class time for physical education and health education, and availability of school facilities for after school physical activity programs.

3. *Assess the school's health policies and programs and develop plans for improvement.* A school health plan is most likely to be effective when it is based on a systematic analysis of existing policies and practices, guided by insights from research, and developed by a school health council that includes teachers, parents, school administrators, students, and the community.

4. *Routinely revisit and strengthen the school's nutrition and physical activity policies.* School policies can dictate how often students attend physical education, which items go into school vending machines, which topics and skills are taught in health education, which foods are served in the cafeteria, and much more. School policies directly affect students' opportunities for physical activity and healthy eating and can support the implementation of other related strategies.

5. *Implement a high-quality health promotion program for school staff.* Staff wellness programs provide opportunities for school staff members to participate in health assessments, nutrition classes, physical activity programs, and other health promotion activities. These opportunities can contribute to improvements in physical and mental health outcomes; increases in morale, productivity, and positive role modeling; and decreases in absenteeism and health insurance costs.

6. *Implement a high-quality course of study in health education.* Health education provides formal opportunities for students to acquire knowledge and learn essential life skills that can foster physical activity and healthy eating. Taught by qualified teachers, quality health education includes instruction on essential topics that protect and promote physical, social, and emotional health and safety and provides students with ample opportunities to practice health-enhancing skills. State-of-the-art health education features a sequential curriculum consistent with state or national standards and adequate instructional time.

7. *Implement a high-quality course of study in physical education.* Physical education is the cornerstone of a comprehensive approach to promoting physical activity through schools. All students, from prekindergarten through grade 12, should participate in quality physical education classes every school day. Physical education not only provides opportunities for students to be active during the school day, but also helps them develop the

knowledge, attitudes, skills, behaviors, and confidence needed to be physically active for life.

8. *Increase opportunities for students to engage in physical activity.* The school setting offers multiple opportunities for all students, not just those who are athletically inclined, to enjoy physical activity outside of physical education classes: walking to and from school, enjoying recess, physical activity clubs and intramural sports programs, and having classroom lessons that incorporate physical activities. These opportunities help students learn how to weave physical activity into their daily routines.

9. *Implement a quality school meals program.* Each school day, millions of students eat one or two meals that are provided as part of the federally funded school meals program. These meals have a substantial impact on the nutritional quality of students' overall dietary intake and provide a valuable opportunity for students to learn about good nutrition. The CDC supports the efforts of the USDA to ensure that meals served through the National School Lunch Program and School Breakfast Program are safe, nutritious, and balanced.

10. *Ensure students have appealing, healthy choices in foods and beverages offered outside of the school meals program.* Most schools offer foods and beverages to students through a variety of channels outside of the federally regulated school meals program: vending machines, school stores, concession stands, after-school programs, fundraising campaigns, and class parties. These offerings have dramatically increased student access to high-fat or high-sodium snacks and non-nutritious, high-calorie beverages. Although federal regulations on these foods and beverages are limited, many states, school districts, and schools are establishing strong policies and innovative marketing practices to promote the sale of healthier foods and beverages.

■ REFERENCES

Centers for Disease Control and Prevention. (2010a). Adolescent and school health. Summary of adolescent and school health tools. Retrieved June 6, 2010, from http://www.cdc.gov/healthyyouth

Centers for Disease Control and Prevention. (2010b). The association between school-based physical activity, including physical education, and academic performance. Retrieved June 6, 2010, from http://www.cdc.gov/HealthyYouth/health_and_academics/index.htm

Centers for Disease Control and Prevention. (2011). Division of Nutrition, Physical Activity and Obesity, National Center for Chronic Disease Prevention and Health Promotion. Retrieved June 7, 2011, from http://www.cdc.gov/obesity/childhood/data.html

Dietz, W. (1998). Health consequences of obesity in youth: Childhood predictors of adult disease. *Pediatrics, 101*, 518–525.

Eaton, D. K., Kann, L., Kinchen, S., Ross, J., Hawkins, J., Harris, W. A., et al. (2006). Youth risk behavior surveillance—United States 2005. *Journal of School Health, 76*, 353–372.

Epstein, L., Myers, H., Raynor, B., & Saelens, B. (1998). Treatment of pediatric obesity. *Pediatrics, 101*, 554–570.

Finkelstein, E., Trogdon, J., Cohen J., & Dietz, W. (2009). Annual medical spending attributable to obesity: Payer- and service-specific estimates. *Health Affairs, 28*(5), 822–281.

Freedman, D. S., Mei, Z., Srinivasan, S. R., et al. (2007). Cardiovascular risk factors and excess adiposity among overweight children and adolescents: The Bogalusa Heart Study. *Journal of Pediatrics, 150*(1), 12–17.

Golan, M., & Crow, S. (2004). Parents are key players in the prevention and treatment of weight-related obesity. *Nutrition Reviews, 62*(1), 39–50.

Guthrie, J. F., Lin, B. H., & Frazao, E. (2002). Role of food prepared away from home in the American diet, 1977–78 versus 1994–96: Changes and consequences. *Journal of Nutrition Education and Behavior, 34*(3), 140–150.

Kaiser Family Health Foundation. (2010). Generation M^2: Media in the lives of 8–18 year olds. Retrieved June 6, 2010, from http://www.kff .org/entmedia/8010.cfm

Mayer-Davis, E. J., Bell, R. A., Dabelea, D., et al. (2009). The many faces of diabetes in American youth: Type 1 and type 2 diabetes in five race and ethnic populations: The SEARCH for Diabetes in Youth Study. *Diabetes Care, 32*(Suppl. 2), S99–S101.

Ogden, C. L., Carroll, M., Curtin, L., Lamb, M., & Flegal, K. (2010). Prevalence of high body mass index in US children and adolescents 2007–2008. *Journal of the American Medical Association, 303*(3), 242–249.

Ogden, C. L., Flegal, K. M., Carroll, M. D, et al. (2002). Prevalence and trends in overweight among US children and adolescents, 1999–2000. *Journal of the American Medical Association, 288*(14), 1728–1732.

Olshansky, J., Passaro, D., Hershow, R., Layden, J., et al. (2005). A potential decline in life expectancy in the United States in the 21st century. *New England Journal of Medicine, 352*(11), 1138–1144.

Pi-Sunyer, F. X. (1993). Medical hazards of obesity. *Annals of Internal Medicine, 119*, 655–660.

Rofey, D., Kolko, R., & Losif, A. (2009). A longitudinal study of childhood depression and anxiety in relation to weight gain. *Child Psychiatry and Human Development, 40*, 517–526.

Singh, A. S., Mulder, C., Twisk, J. W., et al. (2008). Tracking of childhood overweight into adulthood: A systematic review of the literature. *Obesity Reviews, 9*(5), 474–488.

Strauss, R. S. (2000). Childhood obesity and self-esteem. *Pediatrics, 105*(1), e15.

Trasande, L., & Chatterjee, S. (2009). Corrigendum: The impact of obesity on health service utilization and costs in childhood. *Obesity, 17*(9), 1749–1754.

White House Task Force on Childhood Obesity. (2010). Solving the problem of childhood obesity within a generation. Report to the President. Retrieved June 6, 2010, from http://www.letsmove.gov/tfco_fullreport_ may2010.pdf

Research Review

Promoting Healthful Food Choices Among Students in Grades K–12

Avital Pato Benari

One of the ultimate nutrition goals of school health educators is to improve the food choices of their students. Health educators' efforts should focus on a few key aspects of their students' diet, like making sure that the diet is composed of mostly **nutrient-dense foods** and is low in **high-energy, low-nutrient foods**. This article will provide some suggestions on how best to promote healthful food choices in the schools by summarizing the most current studies, which discuss school-related nutrition topics. Health educators could use this information when planning nutrition lessons in schools; using reliable and valid data and researchers' recommendations is an effective strategy for teaching this content.

■ BACKGROUND ABOUT DEFINING FOOD CHOICES

Over the past few decades, recommendations for sound nutrition choices have constantly changed. One prime example would be the food guide pyramid. In April 2005 the U.S. Department of Agriculture (USDA) released its new food guidance system based on the 2005 Dietary Guidelines for Americans. The new pyramid replaced a food guide that had provided guidance to Americans since the early 1980s. In the new pyramid, food is still categorized into food groups just like in the old one, but now the representation of the groups is vertical rather than horizontal. Serving recommendations are no longer included. Instead, daily servings are left to the individual to determine. Determining the appropriate number of servings for the food groups depends on several variables, including an individual's daily energy expenditure (how many calories he or she needs per day). Servings also are determined by variables such as age, weight, height, and gender. These changes can be very confusing for the public and also for health professionals. Amid the frequent changes, one recommendation has remained steady throughout the years: the recommendation to consume more fruits and vegetables. Although increasing fruit and vegetable consumption has been the

target of nutrition education in schools in the last few years, the reality is still grim. Currently, less than 50% of students ages 4–18 years meet the recommendation of five daily servings of fruits and vegetables (Robinson-O'Brien, Story, & Heim, 2009).

Studies have established the importance of fruit and vegetable consumption in adults, but it is even more important to pay extra attention to these eating habits in childhood. Birch and Fisher (1998), in their article "Development of Eating Behaviors Among Children and Adolescents" emphasize the importance of developing eating habits that include regular servings of fruits and vegetables during childhood, because establishing these habits during childhood can influence food preferences and eating habits later in life. The eating patterns that develop during childhood and adolescent years likely will continue through adulthood. Therefore, it is crucial to develop effective nutrition intervention in order to increase consumption of fruits and vegetables during these formative years, so children develop healthful eating habits for life. It is never too early to start. Increasing consumption of fruits and vegetables among children as an effort to reduce childhood obesity rates should be a high public health priority, according to researchers such as Vadiveloo, Zhu, and Quatromoni (2009). Therefore, when discussing a student's menu, for any age or grade, increasing fruit and vegetable consumption should be the focus of attention. At the same time, there are items that should be eliminated from students' menus, or at least reduced. Recently, researchers have warned that consumption of beverages high in sugar and energy-dense foods that are low in nutrients—in other words, empty-calorie foods—are directly related to children's weight and health (Briefel et al., 2009). Researchers, professionals, and educators should continuously look for creative, innovative, and effective methods to improve children's and adolescents' eating habits.

■ THE SCHOOL FOOD ENVIRONMENT

There is a dire need for environmental and policy changes in order to improve students' nutrition and dietary habits. Children spend the majority of their time in school and consume about one-third of their food in school, so it makes sense that intervention should take place there. In an article called "School Food Environments and Practices Affect Dietary Behaviors of US Public School Children" that was published in the *Journal of the American Dietetic Association*'s supplement, "School Food Environment, Children's Diets, and Obesity" (Briefel et al., 2009), the researchers state that in addition to school-provided meals, children face an array of food choices during school hours, from vending machines in the hallways to snacks sold at sporting events. These foods are known as **competitive foods**, and they are a key to understanding what influences children's eating habits in school and to improving a school's food environment. Competitive foods are "foods that are available in schools but are not part of U.S. Department of Agriculture school meals. These include foods and beverages sold in schools through vending machines, a la carte purchases in cafeteria lines, school stores, and snack bars. Other sources include foods used in fundraising and other school activities, or provided by teachers" (Briefel et al., p. S92). Other factors that shape a school's food environment include characteristics of the school meals, nutrition education programs, and school activities generated by the school to promote

healthy eating patterns. In higher grades, yet another factor comes into play: whether students are permitted to leave the school premises and get lunch outside.

In 2004, the Child Nutrition and WIC Reauthorization Act mandated that beginning with the 2006–2007 school year, schools should address nutrition and well-being in school by providing a healthy school environment. The federal mandate could be an aid in the effort to increase wellness in schools, as could state laws and guidelines for foods served in school. However, laws and regulations, as important as they can be, are not enough. Other factors within a school itself can either facilitate or hinder a school's general level of wellness and the eating habits of the students. Some of these variables come from sources that are not directly related to a school's health education program or food service program. For example, a school's desire to raise money by hosting bake sales may bring in important income, but it also raises the availability and consumption of high-sugar, high-calorie products at school. Teachers and administrators might be unwilling to devote time and effort to wellness programs when they feel pressured to meet the demands of No Child Left Behind (Longley & Sneed, 2009).

The School Food Environment and Children's Diet

Findings from the **third School Nutrition Dietary Assessment (SNDA III)** confirm what practitioners and everyone who works with children already know—that school-age children do not make healthy choices most of the time. Gordon et al. (2009), after summarizing the implications of the third SNDA, indicate there is a dire need for both wellness polices in schools and nutrition education geared towards students, parents, and communities in order to promote healthy choices among students. As with other aspects of education, when it comes to diet and nutrition, it is important to distinguish among elementary, middle school, and high school students. Briefel et al. (2009) explain that as children move from elementary to middle school and high school, competitive foods and beverages become more accessible. These researchers report that when the consumption of sugar-sweetened drinks in schools was studied, the findings indicated that children in high school consumed about 10 times more sugar-sweetened beverages from school sources than elementary school children did. In evaluating fruit and vegetable consumption, studies found similarly deteriorating food choices as students aged. Consumption of fruits, vegetables, and pure fruit juice declined as students progressed through school. By high school, french fries were what most often passed for vegetable servings. In middle school and high school, if students did not have the option to purchase foods or beverages from a store or a snack bar, the consumption of sugar-sweetened beverages declined. In middle school, the most influential factor in increasing consumption of vegetables in school was the exclusion of low-nutrient energy-dense foods a la carte. In high school, the most influential factor in increasing consumption of vegetables in school was not having an open-campus policy.

The third SNDA provides up-to-date information about the association between these policies and practices and students' body mass index (BMI), which is calculated as kg/m². The results of the SNDA III indicate that students are more likely to be obese in elementary schools that serve french fries more than once a week in school lunch. The same results were found in elementary schools that offer desserts more than once a week. In middle schools, vending machines are the culprit. Students who attend schools that offer empty-calorie foods in vending machines were more likely to have a higher BMI (Gordon et al., 2009).

Among elementary school children, the types of foods offered by the school influenced whether the children consumed healthy foods at school. The healthier the food at lunchtime, the less energy-dense, low-nutrient foods—empty-calorie food—consumed by the students in school. When schools offered fresh fruits and vegetables daily and did not offer french fries, children consumed more produce daily (Briefel et al., 2009).

■ SUGGESTIONS FOR GRADES K–3: PLAYING WITH FOOD

In August 2007, the *Journal of the American Dietetic Association* volume was titled "Pathway to Healthful Eating." Karen Stein wrote an article for this issue, called "Playing with Food: Promoting Food Play to Teach Healthful Eating Habits." In this article, Stein advocates playing as the best approach to teaching young children healthy eating habits.

Early-childhood educators know that children learn, explore, and develop through play. Play is necessary to developing reading and math concepts, to developing social skills, and to absorbing new information about their surroundings. Because eating is part of a child's world, acquiring healthy eating habits is no different than any other skill—learning through play is the most effective method. Pretend food is abundant in the toy store, where play foods are an integral part of children's play toys. Observing children at play, it is evident that they enjoy playing with kitchen sets, tea sets, and toy foods. Decades ago, the toy foods available represented basic pantry items, including cereal, fruits and vegetables (either fresh or canned), dairy and meat products, breads, oils, and a few unique items like pizza slices and ice cream cones. Today, however, the availability of play foods goes far beyond the basics; it is easy to find toy versions of sushi kits, Hispanic food items, and spice collections. Make-believe kitchen utensils, appliances, and food selection are eclectic, diverse, and readily available. Children who play with these items by shopping, storing, preparing, cooking, and eating the "food" learn basic life skills. Health professionals could use the same toys and games to teach young children—and their caregivers—healthy eating habits (Stein, 2007).

In order to be educational, this food play should be guided. One way to direct the games toward the desired outcome, according to Stein (2007), is to make sure the children have a "well-stocked pretend kitchen." The kitchen should include an array of ethnic foods to encourage children to discuss the foods they eat and to expose them to new food items. The kitchen should include fruits and vegetables, preferably the kind that can be peeled and cut, so the children will have fun playing with them. Other suggestions for guided play include pretending to prepare a meal and using this game as an opportunity to discuss what foods make up a balanced meal.

Educators who work with young children know the importance of involving parents in everything the children do. Young children tend to follow their parents' eating habits, and so it is important to instruct the parents in the principles of healthy nutrition. Parents, when purchasing pretend food for their children, could easily choose to purchase a "fast-food drive through play set" (Stein, 2007, p. 1285). With the right guidance, parents could be influenced to provide healthy food representations for their children's

play. Parents can get directly involved in guided play by asking the children to prepare healthy pretend meals and requesting healthy options while pretending to prepare, eat, and shop for food.

Pretend food is not the only way to teach about food. Parents, educators, and children can all benefit from letting children, including very young children, play with real food. Participating in grocery shopping, following recipes to prepare foods, cutting, peeling, and playing with food could reap even greater benefits.

■ SUGGESTIONS FOR GRADES 4–12: GARDEN-BASED EDUCATION

Fruit and vegetable gardens can be a great addition to any schoolyard and a wonderful way to establish a healthy school culture. In addition to helping to shape the school environment with healthy nutrition principles, garden-based nutrition education in school also provides students with excellent hands-on experiences. Students have the opportunity to plant, harvest, prepare, and cook various herbs, vegetables, and some fruits, like berries and melons (Robinson-O'Brien et al., 2009). Garden-based education could be integrated into a wellness curriculum because it might lead to increased consumption of fruits and vegetables and also would increase students' exposure to new foods (Robinson-O'Brien et al., 2009).

In their article, "Garden-Based Nutrition Education Affects Fruit and Vegetable Consumption in Sixth-Grade Adolescents," McAleese and Rankin (2007) discuss school gardens as an educational tool to promote healthy food choices. The researchers investigated how a school-based garden impacts the eating habits of 10- to 13-year-old students. A school garden in southeast Idaho was "approximately 25 by 25 feet with two raised strawberry beds, a large herb garden, and a variety of fall crops including potatoes, corn, peppers, peas, beans, squash, cantaloupes, cucumbers, broccoli, tomatoes, spinach, lettuce, and kohlrabi" (McAleese & Rankin, 2007, p. 663). The sixth graders who participated in the study worked in the garden over 12 weeks. They planted, watered the garden, weeded, and harvested. After harvesting, the students also participated in preparing food using fruits, vegetables, and herbs harvested from their garden. They prepared salsa, created a cookbook, dried herbs, and engaged in other food preparations and experiences.

There are some obvious benefits to the school garden. Students learn about crops from this experience, and engage in hands-on activities regarding science, agriculture, and the environment. They also get exercise and move around during the school day. Moreover, as McAleese and Rankin (2007) demonstrate in their study, students who engage in school gardens also improve their fruit and vegetable consumption. According to the researchers, students in the schools that combined the garden with their nutrition-education curriculum more than doubled their consumption of fruits and vegetables from less than two servings per day to more than four per day.

■ CONCLUSION

Health educators in schools are facing a tough reality. They advocate for healthy food choices, and yet the school's food environment can sabotage all the positive work going on within the health classroom by providing unhealthful choices in the form of vending machines, french fries for lunch, and daily desserts. In order to succeed in improving students' food choices, teachers should look

for solutions outside the classroom as well as within (Briefel et al., 2009, p. S93). Teachers can influence many aspects of children's food choices. They can advocate for a healthier food environment by encouraging the availability of more nutritious food choices, and by marketing wellness throughout the school culture. They also can help guide children's food choices by influencing factors that are not directly related to the school food environment, like parents' beliefs, attitudes, and practices regarding children's diets. They can spur interest and learning in very young students by setting up a pretend healthy food area that includes "shopping," "preparing," "ordering," and "sharing a meal" involving healthy food items. As students grow and can take an active role, creating a school garden can be the perfect addition to any school interested in improving students' eating habits. The school garden can help to shape a better school food environment that will contribute to a better diet and healthier food choices for the entire student body.

For parents and teachers—and especially for health educators—leading by example is an effective and influential way to teach children lessons in healthy eating. This single, individual effort requires no funding, planning, or stamp of approval. By practicing healthy dietary habits themselves, teachers, coaches, and administrators can make a huge difference in their students' choices. Remember, students learn best by doing, participating, and practicing.

■ KEY WORDS AND DEFINITIONS

competitive foods "Foods that are available in schools but are not part of U.S. Department of Agriculture school meals. These include foods and beverages sold in schools through vending machines, a la carte purchases in cafeteria lines, school stores, and snack bars. Other sources include foods used in fundraising and other school activities, or provided by teachers" (Briefel et al., 2009, p. S92).

high-energy, low-nutrient food Foods high in sugar and/or fat content, which contribute to their high-energy content. These foods are usually low in other nutrients, and are often referred to as empty-calorie foods or junk food. Examples of high-energy, low-nutrient foods include cookies, potato chips, and sugared soda drinks (Wardlaw & Hampl, 2007, p. 41).

nutrient-dense food Foods that provide relatively high quantities of nutrients for a small amount of energy (compared with other food sources). The more nutrient-dense the food is, the better it is as a nutrient source. Examples of nutrient-dense foods include low-fat milk, beans, berries, dark-green leafy vegetables, and whole-grain bread (Wardlaw & Hampl, 2007, pp. 40–41).

Third School Nutrition Dietary Assessment Study A study conducted in 2004–2005; the researchers collected data from 2300 students in 287 schools that participated in the National School Lunch Program. The researchers reviewed menu data, observed competitive food options, collected 24-hour dietary records, and interviewed parents. The researchers also measured heights and weights of students. SNDA III, therefore, provides the most widespread and recent information about the food provided by schools, competitive foods, and the general school food environment in elementary, middle, and high schools (Story, 2009).

■ DISCUSSION QUESTIONS

1. What factors might shape a school's food environment? Think about school activities, such as PTO events, birthday celebrations, and fundraisers. Do these events include food? What kind of food? What do you think can be done to use these events to create a better food environment in schools?

2. Do you think it is important to involve parents and the communities when planning and implementing nutrition education in schools and planning a curriculum that promotes healthy choices among students? Why or why not? Give examples.

3. What do you think about cooking classes in elementary school? What might be some advantages, and disadvantages, of integrating cooking classes within the curriculum?

4. Garden-based education could be integrated into a wellness curriculum. What other classes could enjoy the benefits of garden-based education? Which other subjects taught in school could be enhanced by the hands-on activities in the garden?

5. Can you think of alternatives to a garden in urban schools that don't have the space or resources to create a garden within a schoolyard?

■ REFERENCES

Birch, L. L., & Fisher, J. O. (1998). Development of eating behaviors among children and adolescents. *Pediatrics, 101*(3), 539–550.

Briefel, R. R., Crepinsek, M. K., Cabili, C., Wilson, A., & Gleason, P. M. (2009). School food environments and practices affect dietary behaviors of us public school children. *Journal of the American Dietetic Association, 109*(2 Suppl), S91–S107.

Gordon, A. R., Crepinsek, M. K., Clark, M. A., & Fox, M. K. (2009). The Third School Nutrition Dietary Assessment Study: Summary and implications. *Journal of the American Dietetic Association, 109*(2 Suppl), S129–S135.

Longley, C. H., & Sneed, J. (2009). Effects of federal legislation on wellness policy formation in school districts in the United States. *Journal of the American Dietetic Association, 109*(1), 95–101.

McAleese, J. D., & Rankin, L. L. (2007). Garden-based nutrition education affects fruit and vegetable consumption in sixth-grade adolescents. *Journal of the American Dietetic Association, 107*(4), 662–665.

Robinson-O'Brien, R., Story, M., & Heim, S. (2009). Impact of garden-based youth nutrition intervention programs: A review. *Journal of the American Dietetic Association, 109*(2), 273–280.

Story, M. (2009). The Third School Nutrition Dietary Assessment Study: Findings and policy implications for improving the health of US children. *Journal of the American Dietetic Association, 109*(2 Suppl.), S7–S13.

Stein, K. (2007). Playing with food: Promoting food play to teach healthful eating habits. *Journal of the American Dietetic Association, 7*(8), 1284–1285.

Vadiveloo, M., Zhu, L., & Quatromoni, P. A. (2009). Diet and physical activity patterns of school-aged children. *Journal of the American Dietetic Association, 109*(1), 145–151.

Wardlaw, G. M., & Hampl, J. S. (2007). *Perspectives in nutrition* (7th ed.). Boston: McGraw-Hill Higher Education.

CHAPTER 4

The *Content* in the Triad of Teaching and Learning (Teacher-Student-Content)

■ CHAPTER OVERVIEW

In addition to *how* you teach, *what* you teach will play an integral role in cultivating a positive physical education environment. Your curriculum, or blueprint, for what is taught should take into consideration the needs of your students, regardless of what age, grade, or level you may teach. What type of curriculum will encourage a student of any level to enjoy physical education? Which curriculum model would benefit your students the most: multiactivity, fitness education, Adventure Education, Sport Education, or all of the above? The first article provides a thorough primer on the types of curriculum models you can use to engage students and streamline your curriculum, instruction, and assessment process.

The second article provides an example of how to implement a Fitness for Life unit that includes physical health components and nutrition. Students learn how to incorporate the five physical health components into their lives to improve their overall fitness level, allowing them to reach their fitness goals. Students also will be able to reflect upon their own nutritional knowledge and fitness goal progress while participating in diverse physical activities. When considering what nutritional information should be included in a Fitness for Life unit, a physical educator should first examine which healthy meal programs and wellness policies have been implemented at the federal level, such as the School Breakfast Program (SBP) and the National School Lunch Program (NSLP).

At the secondary level it is common for some physical educators to also be coaches, either at their own school or at another school or organization. Like physical educators, coaches can influence their students/players, so it is important for those in athletic leadership roles to consider what the most important responsibilities are when coaching. The third article in this chapter discusses the Youth Development Approach, which identifies how young people, especially in their adolescent years, have some key developmental needs that should be addressed in appropriately structured physical activity programs. The Youth Development Approach stresses similar themes as those seen in physical education, such as the development of empowerment, relationship building, integration, and teaching for transfer.

One curriculum model in particular—fitness education—can be used to teach students the why and the how of becoming fit for a lifetime. This model is described in an online article available at **go.jblearning.com/ciccomascolo**. One approach to teaching fitness education is to use concepts-based fitness and wellness education, which teaches the students the how and the why of fitness and wellness. This model is typically taught at the secondary level and combines a lecture and lab approach to produce a realistic plan for helping students to develop the knowledge and skills necessary to adopt and maintain physical activity for a lifetime. As students transition from middle to high school or high school to college or the workforce, they can take what they have learned about the process of becoming fit and well and continue to use their skill and knowledge base in a health-club or fitness setting.

Teaching Model-Based Physical Education

Gay L. Timken and Jeff McNamee

This is an era of standards-based education, where creating curriculum and program outcomes that align with national and/or state content standards is no longer optional. This is also the age of accountability, a time when we must demonstrate with formal assessment documentation the substantive impact physical education has on student learning and achievement relative to standards and program outcomes.

Meeting these pressing requirements—those of standards, outcomes, and accountability via assessment data—requires physical educators to think differently about creating and delivering curriculum. Following a model-based perspective when designing curricula will help teachers with this process, as the curriculum, instruction, and assessment process becomes more unified and streamlined, with long-term learning outcomes at the center. **Curriculum and instructional models**, in essence, are blueprints for teaching and learning. Models have a theoretical framework; have specific learning goals and outcomes that meet standards and can be measured (i.e., assessment); and provide specific language, teaching strategies, methods, and instructional guidance that lead to faithful implementation of the model (Metzler, 2005). **Table 4-1** demonstrates features of the models presented in this article. For example, Adventure Education is framed by experiential education (a theoretical teaching model first proposed by Dewey, 1938), in that much of one's education comes through experiences. Common outcomes of Adventure Education are to improve group cohesion and social interaction and increase personal confidence, all through the medium of physical activity. These outcomes fall within the educational domain known as the affective domain. Affective domain outcomes clearly meet the National Association for Sport and Physical Education (NASPE) Standards 5 and 6 and can be measured via group processing and student reflections or journaling. Physical competence, NASPE Standard 1, can be measured but is certainly more secondary to the social and emotional outcomes.

TABLE 4-1   Basic Components of Models

	Theory	Goals/Outcomes	NASPE Standards	Teaching Strategies and Specific Language
Adventure Education	Experiential education (Dewey)	Improved group cohesion; personal confidence; reflective learners; engaged members of society.	Primary: 5 and possibly 6 Secondary: 1	Facilitation; experiential learning cycle; challenge by choice; full value contract
Outdoor Education	Experiential education (Dewey)	Personal and group development; skill development; participation in physical activity.	All standards can be met, depending on activity	Teaching in the natural environment; can use experiential learning cycle if and when appropriate; leave no trace
Personal and social responsibility	Piaget's Stages of Cognitive Development; Kohlberg's Stages of Moral Development	Personal empowerment to be responsible for self and others; citizenship.	Primary: 5 Secondary: 1, 2, 3, 4, and 6 (all a medium by which to achieve Standard 5)	Counseling time; awareness talks; group meetings; reflection time; goal setting; modified tasks; self-paced challenges; self-grading
Sport Education	Play theory (Johan Huizinga; Roger Caillois)	Develop competent, literate, and enthusiastic sportspeople; learning about the concepts and conduct of sport (Metzler, 2005).	All standards can be met	Seasons; team affiliation; formal competition; culminating event; record keeping; festivity
Tactical games	Constructivist theory (Piaget, 1973); situated learning (Lave & Wenger, 1991)	Improved understanding of the tactical components of the game leads to skillfulness in game play.	Primary: 1 and 2 Secondary: 3, 6, and possibly 5	Tactics drive lessons; skill learning is embedded in and surrounded by a tactical understanding of the game; game, question series, practice task, game; games classification system

The facilitation process, which is more about guiding students through activity than actually leading or using direct instruction, is guided by Kolb's (1984) experiential learning cycle. Challenge by choice and the full value contract (Project Adventure®) are strategies to encourage a sense of safety, participation, and social interaction. As with all models, failure to deliver the model faithfully and with the intended instructional processes may negatively impact student learning and involvement (Lund & Tannehill, 2010). The blueprints for teaching various models are essential to help teachers balance the planning, implementation, and assessment tasks needed for student learning to occur (Metzler, 2005).

The key to teaching from a model-based perspective is to know which model to select for particular student outcomes and a particular group of students. Carefully choosing a model and placing it strategically within a curricular framework takes considerable planning and a depth of understanding of each model. Taking into account the following factors prior to selecting a model is requisite to good planning and instruction that is model-based (Metzler, 2005):

1. Standards and outcomes
2. Assessment of outcomes
3. Learning context and environment
4. Student developmental levels and learning preferences
5. Learning domain priorities
6. Development and sequencing of lessons and tasks within lessons

There must be purpose and intent in the curriculum development process beyond facilities and equipment and personal likes/dislikes. Merely placing various models throughout the school year without considerable thought and reflection on why, how, when, and which model is most appropriate will achieve little in terms of student learning.

The purpose of this article is to briefly describe five models that can be used with students at virtually all levels, assuming teachers will make modifications to meet the needs and developmental levels of students. Because of the brevity in explaining each model, the recommendation we make is to access resources, attend conferences, take special classes and/or workshops, and spend considerable time learning a model prior to teaching. Additionally, when teaching a model for the first time, try to work with a teaching buddy, start small, use the activity most familiar to you, and choose the right class.

■ ADVENTURE EDUCATION

One often connects Adventure Education with Project Adventure® and other similar entities that use challenge or high ropes courses to deliver curriculum. Undoubtedly facilities such as high ropes courses serve a curricular purpose, but low ropes courses and gym-based activities (even with minimal equipment; see Affordable Portables by Cavert, 1999) also help students meet specific goals and outcomes of Adventure Education. Essentially, the teacher, who acts more like the facilitator, attempts to create challenges that meet students at their level and then engage them in interdependent or collaborative activities whereby students need one another to complete a task. Although there is value in the activity, the value is extended during the processing and reflection of the activity, whereby participants think back on what happened during the activity, the inherent meaning in what happened, and how they can take what they learned into the future (i.e., future activities, life in general).

Theory

John Dewey (1938) is considered the "father" of experiential education, believing that experience is the master teacher, and in order to gain anything from experience, one must be able to reflect on that experience. Learning requires involvement (planning, execution, reflection) and commitment (physically, mentally, emotionally) by participants, something that is achievable through quality planning, sequencing, and facilitation. The activities common to Adventure Education are specifically designed to encourage involvement and commitment, and the guided reflection that follows turns the experience into experiential education (Dyson & Brown, 2010).

Goals and Outcomes

The holistic development of the student, or the development of the total person, is at the center of Adventure Education—that is, developing the social, emotional, mental, and physical capabilities of each student. Activities are specifically designed and sequenced so that students meet pre-established outcomes focused on trust, cooperation, communication, goal setting, risk taking (emotional as well as physical), meeting challenges, and problem solving. These outcomes are often reached collaboratively, so the social dimensions of learning and working with others (e.g., sharing ideas, being a good listener, being good leaders and good followers) is clearly a focus. In order to successfully complete adventure activities, students must work together to meet a common goal. And in order to work together, students must demonstrate good communication skills to solve the problem at hand; set goals as a team to meet the challenge; trust one another in order to take risks; and keep everyone safe not only physically, but also mentally and emotionally. Long-term or broad goals include helping

students become more reflective learners who are civic minded and engaged in their schools and communities (Dyson & Brown, 2010).

Connection to NASPE Standards

The link to standards is based on programmatic goals and outcomes, but, as Dyson and Brown (2010) point out, the primary standards tend to be Standards 5 and 6, due to the link to personal and social behavior. Meeting Standard 5 means students need to behave in pro-social ways, providing positive support and feedback and taking on personal responsibility to help the group achieve its goals. Adventure activities provide social interaction, self-expression, challenge, and enjoyment (i.e., Standard 6), and students can learn to reflect on these aspects of participation in journals and group debriefs. Though not a primary focus, students can be held accountable for demonstrating physical competence while participating in adventure activities. However, physical activity and related skills are merely a medium through which to learn in the affective domain.

Teaching Strategies and Guidelines

It is important to understand the need for professional certification when working in a challenge course setting. Working with Project Adventure and/or the Association for Challenge Course Technology (ACCT) is a step in the right direction.

Teaching via direct instruction and providing cues and feedback works in many physical education settings, but is less applicable when facilitating adventure activities. The word *facilitate* and the process of facilitation are important to distinguish from teaching, because facilitation requires a different skill set. **Facilitation** means setting the problem and defining the rules clearly and completely, but not providing a model or answer. Connecting to the theory of experiential education, setting the problem without the answer helps engage and involve students as they analyze, plan, execute, reflect, and assess (possibly multiple times) in their attempt to complete the task. Allowing this process to occur can be difficult, which is why we encourage teachers to attend workshops and conferences. Another difficulty we have seen with physical education teachers while implementing Adventure Education is the focus (conscious or unconscious) on competition, which is inappropriate and counterproductive to the outcomes of this model. Remember, the focus is on the process, or how students go about completing the activity, the problem solving, the trust, and the like; the outcome of the activity (who finished first, for example) is relatively inconsequential.

The scope and sequencing of activities must be thoughtful and deliberate, with group initiatives and team building activities coming before activities of higher risk (again, emotional or physical) and level of difficulty, and low element activities (e.g., activities located near ground level) occurring prior to high element (e.g., activities 20 to 40 feet above ground). To order activities out of sequence is to sabotage the experience. Again, the process and processing remain the focus, with the activities the means and medium.

As Dyson and Brown (2010) explain, engaging students in the experiential learning cycle of reflection and using the full value contract (FVC) and challenge by choice are three strategies that distinguish Adventure Education from other models in physical education. The FVC is a written or verbal social contract that identifies how students and facilitators should behave and interact. To maximize its impact, students should have some say or ownership in how the FVC is drafted—the language, expectations, and

guidelines. For example, "put forth your best effort," "only use put-ups," and "keep everyone safe" are part of a FVC. The facilitator then uses the FVC as a reminder when necessary but *not* as a disciplinary tool.

To maximize participation and minimize mental and emotional risk, facilitators can use challenge by choice. Challenge by choice gives students options for participation relative to their personal comfort level and perceived physical and emotional safety. Students may *not* opt out of an activity, but instead participate in a challenging activity at a level they can handle. Students are never to be forced into uncomfortable and/or unpleasant situations, but instead empowered to choose a level of participation and risk taking in an environment that encourages taking risks. For example, a student may opt out of participating in a trust fall from a height of 3 to 6 feet, but he or she could drop back from the ground, or he or she might opt to only be a "catcher" instead of a "faller." Challenge by choice coupled with FVC helps create a safe and caring environment in which students can attempt a challenge regardless of the outcome.

The experiential learning cycle is a four-stage model consisting of the following stages: the experience or activity, observations and reflections participants make about the experience, generalizations, and finally, application (Kolb, 1984). This cycle is designed to engage a small or large group of participants in the process of reflection after an activity. The role of facilitator is key—asking (but not answering your own) questions being the task. The first step, reflection, is typically started by asking, "What happened?" This question begins the reflective process by getting participants to identify, describe, and interpret what occurred (what they heard, saw, and experienced) during the activity. Additional probing questions may be necessary, and they should be thoughtfully and carefully crafted and placed within the context of discussion.

The next step, generalizing, helps participants connect ideas, feelings, and experiences in an attempt to describe what made the activity successful. This step is considered the "So what?" step. The final step, "Now what?," encourages students to find the take-home message—the application and transfer of what was learned to new experiences and settings.

■ OUTDOOR EDUCATION

Outdoor Education is becoming more popular in physical education due to the appeal it has with students and teachers. Imagine learning to surf, snorkel, downhill and/or cross-country ski, mountain bike, kayak, backpack, or climb mountains in physical education. These activities offer real challenges in a natural environment and have more to do with meeting such challenges than winning or losing. The excitement that builds from such novel activities may seem more enticing than another year of the same sport.

We know that adults engage in activities that are rarely competitive and are based more on lifetime activity. Researchers found that exercise such as aerobics, walking, and biking are most popular among adults, followed by activities such as dancing, fishing, and hiking. Few people participate in a traditional sport (Ham, Kruger, & Tudor-Locke, 2009). Teaching sport can be very positive for students, and we suggest offering a few, but filling a physical education curriculum full of traditional sports doesn't seem to set students up for a lifetime of activity. As explained by Stiehl and Parker (2010), including outdoor activities extends and enriches the curriculum; it is meant to supplement, not supplant.

For the purpose of this article, we choose to differentiate between Adventure Education and Outdoor Education (see **Table 4-2**). Although there can be similarities in outcomes,

TABLE 4-2 Unique Characteristics of Outdoor Education and Adventure Education		
	Outdoor Education/ Outdoor Pursuits	**Adventure Education**
Primary focus	Skill development (e.g., wet exit in kayaking)	Personal/group development (e.g., team building, group initiatives)
Primary setting	Occurs in the natural environment (e.g., forest, lake, river, mountains)	Can occur in a natural environment, but the area is developed specifically for AE (e.g., challenge course)
Risk	Actual, not invented—little to no control over the natural environment (e.g., weather, animals, insects)	Perceived and created (physical, emotional, and social)—controlled environment in which risk is sometimes fabricated to encourage participants to confront an issue (e.g., activities occur in a predetermined order with requisite safety equipment)
Teachers	Requires both skill and safety training and expertise to teach many activities, particularly those that venture into the back country (e.g., overnight backpacking trip, mountaineering, mountain biking)	Requires both safety and facilitation training and expertise (e.g., front loading, facilitating group-processing postactivity)

like teamwork and trust when white water rafting on a river, there are significant differences. The primary focus in Outdoor Education is skill development, whereas in Adventure Education it is personal and group development. The primary setting for Outdoor Education is the natural environment, whereas for Adventure Education it is in developed or structured settings, such as a challenge course. Risk in outdoor activities is real (e.g., weather, insects, uneven terrain), but in adventure activities the risk is perceived, because they are often held within a more structured or controlled environment (J. Stiehl, personal communication, March 2010).

Theory

Outdoor Education is framed by Dewey's (1938) theory of experiential education, which states that students can gain more from direct or genuine experiences. In essence, students take an active role in their education by doing! For example, a student is likely to learn more about kayaking from being in a boat on the water than from reading about it. That said, the experience students receive still needs structure and leadership, and a time for reflecting on what has been learned.

Goals and Outcomes

Goals and outcomes in Outdoor Education largely depend on the intent the teacher has set for the activity. There will likely be primary and secondary outcomes, but what is essential is that teachers have clearly defined learning outcomes and have linked those outcomes with standards.

Connections to NASPE Standards

Again, the primary focus of Outdoor Education is skill development. Therefore, skill development (Standard 1) and the application of principles and concepts (Standard 2) will apply to virtually all outdoor activities. Although skill development is often the primary outcome, what might prove helpful is an example of how Standard 1 may play a secondary role while Standard 2 plays a primary role. Orienteering doesn't necessarily require the learning of a new skill (most students already walk, jog, or run), but it does require an understanding and application of orienting the body, a compass, and a map (or GPS unit) to an outdoor setting. The application of those skills makes Standard 2 more of a focus (Stiehl & Parker, 2010). Nearly all outdoor activities require students to be physically active (Standard 3), which in turn helps students achieve a health-enhancing level of physical fitness (Standard 4), but again, these standards may be secondary to others. It is also appropriate to build in concepts of health-related physical fitness and help students make the connection between outdoor activities and lifetime activity. Standard 5, being respectful and responsible participants, is easily met in all outdoor activities. Being responsible for oneself and/or a partner while respecting and caring for the natural environment (**leave no trace**) are two main examples. Students can meet Standard 6 (value of physical activity) as they participate (i.e., are active learners) in a wide variety of activities that are new and challenging.

Teaching Strategies and Guidelines

We would be remiss to not provide a word of caution for teaching outdoor activities. The technical expertise required to deliver many outdoor activities (e.g., rock climbing, canoeing or kayaking on open water, mountain biking, mountaineering, and scuba diving, all of which we know to be taught in schools) cannot be underestimated, so we urge teachers to receive specific training (e.g., National Outdoor Leadership School [NOLS], Outward Bound), earn a wilderness first aid certificate, and/or include local experts in the curriculum and instructional process. A misstep by the teacher while teaching basketball is not the same as when teaching rock climbing. Completing the level of planning required, such as carefully considering budgetary restrictions, local resources, the amount of equipment that is also in safe working condition, correctly sized equipment, scheduling and time, transportation, the student/teacher ratio, the number and expertise of chaperones, safety and first aid, and the physical condition and technical skills of students required for the activity is critical to the success of the unit. And a teacher and his or her students should always be mindful of the impact they have on the environment, and do their best to preserve and protect natural resources and the beauty of the landscape (see www.lnt. org for guidance).

When preparing to add Outdoor Education to the curriculum, it is necessary to be mindful of the immediate surroundings and available resources. Activity selection should be based on what is realistic for the area and in the realm of the teacher's expertise. Even with all the challenges, the teachers we know who integrate Outdoor Education into their program report the benefits to students and themselves far outweigh the obstacles.

As with many activities included in the physical education curriculum, skill development is of primary concern in Outdoor Education. The technical skills required for most outdoor activities, again, call for a level of teacher expertise not often required for traditional physical education content. The further into the wilderness teachers take students, the more mentally, emotionally,

and physically prepared students must be to handle highly variable conditions. As a result, Stiehl and Parker (2010) have outlined nine skills and competencies for teachers of outdoor activities:

1. Technical skills (knot tying, belaying)
2. Outdoor living (cooking, orienting map and compass)
3. Safety considerations (water treatment, risk management/emergency procedures)
4. Environment impact (leave-no-trace principles)
5. Organizational considerations (securing permits, meals)
6. Instruction (teaching progression, assessing learning)
7. Facilitation (conflict resolution, group cooperation)
8. Leadership (sharing decision making)
9. Environmental ethics (sustainability efforts)

The ability to integrate environmental science, ecology, the flora and fauna of the area, geology, and other disciplines would only enhance students' experiences.

■ PERSONAL AND SOCIAL RESPONSIBILITY

Plato said, "You can discover more about a person in an hour of play than in a year of conversation." This quote seems to capture something extraordinary about the nature of play (and physical activity). An individual's moral character, ethical behavior, responsibility, and level of respect for others and the game itself become clearly visible during play. Given this, it might then be true that one can develop moral character, ethical behavior, responsibility, and respect through play. This is certainly what Hellison (2003) realized in his work teaching physical education to underserved and at-risk youth. His students needed more than just physical activity, games, and sport because of their life history with gangs and violence; they needed to learn to take more responsibility—for themselves and for others. Physical activity was the perfect medium. As a result of his work with underserved youth, the Teaching for Personal and Social Responsibility (TPSR) model was created for use in physical education.

It should be noted that, while TPSR was created for inner-city students who face unique societal and environmental challenges, this model should not be viewed as a deficit model—that is, only to be used in urban settings and/or with students who are having problems (Metzler, 2005). We would all do well if TPSR were implemented from Day One with all students in all classes in all schools, which is another way of saying that a form of TPSR should be integrated throughout the school as well as in physical education.

Theory

TPSR can be viewed through the theoretical lens of moral development—the ability to make moral decisions and take actions that are appropriate,with a sense of compassion and empathy (Parker & Stiehl, 2010). The work of Piaget (1962) was extended by Kohlberg and Mayer (1972) to include six stages of moral reasoning that people may progress through in their lifetime, though not all individuals may reach the highest stages. There seems to be a clear understanding that moral development does not happen automatically, which provides a rationale for specifically targeting moral development through structured learning experiences (Berman, 1998).

Goals and Outcomes

The main learning goals of TPSR are based on the need for students to learn to assume both personal and social responsibility in their lives (Hellison, 2003). What does this look like, and how do we go about helping students learn and ultimately internalize these attitudes and behaviors? It is easy to use global terms like *responsibility*, *teamwork*, *sportsmanship*, and *fair play*, but clearly defining these terms into observable behaviors for children and youth is more challenging. What does it look like, sound like, and feel like to be responsible, and does responsibility have different meanings in various contexts? Do we want students to:

- Solve problems?
- Resolve conflict peacefully?
- Not inhibit others opportunities to participate and/or learn?
- Be accountable for themselves and their actions?
- Live up to their obligations?
- Help and care for others?
- Be self-directed?
- Be responsible for their health and well-being?
- Be good leaders and good followers?

The goals and outcomes for becoming responsible are many, so the caution is to be clear with students about expectations and to provide ample opportunity for practice.

Connection to NASPE Standards

Because TPSR is delivered in the context of physical education, meeting all standards is not only an achievable outcome but also a necessary one. While Standard 5 is the primary focus for TPSR, students should become skillful movers (Standard 1) and understand and apply various concepts to their movement patterns (Standard 2). Physical activity and fitness (Standards 3 and 4) may be secondary outcomes due to participation in games and activities, and Standard 6 can be achieved as well. How each outcome is met largely depends on the intent of the teacher, the activity, and the students, but what Hellison (2003) makes clear and Parker and Stiehl (2010) also suggest is that the standards are best met when integrated.

Teaching Strategies and Guidelines

This is where the rubber meets the road, for it is easy to talk about teaching responsibility but the difficulty lies in getting the thoughts and concepts off of the page. As Hellison (2003) points out, the need for competent instruction in physical activity is "the central and most visible feature" of any program implementing TPSR (p. 56). Incompetent planning and instruction in any given activity/unit decreases the chance for student success, and planning and instruction in TPSR is even more critical. Planning for multiple outcomes in a given lesson is not an easy task. We often see teachers whose espoused outcome is something akin to personal and social responsibility, when in reality there is little going on beyond learning a particular skill or game. The ability to attend to multiple outcomes (psychomotor and affective) and maximize those opportunities presented for students to expand on personal and social goals is not an easy task for teachers. Therefore, teachers must be mindful of which particular outcome is most important at any given moment, and how that outcome impacts the others for the lesson and unit (Metzler, 2005).

Four main themes must frame TPSR instruction: integration, transfer, empowerment, and teacher–student relationship (Hellison, 2003). As mentioned previously, TPSR must be integrated with physical activity instruction, and clear outcomes must be established for both. The goal of transfer is to help students apply TPSR principles from physical education into their life. This happens more easily when students become empowered and self-determined—when they recognize how they *do* have control over much of their life. The student–teacher relationship is essential to helping students develop into self-determined individuals. The teacher must make the time and effort to build relationships with students based on trust, respect, honesty, and open communication. This may seem ominous given class sizes of today, and, while the student–teacher relationship is important, one cannot dismiss the power of the student–student relationships that develop. How the learning environment is created and feels to students will have a direct impact on how well students do.

The learning environment must be student-centered, with choice and student input as central features. Students cannot (or will not) learn to be responsible in an authoritarian environment where obedience is the hidden agenda. There must be a gradual shift of responsibility from teacher to students, and the teacher must be willing to listen and put into action student ideas. Students can smell a fake choice from a real one, so offering real choices at an appropriate level of challenge helps them learn to take more responsibility. As Parker and Stiehl (2010) mention more often than not, we tell students to be responsible without actually given them the opportunity to do so. Students actually need to practice making and reflecting on the choices made. Students will make mistakes, likely many. How these mistakes are interpreted and handled sets the tone. A learning environment where mistakes are viewed as a natural part of learning creates an environment where students can feel safe to make repeated attempts at a skill, even a responsibility skill.

Hellison (2003) has outlined some instructional strategies for teachers to follow. For example, a lesson may start with counseling time, during which students are doing the warm-up on their own (choice) while the teacher counsels with individual students. The class then comes together for an awareness talk to discuss a particular concept (e.g., fair play, peaceful conflict resolution) relative to the activity for the day and possibly reflect on previous lessons. Student voice and input are important, so teachers beware— lecturing about an expected behavior is not necessarily a responsible teacher behavior! Students can then participate in the physical activity lesson, which may be framed by modified and/or self-paced tasks and possibly peer teaching and peer assessment. The lesson concludes with a group meeting and reflection time.

Hellison (2003) illustrates levels of responsibility in TPSR that help define responsible behavior for students. While the levels can be structured to meet any context, they are generally similar in nature. On any given day, students may range from Level 0 (irresponsibility) to Level 5 (transfer). An example of one author's modification to levels for a college Sport Education class is as follows. Level 1 is self-control, and students at Level 1 may need more reminders about playing under control or helping with equipment, but they do not hinder others' opportunities to learn. Students at Level 2 (involvement) are willing to try new activities and only occasionally need a reminder to stay focused. Level 3 (self-responsibility) is when students are becoming independent learners who are supportive of classmates with words and actions and are willing to help others. Caring is Level 4, in which students can take

those positive and supportive behaviors out of physical education and into the hallways. Students at Level 4 are helpful without being asked. Teachers help students connect with the behaviors at each level, striving to reach the higher levels of responsibility. Teachers also help students monitor their levels, even with a question as simple as 'What level are you at right now?' Teachers also should monitor their own levels because it is likely difficult to be a responsible student when the teacher is behaving in less-than-desirable ways.

Most importantly, TPSR outcomes are not just for Mondays or for just one unit. TPSR can and should be infused daily and in every unit with all models. The impact on the learning environment and on student learning should really be all it takes to convince teachers to use TPSR.

■ TEACHING GAMES FOR UNDERSTANDING

What does it take to be a solid games player? What must a player understand about a game in order to successfully engage? What kinds of decisions do players need to make at any given moment in a game to be successful? And how do we help students in physical education become better games players when it seems they are unmotivated to even participate in games? We argue that rethinking how games are taught, and in effect learned, is the key. One only needs to watch a few physical education classes to see students regularly failing to transfer what they've learned from the traditional skill/drill types of practice tasks into game settings; and they typically lack a deeper understanding of the game to know when to use a given tactic and skill at the most appropriate time. What fun can that be? Furthermore, we often hear teachers complain how students are just not ready to understand tactics and/or need more time practicing the skill, so a teacher failing to believe in their students' capabilities to learn "hard stuff" can also stifle motivation.

What has been suggested by David Bunker and Rod Thorpe (1982) and Mitchell, Oslin, and Griffin (2006) is that teaching *through* games (i.e., learning via modified game play) instead of strictly teaching *for* games (i.e., the skill/drill approach followed by tournament play) provides students the opportunity not only to increase their depth of understanding about a game, but also to improve their *skillfulness* and game sense in game play. Learning tactically is more about understanding the underlying principles and structure of the game, and during game play learning to choose the best response for a given situation. Students *can* do this, even students in grade two, if their teachers will give it a go. Even better, students get to play a game, which is much more enjoyable and motivating than engaging in those seemingly endless repetitious drills. It's all in the approach, from belief in students to the lesson structure and instructional process. This model can also be used to plan curriculum, to improve transfer of learning between games that have similar tactics (e.g., basketball, team handball, soccer, pickleball, badminton, tennis, volleyball).

Theory

Two learning theories frame these Teaching Games for Understanding (TGfU) and Tactical Games model (TGM)—constructivist theory and situated learning theory. Constructivist theory (Piaget, 1973) posits that student learning is enhanced when previous experiences and information are used in the development of new learning. Students are constantly building new understandings from previous knowledge and experiences. Teachers are constantly and deliberately placing students in specific modified game situations to help them learn what to do when—that is, what tactical maneuvers and skills are best applied in given situations. In this case, developing a cognitive understanding of *what* to do comes before the *how*, or the skills required to carry out a task. Students are constantly building on previous experiences (lessons) as they learn new information. The information in TGfU and in TGM is almost always placed in game context; that is, learning is always embedded in a game form, and most often with others (e.g., small-sided games, 3v3 soccer), which specifically illustrates the need for particular tactics and skills. Learning in the context of the game, and not in isolation from it (isolated skills and drills), fits with situated learning theory (Lave & Wenger, 1991).

Goals and Outcomes

The outcomes of both models, which are inherently similar, are about developing good games players—players who are skillful and who understand the game well enough to make good decisions. To do so, students must come to understand the tactics of the game and, again, know *what* to do prior to *how*. What is commonly seen in youth soccer is what one might call "beehive" soccer, as the children, even offensive players, move in a swarm around the ball and fail to understand the need to create space for an attack. What is required is an understanding of the need to move off or away from the ball in order to create space, to open the field of play, to draw defenders away from the ball. Developing this tactical understanding, being cognizant of this during game play, and then actually moving away from the ball is an example of an outcome. Coming to understand the tactical complexities of a game, and then applying those tactics and skills in game play are definable outcomes for these models.

Connection to NASPE Standards

The focus of these models is on movement competence and application of tactics (Standards 1 and 2) and enjoyment of participation (Standard 6), with a secondary focus on physical activity (Standard 3) (Mitchell & Oslin, 2010). Students can demonstrate competent movement during game play as they, for example, choose to hit a lob shot in badminton because their competitor is up at the net. A teacher can assess the students' lob technique as well as their tactical decision to hit a lob, and can assess for transfer during tennis or pickleball. Developing a greater understanding of

the tactical components and structure of a particular game is assumed to lead to greater enjoyment due to increased physical competence and possibly even the social interaction, challenge, and competition that ensues (Standard 6). And it is assumed that better games players play more often, leading to more physical activity (Standard 3). Mitchell and Oslin (2010) suggest that Standard 5 can be met, because most often students are placed in small-sided games (2v2; 3v3) and must play with and against others. Learning to be respectful games players is essential to learning to play the game.

Teaching Strategies and Guidelines

The games classification system (see **Table 4-3**) helps us think differently about games. Although this system doesn't apply to all games and sports (e.g., track and field, swimming), it

TABLE 4-3 The Games Classification System			
Invasion	**Net/Wall**	**Striking/Fielding**	**Target**
Basketball (FT)	*Net*	Baseball	Golf
Netball (FT)	Badminton (I)	Softball	Croquet
Team handball (FT)	Tennis (I)	Kickball	Bowling
Soccer (FT)	Table tennis (I)	Rounders	Lawn bowls
Field/ice/floor hockey (FT)	Pickleball (I)	Cricket	Pool
	Volleyball (H)		Billiards
Lacrosse (FT)	*Wall*		Snooker
Water polo (FT)	Racquetball (I)		
Speedball (FT/OET)	Squash (I)		Shuffleboard
	Handball (H)		
Rugby (OET)			
Football (OET)			
Ultimate Frisbee (OET)			

Note: FT, fixed target; I, implement; OET, open ended target; H, hand.

Source: Adapted from Almond, L. (1986). Reflecting on themes: A games classification. In: Thorpe, R., Bunker, D., & Almond, L. (Eds.), *Rethinking games teaching* (pp. 71–72). Loughborough, UK: University of Technology.

applies to many. Invasion games are all about one team invading another team's territory to score. These games have similar tactics, including movement with the ball, movement off the ball, creating space in the attack, ball control (e.g., shooting, passing), starting and restarting play, and guarding/marking. Yes, some elements of the games differ, but there are many more similarities, and when those similarities are deliberately taught, especially when similar game units are delivered in succession (i.e., Ultimate Frisbee, soccer, speedball), students learn more about many games instead of just one.

Teachers have some incredible resources at their fingertips, such as books including multiple lessons for multiple games in each class (Mitchell, Oslin, & Griffin, 2003, 2006). There is a clear delineation of tactical complexities for each game, resulting in lessons by levels; that is, lessons are developmentally sequenced (five to six lessons to one level, anywhere from three to six levels) for maximum transfer of learning. Thinking back to constructivist learning theory, students learn specific tactics in a sequential order, which should positively impact later learning experiences in future lessons. For example, in a typical volleyball unit students learn the forearm pass, then the set, and finally the spike. However, Mitchell et al. (2006) suggests that students learn the tactical need (and the skill) for the forearm pass and the tactical need (and skill) for the spike. Why? If students come to understand how a good spike translates into a point, they may develop a better appreciation for the importance of, and ultimately better skills for, a good solid set.

Considering scope and sequence of a games unit is essential to delivering the model. What is required for teachers to create their own unit is a deep understanding of the game or a game similar in tactical components. For example, teachers can use their understanding of basketball and soccer to develop a tactically based unit for team handball. Identifying each tactical problem and solution is an initial step in the process of developing a unit.

Following the lesson structure designed by Mitchell, Oslin, and Griffin (2003, 2006) is essential to teaching for greater tactical understanding and improved skillfulness. Lessons always begin with a modified game, followed by a series of questions to get students thinking about the tactical problem to be solved and the accompanying skills required to carry out that tactical maneuver. At this point, students participate in some form of skill development task, be it isolated practice or modified game format. This isolated technique practice is a unique feature of TGM because the authors feel at times it may be necessary to work on isolated skills, but only after a tactical awareness has been developed. After the practice task(s), students return to the original game, to emphasize the tactics and skills once again. Naturally, closure is put on the lesson with questions, discussion, demonstration, and the like. This lesson structure is highly effective in engaging students in critical thinking and problem solving, leading to improved decision making, learning, and performance, which results in more enjoyable game play.

We suggest using TGM during the process of curriculum design, whereby games within one classification are stacked as units, such as teaching throw tennis, then pickleball, and then volleyball, one following another. Although the skills differ somewhat, this unit stacking process creates continuity in learning tactics that are similar, allowing for greater transfer of learning. From a student learning perspective, the overall time spent in two to three stacked units allows students more opportunities to practice and demonstrate learning. From a teacher perspective, assessment becomes more streamlined and, in a sense, easier. Similar outcomes cross each game, which means similar assessment tools can be used. If a student is not returning to home position in throw tennis, he or she can continue to work on that in pickleball and volleyball. Imagine the frustration of a student who is just starting to understand and demonstrate correct tactics and skills, only to start another unit on a completely different game. Teachers often complain of a lack of time in physical education to truly develop learning in students, but using the games classification system when designing curriculum alleviates this problem.

■ SPORT EDUCATION

There is evidence to suggest that physical education is dominated by competitive team sport, and not just at the secondary level (Fairclough, Stratton, & Baldwin, 2002; Quick, 2007; U.S. Department of Health and Human Services, 2000). Lower skilled students and girls are often dominated by higher-skilled students and boys, resulting in feelings of frustration and marginalization (Ennis, 1996, 1999). Students who fail to thrive in such situations may find physical education meaningless and refuse to participate. (Who can blame them?) It doesn't take a rocket scientist to determine the long-term consequences of such negative experiences. Sport will likely continue to play a role in the physical education curriculum, so how, then, can sport be delivered more authentically and with more positive results? Most of those in the world of physical education have experienced the power of sport, how it brings people together, and how it develops community. So, too, can Sport Education, if planned

for, structured, and delivered thoughtfully and with consideration toward the overarching goals and outcomes. As Metzler (2011) suggests, Sport Education is not just about learning the physical aspects, skills, techniques, tactics, and strategy of sport—more importantly, it is about learning the "concept and conduct of sport," the essence of spirit through affiliation, etiquette, traditions, values, and structure (p. 264).

Research demonstrates that the Sport Education model (Siedentop, 1998; Siedentop, Hastie, & van der Mars, 2011) provides the blueprint and teaching strategies and guidelines whereby students, particularly those who are lower skilled and those who do not participate, can have positive experiences. Again, delivering the model faithfully is key here because, like any model, Sport Education can be delivered in such a way as to marginalize rather than empower students.

Theory

According to Metzler (2011), the theoretical underpinnings of Sport Education is Play Theory (influenced by Huizinga and Caillois), as Siedentop and others saw sport and play as constituting an important place worldwide historically, sociologically, and culturally. We recognize movement play as a form of meaning making for infants, toddlers, and young children, but this also can be true for adolescents and even adults. As such, play should continue to be a valued part of society and formalizing play and sport through Sport Education makes this model unique. While not an educational theory, it should be noted that Siedentop (1998) was disillusioned with what he was seeing in school physical education—students not learning much in terms of skill or knowledge development, students feeling disenfranchised and unmotivated, students not coming to value what sport has to offer. As a result, the idea of Sport Education was born.

Goal and Outcomes and Connection to NASPE Standards

There are three major goals for Sport Education that Siedentop (1998) expressed in his initial publication—that of developing *competent*, *literate*, and *enthusiastic* sportspeople. The *competent* individual has the skills and understands and executes the strategies and tactics to play successfully (success does not necessarily mean winning); they are a knowledgeable and skillful games player. The *literate* sportsperson can distinguish between good and bad sporting practices, as both a player and fan/spectator, because they come to value the rules, rituals, and traditions of sport. The *enthusiastic* sportsperson preserves, protects and enhances the sporting culture through values and actions, through continual involvement at various levels of sport (youth and beyond). Additionally, Siedentop (1998) outlined 10 specific learning objectives for student learning, and these have been modified by van der Mars and Tannehill (2010) to demonstrate connection with the three major goals and also NASPE Standards (p. 301):

Competency
1. Develop techniques, tactics, and fitness specific to particular sports (Standards 1, 3, and 4)
2. Appreciate and be able to execute strategic plays specific to particular sports (Standards 1 and 2)
3. Participate in game contexts appropriate to their stage of development (Standards 1 and 3)
4. Work effectively within a group toward common goals (Standard 5)

Literacy
5. Develop and apply knowledge about officiating/refereeing and scorekeeping (Standard 2)
6. Provide responsible leadership (Standards 2 and 5)
7. Develop the capacity to make reasoned decisions about sport issues (Standard 2)
8. Share in the planning and administration of sport experiences (Standard 5)

Enthusiasm
9. Understand and appreciate the rituals and conventions that give sports their unique meanings (Standard 6)
10. Decide voluntarily to become involved in sport beyond school (Standard 6)

Through developmental and appropriate practices when teaching Sport Education, these goals and objectives help students not only become better games players but also uphold the essence of sport in its unadulterated form, the form that contributes to those fun experiences many of us have had.

Teaching Strategies and Guidelines

Siedentop (1998) suggested longer seasons to allow for greater depth of coverage and an expanded set of content goals. Essentially longer seasons allow more time to learn a sport thereby increasing the potential for knowledge and skill development. Additionally, because Sport Education is a more authentic or complete sporting experience within physical education, there is much more to learn (expanded content goals) not just about the game but also about the culture of sport.

The culture of sport is found in the following features delivered in Sport Education: (1) seasons (pre-, in-, and postseason), (2) team affiliation (membership, roles, and responsibilities), (3) formal competition (season schedule, progressive competition), (4) record keeping (statistics, league standing), (5) culminating event (postseason play, championship games), and (6) festivity (ceremony, rituals). Merely making teams and engaging in tournament play does not constitute Sport Education; each feature, however large or small and however graded developmentally, is critical to learning the culture, concept, and conduct of sport (Metzler, 2011), thereby contributing to developing competent, literate, and enthusiastic sportspeople.

Sport Education differs from youth- or school-based sport in three distinctly important ways that help contribute to the authentic student experience.

1. Equity of play regardless of skill/ability level is a key element to encouraging participation and learning, and preventing dominant play. Both practice and competition are designed around small-sided games (e.g., 1v1, 2v2) to enhance play. Non-elimination tournament play keeps everyone involved.
2. Practice and game play are modified to be developmentally appropriate; in other words, the parent game is rarely, if ever appropriate. For example, field size is modified to fit small team play; rules are modified, as are skill requirements for some students (e.g., a serve in volleyball is a rainbow toss not an actual serve, players may choose to be pitched to or use the batting tee).
3. Students take on various roles beyond the player role by learning to be a coach, referee, personal/fitness trainer, manager, statistician, sports information director, scorekeeper, and the like—all the roles seen in sport can apply to a Sport Education season (van der Mars & Tannehill, 2010).

There are some basic principles to follow to make Sport Education the **student-centered** approach it is designed to be. A student-centered approach empowers students to take more responsibility, individually and collectively, for their learning experience. During a Sport Education season, as it becomes age and developmentally appropriate, the responsibility gradually shifts from teacher to students, and various roles are carried out with teacher guidance but not teacher direction. Bear in mind the need for modifications based on developmental level of students. Sport Education is delivered at the elementary level, but roles and responsibilities are modified such that students can successfully complete those roles. In addition, teachers may have more direct instruction time with elementary students, particularly at the beginning of a season, and gradually shift some practice-type responsibilities to team coaches.

Success depends on the amount and type of planning and preparation by the teacher such that students learn to carry out managerial tasks during each lesson. When done well, the teacher is more able to actively instruct and cover more content. The teacher must plan and prepare for the following, as outlined by Siedentop, Hastie, and van der Mars (2011):

- Season context, including age group and sport
- The season objectives and content that leads to learning outcomes
- How students will be assessed for learning and their roles
- Team construction and development
- Roles for students to complete
- Class rules, routines, and expectations, including fair play
- How to structure festivity within the season

- How to design the season, including pre-, in-, and postseason play
- Record-keeping procedures during lessons and game play
- If and to what degree more features of sport can be included, such as media guides, trading cards, and/or newsletters.

An important note here is how models can be combined to create a more powerful learning experience. For example, lessons can be taught tactically within Sport Education, for there is no reason not to teach tactically based lessons to enhance transfer of learning. Due to the level of responsibility students assume, the TPSR model would be appropriate in helping students learn to take more responsibility. Individual and group counseling time as well as awareness talks can be implemented to improve levels of fair play.

Teachers should begin a Sport Education season with their most familiar sport and start small, with one class and only a few key features. As a teacher gains confidence and a certain comfort level, he or she can include other features. The ability to allow students to take, at times and with some classes, a great deal of control during each lesson of the season can be uncomfortable for some teachers. However, the stretch is worth it, for taking an active role (e.g., duty team, coach, official) in a sporting season can be empowering for students, thereby increasing motivation and learning.

■ CONCLUSION

Aligning curriculum, instruction, assessment, and standards is now a focus for physical education teachers and programs. Teaching to standards and demonstrating student learning to various constituents is no longer optional. We must verify learning and substantiate physical education as a worthy educational endeavor or risk losing more curricular ground. Planning curriculum and teaching from a model-based perspective has enormous potential to lead to positive developments for our profession. Becoming a model-based teacher who creates a model-based program requires effort and persistence for teaching in a new way. This requires a departure from business as usual and will push teachers out of their comfort zones. However, this push is necessary, and this departure a step in the right direction for students, teachers, and physical education.

We suggest reading more thoroughly about each model in their specific texts, along with the various chapters on models in books by Metzler (2011) and Lund and Tannehill (2010). Additionally, we suggest looking for ways to connect with other like-minded teachers during both exploratory and implementation phases, for a teacher's own community of learners can be supportive and affirming.

■ KEY WORDS AND DEFINITIONS

curriculum and instructional models Blueprints for teaching and learning.

facilitation A process of leading individuals and/or groups through activities and reflection such that participants gain the most from the experience.

leave no trace A program designed to help people take responsibility for the wilderness areas in which they travel, such that their impact in minimized.

model-based instruction A way of creating and then delivering a coherent physical education program.

student centered When a curriculum, unit, and/or lessons are developed and implemented with the focus on students and their learning instead of teachers.

■ DISCUSSION QUESTIONS

1. What model(s) defined in this article seem to fit with your philosophy of physical education? Why?
2. What are four or five benefits of both learning and teaching from a model-based perspective?
3. What are the key features and specific goals of each model presented in this article?
4. Why would a teacher design their curriculum around models? What would it offer students and teachers?
5. What model(s) might a teacher use to start the school year? How would that create long-term (think school year) benefits for students and the learning environment?

■ REFERENCES

Almond, L. (1986). Reflecting on themes: A games classification. In R. Thorpe, D. Bunker, & L. Almond (Eds.), *Rethinking games teaching* (pp. 71–72). Loughborough, UK: University of Technology.

Berman, S. H. (1998). The bridge of civility: Empathy, ethics, and service. *School Administrator, 55*(5), 27–32.

Bunker, D., & Thorpe, R. (1982). A model for the teaching of games in secondary schools. *Bulletin of Physical Education. 18*(1), 5–8.

Dewey, J. (1938). *Experience and education.* New York: Collier.

Dyson, B., & Brown, M. (2010). Adventure Education in your physical education program. In J. Lund & D. Tannehill (Eds.), *Standards-based physical education curriculum development* (2nd ed., pp. 218–245). Burlington, MA: Jones & Bartlett Learning.

Ennis, C. D. (1996). Students' experiences in sport-based physical education: (More than) apologies are necessary. *Quest, 48*, 453–456.

Ennis, C. D. (1999). Creating a culturally relevant curriculum for disengaged girls. *Sport, Education and Society, 4*, 31–49.

Fairclough, S., Stratton, G., & Baldwin G. (2002). The contribution of secondary physical education to lifetime physical activity. *European Physical Education Review, 8*, 69–84.

Ham, S., Kruger, J., & Tudor-Locke, C. (2009). Participation by U.S. adults in sports, exercise, and recreational physical activities. *Journal of Physical Activity and Health, 6*(1), 6–14.

Hellison, D. (2003). *Teaching personal and social responsibility through physical activity.* Champaign, IL: Human Kinetics.

Kohlberg, L., & Mayer, R. (1972). Development as the aim of education. *Harvard Educational Review, 42*(4), 449–496.

Kolb, D. (1984). *Experiential learning.* Englewood Cliffs, NJ: Prentice-Hall.

Lave, J., & Wenger, E. (1991). *Situated learning: Legitimate peripheral participation.* Cambridge, UK: Cambridge University Press.

Lund, J., & Tannehill, D. (2010). *Standards-based physical education curriculum development* (2nd ed.). Burlington, MA: Jones & Bartlett Learning.

Metzler, M. W. (2005). *Instructional models for physical education* (2nd ed.). Scottsdale, AZ: Holcomb Hathaway.

Mitchell, S. A., & Oslin, J. L. (2010). Teaching games for understanding. In J. Lund & D. Tannehill (Eds.), *Standards-based physical education curriculum development* (2nd ed., pp. 270–295). Burlington, MA: Jones & Bartlett Learning.

Mitchell, S. A., Oslin, J. L., & Griffin, L. L. (2003). *Sport foundations for elementary physical education: A tactical games approach.* Champaign, IL: Human Kinetics.

Mitchell, S. A., Oslin, J. L., & Griffin, L. L. (2006). *Teaching sport concepts and skills: A tactical games approach* (2nd ed.). Champaign, IL: Human Kinetics.

National Association for Sport and Physical Education. (2004). *Moving into the future: National standards for physical education.*

Reston, VA: National Association for Sport and Physical Education.

Parker, M., & Stiehl, J. (2010). Personal and social responsibility. In J. Lund & D. Tannehill (Eds.), *Standards-based physical education curriculum development* (2nd ed., pp. 162–191). Burlington, MA: Jones & Bartlett Learning.

Piaget, J. (1962). *Play, dreams, and imitation in childhood.* New York: Norton.

Piaget, J. (1973). *To understand is to invent.* New York: Grossman.

Quick, S. (2007). *2006/07 school sport survey (Research report DCSF-RW024).* Report prepared for the Department for Children, Schools and Families. Retrieved June 30, 2011, from https://www.education.gov.uk/publications/RSG/Subjects/Page6/DCSF-RBW024

Siedentop, D. (1998). What is Sport Education and how does it work? *Journal of Physical Education, Recreation and Dance, 69*(4), 18–20.

Siedentop, D., Hastie, P., & van der Mars, H. (2004). *Complete guide to sport education.* Champaign, IL: Human Kinetics.

Stiehl, J., & Parker, M. (2010). Outdoor education. In J. Lund & D. Tannehill (Eds.), *Standards-based physical education curriculum development* (2nd ed., pp. 246–269). Burlington, MA: Jones & Bartlett Learning.

U.S. Department of Health and Human Services. (2000). *School health policies and programs study.* Retrieved August 30, 2009, from http://www.cdc.gov/shpps/index.htm

van der Mars, H., & Tannehill, D. (2010). Sport education: Authentic sport experiences. In J. Lund and D. Tannehill (Eds.), *Standards-based physical education curriculum development* (2nd ed., pp. 296–331). Burlington, MA: Jones & Bartlett Learning.

The authors want to acknowledge Mike Metzler's (2005) work on instructional models as a guiding force for this chapter as well as the various chapter authors in Lund and Tannehill's (2010) book on standards-based curriculum development. Both books are valuable resources for teachers who wish to teach from a model-based perspective.

Benefits and Implementation: A Fitness for Life, Physical Component, and Nutrition Unit

Kate Balestracci

Nutrition and physical education are both essential for a student's healthy lifestyle, especially at the secondary level where middle school students will be transitioning to high school, and high school students will be transitioning to college, the workforce, or elsewhere. Therefore, a secondary physical education and health curriculum should focus on the importance of adopting and maintaining enjoyable, lifetime physical activities and understanding how to eat a nutritionally balanced diet. An effective secondary school physical education and health curriculum provides opportunities for students to be introduced to physical activities and healthy eating habits that will enhance their health and well-being.

Participation in physical activity and physical education is declining in adolescents. One way to reverse this unhealthy trend is to implement a more progressive type of physical education curriculum referred to as the "New PE." The objective in implementing the New PE is to provide secondary students the opportunity and education to participate in lifetime fitness. Lifetime fitness activities and Fitness for Life classes can be done regardless of the student's ability level. In more progressive physical education curriculums, activities such as yoga, fitness training, cooperative games, and fitness walking are being taught in addition to the more traditional sport activities.

In 2001, the Surgeon General's *Call to Action to Prevent and Decrease Overweight and Obesity* was released. This report encouraged schools to provide health education to students for the development of knowledge, attitudes, skills, and behaviors that they will carry with them throughout life. It helped to promote improved access to nutritious foods by ensuring meals offered meet standards and the *Dietary Guidelines for Americans*; that vending machines, school stores, and other venues offer only healthy options and do not compete with meals provided; and that students are allocated an adequate amount of time to eat meals (U.S. Department of Agriculture [USDA], 2001). Since this report was released, the U.S. Congress produced the **Child Nutrition and WIC Reauthorization Act of 2004 (CNR)**. The CNR mandates that local education agencies adopt and implement a local wellness policy (U.S. Department of Health and Human Services [USDHHS], 2001). The wellness policy must include goals for nutrition education, physical activity, and other school-based activities that promote wellness; nutrition guidelines for foods available in schools during the school day; and a way to measure implementation and who will be involved in the policy (Moag-Stahlberg, Howley, & Luscri, 2008).

In order to meet the CNR mandate, physical educators can implement a wellness policy at a middle and/or high school that includes fitness walking, a physical health component, and a nutrition unit. Students can benefit from this type of unit because they are activities that accommodate students of differing abilities, require little to no equipment, can be adapted to various school environments, and can initiate socialization between different student groups. Secondary physical education teachers can develop a fitness-based unit by using a fitness education curriculum model with a Fitness for Life approach. The aim of this Fitness for Life curriculum model is to improve and maintain physical fitness and learn more about basic nutrition by using a curriculum that focuses on physical activity (using one or all of the five physical health components) and nutrition. It also strives for individual fitness goals, fitness self-assessments, and decision-making skills, including nutrition topics, to continue students' fitness and health throughout life.

When developing a curricular unit using the Fitness for Life approach, the following four objectives should be considered:

1. Students learn what the five physical health components are (cardiovascular fitness, muscular endurance, muscular strength, flexibility, and body composition) and how to incorporate them into their lives.
2. Students set realistic, individual fitness goals.
3. Students discover which physical activities can improve their overall fitness level, allowing them to reach their fitness goals.
4. Students reflect on their own nutritional knowledge and fitness goal progress while participating in the physical activity.

When considering what nutritional information should be included in a Fitness for Life unit, a physical educator should first examine which healthy meal programs and wellness policies have been implemented at the federal level. For example, the U.S. Department of Agriculture (USDA) regulates the nutritional content of foods sold in the national school breakfast and lunch programs. The **School Breakfast Program (SBP)** was permanently instituted in public and nonprofit private schools up to and including high school in 1975. At the start of the program, 1.8 million children participated. By 1985, 3.4 million children took advantage of the school breakfast. By 2000, 7.5 million children participated, and in 2007, 10.6 million children were having school breakfast (USDA, 2010). Many of the students receive it at a free or reduced rate. Some schools offer the Universal Free Breakfast program, which is free breakfast for any student in the school.

The **National School Lunch Program (NSLP)** began in 1946. It serves the same population as the SBP, and provides lunch as well as snacks. The NSLP offers meals for no cost to those who are at or below 130% of the poverty level, and for a reduced price for those who are at or below 185% of the poverty level. At the start of the program in 1946, 7.1 million students participated; in 1970, 22 million were participating. By 2007, 30.5 million students were participating (USDA, 2009). Both programs follow the *Dietary Guidelines for Americans*, which includes no more than 30% of calories from total fat and less than 10% from saturated fat; one-fourth of the Recommended Dietary Allowances of protein, vitamin A, vitamin C, iron, calcium, and calories must be provided by breakfast and one-third by lunch. Therefore, a child receives more than half of his or her total calories and nutrient needs for a day at school.

Physical educators should also discuss with students a serious issue in regard to food in school—competitive foods. The USDA defines competitive foods as those offered in school that compete with the SBP, NSLP, or after school programs (USDA, 2001). Locations of competitive foods include vending machines, the school store, fundraisers, canteens, or snack bars. The National 2006 School Health Policies and Programs Study (SHPPS), conducted by the Centers for Disease Control and Prevention (CDC), found that 32.7%, 71.3%, and 89.4% of elementary, middle, and high schools, respectively, had vending machines, a school store, a canteen, or a snack bar (CDC, 2006). Sports drinks, sodas, and fruit drinks (not 100% juice) were the most common drinks; the most common foods were high-fat and salty snacks. Although a high percentage of schools offer these competitive foods, there has been improvement since the 2000 SHPPS. Unlike for school meals, the USDA has very little regulatory control over competitive foods. It is up to the states and wellness committee of the school system to set regulations. There has been an increase in the percentage of states that prohibit schools from offering high-calorie, low-nutrient-dense foods and beverages as a la carte selections during breakfast and lunch periods (from 20% to 42% of states); in school stores, canteens, or snack bars (from 6% to 32% of states); and in vending machines (from 8% to 32% of states) (O'Toole et al., 2007).

The USDA further defines those foods with minimal nutritional value (FMNV). FMNV are often low in nutrient density, but relatively high in fat, sugar, and calories (USDA, 2001). Schools that allow FMNV, yet teach about the value of healthy snacks in health class, are providing a mixed message to the students that good nutrition is just a part of an academic exercise and does not need to be practiced. In addition to food alterations and limitations, other food-related changes have been made. One improvement was an increase in the percentage of schools that recommended the discouragement of using food or food coupons as rewards (from 13.0% to 45.1%). Another was an increase from 32.7% to 44.0% of districts that provided schools with ideas on how to involve school nutrition services staff in classrooms to teach students about nutrition or healthy eating (USDA, 2009).

Current issues in nutrition, such as competitive foods, are just one reason why nutrition should be a key component in a Fitness for Life unit. Interactive activities in which the students are learning one or two concepts at a time help to teach the topic most effectively (Rhode Island Department of Education [RIDE], 2009). Further, it is important for physical educators to be knowledgeable about these recommendations for students. Nutrition can be a difficult subject to cover because there is a great deal of media hype and incorrect information available. Teaching the importance of a reliable resource allows the students to decipher when information is accurate or just an opinion, hoax, or fad. It also is important to teach that all foods can fit into any diet; the important point to stress is moderation. Dietitians do not view foods as "good" or "bad" but more as "healthy" and "less healthy."

■ DEVELOPING AND IMPLEMENTING A PHYSICAL EDUCATION AND NUTRITION FITNESS FOR LIFE UNIT

Teachers can use a lecture and lab approach when implementing a Fitness for Life physical education and nutrition unit, more specifically a fitness walking, health component, and nutrition unit. For example, teachers can lecture on or discuss topics such as motivation, barriers in adopting and maintaining physical activity, stretching, proper walking form, and the health benefits of fitness walking, muscular strength, and so forth. Depending on the class length, the physical educator can hold a shorter or longer lecture or discussion. The remainder of the class, or the lab, should be dedicated to the fitness and nutrition goals that the students will set. For example, students could choose to walk for 30 minutes, play Ultimate Frisbee, or do a yoga DVD during the lab portion of the unit. Teachers can use more time if needed during both the lecture and lab sections, especially if their school uses block scheduling.

On the first day of instruction, the teacher should inform the students of the purpose of the unit and have the students complete a fitness walking and/or physical health component goal sheet where students will write their goals for the lab portion of the class. Students' goals should be realistic and should be reviewed by the teacher. For example, a student can write, "At the end of the 4-week fitness walking, physical health component, and nutrition unit, I will have walked 2 miles in 30 minutes," or "I will have done 10 push-ups every day," or "I will have participated for the entire PE class while playing Ultimate Frisbee." If the physical education program has pedometers, students can choose a walking goal or an exercise goal of a certain number of steps completed within the class time. Students also should choose a fitness walking or exercise buddy who they can email, call, or communicate with if they need or want support in adhering to their fitness walking or exercise goals. Further, a student should fill out a nutrition goal sheet that, much like the exercise goals, should be realistic and reviewed by the teacher. Finally, students will need to use a journal to keep track of their fitness walking or exercise progress, or lack thereof, both inside and outside of class. Physical education teachers can decide whether the journal is written on a piece of paper, in a notebook, or typed if students have access to a computer.

STRUCTURE OF THE FITNESS WALKING, PHYSICAL HEALTH COMPONENT, AND NUTRITION UNIT

The following is a sample curriculum for a 4-week fitness walking, physical health component, and nutrition unit for a ninth-grade class. In this example, the physical education class meets twice per week for 60 minutes. The physical education teacher can use his or her discretion to structure the lecture and the lab portions of the Fitness for Life class accordingly because, clearly, every school will be different in terms of class time, space, facilities, and so forth.

Sample Fitness Walking, Physical Health Component, and Nutrition Unit

See **Box 4-1** for an example of eight class lectures in this unit.

Box 4-1   Class Lectures 1-8

CLASS ONE

Lecture/Discussion

The purpose of the fitness walking, physical health component, and nutrition unit is to:

- Learn the proper walking techniques (e.g., proper fitting shoes, stretching, correct walking form).
- Learn all five of the health components.
- Learn how to calculate your target heart rate.
- Learn how to use and complete your fitness walking goal sheets *and* nutrition goal sheet.
- Learn the definition of cardiovascular endurance and what activities can be done to improve this fitness component.
- Discuss and recognize activities that will enhance the development of cardiorespiratory endurance.

Definition: Cardiovascular endurance is the ability to be active for a prolonged period of time at a moderate to high intensity level and is aerobic (needing oxygen) in nature. In endurance training, one's heart becomes stronger (just like any other muscle that is "worked out") and daily activities can be done with less effort. Heart-healthy people live longer, healthier lives!

Nutrition

Define whole grain and discuss which foods are considered whole grains and why they are important to overall health.

Definition: A whole grain is a carbohydrate that includes all three parts of a grain: the bran (brown outside shell that provides the fiber), germ (provides a small amount of fat and vitamins and minerals), and endosperm (the white, carbohydrate portion). Foods include whole wheat bread, brown rice, popcorn, and whole wheat tortillas. Whole grains contain fiber, and fiber helps to lower cholesterol, keep you full longer, and keep your bowel movements regular.

Lab

30 minutes of fitness walking or jogging *and/or* 30 minutes of an aerobic activity (e.g., jumping rope, dancing, team handball, Ultimate Frisbee).

CLASS TWO

Lecture/Discussion

Learn about proper walking technique and safety, define muscular strength, and discuss what activities can be done to improve this fitness component.

- Sneakers (or shoes with a flexible sole and cushioned heel) should be worn at all times for comfort and safety.
- Eyes should look at least 6 feet in front; arms relaxed and swinging from the shoulders.
- Tight abdominal area; stand straight, do not arch the back.
- Plant the heel of your front foot while pushing off with the toes of your back foot.
- Carry ID when walking outside of class and tell parents and/or friends where you'll be walking. Walk on sidewalks or walk facing oncoming traffic.

Definition: Muscular strength is the amount of force one can produce at a single time (e.g., performing a chest press or push-up). Muscular strength is important for posture (keeps one from slouching), can increase metabolism (in addition to cardiovascular exercise), is important in performing everyday activities (getting up from a chair or out of a car), and helps in physical activity (kicking a soccer ball farther).

Nutrition

Role of dietary protein and muscles. Dietary protein helps build muscle when you work on muscular strength. *Definition:* Dietary protein is in food sources such as meats, poultry, fish, eggs, nuts, beans, and seeds. Choose lean meats and skinless chicken. Choose to grill, bake, or broil instead of frying. Peanut butter, nuts, and seeds make great additions to snacks.

Lab

30 minutes of fitness walking or jogging and/or aerobic activity (e.g., jumping rope, dancing, team handball, Ultimate Frisbee) *and/or* push-ups, sit-ups, pull-ups, squats, lunges, step-ups, and wall sits.

CLASS THREE

Lecture/Discussion

Learn the benefits of fitness walking and define muscular endurance and what activities can be done to improve this fitness component. Fitness walking:

- Is easy to do, regardless of athletic or skill ability.
- Helps in weight management.
- Lessens anxiety levels.
- Improves stamina and energy.
- Is easier on your joints than jogging or running.
- Can be done in short or long sessions and with friends.

Definition: Muscular endurance is the ability to use one's muscles repetitively over a certain period of time rather than at a single time. Muscular endurance is important in performing daily activities in sport and physical fitness, such as keeping one's arms raised on defense during a basketball game and keeping one's legs going while jumping Double Dutch.

Nutrition

Importance of calcium in bone strength. Along with weight-bearing exercise, consuming enough calcium (3–4 servings each day) will help keep bones strong and help prevent osteoporosis later in life.
Definition: Dairy products are an excellent source of calcium. Try 1% or skim milk and low-fat yogurt and cheese. Nondairy sources of calcium include broccoli, spinach, and fortified cereals.

Lab

30 minutes of fitness walking or jogging and/or aerobic activity (e.g., jumping rope, dancing, team handball, Ultimate Frisbee) *and/or* curls-ups, push-ups, mountain climbers, squats, and playing flag football.

CLASS FOUR

Lecture/Discussion

Learn about flexibility, define flexibility, and discuss what activities can be done to improve this fitness component.

- The benefits of being flexible include good joint health, prevention of lower back pain, and relief of muscle cramps, and it promotes good posture.
- Increase flexibility through proper stretching; static stretching.
- Demonstrate proper stretches for the lower body.
- Technique: No bouncing; don't stretch to the point of pain; hold stretch for 15–30 seconds.

Definition: Flexibility is the ability of a joint to move through a full range of motion or movement. Flexibility is important in order for one not be stiff when moving or hurt after being active (muscle soreness). Lower back or knee pain can also be caused by inflexibility.

Nutrition

Fat is necessary for our bodies, but choose "healthy" fats, called unsaturated fats, like those found in peanut butter, nuts, avocados, and canola and olive oils.

Lab

30 minutes of fitness walking or jogging and/or aerobic activity (e.g., jumping rope, dancing, team handball, Ultimate Frisbee) and/or a yoga, Pilates, or sports stretching, balance, or core strength DVD.

CLASS FIVE

Lecture/Discussion

Discuss the barriers in adhering to the fitness walking and exercise goal(s).

- Check to make sure students are keeping up with journal entries.
- Discuss any barriers students are experiencing. Other students can share their ideas for success and/or motivation with classmates. Include nutrition barriers in conversation.
- Discuss the importance of teamwork and social support while becoming physically fit.
- If feasible, students could complete a self-assessment reflection paper due at the end of the unit, focusing on the students' success or lack thereof using these questions:
  - Were you able to adhere to the fitness walking and exercise goals that you set at the beginning of the unit? If yes, list three things that helped you. If not, what were the barriers that did not allow you to reach your goals?
  - What did you like and/or dislike about the fitness walking and exercise unit?
  - Will you consider walking or doing other exercises once this unit is over? If so, why? If not, why not?

Why teamwork and social support are important in becoming physically fit: Reasons include having fun with friends, a feeling of belonging, gaining more confidence in learning a new skill or activity, feeling more security in trying a new activity, learning the skill or new activity more quickly, and learning how to communicate more effectively with friends.

Potential nutrition barriers (and potential remedies): Student does not do the shopping or cooking (ask to help with the shopping/cooking); healthy food is expensive (not necessarily, look for sales, frozen items, and make a list before shopping); and there are no good choices at lunch (avoid the fried foods, try adding a salad to your lunch).

Lab

30 minutes of fitness walking or jogging *and/or* aerobic activity (e.g., jumping rope, dancing, team handball, Ultimate Frisbee) *and/or* a yoga, Pilates, sports stretching, balance, or core strength DVD.

CLASS SIX

Lecture/Discussion

Weight management and fitness walking.

- Explain and calculate students' body mass index (BMI).
- Discuss how to calculate a target heart rate and use a pedometer.

Nutrition

Discuss societal influences on being overweight (i.e., lack of activity, fast food, emotional eating, bigger portion sizes, driving when you're able to walk). Explain the "energy balance" equation (i.e., calories in vs. calories out) and how fitness walking contributes to calorie expenditure. Provide appropriate caloric intake for male and female sedentary and active adolescents.

Lab

30 minutes of fitness walking or jogging *and/or* aerobic activity (e.g., jumping rope, dancing, team handball, Ultimate Frisbee) *and/or* a yoga, Pilates, sports stretching, balance, or core strength DVD. *This time, if possible, have students track the number of steps they took in their 30 minutes of activity by using a pedometer.*

CLASS SEVEN

Lecture/Discussion and Nutrition

Nutritional basics and hydration.

- The six essential nutrients are carbohydrates, proteins, fats, vitamins, minerals, and water.
- It is important to stay hydrated every day as well as when fitness walking or performing any type of physical activity.
- Water is a better alternative than soda.
- Soda fills you up, which is not good when you are exercising.
- Soda provides "empty calories"; that is, for the calories it provides, it has very little nutritional value.
- You only need sports drinks if exercising intensely for more than 60 minutes.
- Discuss the symptoms of dehydration (e.g., dizziness, fatigue, constipation, headaches).
- Low-fat milk is a great postworkout drink. It provides protein for muscle repair, carbohydrates to replenish the stores used in the workout, and some sodium to replenish salt lost while sweating. Milk also contains calcium, which is important for strong bones.

Lab

30 minutes of fitness walking or jogging *and/or* aerobic activity (e.g., jumping rope, dancing, team hand-ball, Ultimate Frisbee). *While wearing pedometers, separate students into groups for the aerobic activities and challenge them to see which group can get the most steps during their 30 minutes of activity.*

CLASS EIGHT

Lecture/Discussion

Final day of fitness walking, health component, and nutrition unit.

- Students submit three assignments: (1) fitness walking or exercise goal sheet, (2) nutrition goal sheet, and (3) fitness walking or exercise journal (or the teacher may already have them if done in e-journal format).
- Remind students to complete their self-assessment reflection paper for the next class.
- Students discuss how having a fitness walking buddy affected or did not affect their adherence to their fitness walking and exercise goal(s).
- Students discuss whether having a nutrition goal changed or did not change their nutrition habits.
- If necessary, announce a future written exam or reflection on the information taught during the unit.

Lab

30 minutes of fitness walking or an alternative aerobic activity (e.g., Capture the Flag, fitness scavenger hunt, an activity that combines health components, fitness walking, and possibly using walking maps in trying to find a "treasure"). *Students can also calculate how many steps they've taken throughout the activity.*

■ CONCLUSION

The physical education curriculum should focus on the importance of adopting and maintaining enjoyable, lifetime physical activities as well as understanding the importance of sound nutritional habits. Most students spend six or more hours a day for 180 days out of the year in school; as a result, there is an opportunity to influence healthy behaviors such as diet and physical activity. Physical educators can create a Fitness for Life unit that can promote a healthy lifestyle that includes not only physical activity, but also sound nutritional choices. The sample unit provided here is just one example of what physical educators, health educators, and sport professionals could implement to

teach the benefits of nutrition and physical activity, and ultimately how to lead a healthy lifestyle.

■ KEY WORDS AND DEFINITIONS

Call to Action to Prevent and Decrease Overweight and Obesity The Surgeon General's report that encouraged schools to provide health education to students for the development of knowledge, attitudes, skills, and behaviors that they will carry with them throughout life.

Child Nutrition and WIC Reauthorization Act of 2004 (CNR) Produced by the U.S. Congress; mandates that local education agencies adopt and implement a local wellness policy (USDHHS, 2001).

National School Lunch Program (NSLP) A program that provides lunch and snacks to low-income children that was permanently instituted in public and nonprofit schools in 1946.

School Breakfast Program (SBP) A program providing breakfast to low-income children that was permanently instituted in public and nonprofit private schools up to and including high school in 1975.

DISCUSSION QUESTIONS

1. Should a physical education teacher be aware of what he or she eats when around students?
2. Should a school remove its vending machines to rid the school of competitive foods?
3. Why is a Fitness for Life curriculum beneficial for students at the middle or high school level?
4. Do you find it more helpful to work out with an "exercise buddy," either at school or at home?
5. The School Breakfast Program (SBP) was permanently instituted in public and nonprofit private schools up to and including high school in 1975. How has the SBP helped students to work toward a healthy lifestyle overall?

REFERENCES

Centers for Disease Control and Prevention. (2006). School health policies and practices study. Retrieved September, 22, 2009, from http://www.cdc.gov/HealthyYouth/shpps/index.htm

Moag-Stahlberg, A., Howley, N., & Luscri, L. (2008). A national snapshot of local school wellness policies. *Journal of School Health, 78*(10), 562–568.

Rhode Island Department of Education (RIDE). *Thrive: Component health education.* Retrieved August 31, 2009, from http://www.thriveri.org/components/health_education.html

U.S. Department of Agriculture Food and Nutrition Service. (2001). *National School Lunch Program: Foods sold in competition with USDA school meal programs.* Retrieved August 31, 2009, from http://www.fns.usda.gov/cnd/lunch/_private/CompetitiveFoods/report_congress.htm

U.S. Department of Agriculture Food and Nutrition Service. (2004). *Section 204 of Public Law 108–265—June 30, 2004, Child Nutrition and WIC Reauthorization Act of 2004.* Retrieved August 26, 2009, from www.fns.usda.gov/tn/healthy/108-265.pdf

U.S. Department of Agriculture Food and Nutrition Service. (2009). *National School Lunch Program.* Retrieved July 31, 2009, from www.fns.usda.gov/cnd/Lunch/AboutLunch/ProgramHistory.htm

U.S. Department of Agriculture Food and Nutrition Service. (2010). *School Breakfast Program.* Retrieved July 31, 2010, from http://www.fns.usda.gov/cnd/breakfast/Default.htm

U.S. Department of Health and Human Services. (2001). *The Surgeon General's call to action to prevent and decrease overweight and obesity.* Rockville, MD: US Government Printing Office.

High School Coaching and a Youth Development Approach

John McCarthy

What is the purpose of high school sport? Often it is assumed that key life lessons are learned through the vehicle of sport. We know, however, that all sport experiences are not positive and that sport does not always lead to the healthy social or emotional development of high school athletes. Unlike youth sport, where children are most likely to take their cues and measure from their parents, the high school athlete often looks to other significant adult mentors for their cues, particularly their coaches. High school coaches are key figures in the lives of these adolescent athletes (Yeager et al., 2001). Given the power and influence the high school coach has over his or her charges, it is important for those in athletic leadership roles to consider what the most important responsibilities are of these coaches.

In this article, a **youth development approach** for high school coaches is presented. Hellison and Cutforth (2000) identified how young people, especially in their adolescent years, have some key developmental needs that can be addressed in appropriately structured physical activity programs. The things that young people grapple with, such as developing social competencies, a sense of belonging, and learning to be in control of their future, are particularly salient. Therefore, this article will discuss how Hellison and Cutforth's youth development approach, which stresses the themes of youth development of empowerment, relationship building, integration, and teaching for transfer, could also be embedded in team sport settings.

The youth development approach is consistent with the humanistic coaching philosophy espoused by Lombardo (1987). Lombardo focused on the holistic development, well-being, and success promotion of the athlete by using coaching methods that promote autonomy and learning for all participants. In short, Lombardo (1987) argued for an alternative to the **professional model of sport leadership**. Coaches and sport leaders that implement a youth development approach are likely to consider educational outcomes as much as winning games and championships. A discussion about the professional model of sport leadership is presented prior to elaboration of the youth development approach. Related to this professional model of coaching, we will explore some of the forces that seem to be driving the current win-at-all-costs trend in sports. Coach happiness and job satisfaction will also be considered. Prior to describing today's sporting environment, which in many schools is antithetical to a youth development approach, it is important to emphasize that there are two major reasons that warrant such an approach.

First, given that high school sport happens within the context of a school, we should aim to infuse sport with a broader educational intent (Lombardo, 1987), and therefore we should train our sport coaches to be educators (Jones, 2006). Athletic leadership needs to ensure coaches widen their focus from the beating-others value. Second, the high school coach, as a **caring adult mentor**, has the responsibility to ensure that sport adds real value to the educational experience of their charges. Engagement in sport should not only increase students' athletic competencies, but also should have a positive impact on their cognitive, social, and emotional development. The coaches today that adopt a professional model of sport leadership often ignore fulfilling the legitimate roles as caring adult mentor and sport coach as educator. Ultimately, this article will attempt to persuade athletic leadership as well as coaches of high school sport to consider using a youth development approach as part of their overall philosophy.

■ SOCIAL SYSTEM OF HIGH SCHOOL SPORT: PROFESSIONAL MODEL OF SPORT LEADERSHIP

In every sport setting there are several interlocking social systems that influence what happens in that sporting environment. All these systems inform and can influence how high school sport teams orient themselves. The high school sport team operates within the purview of the school, which has its own culture and traditions. A school is situated in a community that also has certain cultural and historical traditions and values. That community is situated in our larger society and has a sporting culture and ethics associated with that culture.

There are a few ways in which the larger sport culture has changed that contributes to how coaches conduct their work. For example, in our broader society we have an ever-increasing need for a quick fix. In professional sport, coaches are often fired after their first year on the job if their teams do not have instant success on the field. As a result, in some communities pressures exist at the high school level that closely mirror those seen at the professional level. The extent to which high school administrators succumb to such pressures is not fully known. But to be sure, there are a few identifiable trends that work counter to high school sport becoming the educational vehicle that most school administrators and parents might hope for.

First, at a time when budgets for sport in schools seem to be shrinking, there is pressure on high school administrators to find revenue and become more commercially driven. Second, most young people get involved in sport for its own value. At the beginning, at least, young people want to get involved in sport because they find it intrinsically motivating. Oddly, our sport system seems to place heavy emphasis on external rewards. It is difficult to determine who or what is responsible for placing such a high value on such rewards, but high school sport is replete with them.

All-star teams, academic all-star teams, media attention, and scholarships are things that are valued in the high school sport world. The social status that athletes obtain is perhaps not surprising. What is a bit more troubling is that parents, coaches, and school leadership seek to validate themselves through these external rewards. Unfortunately, one consequence of such an approach is that it can lead to the objectification of the athlete. In our present scheme, the coach, in particular, is susceptible to promoting one athlete to gain prestige and attention to their team and themselves. This is especially problematic if they choose to favor one athlete over others. A third trend is the overall mentality of impatience that surrounds high school sport. Sport activities are developmental in nature, and most sensible people can see that learning to do anything well is a gradual process. But in our sport culture we are constantly on the lookout for the next superstar or athletic genius. In an effort to be associated with such fame and fortune, some parents are seduced into compelling their children to get serious about sport at tender ages. These three trends are part of the backdrop of high school sports.

Sport Is Commercially Driven

For more than 25 years, there has been a television sports network (ESPN) playing around the clock. During this time, big-time college sport has become increasingly more commercial and part of a huge media, entertainment, merchandising, and gambling industry. Increased pressure to have state of the art facilities, equipment, scoreboards, and video-editing systems, and to travel to play high profile opponents are just a few of the costs that put athletic leaders in search of funding to offset the costs of being in today's game. Both public and private high schools are engaged in a sort of arms race to keep pace with their competitor schools. The attractiveness of their schools is linked to the quality of their facilities. Fundraising is time consuming and distracting to all the adult stakeholders in sport, with the result that financial issues can take precedence over human needs.

Objectification of Athletes and Coaches

The growth of championship systems, statistical analysis, fantasy leagues, rankings, scouting, and product endorsements has created an environment that looks at athletes and even coaches as commodities. You are either "hot" or "not." Professional and elite athletes and coaches often operate in the same firmament as supermodels, rock musicians, rap stars, actors, and politicians. Some might argue that this is only in the world of professional sport, but elements of these systems are fast developing around high school athletes.

For many years now, high school football and basketball teams have been ranked nationally by newspapers like *USA Today*. And this has been widened to include girls' sports in the last few years. Like scouting at the professional level, recruiting has become a high stakes game for big-time college sport programs. In an effort to identify the next great players, an entire industry has grown up around identifying and recruiting talent. A host of websites ranks individual athletes from various high school sports. High school players and even grade-school-aged players in some sports like basketball are evaluated and ranked by various recruiting services and media outlets. Global corporations that sell athletic gear, like Nike and Adidas, spend millions of dollars to have powerful networks (Wetzel & Yeager, 2000) to identify tomorrow's superstars. Shoe companies in search of the next Michael Jordan or LeBron James run camps, showcases, and combines that aim to identify athletes who are a "hot commodity" and seek to create brand loyalty. And coaches who can get "free" shoes and gear are willing participants in the scheme.

Sadly, whether they would admit it or not, parents and coaches treat their young athletes as an object or a commodity. They want their own children to be "the next" or "the chosen one" for a college scholarship. Given the high cost of college education, this has become a high stakes game for parents. There are countless examples of athletes who have been pushed at young ages to be successful. Tiger Woods and Andre Agassi are well-publicized examples of the eventual cost of sacrificing a childhood in exchange for external rewards. Not surprisingly, some schools and athletic leadership are also tempted to bend their school's purposes to bring positive publicity to their school through sport success.

Impatience

The harsh downside of the professional model of sport leadership is that on-the-field success trumps all other goals. When coaches aim to get to the top of the ladder, they feel pressure to discard those athletes who cannot help them get there, in particular injured players and those who are not developing as planned. Athletes who are star performers often get help and "breaks" in their academics from teachers and coaches because they are athletes. In some schools, high school athletes barely achieve minimum eligibility requirements and are passed along because they can help their teams succeed. This mirrors what happens at the college level as well. Many universities have struggled to maintain their integrity as academic institutions as they ramp up to compete in big-time sports in hope of big payoffs. Payoffs can come in the form of being nationally recognized and financial boons. Though there has been a big push by the National Collegiate Athletic Association (NCAA) for coaches and their schools to be held accountable for the academic progress of their players (Christianson, 2009), there are countless sad stories of how the sport system is not serving the athlete. For example, in a 5-year stretch under Coach Bob Huggins, the University of Cincinnati men's basketball program did not graduate a single player (Rozin, 2007).

Why are we discussing big-time collegiate sport and professional sport when this article is focused on high school coaching? We talk about big-time collegiate and elite sport because high school coaches' values are influenced by the values of big-time sports: What is important to *them* can become important to *me* as the coach. Our understanding of what it takes to be a coach is in part defined by the values espoused by high profile coaches and athletes. The social currency that comes with winning for the big-time or professional coach is status, fame, and wealth. All of these external values are associated with the professional model of sport leadership. In many cases, high school coaches are products of a sport system that is professionally oriented. That is to say, coaches often gain their standing because they have status as former high-level athletes themselves, and they will increase their standing by producing championship teams.

What is the professional model of sport leadership? It essentially encompasses valuing winning above all else in sport. To this end, almost any means is justified. Although few coaches would admit that they embrace such a model, in many cases their actions suggest otherwise. Tinning, Kirk, and Evans (1993) describe a teacher's "method" as an expression of "principles in action." For example, if a coach wants to help his or her players to learn to make "good decisions" on and off the field, then why do those same coaches make nearly all the technical, tactical, and planning decisions for their players? Is not decision making, like dribbling or rebounding, also a skill that takes practice?

In the pursuit of victory, with the uncertainties of extracting performance out of teenagers, coaches feel compelled to take control of any and all aspects that can ensure their teams will perform better in the short term (Cassidy, Jones, & Potrac, 2007). This is not too surprising because high school coaches are expected by parents, fans, boosters, alumni, and administrators to win. Consequently, coaches tend to use methods that compel their athletes to act in certain ways that would be considered overconformist and submissive in other educational settings. For example, some coaches do not ask legitimate questions of their athletes (Lombardo, 1987). In this sort of environment, questions from the athletes are not encouraged either. This sort of approach to teaching and learning is antithetical to the development of even the most basic critical thinking skills.

Coaching is a complex endeavor, and trying to characterize or pigeonhole all the different ways people coach would be overly simplistic. On a continuum, however, there are some coaches at one end who are very "coach-centered"; at the other end would be those who are more "athlete-centered" in their approach. Coaches that are very coach-centered in their approach might be more likely to use authoritative, directive methods towards achieving their goals. An athlete-centered coach may be more in tune with the goals of their players and use methods in line with transferring responsibility to the athlete. There are many types of coaches out there, so it would be fallacious to say that coach-centered coaches are bad and athlete-centered coaches are good. In action, athlete-centered coaches who are overly friendly, do not set limits for their young charges, or do not ensure their athletes understand the consequences of their actions are not likely to be helpful to the evolving young person. On the other hand, some coaches could be considered coach-centered in their approaches to coaching and are also deeply concerned about the positive growth and development of their athletes.

Presently, where do coaches look to find out how to coach? Far too often the models for high school coaches are those that can be found in the big-time and professional ranks. Unfortunately, in those settings the objectives are decidedly not educational in intent. Because professional coaches are expected to produce results, they often resort to outlandish methods of control, intimidation, and coercion. Bob Knight, the most winning Division I college basketball coach, despite his obvious tactical wizardry, became a glaring example of the downside of the professional model of sport leadership. His tactics of bullying and intimidation are now legendary.

A traditional approach to coaching that is essentially authoritative places little power in the hands of the athlete. Consistent with this power structure, authoritative coaches sometimes can have an "I'll tell you what is good for you" mentality that shows little regard for or confidence in the developing cognitive, social, and emotional abilities of their players. And using such methods do little to reinforce what unique individual talents each player brings to the team. Defenders of an overly controlling approach justify their method by saying that it works. But what if a coach was actually measured on what kind of progress their athletes made on some alternate scale? Joe Ehrmann, former Pro Bowl professional football player with the Baltimore Colts turned high school coach, is a startling example of how coaches can see the power of their position as a platform to teach other things. Core to his philosophy in working with high school boys is how they can become a "man built for others" as he teaches them to be more concerned with how well they are doing in their roles of son, brother, and boyfriend, and to measure their worth based on their commitment to each other (Marx, 2003). Not surprisingly, the teams he coaches also win a lot of games. Ehrmann believes that such an approach is not confined to boys; coaches of girls should teach girls to be "a woman built for others."

In professional sport, fans and owners demand that coaches and players win or they are replaced, regardless of what other redeeming qualities they may possess. Such pressures are not new to power sports like football (e.g., Bissenger, 1990) and other major team sports. We are beginning to see the same trend in high school sport, including coaches of girls' sports. For those who doubt whether such impatience exists at the high school level, there is much evidence to suggest that this ethic is even present at the games of much younger children. Few who have watched youth sport carefully for any extended period of time would deny that this win-at-all-costs mentality has also crept into the youth sport culture surrounding even the youngest age groups playing sports. The "professional" mentality can be seen and heard from adults (parents and coaches) on the sidelines of games in which 6 and 7 year olds "compete." Given this mentality in our sporting culture, would it be any surprise that the expectations are ratcheted up even higher for high school athletes and coaches? (Using a professional model of sport leadership should not be confused with showing professionalism in one's work. Professionalism is associated with being courteous, conscientious, and ethical, which certainly are positive qualities for any coach.)

lessons to their sporting experiences. Indeed, some attribute transformational experiences directly to the influence of their coaches (Lewis, 2006).

Sport has been a staple of school culture in secondary schools in the United States for decades. The purpose of sport has been to nurture the good character habits of developing young men and women. It is a widely held contention that sport provides the locus to teach a variety of important life skills. It is not difficult to name several of these skills: resilience, teamwork, hard work, discipline, and appreciating differences in others. Many believe that sport encourages a culture of striving for achievement that can carry over into other domains like academics. Sometimes these are referred to as **transferable life skills**. At its best, high school sport offers a sense of identity and belonging to a wider community (Petitpas, Cornelieus, Van Raalte, & Jones, 2005).

■ WHAT IS THE PURPOSE OF HIGH SCHOOL SPORT? (THE IDEAL)

What currently is the purpose of high school sport? Is our goal to blindly follow the lead of the professional model of sport leadership? Should the high school coach only celebrate the athletes who can help them be successful in the "W" or win column? Clearly much more potential good can come out of high school sport than just a focus on the results of matches and games. Most current high school coaches are in the business to do good, going beyond their personal win–loss record. Even though many current coaches probably would claim their high school sport experience was less than idyllic, many of our society's current leaders from many fields in the last 50 years attribute important life

■ WHAT ACTUALLY HAPPENS IN HIGH SCHOOL SPORT? ("IT DEPENDS")

One coach educator, Mike Luke, summed it up nicely when asked whether high school sport is beneficial. He replied, "*It depends.*" He described what goes on out there as "random acts of coaching." Whether good things are happening for the participants of any level of sport, he explained, "... depends upon what coaches are trying to accomplish, what methods they employ, and how well prepared they are to help the athletes reach those goals" (Luke, personal communication, September 12, 2009). There is no doubt that countless high school coaches take their role in the development of their athletes seriously. But there is mounting evidence that by any measure we might be missing the mark on realizing the educational potential of the sport experience.

As early as 1987, Lombardo called into question whether we are having positive effects on the development of participants in high school programs. He states, "Attainment of these outcomes are not automatically guaranteed simply because the individual enters the sport program. The effects of athletic experience vary greatly, dependent mainly on the specific athletic leadership provided" (p. 30). Recent trends have raised the specter that sport programs of many schools, in fact, carry fewer benefits to fewer students than is acceptable in a school setting. All too often athletes learn attitudes in the sport setting that will *not* serve them well in the long term. In some schools, athletes develop an inflated sense of self-importance and entitlement, which sets the stage for many social ills (Bissenger, 1990). Parents who are overly invested in their child's athletic success help to further feed self-centeredness in young people. Administrators and coaches fail to ensure that sporting environments are structured to ensure attainment of any educational goals. How is it possible that sport can potentially offer so much and in many cases deliver so little? What can be done to work towards the ideal with our sports programs?

■ THE YOUTH DEVELOPMENT APPROACH (WHAT IS STILL POSSIBLE)

The youth development approach is derived from humanistic (now called positive) psychology, which emphasizes the human desire for self-direction and authenticity and values the dignity of all human beings (regardless of skill level). Coaches who use a youth development approach would be recognizable for their adherence to a few basic themes. First, they would try to use strategies of empowerment with their athletes. By allowing them to make choices and giving them lots of opportunities to make decisions, coaches enable athletes to practice making choices and to find their voices to influence their own direction and that of their team. This does not mean that coaches "hand over" the team to the athletes. Quite to the contrary, a caring coach will ensure that athletes build the skills to be successful. This sort of coach gradually shares leadership roles and scaffolds early choices so that the athletes can gain the necessary confidence to become more independent.

Second, a coach who uses a youth development approach aims to leverage the sport activity to teach valuable lessons; therefore, they are always seeking "integration" of learning into the activity. Instead of weaving lessons throughout the sport experience, some coaches cannot resist lecturing their athletes and use standalone meetings to hammer home messages that actually could be better learned directly through the activity. Most adolescents learn a lot more from being asked to reflect on whether they just made "good effort" or not, than they do from someone telling them they did not measure up afterwards.

Third, a coach who genuinely and actively does "relationship building" in the role of caring adult mentor provides an important resource to the developing adolescent. Studies have pointed to at least one caring adult mentor as being crucial in the development of resilient people. Resiliency studies (e.g., Brooks, 2006) examine those who have thrived even while overcoming significant difficulties in their lives. This is not to say that a relational coach is all of a sudden overly friendly with their players.

Young people do not need their coaches to be their buddy or their best friend. And yet, the coach can be friendly, real, and knowledgeable about the athlete's life without being inappropriate. This also does not imply that coaches shirk other legitimate coaching roles they can fulfill, such as being limit setters or disciplinarians. Coaches who are confident in what their legitimate roles and responsibilities are act as a consistent presence in the young person's life and serve as models for many qualities that the athlete may want to emulate. The coach, as such, can be authentic and caring as well as being tough-minded and disciplined. All genuine mentoring relationships have that two-way quality to them. If coaches are open they can also learn and benefit from their association with their players. These sorts of relationships have at their core a mutual respect based on human qualities rather than utility.

Fourth, a key aspect of the youth development approach is teaching athletes to apply lessons learned in the sport setting elsewhere. The coach that **teaches for transfer** is perhaps delivering on the "holy grail" of the youth development approach, especially because teaching such life skills is more of a process than any one single act. To teach for transfer well assumes the athlete is learning something in the sport setting that could be transferred in the first place. For example, learning to give your best effort even when you may be tired in practice can be transferred to one's late night academic work. To structure successful athletic experiences is difficult enough on some days, but to get the athletes to consider how they can take what they are learning on the field or court and transfer that to school or to the street is a longer term and more challenging endeavor. Such social and emotional learning should be, however, at the heart of the work of the coach in a high school setting.

Detractors of such an approach typically are so wedded to the professional model of sport leadership in their mindset that they do not even consider that not all high school athletes have the desire to be a scholarship athlete or to play professional sport. Some coaches may be hesitant to implement an alternative approach because it may seem too "athlete-centered" (Kidman, 2005). This is curious because for years now educators have been trying to make schools and more specifically teaching approaches more student-centered. There are many pedagogical and motivational reasons that teacher educators have advocated this shift, but competitive sport coaches have been slow to adopt a similar framework. Because the high school sport coach should be a key asset in the educational process and sporting experiences, there should be deep learning experiences; it is time for coaches to embrace an approach that is in keeping with larger educational aims.

How does this valuing of winning at all costs impact the high school coach? If coaches subscribe to the professional model of sport leadership, they will hold themselves to the same standard as our sport culture will—if they do not win they are a failure. This approach limits the potential happiness and job satisfaction of the coach in many ways. Two concepts are central to the mental health of the coach: control and motivation. First, the authoritative coach feels compelled to make his or her players act a certain way. Instead of allowing each athlete's individual personality to flourish and add to the creative strength of the group, the traditional model aims to create an image of what a person *should be*. In this mode, the coach spends much of his or her energy trying to get athletes to conform to the coach's worldview. Anyone who has worked with teenagers can see the inherent difficulty with this scheme. Second, some coaches feel they must "motivate" their players. The underlying assumption is that their players are lazy and unmotivated, so based on this premise coaches often find themselves responsible for motivating people to do things they do not necessarily want to do.

A coach who adopts a youth development approach assumes that players want to play because the game is intrinsically motivating in the first place. This coach would spend more time and energy trying to get to know the player to help them recognize their strengths to become more attuned to their own goals and how to reach those goals.

In much of the last century teachers coached high school sports. Many were physical education teachers, but some were math, science, English, and history teachers. Today, the coaching landscape has changed. Often the coach is hired from outside the school. This in and of itself is not a bad thing. But the result of such arrangements is that the coaches often do not know their athletes as people or even students first. The athlete becomes an object to advance the coach's success. If the athlete is a legitimate athletic prospect for their team, then they warrant the coach's attention. Even if the coach in this situation is well intentioned he or she cannot have as many opportunities to influence young people, to view them outside the athletic arena, and to come to know and appreciate them as people. Perhaps even more egregious is when a school will hire a teacher who in truth is selected for his or her supposed coaching ability. In this case, you have the same professional model coach but also may have an inferior teacher of math, English, science, or another subject. To avoid this scenario, teachers should be hired based on their teaching skills and commitment to the development of young people. After that, they could apply to coaching positions for which they are qualified.

■ CONCLUSION

School leadership and administrators—especially athletic directors—have a great deal of power to address some of the key issues to help coaches fully understand their role in the educational goals of the school. These school leaders and administrators can emphasize how the coach has a profound effect on their athletes, but specifically they could ensure that their sport coaches adhere to the four themes of youth development proposed in this article. In schools, the responsibility and authority to shape how coaches structure the athletic experience usually rests largely with the athletic director. In some schools it may be up to the principal or headmaster, who is usually up to his or her ears in seemingly more pressing issues.

Unfortunately, trends that extend the work of the athletic director into areas of fundraising, facility management, parent management, and a myriad of other tasks means that often athletic directors have less time to pay attention to and ensure that coaches' work is aligned with the educational goals of the school. To change this environment, school leadership must take some simple but not easy steps towards reclaiming the educational purpose of sport.

First, athletic directors and school leadership must clearly define what outcomes the coaches are going to be held accountable for. This exercise helps coaches know what is expected of them and will help them see that the athletic director and other key administrators are allies in the process of fielding competitive teams. Sometimes pressure on the coach is more perceived than real, and the coach is caught up in the professional mentality that exists in the sport culture at large. Key administrators can re-emphasize to the coach that the educational goals are the main markers of success. Defining the key areas developed by each school can help guide how coaches conduct their daily work and can help administrators and coaches to assess what areas need improvement. Second, athletic directors and school leadership must develop some way of delivering training and development for their coaches to become the sorts of coaches they hope to have at their school. This process is complex because training for coaches is not a one-size-fits-all affair. An inexperienced coach may need assistance in several areas of development: techniques, tactics, philosophy, and communication skills, to name a few. More experienced coaches might need work on different aspects of their coaching. An overall commitment to continually work with coaches to do their job better is critical to the development of athletic programs that offer educational value to the participants. Finally, incorporating a youth development approach into the culture of an athletic department might help guide young coaches, in particular, to develop methods of coaching that meet the needs of the athletes while keeping in sight some broader educational goals.

■ KEY WORDS AND DEFINITIONS

caring adult mentor   An adult who serves an important role in the life of a child or young adult: The caring adult mentor provides a sense of personal connection and value to the life of the youth/young adult.

professional model of sport leadership   A method of coaching in which the goal is to win, regardless of the process or method. Typically, such methods rely on coercion, intimidation, and control for success.

teaching for transfer   When a coach, who values teaching transferrable life skills, prioritizes helping his or her athletes take lessons learned in sport and apply them to other important areas of their life—particularly academic pursuits.

transferable life skills   From the high school sport perspective, skills that the athlete learns in sport that can be used in other aspects of his or her life. Some examples include respect and being on time.

youth development approach   A coaching philosophy that emphasizes the holistic development, well-being, and success of their athletes.

■ DISCUSSION QUESTIONS

1. What did you learn from your high school sport experience? What transferable life skills did you learn? What did you not learn that you wish you had?
2. Specifically, if a coach helped you learn transferable life skills, how did that happen? What could your coaches have done differently to make sure you had an optimal learning experience?
3. Did any of your coaches fit the description of caring adult mentor? What sorts of things did they do or what ways did they act that signaled that they were that caring adult mentor to you? What are some ways you could become that person for your future athletes?
4. Develop three specific teaching strategies that you could use to help your coaching philosophy move from a professional model towards a youth development model of coaching.

5. What can school and athletic leadership do to ensure that coaches focus on educational goals as much as athletic goals?

■ EXTENSION ACTIVITIES

1. Have students work in small groups (three to five students per group) to reflect back on their sports experiences in high school. Have them describe their coaches, considering both the professional model and youth development approach.
2. Have students write a letter to their favorite coach describing what they learned from that coach. Ask them to thank the coach for teaching them some key life lessons.
3. Have students list all the negative things they have learned or experienced in sport (particularly high school sport) and to consider how they could have set up the sporting environment differently.
4. Outside class activity: Have students observe a coach, other than someone they have been coached by. Have them try to describe the methods or approach of the coach they observe. Were they using any youth development approaches or was it more of a professional model of sport leadership?

■ REFERENCES

Bissenger, H. (1990). *Friday night lights: A town, a team and a dream.* Cambridge, MA: DaCapo Press.

Brooks, J. (2006). Strengthening resilience in children and youths: Maximizing opportunities through the schools. *Children & Schools, 28*(2), 69–76.

Cassidy, T., Jones, R., & Potrac, P. (2007). *Understanding sports coaching.* New York: Routledge.

Christianson, E. (2009). *Baseball, basketball, football improve their grades.* National Collegiate Athletic Association, News Release. Retrieved July 20, 2011, from http://fs.ncaa.org/Docs/PressArchive/2009/Academic%2BReform/20090506%2BAPR%2BRelease.html

Jones, R. (2006). *The sports coach as educator: Re-conceptualizing sports coaching.* New York: Routledge.

Kidman, L. (2005). *Athlete-centered coaching.* Christchurch, NZ: Innovative Print Communications.

Lewis, M. (2005). *Coach: Lessons on the game of life.* New York: Norton.

Lombardo, B. (1987). *The humanistic coach: From theory to practice.* Springfield, MA: Thomas.

Marx, J. (2003). *Season of life.* New York: Simon and Schuster.

Petitpas, A., Cornelius, A., Van Raalte, J., & Jones, T. (2005). A framework for planning youth sport programs that foster psychosocial development. *The Sport Psychologist, 19*, 63–80.

Rozin, S. (2007). The basketball coach vs. the college president. *Wall Street Journal* Digital Network, Sports. Retrieved December 14, 2009, from http://online.wsj.com/article/SB114367599328911693.html

Tinning, R., Kirk, D., & Evans, J. (1993). *Learning to teach physical education.* London: Prentice Hall.

Wetzel, D., & Yeager, D. (2000). *Sole influence: basketball, corporate greed, and the corruption of America's youth.* New York: Warner Books.

Yeager, J., Buxton, J., Baltzell, A., & Bzdell, W. (2001). *Character and coaching: Building virtue in athletic programs.* Port Chester, NY: Dude.

Research Review

Examining Skills-Based Health Education in Select Secondary Schools

Sarah Sparrow Benes

The primary purpose of this study was to examine the implementation of **skills-based health education (SBHE)** in select Massachusetts secondary schools. Purposeful sampling was conducted to obtain subjects/teachers ($n = 3$) implementing SBHE in quality health education programs. A secondary purpose was to develop and use a classroom observation form (COF) (Sparrow, 2010) for collecting data in an SBHE classroom.

A mixed method design was used with a focus on qualitative data collection methods. The researcher observed 10 class periods of three health educators for a total of 26 hours of observation. Qualitative data collection procedures included a COF (Sparrow, 2010), field notes, and interviews with the subjects. The quantitative procedure was an evaluation of two assessments completed by students in one select class of two subjects (four assessments total).

Due to the large amounts of data collected in this study, selected results are presented here that best represent the primary purpose of this study and the themes of this textbook. The results are presented in this order: lesson content data, themes from field notes, and themes from interviews with health educators and data from student assessments. A short discussion of the results follows the data, to provide further insight into the significance and potential application of the results.

Lesson Content Data

The data in **Figure 4-1**, **Figure 4-2**, and **Figure 4-3** represent the types of activities (or lesson content) that were observed during the lessons. The researcher recorded all activities that occurred during the lessons, then, using an emergent approach, determined the categories of lesson content, which are presented in the figures; the data for lesson content are presented by teacher or subject number.

The COF provided a majority of the data regarding the health educators' methods of implementation. As presented in the figures, the health educators used a variety of lesson content, including skill-related activities, student presentations, direct instruction, discussion, role play, video, demonstration, and non-skill-related activities. All three health educators used three types of lesson content: skill-related activity, direct instruction, and student presentations. Another type of lesson content that was important, and that has important implications for practice despite only being used by one health educator, is reflection. These four categories of lesson content will be discussed here to provide further information about each in hopes that it can inform your future practice and knowledge of health education.

Skill-related activity was a category description created by the researcher to encompass a variety of activities observed

FIGURE 4-1 Lesson content for health educator A (HEA).

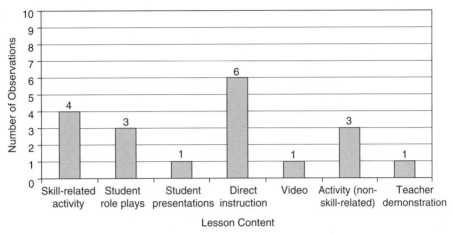

FIGURE 4-2 Lesson content for health educator B (HEB).

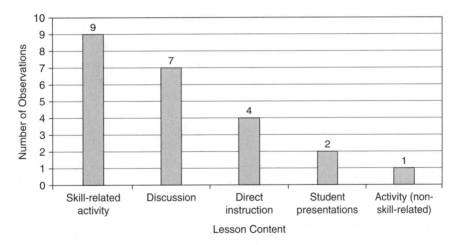

during implementation. The defining characteristic of all of these activities was that they *directly related* to the current skill being taught and provided opportunities for students to use the skill. Some examples of skill-related activities observed include time in the computer lab for an accessing information project, time in class to develop personal goals for a goal-setting project, time in class to work on prompts and role plays (which

FIGURE 4-3   Lesson content for health educator C (HEC).

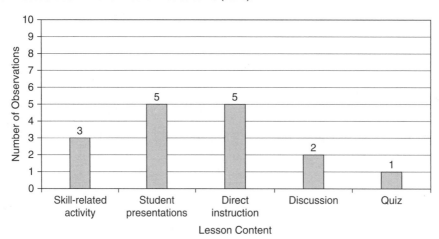

related to skills being taught), and mock scenarios in which students acted out refusal skills. Note that the skills in the skill-related activities were all based on the National Health Education Standards (NHES), which present seven health-related skills that students should have: decision making, goal setting, advocacy, interpersonal communication, self-management (practicing healthy behaviors and avoiding risky behaviors), analyzing influences, and accessing information (Joint Committee, 2007).

The ultimate goal of health education is to produce students who engage in healthy behaviors and who are able to apply what they have learned in health-enhancing ways (Tappe et al., 2009). Implementation of skills-based curricula should provide students with the opportunity to practice skills learned. Despite the consistent use of the word *practice* in much of the literature examining skills-based health education, what the word *practice* actually means in terms of implementation in skills-based health education is not as clear. For example, Kirby et al.

(1994) discussed that skill practice was an area that had inconsistencies surrounding its effectiveness, and one of the reasons was due to the difficulty in determining time spent on skill practice. The difficulty in determining time on skill practice could be related to many things; in this study, it was challenging to definitively categorize certain activities that occurred in the classroom due to a lack of clarity about what skill practice is in a skills-based health education classroom. However, the take-away from this is that students should have the opportunity to be directly engaged with the skills being taught in the classroom, no matter what term is used for those opportunities.

The second method of implementation that was used by all three health educators was **direct instruction**. In order to determine which activities should be categorized as direct instruction, the following definition was used: teacher-directed lesson content including lecture, question and answer, and explanation. Results revealed that the health educators used a variety of types of direct instruction, but they all used direct instruction to disseminate functional health knowledge rather than fact acquisition. Examples include a lecture about risk factors that threaten health (controllable and uncontrollable), explaining the steps to analyze an advertisement, using question and answer to review information for a quiz, and explaining the fact that alcohol can cause one to become uninhibited and the consequences of this. The use of direct instruction might seem, on some level, to be a little counterintuitive due to the "student-centered, interactive, and experiential" instruction that should be a hallmark of effective health education (Centers for Disease Control and Prevention [CDC], 2008). In fact, direct instruction was not included as an effective instructional strategy for health education by either the CDC or the World Health Organization (WHO), and is not usually associated with an interactive instructional style (CDC, 2008; WHO, 2003). However, the opposite is true in the case of these three health educators because all health educators found ways to have students engaged and involved during direct instruction. For example, one health educator provided students with content sheets to fill in information that was being provided during the PowerPoint lectures and asked students questions about the slides and the content during the lecture. Using these types of techniques can assist the health educator in creating a social learning environment where there are higher levels of social interactions between the health educators and students as well as between students. The social context of learning is important to skills-based health education, and the health educators in this study adapted a more traditional instructional strategy, which in general is not associated with an interactive style, to support their skills-based approach (Borders, 2009). The findings support the

inclusion of direct instruction in a skills-based health education classroom if these or other methods are used that encourage student participation and enhance the social aspect of the learning environment.

The last method of implementation that was consistent for all three health educators was the use of student presentations. Of note, all of the student presentations were of projects in which students had to use a skill (one of the NHES) to create the projects. The skills included in observed student presentations were advocacy, goal setting, accessing information, and analyzing influences. Many of the presentations also provided functional knowledge as well as a chance for students to personalize information and to be engaged in the material—all aspects of effective health education (CDC, 2008). Including student presentations in class can assist health educators to achieve multiple goals: (1) assess students on their mastery of skills, (2) engage students, (3) provide students with functional knowledge, and (4) allow students some level of ownership of their learning. This type of instructional strategy was not specifically mentioned in the literature reviewed for this study, but it could be an effective way for health educators to achieve the goals mentioned earlier and implement characteristics of effective health education.

The last type of lesson content to discuss is **reflection**. Reflection was a part of almost every lesson observed in health educator B's (HEB's) classroom. The main form of reflection was a question that HEB posted on the board for students to answer in their journals at the beginning of class. The questions were usually related directly to the topic of the day and could refer either to content or skills that were being learned. Upon examination, the researcher found that reflection can have an impact on metacognition, which can influence student learning and **transfer**. Ultimately, the hope is that students are able to apply what they have learned in the classroom in new contexts and in new situations in their actual lives (transfer). Implementing methodologies, like reflection, that have the potential to enhance transfer can be a meaningful tool for health educators to help students lead healthy lives.

■ THEMES FROM FIELD NOTES AND INTERVIEWS

Table 4-4 displays the themes that emerged from the field notes recorded by the researcher during the observations, and **Table 4-5** shows the themes that emerged from analysis of interviews with the health educators. All themes discovered through the data analysis are significant when examining skills-based health education; however, for the purposes of this article, the discussion will focus on the following themes: learning environment; student involvement/student centered; and connections, questioning, and relevance. The themes of student understanding/learning and variety of teaching methods shown in Table 4-4 are not as relevant in the context of providing key information from the research.

Learning environment is not prominent in the literature about skills-based health education, but was a very prominent theme from both the field notes and the health educator interviews. It seems that the learning environment is an essential aspect of skills-based health education due to the interactive and experiential methods that are parts of skills-based health education and the significant role peer pressure and peer acceptance play in the lives of adolescents. In this study, all health educators attempted to create positive learning environments mainly through good rapport with students and providing clear expectations. The health educators identified clear expectations as very important, as evidenced

TABLE 4-4 Themes from Classroom Observation Field Notes		
Examples from Data for HEA	**Examples from Data for HEB**	**Examples from Data for HEC**
Learning Environment		
Relaxed atmosphere. Students appear comfortable in class. Jokes with students. Provides clear directions.	Relaxed, comfortable atmosphere. Student work hung around room. "Be a nice, little, happy health family." "This is what I am looking for."	Good rapport with students. Gives positive feedback often. Shares her experience/ thoughts with students.
Student Involvement		
Almost always defers questions back to students. During PowerPoint asks students questions about the slides/content.	Students ask questions throughout class. HEB allows flow of class to be directed by students. Students read from handouts.	Provided students with advertisements so they are involved during presentations. Asks questions of the group during student presentations.

TABLE 4-4 Themes from Classroom Observation Field Notes (continued)		
Examples from Data for HEA	**Examples from Data for HEB**	**Examples from Data for HEC**
Connections		
During stress unit, made connections back to cycle of addiction content. "I was hoping you could use accessing information." "Use experiences from class . . . make healthier decisions when time does come."	"The way to figure out whether the cereals that claim they are whole grains are you need to look at ingredients on the nutrition label" [content covered previously]. "So they are constantly updating information on the website. And that is a good indication that this is a good place to go to for info."	"You have analyzed the media for influences . . . you have already practiced the skill." "That is one thing we can pick out if we have knowledge about weight loss." "If someone is passed out . . . need to call 9-1-1." Points out the importance of advocating because "you know what to do to stand up for yourself."
Questioning		
"What factors made the situation high risk?" "What bad decisions were made in the video?" "What type of communication style?"	"What are the things you should look for?" [on a food label] "Anyone heard of the word *epidemic* . . . what does epidemic mean?" "What other parts of the website make it look like maybe . . . accurate source?"	"Why is it important to seek out information?" "What is a key symptom of stroke?" "Why could a .org be reliable?" "What is the effectiveness of the birth control pill?"
Relevance		
"We want you to know how to make smart decisions because what you do now will influence/ impact you later." "Make sure you use strategies to protect yourself." "Decisions you make now affect life later."	Changed plans to include lessons about bullying assembly. "This is just the sort of a skill you need to develop throughout your life." "It is talking about the skill and the reason why we are doing this project—and that is being able to access valid and reliable health information."	"If you are sitting with a friend . . . withdrawn . . . need to take action, want to get them professional help." Provides students with scenarios that are relevant to real-life situation. "We address this throughout the semester, I want you to think about it" [society's acceptance of alcohol]. "Most important information to give you is how to prevent."

TABLE 4-5	Themes from Health Educator Interviews
Themes	**Examples**
Student centered	"Guidance reports had been showing more and more kids coming down, talking to them just about how stressed they were." " . . . just to let everybody have that, you know, develop a relationship with . . . a trusted adult." "Honestly, I put myself in their shoes." " . . . put that in the hands of the kids and have them sort of learn it . . . as individuals as they kind of go through practicing the skill."
Relevance	"Because we do cover . . . binge drinking and some just basic, you know, you come across this type of situation?" "That's our goal, is to make them self-sufficient, to go out in life. . . ." " . . . when you think about all the different skills, influences, accessing information, communication, decision making, goal setting, and so on, it is just what they need to know for their future." "And so those are the things that come back to you and say, 'Hey! That is making a difference.' These kids, some of them, not all of them, some of them are making some better choices because of having been through this program."
Learning environment	" . . . it needs to be a smaller environment. . . . is that ability for the kids to feel comfortable, getting to know them, developing that rapport with class." " . . . you've got to have, you know, the teacher actually believing in what they're doing." " . . . just brings some sort of activity to the class, you know, getting up and moving around." "The skills posted in the classroom. Evidence of students' work around the classroom." "But when I finally showed them what the final thing that I was looking for, it just made a huge difference." " . . . keep the kids having fun. . . . I don't know that they realize that they are learning, having fun at the same time."
Student understanding/ learning	"I want them [students] to tell me, 'Well,' you know, ' . . . why is it important for us to advocate for . . .' whatever the topic that I'm doing." "They [students] actually get that opportunity to, you know, create a skit around . . . advocating against why it's bad to discriminate against gays." " . . . able to see the students, you know, performing skills, that they are able to, you know, perform it with confidence and . . . actually demonstrate to me and the rest of the class. . . ." " . . . it's important to assess how they are doing, not just to give them some sort of grade to pass the course but really, for them to see, did I successfully achieve the skill or not?"

TABLE 4-5	Themes from Health Educator Interviews (continued)
Themes	**Examples**
Variety of teaching methods	"But, you know, lecture, role play, activity-based . . . those are the big three that . . . I try to incorporate." " . . . so a visual is good. Explanation is good. And then practice would also be important with the method." "I would say direct instruction and then discussion. Pre-assessment, direct instruction, and discussion." "The teacher's role is to provide guidance about the skill." " . . . technically you can consider it like the kids are teaching the class about content and the skill combined." "But also, we are giving them a lot of opportunity to practice those decisions and go through the process of making those decisions with lots of different content." "I think I mainly explain the skill and then we try to match up activities to go with the skill so that they are learning the skill through the activities." "I guess it would be ideal to have a variety of approaches and a variety of activities that they can participate in."

by the following quotes: "But when I finally showed them what the final thing that I was looking for, it just made a huge difference . . .", "And when you give them the rubric and they can see, 'Oh, I need to do this and this and this . . . ,' And they learn it. And that's huge", and " . . . telling them to be very specific about what you want. Like, you can't be vague in telling them. Our directions have gotten so much more elaborate . . . thinking like a 14-, 15-, 16-year-old kid, you've got to be very explicit." Creating a positive learning environment through developing good relationships with students and through providing clear expectations appears to be an important theme of implementing skills-b educator interviews). They are discussed together here because there is a great deal of overlap between the two, even though they have slightly different titles. The theme of student involvement emerged from field notes and relates mainly to the instructional strategies that were used by all health educators in which students were active participants in the class. All three health educators used instructional strategies to engage students and keep students involved in the lessons. The student-centered theme was defined as statements or ideas from the interviews relating to the needs of students, putting the students first, accounting for what students are going through in their lives, meeting the needs of students, and providing students with knowledge/skills they need in their lives. HEA and HEC both discussed how their curriculum was developed based around the needs of the students at their schools and can be best summarized by the following quote: " . . . it's all driven around the kids and what they need." HEB has a slightly different approach, which was teacher as guide; she explains:

The teacher's role is to provide guidance about the skill but to kind of put that in the hands of the kids and have them sort of learn it, based on my guidance and through their projects, as groups, as individuals . . . they kind of go through the skill . . . you can consider it like the kids are teaching the class about content and the skill combined.

Regardless of the method, results suggest that implementation of skills-based health education should be centered around the needs of the students and should keep students involved and engaged.

Three other themes that emerged from the field notes data were connections, questioning, and relevance. These are referenced together because these themes all seem to be strategies that have the potential to enhance transfer. Connections referred to instances where the health educator made specific connections to concepts, skills, or the real world during the observations. All three health educators used questioning during their teaching, with the questions relating mainly to concepts and skills. Lastly, the theme of relevance was identified by the health educator, referring to the relevance or usefulness of a skill or concepts being learned, or the importance of the health education class in general.

Transfer of learning can be influenced by many factors, but the ones that are most relevant for this discussion include context of learning, the need for prompting, and motivation to learn (Bransford et al., 2000). Bransford et al. suggest that the context in which knowledge is acquired can affect levels of transfer, and in order to facilitate transfer, educators should help students learn in multiple contexts. The health educators in this study seem to address this by making connections for students. The connections help students see not only how certain content is connected, but also ways that these skills can be used in different settings or different scenarios (e.g., they learn about decision making regarding birth control, but they will also have to use decision making to choose colleges in the future). Bransford et al. also explain that prompting can be used to improve transfer.

In this study, the health educators seemed to use questioning to prompt students to transfer their learning, and in some cases to engage their prior knowledge. Lastly, the theme of relevance that emerged is related to motivating students to learn (Bransford et al., 2000). Students are more motivated to learn when they can see "the usefulness of what they are learning" (Bransford et al., 2000, p. 61). All three health educators discussed with students the relevance of information and skills they were learning in class to their lives both now and in the future. This might help students see the usefulness of the class and the content they are learning, make them motivated to learn, and increase their levels of transfer. If students are more motivated to learn, they might also become more involved in class and in activities, which will not only help to further increase their learning, but also help the health educator implement the interactive, experiential techniques of skills-based health education.

In conclusion, the tables present the themes that emerged from analysis of both field notes data and data from interviews with the health educators. These themes reveal many key aspects of skills-based health education implementation and can help health educators in their practice. Future research should be done to further examine these themes and their application to and impact on skills-based health education implementation.

■ STUDENT ASSESSMENT

This last section will provide summary data from analysis of four student assessments, two from one of HEA's classes (see **Figure 4-4**) and two from one of HEB's classes (see **Figure 4-5**).

These figures demonstrate that students in HEA's and HEB's classes achieved similar levels of learning. If the scores are averaged for each health educator, HEA's students averaged 2.90 on concepts and 3.12 on skills. HEB's students averaged 3.13 on concepts and 2.88 on skills. These numbers

FIGURE 4-4   Average scores for concepts and skills on both assessments for health educator A (HEA).

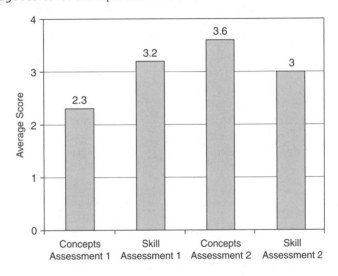

FIGURE 4-5   Average scores for concepts and skills on both assessments for health educator B (HEB).

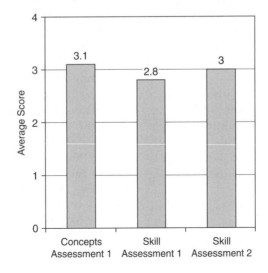

indicate that students in both health educators' classes achieved appropriate levels of learning. A four-point rubric was used to evaluate the students' work, with 4 being the best score. Based on this rubric, "appropriate levels of learning" were defined as scores of 3 or 4. When the averages for each health educator are rounded to the nearest whole number, students in both classes averaged 3 out of 4 on both concepts and skills. This might suggest that, despite the differences in implementation, students are learning skills and concepts in both classrooms. It could also suggest that, in a skills-based classroom, a variety of methods can be used to achieve student learning. Lastly, it might also suggest that **home-grown curricula** (curricula developed locally), as observed in this study, can lead to positive student outcomes.

■ CONCLUSION

The following are the key points that summarize the findings from this study. Key points from all aspects of the study, not just the items presented in this article, are presented here to provide the reader with an understanding of the scope of this study:

- There were significant differences in time allotted for health education at each site (65 hours versus 28).
- The health educators in this study each developed their own home-grown curriculum, which is a curriculum developed locally. The curricula in this study were built around the NHES with health-related concepts integrated into the skills.
- All three health educators used skill-related activities, direct instruction, and student presentations as main methods of implementation. Discussion, role play,

reflection, and non-skill-related activities were also methods used often by the health educators.

- Skill practice is an issue in the implementation of skills-based health education.
- Direct instruction, in this study, was an interactive instructional strategy in which students were involved and engaged.
- Overall, the implementation of the skills-based curricula in this study was interactive with a focus on skill-related activities.
- The following themes emerged from field notes as significant to the implementation: student involvement, learning environment, connections, questioning, and relevance.
- The themes of connections, questioning, and relevance seem to be strategies that can aid in the transfer of learning in the skills-based health education classroom.
- Skill teaching and review is a central aspect of implementation that was performed in varying ways by the health educators, but that was mainly aligned with the model for skill development presented in the NHES.
- Data from the health educator interviews support themes of student centered, learning environment, student understanding/learning, and variety of teaching methods as a part of implementation. Learning environment, student centered, and variety of teaching methods were supported by field notes and COF data.
- Direct instruction and activities (both skill-related and non-skill-related) were identified by the health educators as main methods of implementation and were supported by the lesson content data.

- The health educators in this study felt that the content being taught was both relevant and important to students' lives.
- The health educators believed in the efficacy and importance of a skills-based approach to health education.
- Students were achieving appropriate levels of learning in the classrooms of two subjects in this study despite differences in implementation.

Key Recommendations for Health Educators in the Field

Preliminary recommendations for ideas to assist health educators in the field implementing skills-based health education, based on the findings of this study, are:

- Provide health educators with training about the skills included in the NHES. Specifically, these trainings should provide health educators with clear definitions of the skills, steps of skill development, opportunities to practice the skills, characteristics of effective and ineffective performance of the skills, and how to assess and provide feedback regarding skills. These trainings should include discussion about the relationship among all of the skills and how to effectively integrate all skills into the curriculum.
- Discuss the importance of revising health education curricula to be developed around the NHES with health-related concepts integrated into the skills. Professional development should focus not only on the flexibility of this approach and the ability for health educators to include a variety of health-related concepts, but also that a curriculum developed in this fashion can be modified to meet the needs of students.

- Provide health educators with training about how to effectively include role play as an instructional strategy in skills-based health education classrooms.
- Provide opportunities for health educators to brainstorm and share ideas about lesson content, instructional strategies, ideas for activities, and other aspects of skills-based health education to assist them in implementing successful, effective skills-based health education programs.
- Provide training on skill development with special attention to skill practice. Additionally, provide guidance on effective methods of skill development for various amounts of class time because schools have different amounts of time allotted for health education.
- Include discussions and provide information about the relevance of the skills-based approach.

■ KEY WORDS AND DEFINITIONS

direct instruction   In the context of this study, a teacher-directed instructional strategy that included high levels of student involvement and engagement. It can be one method used in a skills-based health education classroom to help meet the characteristics of effective health education outlined by the CDC and promote a social learning environment.

home-grown curriculum   A curriculum developed locally that can be compiled from a variety of resources. All health educators in this study were implementing home-grown curricula.

learning environment   The atmosphere of the classroom, which can influence student learning. In this study, health educators attempted to create a positive learning environment by developing a good rapport with students and by providing clear expectations. There are many ways in which a health educator can create a positive learning environment, but ultimately, data from this study suggest that the learning environment is a very important part of implementing a skills-based health education program.

reflection   A type of lesson content used in this study that provides students with an opportunity to examine how the health content and skills learned are meaningful in their own lives. Lesson content was designed to personalize student learning and to allow for some introspective examination. Research suggests this strategy can enhance both metacognition and transfer.

skill-related activity   A category of lesson content that emerged from the data. Includes activities implemented in the classroom that were *directly related* to skills being learned in the class. The term *skill practice* was not used because of the ambiguity and lack of clarity about what skill practice is in a skills-based health education classroom.

skills-based health education   A curriculum designed around teaching students skills in the context of health. This includes teaching specific sets of skills, establishing beliefs and attitudes towards health that are health enhancing, and providing students with the knowledge they need to apply the skills and be healthy. This is similar to the definition of health education, but the key point to remember is *the focus is on skills*; the planning should start with expected behavioral outcomes based on

health-related skills and then specific content should be included.

transfer   The ability to use knowledge and skills learned in class in other contexts and situations. The ultimate goal of health education is to help students learn what they need to lead healthy lives *outside of the classroom and in their own lives*; in other words, to help students learn and then transfer their learning into their real lives outside of school.

■ DISCUSSION QUESTIONS

1. What were the two primary purposes of this research study? What type of research design was used? What were the key methodological procedures in this study?
2. List and explain the four types of lesson content discussed in this article.
3. What do you think are the two most important themes of implementation of skills-based health education?
4. How can current health educators apply this information? How can future health educators apply this information?
5. What are the most important concepts presented here for skills-based health education?

■ REFERENCES

Borders, M. J. (2009). Project hero: A goal-setting and healthy decision-making program. *Journal of School Health, 79*(5), 239–243.

Bransford, J. D., Brown, A. D., Cocking, R. R., Donovan, M. S., & Pellegrino, J. W. (Eds.). (2000). *How people learn: Brain, mind, experience, and school.* Washington, DC: National Academy Press.

Centers for Disease Control and Prevention. (2008). *Characteristics of an effective health education curriculum.* Retrieved January 20, 2010, from http://www.cdc.gov/HealthyYouth/SHER/characteristics/index.htm

Joint Committee on National Health Education Standards. (2007). *National health education standards: Achieving excellence* (2nd ed.). Athens, GA: American Cancer Society.

Kirby, D., Short, L., Collins, J., Rugg, D., Kolbe, L., Howard, M., et al. (1994). School-based programs to reduce sexual risk behaviors: A review of effectiveness. *Public Health Reports, 109*(3), 339–360.

Sparrow, S. L. (2010). *Examining skills-based health education in select secondary schools.* Unpublished doctoral dissertation. Boston: Boston University.

Tappe, M. K., Wilbur, K. M., Telljohann, S. K., & Jensen, M. J. (2009). Articulation of the National Health Education Standards to support learning and healthy behaviors among students. *American Journal of Health Education, 40*(4), 245–253.

World Health Organization. (2003). *Skills for health: Information series on school health, document 9.* Retrieved July 5, 2007, from http://www.who.int/school_youth_health/media/en/sch_skills4health_03.pdf.

CHAPTER 5

Assessment Measures

■ CHAPTER OVERVIEW

Two real-life scenarios for physical education accountability and the perception of physical education curriculum and teachers set the stage for the first article in this chapter. The difference among evaluation, assessment, and grading is then defined and discussed, with specific deliberation about the importance of assessment in physical education. The reader learns about the types of assessment and becomes familiar with the terminology of formative, summative, formal, informal, alternative, and authentic assessment. There are five tables and charts of specific assessment examples that illustrate assessment measures. Finally, a list of important considerations for assessment in physical education is included.

By writing in first person, the author of the second article in this chapter bridges the gap between the theory and practice of assessment for practitioners. She reflects back on her undergraduate education and teaching years. The true meaning of grading in physical education is discussed, with real-life assessment examples and discussion. She successfully informs the reader about how she worked within the school to make significant changes for the better of her students. Rubrics, curriculum changes, the affective domain, administrative issues, and technology are all addressed in the article. The title of the article clearly outlines the scope of the content: the debate as to whether assessment should be our friend or foe.

The move away from traditional to more authentic and alternative assessment is the theme of the third article. Types of alternative assessments, such as the use of rubrics, peer assessment, journals, and portfolios, are defined with some specific examples. Although the reader is exposed to alternative assessments in physical education, the author reinforces the need to implement multidimensional assessments in order to effectively assess our students in physical education.

The role of the teacher as an assessor, the components of high quality assessment, and how assessment affects student self-esteem and motivation are the subject matter of the fourth article in this chapter. A pretest on assessment cleverly allows the reader to reflect on his or her knowledge about quality assessment. Then, the author uses the content from the test questions to talk about teachers as assessors, high quality classroom assessment, the impact of assessment on students, and assessment literacy. Most importantly, the meaning of assessment *for* learning versus assessment *of* learning is defined, discussed, and emphasized.

Physical Education Assessment: A Primer for Beginning Teachers

Lori E. Ciccomascolo

Scenario 1: Mrs. Cocchiola, principal at Ocean Middle School, asks one of her physical education teachers, Mr. Harris, to come to her office to discuss a student's grade. The student, Ashley, received a *B* in physical education during the third quarter of the school year. Ashley's mother is upset by the grade and wants to meet with Mr. Harris to review the criteria on which he graded Ashley. When Mrs. Cocchiola asks Mr. Harris what criteria he uses when assessing a basketball unit, he states, "I look to see if the students know how to execute the basic skills that I teach them. I also write down if the students dress for PE and if they put a lot of effort into whatever activity they are performing." Mrs. Cocchiola then asked, "How do you know how much effort Ashley is putting into her activity? How can you tell if she and other students are actually learning the skills? Are you using tests, rubrics, checklists, or any other type of assessment that uses data or performance compared to standards or benchmarks?" "No," replied Mr. Harris, "I can just 'eyeball' the students' performance and assess if they are learning."

Scenario 2: It is Back to School night at West End High School, where parents and guardians visit their child's teachers and examine what the students have been learning in each class. When parents and guardians meet with the chemistry teachers, they find periodic table projects that each student had to complete. The chemistry teachers explain how their students are assessed and how these assessments evolve into final grades for each quarter. In another part of the school, English teachers proudly demonstrate essays their students have written. One of the English teachers explains to the parents that he assesses his students' writing on aspects such as clear voice, organization, and proper mechanics and grammar, among other things. When parents and guardians visit the physical education teachers, what types of assessments will they see? Tests? Quizzes? PowerPoint or multi-media presentations of the types of activities that the students perform? Will there be any assessments to showcase or will the equipment room be the highlight of the PE faculty's assessments?

The first scenario deals with the issue of accountability in assessing students' performance in physical education. Too many times physical education (PE) teachers use a type of informal assessment known as "teacher observation" to assess whether their students are learning what they are being taught in class. The principal, Mrs. Cocchiola, asks a pointed and important question to the PE teacher, Mr. Harris, about his assessment techniques. He submits that he "just knows" how his students are performing in his class. Either Mr. Harris has superhuman powers to gather assessment data on all of his students or he is not taking the time to properly assess his students. Quite frankly, he would not have a strong case in explaining to either Ashley, her mother, the school principal, or anyone how her performance in PE was assessed and then ultimately graded for the quarter. As a result of Mr. Harris's lack of evidence (and credibility), Mrs. Cocchiola might further investigate whether the PE program at her school is worthwhile because there is no indication that learning is taking place. In a budget crisis, when PE programs are being eliminated, teachers like Mr. Harris who do not adequately assess their students are not helping the case for keeping PE in schools. With the move toward increased accountability and standards-based curricula, physical education teachers must assess in a more structured way to prove that PE is a viable and important discipline.

The second scenario deals with how parents/guardians and other teachers in the school might view PE and PE teachers. When it comes to showcasing what students in PE actually do, what is there to demonstrate? Too many times physical education class is mistaken for structured recreation or recess with little to no educating being done. Years of stereotypical "gym" teachers who do not even educate, never mind assess lessons, have made it difficult for other effective, diligent, focused, professional, and caring physical educators to be taken seriously. Forward thinking physical educators can account for how their students learn and improve skill development, physical fitness, and attitudes about physical activity.

■ EVALUATION, ASSESSMENT, AND GRADING: WHAT'S THE DIFFERENCE?

On a daily basis, teachers have to make evaluations about what is best to teach students. Teachers also have to assess student learning and then provide a final grade for the student assessment; therefore, evaluation, assessment, and grading are not the same. **Evaluation** is the process of collecting and analyzing data that leads to a judgment about what should be taught and how it should be taught. **Assessment** is any planned technique used to measure or judge a student's achievement on a task. Finally, **grading** is the act of assigning a symbol to denote student progress, decline, or achievement. An example of how all three concepts connect would look like this: On the first day of a softball unit, a PE teacher would evaluate the throwing, catching, and fielding skills of his or her students. The PE teacher would determine the ability levels of students and reflect upon how he or she has planned to teach and assess his or her students. The PE teacher would then create different ways to assess the students (e.g., tests, quizzes, journals) at the beginning, middle, and end of the softball unit. Finally, the PE teacher would assign a grade according to how each student performed on each of the assessments.

■ WHY IS IT IMPORTANT TO ASSESS IN PHYSICAL EDUCATION?

Physical educators need to use assessment in their discipline because it establishes credibility and because it allows them to demonstrate if students are learning what they teach. Outcomes and assessment are becoming more and more important parts of education, especially in an age of standardized testing and the need for a solid PE curriculum to combat childhood obesity. Further, assessment demonstrates improvement from grade level to grade level and places accountability on the physical education teachers to not only assess but also create a form of remediation if there is no improvement in the student's performance. It is important to note that improvement should not be the only way to grade because performance tasks need to be taken into consideration for the final grade. Two common challenges physical educators find when effectively implementing assessments in physical education classes are a lack of time and overcrowded physical education classes (Gallo et al., 2006). Length of class time (an elementary PE class may only be 30 minutes long), lack of proper equipment, and lack of cooperation from colleagues may be reasons why assessment is not done as readily as it should be before, during, and after a PE unit. It is still vital—even in the midst of these time and space challenges—to effectively assess a PE class.

■ TYPES OF ASSESSMENT IN PHYSICAL EDUCATION

There are a number of different methods with which to assess students' performance in PE. **Summative assessment** tends to collect information at the end of a unit, from which physical education teachers can gain insight into how their students learned, or did not learn, the material they taught (Capel, 2004). **Formative assessment** is embedded in a lesson or lessons and is part of the scope (depth) and sequence (breadth) of the lesson or lessons. More specifically, daily lessons that students are taught are reflected in how they are assessed (Cape, 2004). For example, a formative assessment in PE could be an assignment in which a student reflects on his or her effort and sportspersonship for the day, or it could an assignment in which students assess themselves individually in volleyball skills on a daily basis (Rink, 2010).

Summative and formative assessments can be either formal or informal. For example, tests and quizzes given at the end of a unit (summative) or a rubric or checklist given during the unit (formative) can be considered formal assessments. **Formal assessment** is the practice of using a more standardized way of measuring student learning or performance. Formal assessments can include rubrics, checklists, papers, tests, and quizzes (McCracken, 2001; Mohnsen, 2003). **Informal assessment** is less methodical or uniform than formal assessment. A common type of informal assessment is teacher observation, or "eyeballing" a student's performance without recording any particular data. Another type of informal assessment is feedback, which can be corrective and/or positive (e.g., "Make sure you follow through after you hit a backhand"). Although teacher observation is used in a PE setting, it should not be the primary assessment used in measuring student outcomes.

A **rubric** (see **Table 5-1**) is a subjective type of formal assessment that includes a set of criteria aligned to standards-based learning objectives and that is used to measure a student's performance in a particular task or activity (Graham, 2008). A teacher can use a holistic rubric in which a level of performance is assigned by assessing performance across multiple criteria as a whole, or a teacher can use an analytic rubric that reviews each aspect of a performance or product (Mohnsen, 2003).

A checklist (see **Table 5-2**) is a type of formal assessment that includes a list of outcomes or standards-based learning objectives against which student work or performance is measured.

An **alternative assessment** is a less traditional form of a summative or formal assessment. Alternative assessments in physical education can take many forms, such as

TABLE 5-1	Example of a Holistic Rubric for Proper Dribbling/Ball Handling
Rubric Number	**Rubric Criteria**
4 = excellent, exceeding standard	Eyes and head always looking up Positive contribution to group effort Always protects the ball with body Dribbles well with both hands Dribbles with fingertips and pads of hands waist high
3 = proficient, above average	Eyes and head frequently looking up Positive contribution to group effort Frequently protects the ball with body Dribbles better with dominant hand but can dribble with nondominant hand Dribbles with fingertips and pads of hands waist high
2 = satisfactory, average	Eyes and head at times are looking up Some positive contribution to group effort Sometimes protects the ball with body Dribbles best with dominant hand Dribbles with fingertips and pads of hands waist high
1 = unsatisfactory, below standard	Rarely looks up when dribbling No contribution to group effort Dribbles ball with only dominant hand, palm too far out in front of body; easily stolen
0 = incomplete	Unable to perform necessary skills to master dribbling a ball No contribution to group effort Chooses not to participate

TABLE 5-2	Example of a Checklist for Dribbling a Basketball Properly

Student Name	Controlled dribble; not out in front so ball isn't easily stolen	Dribbles using fingertips; doesn't slap at the ball	Dribbles with knees bent	Dribbles with head up; looks down court

Note: *, has not mastered skill; **, is beginning to master skill; ***, has mastered skill.

a videotaped public service announcement (PSA) promoting regular physical activity or a poem or poster project detailing the benefits of being active in an outdoor setting, such as kayaking or hiking. Students meeting the standards-based learning outcomes of an alternative assessment can do so in a creative manner. An alternative assessment is ideal for students of varying ability levels and for those students who have difficulty performing well on tests.

An example of an alternative assessment in a fitness unit, for example, would be encouraging students to adopt and maintain regular physical activity using the Stages of Change model of health behavior change (Prochaska & DiClemente, 1983). At the beginning of a fitness unit students can choose what stage they are in and examine whether their stage has changed upon completion of the unit.

Or, teachers can track students' stages each week to assess changes in behavior and what influence, if any, the unit curriculum had on the students' stage change (Ciccomascolo & Riebe, 2008). At the end of the fitness unit, students can also write a reflection paper on the barriers they may have encountered in advancing through the stage of change.

Authentic assessment is a way to assess students in a "real-life" situation. More specifically, the tasks used in an authentic assessment often simulate actual issues or problem-solving opportunities and application of knowledge and skills. A PE teacher could use an authentic assessment in an outdoor education unit to assess whether his or her students are putting into action what they were taught throughout the unit (e.g., kayaking techniques; see **Table 5-3**). It is important to note that authentic assessment

TABLE 5-3 Authentic Assessment in a Kayaking Unit			
Proficient = 4	Competent = 3	Advanced Beginner = 2	Beginner = 1
Consistently makes sure to secure the kayak before getting in	Frequently makes sure to secure the kayak before getting in	Occasionally makes sure to secure the kayak before getting in	Rarely makes sure to secure the kayak before getting in
Consistently grasps the paddle with both hands and uses torso, not arms, to paddle	Frequently grasps the paddle with both hands and uses torso, not arms, to paddle	Occasionally grasps the paddle with both hands and uses torso, not arms, to paddle	Rarely grasps the paddle with both hands and uses torso, not arms, to paddle
Consistently checks equipment (skirt, map, wet bag) prior to paddling	Frequently checks equipment (skirt, map, wet bag) prior to paddling	Occasionally checks equipment (skirt, map, wet bag) prior to paddling	Rarely checks equipment (skirt, map, wet bag) prior to paddling
Consistently remembers to wear life jacket without reminding	Frequently remembers to wear life jacket without reminding	Occasionally remembers to wear life jacket without reminding	Rarely remembers to wear life jacket without reminding
Consistently writes in outdoor education journal	Frequently writes in outdoor education journal	Occasionally writes in outdoor education journal	Rarely writes in outdoor education journal

should not be done only at the end of a unit because it is vital to assess whether a student has grasped key concepts, skills, and knowledge prior to the conclusion of the unit.

IMPORTANT CONSIDERATIONS FOR ASSESSMENT IN PHYSICAL EDUCATION

When assessing a lesson and/or unit plan it is important that the assessment is aligned with the teacher's standards-based objectives and is appropriate for the grade and skill level being taught. In addition:

- Assessment should be done before, during, and after a lesson or unit plan. If a teacher assesses at the beginning of a unit plan, he or she can understand the baseline from which the student is starting. Doing an assessment at the beginning and end of a unit, in a pre/post manner, can provide a teacher insight into how the student progressed through a task from day one to the last day of the unit. Further, if a teacher waits until the last day of a unit to administer an assessment to a student, it might be too late to introduce any type of remediation if the student does not score well on the assessment or meet the objectives of the lessons and unit plan.
- It is critical that a teacher assess students on what they are actually learning! Teachers need to align their standards-based objectives with their assessment techniques.
- Assessments should be transparent; that is, discuss with students the parts of a rubric so they will know what is expected of them. In some cases, as with a rubric or a checklist, it might be helpful to have the students work on the criteria of an assessment so they feel a type of

"ownership" on the measure of assessment. It is not fair to the student if a teacher does not first share the criteria for an assessment and then penalizes a student for not meeting the criteria. How is the student to know what is expected of him or her? The act of assessment should not be covert, but rather an overt process that builds trust between teacher and student and enhances communication between teacher and parent or guardian.

- Students learn in different ways, so it is important to use different types of assessments in a lesson or unit plan. For example, teachers should include an authentic assessment for those students who can perform at a more advanced skill level, but also include a writing assignment for those students who excel at writing but perhaps not at skill acquisition.
- Assessments need to be developmentally appropriate; therefore, it is not considered good practice to use the same test for a sixth grade class and an eighth grade class, because they would be performing at different skill and cognitive levels. Further, be sure to create assessments for all ability levels and accommodate students with disabilities by working with the students' adapted physical education teacher or aide so that every child is assessed in a fair and reasonable manner.

CONCLUSION

It is critical that physical educators continually search for new ways to assess student learning and performance. Although a number of teachers rely on observation as a form of assessment, more objective measures provide better information regarding student outcomes. Effective assessment lends credibility to a physical education program because it demonstrates that teachers have structured student goals in the objective of the physical education curriculum. Using a method of eyeballing to assess a physical education class cannot provide the much-needed evidence that formal, informal, alternative, and authentic assessment can provide in demonstrating whether students are learning and mastering what is being taught in a PE setting. Finally, it is important that both successes and areas for improvement of students' performance are recorded in order for PE teachers to hold themselves and their students accountable for meeting state and national standards for physical education.

■ KEY WORDS AND DEFINITIONS

alternative assessment A less traditional form of a summative and/or formal measure of learning that can include creative ways to assess including the creation of a journal, public service announcement, or booklet (i.e., not a traditional test or quiz).

assessment Any planned technique used to measure or judge achievement on a task.

authentic assessment A measure of learning while students are in a "real-life" situation.

evaluation The process of collecting and analyzing data that leads to a judgment.

formal assessment The practice of using a more standardized way to measure student learning.

formative assessment A measure that is embedded in a lesson or lessons.

grading The act of assigning a symbol or number to demote student progress or decline.

informal assessment The practice of using less methodical ways to measure student learning.

rubric A subjective type of formal assessment that includes a set of criteria.

summative assessment A collection of information at the end of a unit.

■ DISCUSSION QUESTIONS

1. In your elementary or secondary (middle and/or high school) PE classes, did your physical education teachers assess your skill acquisition, physical fitness level, effort, attitude, or any other task in a lesson or unit? If so, what types of assessments were used? If not, why do you think your physical education teacher chose not to assess the performance of his or her students?

2. Is it fair to grade on improvement when your students may only have PE twice a week in a 6- to 8-week unit?

3. What type of remediation should a physical education teacher provide if a child fails an assessment (e.g., test, quiz, is unable to perform a skill at the end of unit)?

4. Create a scenario with a physical educator explaining the right way to assess students in physical education. Write one for elementary, middle, and high school.

5. Think ahead to 2050. What will PE assessments look like in the future at the elementary and secondary levels (e.g., technology, data driven)?

■ REFERENCES

Capel, S. (2004). *Learning to teach physical education in the secondary school: A companion to school experience.* New York: Routledge.

Ciccomascolo, L., & Riebe, D. (2008). Stages of change and physical education assessment. *Journal of Physical Education, Recreation, and Dance, 82*(3), 11–18.

Gallo, A., Sheehy, D., Patton, K., & Griffin, L. (2006). Assessment benefits and barriers: What are you committed to? *Journal of Physical Education, Recreation, and Dance, 77*(8), 46–50.

Graham, G. (2008). *Teaching children physical education: Becoming a master teacher.* Champaign, IL: Human Kinetics.

McCracken, B. (2001). *It's not just gym anymore: Teaching secondary school students how to be active for life.* Champaign, IL: Human Kinetics.

Mohnsen, B. (2003). Teaching middle school physical education: A standards-based approach for grades 5–8. Champaign, IL: Human Kinetics.

Prochaska, J. O., & DiClemente, C. C. (1983). Stages and processes of self change of smoking: Toward an integrative model. *Journal of Consulting and Clinical Psychology, 51*, 390–395.

Rink, J. (2010). *Teaching physical education for learning.* New York: McGraw-Hill.

Assessment: Friend or Foe?

Ann Marie Gallo

As a novice physical educator, I learned of the gap between theory and practice upon graduating from a college physical education teacher education program. My first encounter with the theory–practice gap was at the end of the first quarter of my initial year of teaching. At the time, I held a position as an elementary physical educator in a Catholic elementary school. The students were assigned to physical education one time per week. At the end of the first quarter, the students had attended seven physical education classes. I read through the class rosters, still uncertain of students' names, glancing at the grading options: "Unsatisfactory or Satisfactory." I had to consider what would classify as "unsatisfactory." In second grade we had practiced throwing repeatedly week after week. The students must have been satisfactory.

Certainly, I had an undergraduate course in tests and measurements in physical education. The content of that textbook did not include class sizes of 32 students and class meetings of once a week for 35 minutes, in the church hall. For lack of a better resource, I jotted down notes when students experienced difficulty with a skill. Yet I lacked a method of defining to what degree the student experienced difficulty. I spent my initial 4 years as a K–8 physical educator trying to define "unsatisfactory."

When I obtained a position as a secondary physical educator in a vocational high school, I felt confident because this was my licensure area. At the end of the first quarter, however, I was in a very familiar position with regard to assigning grades. I remember initially thinking, "It should be easier to grade high school students." Contrary to my optimistic outlook, the task of producing student grades became a long tedious process.

The challenge included that the physical education curriculum at that time involved 2-week activities where teachers would get new classes every 2 weeks. I vividly remember walking out to the tennis courts of the eighth tennis lesson planning to cover the serve. When I approached the tennis courts, a group of unfamiliar students were at the gate. I looked at the students and inquired, "Who are you?" They replied, "We are your new class." Confused, I asked, "Where is my 'old' class?" The students took great pride in informing me, the new teacher, that my old class was playing soccer with another teacher. In addition to my initial surprise, I recall feeling troubled at the notion that my students left tennis without learning how to serve. When faced with the paramount task of grading the students again, I realized that the serving issue was less significant.

For each of the eight sections of physical education that I taught, I had three rosters. The task was to assign the students a "grade" for tennis and pass the rosters along to the next instructor who would do the same for soccer, and the third instructor would follow suit grading the students in flag football. Evidently, I held up the entire grading procedure trying to make sense of the process and figuring out student names. Staring at the rosters, I contemplated, "I taught 720 students tennis?" Quickly, I submitted to the fact that 720 students were *exposed* to tennis. But how do you grade a student on exposure? The brief 2-week meeting period left no time for formal testing, or adequate practice. This grading paradox, absent from the test and measurement lessons in my college course, was layered with complexity and far from "best practice." At this point in my novice teaching career, I felt that returning to the elementary level to define "unsatisfactory" would be substantially easier.

To complicate the issue further, the vocational school awarded two grades to each student, one for "task" and one for "work." The rationale was that the student can be exemplary in the task (academic or vocational) but be marginal in work ethic. Would this match the student who performed skillfully in tennis but lacked in the area of etiquette or was "off task" during practice sessions? At the time, I couldn't move beyond the fact that I had to grade each student twice!

Perhaps what is more perplexing than the prior events is that the following statement, written 33 years ago by Solley (1967), is an accurate account of the gap between theory and practice:

> *The theorists fail to give attention to obstacles universally found at the local school level. The local teacher, on the other hand, accepting limitations as irrevocable, has rejected the grading systems of the theorist, the result is compromise, mediocrity, and an inadequate job of evaluating and reporting pupil progress and achievement. (p. 35)*

I worked in a situation of "compromise ... and inadequately reporting pupil progress and achievement" (Solley, 1967, p. 35). Yet, it was unsettling to know that the problem of the gap between theory and practice had been so clearly defined in 1967, but I was consumed by the same problem in 1991. If 24 years of research in physical education and teacher education hadn't been able to provide a solution, where did that leave me, the new teacher?

As the newest teacher in the physical education department, I carefully weighed a few different action plans to begin rectifying the situation. Quite aware of the hierarchy and the echoing reply to every question that I asked—"This is the way we have always done it"—my suggestions would clearly alter the status quo. I thought deeply about the implications of making any changes to what had become so very comfortable for my colleagues in their veteran years of teaching.

Would I fall into the trap of "Go along to get along" (Helion, 2009, p. 5)? I struggled with the notion of what to do as the second quarter flew past, and it was that dreaded time of the year for me, time to assign student grades again.

Having to complete the countless grade rosters and pass them along to the next instructor helped me to realize that I couldn't bear the thought of "grading students" this way one more year. Therefore, I needed to initiate change. Fortunately, the topics of best practice, changing the "recreational approach" to physical education, and that I, as a professional should "stand for something" were covered in my teacher education courses. Absent from the course work, however, was how to actually make change happen. So I stood in front of the physical education director's desk and respectfully said, "I want to keep my students all year; I don't want to switch classes every 2 weeks." She looked at me, paused, and then simply asked, "Why?" I sat down and began the long list of reasons (see **Table 5-4**).

TABLE 5-4   Responses to the Question "Why?"

I don't have enough time to teach all the necessary skills.

I taught a tennis "unit" without the students learning how to serve; actually, I didn't teach tennis, I exposed students to the activity of tennis.

I don't even know my students' names.

I can't make any connections with the students because I don't spend enough time with them.

I have no idea what to do with the grading system.

I can't legitimately assess student learning and/or honestly assign "real grades."

As I paused before continuing, she stopped me. For a very long moment, I wondered if I would still have a job, but she replied, "Okay, let's try it." The few minutes that had just transpired would be the easiest part of the paradigm shift that would take place.

At the next physical education department meeting, the director announced that we would no longer switch classes after 2 weeks; instead, students would select to take a course and stay with the same instructor for the entire quarter. To summarize how the rest of the department reacted, I would use the term, "disgruntled." The notion that the students would grow bored if we didn't switch classes every 2 weeks and that it would "make things more complicated" were recurring objections. Quietly I sat, thinking to myself, "More complicated?"

I sighed with relief after the first 2 weeks of the quarter had passed and I recognized all the students in my class. I had more time to pay attention to each student and all the pertinent details necessary for a positive class climate. As I attempted my first try at implementing a formal assessment, I encountered a new challenge. I couldn't define what was important or worthy of assessing. Pulling the "tests and measurements" textbook off the bookshelf, I reviewed the volleyball assessments. It didn't seem to matter how many times a student was able to hit a forearm pass against a wall in 60 seconds because that is not how volleyball is played. Nor did it matter to me the number of times a student could pass the ball into a target area in 30 seconds. I longed for something different, practical, and meaningful.

Before my search revealed any miraculous evaluation tool, the third quarter had come to a close. "Grading the students should be easier this time," I thought, "because this quarter I had just one roster for each class that I taught and I knew all the students."

Knowing the students' names certainly helped, but I struggled with quantifying their learning experiences and delineating the two different grades for each student, one for "task" and one for "work."

My class rosters included the date of the lesson, the topic, a check mark or zero denoting whether the student had changed and participated, and some points for written assignments that the students had completed. I referred back to the physical education grading policy, and it described the system for students who accumulate zeros. The policy stated that after the third zero, the student is assigned a detention, after the fourth zero the student is sent to the physical education director, and upon the fifth zero the student's parent is contacted by phone. Luckily only a few students accumulated three zeros in my classes. I recall a student's response when I, in a very neutral tone, informed him that he would need to serve a detention for his third zero. He responded in the same neutral tone, "There is a long list before I can serve yours." How does a teacher respond to such an answer? Since I am a patient person, I said, "Thank you, I'll wait." But this dialogue demonstrated that the value of the policy was insignificant to the students and me. Therefore, weighing the zeros against the time the student participated seemed irrelevant.

The student's skill level surfaced as an important component of the student's grade to me, but the motor learning lecture about **abilities** and genetic traits from my undergraduate work made me wonder if grading my students on the "genetics passed on from their parents" was an unjust action. I knew more about the students who were challenged by the motor components than the students who were proficient, yet it still wasn't quantifiable. I did have graded written assignments, but would they be categorized as task or work grades? For some reason,

I continued to associate the work grade with the student's etiquette, sportspersonship, and "attitude." Yet, how would I judge the degree of the student's success or shortcomings in the previous areas?

I started with the most unskilled students in both areas: motor skills and attitude. Therefore, the students who kicked the volleyball during instructional time, traveled away from their station to socialize, and/or complained about the teams or the officiating were not going to receive *A*'s. Hours passed, and I found myself drifting back to my undergraduate training, where I was forewarned of Judy Placek's findings in her landmark manuscript, "Conceptions of Successful Teaching: Busy, Happy, and Good?" (1983). I asked myself, "What exactly happened this quarter?" The final quarter of the year seemed the quickest of the four, and this quarter the task included combining all four grades into a final grade. Feeling even more unsettled with the results, I spent hours being extremely careful, knowing that this grade would be permanent on each student's official transcript. Additionally, physical education was a requirement for graduation. I, of course, agreed with the graduation requirement, but would I be able to defend inquiries about a student's physical education grade?

The closing of school left me feeling frustrated. I had detailed lesson plans with objectives, dissections of skills, and practice stations, but little proof that students were learning. Despite the large class sizes, I felt strong connections to my students, and was pleased that my classes were organized; the prior positive aspects of my teaching surely would have gained the approval of my college supervisor. Yet, at the end of each quarter I felt tormented by the grading process.

Over the summer and the next academic year, I tried to obtain as much information about assessing student learning as possible. Initially, most of the information aligned with academic subjects such as English, math, and science. Despite the status of the physical education program, the high school was progressive and offered excellent workshops for faculty. None of the content, of course, related to physical education. I kept asking myself the question, "How can I transfer this information to physical education?" My inquiries and questions left me wanting to expand my knowledge. Enrolling in graduate school while I was teaching and coaching three sports seemed to be a decision that demonstrated lack of foresight. However, when weighing the distress of grading students each quarter, I was prepared for a tight schedule and lack of sleep.

I found literature that told me why physical educators don't assess their students, but a limited amount related to fixing the problem. The work of Mary Lou Veal (1995) inspired me at the time because her work presented different types of assessments to use with real students in physical education classes. I began using some **rubrics** in my classes. As the literature stated, it took time to assess the students during class, the class size was not optimal, and the number of papers was cumbersome (Hensley et al., 1989; Hensley, Morrow, & East, 1990; Imwold, Rider, & Johnson, 1982; Veal, 1988; Wood & Safrit, 1990). Solley (1967), however, provides an adequate summary of the number of evaluations involved in calculating student grades.

Teacher A with 300 pupils, who grades each student in the four major objectives— physical fitness, skill and/or ability, knowledge, and personal social traits— makes a minimum of 1200 separate estimates or measurements of pupil status. When such evaluations are repeated in six activity units (paralleling six grading periods as established in some states), the yearly requirement reaches 7200 evaluations. Add this to 600 additional tasks in computing semester and final grades! What teacher is not overwhelmed with the magnitude of making 7800 separate evaluations in the school year for the purpose of grading? (p. 36)

This explanation gave merit to my experiences at the end of each quarter and the overwhelming task of assigning grades to students.

My quest for simplifying the grading process revealed a new finding and potential stumbling block. Most of my students were not improving in the area of motor skills. I began looking at this "new" phenomenon by watching students move in class as well as the curriculum offerings. The question, "What do you want your students to know and be able to do?" (National Association for Sport and Physical Education [NASPE], 1995, 2004) led me to the realization that the entire curriculum needed revisions. Fearful of the reactions of my colleagues that we would undertake such a task together, I started "sketching" some ideas. In the meantime, the quarter ended and I finally had motor skill evaluations of my students that I had designed. Certainly, I didn't have a formula for calculating the grade, but I felt better struggling with how to combine all the information rather than my prior experiences of lacking information.

Beyond trying to master the grade-reporting component, using assessment in my classes began changing the way I taught and eventually the entire curriculum. How many times in a student's tenure would a volleyball unit begin with the introduction of the forehand pass? If the students are seniors, shouldn't they be proficient in the forearm pass? Perhaps the question that gave me the most direction was, "How many times should a student experience volleyball in 4 years?"

Fortunately, the next faculty in-service (1994) included the restructuring of the entire school's curriculum using **outcome-based education**. We were charged with creating the end result before we worked on the details of the beginning stages. Listening carefully to the superintendent explain the process, I developed my own vision for the physical education program. After his explanation, each department was given a life-size drawn model of a student on newsprint paper and directed to draw and write what skills a student that completed their 4-year program would possess. That exercise helped me visualize all that our student would learn and led me to believe the one approach for organizing the curriculum would be by grade level. The curriculum would include basic water safety and fitness concepts for grade 9, lifetime activities for grade 10, team sports for grade 11, and **cross-training** for grade 12. Our students would spend the entire year with one physical educator and experience approximately six units in lifetime, team, and cross-training courses throughout the year.

Each department divided the curriculum work among their members and eventually the director of each department would review the work and pass it along to division coordinators. At the time, I became immersed in the work and in my excitement I didn't realize that I somehow wrote most of the curriculum and the assessments. Proud of the paper copy of the curriculum and knowing the assessments needed improvement, I faced the next challenge of implementation. Could we teach to this curriculum?

Certainly, we would need smaller class sizes (especially for teaching in the pool) and perhaps some teacher training or retraining. I felt as if the prior "needs" were out of my immediate control; after all, the physical education department didn't schedule the students for classes and who would "train" our department? The curriculum, however, dictated our needs, and the principal agreed to meet with the physical education director, the guidance department, and me to discuss scheduling. We had two pressing points. First, we requested consistency among the enrollment of sections. The common practice of 8 students assigned to one section and 39 to another surfaced as an obvious undesirable option. Second, we addressed the issue of safety in the pool and the instructor-to-student ratio. If the school administrators embraced the notion of every student becoming water safe by taking the American Red Cross Basic Water Safety Course, then they needed to provide us with smaller class sizes. Similarly, for the curriculum to be implemented and for student learning and assessment to occur, physical education needed the same class sizes as the other academic courses.

Much to my surprise, the deal we received included freshman classes not to exceed 18 students and the optimum size for the other grade levels would be 24 students. However, the freshmen would only spend a half-year in physical education and the other half in a computer literacy course. Interestingly, there were only 18 computers in the technology lab. We accepted the deal and promised to return to the table to discuss a full-year experience of physical education for the freshmen. Before we left the meeting, the guidance department requested one contact person to discuss students adding and dropping sections of physical education. I could tell by the look on my physical education director's face that she had little time in her day for such dialogue because she also fulfilled the role of athletic director and served on various other committees. I volunteered and let the guidance department know that they could call me with questions.

During the next academic year, when I was in my office, I answered phone calls from the guidance department and filled my trash barrel with drafts of assessments that needed improvements. In November, a guidance counselor called to ask if she could add a twenty-fifth sophomore student into a class because the student read at a fourth-grade level and needed to enroll in the accelerated reading course. It was my section of physical education, so I agreed. When I hung up the phone, I realized that a shift in power had occurred; we were in charge of our own destiny. I felt a sense of empowerment until the first quarter ended and grades were due. Grading the freshman students in basic water safety was actually easy! The combination of written exams and practical skills resulted in simple mathematics. The practice skills in the course are adaptable to the student's comfort level in shallow and/or deep water and the student earns a pass or fail, lacking a rating of the degree to which they performed. Computing grades for the students in the lifetime activities course, however, challenged me in the area of motor skills. Additionally, I still hadn't entirely figured out the work grade issue.

Meanwhile, the physical education director assigned each of my colleagues to the fitness concepts course to team-teach with me. I felt unsettled about this because they had more years of teaching experience than me. Surprisingly, they were not resistant; they were compliant and moderately interested. At the close of the second quarter, I found grading the students for the fitness course less cumbersome because I had decided in advance to weight more of their grade on their fitness project than their performance. My rationale for the decision was that one quarter was not enough time to adequately measure gains in fitness. Once again, however, the work grade troubled me. The question

at the time was, did it trouble me *enough* to pursue my doctorate?

During the summer I was accepted into a doctoral program in educational leadership and change. I chose a distance-learning program so that I could remain teaching at the high school level during the day. For the years that followed, my gymnasium turned into a laboratory for trying different assessment instruments and using various instructional models. My students gave me immediate feedback on the trials and were quite accustomed to the new adventures that we would explore together. I attribute their flexibility to the strong connections that we had developed over the years. I would smile coming up the stairs to the gymnasium when I would hear one student inform the class, "She has the clipboards today, some assessment thing is gonna happen." They knew "the drill" and participated willingly.

The focus of my studies, due to my interest in teaching the whole student and my career experiences, included "Assessing the Affective Domain" (Gallo, 2003) and revealing the answer to that work grade quandary. With the help of a task force, I designed a simple instrument that assessed student actions and interactions that I would use to assess my students in November and May (Gallo, 2003). During the other two grading periods, students had the opportunity to practice attributes such as fairness, positive communications, and other dispositions that warranted ample time for making change and improving. I finally had a legitimate work grade to record. Although conquering the work grade issue provided a sense of personal victory, I felt unsettled about the motor domain.

As the quarters and academic years passed, the task of grading students became easier and streamlined by the use of a schoolwide grading system called the Bobbing Gradebook (http://www.bobbingsoftware.com). The system was a teacher-friendly spreadsheet for entering the results of exams, projects, and performance assessments. This simplified the calculations and weighting of grades to simply pressing the Enter key. Due to the record keeping and calculating features, I could also print an individual student's progress for a parent meeting and even show a comparison to the class norm. Using the grading system permitted me to keep the weight of the motor domain lower, based on my internal struggle with genetic abilities.

My combined experiences of 4 years as an elementary physical educator, 10 years as a high school physical educator, and 11 years as a college physical educator of teacher education has allowed me to witness the gap between theory and practice. I contend that the theory courses inside the walls of a college classroom or gymnasium, prepracticum/field experience hours, and 300 hours of student teaching required in physical education teacher education programs are unable to replicate the dynamic, ever-changing, yet stagnant culture of schools filled with human beings. The answers to many of the challenges that new physical educators face are related to acknowledging that "things aren't right" and combining the preservice training with the instinctive feeling of how to "make things right." Initiating change is about leadership and perseverance. In the absence of a template with step-by-step instructions, change occurs when individuals believe in something and endure the work that accompanies the fulfillment of a vision. The road to the fulfillment of a vision is not a direct path, of course; therefore, leaders must be patient and use every available resource. Available to all new physical educators are the National Association for Sport and Physical Education (NASPE) PE-Metrics: Assessing the National Standards Standard 1 Elementary (2008), the answer to my assessment challenges in the motor domain. The instruments have been tested in physical education settings on school-aged children. Now motor assessments are available to physical educators in print and on CD for immediate implementation.

When I entered the field to find the discipline of physical education imperfect and not packaged quite the way I had expected, I had three choices. First, I could have accepted the package and quietly complied with the status quo, listening when I was told, "We don't do things that way here" (Helion, 2009, p. 5). Second, I could have spent 14 years complaining about large class sizes, limited time with students, and inadequate facilities (Hensley et al., 1989, 1990; Imwold, Rider, & Johnson, 1982; Veal, 1988; Wood & Safrit, 1990). Or third, I could have acknowledged the challenges and one by one chipped away at making improvements. If I may return to the original question at the beginning of this chapter, "Where did that leave me, the new teacher?"—the answer is in a position of power to make one decision that would dictate my future and the potential of the physical education program. Having made the third choice led to making countless other choices, but the original decision to acknowledge and take action was the prominent decision. With this topic of assessment of student learning in physical education, *my biggest rival* became *my best friend*, simply because it directed all the decisions I ever made about teaching and curriculum.

■ KEY WORDS AND DEFINITIONS

abilities ". . . genetic traits that are a prerequisite for skilled performance" (Coker, 2009, p. 15).

cross-training A teacher-made course that included 30 minutes of cardiovascular activity and 30 minutes of a team or individual sport.

outcome-based education According to Spady (1991), this includes three basic ideas: First, all students can learn and succeed (but not on the same day and/or in the same way); second, success breeds success; and third, schools control the conditions of success.

rubric A scoring device that includes the criteria and standards used to evaluate student work and/or performance (Lund, 2000).

◼ DISCUSSION QUESTIONS

1. What is unsatisfactory? Does it have universal meaning?
2. Discuss the pros and cons of teaching students shorter units as opposed to longer units.
3. As a new physical educator in your first teaching position, describe how you would respond to the statement, "This is the way we have always done it."
4. Create other possible strategies the author could have used to initiate change, and predict whether those strategies would have resulted in a positive outcome.
5. Describe the components that you feel are necessary to produce a legitimate grade for a student in physical education. In the description, prioritize the components into what you deem as most important (largest percentage of the grade) to least important (smallest percentage of the grade). Provide a rationale for each part of your response.

◼ EXTENSION ACTIVITIES

1. Number of Students vs. Number of Minutes
   This activity will bring to life the paradox that many physical education programs face: increasing class size rather than reducing the number of minutes of physical education per week. Divide the students into three groups.

   - *Group 1* will represent the physical educators of an elementary or secondary school. Their position is creating a strong recommendation for smaller class sizes and maintaining the same number of minutes per week that students are assigned to physical education. Prepare, however, for the ultimatum, "More students and the same amount of minutes, or less students with less meeting time per week, or more students and less meeting time per week."
   - *Group 2* will take the role of the administration. Their position is to increase student learning in the academic areas of math, science, English, and social studies to produce high performance scores on state-mandated exams. Protecting the academic reputation of the school and, in some states, their administrative position prevails as a concern.
   - *Group 3* will be the guidance department. Their position is a scheduling dilemma. They can't fit the necessary amount of time for academic courses into students' schedules without having to take time from a "nonacademic" course.

2. Busy, Happy, and Good: Is It Still Relevant in Physical Education Today?
   Read Dr. Judy Placek's (1983) "Conceptions of Success in Teaching: Busy, Happy, and Good?" In T. Templin and J. Olson (Eds.), *Teaching in Physical Education*. Compare Dr. Placek's findings to your secondary physical education experience and address whether the concept of "busy, happy, and good" was evident in your physical education program.

■ REFERENCES

Coker, C. (2009). *Motor learning and control for practitioners* (2nd ed.). Scottsdale, AZ: Holcomb Hathaway.

Gallo, A. M. (2003). Assessing the affective domain. *Journal of Physical Education, Recreation and Dance, 74*(4), 44–48.

Helion, J. G. (2009). Professional responsibility. *Journal of Physical Education, Recreation and Dance, 80*(6), 5–6, 62.

Hensley, L. D., Aten, R., Baumgartner, T. A., East, W. B., Lambert, L. T., & Stillwell, J. L. (1989). A survey of grading practices in public school physical education. *Journal of Research and Development in Education, 22*(4), 37–42.

Hensley, L. D., Morrow, J. R., & East, W. B. (1990). Practical measurement to solve practical problems. *Journal of Physical Education, Recreation and Dance, 61*(3), 42–44.

Imwold, C. H., Rider, R. A., & Johnson, D. J. (1982). The use of evaluation in public school physical education programs. *Journal of Teaching in Physical Education, 2*(1), 13–18.

Lund, J. L. (2000). Creating rubrics for physical education. In National Association for Sport and Physical Education (NASPE) (Ed.), *Assessment series K–12 physical education: National standards for physical education a guide to content and assessment.* St. Louis, MO: NASPE.

National Association for Sport and Physical Education. (1995). *Moving into the future: National standards for physical education, a guide to content and assessment.* St. Louis, MO: NASPE.

National Association for Sport and Physical Education. (2004). *Moving into the future: National standards for physical education* (2nd ed.). Reston, VA: Author.

National Association for Sport and Physical Education. (2008). *PE-Metrics: Assessing the national standards.* Reston, VA: Author.

Placek, J. H. (1983). Conceptions of success in teaching: Busy, happy, and good? In T. Templin & J. Olson (Eds.), *Teaching in physical education* (pp. 46–56). Champaign, IL: Human Kinetics.

Solley, W. H. (1967). Grading in physical education. *Journal of Health, Physical Education, and Recreation, 38*(5), 34–36.

Spady, W. G. (1991). Beyond traditional outcome-based education. *Education Leadership, 2*(49), 67–72.

Veal, M. L. (1988). Pupil assessment perceptions and practices of secondary teachers. *Journal of Teaching Physical Education, 7*(4), 327–341.

Veal, M. L. (1995). Assessment as an instructional tool. *Strategies, 8*(6), 10–15.

Wood, T. M., & Safrit, M. J. (1990). Measurement and evaluation in professional physical education: A view from the measurement specialist. *Journal of Physical Education, Recreation and Dance, 61*(3), 29–31.

Using Alternative Assessment in Physical Education

Kelly Nelson and Justine Boisvert

As the learning landscape has changed in the United States, educators have shifted their focus to a style of testing that measures how well a student *understands* a concept versus how well a student can *memorize* a concept. Instead of solely offering a number of multiple-choice options, educators are now tasked with formulating assessments that gauge a student's analytical thinking skills and knowledge of a specific subject matter.

The use of a multitude of assessment techniques, including alternative assessment, allows educators to fully assess student knowledge, growth, and achievement.

TRADITIONAL VERSUS ALTERNATIVE ASSESSMENT

For a long time students were evaluated using primarily **traditional assessments**, such as written tests on game rules, skills performance, and teacher observations (McCracken, 2001). However, these types of evaluations were often lacking and did not necessarily measure class material and student activity levels. For instance, at the end of a soccer unit, a student may have been assessed by a skills test in which they had to shoot 10 penalty shots. Their grade would be based on the number of shots they successfully completed. This traditional form of assessment is inconclusive on many levels. First, this traditional skills assessment measures only one aspect of the game versus an assessment that measures multiple aspects or overall game play. Second, skills tests do not measure a student's knowledge of concepts, sportsmanship, game etiquette, and strategy. Lastly, skill assessment is often discouraging to students with lower skill levels and performance anxiety (Lacy & Hastad, 2003).

Alternative assessment refers to any type of assessment that differs from a traditional standardized test. Examples of alternative assessments include interviews, journals, demonstrations, and checklists (Lacy & Hastad, 2003). The use of alternative assessment has become increasingly popular in physical education as teachers seek to assess students in multiple contexts including critical thinking and analytical skills. Unlike traditional assessment, while using alternative assessment tools such as portfolios, logs, and journals, students must analyze their own performances by assessing their own skills and strategies instead of their skill performance (McCracken, 2001).

DESIGNING ALTERNATIVE ASSESSMENTS

While designing meaningful alternative assessments of student performance, educators must take course goals and objectives into consideration. It is essential that teachers establish a clear purpose, identify observable criteria, provide an appropriate setting, and score the performance (Airasian, 1997). Properly designed assessments can be used to evaluate student progress and achievement, to recognize integral steps towards a goal, to assign a grade, or to create a portfolio (Santrock, 2001).

TYPES OF ALTERNATIVE ASSESSMENTS

There are a number of alternative assessments that a physical educator can use in his or her classroom. Choosing which type of alternative assessment to use depends on the class size and the age and grade level of students; however, the following types of alternative assessment can be easily adapted to varying ages, grades, and abilities.

Rubrics

In physical education classes, grades must be based on more than just teacher observation in order to establish credibility for the program. A **rubric** is an assessment instrument used to guide teachers in determining scores and grades (Lacy & Hastad, 2003). Rubrics describe the standards being taught and the techniques needed to attain proficiency at each level of scoring. Rubrics help students understand how they are being graded and exactly what is expected of them while eliminating teacher subjectivity and ambiguity. In return, students will be more focused on the task at hand because expectations and criteria associated with scoring have been clearly defined (Lund & Kirk, 2002). Before an assignment, game play, or skills testing takes place, the teacher should discuss in detail the rubric with the students.

Rubrics are often in a table form with the standards being assessed listed either along the top or down the left side. The students' names are listed either across or down depending on where the standards are located. The point scale for scoring should be described either above or below the table.

Table 5-5 shows a rubric designed for assessing the Tanko-Bushi dance. This is a Japanese folk dance that may be taught during a dance unit for a fourth grade class. The grading scale is described on the top and the amount of points needed to achieve each grade is shown. Across the top of the table are the skills of the dance required to be performed. The teacher observes the student performing the Tanko-Bushi and for each category of the dance, points are allocated on a scale of 5 (performs this every time), 3 (performs this most of the time), 1 (having difficulty), and 0 (off task, did not observe). All the points are then added up to determine the final grade.

Peer Assessment

Peer assessment is a helpful tool in assessing students' development. Peer assessment often takes place in the form of a rubric or checklist with one student evaluating another. It can be used as a formative assessment, which is often not graded but instead

used to check for progress and to determine the current level of proficiency. In order to develop skills, students need feedback. Due to factors such as class size, space, equipment, and safety considerations, it is not always feasible for physical educators to give feedback when necessary (Johnson, 2004). With peer assessment, the student receives instantaneous feedback and the teacher is able to increase instructional time (Pangrazi, 2004). It is beneficial for teachers to use predetermined mixed grouping strategies while students participate in peer assessments. Students who are more skilled can become models for those who are less skilled, and students with low self-esteem feel lessened anxiety due to peer observation versus teacher evaluation. The use of this type of alternative assessment allows students to receive feedback, to develop increased responsibility, to exhibit social skills, and to self-reflect (Johnson, 2004).

Table 5-6 shows an example of a peer assessment used in a lesson on foul shooting for a sixth grade class. One student will shoot 10 foul shots. The observer will be looking for proper technique of the shot using the determined rubric. With each shot taken, the observer will put an X in the box or boxes of the categories that were completed successfully. Points are calculated (1 point for each box) to conclude skill level.

Journals

Another effective form of alternative assessment is the use of **journals**, a type of written assessment in which students record, respond, and reflect on various class materials and topics. If used correctly, journals can be an excellent contribution to the evaluation of the affective and cognitive domains of student learning (Lund & Kirk, 2002). Structured journals provide students with

TABLE 5-5   Dance: Tanko-Bushi (fourth grade)

Student:

Class:

Date:

Student Performance Levels—Total Points: 55

A: Exceeding standards (advanced): 41–55 points

B: Meeting standard (proficient): 24–40 points

C: Making progress toward standard (partially proficient): 10–23 points

U: Standards not met (unsatisfactory): 0–9 points

ME: Medically excused from this assessment

MS: Student has had standards modified

Performing with music:
5 points: Performs this every time
3 points: Performs this most of the time
1 point: Having difficulty
0 points: Off task/did not observe

Student Name or Number	Dig, dig (R)	Dig, dig (L)	Shoulder (R)	Shoulder (L)	Back (L)	Back (R)	Push (R)	Push (L)	Open	Chochon-ga-chon	Fitness Check	Total Points
1												
2												
3												
4												
5												
6												
7												
8												
9												
10												

TABLE 5-6	Foul Shooting: Peer Assessment (sixth grade)

Shooter's Name:

Observer's Name:

Date:

Class Section:

Directions: As the shooter takes 10 shots lined up from the foul line, you (the observer) should mark an X in the appropriate box for each technique that is properly executed during each shot.

Shot	1	2	3	4	5	6	7	8	9	10	Total
Student's knees are bent.											
Student's eyes are on the rim.											
Student's dominant elbow is at 90 degrees.											
Student's nondominant hand is on the side of the basketball as a guide.											
Student follows through toward intended target.											

To receive a final score, add up one point for each box with an X in it.

Total Points

Exemplary: 40–50 points
Accomplished: 30–39 points
Developing: 20–29 points
Beginning: 0–19 points

the opportunity to safely reflect on and express feelings, struggles, and achievements in a private environment. In order to ensure students take responsibility for their learning and complete their journals, teachers must effectively communicate expectations and share grading rubrics and/or criteria for grading with students (Gregg, 2009).

Table 5-7 shows an example of using a journal during a fitness unit incorporating pedometers in an eighth grade class. This journal requires students to wear pedometers for the entire duration of the school day for 2 weeks.

Portfolios

Portfolios are a collection of student work that is compiled over a period of time such as an academic quarter, a semester, or a year and is reviewed against predetermined criteria. Portfolios incorporate completed work, works in progress, teacher and peer feedback on assignments, and self-reflection pieces (Lacy & Hastad, 2003). Portfolios, a multidimensional assessment technique, document student growth throughout a period of time, areas of improvement, progress towards goals, and reflection on the learning process (Lund & Kirk, 2002). Teachers can use

TABLE 5-7	Journal (eighth grade)

Step Log: Record your number of steps at the end of each day.

	Date	Number of Steps
Day 1		
Day 2		
Day 3		
Day 4		
Day 5		
Day 6		
Day 7		
Day 8		
Day 9		
Day 10		
Total		

Day 1	1. How many steps did you take today? 2. Do you think wearing the pedometer will increase your activity level? Explain.
Day 2	What is motivating you to increase your daily steps?
Day 3	So far, what is your favorite part of using the pedometers? Explain.
Day 4	List and explain two ways you can improve your number of steps during the remaining days of this project.
Day 5	1. Which day did you move the most this week? Circle one: Monday Tuesday Wednesday Thursday Friday 2. What did you do on this day to increase your activity level?
Day 6	1. What physical activity did you participate in over the weekend? 2. Set a goal for how many steps you would like to take tomorrow.
Day 7	1. Did you reach the goal you set yesterday? Circle one: Yes No 2. What physical activity did you participate in today?
Day 8	1. List four types of physical activity you participate in outside of school. 2. Which is your favorite? 3. Draw a picture below of you participating in your favorite type of physical activity.
Day 9	On Day 4 you listed two ways you could increase your number of steps. Have these ideas helped you? Why or why not? Explain.
Day 10	Did you enjoy participating in this project? Why or why not? Be honest!

At the end of the 2 weeks, students can total their number of steps and calculate the number of miles they completed by first determining their stride length. Then, interdisciplinary connections can be formed by relating distance traveled to a local marathon or road race, a specific geographical area students are studying, or the like.

software programs or work with the technology director of the school to have students use web-based portfolios so they could even write about their experiences during school hours or at home on the computer.

■ CONCLUSION

In addition to using traditional types of assessment in physical education, it is important to include alternative assessments as well. The use of a multitude of assessment techniques, including alternative assessments, allows educators to fully assess student knowledge, growth, and achievement. Portfolios, journals, and peer assessment are just a few samples of what types of alternative assessments physical educators can implement in their classes. It is important to realize that assessment in physical education is as important as it is in any other discipline. Whether a teacher uses traditional, alternative, or another type of assessment, it is critical that assessment plays an integral role in recognizing whether students are learning the skills and information that is taught in physical education.

■ KEY WORDS AND DEFINITIONS

alternative assessment Any type of assessment that differs from a traditional assessment. Examples of alternative assessments include rubrics, peer assessments, checklists, journals, and portfolios.

journal Type of written assessment in which students record, respond to, and reflect on various class materials and topics.

peer assessment The assessment of one student completed by a classmate. Peer assessments may be completed in rubric or checklist form and assess class material and development.

portfolio A collection of student work that is compiled over a period of time such as an academic quarter, a semester, or a year and is reviewed against predetermined criteria.

rubric An assessment instrument that describes the standards being taught and the techniques needed to attain proficiency at each level of scoring. Rubrics help teachers to objectively determine scores and grades.

traditional assessment The type of assessment previously used in physical education. Types of traditional assessments include tests on game rules, skills performances, and teacher observations.

■ DISCUSSION QUESTIONS

1. List and describe the differences between traditional assessment and alternative assessment. As a teacher, what are the benefits of using alternative assessment in your physical education classes?
2. Design a rubric to assess the forehand stroke in tennis. Make sure to include all criteria and a measurable rating scale.
3. Describe the benefits of using peer assessment in addition to teacher evaluation.
4. Why is it important for the teacher to provide clear expectations when assigning journals?
5. Which type of alternative assessment strategy would you use to assess student fitness levels throughout the school year? Explain.

■ REFERENCES

Airasian, P. W. (1997). *Classroom assessment* (3rd ed.). New York: McGraw-Hill.

Gregg, A. (2009). Journal assignments for student reflections on outdoor programs. *Journal of*

Physical Education, Recreation and Dance, 80(4), 30–38.

Johnson, R. (2004). Peer assessments in physical education: Peer assessments benefit students and teachers alike, but they can be tricky to implement. This guide will ease the process. *Journal of Physical Education, Recreation and Dance, 75*(8), 33.

Lacy, A., & Hastad, D. (2003). *Measurement and evaluation in physical education and exercise science* (4th ed.). New York: Benjamin Cummings.

Lund, J. L., & Kirk, M. F. (2002). *Performance-based assessment for middle and high school physical education.* Champaign, IL: Human Kinetics.

McCracken, B. (2001). *It's not just gym anymore: Teaching secondary school students how to be active for life.* Champaign, IL: Human Kinetics.

Pangrazi, R. P. (2004). *Dynamic physical education for elementary school children.* Boston: Pearson Education.

Santrock, J. W. (2001). *Educational psychology.* Boston: McGraw-Hill.

The Assessment-Literate Teacher

Susan Metzger Gracia

Having come as far as you have in your educational career, you are undoubtedly quite familiar with the term *assessment*. You have taken numerous classroom assessments and district, state, or national standardized tests, and you have completed performance assessments such as projects, reports, presentations, and demonstrations. But, have you given much thought to your future role as an assessor in health and/or physical education, to what constitutes high quality assessment, and to how assessment affects student self-esteem and motivation? These are the major themes of this chapter on assessment literacy.

To get you in the "assessment frame of mind," think about the main ideas of this chapter and explore how much you already know about high quality assessment. Please take the following short assessment quiz, a traditional multiple choice assessment requiring you to select one correct response per question.

■ PREASSESSMENT QUIZ

1. At a minimum, teachers spend approximately how much of their professional time in assessment-related activities?
   a. 1/8
   b. 1/6
   c. 1/4
   d. 1/2

2. Which of the following is *not* a characteristic of high quality classroom assessment?
   a. Students know the learning goals they are aiming toward.
   b. Students are trained in self-assessment.
   c. Students receive feedback about their current performance and what they need to do to improve.
   d. Students equate assessment with grades and test scores.

3. Which of the following strategies is most likely to motivate students to learn?
   a. Not telling students what's coming on the next test in the hope that uncertainty will compel them to study broadly and learn more
   b. Consistently communicating with students about learning targets and their progress in relation to them
   c. Keeping students guessing about what grade they will receive on their report cards and leaving them wondering what that grade means when they finally get it
   d. Learning in a classroom culture that focuses on rewards, gold stars, grades, or class ranking
4. Who benefits most from sound classroom assessment practices?
   a. Low achieving students
   b. Average achieving students
   c. High achieving students
   d. All students
5. Among other things, a teacher who is "assessment literate:"
   a. Understands what assessment methods to use in order to gather dependable information about student achievement
   b. Communicates assessment results effectively, whether using report card grades, test scores, portfolios, or conferences
   c. Understands how to use assessment to maximize student motivation and learning by involving students as full partners in assessment, record keeping, and communication
   d. All of the above

How do you think you did on the assessment quiz? Read on to see if your responses match current thinking in the assessment field.

■ TEACHERS AS ASSESSORS

Assessment may be defined as the activities undertaken by teachers, students, and other entities (e.g., schools, districts, states) that provide information to be used as feedback to modify teaching and learning activities or to make a judgment about achievement. A conservative estimate of the proportion of the time in which teachers engage in assessment-related activities is 25%, or one-quarter of the time (Stiggins, 2007). However, the actual figure may be even larger, with international researchers such as Black and William (1998) estimating that pre-K through twelfth grade teachers spend approximately one-third of their time in assessment-related activities. Additionally, there is no sign that the role of assessment in teachers' professional roles is diminishing in the present era of accountability and standardized testing (Popham, 2004).

Clearly, assessment is not a trivial component of a teacher's day-to-day responsibilities. Yet, research suggests that this is an area in which preservice teachers tend to be underprepared (Black & William, 1998; Popham, 2004; Stiggins, 2002; Volante & Fazio, 2007; Zhang & Burry-Stock, 2003). Until fairly recently, few states required competence in classroom assessment for teacher certification. As recently as 1999, in fact, 25 U.S. states had no expectation of competence in assessment (Trevisan, 2002). Given the fact that state teaching certification requirements are significant determinants of teacher education program content, many practicing teachers and teacher educators have little grounding in sound assessment practice.

Even now, most teacher education programs offer little assessment coursework during training, with most programs aiming to integrate assessment concepts and practices into existing methods or other courses. However, the depth and breadth of integrated assessment content is uneven. It is therefore not surprising that many teacher education candidates and practicing teachers feel underprepared in the area of assessment (Black & William, 1998; Mertler, 1999; Volante & Fazio, 2007). Without a solid assessment foundation, many teachers mimic the assessment practices they themselves experienced as students and end up perpetuating poor assessment practices, such as implementing assessments that encourage rote and superficial learning; assessing quantity of work and presentation, rather than quality of learning; overemphasizing grading and underemphasizing the giving of useful feedback; and fostering a competitive atmosphere that decreases the self-confidence of low-achieving students (Black & William, 1998).

■ HIGH QUALITY CLASSROOM ASSESSMENT

At this point, it is important to distinguish between four different, yet related, notions: formative assessment, summative assessment, assessment *of* learning, and assessment *for* learning. Assessments have traditionally been classified as either formative or summative. **Formative assessment** refers to assessment that takes place during instruction, yielding information teachers use to track student progress on standards and plan instruction. Teacher observation, performance tasks, homework assignments, and periodic quizzes can all be used as formative assessment. In contrast, **summative assessment** takes place at the end of instruction, to make a judgment about achievement and/or to assign a score or grade. Summative classroom assessments

include end-of-chapter tests, final exams, classroom grades, and other measures.

Black and William (1998) coined the important phrases assessment *of* learning and assessment *for* learning. **Assessment *of* learning** is essentially the same as summative assessment: assessment of how much learning has taken place at a specific point in time. **Assessment *for* learning** is formative in nature, but it goes beyond the traditional view of formative assessment as information that is used by teachers to track student progress on standards and plan instruction. Assessment for learning includes teachers providing descriptive (rather than evaluative) feedback to students and student actions such as self-assessment and goal setting, tracking learning, analyzing progress, and describing learning to others (FairTest, 2007). The notions of descriptive feedback and student involvement are key to assessment for learning and differentiate it from the typical notion of formative assessment. Further, recognizing the qualities of assessment for learning is crucial to understanding and using high quality assessment strategies in the classroom.

Building on the work of Black and William (1998) and others, Stiggins, Arter, Chappuis and Chappuis (2007) identified the following seven strategies for sound assessment for learning:

1. *Provide a clear and understandable vision of the learning target.* This includes sharing with students the target(s), goal(s), or objective(s) in advance of a lesson, unit, or class. Targets should be expressed in language students can understand. The teacher should facilitate discussion around what high quality looks like. The scoring guide or rubric should be shared with students, or students should have the opportunity to develop scoring criteria with the teacher.

2. *Use examples and models of strong and weak work.* Strong and weak examples of anonymous student work should be shared with students so they can analyze the work against the scoring criteria. This will help them visualize what high quality work looks like.

3. *Offer regular descriptive feedback.* If work is submitted for practice, it is better to offer descriptive feedback rather than a grade. Descriptive feedback should focus on the strengths and weaknesses of the work with respect to the learning target(s) and what the student should focus on next.

4. *Teach students to self-assess and set goals.* Self-assessment helps students answer the question, "Where am I now?" and is essential for them to identify next steps in their own learning. Strategies for helping students become comfortable with self-assessment and goal setting include asking them to analyze their own work using a rubric, having them assess their peers' work, and keeping a journal or log describing what they are learning and questions they have.

5. *Design lessons to focus on one aspect of quality at a time.* This involves analyzing student learning targets for various aspects of quality and teaching them one at a time, while emphasizing that all aspects must be included in a quality product. By focusing on and offering feedback on one aspect of quality at a time, the students' task becomes more manageable and less overwhelming.

6. *Teach students focused revision.* Before asking students to revise their own work on a single aspect of quality, it is important for the teacher to model how this is done for a sample piece of work. Then, students should be offered a multitude of opportunities (individually and in pairs/groups) to analyze work for specific aspects of quality and offer suggestions for improvement. When that work has been revised, they should analyze it again for another aspect of quality. This will give them experience and practice in the revision process.

7. *Engage students in self-reflection, and let them keep track of and share their learning.* Activities should be incorporated that require students to reflect on what they are learning, analyze their growth, and share their progress with parents and teachers. This can take place through conferences with parents and/or teachers and written reflections on the learning process (Stiggins et al., 2007).

Use of these strategies will help students address these three questions: Where am I going?, Where am I now?, and How can I close the gap? (Stiggins et al., 2007), making them stronger and more independent learners.

■ IMPACT ON STUDENTS

The ability to implement high quality classroom assessment for learning strategies is more than just a nice idea. Research has demonstrated that high quality assessment for learning has a significant impact on student learning. In a review of more than 20 studies focusing on the impact of high quality classroom assessment on students, Black and William (1998) concluded that innovations that include strengthening assessment for learning practices yield significant and substantial learning gains. In fact the typical effect sizes (a ratio of the learning gains for students involved in assessment interventions compared to the learning gains for students not involved in assessment interventions) were larger than for most other educational interventions. In practical terms, improving the quality of classroom assessments translated to learning gains of three to four grade levels or 15 to 20 percentage points. Further, improving the quality of classroom assessment helped low achieving students more than other students, representing a promising strategy for closing achievement gaps.

Finally, the use of assessment for learning strategies is linked to increased student motivation. An exclusive emphasis on assessment of learning (e.g., grades, test scores, class ranking) can cause students to focus on obtaining high scores or grades rather than improving their learning. Those who do not typically do well often "tune out" and lose confidence in their ability to succeed. Furthermore, they do not have a clear roadmap of what they need to do to improve and lose confidence in their ability to do so. Assessment for learning, with its focus on illuminating targets, providing models and descriptive feedback, involving students in goal setting and self-assessment, tracking their own progress, and communicating their learning to others, increases the chances of student success. With success comes self-confidence (Stiggins, 1999a).

■ ASSESSMENT LITERACY

The previous section underscores the importance of **assessment literacy** for all teachers. Assessment literacy has been defined as

> ... *understanding what assessment methods to use in order to gather dependable information about student achievement; communicating assessment results effectively, whether using report card grades, test scores, portfolios or conferences; and*

> *understanding how to use assessment to maximize student motivation and learning by involving students as full partners in assessment, record keeping, and communication. (Chappuis, Stiggins, Arter, & Chappuis, 2004, p. 233)*

Numerous assessment experts, researchers, and practitioners have attempted to make explicit the performance expectations of assessment-literate teachers. In 1990, the American Federation of Teachers (AFT), the National Council on Measurement in Education (NCME), and the National Education Association (NEA) joined forces to draft the Standards for Teacher Competence in the Educational Assessment of Students. These standards were designed as:

- A guide for teacher educators as they design and approve programs for teacher preparation
- A self-assessment guide for teachers in identifying their needs for professional development in student assessment
- A guide for workshop instructors as they design professional development experiences for in-service teachers
- An impetus for educational measurement specialists and teacher trainers to conceptualize student assessment and teacher training in student assessment more broadly than has been the case in the past (AFT, NCME, & NEA, 1990)

According to the seven Standards for Teacher Competence in the Educational Assessment of Students, assessment literate teachers are skilled in:

1. Choosing assessment methods appropriate for instructional decisions
2. Developing assessment methods appropriate for instructional decisions

3. Administering, scoring, and interpreting the results of both externally produced and teacher-produced assessment methods
4. Using assessment results when making decisions about individual students, planning teaching, developing curriculum, and making school improvements
5. Developing valid pupil grading procedures that use pupil assessments
6. Communicating assessment results to students, parents, other lay audiences, and other educators
7. Recognizing unethical, illegal, and otherwise inappropriate assessment methods and uses of assessment information (AFT, NCME, & NEA, 1990)

In 1992, the Interstate New Teacher Assessment and Support Consortium (INTASC) identified knowledge, skills, and dispositions related to a teacher's ability to use assessment strategies to evaluate and ensure the continuous intellectual, social, and physical development of the learner. The INTASC assessment indicators overlap significantly with the Standards for Teacher Competence in the Educational Assessment of Students; however, they include a greater emphasis on key components of assessment for learning. According to INTASC, key indicators of the assessment-literate teacher include:

• Selecting, constructing, and using assessment strategies appropriate to the learning outcomes
• Using a variety of informal and formal strategies to inform choices about student progress and to adjust instruction (e.g., standardized test data, peer and student self-assessment, informal assessments like observations, surveys, interviews, student work, performance tasks, portfolios, and teacher-made tests)

• Using assessment strategies to involve learners in self-assessment activities to help them become aware of their strengths and needs, and to encourage them to set personal goals for learning
• Evaluating the effects of class activities on individuals and on groups through observation of classroom interaction, questioning, and analysis of student work
• Maintaining useful records of student work and performance and communicating student progress knowledgeably and responsibly
• Soliciting information about students' experiences, learning behavior, needs, and progress from parents, other colleagues, and students (INTASC, 1990)

The INTASC standards are currently under revision once again and will reflect new developments in the field of assessment and new understandings of assessment literacy. These and other standards serve as an ongoing guide to the assessment-related skills, knowledge, and dispositions of professional teachers.

◼ YOUR PREASSESSMENT QUIZ

Look at your original answers to the short assessment quiz at the beginning of this chapter. Did you change any answers as you read the chapter? Are you able to confidently answer all of the questions now? Just to make sure, here are the correct answers: (1) c; (2) d; (3) b; (4) a; and (5) d.

The purpose of the quiz was to highlight some important concepts about assessment and to have you start thinking about the health and/or physical education teacher's role as an assessor, the characteristics of high quality classroom assessment, the relationship between assessment and student motivation, the impact of sound classroom assessment on students, and the notion of assessment literacy—key concepts in this chapter.

■ CONCLUSION

Teachers spend a significant portion of their professional lives engaged in assessment-related activities. The impact of high quality classroom assessment strategies is not trivial and has a research base linking it to improved student learning outcomes and motivation. Recognizing the qualities of assessment for learning is crucial to understanding and using high quality assessment strategies in the classroom. Given the important role of classroom assessment for teachers, it is crucial that teachers develop assessment literacy, which involves understanding and using sound assessment methods, communicating assessment results appropriately to various audiences, and using assessment to motivate and empower students rather than discourage or punish them. The Standards for Teacher Competence in the Educational Assessment of Students and the Interstate New Teacher Assessment and Support Consortium (INTASC) standards have been developed to make explicit the evolving performance expectations of assessment-literate teachers.

■ KEY WORDS AND DEFINITIONS

assessment   Activities undertaken by teachers, students, and other entities (e.g., schools, districts, states) that provide information to be used as feedback to modify teaching and learning activities or to make a judgment about achievement.

assessment *for* learning   Goes beyond the traditional view of formative assessment as information that is used by teachers to track student progress on standards and plan instruction. Assessment for learning includes teachers providing descriptive (rather than evaluative) feedback to students and student actions such as self-assessment and goal setting, tracking learning, analyzing progress, and describing learning to others.

assessment literacy   Includes understanding what assessment methods to use in order to gather dependable information about student achievement; communicating assessment results effectively, whether using report card grades, test scores, portfolios, or conferences; and understanding how to use assessment to maximize student motivation and learning by involving students as full partners in assessment, record keeping, and communication.

assessment *of* learning   Also called summative assessment; it takes place at the end of instruction, to make a judgment about achievement and/or assign a score or grade. Examples are standardized tests used for accountability purposes, student assessments designed to determine mastery of standards, and classroom grades.

formative assessment   Assessment that takes place during the process of learning and teaching, yielding information that is used by teachers to track student progress on standards and plan instruction.

summative assessment   Assessment that takes place at the end of instruction, to make a judgment about achievement and/or assign a score or grade. Summative assessment is also known as assessment of learning.

■ DISCUSSION QUESTIONS

1. Does your state require competence in classroom assessment for teacher certification? Go to your department of education's website (or other pertinent resources) to find out. If assessment competence is required, what type(s) of competence are needed? How does this compare with the content in the Standards for Teacher Competence in the Educational Assessment of Students? If competence in assessment is not required for teacher certification in your state, why do you think this is the case?

2. Interview a faculty member in your teacher preparation program to find out how training in assessment competence is integrated into your program. Questions to ask include: What kind(s) of assessment competence are expected of successful candidates? Where do these expectations come from? How/where is training in assessment integrated into the program? Is assessment training woven into a candidate's coursework, or are there specific courses on assessment? How is assessment literacy developed in the program? (You may have to define assessment literacy for the faculty member.) How does the program measure whether candidates have achieved the required level of assessment competence?

3. Analyze assessment practices in this course or another course you are currently taking. How is assessment *of* learning being implemented? What methods are being used? How is assessment *for* learning being implemented? And what does that look like? Compare and contrast the two methods of assessment in terms of how they make you feel as a learner.

4. What are some ways in which the seven strategies of assessment for learning can be incorporated into health and physical education instruction? Provide examples.

5. Describe the best and worst assessment experiences you have ever had as a learner. Analyze them in terms of the main ideas of this chapter. For each experience, classify it as formative *or* summative assessment and as assessment *for* learning or assessment *of* learning. Explain why you classified it the way you did. How did each experience affect your self-esteem or motivation to learn?

6. Using the Standards for Teacher Competence in the Educational Assessment of Students or the INTASC key assessment indicators, evaluate your own assessment literacy. In which areas do you feel strong? In which areas do you still have more to learn? How will you go about improving the skills or knowledge areas you have identified for improvement?

■ REFERENCES

American Federation of Teachers, National Council on Measurement in Education, & National Education Association. (1990). *Standards for teacher competence in educational assessment of students.* Retrieved January 15, 2010, from http://www.unl.edu/buros/bimm/html/article3.html

Black, P., & William, D. (1998). Inside the black box: Raising standards through classroom assessment. *Phi Delta Kappan, 80*(2), 139–148.

Chappuis, S., Stiggins, R., Arter, J., & Chappuis, J. (2004). *Assessment for learning: An action* guide for school leaders. Portland, OR: Assessment Training Institute.

FairTest. (2007). *The value of formative assessment.* Retrieved July 7, 2011, from http://www.fairtest .org/value-formative-assessment-pdf

Interstate New Teacher Assessment and Support Consortium. (1990). *Model standards for beginning teacher licensing, assessment and development: A resource for state dialogue.* Washington, DC: Council of Chief State School Officers.

Mertler, C. A. (1999). Assessing student performance: A descriptive study of the classroom assessment practices of Ohio teachers. *Education, 120*(2), 285–296.

Popham, W. J. (2004). All about accountability/ Why assessment illiteracy is professional suicide. *Educational Leadership, 62*(1), 82–83.

Stiggins, R. J. (1999a). Assessment, student confidence, and school success. *Phi Delta Kappan, 81*(3), 191–198.

Stiggins, R. J. (1999b). Evaluating classroom assessment training in teacher education programs. *Educational Measurement: Issues and Practice, 18*(1), 23–27.

Stiggins, R. J. (2002). Assessment crisis: The absence of assessment for learning. *Phi Delta Kappan, 83*(10), 758–765.

Stiggins, R. J. (2007). Five assessment myths and their consequences. *Education Week, 27*(8), 28–29.

Stiggins, R. J., Arter, J., Chappuis, J., & Chappuis, S. (2007). *Classroom assessment for learning: Doing it right—using it well.* Upper Saddle River, NJ: Pearson Education.

Trevisan, M. S. (2002). The states' role in ensuring assessment competence. *Phi Delta Kappan, 83*(10), 766–771.

Volante, L., & Fazio, X. (2007). Exploring teacher candidates' assessment literacy: Implications for teacher education reform and professional development. *Canadian Journal of Education, 30*(3), 749–770.

Zhang, Z., & Burry-Stock, J. A. (2003). Classroom assessment practices and teachers' self-perceived assessment skills. *Applied Measurement in Education, 16*(4), 323–342.

Research Review

Effect of Wellness and Fitness Curriculum on College Students' Behavior Change

Lori E. Ciccomascolo

The goal of many adults is to live a healthy, productive life; however, living well, more often than not, requires that individuals adopt and maintain healthy behaviors. Participation in regular exercise, maintaining well-balanced nutritional habits, and persevering toward a positive balance and interaction among one's physical, emotional, mental, and social dimensions are all examples of healthy behaviors. Regular exercise, for any population, is an important component in the prevention of a wide variety of diseases and conditions influencing the physical, emotional, mental, and social health dimensions. Regular exercise can help prevent coronary heart disease, osteoporosis, diabetes, hypertension, and depression.

Despite the positive long-term physiological and psychological effects of exercise, "The Surgeon General's Vision for a Healthy and Fit Nation 2010" (U.S. Department of Health and Human Services [USDHHS], 2010) report suggested that inactivity is prevalent among young and older adults. For example, the prevalence of obesity has increased from 13.4% in 1980 to 34.3% in 2008 among adults and from 5% to 17% among children during the same period. Furthermore, 35% of students on college campuses are overweight or obese (American College Health Association, 2006). In addition, college students have become less active to the point where the number participating in regular physical activity has decreased to 36.6% (Centers for Disease Control and Prevention [CDC]), 2006.

Balancing physical activity and proper nutrition does not happen by accident; instead, individuals need to plan and prepare when they are going to exercise and what they will eat. Spending more time at the workplace may increase an individual's prevalence of turning to fast food as an option instead of planning healthy meals (USDHHS, 2010). Some choices that adults, adolescents, and children can make to be healthier include being more regularly active, and decreasing soft drink, sugar, and fat intake while increasing fruit, vegetable, and water consumption (USDHHS & U.S. Department of Agriculture, 2005).

College students comprise a population that could benefit from learning the importance of making appropriate lifestyle/health decisions through interventions because they are not meeting dietary or physical activity guidelines (Butler et al., 2004; Huang et al., 2003; Lowry et al., 2000). College students need to partake in regular exercise, make sound nutritional choices, and balance their emotional, physical, and mental well-being with their social lives. Students at the college and university level generally have access to exercise facilities and training opportunities (e.g., physical education class, intramural sports teams). The majority of college students are faced with time pressures from class schedules and the demands of social activities; however, they need to understand that regular exercise contributes to self-protection against progressive, degenerative diseases.

Making sound choices about health-enhancing behaviors may be difficult because students may be used to relying on others for such information including peers and the media. Although several agents (e.g., parents, media, friends) may influence the adoption and maintenance of college students' health-enhancing behaviors, it is important to realize that school systems, including colleges, appear to have the greatest influence in helping them to do so. As a result, it is important that physical educators and other allied health professionals address the impact of their institution's physical education curriculum in promoting students' health-enhancing behaviors.

Interventions used to promote college students' physical activity have only produced moderate effects. Keating et al. (2005) suggest that the primary issues with the current research on this topic is that college students' physical activity levels have not been studied as readily as they should have. Further, the authors state that when physical activity levels of college students are studied, there is a lack of a multiple-level approach in doing so.

Most higher educational institutions offer general health, fitness, or wellness classes.

The two most common types of undergraduate physical education classes are general health/fitness and wellness. General physical education classes have commonly focused on teaching students how to obtain physical health. Contemporary goals of general physical education classes have included improving students' abilities to demonstrate a sport or fitness skill. **Wellness** classes, in contrast, have focused on a more holistic approach to physical education by including mini health lectures combined with physical activity. The overall goal of a wellness class is to stress the importance of physical activity as well as to teach health behaviors that affect the emotional, mental, and social dimensions in a student's life such as stress management, nutrition, and interpersonal communication.

In adopting and maintaining physical activity, many individuals seem to go through various stages as they change their behavior. One indicator of exercise behavior change is the **Stages of Change model**, which includes five stages: (1) precontemplation (not intending to make a change), (2) contemplation (considering a change), (3) preparation (making small changes), (4) action (actively engaging in the new behavior), and (5) maintenance (sustaining the change over time) (Prochaska & DiClemente, 1983). The Stages of Change model suggests that individuals change their behavior in a more cyclical manner versus a linear pattern; as a result, it is important to note that several attempts at changing an individual's behavior may take place before a goal is achieved. In addition to exercise adoption and maintenance, the Stages of Change model has been successfully applied to smoking cessation, assessment in physical education, weight control, and dietary intake of college students (Ciccomascolo & Riebe, 2008; Snelling, Adams, Korba, & Tucker, 2006). The Stages of Change approach

has been applied to weight control and to dietary intake in samples of college students. However, there is a paucity of research on the application of the stage-intervention approach to exercise behavior in college-level *physical education* classes.

■ PURPOSE OF STUDY

The purpose of this study was to compare the effects of two types of undergraduate physical education courses, wellness and fitness, on health behaviors of college students. More specifically, this study investigated pre and post changes (movement from stage to stage) in the students' Stages of Change. To examine this problem, the following research question was posed: Will wellness courses prompt college students to change stages in the Stages of Change model compared to fitness courses?

■ METHODS AND PROCEDURES

The study was conducted at an urban university in the Northeast with an enrollment of approximately 11,500 students. Presently, 64% of the student population is female and 36% is male. Approximately 75% of the student population is white, non-Hispanic; 10.6% is black; 5.2% is Hispanic; 5.2% is Asian; and the remaining approximately 5% was composed of other ethnic backgrounds.

One hundred and fifty-six students, ranging in age from 18–35 years (mean age 21.2 ± 3 years), participated in this study. Each subject was a non-physical education major enrolled in a wellness, fitness walking, or aerobics course as a university-wide requirement. There were four sections of the wellness course, one section of the aerobics course, and two sections of the fitness walking course. Because there were similar educational objectives in the fitness walking and aerobics classes, the researcher combined both courses under the name of "fitness group." There were 102 subjects in the wellness group and 54 subjects in the fitness group.

The university requirement for physical education is completion of two physical education courses. These courses may be taken in any semester, and two courses may be taken in the same semester. It is important to note that subjects chose to enroll in the classes although they had other skill-type classes from which to choose.

None of the students received compensation, academic or otherwise, for participating in the study. Prior to participation in this study, subjects signed an informed consent form stating that they were made aware of the conditions of the tests and that all questions about the tests had been answered to their satisfaction by the researcher. Also, subjects were told that they could drop out of the study at any time during the semester without any consequence. Subjects were informed that all information generated from this study would be treated as privileged and confidential.

All classes met in the Athletic Field House where subjects were able to use the facilities. The Athletic Field House contains an indoor and outdoor quarter-mile track, a pool, and a weight room complete with free weights, machine weights, treadmills, stationary bikes, and a flexibility mat. Class time was used to teach the subjects how to properly and safely use each piece of equipment.

The wellness course was made up of two 0.5-credit, 8-week courses that were to be taken consecutively in the same semester. The two courses, called Fit for Life I and II, contained lecture as well as laboratory activities. Each section of the course met for 150 minutes/week. The purpose of the wellness course was to provide the students with a systematic plan that included health-related physical fitness, self-responsibility and self-management, nutrition, weight management, lifestyle choices, and stress reduction. In addition, this course taught the importance of the mind–body connection in a long-term healthy approach to living.

The main objectives for the wellness course were as follows: (1) participate in a planned, goal-specific exercise program throughout the semester; (2) understand the importance of safety precautions and appropriate skill progressions while preparing for and participating in physical activity; (3) evaluate activities that promote the health-related components of physical fitness; (4) identify good nutritional habits and develop a long-range plan for a healthy diet; (5) understand and implement stress management techniques; and (6) identify at least three behavioral and lifestyle changes to be initiated as a result of the course.

The fitness walking course was a 1.0-credit, 16-week course taken in one semester that met for 150 minutes/week. The purpose of the course was to provide the student with an opportunity to maintain health and fitness through walking while learning about the effects of the F.I.T.T. principle (frequency, intensity, time, and type of exercise) on their health. In addition, this course emphasized the proper way to walk to achieve maximum benefit of the exercise. Overall, the goal of the course was to encourage students to continue the healthy behavior of participating in physical activity after the semester was completed. The main objectives for the fitness walking course were as follows: (1) participate in a planned, goal-specific walking program throughout the semester; (2) understand the importance of safety and proper skills while preparing for and participating in fitness walking; (3) understand and implement the F.I.T.T. principle in a goal-specific walking program; and (4) understand how to accurately take one's resting and target heart rates.

The aerobics course was a 1.0-credit, 16-week course that met twice a week for one semester. Subjects in the aerobics class devised and organized an aerobic lesson that included using high-impact, low-impact, mixed-impact, and step aerobics as well as floor exercise. The overall goal of the course was to understand why aerobic exercise is of value. The main objectives for the aerobics course were as follows: (1) know how to prevent injury and enhance health during an aerobics class by using proper warm-up and cool-down routines; (2) be able to organize and demonstrate an aerobic lesson; and (3) understand how to accurately take one's resting and target heart rates.

Each person in the wellness course had devised an individual fitness program in the third or fourth week of class that included a certain type, frequency, intensity, and time of exercise. The planned exercise program was to be goal-specific, and could include weight loss, increased endurance, decreased body weight or body fat, or increased muscle tone. Each subject was asked to be as specific as possible. For example, if the subject's goal was to lose weight, they were asked to write how many pounds they wanted to lose, and the time line of the long-term goal as well as monthly short-term goals. Subjects were encouraged to choose an activity that they would enjoy participating in for the semester.

Prior to this assignment, the instructor of the wellness course provided accurate information about the time, intensity, and type of exercise suitable for each individual. For example, the guidelines for weight loss, endurance training, or other types of exercise-related goals were established by using the guidelines of the **American College of Sports Medicine (ACSM)**. The ACSM is the primary, and most reputable, institution that governs exercise science–related research and creates exercise guidelines and recommendations for individuals based on the results of its studies. Subjects were encouraged to present their planned exercise programs to their instructor, who examined them to ensure the goals were realistic and accurate. In addition, subjects were encouraged to choose a person, or a "buddy," to provide additional support toward goal adherence throughout the semester.

Subjects in the fitness walking course devised similar planned exercise programs as subjects in the wellness course; however, the programs were more focused around walking. For example, a goal-specific program could include walking for cardiorespiratory fitness, decreased body fat, or increased quadriceps strength. Subjects in the aerobics course devised and organized an aerobic lesson, and also learned how to prevent injury and enhance health, including using proper warm up/cool down exercises.

On the first day of class, subjects were given a questionnaire that asked them to select their initial Stage of Change, or readiness to become involved in exercise. The same questionnaire also asked what type of exercise program subjects were following, if any. The subjects' Stage of Change was measured using Prochaska and DiClemente's (1983) Stages of Change Questionnaire. The questionnaire measures an individual's movement through various stages as he or she changes his or her behavior in the adoption and maintenance of physical activity. Subjects were asked to choose the stage (1 = precontemplation through 5 = maintenance) that best described their readiness for involvement in exercise.

Also on the first day of class, subjects were given a 4-month calendar and were asked to accurately record any exercise they performed outside and inside of class. Subjects were asked to fill in information about their exercise programs because the researcher needed to know what physical activity, if any, they were doing or planned to do over the semester. The researcher was to take this information and use it in measuring exercise adherence both inside and outside of class.

A modified version of the Stages of Change questionnaire was given on the last day of class. This questionnaire did not include the exercise portion of the initial questionnaire. Also, the modified Stages of Change questionnaire included only four stages. The maintenance stage was not included because the semester was only 16 weeks long; maintenance is defined as exercising on a regular basis for longer than 6 months.

The researcher investigated the following **hypothesis**: There will be no statistically significant difference in subjects' pre– and post–Stages of Change scores measured in the wellness group compared to the fitness group. The following statistical tests were used: (1) paired t tests, (2) unpaired t tests of d scores (difference score between posttest and pretest measures), and (3) one sample analysis of variance (ANOVA) for d scores of both the wellness and fitness groups. If statistical significance was found for either the wellness or fitness group, an ANOVA was computed to examine possible gender and/or instructor differences. The level of significance was set at 0.05.

RESULTS

One hundred fifty-six subjects (mean age 21.2 ± 2.6 years) participated in this study. The mean age for the wellness group was 21.5 ± 3.0 and the mean age for the fitness group was 20.7 ± 1.7. The ages in the wellness group ranged from 18–35 years and for the fitness group ranged from and 18–25 years. There were 67 females and 35 males in the wellness group. There were 39 females and 15 males in the fitness group. Both groups consisted of a mixture of freshman, sophomores, juniors, and seniors. The largest number of students in both the wellness and fitness groups were seniors (52 and 20, respectively).

The hypothesis stated that there would be no statistically significant differences in subjects' Stages of Change measured in the wellness group compared to the fitness group. There was a significant difference in the d score for the Stages of Change in the wellness group versus the fitness group ($p = 0.0271$). Because significance was set at 0.05, the null hypothesis was rejected.

DISCUSSION

Research suggests that the relationship between physical education curricula and subjects' health behaviors is unclear. The purpose of this study was to compare the effect of two types of undergraduate physical education courses, wellness and fitness, on health behaviors of college students; more specifically, this study investigated pre and post changes in the students' Stages of Change. A Stages of Change questionnaire and exercise program were administered to all 156 subjects in the fitness and wellness courses in the beginning of the fall semester.

The researcher's hypothesis stated that there would be no statistically significant differences in subjects' Stages of Change in the wellness group compared to the fitness group. However, there was a significant mean difference in the d score for the Stages of Change in the wellness group versus the fitness group ($p = 0.0271$).

The overall result of this study showed that for this population, there was an increase in the wellness group's Stages of Change compared to the fitness group. Prior research findings on wellness curricula have supported positive effects on students' health behavior and attitudes. Subjects' Stages of Change may have improved since the beginning of the semester in the wellness group because these types of classes focus on the importance of lifelong activity. Wellness courses focus on other dimensions beyond the physical; therefore, students are informed about how to deal with issues in their lives including stress management and decisions about sexual behavior and/or drug use. Students in wellness courses learn *why* they should balance their physical, social, and emotional dimensions in life and not just *how* to do so. Conversely, the focus of activity- or fitness-based courses is on the physical dimension alone. Mack and Shaddox (2004) suggest that college students can increase their attitudes in wellness and physical activity even after a one-semester university personal wellness course.

Perhaps subjects were able to move through the Stages of Change in the wellness group because they were given reasons regarding why they should exercise and not just told how to exercise. Subjects could have made better decisions about exercising because the information in the curriculum provided an impetus to do so. Subjects could have reflected on the knowledge that they acquired during the lecture part of the lecture/lab class and subsequently reduced their "cons," therefore changing their behavior.

During the first week of class, subjects in the wellness group were asked to evaluate their health and lifestyle. In addition, during week 5, subjects were asked to write an attainable goal/objective in one or two dimensions in life (physical, emotional, spiritual, other) that they would give to their instructor to evaluate. Furthermore, during weeks 8–12, subjects met with the instructor for individual questions, guidance, and overall help/motivation. Finally, subjects were asked to look at their accomplishments over the semester on week 14. These events are all examples of the type of interaction between subjects and their peers and instructors that did not occur in the fitness group. Moreover, although subjects in the wellness group had help from their instructor, they had to be proactive and self-manage their exercise both inside and outside of class.

Other elements of the course that were taught in addition to the five components of physical fitness included coping with stress, meditation, organizational skill, and optimal nutritional guidelines. The wellness curricula provided a balanced content that allowed subjects to learn and reflect upon other dimensions of their lives. As a result, perhaps subjects focused less on the cons of physical activity and focused more on the pros because exercise improved their mood, gave them energy, or motivated them to feel as if they could accomplish their goal.

■ CONCLUSION

Based on the findings and within the limitations of this study, this study demonstrates that a wellness course has an effect on subjects' Stages of Change. The fitness courses did not show the same effect. Therefore, it appears that fitness courses do not automatically improve one's attitudes or behavior toward exercise.

The present study has added to the fundamental understanding of how two types of curricula do or do not affect students' health behaviors. To increase the understanding in this topic, the following recommendations for future study can be made: (1) inquire why the individual enrolled in a particular physical education course, (2) inquire whether students live on or off campus; (3) investigate whether students are enjoying what they are doing in physical education classes; (4) replicate this study at many different colleges and universities and compare to the results of this study; and (5) research the demographics and background of the college students in a study similar to this one to determine whether past experiences impacted change.

■ KEY WORDS AND DEFINITIONS

American College of Sports Medicine (ACSM) The primary, and most reputable, institution that governs exercise science–related research and creates exercise guidelines and recommendations for individuals based on the results of its studies.

hypothesis A specific, testable prediction about what one expects to happen in a scientific study.

Stages of Change model A model for behavior change that includes five stages: precontemplation, contemplation, preparation, action, and maintenance.

wellness An active process of becoming aware of and making choices toward a more successful life through balancing the social, physical, and emotional dimensions of life.

■ DISCUSSION QUESTIONS

1. Do you think college students should have to take a required PE or wellness class? Why or why not?

2. What are some barriers that college students experience in adopting and maintaining regular exercise?

3. What would motivate college students to be more active, especially if they are living away from home for the first time in their lives?

4. Do you think exercising or being physically active with a friend helps you to adhere to an exercise program compared to exercising by yourself?

5. If you had to choose a Stage of Change for yourself regarding exercise, what stage would you choose?

■ REFERENCES

American College Health Association. (2006). *American Health Association National College Health Assessment (ACHA-NCHA) web summary*. Retrieved July 7, 2011, from http://www.acha-ncha.org/data_highlights.html

Butler, S. M., Black, D. R., Blue, C. L., & Gretebeck, R. J. (2004). Change in diet, physical activity, and body weight in female college freshman. *American Journal of Behavior, 28*(1), 24–32.

Centers for Disease Control and Prevention. (2006). *Health, United States, 2006.* Retrieved February 7, 2006, from http://www.cdc.gov/nchs/data/hus/hus06.pdf#highlights

Ciccomascolo, L., & Riebe, D. (2008). Stages of change and physical education assessment. *Journal of Physical Education, Recreation and Dance, 79*(1), 13–16.

Huang, T. T-K., Harris, K. J., Lee, R. E., Nazir, N., Born, W., & Kaur, H. (2003). Assessing overweight, obesity, diet, and physical activity in college students. *Journal of American College Health, 52*(2), 83–86.

Keating, X. D., Guan, J., Piñero, J. C., & Bridges, D. M. (2005). A meta-analysis of college students' physical activity behaviors. *Journal of American College Health, 54*(2), 116–126.

Lowry, R., Galuska, D., Fulton, J., Wechsler, H., Kann, L., & Collins, J. (2000). Physical activity, food choice, and weight management goals and practices among U.S. college students. *American Journal of Preventative Medicine, 18*(1), 18–27.

Mack, M., & Shaddox, L. (2004). Changes in short-term attitudes toward physical activity and exercise of university personal wellness students. *College Student Journal, 38*(4), 587–594.

Prochaska, J. O., & DiClemente, C. C. (1983). Stages and processes of self change of smoking: Toward an integrative model. *Journal of Consulting and Clinical Psychology, 51*, 390–395.

Snelling, A. M., Adams, T. B., Korba, C., & Tucker, L. (2006). Stages of change algorithm for calcium intake by male college students. *Journal of the American Dietetic Association, 106*(6), 904–907.

U.S. Department of Health and Human Services. (2010). *The Surgeon General's vision for a healthy and fit nation.* Rockville, MD: U.S. Department of Health and Human Services, Office of the Surgeon General.

U.S. Department of Health and Human Services & U.S. Department of Agriculture. (2005). *Dietary Guidelines for Americans, 2005* (6th ed.). Washington, DC: U.S. Government Printing Office.

CHAPTER 6

Keeping Up with Technology

■ CHAPTER OVERVIEW

The first article in this chapter provides an overview of the world of technology in education today, with specific examples of how to teach with technology, benefits for student learning, and the challenges with teaching and learning online. To succeed in this fast-paced digital information age, educators, especially physical and health educators, need to teach their "digital natives" or the "Net Generation" (Prensky, 2001) while continuing to stay up-to-date with technology.

The second article discusses how using technology in physical education raises the level of teacher and student accountability and provides a more objective means of assessing student performance and effort not often seen in traditional physical education curriculum. In the "new" physical education curriculum, compared to the traditional, technology such as pedometers and heart rate monitors—in addition to smart phones, MP3 players, tablets, and gaming consoles—are used to collect data during physical education class.

Teaching and learning online are now viable components in all areas of education, even in our discipline. The third article presents some introductory information about web-enhanced, blended, and online learning. Supporting research about online education, online course development, and implementation is presented. Blended or hybrid courses and virtual schools are discussed as well as why we need to become more proactive in our approach to using technology to teach and learn in physical and health education.

The importance for educators to embrace technology and feel confident and comfortable while using it is the subject of the fourth article. Beginning teachers will learn that although technology can play a significant role in enhancing their physical education and health education classes, technology alone cannot create a perfect classroom. Furthermore, beginning teachers will need to learn to solve problems such as how to replace a bulb that has burned out when using an LCD projector, how to reboot an Internet page, or how to handle a simple mistake of leaving a necessary cord at home. Finally, the author shares some insight into gaming technology for physical education.

Technology in Education

Swapna Kumar

The Internet has transcended political, economic, social, and cultural barriers and has brought about momentous changes in our professional and personal lives today. The advancement of communication technologies has led to radical changes in the workplace, to jobs being outsourced, and to teams working together remotely from different parts of the globe. On the personal front, we use the Internet to book tickets, to shop, to find good restaurants, to get directions to a destination, to research medical problems, to communicate with our families, and to share photographs and special moments. In this ubiquitous technology environment, K–12 educational institutions and higher education are also investing in and implementing online technologies in the form of wireless networks, laptop and tablet computers, interactive whiteboards, school websites, course websites, and online admissions. Even online degrees and virtual schooling are a reality today. Within this world of expanding technological advances, teachers are expected to understand and integrate technology into their classrooms in order to engage and motivate students who have grown up in a digital age. Teachers, along with parents and caregivers, must face the challenge of preparing students for a digital society that will be very different from the one we know today.

■ DIGITAL NATIVES AND DIGITAL CITIZENSHIP

Students who were born after 1980 and have grown up with digital technologies are called the **Net Generation** or **digital natives**

(Tapscott, 1998; Prensky, 2001). Prensky claimed that digital natives have certain characteristics—they multitask, access information in a nonlinear manner, prefer active learning, and are heavily networked. As compared to digital immigrants (people who did not grow up with digital technologies), digital natives can process information very quickly and have an expectation that the technologies available in their daily lives will also be used in their education. According to the Pew Internet and American Life Project (2007), 93% of teenagers in the United States use the Internet and 64% have created content on the Internet. In surveying 2000 students born after 1980 in Australia, Kennedy et al. (2006) found that 96% had unrestricted access to a mobile phone, 69% to an MP3 player, 76% to a digital camera, and 63% to a laptop computer.

Although it is common to hear parents and teachers express wonder at students' use of new gadgets and new technologies, familiarity with technology use and access to a variety of gadgets does not automatically translate to responsible use of technology by students, or to the effective use of technology for learning. Acknowledging the importance of preparing students for a digital society, the International Society for Technology in Education (ISTE) included Digital Citizenship as one of the six National Educational Technology Standards (NETS) for students in 2007. As **digital citizens**, students should "understand human, cultural, and societal issues related to technology and practice legal and ethical behavior" (ISTE, 2007). In order to help students become digital citizens and to responsibly use technology, teachers have to "model digital citizenship and responsibility" and "design and develop digital-age learning experiences and assessments" (ISTE, 2008).

Educators and critics argue that teaching practices and schools do not reflect the prevalence of technology in other parts of our lives, and that teachers will have to be trained to teach with technology. There is continuing discussion about how technology is currently used for teaching, and should ideally be used for teaching. Among the questions being raised are: How can teachers exploit the potential of students' online connectivity, mobile phones, digital cameras, and MP3 players to help them learn better? Is the use of such technologies more distracting than useful? How can teachers stay up-to-date with these technologies and implement them in the prescribed curriculum? How can new projects and assignments that students complete using new technologies be assessed in the standards-based environment of today? These are some questions that educators also ask themselves as they experiment with new technologies. The articles in this chapter do not aim to answer all of these questions, but will provide some insight into the different aspects of the use of technology in education today.

■ TEACHING WITH TECHNOLOGY

The use of technology in education is not new—radio, television, videos and DVDs, and more recently computers, have been used in formal and informal education settings for many decades. Some educational technologists even consider the chalkboard and chalk as a technology that is used for teaching (i.e., instructional media). **Instructional media** refers to media that are used to deliver instruction, such as CDs or videos.

The term is often confused with **educational technology**, which is "the study and ethical practice of facilitating learning and improving performance by creating, using, and managing appropriate technological processes and resources" (Association for Educational Communications and Technology [AECT], 2004, p. 3). Instructional media refers to the actual tool, whereas educational technology represents the process of creating and implementing those tools to enhance the learning environment and to facilitate learning.

When people speak of a technology as being extremely effective for teaching or learning, they are usually referring to instructional media. However, most technologies were not originally developed for teaching purposes—they have to be adapted to the classroom environment, the subject being taught, and class goals. Two different standpoints toward instructional media formed the basis of the "media versus methods" debate during the 1980s and 1990s when Clark (1983) likened media to a grocery truck that delivers groceries but does not change people's nutritional habits. He argued that good instruction could help students learn regardless of the technology that was used. On reviewing research that compared traditional instruction (without technology) to instruction in which the technology of the time was being used, he stated that "no learning benefits were to be gained from employing any specific medium to deliver instruction" (p. 445). Kozma (1991), on the other hand, argued that the type of technology used to teach could make a difference if the technology was not used only for presentation, and if learners actively engaged with the media. More recently, the inclusion of interaction in the form of student–content interaction, student–student interaction, and student–teacher interaction has become important to the design of any instruction that uses technology (Moore & Kearsley, 1995).

Although some educators continue to debate whether technology-enhanced teaching is more beneficial to students than teaching without technology, others argue that there is no longer the option of teaching without technology—educators have to focus on *how best* to teach with technology.

In considering this question, variables that influence the successful implementation of technology in teaching practice—the infrastructure available at an institution, teacher and student access to hardware and software outside the classroom, time for teachers to plan and implement a curriculum that integrates technology, institutional as well as technical support, and the training that teachers receive in the use of technology—should be evaluated. Preservice teachers usually complete at least one educational technology course during their teacher education or teacher certification program, and many opportunities for technology development are available to in-service teachers in the United States. Today, however, the technology available is advancing at such a pace that it is difficult to take the time to evaluate the effectiveness of each practice in an education setting, before it is succeeded by another.

■ BENEFITS FOR STUDENT LEARNING

So what are some benefits to student learning from the use of instructional media in the curriculum? Research has established that the effective use of instructional media can engage learners, make learning more relevant, simulate reality, foster higher-level understanding, encourage student-centered practices, individualize instruction, address multiple learning and cognitive styles, motivate learners, and increase collaboration and critical thinking (Bethel, Bernard, Abrami, & Wade, 2007; Duffy & Cunningham, 1996; Dwyer, 1994; Jonassen, Campbell, & Davidson, 1994; Kozma & Johnston, 1991; Waxman, Connell, & Gray, 2002). The Internet allows students to experience other worlds first-hand and collaborate with students or experts in other parts of the world. For example, in a class about ancient Egypt, they can explore an archaeological site or a pyramid in an online simulation provided by a museum, view original manuscripts and translations of hieroglyphics, view short video clips from well-researched documentaries, read related material on their topic of interest, read a blog by an eminent archaeologist, and email an expert or an archaeologist with their questions. They are more motivated, can learn more about topics that interest them, engage in dialogue, and have real-world experiences sitting in their homes or classrooms. For class projects, students can create a podcast, an interactive presentation, or a blog that they can share not only with their teacher but also with anyone in the world, making the classroom truly global.

The use of technology also provides students with opportunities to learn according to their preferences for visuals, audio, or text. Giving students the option of listening to podcasts about physical education, health, nutrition, or assessment practices, as well as providing them with a transcript of the podcasts, can help students who prefer to read or listen. Videos have been popular in physical education for over a decade—teachers and students have often used them to explain techniques or physical skills and to analyze team behavior. The ubiquity of cell phone cameras and ease of upload to the Internet make it possible for teachers and students anywhere to share videos today. PDAs, iPhones, Wiis, and Xboxes have made it possible for individuals to develop and monitor exercise plans, track their progress, and share their experiences with others.

If you reflect on your own school and college experiences, there may have been projects or topics that you learned better because you watched a movie or created a web-based resource.

On the other hand, the required use of a technology to complete an assignment can be difficult for a student if the teacher is not familiar with the technology, if there is no support in the classroom, or if the student does not have access to a computer or software needed for the assignment. When using any type of technology in teaching, it is extremely important to first ascertain whether all students have access to the technology and that they know how to use the hardware and applications needed to complete activities. In order to teach successfully with technology, it is also important for the teacher to be familiar with not just technological applications but also the challenges students might face when trying to work with the technology.

■ CHALLENGES WITH TEACHING AND LEARNING ONLINE

Given the large and overwhelming amounts of rich information available on the Internet, both teachers and students in the twenty-first century have to learn to be critical of information sources, to extract relevant information for their individual needs, and to use and apply web-based resources thoughtfully. As opposed to older media such as books, videos, or CD-ROMs, the World Wide Web is flexible and easily accessible but also unreliable and uncensored. Teachers who assign web-based work or use web-based activities have to be aware of problems associated with the authorship, credibility, and reliability of information on the Internet. Students have to learn to assess the credibility and veracity of web-based resources; for example,

who is the author of a website and what is his or her expertise in that topic? Students have to also learn to compare online content with other websites for accuracy and bias. An excellent resource to use with students for this purpose is Kathy Schrock's evaluation surveys at http://school.discovery.com/schrockguide/eval.html.

Students using the Internet at every stage of their research or projects also have to learn not to plagiarize what they find online. Many are under the misconception that it is possible to use images or text from the Internet in a paper or on their own website. Guidelines for fair use of copyrighted material that covers educational use of copyrighted text, images, music, or film can be found at http://www.halldavidson.net/chartshort.html. An increasing number of educators have begun using **Creative Commons** materials—materials that have been in existence since 2001 and are more flexible, where the author of a product can specify the terms of use. Even when using an image or song licensed under Creative Commons, students should be taught to read the terms of the license and use it accordingly. When students create movies, podcasts, websites, and blogs for educational purposes, they are available to a larger audience than just their class, teacher, or school. Cultivating fair use and copyright principles prepares them for the real world where they will create such products and be accountable for them.

■ PREPARING STUDENTS TO BE DIGITAL CITIZENS

In order to guide their students to critically evaluate information, and to help them succeed in the information age, it is important that teachers are facile at using online technologies to find good quality web-based materials and to foster critical thinking. They can, for instance, use instructional activities like WebQuests, where students learn to find and evaluate information on the Internet, cite the sources used, synthesize information, justify their decisions to use or omit information, and work collaboratively in groups. Such activities do not just contribute to the depth of a student's knowledge about a subject, but also simulate the wisdom that students will need in the real world, that now includes the cyber world. In addition to being conversant with the gathering and use of online information, teachers and parents should be aware of the challenges of using online technologies.

The Internet is an important medium that provides students with easy access to information, but it also gives them easy access to communication technologies that allow anonymity, that make it possible to violate privacy, and that facilitate interactions that cannot be moderated by adults. **Cyberbullying**, the use of "email, instant messaging, web sites, voting booths, and chat or bash rooms to deliberately antagonize and intimidate others" (Beale & Hall, 2007, p. 8), is increasingly prevalent among K–12 students. Teachers and parents should be aware of school policies against cyberbullying, and furthermore, make such policies transparent to students and directly address such issues in conversations with students. Students often do not realize that web-based materials and communications can be archived and available for a very long time, and that their web-based activities in their younger years can influence their future careers and reputations.

■ CONTINUOUS LEARNING FOR TEACHERS

How can teachers learn about new technologies, decide whether they are useful or appropriate for their classes, and educate

their students to be critical of online information? Teachers do not always have the time to attend classes or courses, and not every school has a culture of sharing and professional development for teachers. Fortunately, the Internet and communication technologies available today have made it possible for teachers to share experiences and educational materials, and learn from each other regardless of social, political, and geographical barriers. **Teacher portals** are large websites that provide lesson plans, ideas, and solutions to learner problems that teachers can adapt to their individual contexts. Social networks, blogs, and wikis enable teachers from different schools, districts, states, and even countries to share and discuss their use of technology, teaching methods, and different instructional and institutional problems. Not only beginning teachers, but also teachers with many years of experience have reported benefiting greatly by becoming members of these communities. For example, http://www.pbs.org/teachers or http://www.teachers.net provide excellent educational technology resources for teachers. Classroom 2.0 at http://www.classroom20.com details how different teachers use Web 2.0 tools in their teaching, and is a great place to get ideas for teaching a subject with new technologies. For teachers who prefer to listen to how new technologies can be used, http://www.teacherspodcast.org provides podcasts that can be downloaded to an MP3 player and listened to in the car or the gym. There are many more such websites on the Internet for teachers of specific subjects or grade levels.

Despite the long history of technology use in education, the benefits to students, and the increasing prevalence of technology in our daily lives, there is often discussion around the problems with using technology, whether using technology is 'better," or whether a new technology should be learned or integrated into teaching. Online communities or portals and professional development are a great way for teachers to judge the usefulness of a technology. They can learn from peers' use of a certain application or technology, and make an informed decision about whether that tool or online application will correspond to her or his class, course goals, students' needs, infrastructure, and teaching style. Given the dynamic nature of the Internet and the daily emergence of new technologies and applications, portals also provide exposure to the latest and most useful tools for teaching. Some applications that are currently popular with teachers and have been reported as useful for student learning (e.g., blogs, wikis, social bookmarking) are described in a later article in this chapter.

The lack of censorship, the high level of anonymity, and easy access to harmful information on the Internet make it necessary for schools and communities to teach students to use technology wisely and to cultivate cyber ethics so that students become good digital citizens. Teachers of today may not know what new technologies will shape future environments in which their students will live and work, but they can try to stay current with new technologies and apply those technologies in their teaching whenever appropriate and in a manner that simulates real life. Students would then be more capable and competitive in the global economy and in virtual working environments, and could assume responsibility for their interactions in the cyber world of tomorrow.

■ KEY WORDS AND DEFINITIONS

Creative Commons A nonprofit organization that releases licenses that allow the author of a product to specify the terms of use (which rights they reserve or waive).

cyberbullying The use of "email, instant messaging, websites, voting booths, and chat or bash rooms to deliberately antagonize and intimidate others" (Beale & Hall, 2007, p. 8).

digital citizens People who "understand human, cultural, and societal issues related to technology and practice legal and ethical behavior" (ISTE, 2007).

educational technology "The study and ethical practice of facilitating learning and improving performance by creating, using, and managing appropriate technological processes and resources" (AECT, 2004, p. 3).

instructional media Media used to deliver instruction, for example, CDs or videos.

Net Generation or digital natives Students who were born after 1980 and have grown up with digital technologies (Prensky, 2001).

teacher portals Large websites that provide lesson plans, ideas, and solutions to learner problems, which teachers can adapt to their individual contexts.

■ DISCUSSION QUESTIONS

1. Would you term yourself a digital native or a digital immigrant? Why?
2. What does the term *digital citizen* mean for you? How could you prepare students to be digital citizens within the scope of your teaching?
3. Share with your peers one example of a good use of technology that helped you learn in the past. Reflect on whether it was the technology or the way it was used (media versus method) that helped you.
4. Discuss one way in which (a) videos and (b) podcasts can be used effectively to teach physical/health education.

5. Given your experiences as a student and teacher, what are three important considerations for you, personally, when you use a particular technology to teach?

■ REFERENCES

Association for Educational Communications and Technology (AECT) Definition and Technology Committee (2004). *The meanings of educational technology.* Retrieved September 1, 2010, from http://www.indiana.edu/%7Emolpage/Meanings%20of%20ET_4.0.pdf

Beale, A., & Hall, K. (2007). Cyberbullying: What school administrators (and parents) can do. *The Clearing House, 81*(1), 8–12.

Bethel, E., Bernard, R., Abrami, P., & Wade, C. (2007). The effects of ubiquitous computing on student learning: A systematic review. In T. Bastiaens & S. Carliner (Eds.), *Proceedings of World Conference on E-Learning in Corporate, Government, Healthcare, and Higher Education* (pp. 1987–1992). Chesapeake, VA: AACE.

Clark, R. E. (1983). Reconsidering research on learning from media. *Review of Educational Research, 53*(4), 445–459.

Duffy, T. M., & Cunningham, D. J. (1996) Constructivism: Implications for the design and delivery of instruction. In Jonassen D. H. (Ed) *Handbook of Research for Educational Communications and Technology* (pp. 170–198). New York: Simon & Shuster.

Dwyer, D. (1994). Apple classrooms of tomorrow: What we've learned. *Educational Leadership, 51*(7), 4–10.

International Society for Technology in Education. (2007). *National educational technology standards for students.* Retrieved July 22, 2009, from http://www.iste.org/Content/NavigationMenu/NETS/ForStudents/NETS_for_Students.htm

International Society for Technology in Education. (2008). *National educational technology standards for teachers.* Retrieved July 22, 2009, from http://www.iste.org/content/navigationmenu/nets/forteachers/2008standards/nets_for_teachers_2008.htm

Jonassen, D. H., Campbell, J. P., & Davidson, M. E. (1994). Learning with media: Restructuring the debate. *Educational Technology Research and Development, 42*(2), 31–39.

Kennedy, G. E., Judd, T. S., Churchward, A., Gray, K., & Krause, K. L. (2008). First year students' experiences with technology: Are they really digital natives? *Australasian Journal of Educational Technology, (24)*1, 108–122.

Kozma, R. B. (1991). Learning with media. *Review of Educational Research, 61*(2), 179–211.

Kozma, R. B., & Johnston, J. (1991). The technological revolution comes to the classroom. *Change, 23*(1), 10–23.

Lenhart, A., & Madden, M. (2007). Teens and social networking, Pew Internet. Retrieved January 16, 2008, from http://www.pewinternet.org/pdfs/PIP_SNS_Data_Memo_Jan_2007.pdf

Moore, M. G., & Kearsley, G. (1995). *Distance education: A systems view.* Belmont, CA: Wadsworth.

Prensky, M. (2001). Digital natives, digital immigrants. *On the Horizon, 9*(5), 1–6.

Waxman, H. C., Connell, M. L., & Gray, J. (2002). *A quantitative synthesis of recent research on the effects of teaching and learning with technology on student outcomes.* Naperville, IL: North Central Regional Educational Laboratory. Retrieved January 18, 2008, from http://www.ncrel.org/tech/effects

Technology Use in Physical Education and Health Education

Shawna J. Southern

The use of technology in the classroom or gymnasium is necessary in today's physical education and health courses. It is important for educators to embrace technology and feel confident and comfortable while using it. When used properly, technology can help educators motivate students to participate in physical activity and maintain healthy behaviors. In a physical education or health class, technology can be used by the teacher to facilitate learning, and it can be used by the student to inform, set goals, make decisions, and provide evidence of knowledge and understanding of certain concepts. Technology also can aid in assessment of student learning. School districts are becoming more interested in data, which can be collected with the use of technology, because data drives decisions made in reference to funding, scheduling, and other allocations of resources.

Teachers can use the relationship between one's fitness levels and how one performs academically as an advocacy tool. Using fitness software to assess student fitness is one way to cultivate the data from students' activity levels. If the physical education teacher can demonstrate and document growth in fitness levels by using fitness assessment software, that data can be used to advocate for more technology equipment for the physical education program.

Although there are many advantages to its use, caution needs to be exercised when using or requiring the use of technology.

Technology is not perfect; it does have flaws. A bulb could burn out when using an LCD, filters may prohibit certain webpages from working properly, or a cord may have been left at home and is not available for use. Both teachers and students should be prepared to continue with their presentation/performance task if the technology does not work. Educators may also find that technology is not available to them because they might not have a budget for it or perhaps there is little or no setup in the school to support its use. Further complicating matters is when technology is made available to PE teachers and they are too intimidated to use it to their advantage. Regardless of the advantages and disadvantages, technology in health and physical education needs to be on par with every other discipline. If technology money is budgeted for math, literacy, and science, then it should also be budgeted for health and physical education. If it is not budgeted, then the teacher needs to begin advocacy efforts to be able to bring health and physical education programs and students into the twenty-first century.

In addition to teachers, the availability of technology for students should be well noted. It is important that physical and health educators understand which of their students have access to the necessary technology for assignments, but this must be done without labeling or signaling out students. Some students have access to laptop and/or desktop computers, the Internet, and basic computer software whereas others do not. This can make it difficult to ask students to perform technological tasks if they have nothing at home with which to complete the assignment. If students do have access to various modes of technology, physical and health educators must learn how to handle issues such as cheating, plagiarism, software piracy, and obtaining false information online from disreputable websites when doing research for a report or project. An option could be for a physical or health education assignment that requires the use of technology to be completed in collaboration with the technology class at school.

■ EDUCATIONAL TECHNOLOGIES: GETTING STARTED

In most educational settings in which computers and the Internet are used, the user must sign an **acceptable use policy (AUP)**. The AUP provides guidelines for the user and will differ depending on the school. Penalties could be incurred by the user if the AUP code of conduct is not followed. School community members should be aware of the specific AUP in their school district.

The use of educational technologies will vary depending on the user. If the teacher does not have much experience with technology it is important to start small. The teacher should practice using the technology before demonstrating it and using it with students. Familiarity and preparation will make all the difference in a teacher's confidence level when teaching or using technology. It is recommended that teachers keep the owner's manual/directions close at hand, and if difficulty persists, teachers can access help sites or chat forums on the Internet that will provide some assistance. In fact, most products do not even come with written directions

any more, and user guides are accessed on the web. Educators are continually problem solving ways to improve software programs they may already be using. Glitches and possible improvements in those programs can often be addressed by reporting them to the software company. In some cases, new information can be downloaded by visiting the website and following the directions. In other cases, the teacher may have to wait until a new and improved technology is developed.

It is recommended that teachers begin using the new technology with only one class. Once proficiency using the technology has been achieved with that class, the teacher will be able to use it to provide more efficient and effective feedback to more students. As a beginner, it is imperative not to become overwhelmed and disillusioned with technology. It is a process, and it takes time and practice. The experienced user will continue to seek out new kinds of technology and become proficient in its uses to benefit the learning community.

■ VARIOUS TECHNOLOGIES FOR TEACHER USE IN PHYSICAL AND HEALTH EDUCATION

New technologies are continually being developed as new ideas, methods, and information lead to new experiences and expectations. Technology is a wonder that has become the norm. It can also be described as a work in progress, because it is always changing to better serve its users.

There are a number of ways in which physical and health educators can implement technology in their classrooms. Technology can be used by teachers to increase student motivation, make both assessment and grade keeping easier, develop rubrics, access information, compile individual student and class reports, and prepare newsletters, among other uses. Using technology to assess and inform students about physical fitness is an integral part of helping them understand health-related fitness concepts. The health and physical educator needs to employ strategies the students will enjoy and use, such as a digital camera to take pictures of a health career day, heart rate monitors to teach about heart rate zones, pedometers to encourage students to move more, or nutrition software to track and analyze daily food intake. If students find no value in something, they will have little interest in it.

Another way to use technology in the classroom is to have students obtain and provide factual information regarding topics such as disease prevention, human growth and development, and mental health. In fact, the intent of standard three of the National Health Education Standards (Centers for Disease Control and Prevention, 2009) is to prepare the student to demonstrate the ability to access good information, products, and services to improve health. One way to facilitate student learning in meeting this standard and also infuse technology into the health education classroom is to teach the skills needed to select valid websites. The teacher should facilitate learning about how to access resources, including but not limited to using information from various websites. However, before using the information from the websites it is important to teach how to make sure the websites are valid. The last few letters of the **uniform resource locator (URL)** can supply information as to whether the site is a commercial website (.com), a nonprofit organization (.org), an educational institution (.edu), a network (.net), and so on. The website may include information such as when it was

last updated, the author's qualifications, the purpose of the website, and at least one method of contacting the website author. These are important in evaluating the validity of a website. Any teacher, but especially one who teaches students at the elementary level, needs to find and evaluate specific thematic websites before using them with students. The teacher should present them to the students to facilitate learning about how to validate a website, which will enable students to examine examples of specific aspects of website validity.

Purchasing physical education and health education technology tools to use with students is another option for teachers. Tools such as pedometers, activity monitors, heart rate monitors, body mass index (BMI) calculators, treadmills, and Dance Dance Revolution (DDR), Wii, X-Box, and most other interactive game software will motivate and enhance teaching and learning, making it authentic, interesting, and fun. Use of tools such as these can lead to lessons designed around goal setting and decision making, developing and maintaining personal fitness plans, and helping students learn how to stay fit and live a health-enhancing lifestyle. Students should be educated on how to take the information gathered from the technology and analyze it to improve their personal fitness and wellness plan at regular intervals. Self-advocacy and the ability to access information are extremely important skills in both health and physical education. If the physical education teacher does not receive a budget to use for physical education tools, there are still ways to raise funds to purchase different types of technology. Writing grants, making connections with school business partners, and searching for businesses to make equipment or financial donations can all help to add technology to any program. Purchasing equipment from online auction websites is a great way to spend very little money on equipment that can help get your students moving.

Interactive video games, like those for the Wii and Xbox, are yet another way to use technology in physical education and health education classes. In addition to the video game console and a marketed CD game, all that is needed is a television or large monitor with an **A/V port**. The game cable plugs into the A/V port, and the game is ready to be used. This technology can usually be used by one or two students at a time, or an entire class following the actions on a screen. This kind of technology, because it is fun and interesting, can also be used as a reward as a classroom management tool to help improve student behavior. Another benefit to video games is that because the students have had the opportunity to learn how to use this technology, they may use it at home instead of sitting and playing other kinds of video games that may reinforce an unhealthy, sedentary lifestyle.

Interactive video games, also referred to as **active gaming technology** (e.g., DDR, Step Mania, iDance), can be used in conjunction with physical education classes to offer the student the opportunity to be active most days of the week throughout the year. This is important in districts where students do not have physical education every day because of scheduling. Using these interactive technologies can also help students advocate for better health with family members and friends. The benefits of using active gaming technology include a steady increase in heart rate and step counts during a physical education class as well as a "persistence to game" mentality while playing the game (Mears & Hansen, 2009). By using active gaming technology, a physical educator can involve students in an activity that is fun and challenging, and differs from a traditional sport skill activity.

In addition to active gaming technology, music is a popular way to motivate students to participate in physical education or health

education class. Music can be used both before and during the physical education or health class for a warm-up or to motivate students. Teachers can purchase and download songs from iTunes or another site to be put on an MP3 player for a dance class or a health lesson on a particular topic mentioned in the song. Using a remote control with the MP3 player allows the teacher to change songs from any vantage point in the gymnasium.

■ INTERDISCIPLINARY USES OF TECHNOLOGY

Teachers can also use technology to integrate health and physical education with other disciplines. When providing a **criteria chart** for a standards-based performance task, students can use technology to present knowledge and skills. If students have the opportunity to integrate what they are learning in health or physical education with music, art, and any other discipline, the learning that takes place will mean more to the student and reinforce concepts from other disciplines.

Pedometers can be used in physical education class and integrated with many other disciplines. Adding total number of steps, averaging daily steps, and converting steps to miles are a few ways to integrate physical education and technology with mathematics. Converting steps to miles can also be used during geography lessons. Students can add steps together and virtually walk to different places around the globe. Social studies concepts can be integrated with physical education by reaching a virtual destination and learning about that country or designated city. In high school, students with access to heart rate monitors can use them to compare the activity levels of people with different jobs based on time in the target heart rate zone during the course of their work. Comparisons by job in relationship to being sedentary or active can follow. Further, middle school students can use technology to present information about drug abuse to younger students and work on health literacy standards while creating newsletters, flyers, or even websites. Elementary school students can use the Internet to research the health problems of people in different parts of the world, during different time periods, to compare health problems and concerns. The connection between science and technology can become richer as the teacher introduces different software programs that analyze the nutritional value in diets, convert physical activity to calories, or analyze sport movement for students.

The following is an example of an actual interdisciplinary use of technology at the elementary level. During an elementary health education class, a performance task was given to students in grades four and five. The students, after receiving information about gangs and gang behaviors, were to provide information to educate others about gangs, their behaviors, and gang prevention. Each student had the opportunity to prove what he or she learned by using any medium within the constraints of the criteria chart. Reports, bumper stickers, placemats, interviews, writing a newspaper article, and many other options were possibilities. Two students partnered together to write new lyrics to a popular song. The students practiced the song and approached the music teacher to find out if it could be recorded onto a CD. The music teacher worked with the students and a CD was completed and turned in for their performance task. The students then performed the song at the end of the year music celebration and educated others about gang violence. The music teacher also provided the students with a CD of the song for their portfolio. Some might suggest that the students did not use technology; the music teacher used the technology. That may be correct; however, the students knew that specific technology was available

for their use and they knew who to contact to access the technology. These students demonstrated to the teacher that they knew how to access the technology service to educate others on how to enhance their health. It is becoming increasingly easier to use technology to create music and even videos. Digital cameras and cell phones have video capability, and the video can be downloaded to the computer, and then played and shared with students.

Rich in multimedia, electronic portfolios are another way to exhibit learning through an interdisciplinary progression over time. Some performance tasks that can be included in electronic portfolios are students videotaping interviews, writing newspaper articles, completing PowerPoint presentations, compiling databases, and other authentic learning opportunities. Electronic portfolios are an excellent example of providing evidence of learning for all in the school community. Teachers can use electronic portfolios to assess student learning, students can use them to prove authentic learning, and parents/guardians can use them to understand the progression and/or depth of learning.

■ CONCLUSION

Regardless of whether one is a physical and/or health education student or teacher, technology is here to stay. Efforts should be taken to become proficient in the kinds of technologies that make your professional, educational, and personal lives easier. Obtaining technology professional development should be a part of every teacher's educational goal, as well as effectively implementing the learned technology in the gymnasium or classroom. Best practices in health and physical education should include using technology. There are numerous ways in which students can use technology, so it is up to the teacher to keep the students informed and challenged. Both teachers and students should have opportunities to learn and practice new technology skills. Turning away from technology and the many possibilities it holds for both personal and professional use will leave the nonuser in less of a position to use modern means to teach and motivate students to adopt and live a healthy lifestyle.

■ KEY WORDS AND DEFINITIONS

acceptable use policy (AUP)   Provides acceptable guidelines for an individual using technology; will differ depending on the provider.

active gaming technology   An interactive video game system such as a Wii or video game such as DDR that provides students with physical activity in a fun and challenging manner.

A/V port   The input/output path on audio and video devices.

criteria chart   A learning tool used to clearly communicate to students what a particular task or assignment requires of them.

uniform resource locator (URL)   The address of a website.

■ DISCUSSION QUESTIONS

1. Why should physical and health education teachers remain current with technology?
2. Would you give your students your home or work email address? Would you allow your students to Facebook or IM you?
3. Why do you think some physical education and health teachers are resistant to learning about how to use technology in their classes?
4. Do you think using music technology helps to motivate and focus students in physical education class?
5. What steps can you take as a future physical education and health educator to limit the number of technological glitches that may occur while using technology during a physical education or health class?

■ REFERENCES

Centers for Disease Control and Prevention. (2009). *National health education standards*. Retrieved August 16, 2009, from http://www.cdc.gov/healthyyouth/sher/standards/index.htm

Mears, D., & Hansen, L. (2009, November/December). Active gaming: Definitions, options, and implementation. *Strategies*, 26–29.

Supporting New PE with Technology

Emily Clapham

Due to the rise in childhood obesity, physical education classes during school hours and physical activity after school hours are becoming significantly more important.

Being overweight is a serious health concern for children and adolescents. The most recent data indicate that in the United States about 16% of children ages 6 to 19 are overweight

(Centers for Disease Control and Prevention [CDC], 2008). Since the 1970s, overweight has doubled among young children ages 2 to 5 years and tripled among school-aged children ages 6 to 19 years (Ogden, Carrell, Curtin, et al., 2006). Technological devices such as **heart rate monitors (HRMs)** and **pedometers (PEDs)** play an important role in increasing physical activity levels.

■ THE NEED FOR PHYSICAL ACTIVITY AND TRACKING ACTIVITY LEVELS

Physical activity and fitness are generally recognized as factors that enhance physical and mental health as well as helping to prevent a number of diseases and other problems later in life (Blair et al., 1989). In fact, physical inactivity is recognized as a risk factor for chronic diseases such as coronary heart disease, type 2 diabetes, and certain cancers. Data from two National Health and Nutrition Examination Surveys (NHANES) (1976–1980 and 2003–2004) show that the prevalence of overweight is increasing: for children ages 2–5 years, prevalence increased from 5.0% to 13.9%; for those ages 6–11 years, prevalence increased from 6.5% to 18.8%; and for those ages 12–19 years, prevalence increased from 5.0% to 17.4% (CDC, 2008). The focus on youth physical activity has led to the creation of physical activity guidelines and recommendations specific to adolescents and children.

Children, ages 6 to 17, need to accumulate at least 60 minutes or more of physical activity a day in order to be healthy (CDC, 2011). This should be a combination of three different types of physical activity: muscle strengthening, bone strengthening, and aerobic activity (CDC, 2011). Muscle strengthening activities include exercises like push-ups, sit-ups, and triceps dips. Bone strengthening activities include jumping rope, jumping jacks, and running. Aerobic activities include moderate- to vigorous-intensity exercises like running, cycling, and swimming laps. These three different types of activities should be done at least three times a week (CDC, 2011).

Other methods of tracking the amount of physical activity include using pedometers to record the number of steps taken each day. Girls should accumulate 11,000 steps per day and boys should accumulate 13,000 steps per day (President's Council on Physical Fitness and Sports, 2002). Quality physical education programs help children acquire some of the required number of steps. Steps that can be counted also include those that are part of recess and walking to and from school as well as those during organized sports, recess, or other physical activities during and after the school day. In some cases, the physical activity that students receive during school is the only exercise they receive all day.

■ ISSUES WITH THE LACK OF PHYSICAL ACTIVITY

Concern about the epidemic of overweight and obese children, and the question of whether this pattern will continue into adolescence and eventually to adulthood, also suggest the benefits of physical activity among children and youth (Sallis, Prochaska, & Taylor, 2000). The Centers for Disease Control and Prevention (CDC) stated that declining physical activity may be evident by ninth grade and recommended interventions to increase physical activity targeted at school-aged children to help eliminate the sedentary lifestyles that currently exist. According to the CDC (1996), nearly half of American youths ages 12 to 21 years are not vigorously active on a regular basis.

The minimum amount of physical activity recommended for adults by the CDC is 2 hours and 30 minutes (150 minutes) of **moderate-intensity aerobic activity** every week and muscle strengthening activities on 2 or more days a week that work all major muscle groups (legs, hips, back, abdomen, chest, shoulders, and arms) (CDC, 2011). Most adults do not achieve the minimum amount of physical activity; therefore, childhood has been identified as a critical period for nurturing lifetime activity behavior. Further, school physical education is a key opportunity to promote active lifestyles. The results from Carrel and colleagues' (2005) study, which included 55 children with a body mass index (BMI) above the ninety-fifth percentile for their age, demonstrated that measurable health benefits were achieved with modifications of the school's physical education curriculum. They suggest that a school curriculum could be effective in improving cardiovascular fitness, reducing body fat, and improving insulin sensitivity. Whether someone is overweight or obese is often determined by using BMI, which is measured by dividing weight in kilograms by height in meters. BMI can be defined as a measurement of the relative percentages of fat and muscle mass in the human body (CDC, 2007). In this study, even a small change in the amount of physical activity showed beneficial effects on body composition, fitness, and insulin levels in children (Carrel et al., 2005).

Schools should take the lead and strive to make an impact on children's physical activity and fitness levels. Schools offer a unique environment in which to influence the area of fitness in that they can develop health-related activities and assessment programs designed to promote proper physical activity and assess the changes in children. Physical education and health education professionals are trained to teach children how to be physically active and eat right. Furthermore, the partnering with school districts should be a part of a public health approach to improving the health of overweight children (Carrel et al., 2005).

Physical educators have the opportunity to influence the activity patterns of children and adolescents through developmentally appropriate instructional programs (Buck, 2002). Historically, there have been assessment and grading issues in traditional physical education classes (James, Griffin, & France, 2005). Traditionally, students have been graded on their attendance and whether they were appropriately dressed for class, not on their level of activity during physical education class time (James et al., 2005). Limited research has shown that **authentic assessment** should be the preferred means of assessment in physical education settings because it capitalizes on the "real" work of the student (Chittenden, 1991), but even authentic assessment measures often do not quantify the level of activity for students.

■ THE NEED FOR TECHNOLOGY IN THE GYMNASIUM

Research demonstrates that the use of Internet assessment tools for health-related fitness allows students to interact with the content and apply their knowledge to authentic tasks (Thornburg & Hill, 2004). Researchers found that technology applied in the physical education curriculum can provide an opportunity for improved instruction and enhanced student learning in physical education (Thornburg & Hill, 2004, p. 54). The use of technology within the physical education program seemed to motivate students to engage with the material presented. The students also expressed positive attitudes toward the use of technology in their physical education class (Thornburg & Hill, p. 55).

The use of technological devices could be used to obtain the data and feedback necessary for a successful physical education program. "Making students accountable for their own nutritional and physical activity habits may assist in changing behaviors" (Thornburg & Hill, 2004, p. 53) and could be the answer to problems with motivating and assessing youth in physical education settings.

The limited use of technology in physical education programs is generally restricted to software and equipment that assess students' fitness or to the Internet as a means to obtain and share information (Ladda, Keating, Adams, & Toscano, 2004). Heart rate monitors (HRMs) and pedometers (PEDs), once considered to be primarily research tools with little instructional value, are now frequently used by students in physical education classes (Ladda et al., 2004). These technologies provide augmented feedback and further instruct the students in quantifying their exercise experience. Both tools are appropriate to use with children (Welk, Corbin, & Dale, 2000).

■ THE NEW PHYSICAL EDUCATION USES TECHNOLOGY

The New Physical Education curriculum, or the New PE, as compared to the traditional program, is designed to allow every student to succeed. To address the growing concern for the long-term health and well-being of Americans, many physical education programs are undergoing radical transformations. In schools where physical education has managed to survive the budget cuts, enlightened teachers are introducing students to new national standards-based activities they can take with them through their adult years. The traditional (old) physical education emphasizes competition and team sports, which has little application outside the physical education class. In contrast, the New PE stresses cooperation and application to physical fitness outside of the school day (Sherman, 2000). The New PE focuses on pursuits that students can use in the real world for fun and fitness, such as fitness walking, inline skating, cross-country skiing, whitewater kayaking, dancing to Latin music, juggling bowling pins, learning to manipulate wheelchairs, maneuvering mountain bikes, balancing on unicycles, and bouncing on pogo sticks. The traditional physical education was geared for the physically gifted athlete. The New PE is designed to allow every student to be physically active.

HRMs and PEDs bring a new awareness of individual physical activity measures and goals and represent the New PE tools. Current research on using PEDs and HRMs, as a part of the New PE, presents many implications for practice in the field of physical education. Using HRMs and PEDs individualizes instruction to meet the needs of all students because activities are focused on time spent in the target heart rate zone and how many steps they are accumulating during PE class time. These technological devices motivate students and build self-confidence because students receive instant feedback about their level and amount of physical activity during physical education class.

HRMs and PEDs also raise the level of teacher and student accountability, provide a more objective means of assessing student performance and effort, and help students understand how physical, mental, and emotional challenges affect their heart rate and number of steps taken. HRMs and PEDs help students achieve optimal and safe workouts. In addition, the teacher is able to build a report for each student to grade their individual effort using heart rate and step data. The reports can be used to validate the curriculum and act as a resource to justify why technology is needed. Grades could be based on how long students exercise in their target heart rate zone and how many steps they take during class time instead of the traditional measures of attendance and skill tests.

■ THE USE OF HEART RATE MONITORS IN THE GYMNASIUM

Heart rate is a key indicator for estimating cardiovascular fitness. The use of heart rate monitors has become more popular with teachers seeking new techniques to educate and motivate students regarding cardiovascular fitness. HRMs were originally used with athletes, specifically runners, and then moved to fitness centers and gyms nationwide. In a private telephone interview with Polar Sales Representative Matthew Zuccarello, he noted that "10,000 schools are using heart rate monitors nationwide." The technological devices are growing tremendously in popularity (Clapham, 2008).

HRMs provide opportunities to demonstrate heart rate changes during various kinds of physical activity, verify palpitation, and monitor intensity of exercise (Buck, 2002). An electronic HRM device allows a person to determine heart rate without stopping and manually counting and, therefore, has the potential to provide a more accurate assessment of heart rate (Buck, 2002). HRMs now come in a new and improved downloadable version. Upon hooking the apparatus up to a computer, the user is able to obtain a printout of the time in which the HRM was worn, depicting the user's heart rate information.

Heart rate monitoring has been identified as a valid means of estimating energy expenditure and intensity of physical activity

with young children from different ethnic and gender groups (Durante et al., 1992). The use of heart rate monitors has also been compared to the use of an EKG (Karvonen, Chwalbinska-Moneta, & Saynajakangas, 1984). An EKG is a test that measures the electrical activity of the heartbeat. With each beat, an electrical impulse (or "wave") travels through the heart. This wave causes the muscle to squeeze and pump blood from the heart. The two methods, HRMs and EKGs, were shown to be equally valuable for measuring heart rate during activity.

It is difficult for physical education teachers to know how hard students are working during physical education class using observation. Some students who appear to be working vigorously may barely increase their resting heart rate and vice versa. Changes need to be made in physical education to ensure all students are working equally as hard and within their target heart rate zones. Some methods that ensure success include switching from the mile run to a timed run and having students set personal goals for working within their target heart rate zones for a certain amount of time during each physical education class.

Caution should be exercised in interpreting heart rate information because heart rate is susceptible to a variety of factors, including the environment, type of exercise, and individual variables (Buck, 2002). Increased understanding of the response to physical activity creates opportunities for interdisciplinary assignments and experiences that contribute to the overall literacy of the students (Buck, 2002). Students whose level of exertion must be controlled to exercise safely can use an HRM for this purpose. Students' use of HRMs in a physical education setting and completion of assignments using the data collected contribute to student literacy in technology.

■ PEDOMETERS IN THE GYMNASIUM

Other technological approaches such as using PEDs and accelerometers to measure the physical activity levels of children and youth have also become popular (Le Masurier & Tudor-Locke, 2003). These methodological advances in physical activity measurement are poised to improve the quality of physical activity surveillance of America's youth (Le Masurier, 2004). A PED is a device that measures vertical movement as steps or counts while an accelerometer is a device that measures vertical acceleration and energy expenditure.

Research suggests that the most significant benefit of wearing a PED may not be its ability to monitor the actual amount of activity in any given day, but rather to provide immediate feedback for participants, serving as a behavior modification tool. Sequira and colleagues (1995) suggest that the PED can be worn without major inconvenience, requires little effort on the participant's part, and is compatible with most daily activities, making it a practical and socially acceptable measure of physical activity in large free-living populations. A study of 400 women—with a mean age of 42.1 and who wore PEDs for each entire day throughout the research—demonstrated significant improvements in self-efficacy, were more likely to be aware of the level of exercise needed to benefit their health follow-up, and were more likely to increase the awareness of their own level of activity (Rooney, Smalley, Larson, & Havens, 2003). This research (Sequira et al., 1995) reinforces the notion that PEDs bring a new awareness of the amount of physical activity to participants.

Using PEDs to assess physical activity level has been validated and is widely used as a research tool (Arizona Department of Health Services, 2003). "Using a PED as a physical activity measurement tool allows for small increases in ambulatory movement to be detected and accumulated throughout the day" (Schofield, Mummery, & Schofield, 2005, p. 1119). A number of studies have validated the use of PEDs in physical activity settings (Beets, Patton, & Edwards, 2005; Rooney et al., 2003; Schofield et al., 2005). According to Beets et al. (2005), the ability to record ambulatory activity in units of time (i.e., hours, minutes, and seconds) is in agreement with current physical activity recommendations suggesting that children should participate in age-appropriate activities of moderate intensity for at least 60 minutes each day. Furthermore, given the unobtrusive nature of the PED (i.e., it resides on the individual's waistline), low cost per unit, and the concurrent assessment of steps and time, it appears that the PED would be suitable for examining various aspects of health-enhancing physical activity (Beets et al., 2005).

■ OTHER TECHNOLOGICAL DEVICES IN THE GYMNASIUM FOR THE NEW PE

There are several gaming consoles that provide physical activity focused video games for students. These devices are commonly used in fitness centers, weight rooms, the gymnasium, or a classroom. These devices include DDR, Wii Fit, XBox, and PS3. Gaming consoles provide physical activity experiences for children and adolescents that are unique. These devices motivate children and adolescents to be physically active through the experience of participating in a video game.

MP3 players, tablets, and smart phones are efficient technology devices to use for classroom management. Music can be played for classes, tablets can be used for the evaluation of students, and cell phones can be used for emergency calls to the office or 9-1-1. Technology is also used through accessing the Internet and school databases and taking photos and videos of student participation. These devices are the future of physical education classes, but one major issue may be that many gymnasiums lack Internet access.

The new web-based Fitnessgram 9.0, produced by the Cooper Institute (2011), provides a technological approach to fitness assessment in physical education class. After the teacher has assessed students and entered fitness testing scores into the Fitnessgram 9.0 online database, printouts are received with feedback on the students' performance on the test or amount of activity. Teachers are able to access their students' information wherever they have an Internet connection. Further, Fitnessgram reports can be emailed to parents and/or students.

■ GRADING AND ASSESSMENT

The issue of assessment and grading in physical education is challenging for the discipline of physical education. Research suggests that there is a lack of accountability and data-driven grading (Sullivan, 2004). Assessment devices used as motivation in elementary school physical education classes include PEDs, HRMs, tablets, MP3 players, and smart phones. Making students accountable for their own nutritional and physical activity habits may assist in changing behaviors (Thornburg & Hill, 2004, p. 53) and could be the answer to problems with motivating and assessing youth in physical education settings.

There is a growing trend to use authentic assessment measures in physical education (Sullivan, 2004; Clapham, 2008). A large part of grading in physical education is effort-based. How hard students are trying

often determines a daily physical education grade, along with attendance, proper attire, knowledge, and performance. HRMs and PEDs can be used for authentic assessment because they measure the real work of the student by way of their heart rate and actual steps taken. Tablets, MP3 players, and smart phones also can be used for authentic assessment as assessment data can be recorded and stored as the student is performing the task during physical education.

■ CONCLUSION

There are many advantages to the use of HRMs, PEDs, and other devices in physical education settings, including physical education lessons, interdisciplinary lessons, and assessment. The use of HRMs and PEDs in physical education contributes to the New PE philosophy and ensures appropriate assessment in physical education settings in which the actual work of the student is measured and evaluated. Without the use of these devices, authentic assessment would be difficult to obtain accurately and effectively. Physical educators should use HRMs, PEDs, and other technology in their classes regularly and educate students on the importance of using these devices. Physical educators also should use technology for authentic assessment regularly to give physical education accountability and integrity.

■ KEY WORDS AND DEFINITIONS

authentic assessment   ". . . [E]valuates students' abilities in 'real-world' contexts. In other words, students learn how to apply their skills to authentic tasks and projects. Authentic assessment does not encourage rote learning and passive test-taking. Instead, it focuses on students' analytical skills, ability to integrate what they learn, creativity, ability to work collaboratively, and written and oral expression skills. It values the learning process as much as the finished product" (Pearson Education Development Group, 2011). In physical education, authentic assessment includes measuring when students are participating during physical education class activities, not simply during skill tests. Heart rate monitors and pedometers are examples of motivational devices that are authentic assessment measures in physical education.

heart rate monitor (HRM) A device a person can wear that measures and displays heart rate information while participating in exercise. The device has a monitor strap held in place around the chest by an elastic band. The heart rate is displayed on a watch (Buck, 2002).

pedometer (PED) A noninvasive tool that allows for instant feedback regarding a person's activity level. It measures vertical accelerations of the body (steps) and captures a variety of activities that enhance the concept of "lifestyle activity" (Rooney et al., 2003).

■ DISCUSSION QUESTIONS

1. Why is there a need for technological devices such as HRMs, PEDs, tablets, MP3 players, and smart phones in physical education classes?
2. How can HRMs and PEDs be used for authentic assessment in physical education settings?
3. What is the New PE philosophy with respect to the use of technology?
4. What are some ideas for the use of technology that were not presented in this article? Can you brainstorm any innovative and new strategies with technology and the New PE?
5. What are some research studies that should be designed to document the use of technology in physical education or health education?

■ REFERENCES

Arizona Department of Health Services. (2003). Impact of promoting lifestyle activity for youth (PLAY) on children's physical activity. *Journal of School Health, 73*, 317–321.

Beets, M. W., Patton, M. M., & Edwards, S. (2005). The accuracy of PED steps and time during walking in children. *Medicine and Science in Sports and Exercise, 37*, 513–520.

Blair, S. N., Kohl, H. W., Paffenbarger, R. S., Jr., Clark, D., Cooper, K. H., & Gibbons, L. W. (1989). Physical fitness and all cause mortality. A prospective study of healthy men and women. *Journal of the American Medical Association, 262*, 2395–2401.

Buck, M. (2002). Assessing heart rate in physical education: Assessment series K–12 physical education. Oxen Hill, MD: American Association for Health, Physical Education, Recreation, and Dance.

Carrel, A., Clark, R. R., Peterson, S. E., Nemeth, B. A., Sullivan, J., & Allen, D. B. (2005). Improvement of fitness, body composition, and insulin sensitivity in overweight children in a school-based exercise program. *Pediatric and Adolescent Medicine, 159*, 963–968.

Centers for Disease Control and Prevention. (1996). *Physical activity and health: A report of the Surgeon General*. Atlanta, GA: Department of Health and Human Services, Centers for Disease Control and Prevention, and National Center for Chronic Disease Prevention and Health Promotion.

Centers for Disease Control and Prevention. (2007). *Definitions of terms*. Retrieved January 4, 2007, from http://www.cdc.gov/nccdphp/dnpa/physical/terms/index.htm

Centers for Disease Control and Prevention. (2008). *Childhood overweight and obesity.* Retrieved March 24, 2008, from http://www.cdc .gov/nccdphp/dnpa/obesity/childhood/ index.htm

Centers for Disease Control and Prevention. (2011). *Physical activity for everyone: How much physical activity do children need?* Retrieved on June 21, 2011, from http://www. cdc.gov/physicalactivity/everyone/guidelines/ children.html

Chittenden, E. (1991). Authentic assessment, evaluation, and documentation of student performance. In V. Perrone (Ed.), *Expanding student assessment* (pp. 22–31). Alexandria, VA: Association for Supervision and Curriculum Development.

Clapham, E. D. (2008 May). An analysis of physical activity and elementary physical education curricula using heart rate monitors and pedometers. Doctoral dissertation. Boston: Boston University.

Cooper Institute. (2011). FitnessGram 9.0. Retrieved June 20, 2011, from http://www.cooperinstitute .org/youth/fitnessgram/webhost.cfm

Durant, R. H., Baranowski, T., Davis, H., Thompson, W. O., Puhl, J., Greaves, K. A., & Rhodes, T. (1992). Reliability and variability of heart rate monitoring in 3-, 4-, or 5-year traditional children. *Medicine and Science in Sports and Exercise, 24,* 265–271.

James, A. R., Griffin, L. L., & France, T. (2005). Perceptions of assessment in elementary physical education: A case study. *The Physical Educator, 62,* 85–95.

Karvonen, J., Chwalbinska-Moneta, J., & Saynajakangas, S. (1984). Comparison of heart rates measured by ECG and microcomputer. *The Physician and Sportsmedicine, 12,* 65–66.

Ladda, S., Keating, T., Adams, D., & Toscano, L. (2004). Including technology in instructional programs. *Journal of Physical Education Recreation and Dance, 75,* 54–56.

Le Masurier, G. (2004). Health related physical fitness and physical activity trends among American youth. *International Journal of Physical Education, 41,* 48–59.

Ogden, C., Carrell, M., Curtin, L., Lester, R., McDowell, M., Tabak, C., & Flegal, L. (2006). Prevalence of overweight and obesity in the United States, 1999–2004. *Journal of American Medical Association, 295*(13), 1549–1555.

Pearson Product Education Group. (2011). Authentic assessment overview. Retrieved June 26, 2011, from http://www.teachervision .fen.com/teaching-methods-and-management/ educational-testing/4911.html?page=2& detoured=1&for_printing=1

Oliver, M., Schofield, G., & McEvoy, E. (2006). An integrated curriculum approach to increasing habitual physical activity in children: A feasibility study. *Journal of School Health, 76,* 74–79.

Rooney, B., Smalley, K., Larson, J., & Havens, S. (2003). Is knowing enough? Increasing physical activity by wearing a PED. *Wisconsin Medical Journal, 102,* 31–36.

Sallis, J. F., Prochaska, J. J., & Taylor, W. C. (2000). A review of correlates of physical activity of children and adolescents. *Medicine and Science in Sports and Exercise, 32,* 963–975.

Schofield, L., Mummery, W. K., & Schofield, G. (2005). Effects of a controlled PED intervention trial for low-active adolescent girls. *Medicine and Science in Sports and Exercise, 37,* 1114–1120.

Sequira, M. M., Rickenbach, M., Wietlisbach, V., Tullen, B., & Schutz, Y. (1995). Physical activity assessment using a PED and its comparison with a questionnaire in a large population survey. *American Journal of Epidemiology, 142,* 989–999.

Sherman, L. (Fall 2000). The death of dodge ball. *Northwest Education Magazine.*6, 1, 2–13.

Sullivan, E.C. (March 15, 2004). Assessing your teaching behaviors: An introduction to the Teacher Performance Criteria Questionnaire (TPCQ). One-hour presentation at the Massachusetts Association for Health, Physical Education, Recreation, Dance (MAHPERD) state convention. Worcester, MA.

The President's Challenge. (2011). Why these activity amounts. Retrieved June 26, 2011,

from http://www.presidentschallenge.net/
the_challenge/why_activity_amount.aspx

Thornburg, R., & Hill, K. (2004). Using Internet
assessment tools for health and physical education instruction. *TechTrends*, *48*, 53–55.

Ward, P., Martin, B., & Leenders, N. (2005). Physical activity in physical education: Teacher

or technology effects. *Family & Community
Health*, *28*(2), 125–129.

Welk, G. J., Corbin C. B., & Dale, D. (2000). Measurement issues in the assessment of physical activity in children. *Research Quarterly*,
71, 59–73.

Online Education and Virtual Schooling

Swapna Kumar and Erik W. Black

The Internet has permeated almost every teaching and learning environment in the United States today. Not only schools but even courses have websites and many students use the Internet to search for information or to find additional resources to complete their homework. Email between parents and teachers is common, and many students IM (instant message) each other or communicate using social networking applications (e.g., Facebook) while completing assignments and studying for tests. Nevertheless, the concept of studying a subject completely online or taking a course where students never meet the teacher and peers face to face is still foreign and intimidating for most people. Traditionally, distance learning catered to the needs of learners who could not attend school due to other commitments (e.g., family, job) or did not have access to learning opportunities in their environment. In today's fast-paced, technology-rich culture, however, online learning is being chosen by many adults and children as their preferred medium of study. What is online learning? How do students learn in a virtual school?

This article provides a brief overview of distance learning or online learning in K–12 and higher education. It begins with an introduction to terminology often used in online learning, provides some insight into online education and virtual schools, and finally lists some best practices for teaching online.

■ WEB-ENHANCED, BLENDED, AND ONLINE LEARNING

Distance education has a rich history dating back over 100 years in the United States and internationally as a form of instruction for both children and adults. Distance education programs are dependant upon the prevalent communications technology available to the public. Distance education courses were taught by regular paper-based mail, and then radio, television, and video before computers were used. Students living in far-off places would receive materials, gather at a location to listen to a broadcast or listen to it at home, complete and send assignments, and receive feedback from the instructors. Today, all this is accomplished by email and the other communication tools available through the Internet. Because of its expansive power, the Internet has emerged as the contemporary distance learning medium of choice and is expected to increase access to distance education. According to a report by the Sloan Consortium, "over twenty percent of all U.S. higher education students were taking at least one online course in the fall of 2007" (Allen & Seaman, 2008, p. 5).

Classes or courses taught online are referred to by numerous terms: distance education, distance learning, online learning, e-learning, or online education. According to the California Distance Learning Project (1996), *distance learning* includes the following features:

- *the separation of teacher and learner during at least a majority of each instructional process*
- *separation of teacher and learner in space and/or time*
- *the use of educational media to unite teacher and learner and carry course content*
- *the provision of two-way communication between teacher, tutor, or educational agency and learner*
- *control of the learning pace by the student rather than the distance instructor*

Although **online education** refers to instruction that takes place completely or at least 80% online (Allen & Seaman, 2008), educators often combine classroom instruction and online instruction in several ways to enhance teaching and learning. When classroom instruction is supplemented with online resources, an online website, or online activities, it has been termed **web-enhanced instruction**. The completion of a larger component of instructional time and activities online (30–80%) has been termed **blended or hybrid learning** (Allen & Seaman, 2008). Educators strive to find an optimal blend of online and classroom activities in order to leverage the potential of both online and classroom interactions and to address all types of student learning styles.

■ RESEARCH ON ONLINE EDUCATION

Numerous research studies have compared distance education classes with traditional face-to-face instruction. Although some studies found one method to be more effective than the other, researchers who cross-referenced multiple studies (a type of research method called meta-analysis) concluded that there is "no significant difference" because it is possible to have quality online instruction that facilitates learning just as well as face-to-face instruction (Russell, 2001). A review of 68 research papers on online teaching and learning was undertaken by Tallent-Runnels et al. (2006), who concluded that the design and the quality of online courses can be related to student satisfaction and learning outcomes. However, the review also found that there was no one theory that guided the design of online courses in the literature reviewed. The impact of online education on learner outcomes was further highlighted in a recent meta-analysis reviewing research comparing online and classroom instruction in K–12 schools conducted by the U.S. Department of Education (2009). It stated that, "Students who took all or part of their class online performed better, on average, than those taking the same course through traditional face-to-face instruction" (p. 16). It also concluded that teaching with both online and face-to-face components is more advantageous for students than only face-to-face instruction.

Research indicates that online learning may facilitate greater individual student and teacher interactions (Meyer, 2003). Because there is no physical classroom associated with online learning, students who may not normally participate in traditional school settings or who hesitate to interact with the instructor or peers often find themselves able to contribute in an online medium and find it easier to correspond with the instructor or participate in discussions online. The different types of media (video, audio, text, animations) that are used in an online course also serve to make the subject matter more accessible to students with different learning styles or preferences.

■ ONLINE COMMUNICATION

The reduction of distance and the amount of interaction between teachers and students as well as students and their peers is a chief concern for teachers and students in online learning situations (Moore & Kearsley, 1996). Fortunately, new technologies available on the Internet today have made it easier for learners and instructors or learners and learners to communicate. The communications medium is an important component used to maximize the online "presence" of both the teacher and students in a course—how real they seem in the virtual environment contributes significantly to the success of a course (Richardson & Swan, 2003).

Two modes of communication are used in online learning, asynchronous and synchronous communication. **Asynchronous communications** do not happen in real time. In an asynchronous online learning environment, students might post to a message board and have a discussion over several days related to a specific topic. Asynchronous communication removes the restrictions of physical space and classroom time, making students feel less inhibited and allowing students to reflect on and revise their contributions, resulting in the opportunity for rich discourse (Ferdig & Roehler, 2003; Hara, Bonk, & Angeli, 2000). For example, non-native speakers of English can write a response in a text editor, edit the content until they are satisfied, and paste it into an online course discussion. Instructors are able to respond individually to each student, and track the performance or learning of each student online. Educators can also structure asynchronous discussions to achieve certain goals; for example, higher-order thinking can be facilitated by specifically asking students to find solutions to problems or ideas discussed in a course (Meyer, 2003) or providing guidelines and evaluation rubrics for online discussions (Gilbert & Dabbagh, 2005).

Synchronous communications happen in real-time; that is, learners are interacting with each other and the learning environment at the same time. Synchronous interactions can be facilitated in many different ways, using video, audio, and instant messaging or chat applications. Synchronous communication tools make it possible for instructors and students to see each other and speak to each other online. However, it can be difficult to coordinate the schedules of multiple students who are sometimes in different time zones, and it can be problematic to require their participation in synchronous sessions. Activities that involve synchronous and asynchronous communications have to be planned and timed carefully during the development of an online course.

ONLINE COURSE DEVELOPMENT AND IMPLEMENTATION

The Internet allows educators to provide resources and instruction in different formats—video, audio, and visual representations, as well as text. Students with varying learning styles and communication preferences can learn at their own pace and time using whichever type of medium. Unlike a classroom situation, in which teachers can easily gauge whether a student is paying attention or participating, teachers in the online environment have to take steps to encourage students to actively engage with the content, peers, and the instructor to prove participation. Online teachers also have to monitor student progress closely and interact with students to identify gaps in their knowledge. Clearly, ease of access to the online medium and the benefits of integrating online components into classroom instruction are arguments for using some combination of online and classroom instruction in K–12 and higher education. How does an online course function? How can a teacher structure instruction for students who are physically at a distance?

Because online education is "planned learning" it "requires special techniques of course design, special instructional techniques, special methods of communication by electronic and other technology, as well as special organizational and administrative arrangements" (Moore & Kearsley, 1995 p. 2). Online courses often use multimedia and activities that are selected carefully by the instructor and specially designed to facilitate online interactions and learning. Hall, Watkins, and Eller (2003) outlined seven basic components that should be the foundation of online learning design—directionality, usability, interactivity, consistency, adaptability, multimodality, and accountability. Directionality refers to the thoughtful planning of online instruction based on the learning context, learners, and learning objectives. The online content should incorporate basic principles of usability and should have a consistent design for easy use by learners. Further, multiple modalities (i.e., different type of media) should be used to engage learners and to help them interact with online content. Finally, the online content should be adaptable to not only different learning styles and preferences, but also learner abilities, and should include assessment criteria (Hall, Watkins, & Eller, 2003).

The structure and clarity of presentation of content are crucial in an online course if the learner is to understand the content and learn from it in the physical absence of the instructor. Students with no experience of online learning often imagine online learning to entail listening to lectures online or being in an online classroom. Although these are definitely components of online courses, instruction is often asynchronous. A typical online course contains links to readings, video, podcasts, wikis, or other online resources; a space for discussion; a space for assignments and grades; and a virtual classroom. For example, students view videos, listen to podcasts, or read text that is provided online and then respond to a teacher question or contribute their comments on the online discussion forum. They might then meet with the teacher during online office hours in the virtual classroom, or attend a live class meeting to discuss a course topic. Students' access to technology is an important factor to be considered when educators design and facilitate online courses.

TEACHING ONLINE

It often is difficult for teachers to make the transition from the physical classroom to the virtual learning environment. Online material has to be structured differently, activities organized differently, students often need more support, and the time and effort involved can be overwhelming the first time one teaches online. Online instructors have four functions in online courses—a pedagogical function where they facilitate learning, a social function where they create a conducive social environment, a managerial function where they administer different parts of the course, and a technical function where the instructor is comfortable enough with the technology to help the students (Collins & Berge, 1996). To begin with, online teachers have to be skilled in the basic uses of technology and online communication tools. They also need good organizational skills and have to understand the importance of course structure and course pacing for course design. Further, online teachers should not only be responsive to different learning styles, but also motivate students and provide them with opportunities to learn according to those learning styles (DiPietro et al., 2008, Black et al., 2009).

DiPietro and colleagues (2008) and Black and colleagues (2009) make the following suggestions for teachers to model formal communication and manage student interaction in the online environment:

- Monitor venues of public communication in the course. This helps to identify students in personal crisis, or to identify and address inappropriate and abusive behavior of students.
- Model "formal" online communication and monitor their own tone or emotions in online forums and emails.
- Provide timely feedback to maintain students' motivation in the course.
- "Encourage and support communication between students " and "facilitate the formation of community by encouraging content and non-content related

conversations among students" (Black et al., p. 16).

In order to increase students' engagement with the course content and assess their learning, online teachers can:

- Build in course components to reflect the interests of students enrolled in the course
- Use multiple strategies to form relationships that support rich interactions with students
- Motivate students by clearly organizing and structuring content
- Embed deadlines within the content structure to motivate students in self-paced courses to complete course requirements
- Engage students in conversations about content- and non-content-related topics to form a relationship with each student
- Use multiple strategies to assess student learning
- Use alternative assessment strategies that allow students the opportunity to represent their knowledge in ways that are personally meaningful
- Use alternative assessment strategies to accommodate the varying learning styles of their students (Black et al., 2009; DiPietro et al., 2008, p. 16–27)

According to Pearson and Trinidad (2005), instructors have become more comfortable with producing online materials, encouraging students to absorb information from them, and then testing student outcomes based on these materials. There is now a growing movement toward designing an e-learning environment that recognizes how the communicative powers of the Internet support an active and constructive role for learners.

As an increasing number of instructors teach partially or completely online and as new technologies facilitate communications that are more "real life," teaching practices will evolve even further to support active online engagement by learners.

■ VIRTUAL SCHOOLS

Virtual schools and *virtual high schools* are terms that are gaining increasing presence in both households and mainstream media. Although no specific definition exists as to what a virtual school is or is not, the terms are typically associated with a K–12 learning activity or program that uses the Internet or other technologies (Clark, 2001). Virtual K–12 education is a form of distance education. Distance education comprises "formal education in which a majority of instruction occurs while teacher and learner are separate" (Verduin & Clark, 1991).

Although the flexibility of learning anywhere at any time remains one of the main reasons for students to take online classes, certain types of learners prefer the multimedia approach to learning, prefer to self-pace their learning, or prefer virtual interactions to face-to-face interactions. Parents are also increasingly using online classes and curriculum to home-school their children. In the K–12 environment, institutions are usually motivated to establish K–12 online learning programs by expanding course offerings to those unable to access due to geography, disability, or lack of course offering (Mills & Roblyer, 2004; Watson & Ryan, 2007). A prime example of the appeal of virtual schooling is represented by the number of students and parents requesting increased access to foreign language programs, such as Mandarin Chinese and Arabic. Given the shortage of qualified foreign language instructors with specific experience in these languages, online learning offers the opportunity for students to gain access to high quality instructors regardless of their geographic location and the limitations of the course offerings in their brick and mortar high school (U.S. Department of Education, 2007; Watson & Ryan, 2007).

Many states, including Florida, Michigan, Louisiana, and at least 38 others, have commissioned state- or district/county-sponsored virtual schools (Watson & Ryan, 2007). Increasingly, colleges and universities are offering advanced high school students the opportunity for dual enrollment by using the Internet to take college-level courses while completing their high school degrees. States and county regions have used economies of scale by building consortia to offer virtual schooling opportunities to students within their geographic localities (Hassel & Goddard Terrell, 2004). In addition, many public school systems have taken it upon themselves to offer virtual schooling opportunities to supplement educational needs and to reach out to home-schooled students (Hassel & Terrell-Godard, 2004). State-chartered schools and for-profit entities make up the final subset of the virtual schooling community (Clark, 2001). As increasing numbers of students and parents are demanding access to distance education opportunities, the amount of funding allocated to virtual schools has increased along with access.

■ THE FUTURE OF ONLINE EDUCATION

Online education has grown at such a rapid pace in the last 5 years—a 17% increase in online enrollment in higher education from 2007 to 2008 and 21% increase from fall 2008 to fall 2009 (Allen & Seaman, 2009, 2010). Dynamic new online technologies are being developed and are increasingly available free of cost to the public. Online video technologies have already made it possible to see and speak with people at a physical distance, and multi-user virtual environments make it possible for learners and the instructor to interact in virtual spaces using virtual identities.

This article has provided a brief overview of online education and virtual schools—definitions, past research, and the status of online education and virtual schools today. Course design, planned and structured student engagement, and the teacher's role in engaging and mentoring learners will change and evolve based on the technology of the time, but will always make a significant contribution to quality online instruction.

■ KEY WORDS AND DEFINITIONS

asynchronous communication Communication that does not take place in real-time. For example, one person writes an email or online discussion post but the receiver reads it at a later time.

blended/hybrid instruction A substantial component (30–80%) of instructional time and learning activities take place online (Allen & Seaman, 2008).

online education Instruction that takes place completely or at least 80% online (i.e., via the Internet) (Allen & Seaman, 2008).

synchronous communication Two or more persons communicate in real-time with no delay in communication. For example, two people are online at the same time, are logged into the same chat software, and chat with each other.

virtual school This refers to a K–12 learning activity or program that uses the Internet or other technologies (Clark, 2001).

web-enhanced instruction Classroom instruction that is supplemented with online resources, a website, or online activities.

■ DISCUSSION QUESTIONS

1. Conceptualize the practice of online teaching. How do you think it would differ from classroom teaching?
2. Share with your peers one excellent or poor example of how a teacher used online resources or combined classroom instruction with online instruction in a course or class you attended in the past. Why do you think it was effective or not effective?
3. In what way can synchronous communication tools be used to enhance student learning? You can provide examples for any grade level or subject.
4. After reading this article, what do you foresee as some challenges teachers face when communicating with students in the online environment?
5. Can you find and share any examples of a blended/hybrid online course in physical or health education or sport?

■ REFERENCES

Allen, I. E., & Seaman, J. (2008). *Staying the course: Online education in the United States, 2008.* Needham, MA: Sloan Consortium.

Allen, I. E., & Seaman, J. (2009). *Learning on demand: Online education in the United States.* Babson Park, MA: Babson College Survey Research Group. Retrieved February 9, 2010, from www.sloanconsortium.org/publications/survey/pdf/learningondemand.pdf

Allen, I. E., & Seaman, J. (2010). *Class differences: Online education in the United States.* Babson Park, MA: Babson College Survey Research

Group. Retrieved February 19, 2011, from http://www.sloanconsortium.org/publications/survey/pdf/class_differences.pdf

Black, E. W., DiPietro, M., Ferdig, R. E., & Poling, N. (2009). Developing a survey to measure best practices in K–12 online teachers. *Online Journal of Distance Learning Administration, 12*(1). Retrieved January 7, 2010, from http://www.westga.edu/~distance/ojdla/spring121/black121.html

California Distance Learning Project. (1997). *What is distance education?* Retrieved July 15, 2009, from http://www.cdlponline.org/index.cfm?fuseaction=whatis

Clark, T. (2001). *Virtual schools: Trends and issues.* Distance Learning Resource Network. Retrieved November 14, 2004, from http://www.wested.org/online_pubs/virtualschools.pdf

Collins, M., & Berge, Z. (1996). *Facilitating interaction in computer mediated online courses.* Retrieved January 7, 2010, from http://members.fortunecity.com/rapidrytr/dist-ed/roles.html

DiPietro, M., Ferdig, R. E., Black, E. W., & Preston, M. (2008). Best practices in teaching K–12 online: Lessons learned from Michigan virtual school teachers. *Journal of Interactive Online Learning, 7*(1), 10–35.

Ferdig, R. E., & Roehler, L. R. (2003). Student engagement in electronic discussions: Examining online discourse in literacy pre-service classrooms. *Journal of Research on Technology in Education, 36*(2), 119–136.

Gilbert, P., & Dabbagh, N. (2005). How to structure online discussions for meaningful discourse: A case study. *British Journal of Educational Technology, 36*(1), 5–18.

Hall, R. H., Watkins, S. E., & Eller, V. E. (2003). A model of web based design for learning. In M. Moore and B. Anderson (Eds.), *The Handbook of Distance Education* (pp. 367–376). Mahwah, NJ: Erlbaum.

Hara, N., Bonk, C., & Angeli, C. (2000). Content analysis of online discussion in an applied educational psychology course. *Instructional Science, 28*, 115–152.

Hassel, B., & Godard Terrell, M. (2004). *How can virtual schools be a vibrant part of meeting the choice provisions of the No Child Left Behind act?* Virtual School Report. Retrieved January 7, 2010, from http://www2.ed.gov/about/offices/list/os/technology/plan/2004/site/documents/Hassel-Terrell-VirtualSchools.pdf

Meyer, K. (2003). The web's impact on student learning: A review of recent research reveals three areas that can enlighten current online learning. In J. J. Hirschbuhl & D. Bishop (Eds.), *Computers in Education* (11th ed.) (pp. 184–187). New Haven, CT: McGraw-Hill/Dushkin.

Mills, S. C., & Roblyer, M. D. (2003). Implementing online high school programs: An evaluation study. In M. R. Simonson & M. Crawford (Eds.), *26th Annual Proceedings of Selected Papers Presented at the 2003 National Convention of the Association for Educational Communications and Technology* (pp. 311–318). North Miami Beach, FL: Association for Educational Communications and Technology.

Moore, M. G., & Kearsley, G. (1995). *Distance education: A systems view.* Belmont, CA: Wadsworth.

Pearson, J., & Trinidad, S. (2005). OLES: An instrument for refining the design of e-learning environments. *Journal of Computer Assisted Learning, 21*, 396–404.

Richardson, J., & Swan, K. (2003). Examining social presence in online courses in relation to students' perceived learning and satisfaction. *Journal of Asynchronous Learning Networks, 7*(1), 68–88.

Russell, T. L. (2001). *The no significant difference phenomenon: A comparative research annotated bibliography on technology for distance education.* Montgomery, AL: IDECC.

Talent-Runnells, M., Thomas, J., Lan, W., Cooper, S., Ahern, T., Shaw, S., et al. (2006). Teaching courses online: A review of the research. *Review of Educational Research, 76*(1), 93–135.

U.S. Department of Education. (2007). *Innovations in education: Connecting students to advanced courses online.* Jessup, MD: Education Publications Center.

U.S. Department of Education, Office of Planning, Evaluation, and Policy Development. (2010). *Evaluation of evidence-based practices in online learning: A meta-analysis and review of online learning studies.* Retrieved July 20, 2011, from http://www.ed.gov/about/offices/list/opepd/ppss/reports.html

Verduin, J. R., & Clark, T. A. (1991). *Distance education: The foundations of effective practice.* San Francisco, CA: Jossey-Bass Publishers.

Watson, J., & Ryan, J. (2007). *Keeping pace with K–12 online learning: A review of state level policy and practice.* Naperville, IL: North Central Regional Educational Laboratory.

Research Review

Overview of Current Technologies in Education

Swapna Kumar and David Kaufman

A number of technological innovations and free online tools have been adopted in education in the last decade, and others have been developed specifically for teachers and students in K–12 or higher education. Although there is a proliferation of tools and applications that can be used by teachers and students, not every application or tool is appropriate for every teaching and learning situation. Teachers have to carefully choose the technologies that they find most appropriate to their class, teaching style, subject matter, and students' age level. This article provides an introduction to a variety of technologies that are currently popular with teachers and that have been reported as useful for student learning. New technologies and applications are emerging daily, so it is not possible to make a comprehensive list of all useful applications

in this text. You are invited to explore the resources listed here and to find others using the teacher portals described in the first article in this chapter.

■ WEBQUESTS

WebQuests are interactive online lessons where students navigate through different tasks either individually or in groups in order to learn about a specific topic. WebQuests are an excellent way for students to improve their cognitive skills, to learn to work in teams, and to evaluate and synthesize information that they find on the web. Webquest.org (http://www.webquest.org/search/index.php) is an online portal where teacher-created WebQuests can be found according to topic and grade level. To see some examples of

WebQuests specific to physical education and health, go to http://weblinks.morton709.org and choose the link High School, and then Health/P.E. Other fitness WebQuests can be found by typing "Fitness WebQuest" in your preferred search engine.

■ ONLINE VIDEOS

Online videos are a great supplement to text-based readings and can motivate and engage students. Teachers can use videos to model a certain movement and to demonstrate or analyze techniques and team plays. YouTube is a repository of online videos that is blocked in a lot of school districts due to the noneducational nature of some videos. YouTube EDU (http://www.youtube.com/education?b=400) contains videos from colleges and universities, including useful videos for health and physical education. An alternative to YouTube is TeacherTube (http://www.teachertube.com), which many teachers use to post videos for their students. An example of a video posted by university students for a class project can be found at http://teachertube.com/viewVideo.php?video_id=11926&title=Basic_Basketball_Skills.

Some interesting tools for teachers and students to create videos or slideshows and also share or comment on videos and pictures are http://www.voicethread.com, http://prezi.com, http://www.animoto.com, and http://www.photoshow.com/home/start. An example of a student-created VoiceThread can be found at http://voicethread.com/#q+gym+class.b204684.i1076403. Although this presentation was done by one student, VoiceThread has the ability to have multiple contributors to a single project. One student can post information and others can submit their questions and comments. Alternatively, a teacher could post a video

and ask students to comment, pose questions, or synthesize. One great advantage to using tools like VoiceThread and Animoto is that videos can be saved online and used year after year.

■ PODCASTS

A **podcast** (derived from the words iPod and broadcast) is a multimedia file that can be played on computers, MP3 players, or advanced cell phones. Podcasts can be easily created using a microphone and software like GarageBand (Mac) or Audacity (PC) and uploaded to the Internet. It is good practice to provide a question or points of discussion for students as they listen to or watch online videos and podcasts. Students who are asked to create podcasts feel empowered and are often motivated to research their content thoroughly. Having a repository of podcasts to share with students can be a huge time saver for teachers. Students who are absent can listen to podcast lessons that they missed, and students who were in class benefit greatly from seeing or listening to a lesson multiple times. Also, podcasts offer the benefits of learning from a different teacher and changing the pace of the lesson. Podcasts for K–12 can be found at the Education Podcast Network (http://www.epnweb.org) and TalkShoe (http://www.talkshoe.com/talkshoe/web/talkCast.jsp?masterId=3244&cmd=tc). Podcasts by experts on several topics are available from iTunes through iTunes U (http://www.apple.com/education/itunes-u).

The following websites contain interesting podcasts on health and physical education that can be used with students:

- *Health and Physical Education Portal @ Edinboro University:* http://www

.edinboro.edu/departments/hpe/hpe_
podcast_project/hpe_podcast_portal.dot
- *Maggie's Podcast:* http://kelly05.
podomatic.com

■ BLOGS

The word *blog* is derived from web log, which refers to a "set of personal commentaries on issues the author deems important.... Readers can reply easily and thus participate in a discussion in which they share knowledge and reflect on the topic" (Solomon & Schrum, 2007, p. 55). Blogs are easy to use and provide for an equitable educational experience—all students can contribute and have a voice, and the content is open to a global audience. Blogs can also be personally meaningful for students and expose them to resources outside their classroom. For example, students can use blogs by experts as a resource, or can contribute to the blogs of experts by asking questions or posting comments on the blog. Although blogs can be a great starting point for a discussion, students should be cautioned that blogs are subjective and merely opinions.

Anyone can start a new blog free of cost using a number of blogging tools that are available online, such as Blogger (http://www.blogger.com) or WordPress (http://www.wordpress.com). The creator can set controls on who can read and comment on the blogs, thereby restricting access. Two examples of physical education blogs by teachers are Peaceful Playgrounds (http://blog.peacefulplaygrounds.com) and Physical Education Teaching Resource (http://peat-williams.blogspot.com). An example of a blog that uses different software is Get Your Blog in Shape (http://jhh.blogs.com/getyourblog-inshape/). Blogs on any topic can be found at Technorati (http://technorati.com) or Google Blogs (http://blogsearch.google.com).

■ WIKIS

A *wiki* is a collection of web pages similar to a traditional website but that can be created, edited, and managed by multiple users at the same time. Wikis are popular for collaborative projects, peer editing, knowledge sharing, and community building. Wikis, like blogs, can be created free of cost and can be accessed by students and teachers from anywhere. They can be password-protected or open to the public, and users can be given different types of access, such as the ability to read, write, or comment. Anyone can create a wiki using http://www.pbworks.com, http://www.zoho.com/wiki, or http://www.wikispaces.com, to name some wiki applications available online. A repository of educational wikis is available at http://educationalwikis.wikispaces.com/Examples+of+educational+wikis.

■ WEBSITE CREATION AND POSTING

The tried and true website is still alive and well. Websites are easier to create than ever before with the help of online resources like Google Sites (http://sites.google.com) and Webs (http://www.webs.com). Most online web editors have user-friendly interfaces, do not require HTML (a programming language used to build web pages), provide easy-to-use templates, and can be customized as desired. Google Sites, for instance, is useful to educators because it offers settings for accessing and sharing information online. SchoolNotes (http://www.schoolnotes.com) is another free site that is limited in its functionality, but simple to use if you need to post information in a hurry. A paid version is available with more functionality.

A website-creation space popular with teachers is ClassJump (http://www.classjump.com). Aside from creating websites for use in your classroom, there are plenty of websites that are already created and welcome user-posted content. One example is ThinkQuest (http://www.thinkquest.org/en). This web-based learning community claims to be a safe place for students to "collaborate and share knowledge" (O'Hanlon, 2007, p. 42). This site has a competition where students collaborate and compete against others to create innovative websites. Instead of creating a website with multiple pages, some teachers might want to create an attractive web space where they can embed videos, images, and links for students to use. Free online resources, such as http://edu.glogster.com and http://poster.4teachers.org, are easy to use and also can be used by students to demonstrate their learning or their learning artifacts in a class.

■ LEARNING MANAGEMENT SYSTEMS

A **learning management system (LMS)** is software that enables users to deliver, track, and manage instruction. A popular learning management system used in higher education is Blackboard (http://www.blackboard.com), which recently acquired WebCT, another LMS. An LMS is often chosen and installed by a school or educational institution to integrate the administrative, instructional, and assessment functions of online resources in one place. Moodle, an open source learning management system, is increasingly popular with schools and educators. "Open source software is free software that has its code available to the public for adaptations with certain restrictions. The main restriction is that the new software has to also be made available for free as well. This environment promotes collaboration among developers in attempts to create creative and powerful software" (Wikipedia, 2009). Institutions can install Moodle free of cost to create online teaching modules and applications such as forums, wikis, and databases. Another online learning management system (http://www.edu20.org) provides several options and is popular with teachers and educational institutions.

■ SOCIAL NETWORKING

People share experiences and photographs, and can communicate with each other using social networks like Facebook (http://www.facebook.com) and Twitter (http://www.twitter.com). Although these have become an integral part of our social lives, they also are used by educational institutions for admissions, fundraising, and teaching. Teens use these sites at home to share their artistic creations, to blog, and to remix content into their own creations (Lenhart & Madden, 2007). Social networks are open-ended and constructive in nature and could potentially enhance learning in the classroom by enabling students to create, collaborate, evaluate, comment, revise, and constantly think about the curriculum. Many social networking sites provide the capability to communicate with large numbers of people, making them ideal for educational environments. A downside to social networking sites is that the content cannot be filtered easily or protected easily. Although sites like Facebook and Twitter provide settings that allow the user to limit who has access to their content, other users may not filter what they share online, thus providing access to their materials. Privacy and problems with shared content in social networking sites have led educators to be wary of leveraging such applications in their classes.

Twitter is a social network where people can post messages of up to 140 characters that can be viewed by everyone in their network instantly. Others can then comment or respond to those postings. Twitter grew 1,382% from February 2008 to February 2009 (McGiboney, 2009), leading educators to explore the possibility of leveraging the popularity of Twitter in the "real world" in the classroom. Teachers find Twitter useful to share their materials, ask questions, and share progress. When Dean Karnazes, the Ultra-Marathon Man, ran 50 marathons in 50 states in 50 days, some schools incorporated his feat into their curriculum. Students read Dean's blog to keep track of his progress, and some classrooms calculated statistics daily (Williams, 2006). Now with Twitter, which Dean uses, students can read about Dean's progress and interact with Dean and his followers.

Teacher social networks like Teachers Using Technology (http://teachustech.ning.com) or the International Society for Technology in Education (ISTE) community at http://iste.org enable teachers to communicate with each other about their use of technology in their teaching, to attend webinars, and to stay up-to-date on latest events.

SOCIAL BOOKMARKING

Social bookmarking sites like Delicious (http://del.icio.us) and Diigo (http://www.diigo.com) are excellent repositories for students and teachers or groups to share online resources and videos. Delicious is dedicated to sharing Bookmarks (Firefox) or Favorites (Internet Explorer) with others interested in similar topics. This saves people the time and energy they would spend conducting their own searches. If person A has bookmarked a site that person B likes, there is a high likelihood that A will have other bookmarks on similar topics of interest to

B. Diigo, as the website claims, is a place where people can "Highlight and Share the Web!" Any part of any web page can be highlighted or have comments added via sticky notes. Instructors can use Diigo to share bookmarks. Additionally, they can mark up a webpage to make notes for themselves or to point out something to a student or colleague who shares their bookmarks. The social bookmarking site of an expert in your field is a great place to start when looking for resources on subject matter.

COLLABORATIVE APPLICATIONS

Google Docs (http://docs.google.com) and Zoho (http://www.zoho.com) are examples of collaborative, online applications that allow multiple users to edit the same content from multiple locations. It should be noted that this article was written as a collaborative effort between educators in different parts of the United States using Google Docs. It also can be used in the classroom, as described at http://www.google.com/educators/p_docs.html. Within the Google Docs suite, users can create and collaboratively edit documents, spreadsheets, and presentations. Zoho projects (http://projects.zoho.com) even provides a wiki and chat feature to enable users to discuss their work online while working on a project.

INTERACTIVE CLASS TECHNOLOGIES

Interactive class technologies are a broad range of technologies in the classroom that facilitate interaction between the students and the technology. Interactive whiteboards are a widely used technology today in schools. Information displays on a computer screen, with the added benefit of touch screen interactivity. To see some lessons using an interactive whiteboard, go to http://eduscapes.com/sessions/smartboard/. Also, SMART Technologies, a popular provider of this technology, offers many free education resources on its website (http://education.smarttech.com). Automatic response systems or response interactive systems are another popular technology today that allow student feedback to the teacher in real time. Teachers can ask a question of the students and students enter their answer into the response interactive system (RIS) or "clicker" with the click of a button (e.g., Yes or No; A, B, C, or D). An aggregate of students' responses can be displayed on the screen and students can explain why they chose one or the other answer. Teachers find this tool useful to gauge their students' progress and to decide which topics should be repeated or explained again in the curriculum. Teachers also can create quizzes and polls without an interactive whiteboard using a free online resource, http://www.polleverywhere.com, where students can respond using a website, Twitter (http://www.twitter.com), or text messages from their cell phones.

■ MOBILE COMPUTING

Several administrative as well as instructional applications are available online that can be downloaded to smartphones and other mobile computing devices. Students can maintain statistics and scores, track their performance, and manage their schedules using smartphones. iFitness, Nutrition Menu, and iTreadmill are popular on iPhones; Athlete's Diary, Personal Health Tracker, and Target Heart Rate Calculator are some examples of applications for other types of smartphones. When teaching with smartphones, it is extremely important to establish

rules with the students and to review the acceptable use policy for the school where you work.

■ GAMES AND VIRTUAL REALITY

There are many video games to choose from that are relevant to health and physical education. There are traditional sports games like Madden 2010 (available on Xbox 360, Wii, PlayStation 3, PlayStation 2, and PSP), or there are more interactive experiences like Madden 10 NFL for the Nintendo Wii. The Nintendo Wii now offers workouts that focus on yoga, balancing, strength training, and aerobics. Families can create fitness plans in Wii and monitor their progress. Children can learn certain motor skills, play golf or box, and even manipulate the settings and greatly improve their technique long before they actually play sports in real life. Wii games can also be used for team-building and to teach children certain behaviors. Virtual reality and simulations have been used for a very long time to train athletes to perfect a certain technique or to make decisions, but they are much more accessible and available to everyone today.

■ GRADING/PLAGIARISM DETECTION SOFTWARE

With the ease of writing digitally also comes a big side effect: the ease of plagiarism. It takes but a few keystrokes to copy a paper and pass it off as one's own. In order to combat this and ensure academic honesty, software such as Turnitin (http://www.turnitin.com) is available for purchase. A teacher can attach parts or all of a paper submitted by students and the website will check it against its database of papers, online websites, and journals to compare whether the content of the paper has been reproduced from those resources.

■ FINDING FURTHER RESOURCES

The following websites are a good place for finding additional resources in your field:

- *Kathy Schrock's Guide for Educators:* This repository has been active since 1995 and is maintained by Kathy, who is the Director of Technology in her Massachusetts district. Her resources for physical education teachers can be found at http://school.discoveryeducation.com/schrockguide/health/fitness.html
- *Hotchalk LessonPlansPage:* By no means is this the most extensive resource for physical education activities, but it is a good example of the many free sites out there that come complete with pop-ups and advertisements: http://www.lessonplanspage.com/PE.htm
- *Physical Education Lesson Plans:* This website offers some variations of traditional games. These games are great when students get bored with traditional sports and need something to mix it up: http://pazz.tripod.com/lesson.html.
- *P.E.links4U:* This website contains links to resources, games, and websites related to PE and health, and can be used by teachers in both K–12 and higher education: http://www.pelinks4u.org

■ APPROPRIATE USE OF CURRENT TECHNOLOGIES IN EDUCATION

The new online technologies listed in this article have a lot of potential for teaching and learning, but educators also have

responsibilities associated with their use of these applications. Teachers should be the administrator of groups, or at least the co-administrator, to help monitor online interactions and take action if needed. They should also teach their students how to enable privacy settings for a social networking environment and warn students about spending time on social networks to the detriment of their studies. It is the responsibility of the teacher to help students use the Internet appropriately and safely. Students should never assume that, by default, their information is private. Although there can be many positive uses of all of these technologies in education, it is prudent to set safety guidelines with students regarding what they post online. Some important guidelines include:

- Do not post identifiable information about yourself.
- Do not post identifiable information about others.
- Do not chat with anyone that you do not know (Willard, 2002).

Many schools require a parental release form related to the use of online spaces for learning. It is also a good idea to check if all students have access to a computer and the appropriate speed of connection required to run applications used in their classes.

In this digital age, teachers have many resources at their disposal and have plenty of choices for incorporating technology into their classes. It is not possible and might not be appropriate to use every single technology with one class. Although it is easy to be overwhelmed by the wealth of technologies available, and difficult to decide what to use and what to exclude, it is important to remember that applications that do not correspond to the learning objectives, availability of technologies, and background of students will not enhance student learning. When deciding to use technologies with students, some driving questions should be:

- Does this technology assist me in presenting information in an engaging manner?
- Will my use of this technology foster a sense of inquiry among students?
- Will my use of this technology help in engaging all of the students?
- Will my use of this technology facilitate understanding for students with different learning styles?
- Does the technology help cultivate an environment of collaboration?

More often than not, fellow physical education and health teachers will have already tried to integrate different technologies into their teaching. An excellent way to learn from them would be to explore a teacher portal, teacher social network, or blog online.

■ KEY WORDS AND DEFINITIONS

interactive class technologies A broad range of technologies in the classroom that facilitate interaction between the students and the technology.

learning management system (LMS) Software that enables users to deliver, track, and manage instruction.

podcast A multimedia file that can be played on computers, MP3 players, or advanced cell phones (derived from the words *iPod* and *broadcast*).

WebQuests Interactive online lessons where students navigate through different tasks either individually or in groups in order to learn about a specific topic.

wiki A collection of web pages that is very similar to a traditional website, but that can be created, edited, and managed by multiple users at the same time.

■ DISCUSSION QUESTIONS

1. What are some technology tools that you have used during your health and physical education classes? Describe how they were used.
2. Go to http://www.pecentral.com. Which parts of this website do you consider most useful? Explain why.
3. Visit http://idontgive2centsithrowquarters .blogspot.com/2009/05/are-we-burning-our-children-out.html. What are your views on this article? How would your future students react to this article?
4. Are interactive video games a fad? Is there a place for an interactive video game in PE classes? Should children play an interactive video game system or Wii instead of playing the real sport? Why or why not?
5. Of all the tools listed in this article, which three would you use most with your students, in which context, and why?

■ REFERENCES

Lenhart, A., & Madden, M. (2007). *Teens and social media: The use of social media gains a greater foothold in the teen life as they embrace the conversational nature of interactive online media.* Retrieved August 20, 2009, from http://www.pewinternet.org/PPF/r/230/report_display.asp

McGiboney, M. (2009). *Twitter's tweet smell of success.* Nielson Online. Retrieved August 22, 2009, from http://blog.nielson.com/

nielsenwire/online_mobile/twitters-tweet-smell-of-success

O'Hanlon, C. (2007). If you can't beat 'em, join 'em. *The Journal, 34*(8), 38–42.

Solomon, G., & Schrum, L. (2007). *Web 2.0: New tools, new schools*. Eugene, OR: International Society for Technology in Education.

Wikipedia. (2009). *Open source*. Retrieved August 24, 2009, from http://en.wikipedia.org/wiki/Open_source

Willard, N. E. (2002). *Computer ethics, etiquette, and safety: For the 21st-century student*. Eugene, OR: International Society for Technology in Education.

Williams, J. (2006). *School lesson expands beyond the classroom*. Associated Content Society. Retrieved August 22, 2009, from http://www.associatedcontent.com/article/77350/school_lesson_expands_beyond_classroom.html

CHAPTER 7

Diversity

■ CHAPTER OVERVIEW

If a 12-year-old boy falls down during an activity in physical education class, should a physical educator treat the situation the same way as if a 12-year-old girl falls down? Will the physical education teacher tell the boy to, "Shake it off" while telling the girl to, "Get some water and sit down on the bench until you feel better"? It is important for physical educators and all educators—beginning, veteran, and anywhere in between—to reflect upon, understand, and challenge their own value systems regarding gender and gender bias. Physical educators need to understand how they view girls and boys and whether their previously learned gender schemas will affect how they interact with their students as well as the curriculum they develop. The author of the first article in Chapter 7 explores how physical educators can tailor their behavior, communication, and curriculum to create a gender-neutral classroom.

"You throw like a girl." This phrase has been verbalized inside and outside of physical education class, mostly used as an insult describing someone who does not, for example, throw using opposition, has a weak release, and perhaps does not throw with force. With the U.S. Women's Softball National Team winning numerous world and Olympic championships, "throwing like a girl" should be considered a compliment in this day and age. So why does this phrase exist and continue to be used? The author of the second article in this chapter examines discourses, or the ways in which meanings are made, as she asserts that as a future physical educator, it is imperative for the reader to understand how discourses function and why such an understanding will foster social justice in education.

Understanding diversity is the first step to effective teaching, according to the author of the third article. Embracing diversity will help a physical educator to be more thoughtful when planning and executing lessons, accommodating students' skill levels, and teaching to enhance the way in which students learn, among other advantages. Many teachers tend to teach according to their own learning style, but by understanding students' preferences for learning, a physical educator can be aware of how to adjust for all students' styles.

In addition to framing one's curriculum and instruction according to how students learn and how girls and boys perceive physical education, it is necessary for physical educators to accommodate students' physical abilities. Adapted physical education is physical education that has been modified to provide students with disabilities the opportunity to enhance gross motor and manipulative skill development. The fourth article provides a very helpful primer on the purpose of adapted physical education as well as the responsibilities of a person who teaches adapted physical education.

"Girls Can't Do That": Gender and the "Learning Process" in Physical Education

Donna Marie Duffy

A male kindergarten student announced, "Girls can't do that," during a faculty member supervision visit of a physical education student teacher at an elementary school in North Carolina. It was a surprise to hear this young man's remark about his female classmate, who was clinging to the chin-up bar as a part of the Presidential Physical Fitness Test. Even more disappointing and disturbing was that the student teacher did not acknowledge this teaching opportunity. While driving back to the university, the faculty member began to think about the best way to debrief the situation with the student teacher during their weekly meeting. While contemplating this, she was struck with another realization—someone, something, somewhere taught this particular kindergarten student that females were less capable in a physical environment. In his five short years on the planet, the belief that girls are not as skilled or adept as boys certainly resonated with this kindergarten student.

Kirk (2003) suggests that by age 5 or 6, children understand how to participate in social settings based on their learned **gender expectations**. Some scholars contend that it is in early childhood when children receive the message about how they are supposed to behave and act in physical settings, suggesting that boys and girls begin to believe that boys are supposed to be active and girls are supposed to be on the sidelines, watching the boys (Lips, 1999). Further, Lips found that teachers' behaviors and responses to their students add to the "gender-role socialization" (p. 44) immediately upon entering school.

As teachers, we receive students into our learning environments each day who come from diverse family backgrounds with distinct values and beliefs. Although some of these values and beliefs may be grounded in cultural notions, it is imperative that as a part of their undergraduate and graduate experience, preservice teachers are prepared by university faculty to appropriately guide students to challenge their own beliefs and values. We must ensure that preservice teachers can construct a safe learning environment where children can take risks, experience success, develop new skills, have fun, and question and challenge the stereotypical expectations of their own gender.

The American Association of University Women's (AAUW) 1992 report, *How Schools Shortchange Girls*, was a startling pronouncement of how girls are often disregarded in the educational system and how this translates to significant curricular issues and a lack of educational opportunities. The report sounded a warning bell for educators and policy makers to challenge, change, and reform the educational system so that both boys and girls were equally prepared to live and work in their communities. Some may argue, and rightly so, that girls were being left behind, simply because of their sex. In 1972, **Title IX** was a pivotal educational reform, a federally mandated attempt to level the playing field among boys and girls and provide equal access and resources to all learners in educational settings, including sport and physical activities.

Some evidence suggests there has been an increase in opportunities and resources for girls and women in the wake of Title IX in educational settings as well as physical environments. In 1972, only 1 in 27 girls played varsity high school athletics (Lopiano, 2000). In 1998, that number had increased to one in every three girls and today the number of girls who participate in varsity high school athletics remains steadfast. Further, there has been an increase in the number of female Olympic athletes and female professional athletes since 1972 (Lopiano, 2000). According to the National Federation of State High Athletic Associations, in 2009–2010 there were 3,172,637 girls participating on athletic teams at the secondary level. Kirk (2002) suggests that not only have opportunities for girls and women increased, it seems that in contemporary sport and physical activity environments girls and women now participate in sports that were once considered off limits due to the masculine nature of the sport. However, ample evidence suggests that the participation experience of some girls in physical activity settings is still being compromised due to stereotypical gender expectations and biases, as well as historical beliefs and institutional constraints (Boxill 2003; Constantinou, Manson, & Silverman, 2009; Lips, 1999; Sadker & Zittleman, 2005).

■ THE TEACHER AND THE LEARNING ENVIRONMENT

Two years ago, when supervising a student teacher at a high school in North Carolina, the university supervisor observed a lesson plan that the student teacher created with the assistance of the cooperating teacher. It was an innovative lesson that combined a modified version of handball and Ultimate Frisbee. While the university supervisor listened to the student teacher's set induction, she quickly realized that the student teacher was giving two sets of instructions—one for the boys and one for the girls. The girls were allowed to take extra steps with the ball before passing or shooting. A minimum of 3 feet away was required for the boys guarding the girls. The boys, however, could be "right up on" the other boys. (The university supervisor later learned that this rule meant body contact between the boys was permitted during the game.) Boys were allowed to shoot from half court while the girls were only allowed to shoot within the key.

At the end of the lesson, the university supervisor immediately asked to debrief the lesson with the student teacher and the cooperating teacher. She inquired about why there were two sets of rules—one for the boys and one for the girls. The student teacher did not have an answer. The cooperating teacher informed the supervisor that that was the way "she always did it." Stunned, the university supervisor raised the question about the messages these separate rules sent to the students about perceived capabilities and expectations, and what gender stereotyping they were perpetuating and possibly encouraging among the students in the class with regards to acceptable performance expectations among the students. Because the boys were permitted and encouraged to "get right up on" the other boys, were both teachers assuming all boys in the class were comfortable with an aggressive, bodily style of play? And, did they truly believe that all girls in the class were not able to hit the backboard of the basketball hoop to score points for their team outside of the basketball key? Unfortunately, neither teacher really had a response to these questions. "That's the way we do it here," was reiterated several times. After the conversation, the university supervisor left more concerned than ever about the stereotypical gender expectations teachers promote and encourage in their **learning environments**, perhaps due to the way teachers structure their learning environments as well as their lack of knowledge about gender and **stereotypes**.

■ EXPLORING STUDENT OPPORTUNITIES THROUGH TEACHER REFLECTION

Physical education teachers have a tremendous opportunity each day to challenge their students in the psychomotor and psychosocial realms through the very structure of their learning environment and their learning objectives. In recent years, many scholars have suggested that sport and physical activity environments are important spaces for students to learn and practice their physical skills, as well as explore their affective learning domain, which may include learning objectives like respect for the rights and

feelings of others and good decision-making skills (Hellison, 2003; Hellison et al., 2000; Martinek & Hellison, 1998, 2009; Martinek, McLaughlin, & Schilling, 1999). Although most educational progress is typically measured in terms of student development, when addressing gender and gender stereotypes in a learning environment, it is crucial that teachers explore, understand, and challenge their own value systems, biases, and beliefs so they can understand their attitudes and then teach from a place of self-awareness.

■ THE CURRICULUM

Some physical education teachers develop the scope and sequence of their curricula to focus on teaching their students about how to develop healthy lifestyles involving fitness and physical activity. Although these curricular decisions are all well intended and important, Ennis's (1999) work suggests that physical activity environments, specifically physical education, present constraints that deter girls from developing active, healthy lifestyles because of the imposed structure of the practice curriculum in the physical education environment. Ennis believes that it is necessary for girls to have alternatives in a physical setting if they are uncomfortable with the structured environment due to high levels of practiced and imposed masculinity. However, Ennis cautions, "it would be unfortunate if girls were further socialized to reject sport because it was reserved for boys or because boys refused to let them [the girls] participate" (p. 42).

Cockburn and Clarke (2002) examined the complex attitudes that girls hold towards physical education in the United Kingdom. Through in-depth interviews, the researchers determined that girls were disengaged from sport and physical activity for complex reasons such as a lack of enthusiasm and because the girls did not feel like they gain anything from their physical education experience.

■ PHYSICAL EDUCATION TEACHERS AS MESSENGERS

Wright's (2000) study revealed that some physical educators unknowingly convey to their learners through word choices that girls are not as capable as boys. Wright's study also suggested that male and female teachers use different voice tones when they interact and communicate with their female students compared to when they interact with their male students. Kirk (2002) suggests that the students may not make sense of the change in voice tone initially, but that learning is happening all the time and that eventually students will begin to recognize the different ways in which girls and boys are communicated with and treated.

Although students may not be able to determine why boys and girls are spoken to differently by their teachers, they begin to realize that there is a difference, and from that, they begin to make sense of that difference internally. Physical education teachers are practical professionals who teach movement with a purpose. Physical education lessons have learning objectives that are met through a teacher's explicit instructions and demonstrations. However, the implicit lesson objectives, which are commonly referred to as a "null or hidden curriculum," tend to be unintended student learning that is not accounted for through any type of assessment, but may have a significant impact on the learner and the learner's perception of the physical education environment. Lips (1999) contends that a teacher's choice in textbooks and other curriculum materials sends messages to the learners in the class about gender and social expectations of females and males.

Sadker and Zittleman (2005) also suggest that teachers encourage boys to persist and solve problems in learning environments but encourage girls to ask for help. In fact, Lips (1999) and Bartholomew (2003) suggested that teachers respond differently to females and males in the classroom and are less likely to give girls specific feedback regarding their performance. The creation of this type of learning culture can create "self-imposed stereotyping" (Sadker & Zittleman, 2005, p. 30). Self-imposed stereotyping is a process by which girls decide not to participate in what they perceive as "boy stuff" in an educational setting. This can have a significant impact on female participation in a physical education class if teachers are not critical (Ennis, 1999, p. 31) of their curriculum structure, instructional word choices, and motivational techniques. Due to the very nature of a physical education class, girls may perceive physical activity as "boyish" and choose not to participate. This lack of participation can lead to an overall unhealthy lifestyle and may demotivate girls with any curiosity about movement and physical activity.

The question ultimately becomes, "What can physical education teachers do differently to ensure that their own explicit and implicit instructions and demonstrations do not position their students to meet stereotypical gender expectations?" Following is a list of pedagogical considerations for teachers to reflect on when constructing their learning environments and lesson plans:

- Create rules, guidelines, and learner expectations based on skill level, not gender.
- Establish coeducational teams rather than girls versus boys.

- Make sure that the learning space is not arranged into a girls' space and a boys' space.
- Include a variety of activities in the scope and sequence of the physical education curriculum so learners experience a well-rounded curriculum rather than teaching traditional sports that are characteristically associated with male participation (e.g., football).
- Manage the learning environment appropriately and avoid letting certain students dominate the learning environment.
- When decorating the learning area, include pictures of female athletes as well as male athletes.
- When using professional athletes as examples in the learning environment, include female athletes from varied sports.
- Address any stereotypical gender comments made by students in class immediately, regardless of the situation, and reinforce to the students that those attitudes and beliefs are not appropriate in the learning environment.
- Permit girls, as well as boys, to demonstrate for the class.
- Begin each school year with a values inventory that assesses personal biases and learner expectations. Acknowledge and own them and then use them to make pedagogical adjustments.
- When speaking to students, choose words carefully. Avoid saying things like, "I need two strong boys to help me pick up the mats and put the equipment away."

■ TEACHER EXPECTATIONS AND PERCEPTIONS

Many physical education teachers have an "understanding" of how boys and girls are supposed to behave in the learning environment based on their own learned, stereotypical gender expectations. Girls are supposed to be passive, docile, and noncompetitive, whereas the boys are expected to be aggressive and physical. This type of "understanding" of performance based on gender bias is what sets up inaccurate expectations for all students, and consequently may lead to inexact understanding from one gender to the other.

In one study by Lirgg (1993), findings suggested that stereotypical gender expectations and behaviors among the teachers and students were most prevalent in coeducational physical education settings. Given the qualities and characteristics encouraged through structured sport and physical activity by teachers and other learners, like strength, skill, aggressiveness, and assertiveness, there are bound to be perceived contradictions on behalf of the female in the class, if not outright confusion. These contradictions and confusion may lead the girls in the class to become frustrated and anxious, and consequently not interested in physical activity. What may compound matters further is the image that the physical educator portrays, regardless of their sex. Sherlock (1987) found that female physical education teachers may portray masculine characteristics, which may be even more confusing to a female learner in her physical education class.

It has been suggested by several physical education scholars that girls are marginalized, and in some extreme cases completely alienated, in the physical education environment (Constantinou et al., 2009; Ennis, 1999). Research scholars have also found that although some physical education teachers encourage girls to be active in physical education settings, the encouragement is often fleeting because the physical environment is frequently controlled by the dominant male athletes, to the point where even the teachers question their own management of the teaching environment. Ennis (1999) encourages physical education teachers to "think reflectively and critically about girls' experiences in physical education as essential as we work to create spaces where they can overcome traditional societal role constraints and construct an identity that includes an active, healthy lifestyle" (p. 31).

■ RETHINKING THE PHYSICAL EDUCATION LEARNING ENVIRONMENT

One of the main concerns of university faculty in preparing physical education teachers is to identify the ways in which teachers explicitly and implicitly support and reinforce stereotypical gender expectations in their structured learning environments and how these factors become lived pedagogy. Although some may argue that stereotypical gender behaviors come from somewhere, it is important that teachers begin to diffuse stereotypical gendered learning expectations for their students and begin to base their learning constructs around skill levels, fitness levels, and the fun factor. Teachers need to begin to view their students as individuals with different capabilities that are influenced by parents, older siblings, peers, opportunities, and resources rather than gender and learned expectations of what a boy can or should supposedly do and what a girl can or should supposedly do. We are all familiar with the third grade girl who can outrun all of the boys in the class. And we all know the tenth grade boy who would rather sit in the bleachers during his physical education class than participate.

Physical education teachers need to be consistently challenged by colleagues and students to examine their own biases, beliefs, and expectations. There will come a time in all physical educators' careers when they are autonomous decision makers regarding their curriculum and the structure of their learning environment. Therefore, it is imperative that physical education teachers make gender training an important part of their continuous professional development. When physical education teachers attend their local, state, or national professional conferences, it is important that they attend sessions that address topics such as gender and equality in physical activity settings.

■ KEY WORDS AND DEFINITIONS

gender expectations Beliefs about ability based on gender.
learning environment A socially constructed space where the learners and teachers participate in a structured context based on previously established rules and expectations.
stereotype A belief that has been normalized in society, usually about a person or a group of people that embody a certain image.
Title IX An educational reform act passed in 1972 that required all programs and schools receiving federal monies to ensure that all persons, regardless of race or gender, have equitable access and resources in educational settings.

■ DISCUSSION QUESTIONS

1. Have any of your biases and beliefs negatively impacted a student or your expectations for that student?
2. Re-examine the list of pedagogical considerations. Can you add any other teaching considerations to the list? Should

there be separate considerations for the elementary, middle, and secondary education levels?

3. Have you ever created a separate set of performance-based rules for the female and male learners in your class? If so, would you do anything differently now?

4. If you were asked to present a seminar at a local conference, what instructional information would you include for your participants on eliminating bias and inaccurate gender expectations for their learners in physical education settings?

5. Do you have any stereotypes of boys and girls in physical education?

■ REFERENCES

American Association of University Women. (1992). *How schools shortchange girls.* Retrieved July 17, 2011, from http://www .aauw.org/research/upload/hssg.pdf

Bartholomew, C. G. (2003). Examining our beliefs about gender. In C. G. Bartholomew (Ed.), *Gender sensitive therapy: Principles and practices* (pp. 45–55). Prospect Heights, IL: Waveland Press.

Boxill, J. (2003). Title IX and gender equity. In J. Boxill (Ed.), *Sports ethics: An anthology* (pp. 254–261). Malden, MA: Blackwell.

Cockburn, C., & Clarke, G. (2002). "Everybody's looking at you!": Girls negotiating the "femininity deficit" they incur in physical education. *Women's Studies International Forum, 25*(6), 651–665.

Constantinou, P., Manson, M., & Silverman, S. (2009). Female students' perceptions about gender-role stereotypes and their influence on attitude towards physical education. *Physical Educator, 66*(2), 85–96.

Ennis, C. (1999). Creating a culturally relevant curriculum for disengaged girls. *Sport, Education and Society, 4*(1), 31–49.

Hellison, D. (2003). *Teaching responsibility through physical activity.* Champaign, IL: Human Kinetics.

Hellison, D., Cutforth, N., Kullusky, J., Martinek, T., Parker, M., & Steihl, J. (2000). *Youth development and physical activity: Linking universities and communities.* Champaign, IL: Human Kinetics.

Kirk, D. (2002). Physical education: A gendered history. In D. Penney (Ed.), *Gender and physical education: Contemporary issues and future directions* (pp. 24–39). New York: Routledge.

Kirk, D. (2003). Student learning and the social construction of gender in sport and physical education. In S. J. Silverman & C. D. Ennis (Eds.), *Student learning in physical education: Applying research to enhance instruction* (2nd ed.) (pp. 67–81). Champaign, IL: Human Kinetics.

Lips, H. (1999). Gender-role socialization: Lessons in femininity. In C. Forden, A. Hunter, & B. Burns (Eds.), *Reading in the psychology of women: Dimensions of the female experience* (pp. 38–47). Boston: Allyn and Bacon.

Lirgg, C. D. (1993). Effects of same-sex versus coeducational physical education on the self-perceptions of middle school and high school students. *Research Quarterly for Exercise and Sport Science, 11*, 31–46.

Lopiano, D. A. (2000). Modern history of women in sports: Twenty five years of Title IX. *Clinical Sports Medicine, 19*(2), 163–173.

Martinek, T., & Hellison, D. (1998). Values and goal setting with underserved youth. *Journal of Physical Education, Recreation and Dance, 69*(7), 47–52.

Martinek, T., & Hellison, D. (2009). *Youth leadership in sport and physical education.* New York: Palgrave Macmillan Press.

Martinek, T., McLaughlin, D., & Schilling, T. (1999). Teaching responsibility beyond the gym. *Journal of Physical Education, Recreation and Dance, 70*(6), 59–65.

National Federation of State High School Athletic Associations. Retrieved July 18, 2011, from http://www.nfhs.org/content.aspx? id=3282

Sadker, D., & Zittleman, K. (2005). Gender bias lives, for both sexes. *Education Digest, 70*(8), 27–30.

Sherlock, J. (1987). Issues of masculinity and femininity in British physical education. *Women's Studies International Forum, 10(4)*, 443–451.

Wright, J. (2000). Bodies, meanings and movement: A comparison of the language of a physical education lesson and a Feldenkrais movement class. *Sport, Education and Society*, 5(1), 35–50.

What Is Discourse? A Discussion on Discourse, Social Norms, and Physical Education

Melissa C. Wiser

"You throw like a girl." Although the statement appears simple, its social power is vast and complex. Those who say and those who are the recipients of this comment know it is an insult; it is a negative assessment of someone's athleticism. Yet, nowhere in the phrase is there an explicit critique of one's skills. Instead, one is compared to a young female. "You throw like a girl" is an instructive statement that reveals a great deal about gender relations in U.S. society. An analysis of discourse offers students as well as instructors a critical lens with which to assess what social dynamics are present and perpetuated through such phrases as "You throw like a girl."

As a student and a future physical educator, it is imperative for the reader to understand how discourses function, and such an understanding will foster social justice in education. MacDonald, Abbott, Knez, and Nelson (2009) claim, "[i]t is long overdue for physical educators to understand the implications of cultural diversity for their practices" (p. 16). They demand that physical educators "have the skills to analyze the discourses that create crises, quick fixes, and idealized citizenships" (p. 16). Instructors should not oversimplify diversity because they are complex concepts. Oversimplification will not generate meaningful change; it will only obfuscate the issues.

This article is an introduction to the concept of *discourse*; it is not intended to be a definitive piece on the topic. It pulls extensively from the works of Michel Foucault and Judith Butler in order to explain the concepts because their individual works have been highly influential within discursive analysis. Through a basic understanding of discourse, students will be able to start to read and to engage with more complex theorizing and to respond to MacDonald et al.'s challenge. These steps will foster students' abilities to continue to minimize the theory/praxis divide that remains in physical education. First, this article explains discourse, and then relates the concept to *norms*. Finally, there is a relevant example in physical education and sport that illustrates the way to read how discourses operate. There are no solutions included in this article. The extended aim of this piece is to foster creative and insightful conversations. Absolute, or perceived to be absolute, solutions could bring brainstorming to a halt. The reader should follow up on this article and actively engage in on-going dialogues to develop new ideas and approaches. It is essential for even the most concrete thinkers to take part in critical and theoretical dialogues. The discussion questions and extension activity could trigger such conversations.

■ WHAT ARE DISCOURSES?

Discourses are the ways in which meanings are made. Mary Hawkesworth describes discourse as "statements, concepts, categories, and beliefs that are specific to particular sociohistorical formations" (2006, p. 70). These include the structure of language, bodily comportment, the media, and social practice. Discourse is never a standalone tangible object, a statement, or any one idea; it is a system of meaning specific to a particular time and place. Pirkko Markula and Richard Pringle (2006), in a text that details Foucault's central theories and their application within sport studies, *Foucault, Sport and Exercise: Power, Knowledge and Transforming the Self*, describe discourses as a "way of knowing" (p. 31). Discourses frame how one understands or recognizes an object, a thought, a person, and the like, and are processes that often go unacknowledged during daily life.

For example, the symbol for a public restroom operates within discourse. Currently in the United States, the outline of a person with two legs indicates a men's public restroom and the outline of a person wearing a skirt indicates a women's public restroom. One who is already familiar with these facilities will likely instantly understand the meaning of the signs and the function of the rooms behind the doors with the signs. The signs designate more, however, than just men's and women's rooms. For example, they represent that human waste should be contained in public, because bathrooms are behind closed doors; that there are only two sexes to choose from, because there are only two rooms; that the sexes should be separate, because there are two distinct rooms; and that femininity is a female attribute, because the skirt is used as a marker of the female sex. Such restroom signs are not as simple as they first appear.

Although the recognition of a symbol's function is an aspect of understanding how discourses operate, one must dig further and engage with language and objects in order to assess what is often overlooked in daily life. Foucault (1972) advises that discourses should not be treated "as groups of signs" (p. 49), which is how the example of the public restrooms currently remains. According to Foucault (1972), discourse is a practice that consists of a "group of *rules*" (p. 46, emphasis in original). He continues and claims that discourses are "practices that systematically form the objects of which they speak. Of course, discourses are composed of signs; but what they do is more than use the signs to designate things. It is this *more* that renders them irreducible to the language . . . and to speech" (1972, p. 49, emphasis in original). Thus, discourse is a complex concept that this author cannot describe within the confines of language, let alone this article. It is then important to consider even further how the restroom signs function. The symbols designate numerous things, like bodily needs and social expectations about gender conformity. People must learn to place themselves within the discourse of gender to go to the bathroom. So recognition and understanding of the symbols perpetuate meanings.

The signs themselves, however, do not have meaning. They are simply drawings, but society invests meaning in regards to appropriate social behavior in the signs.

Markula and Pringle (2006) provide the productive example of the soccer ball to demonstrate how discourses may operate in a sporting environment. A soccer ball does not have meaning as a "soccer ball," as opposed to any other spherical object or ball, without the existence of soccer and those who accept that the object is indeed a "soccer ball." Those looking at the ball must already be familiar with the idea of "soccer." Those who recognize the ball did not create soccer, nor did they create soccer discourse. Rather, soccer discourses act on and through the ball. They existed prior to the recognition of the ball. Similarly, a soccer player cannot identify as "a soccer player" without the soccer discourses already present.

■ HOW DO DISCOURSES RELATE TO SOCIAL NORMS?

Perhaps the reader is by now eager to understand how this concept of discourse relates to social norms. In the preceding section, the soccer ball illustrates an example of the way in which discourses may relate to objects. To take this concept further, one must be aware that soccer discourses are not limited to the mechanics of the game. Instead, discourses of masculinity, femininity, professionalism, amateurism, health, and so on all act on and through the soccer player. There are multiple and competing discourses within soccer. Of particular interest at this moment are the discourses that relate to social strata and identity. Discourse may relate to social issues through norms. **Norms** are societal expectations of how one is supposed to be or to act; a norm is that which is considered to

be normal and therefore acceptable. Norms generally refer to expectations in regards to race, class, gender, sex, sexuality, ability, religion, and so on in social analyses.

Norms function as regulators in society, meaning people try to adhere to norms in order to be recognized and accepted. The decision to follow norms may not be a conscious one. Butler (1993) notes that "the discursive condition of social recognition *precedes and conditions* the formation of the subject" (pp. 225–226, emphasis in original). A subject does not exist as a definable entity until recognized by another subject. Butler explains, "Indeed, I can only say 'I' to the extent that I have first been addressed, and that address has mobilized my place in speech" (p. 225). One follows norms in order to be an active individual within society, and the following of norms permits society to recognize the individual.

A subject can only be recognized as feminine or masculine in relation to already present gender expectations. Butler explains that the "citation of the gender norm is necessary in order to qualify as a 'one,' to become viable as a 'one,' where subject-formation is dependent on the prior operation of legitimating gender norms" (1993, p. 232). Not only must an "I" be recognized to be brought into discourse, but an "I" must follow gender norms in order to be a subject. "Femininity is thus not the product of a choice, but the forcible citation of a norm" (Butler, 1993, p. 232). No one can choose to be genderless. Can the reader imagine a person with no gender? Societal discourses demand adherence to gender norms, which individuals attempt to fulfill, and, as a result, perpetuate.

Gender discourses, however, are not the only discourses that act on an individual. Kimberle Crenshaw, José Esteban Muñoz, and numerous other cultural and social scholars demonstrate that identity is not compiled of singular categories; those in minority groups do not have more categories than whites, for example. Race, gender, class, and sexuality are present for everyone, even if unnamed. Crenshaw's (1991) influential work concerning the multifaceted structure of identity highlights the complexity of identity. She claims "that the intersection of racism and sexism factors into Black women's lives in ways that cannot be captured wholly by looking at the race or gender dimensions of those experiences separately" (p. 1244). She demonstrates through her theory of **intersectionality** that race, class, gender, and the like operate simultaneously so that one cannot separate a gendered experience from a racial one from a sexuality one. Intersectionality, therefore, calls for a complex understanding of the subject's identity and subjectivity.

Muñoz (1999) importantly asserts that one cannot just include race and ethnicity. Discourses of difference do not act alone; they influence other discourses as they interact with them. Multiple discourses of gender, race, sexuality, and so on intersect with each other. In addition, there is not one gender discourse, one race discourse. Specifically in regards to "sex," Foucault notes that "we are dealing less with *a* discourse on sex than with a multiplicity of discourses produced by a whole series of mechanisms operating in different institutions" (1990, p. 33). Therefore, it is imperative to remember not to overgeneralize and assume that discourses act on all individuals identically or that all individuals within a community are identical because of similar discourses.

■ WHY ARE DISCOURSES IMPORTANT TO PHYSICAL EDUCATION?

Currently in U.S. sport, many participants would likely understand the phrase, "You throw like a girl," and its counterpart, "You could play with the boys." When these statements are uttered, they function within discourse. They are productive examples to illustrate how seemingly simple statements are indeed complex. In order to assess how these statements operate, the appropriate questions one should ask are: What is already understood or assumed in order for the statements to make sense? What social rules enabled these statements to appear? What is the known intent of the statements? What is the outcome, or what is continued through the usage of these statements? What is at stake for different identities? Remember, the statement is like a symbol and a sign. It is not the statement itself that is necessarily relevant; it is how it functions or how it is used.

Men's bodies are considered the norm within U.S. sports. Numerous discourses of men's athletic superiority precede the usage of the statement, "You throw like a girl." For instance, when one speaks about sports, it is assumed the topic of conversation is men's athletics. The phrase is often used in social analyses as an example of women's position in athletics. To begin, it is generally intended as negative or demeaning. To "throw like a girl" is to throw worse than the unmentioned superior thrower or that of a boy. To convey that one is discussing women's athletics, one specifies "women's basketball." The National Basketball Association versus the Women's National Basketball Association is a telling example. Men's athletic superiority is assumed. When "you could play with the boys" functions as a compliment, it also highlights these assumptions. Therefore, to resemble a woman, or even worse a girl, is an indicator of athletic weakness.

In addition to relating to skill and performance, "You throw like a girl" implies certain conceptions of sex, gender, race, and sexuality. An intersectional analysis, or an analysis that uses intersectionality, is relevant here. The recipient of the insult may be a girl or a boy, a woman or a man. When directed towards a man, it implies that he is somehow not masculine enough in his athleticism and, therefore, inferior to more masculine-appearing throwers. A masculine man is normal, and a feminine man is abnormal and undesirable. The undesirability of a feminine man is connected to homophobia within athletics. Eric Anderson (2005) claims that within sports men maintain *hyper*masculinity in order to combat homophobia and accusations of homosexuality. Therefore, the insult carries more weight than just a jab at someone's skill level.

When the comment is directed towards a woman, it is understood among women that it is not acceptable to perform like a woman, or how it is assumed a woman would perform, if she wants to be skilled in athletics. A skilled woman may hear "You could play with the boys," which again points to assumptions of men's superiority in sports. It also places her femininity in question. The comment suggests that she is somehow less of a woman because of her ability. This connection may also situate her sexuality as suspect. Female athletes who are not only skilled but also appear masculine still face social ridicule and accusations of "mannishness." Their rights to womanhood fade as the "threat" of the "lesbian bogeywoman" looms (Griffin, 1998).

Despite the implications that women and feminine persons are inferior athletes, the negative comments do not ban them from sports. Markula and Pringle (2006) demonstrate in their work on rugby in New Zealand that negative comments in regards to women's athletic performance in a male-dominated sport do not exclude women's participation; instead, such comments constrain participation. Similarly, "You throw like a girl" does not say that girls cannot,

or indeed should not, play sports, but it can limit the expectations of their performance. Girls are supposed to be less skilled. These understandings do not reject the existence of feminine men or women in sport, but the statement implies that within society they are not favored in the sporting arena.

Although racial discourses are unnamed in these insults, discourses of normalizing whiteness function in the statements as well. The physically unskilled, feminine body in "You throw like a girl" has been seen as white. Historians Patricia Vertinsky (1994) and Susan Cahn (1994) demonstrate that feminine ideals functioned to limit women's physical activity and participation in organized sports. Cahn argues, though, that African American women's history of physical labor "exempted African Americans from ideals of womanhood that rested on the presumed refinement and femininity of a privatized domestic arena" (p. 127). She claims that white, upper-class ideals of femininity did not apply to African American women in the same way, partially because of the expectation that African Americans conducted primarily physical labor. This historical argument indicates that "You throw like a girl" points to a white, feminine ideal.

Society's attention to the (perceived to be) more physical African American, female body has continued. Jaime Schultz (2005) conducted a cultural studies analysis of Serena Williams's "catsuit" at the 2002 U.S. Open. She argues that "[m]any of the commentaries on Williams's catsuit-clad body reproduce the traditional racialized order in women's tennis" (p. 351). Schultz, also informed by Cahn's argument, concludes that the media's reports on Williams highlight her difference in comparison to her mostly white colleagues. Through the catsuit and its emphasis on Williams's muscular form, the media question: (1) Williams's gender, through comparisons to muscular, men's bodies; (2) her sexuality, through references to her "deviant" (p. 350) attire; and (3) her humanness, through comparisons to the superhero, Wonder Woman. The media construct Williams as different in a manner that questions her rights to womanhood and humanity. Schultz claims "[i]t cannot be denied that Serena Williams is muscular; however, the ways in which muscularity comes to stand in for masculinity affects cultural understandings of female athletes and particularly female athletes of color" (p. 347). Again, the statements do not prevent the possibilities of individuals performing race, gender, and sexuality in a non-normative manner; however, the athletes do so with limited social rewards within the sport community, as demonstrated in Schultz's analysis of Serena Williams.

This example, "You throw like a girl," demonstrates how multiple discourses function within and on relatively simple statements. A remaining question is, does a **hierarchy**, an actual or assumed ranking of individuals or groups that indicates who has power, remain? These discourses of difference are perpetuated through sexism, racism, and heterosexism. The –isms are forms of hierarchy that indicate which social groups are dominant in society. "You throw like a girl" implies a male, white, heterosexual standard in athletics, and the usage of the statement perpetuates that standard.

■ CONCLUSION

One may now wonder how to apply this information about discourse. If everything has discourses acting on it, and everything we say perpetuates social norms, then what are we to do? The idea that discourses always frame language and practice is not intended to render action and activism useless. Instead, an awareness of discourses should draw

attention to the everyday social realities that one takes for granted as "how it is" or "normal." Discourses are not static. Their fluidity and dynamism are evident in how symbols lose and change meaning over time. The symbols that mean something to people today may not have meant anything to individuals 100 years ago. Think about how many women athletes there are now compared to then.

As a future physical educator, the reader must consider this discursive approach in order to engage with cultural diversity. Pat Griffin argues "[i]f education is to live up to its commitments to social justice and educational equity, we need teachers who have an awareness and understanding of how sexism, racism, classism, and other forms of oppression sabotage these objectives" (1991, p. 61). Joy DeSensi notes "[e]veryone in the educational setting (teachers, staff, coaches, administrators, and school boards) is responsible for developing intercultural competence" (1995, p. 42). Thus, all of those in education should interpret discourses in order to be aware of the complexity of identity. First, one should identify what discourses may be operating and to whose detriment, and second, consider these discourses during classroom activities in order to disrupt social hierarchies. Now that the readers have an introduction to discourse, they can begin the thoughtful, involved dialogues that will generate new and creative ideas.

■ KEY WORDS AND DEFINITIONS

discourse   The way in which meanings are made; these meanings are unique to times and places.

hierarchy   An actual or assumed ranking of individuals or groups that indicates who has power.

intersectionality   An approach towards understanding society and individuals that demands that multiple aspects of one's identity be considered in analysis.

norms Societal expectations of how one is supposed to be or to act; that which is considered to be normal.

■ DISCUSSION QUESTIONS

1. In what ways do popular media affect the way we think about and practice organized sport in regards to race, class, gender, and sexuality, in and outside the classroom?
2. How can you extend the "You throw like a girl" and "You could play with the boys" examples in this article to a deeper intersectional analysis to consider social class as well as the existence of more than two sexes?
3. What words do you use to encourage participation in the physical education classroom? Are the words that you use in the classroom different than what you would use as a coach? What is the difference, if any? Why is there one, if there is, and why is or is it not socially acceptable?
4. How should physical education classes be divided? What are the implications of dividing a class based on gender? Who determines who would go in each group? What if a student does not "match" the division?
5. How does the information in this article impact course curriculum? How can you present a variety of activities without marginalizing activities from nondominant cultures?

■ EXTENSION ACTIVITIES

1. Take a day and record the words that you use that reinforce power relations or hierarchies. Do you know what you are saying when you say it? Does it matter

that the meaning you intend does not actually match the meaning of the words you use? What social impact do the words have beyond their immediate usage?

■ REFERENCES

Anderson, E. (2005). *In the game: Gay athletes and the cult of masculinity.* Albany, NY: State University of New York Press.

Butler, J. (1993). *Bodies that matter: On the discursive limits of "sex."* New York: Routledge.

Cahn, S. K. (1994). *Coming on strong: Gender and sexuality in twentieth-century women's sport.* Cambridge, MA: Harvard University Press.

Crenshaw, K. (1991). Mapping the margins: Intersectionality, identity politics, and violence against women of color. *Stanford Law Review, 43,* 1241–1299.

DeSensi, J. T. (1995). Understanding multiculturalism and valuing diversity: A theoretical perspective. *Quest, 47,* 34–43.

Foucault, M. (1972). *The archaeology of knowledge and the discourse on language* (A.M. Sheridan Smith, Trans.). New York: Pantheon Books.

Foucault, M. (1990). *The history of sexuality: An introduction* (Vol. 1, R. Hurley, Trans.). New York: Vintage.

Griffin, P. (1991). The challenge to live up to our ideals: Appreciating social diversity and achieving social justice in schools. *Journal of Physical Education, Recreation & Dance, 62*(6), 58–61.

Griffin, P. (1998). *Strong women, deep closets: Lesbians and homophobia in sport.* Champaign, IL: Human Kinetics.

Hawkesworth, M. (2006). *Feminist inquiry: From political conviction to methodological innovation.* New Brunswick, NJ: Rutgers University Press.

MacDonald, D., Abbott, R., Knez, K., & Nelson, A. (2009). Taking exercise: Cultural diversity and physically active lifestyles. *Sport, Education and Society, 14,* 1–19.

Markula, P., & Pringle, R. (2006). *Foucault, sport and exercise: Power, knowledge and transforming the self.* London: Routledge.

Muñoz, J. E. (1999). *Disidentifications: Queers of color and the performance of politics*. Minneapolis: University of Minnesota Press.

Schultz, J. (2005). Reading the catsuit: Serena Williams and the production of blackness at the 2002 U.S. Open. *Journal of Sport and Social Issues, 29*(3), 338–357.

Vertinsky, P. A. (1994). *The eternally wounded woman: Women, doctors, and exercise in the late nineteenth century*. Urbana, IL: University of Illinois Press. (Reprinted from 1989, Manchester, UK: Manchester University Press.)

Developing a Mindset for Teaching Diverse Learners

Kathy Peno

When you hear the word **diversity**, what comes to mind? Many people immediately think of cultural and racial diversity, and although these are extremely important components, diversity means so much more. Students come to the classroom with many different backgrounds, experiences, abilities, and needs that may or may not result from cultural or racial contexts (Ormrod, 2011). When I talk about diversity in my classroom, I put a visual on the board to help students think more deeply about what diversity really is (see **Figure 7-1**).

By placing a number of circles on the board and filling two of them with *race* and *culture*, students immediately realize there are multiple facets to diversity. *Think for a moment about what you would put in each of the remaining circles.*

My circles include gender, intelligence/learning, special educational needs, language, religion, socioeconomic status, sexual preference, race, ethnicity, and culture. Perhaps you have thought of others. Teaching diverse students can provide many challenges and incredible rewards at the same time. Understanding diversity is the first step to effective teaching. Simply knowing it exists in its many forms will help you be more thoughtful when planning and executing your lessons.

■ DIVERSITY IN THE CLASSROOM

In order to demonstrate how issues of diversity can challenge you as a teacher, two actual cases are provided in the following sections. Although both demonstrate how a student's religious beliefs can affect your classroom, any area of diversity could be substituted. As a physical educator, you may be aware of a student's physical limitations but unaware of a particular student's religion and/or beliefs and the constraints that may affect your teaching. I learned this lesson early on in my career when I worked in a preschool in the summer, and again, as a college professor in a graduate program.

Case 1

When I was 17 years old, I worked in a summer preschool and was in charge of the

FIGURE 7-1 The wheel of diversity.

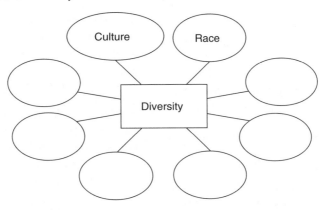

3-year-old children. As a large group activity, we decided we would create a parade for the upcoming fourth of July holiday. We set about making costumes and "floats" that we would pull in wagons around the neighborhood. One day, we were making a "birthday cake" for our nation out of plastic containers that we planned to pull on one wagon. A parent came to pick up her child early that day, and when she saw what we were doing, she informed me that her daughter could not participate in this process in any way. Their religion didn't allow for holiday celebrations of any kind. I was unsure of what to do and asked for guidance from my superiors, but no one had dealt with an issue like this before. I ultimately decided to forget about the parade because I didn't want to leave one child out of the festivities. This decision upset many of the other children who were enjoying the process. *What do you think you would have done?*

Case 2

I have taught a graduate course in adult education for about 12 years. The students typically range in age from about 25–60.

As is tradition, we meet at a restaurant of the students' choice the week after classes end to finish the semester on a positive note and to give students a chance to hand in their final research papers in an informal setting. Most students love the idea (not mandatory) and we have a nice dinner and conversation. One semester, a student approached me and informed me that her religious beliefs prohibited her from being in a restaurant where alcohol was served. Her religion also guided her to be a strict vegetarian. She offered to withdraw from the celebration so that others wouldn't be affected. I took this as a challenge to find a place where all our needs would be met. It took a while but I found a restaurant that was large enough to accommodate us and did not serve or allow alcohol to be brought in by patrons. The restaurant also had a large variety of vegetarian choices on their menu. The food was wonderful and everyone had a great time. *How might you have handled this?*

These two cases demonstrate that, as an educator, issues of diversity can have an impact on your teaching and your classroom. As an educator, I have also had students in class who are visually impaired and hearing impaired. Making sure these students were able to participate in classroom activities and had access to all class materials was of primary importance to me, but challenged me greatly. By simply being aware that issues of diversity exist and must be accommodated, you can better plan and execute your lessons.

This article will focus on the idea that although there are very specific differences among learners, the fact remains, we must think about teaching to diversity of all kinds, all the time, because we may not be aware of all the differences that exist in our students. Rather than looking at strategies to teach to every possible type of student diversity, we will develop a general **diversity teaching mindset** or philosophy.

■ HOW INDIVIDUALS LEARN DIFFERENTLY

One way to think about diversity is in students' learning and in their **learning style preferences** in particular. By focusing on learning diversity, we can take steps to incorporate the needs of all students into a lesson. Sensory learning style preferences refers to the ways in which students prefer to *take in* information via their senses before it goes on for further processing in the brain. Sensory learning style preferences are typically described as auditory, visual, tactile, and kinesthetic (Matthews, 1991). A student's learning style preference can have a powerful effect on their academic achievement in different areas (Gadt-Johnson & Price, 2000; Semple & Pascale, 1984). The following is a general discussion of the different learning style preferences with application strategies for the physical education setting.

Auditory Learners

Students who have an auditory learning preference may not be able to make sense of information unless they hear it presented orally. Therefore, effective strategies to meet the needs of **auditory learners** include lecture, discussions one-on-one and in groups, and debates. Written information may have little meaning until it is heard, which is why some auditory learners prefer to read text aloud and may use a tape recorder to tape lectures or themselves reading text. Auditory learners also tend to pay attention to the underlying meanings of speech by listening to an instructor's pitch, speed, and tone of voice.

Auditory application strategies include:

- When providing instructions for an activity or teaching a skill, make sure they are provided verbally as well as visually through demonstration.
- Repeat instructions if necessary.
- Reduce underlying noise so everyone can hear you.
- Provide verbal feedback about student performance when they are engaged in the activity.

Visual Learners

Those with a visual learning preference learn best by seeing material presented to them in picture form as opposed to text. **Visual learners** may prefer being close to a teacher so they can read their body language and facial expressions to fully comprehend what is being taught. Visual learners may *think* in pictures and learn best from visual displays such as diagrams, illustrated books, overheads, PowerPoint presentations, videos, handouts, and demonstrations. They may take detailed notes during a lecture to best help them absorb the material and may draw pictures in the margin of text to help them summarize what they have just read.

Visual application strategies include:

- Provide a demonstration of and/or model the skill you are teaching while verbally explaining what you are doing.
- Make sure to eliminate any obstructions so all students can see your demonstration.
- Repeat the demonstration several times or as necessary.

Kinesthetic Learners

Kinesthetic learners learn best through active participation in their learning. Their need for movement may cause them to become distracted if they must sit for long periods of time. These learners prefer field trips, exercises, role-play, and other activities.

Kinesthetic application strategies include:

- Engage some students in the demonstration process.
- Allow for sufficient practice of the skill you are teaching.
- Provide feedback so that students can hone their skills during practice.

Tactile Learners

Tactile learners prefer a hands-on approach to their learning. Touching and working with materials, lab experiments, building projects, and the like are preferred to almost any other type of learning. These learners may also have difficulty sitting and passively receiving information for long periods of time.

Tactile application strategies include:

- Engage students in the set-up and tear-down process.

- Provide a variety of materials to teach skills; a bean bag can be used as well as a ball in many activities.
- Make sure all students have an opportunity to participate in the activity.

■ LEARNING STYLES AND INSTRUCTION

For a physical educator to identify and accommodate different learning styles when developing instruction, three strategies have been suggested (Coker, 1996; Sarasin, 1999; Silver, Strong, & Perini, 2000):

1. *Identify your own learning style:* Many teachers tend to teach according to their own learning style, which is not necessarily a benefit to all students. By understanding your own preference(s) for learning you can be aware of how to adjust for all students' styles.
2. *Identify how your students learn:* Use observation, trial and error, and conferences with colleagues to help you accomplish this. Although there are many paper and online learning style inventories or surveys (for example, see the LSI-Dunn; Dunn & Price, 1996) to help identify a student's learning style preference, it may be impractical and expensive to administer them to all students.
3. *Use a variety of instructional strategies:* Although it may be difficult to assess all students' preferred styles, teachers can use a variety of instructional strategies aimed at meeting the preferences of all four learning styles in every lesson.

When mismatches exist between the learning style preferences of most students in a class and the instructional style of the teacher, student attention, learning, and achievement may become negatively affected

(Felder & Brent, 2005; Lovelace, 2005). To avoid these problems, teachers should try to balance instructional strategies as opposed to trying to teach to each student's individual learning style preference. Therefore, some instruction should be provided verbally, some visually, some with simultaneous verbal and visual methods, and then students can be given an opportunity to practice what is being taught (Dunn & Dunn, 1992, 1993). For example, in a physical education class where basketball skills are being taught, the instructor might explain the skill, then demonstrate it while providing verbal explanation, then allow students a chance to practice the skill being taught with verbal and visual feedback provided. In doing so, all four learning style preferences are being accommodated.

With this balancing of instructional strategies for all learning styles, all students will be taught partly in their preferred style and partly in one or more less preferred styles (Reed, Banks, & Carlisle, 2004). This will help students feel more comfortable when taught in their preferred style and will expose them to less comfortable styles, which may challenge them to think in ways they are not used to. This may, in turn, help them to become more comfortable with another learning style. Physical educators who understand the connection between learning differences and effective instruction aimed at those differences can effectively balance instructional activities (Dunn, 1990; Reed et al., 2004). This balancing act is one way a teacher displays the mindset that meeting the needs of all learners is vital.

CONCLUSION

Understanding the depth and breadth of diversity and developing the appropriate mindset about teaching to a diverse group of students will be both challenging and rewarding. By being aware of the potential issues that can present themselves in the classroom, you can respond appropriately to a variety of circumstances. Understanding the differences that exist in students' learning can help you make effective instructional choices when developing and executing lessons to meet the learning preferences of all students.

KEY WORDS AND DEFINITIONS

auditory learners   Those who prefer to learn by hearing information presented.

diversity   Individual differences along the dimensions of race, ethnicity, gender, sexual orientation, socioeconomic status, age, physical abilities, religious beliefs, political beliefs, or other ideologies.

diversity teaching mindset   A personal philosophy or frame of mind regarding teaching a diverse group of students.

kinesthetic learners   Those who prefer active engagement during learning.

learning style preference   The preferred method of taking information from the environment into the senses for further processing.

tactile learners   Those who prefer to be able to touch, feel, and engage with materials used in their learning.

visual learners   Those who prefer to learn with a visual representation of concepts.

DISCUSSION QUESTIONS

1. Given the multiple facets of diversity, what are some of the strategies you might employ when teaching in a diverse physical education classroom?

2. What strategies could you use to address the needs of all students in a physical education classroom where there are students with physical challenges?
3. What is your preferred learning style? How do you think it will affect your approach to teaching?
4. Identify your mindset regarding teaching a diverse group of students. What factors do you think have affected its development?
5. Are there elements of your mindset that may need to be altered? How can you use what you have learned in this article to be a more effective teacher in the future?

■ REFERENCES

Coker, C. A. (1996). Accommodating students' learning styles in physical education. *Journal of Physical Education, Recreation and Dance, 67*(9), 66–68.

Dunn, R. (1990). Rita Dunn answers questions on learning styles. *Educational Leadership, 48*(2), 15–18.

Dunn, R., & Dunn, K. (1992). *Teaching elementary students through their individual learning styles: Practical approach for grades 3–6.* Boston: Allyn and Bacon.

Dunn, R., & Dunn, K. (1993). *Teaching secondary students through their individual learning styles: Practical approach for grades 7–12.* Boston: Allyn and Bacon.

Dunn, R., Dunn, K., & Price, G. E. (1996). *Learning style inventory.* Lawrence, KS: Price Systems.

Felder, R. M., & Brent. R. (2005). Understanding student differences. *Journal of Engineering Education, 94*(1), 57–72.

Gadt-Johnson, C. D., & Price, G. E. (2000). Comparing students with high and low preferences for tactile learning. *Education, 120*(3), 581–585.

Lovelace, M. K. (2005). Meta-analysis of experimental research based on the Dunn and Dunn model. *Journal of Educational Research, 98*(3), 176–184.

Matthews, D. B. (1991). Learning styles research: Implications for increasing students in teacher education programs. *Journal of Instructional Psychology, 18*, 228–236.

Ormrod, J. E. (2011). Educational psychology: Developing learners. Boston, MA: Allyn & Bacon.

Reed, J. A., Banks, A. L., & Carlisle, C. S. (2004). Knowing me, knowing who?: Getting to know your students preferred learning style. *Teaching Elementary Physical Education, 15*(4), 25–27.

Sarasin, L. C. (1999). *Learning style perspectives.* Madison, WI: Atwood.

Semple, E. E., & Pascale, P. J. (1984). An alternative method of grouping for instruction; learning styles/sociometry. *Focus on Learning, 10*, 41–42.

Silver, H. F., Strong, R. W., & Perini, M. J. (2000). *So each may learn: Integrating learning styles and multiple intelligences.* Alexandria, VA: Association for Supervision and Curriculum Development.

Adapted Physical Education: Physical Education for All

Kerri Tunnicliffe

Adapted physical education is physical education that has been modified to provide students with disabilities the opportunity to enhance gross motor and manipulative skill development in the **least restrictive environment (LRE)**. Adapted physical education consists of the development of skill acquisition to actively participate in aquatics, dance, individual sports and activities, and team sports (Adapted Physical Education National Standards [APENS], 2008). The purpose of adapted physical education is to help people with disabilities build a strong foundation to recognize their full potential in the world of physical activity and movement to sustain an active and healthy lifestyle (Sherrill, 2004).

What are the responsibilities of a person who teaches adapted physical education? An adapted physical educator has many roles, which include assessment, planning, teaching, consulting, advocating, and monitoring students with disabilities. The adapted physical educator is the person responsible for determining whether a student needs additional services in physical activity to be successful. This is done by using a formal assessment tool to measure whether a student's gross motor and manipulative skills are on target developmentally with other children his or her age. Once it is determined a student is in need of adapted physical education services, based on the standardized assessment, the next step is to establish what level of services are needed to help the child become successful in the least restrictive environment (LRE). A least restrictive environment is a term defined

in Section 504 of the Rehabilitation Act of 1973, which was created to ensure people with disabilities are in an environment that meets their educational needs.

An adapted physical educator can assist a child with a disability in many ways so he or she becomes successful in physical activity. If a student qualifies for adapted physical education service, the adapted physical educator is responsible for creating goals and objectives to help the student become a more skillful mover. The goals and objectives are part of the student's **individualized education program (IEP)**, which is a legal document required for all students who have been diagnosed with a qualifying disability. The goals and objectives can be implemented in a variety of ways.

The educator could teach a self-contained adapted physical education class. This class would consist of only students with disabilities. The adapted physical educator could go into an inclusion physical education class where students with and without disabilities are participating, and assist the child with the day's activities to modify rules, space, and equipment as needed. The adapted physical educator also could serve as a consultant to the physical education teacher who has students with disabilities. As a consultant, ideas and suggestions would be made to properly modify activities and equipment to make them safe and effective.

The adapted physical educator is also an advocate for each child with a disability to ensure he or she is afforded the same opportunities as the general population of students. The adapted physical educator must monitor the progress of students who qualify for adapted physical education services to ensure progress with their goals and objectives. It is important to note that adapted physical education is a direct service because it is a federally mandated component of special education. Therefore, it can stand alone on an IEP, and cannot be implemented by an occupational or physical therapist because those are related services.

■ HISTORY OF ADAPTED PHYSICAL EDUCATION

Prior to 1970, there were few opportunities for people with disabilities to excel in education. People with disabilities were placed in hospitals and institutions rather than educated in the public school setting. Section 504 of the Rehabilitation Act of 1973 was the first major step for people with disabilities to have equal rights when it came to education, including physical education. The law protects any individual in a program or activity that receives federal funds (U.S. Department of Education, 2007). Section 504 provides that, "No otherwise qualified individual with a disability in the United States . . . shall, solely by reason of her or his disability, be excluded from the participation in, be denied the benefits of, or be subjected to discrimination under any program or activity receiving Federal financial assistance." The intent of the law is to end discrimination by providing all students with disabilities equal opportunities in educational settings. Some of the points relating to physical education include all people with disabilities have the right to access all school programs, including physical education and athletics. Any school receiving federal funds *must* make accommodations for all students to be successful. These accommodations include

adapted physical education (U.S. Department of Education, 2007).

In 1975, the Education of All Handicapped Children Act (EAHC) was enacted. The law allows all students with disabilities to have a free and appropriate public education in the least restrictive environment, including all children 3 through 21 years of age. Examples of the services include adapted physical education or providing physical education in an inclusion class.

The **Individuals with Disabilities Education Act (IDEA)** of 1997 is a modification to EAHC. One of the key components of IDEA is that it removes a child from "regular" class only when supplementary aides and services are not adequate for the child to succeed. Under the law, each person with a disability has equal opportunities in physical education, athletics, intramurals, and recreation. These services must be available in any setting (schools, hospitals, and institutions). The law goes a step further to ensure children can succeed by mandating educational services to children who have the potential to have a disability (are showing signs of a delay compared to similar aged peers) from birth to 2 years and expands services for 3- to 5-year-olds. This means a child could be eligible for early intervention services.

■ FREE AND APPROPRIATE EDUCATION IN A LEAST RESTRICTIVE ENVIRONMENT

Based on Section 504 of the Rehabilitation Act of 1973, all students with disabilities are entitled to a **free and appropriate education** in a least restrictive environment. A *free education* means a child with a disability has the right to go to public school without an associated cost. An *appropriate education* encompasses a variety of scenarios depending on the individual needs of the child, including education in a regular education class, the use of aids and related services in a regular education class, a separate classroom for special education, and/or special services for all or portions of the school day (U.S. Department of Education, 2007).

A least restrictive environment means a child must be placed in a classroom that challenges the child at his or her educational level. This includes children in schools that receive federal funding. The only time a child may be removed from a regular education class is when the severity or nature of a disability is such that even with supplementary aides and services, a child's educational progress cannot be satisfactorily achieved (U.S. Department of Education, 2004).

■ BENEFITS OF AN INCLUSIONARY PHILOSOPHY

Sometimes people with disabilities are not granted the same opportunities as people without disabilities. This is due to society's perceiving a person with a disability as having limitations, as opposed to determining the reality of his or her actual abilities. The word *limitation* by definition means a restriction. Every person has some form of a limitation regardless of his or her physical, cognitive, social, emotional, or intellectual abilities. An example of a limitation could be a student's need for complete quiet when studying or taking a test. The limitation could restrict how well the student does in school. With the proper environment, the student excels in all subjects. It is the job of all educators to look at the whole child rather than just his or her shortcomings. Focusing on a child's abilities, especially when working with a child with a disability, will serve to open more windows of opportunity for the child than ever before.

Seeing a child in a wheelchair or using a walker conjures up unnecessary stereotypes of what a child can and cannot do. Misinformation about disabilities keeps many people with disabilities from being physically educated and active. These attitudes can be easily dismantled as more people with disabilities are incorporated into public school education and extracurricular activities.

■ PRACTICAL SUGGESTIONS FOR BEGINNING PHYSICAL EDUCATORS WHO WILL BE WORKING WITH STUDENTS WITH DISABILITIES

An effective physical education teacher is able to modify instruction for students of diverse ability levels. Therefore, an effective physical education teacher already serves as an adapted physical educator of sorts. Modifications that can be made include:

- *Equipment:* Larger, lighter, colorful, textures, objects with noise.
- *Space:* Decrease size of movement area, increase personal space area.
- *Time:* Short, creative activities with ample practice opportunities.
- *Instruction:* Auditory and kinesthetic demonstration with picture support. Clear start and stop signals, known to unknown progression. Explanations should include short cues, spoken slowly and clearly.

Important characteristics of any educator are the ability to be patient, creative, flexible, energetic, and compassionate while maintaining high expectations and standards. These qualities are the backbone for a quality educator. Teaching people with disabilities can be challenging, yet extremely rewarding. Patience will allow the adapted physical educator to take the time needed to be sure each student reaches his or her full potential. Sometimes, due to lack of experience with a given sport or activity, the individual with a disability may be afraid or apprehensive to participate. The ability of an adapted physical educator to be creative and find new and innovative ways to challenge students will help to ensure a student's success. Being flexible allows the adapted physical educator to stray from the lesson plan as needed to take advantage of teachable moments. The more energetic and compassionate the educator is, the more the student will find the classroom a safe environment in which to learn about and participate in physical activity.

When working with students with disabilities, an adapted physical educator should research information to learn more about the various conditions of each child. It is important that the curriculum for students includes safe, challenging, and appropriate activities based on this research. It is also important that the adapted physical educator take the time to plan a variety of activities, each with many potential modifications. Because each child is different, success in a particular task may be found after several modification attempts. Be a keen observer. Take time to observe how a student moves his or her body to gain valuable insight. Ask questions. The child, his or her parents, and previous teachers and teacher assistants can provide valuable information in a time-efficient manner that will enhance relationship development.

◼ CONCLUSION

The United States has made great strides in including students with disabilities within the public school setting. With the passing of IDEA and other associated laws, students with disabilities have finally been granted the long-deserved right to be educated alongside their peers. The majority of physical education classes today include students with disabilities (Sherrill, 2004). Therefore, it is imperative that teachers are well trained and confident to provide effective instruction for students with a wide range of abilities. The acquisition of fundamental movement and manipulative skills will ensure that children of all abilities have the skills necessary to continue to be physically active for a lifetime.

◼ KEY WORDS AND DEFINITIONS

adapted physical education   Physical education that has been modified to provide students with disabilities the opportunity to enhance gross motor and manipulative skill development in the least restrictive environment.

free and appropriate education   Free means a child with a disability has the right to go to public school without an associated cost. An appropriate education encompasses a variety of scenarios depending on the individual needs of the child, including education in a regular education class, the use of aids and related services in a regular education class, a separate classroom for special education, and/or special services for all or portions of the school day.

individualized education program (IEP)   A legal document required for all students who have been diagnosed with a qualifying disability.

Individuals with Disabilities Education Act (IDEA)   One of the key components of IDEA is that it removes a child from "regular" class only when supplementary aides and services are not adequate for the child to succeed.

least restrictive environment (LRE)   A placement in a classroom that challenges the child at his or her educational level.

■ DISCUSSION QUESTIONS

1. Should the attitude of physical education teachers influence the inclusion of children with disabilities in regular physical education?
2. Should the modifications made in adapted physical education change as the student nears graduation? Explain why or why not.
3. What is the purpose of inclusive physical education? Should there be more than one purpose?
4. What are the varying roles an adapted physical education teacher can hold in a public school setting?
5. How is it possible to provide adequate physical education to a large class of students with diverse learning needs and abilities?

■ REFERENCES

Adapted Physical Education National Standards. (2008). *What is adapted physical education?* Retrieved October 10, 2009, from http://www.apens.org/whatisape.html

Sherrill, C. (2004). *Adapted physical activity, recreation and sport: Cross disciplinary and lifespan.* New York: McGraw-Hill.

U.S. Department of Education. (2004). *Building the legacy: IDEA 2004.* Retrieved October 12, 2009, from http://idea.ed.gov/explore/view/p/%2Croot%2Cstatute%2CI%2CB%2C612%2Ca%2C5%2C

U.S. Department of Education. (2007). *Free appropriate public education for students with disabilities: Requirements under section 504 of the rehabilitation act of 1973.* Retrieved October 12, 2009, from http://www.ed.gov/about/offices/list/ocr/docs/edlite-FAPE504.html

Research Review

A Review of Middle School Students' Attitudes Toward Physical Activity

Furong Xu and Wenhao Liu

Children and adolescents' physical activity behaviors are influenced by many psychological, social, and environmental factors across multiple levels (Sallis & Owen, 2002). The success of promoting children and adolescents' physical activity depends largely on identifying and understanding how these factors influence children's physical activity participation (Sallis, Prochaska, & Taylor, 2000; Subramaniam & Silverman, 2007). Of all the possible factors, children's attitudes are considered to be a key factor influencing their physical activity participation (Biddle & Mutrie, 2001; Hagger, Chatzisarantis, & Biddle, 2002; Solmon, 2003; Subramaniam & Silverman, 2007). As stated by Solmon, attitudes toward physical activity are powerful factors determining the extent to which children choose to participate in physical activity.

Many studies support the notion regarding the relationship of children's attitudes and physical activity participation. Children who have more positive attitudes toward physical activity are found to be more likely to participate in physical activity outside of school (Biddle & Chatzisarantis, 1999; Chung & Phillips, 2002; Hagger et al., 2002; Liu, 2008; Liu & Chepyator-Thomson, 2008; McKenzie, 2003, Portman, 2003) and demonstrate higher physical activity amounts (Hagger, Cale, & Almond, 1995; Liu, 2008; Liu & Chepyator-Thomson, 2008) than those with less positive attitudes. Thus, fostering children's positive attitudes toward physical activity would be conducive to the promotion of children's current and lifelong physical activity participation (McKenzie, 2003; Subramaniam & Silverman, 2007).

Accordingly, children's attitudes toward physical activity have long been a research area attracting many researchers. The research focus has been on identifying factors that may be related to children's attitudes and those that may contribute to developing children's positive attitudes toward physical activity, with the hope of creating more favorable environments to nurture children's positive attitudes, which will in turn contribute to their physical activity promotion. According to Solmon (2003), child characteristics and contextual factors are two major factors related to children's attitudes. This article will provide a review with respect to how these two factors are associated with middle school children's attitudes toward physical activity.

■ CHILD CHARACTERISTICS AND CHILDREN'S ATTITUDES TOWARD PHYSICAL ACTIVITY

Child characteristics refer to children's age, gender, and sports skill. Age is found to be a strong factor impacting children's attitudes toward, or interest in, physical activity participation. Rowland (1998, 1999) provides evidence that the decline of biological drive results in the decline of physical activity levels during the childhood period. That is, during early childhood, daily energy expenditure through physical activity is largely biologically driven. As the child grows, such inherent drive or interest in physical activity declines, which results in the decline of the child's physical activity.

Consistent with Rowland's evidence are the findings of the change in children's attitudes as they grow older. Specifically, elementary children are found to have more positive attitudes than secondary children (Lee, 2004; Martin, 2000; Solmon & Carter, 1995; Xiang, McBride, & Guan, 2004), and children's attitudes become less positive as they progress through their schooling (Biddle & Mutrie, 2001; Lee, 2004; Prochaska, Sallis, Slymen, & McKenzie, 2003; Silverman & Subramaniam, 1999; Subramaniam & Silverman, 2007; Xiang et al., 2004). The findings perfectly match and explain the decline in physical activity level, such that middle school students are less physically active than elementary school students, and high school students are less physically active than middle school students (U.S. Department of Health and Human Services, 1996).

Although in the middle of the course of decline, middle school children's attitudes toward physical activity still remain relatively positive as a whole. In Subramaniam and Silverman's (2007) study, middle school students demonstrate moderately positive attitudes, obtaining a mean value of 70.74 out of a possible 100 points in a survey. A similar finding was obtained by a later study involving middle school students with a different questionnaire (Liu, Wang, & Xu, 2008), confirming middle school students' relatively positive attitudes toward physical activity.

Another child characteristic is gender, which has been reported to be related to middle school students' attitudes toward physical activity as well, although results are not quite consistent. In general, middle school boys demonstrate more positive attitudes toward physical activity than girls (Biddle & Mutrie, 2001; Chung & Phillips, 2002; Colley, Berman, & Van Millingen, 2005). However, in their recent study, Subramaniam and Silverman (2007) did not find significant differences in attitudes between middle school boys and girls. Further, boys are found to be more competition-motivated than girls, and girls are more weight-management-motivated than boys (Kelder et al., 1995; Tappe, Duda, & Menges-Ehrnwald, 1990). In addition, boys have higher levels of self-efficacy (Trost et al., 1996) and perceived competence in physical activity participation than girls (Tappe et al., 1990), whereas girls display more barriers of physical activity participation, such as disliking sweating (Grieser et al., 2006) or spoiling hair and make-up (Leslie et al., 1999; Taylor et al., 1999), lack of sports skill and interest, and fear of injury (Grieser et al., 2006).

The gender differences in attitudes are reflected in middle school students' physical activity preferences as well. It is reported that middle school boys prefer traditional team sports and competitive experiences (Croxton, Chiacchia, & Wagner, 1987), and tend to choose activities like football, hockey, and soccer, which are less chosen by middle school girls (Bradley, McMurray, Harrell, &

Deng, 2000; Prusak & Darst, 2002). Conversely, middle school girls prefer individual physical activities, or activities with more cooperative and less competitive elements such as skating, gymnastics, aerobic dance, yoga, softball, and volleyball (Birtwistle & Brodie, 1991; Bradley et al., 2000; Greenwood, Stillwell, & Byars, 2001; Hill & Hannon, 2008; Kyles & Lounsbery, 2004).

Further, whereas boys are reported to have more positive attitudes than girls toward physical activities, bringing them risk-taking experience and reducing stress, girls are more positive than boys in physical activities with beautiful and graceful movements (Colley, Comber, & Hargreaves, 1994; Ewy, 1993; Hughes, 1994; Hunt, 1995; Parkhurst, 2000). The similar findings are reported that males tend to have more positive attitude scores on competition and strenuous areas of physical activity such as physical and athletic training, whereas females usually get higher attitude scores in social and aesthetic dimensions of physical activity (Brustad, 1996; Duan, 1985; Liu et al., 2008; Smoll & Schutz, 1980). In addition, it is also reported that middle school boys enjoy and are very active in free play, game play, and skill drill, and middle school girls enjoy and are more active during fitness activity (McKenzie, Marshall, Sallis, & Conway, 2000).

Middle school children's attitudes also vary as a function of sports skill levels. Welk (1999) has provided the Youth Physical Activity Promotion model to explain factors influencing children's interests and involvement in physical activity. In Welk's conceptual framework, children's sports skill level is defined as one of the predisposing factors that determine the extent to which a child chooses to participate in physical activity if the opportunity is available. When a child's sports skill is low, the perception of competence will be low. Because children tend to display competence and hide incompetence, children who have low sports skills will feel incompetent in physical activities and may not want to participate in physical activity, even if the opportunity is provided (Welk, 1999). Harter's (1978) competence motivation theory also suggests that children tend to engage in physical activities in which they feel competent and withdraw from activities in which they have low perceptions of ability. Thus, logically, highly skilled children tend to display more positive attitudes than those who have lower skill levels (Solmon, 2003).

This notion has been supported by evidence. Portman (1995) finds that children with higher athletic skills demonstrate more positive attitudes toward participation in physical activity, whereas children with low skill levels display less positive attitudes. Further, the studies investigating field-dependent children's performance in sport-related settings provide evidence as well. Field-dependent children—those who tend to rely more on external reinforcement and learn better through well-structured learning environment—have long been reported to display poorer sports performance, lower athletic ability, slower motor learning rate, more learning problems in the physical education class, and lower physical activity levels compared to their field-independent counterparts (e.g., Ennis, Chen, & Fernandez-Balboa, 1991; Liu, 2008; Meek & Skubic, 1971; Raviv & Nabel, 1990; Swinnen, 1984). Consequently, middle school field-dependent children are usually found to demonstrate less positive attitudes and lower interest in physical activity (Liu, 2008; Liu & Chepyator-Thomson, 2008).

Also, in a recent study examining children's attitudes (Liu et al., 2008), middle school children participating in after-school organized sports were found to display more positive attitudes toward physical activity than those not participating in organized sports. Although sports skills of the children were not examined in this study, it would be readily accepted that organized sports participants usually have higher sports skills than those who do not participate in organized sports.

■ CONTEXTUAL FACTORS AND CHILDREN'S ATTITUDES TOWARD PHYSICAL ACTIVITY

Contextual factors are school environments impacting children's attitudes. For example, quality physical education programs have been reported to be a strong factor influencing children's attitudes toward physical activity. Specifically, children's positive attitudes are likely to be linked with enjoyment, perceived usefulness of the curriculum, and a sense of belongingness (Subramaniam & Silverman, 2002, 2007). Curricula with situational interest, such as those that require students to analyze and design offensive and defensive strategies, may foster students' interests in physical activity (Chen & Darst, 2001). A learning environment that promotes personal meaning is considered to be important to the development of positive attitude (Rink, 2006). Children are also likely to become more positive toward physical activity if they are in a learning environment that makes them comfortable and confident (Hagger et al., 2002). Other studies (Birtwistle & Brodie, 1991; Brodie & Birtwistle, 1990) indicate that, compared with skill-related physical education programs, health-related physical education programs would bring positive changes in children's attitudes toward physical activity.

In general, quality physical education programs, including health-related physical education programs, play an important role in positively impacting children's attitudes toward and intentions to participate in physical activity (McKenzie, 2001; Prochaska et al., 2003). On the other hand, poor physical education programs may impact children's attitudes negatively.

Carlson (1995) indicates that students will become bored if there is a lack of challenge in activities or if the same activities are repeated without taking children's interests into account. Siedentop (2004) also argues that a multi-activity curriculum with a series of short-term units will negatively influence students' attitudes. Biddle and Chatzisarantis (1999) find that it is more difficult for students to maintain interest in traditional team sports than in individual pursuits. It is also reported that too much emphasis on competition in the physical education classes could result in students' negative attitudes toward physical education and physical activity (Carlson, 1995; Ennis, 1996), especially for those who are athletically and physically challenged, because the highly competitive sports typically identify students as "winners" and "losers" (Ryan, Fleming, & Maina, 2003). Additionally, the marginal status of physical education in the school curriculum has a negative impact on students' attitudes (Tannehill et al., 1994). This marginal status includes increasing time for other subjects at the cost of decreasing time for physical education classes, viewing physical education classes and programs as glorified recesses, and problematic and questionable outcomes for physical education students (Strand & Scantling, 1994).

School-based physical activity intervention programs that take the ecological approach, addressing multiple contextual or environmental levels such as intrapersonal, interpersonal, organizational, community, and policy, tend to enhance contexts that foster children's attitudes toward physical activity, resulting in significant physical activity promotion (Ward, Saunders, & Pate, 2007). For example, Sports, Play and Active Recreation for Kids (SPARK), Middle School Physical Activity and Nutrition (M-SPAN), and Child and Adolescent Trial for Cardiovascular Health (CATCH) are well-known school-based physical activity intervention programs that have nurtured children's attitudes toward physical activity (Nader et al., 1999; Rosengard, 1995). As expected, children's physical activity levels in intervention programs were 39% to 70% higher than those of children in control groups in the SPARK (Rosengard, 1995). Moderate to vigorous physical activity increased by 18% during a 2-year intervention in the M-SPAN (McKenzie et al., 2004), and vigorous physical activity levels were 26% higher than those of control groups after a 3-year intervention in the CATCH (Luepker et al., 1996). Further, a tracking study of the original CATCH cohort 3 years after termination of the intervention still indicated 36% more vigorous physical activity minutes than those of the original control groups (Nader et al., 1999).

Another powerful and favorable context that positively impacts children's growth in attitudes and other psychosocial aspects is organized youth programs, including organized youth physical activities (Larson, Hansen, & Moneta, 2006; Roth & Brooks-Gunn, 2003). It is widely reported that participation in organized youth sports contributes to children's development of goal setting, persistence, problem solving, teamwork, managing emotions, and managing time (Danish, Taylor, & Fazio, 2003; Duda & Ntounumis, 2005). One study (Westerstahl, Barnekow-Bergkvist, Hedberg, & Jansson, 2003) suggests that participation in leisure-time sports would contribute to the development of positive attitudes toward physical activity. Another study (Forrester, Arterberry, & Barcelona, 2006) reports that sports involvement in public schools is a predictor of students' attitudes toward sports and fitness activities after graduation. That is to suggest, children getting involved in organized sports in public schools tend to demonstrate more positive attitudes in their university years. It is also reported that children who have more positive attitudes toward physical activity are more likely to participate in physical activity outside of school (Chung & Phillips, 2002; Hagger et al., 2002; McKenzie, 2003; Portman, 2003). Further, a recent study (Liu et al., 2008) reports that middle school children engaging in after-school organized sports display significantly more positive attitudes toward health, enjoyment, and social interaction dimensions of physical activity than those who do not participate in organized sports.

Physical education teachers also are reported by some studies to be an important contextual factor impacting middle school student attitudes toward physical activity. In the participation-identification model developed by Finn (1989), teacher personality and behaviors are listed as a factor that influences students' feelings and motivations. Luke and Sinclair (1991) report that physical education teacher behavior ranks second to curriculum content as a determinant of student attitudes. Specifically, physical education teachers who hold high expectations, focus on learning something, provide contents with challenge, or encourage students despite their low ability will have a positive impact on students' attitudes. By contrast, teachers who evaluate students based on fitness level only or a single skill test, or who provide no chances for students to make choices, will influence students' attitudes negatively (Luke & Sinclair).

It is also reported that physical education teachers who have good physical skills and are friendly with students tend to have a positive impact on middle school students' attitudes, whereas those who cannot relate to students and are partial to skilled students may have a negative impact (Ryan et al., 2003). Similar findings are reported by another study (Stewart, Green, & Huelskamp, 1991). In addition, in developing an instrument to assess students' attitudes toward physical activity, Subramaniam and Silverman (2000) find physical education teachers to be an important factor influencing students' attitudes toward physical activity.

In summary, accumulated evidence indicates that two major groups of factors impact middle school students' attitudes toward physical activity. The first is child characteristics, which include age, gender, and sports skill. The second is contextual factors such as physical education curriculum, comprehensive intervention programs, organized sports programs, and physical education teachers. Due to the logical connection between positive attitudes and physical activity participation and the supporting evidence developing students who value physical activity is one of the six national physical education standards (National Association for Sport and Physical Education, 2004) and has long been a goal of physical education programs (Siedentop & Tannehill, 2000). Thus, it is the duty of current and future physical educators to create fostering environments that contribute to the formation of students' positive attitudes.

■ DISCUSSION QUESTIONS

1. What do you think are the top three items that influence children and adolescents' physical activity behaviors?

2. Why do you think elementary-level students generally enjoy physical activity more than students at the secondary level?

3. What can you do as a physical educator to cultivate positive attitudes in secondary students?

4. How will teaching a sport-skills-only curriculum potentially affect an elementary and/or secondary student's attitudes on physical activity?

5. Do you think an elementary or secondary student's attitude toward physical education is more positive if he or she also plays on a sports team at the school?

■ REFERENCES

Biddle, S. J. H., & Chatzisarantis, N. (1999). Motivation for a physically active lifestyle through physical education. In Y. V. Auweele, F. Bakker, S. Biddle, M. Durand, & R. Seiler (Eds.), *Psychology for physical educators* (pp. 5–26). Champaign, IL: Human Kinetics.

Biddle, S. J. H., & Mutrie, N. (2001). *Psychology of physical activity: Determinants, well-being and interventions.* New York: Routledge.

Birtwistle, G. E., & Brodie, D. A. (1991). Children's attitudes towards activity and perceptions of physical education. *Health Education Research, 6,* 465–478.

Bradley, C. B., McMurray, R. G., Harrell, J. S., & Deng, S. (2000). Changes in common activities of 3rd through 10th graders: The CHIC Study. *Medicine and Science in Sport and Exercise, 32*(12), 2071–2078.

Brodie, D. A., & Birtwistle, G. E. (1990). Children's attitudes to physical activity, exercise, health and fitness before and after a health-related fitness measurement program. *International Journal of Physical Education, 27*(2), 10–14.

Brustad, R. J. (1996). Attraction to physical activity in urban school children: Parental socialization and gender issues. *Research Quarterly for Exercise and Sport, 67,* 316–323.

Carlson, T. B. (1995). We hate gym: Student alienation from physical education. *Journal of Teaching in Physical Education, 14,* 467–477.

Chen, A., & Darst, P. W. (2001). Situational interest in physical education: A function of learning task design. *Research Quarterly for Exercise and Sport, 72,* 285–306.

Chung, M., & Phillips, D. A. (2002). The relationship between attitude toward physical education and leisure-time exercise in high school students. *Physical Educator, 59,* 126–138.

Colley, A., Berman, E., & Van Millingen, L. (2005). Age and gender differences in young people's perceptions of sport participants. *Journal of Applied Social Psychology, 35,* 1440–1454.

Colley, A., Comber, C., & Hargreaves, D. J. (1994). Gender effects in school subject preferences: A research note. *Educational Studies, 20,* 13–18.

Croxton, J. S., Chiacchia, D., & Wagner, C. (1987). Gender differences in attitudes toward sports and reactions to competitive situations. *Journal of Sport Behavior, 10,* 167–177.

Danish, S. J., Taylor, T. E., & Fazio, R. J. (2003). Enhancing adolescent development through sports and leisure. In G. Gdams & M. Berzonsky (Eds.), *Blackwell handbook of adolescence* (pp. 92–108). Malden, MA: Blackwell.

Duan, C. (1985). A study of attitudes toward physical activity among secondary school students in Beijing, China. *International Review for the Sociology of Sport, 20,* 307–319.

Duda, J. L., & Ntounumis, N. (2005). After-school sport for children: Implications of a task-involving motivational climate. In J. Mahoney, R. Larson, & J. Eccles (Eds.), *Organized activities as contexts of development* (pp. 311–330). Mahwah, NJ: Erlbaum.

Ennis, C. D. (1996). Students' experiences in sport-based physical education: More than apologies are necessary. *Quest, 48,* 453–456.

Ennis, C. D., Chen, A., & Fernandez-Balboa, J. M. (1991). Cognitive style differences within an analytical curriculum: Examples of success and nonsuccess. *Early Child Development and Care, 74,* 123–134.

Ewy, S. R. (1993). *Children's attitudes toward physical activity and self-esteem*. Unpublished master's thesis. Hays, KS: Fort Hays State University.

Finn, J. D. (1989). Withdrawing from school. *Review of Educational Research, 59*, 117–142.

Forrester, S., Arterberry, C., & Barcelona, B. (2006). Student attitudes toward sports and fitness activities after graduation. *Recreational Sports Journal, 30*, 87–99.

Greenwood, M., Stillwell, J., & Byars, A. (2001). Activity preferences of middle school physical education students. *The Physical Educator, 58*(1), 26–30.

Grieser, M., Vu, M. B., Bedimo-Rung, A. L., Neumark-Sztainer, D., Moody, J., Young, D. R., et al. (2006). Physical activity, attitudes, preferences, and practices in African American, Hispanic, and Caucasian girls. *Health Education & Behavior, 33*, 40–51.

Hagger, M., Cale, L., & Almond, L. (1995). The importance of children's attitudes towards physical activity. *Kineziologija, 27*(2), 12–16.

Hagger, M. S., Chatzisarantis, N. L., & Biddle, J. H. (2002). A meta-analytic review of the theories of reasoned action and planned behavior in physical activity: Predictive validity and the contribution of additional variables. *Journal of Sport & Exercise Psychology, 24*, 3–32.

Harter, S. (1978). Effectance motivation reconsidered: Toward a developmental model. *Human Development, 21*, 34–64.

Hill, G., & Hannon, J. C. (2008). An analysis of middle school students' physical education physical activity preferences. *The Physical Educator, 65(4)*, 180–194.

Hughes, K. P. (1994). *Influence of conceptually based physical education on student attitudes toward physical activity*. Unpublished master's thesis, Springfield College, Springfield, MA.

Hunt, J. D. (1995). *The impact of a daily physical education program on students' attitudes towards, and participation in, physical activity*. Unpublished master's thesis, University of British Columbia, Canada.

Kelder, S. H., Perry, C. L., Peters, R. J. Jr., Lytle, L. L., & Klepp, K. L. (1995). Gender differences in the class of 1989 study: The school component of the Minnesota Heart Health Program. *Journal of Health Education, 26*, S36–S44.

Kyles, C., & Lounsbery, M. (2004). Project Destiny: Initiating physical activity for nonathletic girls through sport. *Journal of Physical Education, Recreation and Dance, 75*(1), 37–41.

Larson, R. W., Hansen, D. M., & Moneta, G. (2006). Differing profiles of developmental experiences across types of organized youth activities. *Developmental Psychology, 42*, 849–863.

Lee, A. M. (2004). Promoting lifelong physical activity through quality physical education. *Journal of Physical Education, Recreation & Dance. 75*(5), 21–26.

Leslie, J., Yancey, A., McCarthy, W., Albert, S., Wert, C., Miles, O., et al. (1999). Development and implementation of a school-based nutrition and fitness promotion program for ethnically diverse middle-school girls. *Journal of the American Dietetic Association, 99*, 967–970.

Liu, W. (2008). *Adolescents' physical activity levels and behaviors: Examined from perspective of field dependence-independence*. Saarbrücken, Germany: VDM Verlag Dr. Müller.

Liu, W., & Chepyator-Thomson, J. R. (2008). Associations among field dependence-independence, sports participation, and physical activity level among school children. *Journal of Sports Behavior, 31*, 130–146.

Liu, W., Wang, J., & Xu, F. (2008). Middle school children's attitudes toward physical activity. *The International Council for Health, Physical Education, Recreation, Sport & Dance Journal of Research, 3*(2), 78–85.

Luepker, R. M., Perry, C. L., McKinlay, S. M., Nader, P. R., Parcel, G. S., Stone, E. J., et al. (1996). Outcomes of a field trial to improve children's dietary patterns and physical activity: The Child and Adolescent Trial for Cardiovascular Health (CATCH). *Journal of the American Medical Association, 275*, 768–776.

Luke, M. D., & Sinclair, G. D. (1991). Gender differences in adolescents' attitudes toward physical education. *Journal of Teaching Physical Education, 11*, 31–46.

Martin, L. T. (2000, April). *Perceptions of high, average, and low performance second graders about physical education and physical education teachers.* Paper presented at the annual meeting of the American Educational Research Association, New Orleans, LA.

Meek, F., & Skubic, V. (1971). Spatial perception of highly skilled and poorly skilled females. *Perceptual and Motor Skills, 33,* 1309–1310.

McKenzie, T. L. (2001). Back to the future: Health-related physical education. In P. Ward & P. Doutis (Eds.), *Physical education for the 21st century* (pp. 113–131). Lincoln, NE: University of Nebraska.

McKenzie, T. L. (2003). Health-related physical education: Physical activity, fitness, and wellness. In S. J. Silverman & C. D. Ennis (Eds.), *Student learning in physical education: Applying research to enhance instruction* (pp. 207–226). Champaign, IL: Human Kinetics.

McKenzie, T. L., Marshall, S. J., Sallis, J. F., & Conway, T. L. (2000). Student activity levels, lesson context, and teacher behavior during middle school physical education. *Research Quarterly for Exercise and Sport, 71,* 249–259.

McKenzie, T. L., Sallis, J. F., Prochaska, J. J., Conway, T. L., Marshall, S. J., & Rosengard, P. (2004). Evaluation of a two-year middle-school physical education intervention: M-SPAN. *Medicine & Science in Sports & Exercise, 36,* 1382–1388.

Nader, P. R., Stone, E. J., Lytle, L. A., Perry, C. L., Osganian, S. K., Kelder, S., et al. (1999). Three-year maintenance of improved diet and physical activity: The CATCH cohort. *Archives of Pediatrics & Adolescent Medicine, 153,* 695–704.

National Association for Sport and Physical Education. (2004). *Moving into the future: National standard for physical education* (2nd ed.). New York: McGraw-Hill.

Parkhurst, D. L. (2000). *Comparison of attitudes toward physical activity and physical activity levels of sixth grade boys and girls of various ethnic origins* (Master's thesis). Springfield, MA: Springfield College.

Portman, P. A. (1995). Who is having fun in physical education classes? Experiences of sixth-grade students in elementary and middle schools. *Journal of Teaching in Physical Education, 14,* 445–453.

Portman, P. A. (2003). Are physical education classes encouraging students to be physically active? Experience of ninth graders in their last semester of required physical education. *Physical Educator, 60,* 150–160.

Prochaska, J. J., Sallis, J. F., Slymen, D. J., & McKenzie, T. L. (2003). A longitudinal study of children's enjoyment of physical education. *Pediatric Exercise Science, 15,* 170–178.

Prusak, K., & Darst, P. (2002). Effects of types of walking activities on actual choices by adolescent female physical education students. *Journal of Teaching in Physical Education, 21,* 230–241.

Raviv, S., & Nabel, N. (1990). Relationship between two different measurements of field dependence and athletic performance of adolescents. *Perceptual & Motor Skills, 70,* 75–81.

Rosengard, P. (1995). SPARKs are flying. *American Fitness, 13*(4), 40–42.

Roth, J., & Brooks-Gunn, J. (2003). What exactly is a youth development program? Answers from research and practice. *Applied Developmental Science, 7,* 94–111.

Rowland, T. W. (1998). The biological basis of physical activity. *Medicine and Science in Sports and Exercise, 30,* 392–399.

Rowland, T. W. (1999). Adolescence: A "risk factor" for physical inactivity. *President's Council on Physical Fitness and Sports Research Digest, 3*(6), 1–8.

Ryan, S., Fleming, D., & Maina, M. (2003). Attitudes of middle school students toward their physical education teachers and classes. *Physical Educator, 60*(2), 28–42.

Sallis, J. F., & Owen, N. (2002). Ecological models of health behavior. In K. Glanz, B. K. Rimer, & F. M. Lewis (Eds.), *Health behavior and health education: Theory, research, and practice* (3rd ed., pp. 462–484). San Francisco: Jossey-Bass.

Sallis, J. F., Prochaska, J. J., & Taylor, W. C. (2000). A review of correlates of physical activity of children and adolescents. *Medicine and Science in Sports and Exercise, 32,* 963–975.

Siedentop, D. (2004). *Introduction to physical education, fitness, and sport* (5th ed.). New York: McGraw-Hill.

Siedentop, D., & Tannehill, D. (2000). *Developing teaching skills in physical education* (4th ed.). Mountain View, CA: Mayfield.

Silverman, S., & Subramaniam, P. R. (1999). Student attitude toward physical education and physical activity: A review of measurement issues and outcomes. *Journal of Teaching in Physical Education, 19*, 97–125.

Smoll, F. L., & Schutz, R. W. (1980). Children's attitudes towards physical activity: A longitudinal analysis. *Journal of Sport Psychology, 2*, 137–147.

Solmon, M. A. (2003). Student issues in physical education: Attitudes, cognition, and motivation. In S. J. Silverman & C. Ennis (Eds.), *Student learning in physical education: Applying research to enhance instruction* (2nd ed., pp. 147–164). Champaign, IL: Human Kinetics.

Solmon, M. A., & Carter, J. A. (1995). Kindergarten and first-grade students' perceptions of physical education in one teacher's classes. *Elementary School Journal, 95*, 355–365.

Stewart, M. J., Green, S. R., & Huelskamp, J. (1991). Secondary student attitudes toward physical education. *The Physical Educator, 48*, 78–79.

Strand, B., & Scantling, E. (1994). An analysis of secondary student preferences toward physical education. *The Physical Educator, 51*, 119–129.

Subramaniam, P. R., & Silverman, S. (2000). Validation of scores from an instrument assessing student attitude toward physical education. *Measurement in Physical Education and Exercise Science, 4*(1), 29–43.

Subramaniam, P. R., & Silverman, S. (2002). Using complimentary data: An investigation of student attitude in physical education. *Journal of Sport Pedagogy, 8*, 74–91.

Subramaniam, P. R., & Silverman, S. (2007). Middle school students' attitudes toward physical education. *Teaching and Teacher Education, 23*, 602–611.

Swinnen, S. (1984). Field dependence-independence as a factor in learning complex motor skills

and underlying sex differences. *International Journal of Sport Psychology, 15*, 236–249.

Tannehill, D., Romar, J., O'Sullivan, M., England, K., & Rosenberg, D. (1994). Attitudes toward physical education: Their impact on how physical educators make sense of their work. *Journal of Teaching in Physical Education, 13*, 78–84.

Tappe, M. K., Duda, J. L., & Menges-Ehrnwald, P. (1990). Personal investment predictors of adolescent motivation orientation toward exercise. *Canadian Journal of Sport Sciences, 15*, 185–192.

Taylor, W. C., Yancey, A. K., Leslie, J., Murray, N. G., Cummings, S. S., Sharkey, S. A., et al. (1999). Physical activity among African American and Latino middle school girls: Consistent beliefs, expectations, and experiences across two sites. *Women & Health, 30*(2), 67–82.

Trost, S. G., Pate, R. R., Dowda, M., Saunders, R., Ward, D. S., & Felton, G. (1996). Gender differences in physical activity and determinants of physical activity in rural fifth grade children. *Journal of School Health, 66*, 145–150.

U.S. Department of Health and Human Services. (1996). *Physical activity and health: A report of the surgeon general.* Atlanta, GA: U.S. Department of Health and Human Services, Centers for Disease Control and Prevention, National Center for Chronic Disease. Prevention and Health Promotion, International Medical Publishing.

Ward, D. S., Saunders, R. P., & Pate, R. R. (2007). *Physical activity interventions in children and adolescents.* Champaign, IL: Human Kinetics.

Welk, G. (1999). The youth physical activity promotion model: A conceptual bridge between theory and practice. *Quest, 51*, 5–23.

Westerstahl, M., Barnekow-Bergkvist, M., Hedberg, G., & Jansson, E. (2003). Secular trends in sports: Participation and attitudes among adolescents in Sweden from 1974 to 1995. *Acta Paediatrica, 92*, 602–609.

Xiang, P., McBride, R., & Guan, J. (2004). Children's motivation in elementary physical education: A longitudinal study. *Research Quarterly for Exercise and Sport, 75*, 71–78.

CHAPTER 8

Other Dimensions of Physical Education, Health Education, and Sport

■ CHAPTER OVERVIEW

The theme of this chapter, "other dimensions," is characterized by the timely and diverse topics of professional development, service-learning, strength training, and empathy in physical education. Professional development should include continual, relevant, and engaging opportunities that are comprehensive approaches to improving a teacher or principal's effectiveness. The first article in Chapter 8 defines professional development and informs the reader of the need to seek out such opportunities, which could bring change in teacher practices. Six research-based criteria that contribute to effective professional development are discussed. The element of time, a teacher's role in professional development, and the need to develop and implement a professional development plan are presented. Samples of professional learning opportunities, from a self-study and study circles to professional learning communities and training, are outlined. A template of a professional development plan allows the reader to start to successfully plan his or her own professional development path.

The next article clearly defines the meaning and theoretical foundation of service-learning in physical education, examining the integrated triad of academic coursework, reflection, and service. The role of higher education and its connection to service-learning are outlined with definitions, research, examples, and a list of the four traits that characterize service-learning. The alignment of standards to service-learning and the relationship of service-learning to civic responsibility help the reader to acquire a deeper understanding of making a difference and serving others. Anyone who reads this article will leave with a comprehensive view of service-learning and the need to include this as part of a professional preparation pedagogical tool.

The third article in Chapter 8 is strongly research based about strength assessment and resistance training in our youth today. The author begins the article with a discussion about age, physiological factors, and how and when to implement training programs; specific program design guidelines are identified. The different types of programs, including training modalities and plyometric training, are explained. Discussion about assessment measures and the benefits of resistance training is included well. Finally, helpful tips for supervising a youth strength and resistance training program are listed. These eight tips will assist the professional in teaching resistance programs that are safe, individually based, well planned, and supervised by competent adults.

In the final article, the reader examines the need for the affective domain in teaching physical education. There is an informative discussion about factors affecting sociometric status and how students perceive themselves in physical education class. The pattern of learned helplessness, or the perception of someone believing he or she can't perform a task, is explored with application toward teaching. The reader becomes more knowledgeable about identifying and understanding the feelings of others to meet the needs of all students.

Professional Development: More Than Another Workshop

Holly L. Alperin

When you ask teachers how they feel about participating in a professional development day, some might respond, "I am glad to have the opportunity to learn a new skill or idea"; another may say, "I really wish I was not taking time away from the students because there is so little time in health education and physical education as it is"; and yet another might respond, "Great, I can finally catch up on the news I've been missing—I'll be sure to bring my newspaper." Although there are varied opinions about the desire to participate in **professional development**, as an educator, you can expect that you will be required to participate in at least some school-sponsored professional development, and there is little debate over the role quality professional development can play in improving both classroom instruction and student outcomes.

Professional development that is relevant to teacher needs provides on-going opportunities to practice new skills learned, and demonstrates how educators can use the information in their own classroom to have a sustained impact. This, however, must be measured against each individual's willingness to engage in professional development opportunities that challenge their current skill level or way of thinking, offer multiple options for refining and reflecting on the information presented, and require thoughtful implementation at the classroom level.

This article will highlight research supporting quality professional development along with the role each participant chooses in utilizing the knowledge and skills learned in their own classroom. The importance of a professional development plan will be discussed in addition to an example of how to create such a plan for personal use. Each educator has the opportunity to transform student achievement; participation in quality professional development can provide the tools necessary to make that happen.

■ PROFESSIONAL DEVELOPMENT: THINK OUTSIDE THE CLASSROOM

As an educator, participation in many **professional development events** and activities is recommended and often required.

In fact, one may even become responsible for planning quality professional development events for other staff members. To fulfill this, educators need to engage in continual learning opportunities and on-going professional growth through a variety of channels, and not necessarily through a specified "course." Other options may include attendance at a conference/workshop, participation in a **professional learning community** with other school staff, engaging in self-directed study, or involvement in a series of training events. Regardless of the mechanism used to gain professional growth, some key factors determine the quality and usefulness of any professional development experience.

The National Staff Development Council (NSDC) defines professional development as "...a comprehensive, sustained and intensive approach to improving teachers' and principals' effectiveness in raising student achievement" (2008). Additionally, the NSDC believes professional development fosters collective responsibility for improved student performance and must be composed of professional learning that is aligned with rigorous student academic achievement standards, local educational agency, and school improvement goals. The organization further supports professional development that is conducted among learning teams of educators, is facilitated by well-prepared individuals, occurs frequently and ideally multiple times per week, and engages established learning teams of educators in a continuous cycle of improvement.

This definition of professional development, as summarized by the NSDC, outlines professional development as a process that asks learners to be active participants and not passive attendees at a single event or workshop. This highlights the important role that individual learners have in seeking out professional learning opportunities that

are structured to bring about change in personal knowledge, skills, and/or abilities. It is only through participation in well-designed learning opportunities that true professional growth can occur and student achievement can be impacted.

Professional development events designed for maximum results have key criteria in common. Specifically, research has shown that in order for professional development events to bring about change in teacher practice, the following criteria play an important role:

- *Explanation of research/theory behind the topic:* It is important for participants to have a clear understanding of why the information being presented during the event is relevant to their teaching and how it is intended to impact student achievement.
- *Demonstration/modeling of the new strategy:* The workshop presenter holds great responsibility to ensure that participants understand the information presented and are knowledgeable in appropriate methods for implementing the skills or strategies introduced. This is best accomplished when the presenter models the use of the skills or strategies through their own instruction.
- *Practice of the skill under simulated conditions, including receiving feedback:* Just as we know the importance of allowing students to practice a new skill, the same is true for adult learners. The more opportunity an individual has to practice a new skill, especially in an environment that simulates real working conditions, the greater likelihood they have of implementing the skill in the classroom. When this occurs, and authentic feedback is given, individuals are able to make thoughtful adjustments to their classroom implementation.

- *Peer coaching/mentoring:* Education does not occur in a vacuum. Utilizing the knowledge and skills of those who know more than you is invaluable to continual growth. Peer coaching/mentoring allows an individual to work in their school setting while receiving constructive feedback for improvement. Additionally, this strategy may be beneficial in reducing teacher turnover in the long run (Joyce & Showers, 2002).
- *Action planning:* The first step of professional development is attending the event; however, once participants return to their worksite, it is very easy to return to comfortable habits. Having a well-thought-out action plan encourages individuals to set specific and realistic expectations for change in their classroom.
- *Follow-up and support:* Although it is common to see small changes in teacher practice upon return to their classroom, when follow-up to an initial professional development event or on-going support does not occur, the gains are likely to remain small. Well-designed follow-up and support provide the teacher an opportunity to refine their practice with the guidance of a trained practitioner. Additionally, follow-up sessions and support create an on-going dialogue, often resulting in exponential professional growth (Guskey, 1998).

■ HOW MUCH TIME IS THIS GOING TO TAKE?

Professional development that leads to changes in teacher practice and student performance is influenced by many variables, not the least of which is the amount of time individuals spend engaged in their own learning. An analysis of research studies on teacher professional development and its impact on student achievement found that "substantial contact hours of professional development (ranging from 30 to 100 hours in total) spread over six to 12 months showed a positive and significant effect on student achievement" (National Staff Development Council, 2008, p. 2). When the professional development averaged at least 49 hours within a year, student achievement was found to increase by 21% (Wei et al., 2009; Yoon et al., 2007). In addition, studies showed that participation in 5–14 hours of professional development did not have a significant effect on student achievement (Yoon et al., 2007). This research highlights the importance of spending an appropriate amount of time engaging in professional learning opportunities in order to show positive impact on student achievement; however, results from the 2003–2004 National Schools and Staffing Survey (SASS) show that 57% of teachers said they had received no more than 16 hours (2 days or less) of professional development in the last 12 months (Tourkin et al., 2007). Educators must do a better job of both engaging in quality professional development and taking individual responsibility for professional growth and the academic success of students.

Based on his research, Thomas Guskey (1996) proposes a model of teacher change that challenges the "traditional" way of looking at the integration of new ideas and teaching strategies. This model highlights three components (Griffin, 1983; Guskey, 1996):

1. Teachers' beliefs and attitudes
2. Teachers' instructional practices
3. Students' learning outcomes

Guskey asserts that changes in teacher behavior are the first step in changing student learning outcomes and that changes to beliefs and attitudes often follow *after* student learning outcomes have changed.

The premise for this model has roots in teacher assumptions. It is not uncommon for a school administrator to send a teacher to a professional development event for the purpose of learning a new teaching style or strategy, even though the teacher is not necessarily interested in the content. When this is true, the teacher may attend, take the new approach back to their classroom, but not become committed to its effectiveness until *after* they see how students respond and whether the desired academic outcomes are achieved. The end result of looking at professional development through this lens is that events, workshops, and learning experiences need to be developed to enhance the experience of the learner and in turn encourage continual dialogue to ensure the academic achievement of students.

The following, also shown in Figure 8-1, is an example of this concept: During a staff development day, the physical education teachers attend a session on peer assessment strategies. A seasoned teacher questions whether the students actually learn anything by doing this and if they are actually honest in their assessment. Even though the teacher has doubts, he decides to give peer assessment a try in an upcoming class within the volleyball unit.

FIGURE 8-1   A model of teacher change.

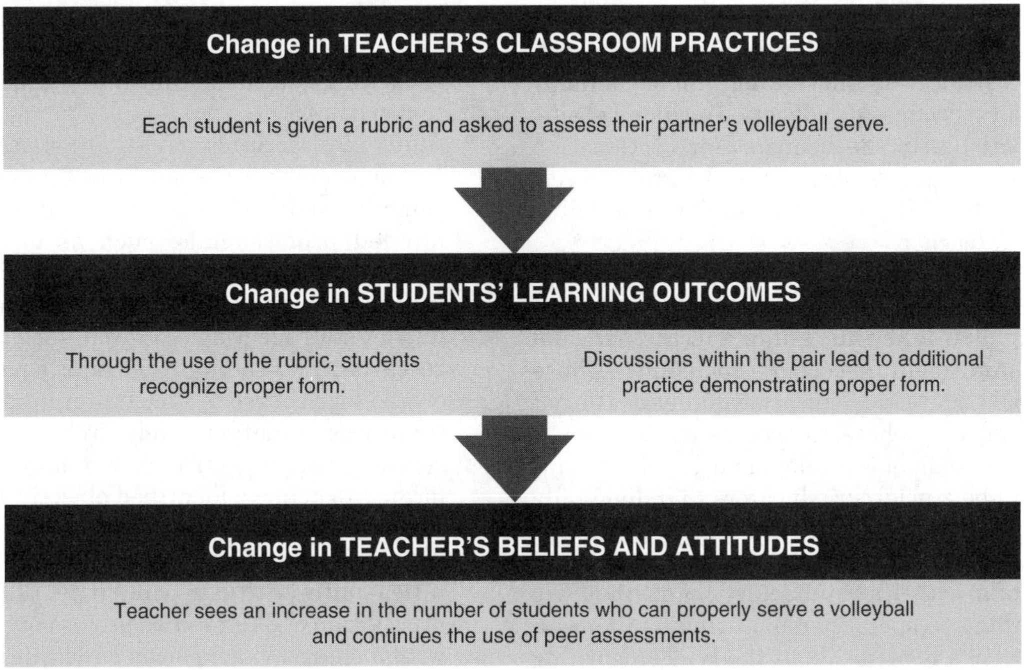

Source: Adapted from Guskey, T. R. (1996). Staff development and the process for teacher change. *Educational Researcher, 15*(5), 5–12.

WHAT IS *YOUR* ROLE IN PROFESSIONAL DEVELOPMENT?

Research highlights the importance of making professional development a standard part of every educator's job responsibilities, but where does professional development fit into an already busy schedule? This section will highlight the importance of establishing a professional development plan, and some of the many different types of professional development activities to consider as you develop your professional development plan.

A **professional development plan** (see **Box 8-1**) is a well-thought-out plan built on personal strengths, areas in need of improvement, and interests of the educator. In addition, consideration should be given to the inclusion of strategic initiatives that the school or district is engaged in and any recertification requirements mandated by the state education agency to ensure that, at minimum, those requirements are being met. Recertification information can be found by visiting your state education agency website, particularly the licensure or certification home page, to learn all of the steps necessary to maintain or advance your standing as a teacher.

Building a professional development plan requires an educator to determine individual **learning goals** and the personal commitment necessary to achieve those goals. State recertification guidelines do not require teachers to receive 30–100 hours of professional development per year, so it will be crucial for educators to individually calculate the number of school-sponsored (or required) hours they will participate in along with the number of hours they are willing to spend personal time on. Once a decision is made about the type of learning opportunities and the amount of time each will involve, a plan can be drafted.

The following is a sample of **professional learning opportunities** to consider for inclusion in a professional development plan. Each of the activities listed varies in its level of time commitment, breadth of information to be learned, and depth of study on the identified skill or topic. When choosing specific learning activities, consider the various factors involved and choose those most appropriate to your identified learning goals.

- *Self-study:* Self-study is achieved by identifying a topic of interest and reading research related to that topic. In addition, self-study may include taking a short quiz at the end of a research article to assess knowledge learned. Self-study exercises tend to be a low impact form of professional development and can often be done in your own home or via the Internet. In addition, some professional organizations offer self-study as a way of earning additional continuing education credits.
- *Study circles:* Study circles are similar to a book club for the purpose of professional growth. Often created with like-minded professionals, such as other middle school health education or physical education teachers, they may be used during staff meetings to discuss a new research article or approach or as a part of a college course to prepare for an upcoming examination. Study circles often serve a discrete purpose, but may be formed to achieve identified objectives.
- *Professional learning communities (PLCs):* Professional learning communities continue to gain popularity. PLCs are a group of like-minded professionals with a shared vision, focus on learning, and commitment to continuous improvement; they are results oriented, and

Box 8-1   **Professional Development Plan**

Name: _____

Subject Area: _____

Date: _____

A. Self-Assessment

What knowledge or skills do I need to learn more about this year?

_____

_____

B. Professional Development Goal(s)

Based on self-assessment data, my professional development goal(s) for this year include:

1. _____

_____

_____

_____

2. _____

_____

_____

_____

3. _____

_____

_____

_____

Skills I Hope to Acquire   **Knowledge I Hope to Acquire**

_____   _____

C. Proposed Learning Activities

I will participate in the following types of activities to meet my professional development goal(s) this year:

_____

_____

Project/Learning Opportunity	**Cost**	**Timeline**
1. _____	1. _____	1. _____
2. _____	2. _____	2. _____
3. _____	3. _____	3. _____

D. Self-Evaluation

Specific measurement of successful completion may include the following:

I will know I am successful if:

_____

_____

Changes I will see in my teaching practice include:

_____

_____

recognize the importance of indentifying and implementing strategies based on best practice. PLCs tend to become part of how a school operates, and team members spend a substantial amount of time over the course of a whole school year working together to embrace and implement skills and strategies targeted at improving student achievement. The PLC may meet once per week, twice per month, or on another predetermined schedule. The PLC may be the mechanism by which attendance at other learning opportunities occurs.

- *In-district trainings or workshops:* Often referred to as "professional development days," a presenter is brought into the school or district to provide all teachers with a designated learning opportunity. Professional development days may be conducted for a whole school, for a content area, or by grade level. The content or information provided may be specific to the subject(s) taught or it may be applicable to a broader view of education. Some professional development days may be offered as a standalone session or as part of a greater professional development plan that includes follow-up and reflection. Many schools offer two to four professional development days per year, and it is expected that all teachers attend.

- *Professional conferences:* Each year, many conferences are offered by a variety of professional organizations. Some of these organizations may be local and affiliated with education professionals in your state; others may be part of a national organization. Conferences tend to be 2–5 days in length and provide the participant with a lot of information on many different topics. Conferences typically do not engage participants in

long-term learning or opportunities for follow-up, but serve an important purpose of exposing individuals to new theories and best practice in the field.

- *Continuous program improvement:* Continuous program improvement is professional development that is not "done to" an individual, but rather "created by" the individual. This approach requires active involvement in research and reviews of current programmatic achievements (perhaps through a needs assessment or other data). That information is used to improve the overall health education or physical education program in the school or district. This may occur through curriculum mapping, policy recommendations to the school committee, implementation of a new curriculum, or further research to indentify gaps in student achievement.

- *Advanced degree courses:* Pursuing an advanced degree will serve to advance current levels of knowledge and skill and may be necessary to continue or advance your teacher certification. While taking courses to receive an advanced degree, look for opportunities to embed new learning into the classroom. This may be a prime opportunity to try something new on a discrete and familiar audience.

- *Research:* One of the best ways to fully understand a phenomenon or the "why" behind a particular behavior or outcome is to research it. Research allows you to determine the question you wish to ask and investigate the underpinnings of an issue. Research does not have to be immensely complex, but can be done in a simple manner. Research may even be conducted by enlisting the help of your students who are interested in a particular issue. Conducting research is one of the best ways to collect valid information to support a change in policy or programmatic structure.

Once the learning activities are chosen and the plan is drafted, compare the stated learning goals with the proposed professional learning opportunities to ensure a logical progression in knowledge and skill development. Reviewing the sequence of learning opportunities is important because change is slow—changes to knowledge, skill level, behavior, and attitudes are a process and require participation in multiple learning opportunities that provide consistent and progressively more complex strategies for implementation. As a learner, allow time for these changes to occur.

Because improving student outcomes is the essential goal of all teacher professional development, the need to support teachers through their journey of exploration through follow-up and reflection-based activities remains a central part of the professional development equation. A well-developed and executed professional development plan is important, but just as follow-up is a key ingredient for quality professional development, self-reflection is a necessary step in on-going professional growth. Although ideally happening on an annual basis, self-reflection and evaluation of progress toward the identified professional learning goals allows for the identification of overlap and gaps in learning. When overlap and gaps are identified, adjustments can be made to further enhance both the learning opportunities chosen in the future and the personal outcomes achieved.

◼ CONCLUSION

Lifelong learning and professional growth is a journey to be taken with care and consideration. Health and physical educators will encounter many professional learning opportunities along their professional journey, but not all of these opportunities will be a valuable use of time or energy. In fact, some of the opportunities will be counterproductive to identified learning goals and will not improve student achievement. Part of the challenge as an educator is to recognize the valuable learning opportunities among those that are crafted to share a small blast of information, but fail to have a positive lasting impact.

The creation of a professional development plan is the first step in truly defining professional goals and achieving those professional outcomes. The plan must be clear and directed in order to avoid some of the common pitfalls, such as too much breadth and too little depth. When care is given and there is time for thoughtful reflection, both the students and the education profession benefit from the dedication and commitment to quality in the classroom.

◼ KEY WORDS AND DEFINITIONS

learning goals   Determined and developed in an effort to guide professional growth. Learning goals should be consistent with desired personal and professional benchmarks.

professional development   A comprehensive, sustained, and intensive approach to improving teachers' and principals' effectiveness in raising student achievement.

professional development event   A structured learning opportunity that has measurable learning outcomes for the participant.

professional development plan   A well-thought-out proposal for professional growth that is built on personal strengths, areas in need of improvement, and the educator's interests.

professional learning community   A group of educators and/or administrators who work collaboratively to address an identified educational concern. Often, they have come together to meet a specific need within a school or content area and result in shared professional growth.

professional learning opportunities Include events or activities that are combined to provide an opportunity for professional growth. Professional learning opportunities may come in many forms and are not necessarily a specific event or single opportunity. Examples include self-study, research, study groups, and advanced degree courses.

■ DISCUSSION QUESTIONS

1. What is the purpose of professional development, and why is it important for educators to engage in?

2. List the key elements of a professional development event. Why is each of these components important?

3. How much time spent in professional learning activities is necessary to impact student achievement? Create a professional development plan that includes this number of hours.

4. Identify at least two forms of professional development you are willing to engage in and explain how these forms of professional development will enhance your identified learning goals.

5. What would be a good research project examining professional development

practices and implementation for physical educators and health educators?

■ REFERENCES

Griffin, G. A. (1983). Introduction: The work of staff development. In G. A. Griffin (Ed.), *Staff development. Eighty-second yearbook of the National Society for the Study of Education* (pp. 8–15). Chicago: University of Chicago Press.

Guskey, T. R. (1996). Staff development and the process for teacher change. *Educational Researcher, 15*(5), 5–12.

Guskey, T. R. (1998). Follow-up is the key, but it's often forgotten. *Journal of Staff Development, 19*(2), 7–8.

Joyce, B., & Showers, B. (2002). *Student achievement through staff development: Fundamentals of school renewal* (3rd ed.). White Plains, NY: Longman.

National Staff Development Council. (2008). *Definition of professional development*. Retrieved August 18, 2009, from http://www.nsdc.org/standfor/definition.cfm

Tourkin, S. C., Warner, T., Parmer, R., et al. (2007). *Documentation for the 2003-04 Schools and Staffing Survey* (NCES 2007-337). Washington, DC: National Center for Education Statistics.

Wei, R. C., Darling-Hammond, L., Andree, A., Richardson, N., & Orphanos, S. (2009). *Professional learning in the learning profession: A status report on teacher development in the United States and abroad*. Dallas, TX: National Staff Development Council.

Yoon, K. S., Duncan, T., Lee, S. W-Y., Scarloss, B., & Shapley, K. (2007). *Reviewing the evidence on how teacher professional development affects student achievement* (Issues & Answers Report, REL 2007-No. 033). Washington, DC: U.S. Department of Education, Institute of Education Sciences, National Center for Education Evaluation and Regional Assistance, Regional Educational Laboratory Southwest. Retrieved September 7, 2009, from http://ies.ed.gov/ncee/edlabs

The Need for Service-Learning in Professional Preparation Programs

Marybeth P. Miller

Service-learning has been identified as a teaching method used by higher education faculty, around the globe, to prepare students for careers in teaching physical education and other related professions (Miller & Nendel, 2011). Having recently written a book on this topic, I wanted to know more specifically about what university students in their first and second year of professional preparation at the college and university level know about service-learning. To help me answer this question, I approached a colleague who at the time was teaching an Introduction to Teaching Physical Education course involving freshman and sophomore students to ask if I could visit the class and informally inquire what they (the students) knew about service-learning. All of the students were physical education majors in a teacher preparation program. A little over half stated that they had heard of service-learning whereas the others had not. Those that had heard of service-learning stated that they heard about it in past jobs, a first-year course at the university, from other students, or they did not remember where they heard of it. Hence, it was all over the place. Their definitions of service-learning included doing a service and learning from it, learning for a purpose, not sure, intrinsic rewards, learning by doing, and helping others. They viewed service versus service-learning as more similar than different, or they stated they were not sure. Their picture of how each was different from the other rested with

service being more helping without a learning component whereas service-learning involved helping and learning by helping or teaching how to help someone.

I then asked the students what they believed the value of service-learning would be in their professional preparation for becoming a physical education teacher. Responses varied from not knowing, to having a better understanding of what they would be doing in the future, gaining new ideas and techniques, doing things outside of the traditional classroom settings, preparing them to aid children in learning, and providing them with a greater opportunity to learn what is expected in the real world. Everyone agreed that service-learning would benefit everyone involved and that service-learning applies to both schools and communities. This was a wonderful informal conversation that provided me with the basis for what I present in this article.

■ WHAT IS SERVICE-LEARNING?

In a traditional education model, most learning occurs within the confines of a classroom. Today's professional preparation of teachers is moving beyond textbooks alone to a pairing of academic content and concepts gleaned from texts with early and more applied real-world experiences. Because teaching is a practice-based profession like medicine, social work, and nursing, one role of higher education professional teacher preparation is to examine and design or redesign applied experiences for greater practice-based training (National Council for Accreditation of Teacher Education, n.d.). Over the past 20 years, professional preparation programs have improved in offering earlier field experiences to explore career possibilities, imprint realistic professional expectations, and increase competency and proficiency in what future professionals should know, value, and do. This improvement is due to the partnerships created between universities and the schools or community organizations where students observe and intern, historically primarily benefiting college students' technical skills, possibly due to no forethought of whether each (the university student and the school/organization site) could intentionally benefit the other.

Duncan and Kopperund (2008) state, "Service learning is a teaching and learning method that upholds a commitment to appreciating the assets of and serving the needs of a community partner while enhancing student learning and academic rigor through the practice of intentional reflective thinking and responsible civic action" (p. 4). They identify four traits that characterize service-learning:

- Commitment to community partnership
- Learning and academic rigor
- Intentional reflective thinking
- Practice of civic responsibility

The academic rigor of a specific course may be associated with service-learning, applying what you've learned in the classroom to the service provided, or more professionally broad, such as what you've learned from a major's club representing the point of view of an academic department's development of professionalism competencies. Intentional

reflective thinking needs to occur before, during, and after the service-learning occurs. This reflective practice connects academic concepts and content to the service being delivered. The practice of civic responsibility challenges students to recognize their roles and responsibilities as citizens living in an ever-changing world, addressing hardships people live with caused by environmental conditions (such as hurricanes and earthquakes) and rising world tensions. In this sense, service-learning is a means of fostering in future professionals the spirit and sense of democracy. I relate this to what the late President John F. Kennedy stated in his January 20, 1961, inaugural address to the United States: "Ask not what your country can do for you—ask what you can do for your country" (Bartleby, 1961, para 25). Serving together to improve the livelihood of others and fostering peace, social justice, and equity are grounded in the democratic process of the human spirit.

■ THEORETICAL FOUNDATION

As a **pedagogy**, physical education instructors may use service-learning as a practical way of linking learning through real world experiences of learning to serve and serving to learn. What's key here is the notion of the experience—the experience of learning while serving. Hence, a popular theory behind service-learning is the Experiential Learning Theory (ELT) developed by educational psychologist Dr. David A. Kolb (1984) that evolved from his research on cognitive development and cognitive style. Kolb developed a four-stage learning cycle using concrete experience (planning, organizing, leading activities, and discussion), reflective observation (recording the service experience, journaling, required writing assignments), abstract conceptualization (course readings based on a service-learning site or program type) to deepen the learning experience, and active experimentation (taking what has been learned from the experience to translate new actions, further planning new actions, solving problems, and making decisions).

Service-learning has an intentional scope and sequence, exercised through the four-stage cycle, that strengthens the bridge between classroom theory and academic content through **reflection**. Experiential learning is the action-based approach to bringing alive concepts and content studied in the classroom. Implementing academic service-learning in physical education may bring alive what is studied in the classroom in a more meaningful manner that can be recognized by students through critical reflection. Hazelbaker (2011) summed this up as "learning results from the synergetic transitions that occur as people interact with their environment, which ultimately creates knowledge" (p. 49).

■ SERVICE VS. SERVICE-LEARNING

During my conversation with students in the Introduction to Physical Education course, I asked them to explain what they knew to be the difference between service and service-learning. Some did not know. Others characterized service as doing something for a cause, acts of kindness, helping others learn, helping someone, or doing it because it's recommended. Their definitions of service-learning included teaching how to help someone, learning by doing, providing learning as a service to children, getting involved in a more hands-on way, and helping target students in need. A common factor that surfaced for both was to help others in need.

Many responses defined service as a means of helping others whereas service-learning was a means of helping others and learning from it. Who learns? What is the link? No service-learning responses addressed the central framework for service-learning: academic coursework, needed service, and intentional reflection.

Although a mission, specific goals, and objectives are needed in both service and service-learning to affect injustice (social change) or solve a pressing problem (civic responsibility), the service-learning model is nested within the integrated triad of academic coursework, needed service, and intentional reflection. The triad is purposeful and carefully laid out by the faculty teaching the course where a service-learning program or project is embedded. It is important for students to know that learning not only benefits them, but also benefits those being served. This two-way street of learning can be evidence-based through intentional reflection before, during, and after a service-learning program in order to examine the impact made upon learning.

An example of a community-based service program is when university students majoring in adapted physical education offer their services, occasionally or regularly, to a community center's adapted aquatics program that has a shortage of instructors. In this model, the primary beneficiaries are the individuals being taught swimming skills by the university students. Although the university students may learn from their experience, the learning is not the intentional outcome of the service they provide in the community. In this situation, the service (an act of volunteerism) is the primary emphasis; the learning is the secondary emphasis.

Let's take the same group of university students majoring in adapted physical education who happen to be enrolled in Introduction to Adapted Physical Activity. The instructor has created a **course-embedded service-learning project** in partnership with a nearby community recreation center that offers an adapted aquatics program that has a shortage of instructors. The university course instructor crafts the initial service-learning program, in which the students enrolled in the course provide adapted aquatics instruction to the clients enrolled in the community aquatics program once a week. The intention of this service-learning project is to link the study of individuals with social-emotional, cognitive, and physical challenges and their unique needs to those being serviced in the aquatics program. While learning styles and dynamic systems of family interaction are being studied as course content in the classroom, they are being witnessed and addressed by the university students' weekly service in the pool.

Prior to the service-learning program starting, the course instructor had the university students write a reflection about their perceived competence to adequately teach aquatics to individuals with special needs—an example of a preprogram reflection. During the service-learning program, these students were to reflect each week by completing a structured journal log and submit it to the course instructor through a technology site where it could be read and responded to—an example of intentional reflection during the service-learning project. Upon the completion of the program, the university students completed a survey designed to address specific components of the service-learning program that reflected the Introduction to Adapted Physical Activity course content and concepts—an example of intentional reflection after the service-learning program has ended. Altogether, in the second example, the learning had primary emphasis and the service had secondary emphasis.

John Miller from Texas Tech University uniquely distinguishes volunteerism from service-learning (Miller, 2011). He states that volunteerism may be best applied as *service*-learning because the primary emphasis is on the service outcomes and the learning is secondary, as is the case of the first community-based adapted aquatics example. In contrast, for university course field experiences and internships, learning outcomes for the benefit of the university students become a primary emphasis, and this may be appropriately titled service-*learning*. However, when a service-learning program's learning outcomes and the service outcomes both are the primary emphasis, and when specific pedagogical strategies are applied to promote reflection, then service and learning become balanced and therefore applied as service-learning, resulting in learning by the university students and those receiving a service. This would be relevant to the second adapted aquatics example provided earlier.

■ LINKING STANDARDS TO SERVICE-LEARNING

Individuals preparing for careers of service, including education, study the importance and value of professional standards. Standards provide a framework for high quality to ensure best practices are executed. Readers of this article who are preparing to become physical education teachers are expected to know, demonstrate, and value the K–12 content standards found in *Moving into the Future: National Content Standards for Physical Education*, Second Edition, published by the National Association for Sport and Physical Education (NASPE, 2004). Preservice teacher candidates study how these standards could be used to shape and revise curriculum in order to provide learners the knowledge, skills, and values needed for lifelong movement habits to remain healthy, and implement these standards when assessing, planning, and teaching.

Although the NASPE content standards help guide physical education best practices, individuals implementing service-learning as a pedagogy at the K–12 grade levels are encouraged to examine and adopt as a best-practice framework the *K–12 Service-Learning Standards and Indicators for Quality Practice* published in 2008 by the National Youth Leadership Council (NYLC). These standards and indicators, yours to discover, provide practitioners implementing service-learning with a direction for designing and implementing a high-quality service-learning program or project with indicators for duration and intensity, linking to curriculum, forming partnerships, and qualifying meaningful service. Further, they help to clarify various roles important to service-learning quality: youth voice (involved with planning, implementing, and evaluating), diversity, reflection, and progress monitoring (assessing service-learning impact). Billig and Weah (2008) identify that these service-learning standards provide a common set of well-defined expectations for high-quality practice, provide a consistent language for in-depth discussion of practice to help educators reflect on and improve their practice, provide a framework for service-learning practice evaluation, and may serve as a compass for professional development opportunities specific to service-learning within a discipline (e.g. embedded service-learning within a therapeutic recreation [TR] course). Together, how can TR and service-learning standards make a difference in the professional growth and development of the service provider and those being served?

■ CULTIVATING CIVIC RESPONSIBILITY

Central to high-quality service-learning is **civic responsibility**. The March 26, 2009, signing of the Edward M. Kennedy Service America Act (H.R. 1388) by the U.S. Senate, which became Public Law No. 111-13 when signed by President Barack Obama, provided increased opportunities for Americans of all ages to serve. As an educator, I believe there is no greater impact than to be self-challenged in examining the ways and means of implementing service-learning as a course-embedded teaching method. Through this, I am able to guide a body of youth—in my case, teacher candidates—to work with me to serve others, all while carefully cultivating their ability to become civically responsible individuals and recognize the meaning of civic responsiblity. I examine how *they* examine their own sense of responsibility to care for others and to contribute to the community through their level of active and direct collaboration. What's more, I examine *their* level of understanding of how they may be impacting the community they are serving (while learning).

Considering the increasingly diverse world we inhabit, both within and beyond the university, integrating a substantive and challenging out-of-classroom experience that offers an in-depth interrogation of social justice issues can help to foster a climate of acceptance and respect long after the students graduate and move on to their careers, to hopefully "pay it forward" to those they teach in schools, programs, and the like. Service-learning projects can provide an excellent opportunity to address issues, such as sensitivity to social differences, systematic injustice, and an orientation toward social action, thus connecting theory and practice in a meaningful way both within and beyond the classroom walls. However, simply stating that service-learning ought to have a socially conscious orientation may, in fact, overlook the entrenchment of the "community service" paradigm that seems omnipresent in a multitude of university service-learning projects. Consider pondering the many ways in which service-learning may foster civic responsibility that may concomitantly cultivate cultural competence.

CONCLUSION

This article presents a very different idea for professional preparation—the use of service-learning as a teaching and learning tool, otherwise known as a pedagogy. Readers may or may not have heard about service-learning, but those who have heard of it may not have a clear understanding of what it is, or how it links to academic preparation within professional development. Service-learning is growing world-wide as a pedagogical tool for teacher preparation inside and outside of health and physical education. Related disciplines of sport management, therapeutic recreation, and adapted physical activity have embraced service-learning (Miller & Nendel, 2011). A recognized and respected teaching and learning method, service-learning can empower students to use their new knowledge to make a difference. It begins with identifying an authentic community need (by instructor and/or instructor-students), and then assessing how finding a solution for that need meets an academic goal. In some cases, service-learning may be course-embedded; in others, service-learning may have a broader professional approach through projects undertaken by members of professional clubs (e.g., PETE Club or FITT Club) that link a professional program's mission, vision, and goals under the supervision of a faculty mentor.

This article provided clarity as to who the beneficiaries are: those serving and those being served. What's more, to facilitate high-quality best practices, service-learning has specific standards to guide practitioners with practice, reflection, evaluation, and discussion using a common service-learning language. Finally, we took a look at the significance of the call for all Americans to serve and become engaged in civic responsibility. Making a difference through a social justice cause may create individuals who work with those different from themselves to become more tolerant and culturally competent.

KEY WORDS AND DEFINITIONS

civic responsibility   An element of high quality service-learning. The service-learning project promotes students' responsibility to care for others and to contribute to the community. By participating in the service-learning project, students understand how they can impact their community.

course-embedded service-learning project   A required or optional project used as a central theme of an academic course. Experiential learning is central to the knowledge development of academic course content and concepts. Service-learning is part of the course practice.

experiential learning theory   A theory developed by Kolb that describes a four-stage learning cycle—experience, reflection, abstract conceptualization, and active experimentation—to explain how knowledge is created.

pedagogy   A teaching method or teaching style; the study of teaching; the practice of teaching.

reflection An element of high-quality service-learning in which students think, share, and produce reflective products individually or as group members. Examples may include but are not limited to discussion, journal writing, and surveys.

service-learning A teaching method that combines academic instruction, meaningful service, and critical reflective thinking to enhance student learning and civic responsibility.

■ DISCUSSION QUESTIONS

1. Discuss the difference between service and service-learning, and present examples.
2. Identify a course in your program of study and picture how the triad would be completed.
3. Discuss what role standards have in service-learning.
4. What other types of experiential learning could exist, and how might they be different than service-learning?
5. What role does service-learning play in developing civically responsible individuals?

■ EXTENSION ACTIVITIES

To complete these activities, you will need to have the NASPE 2004 physical education national content standards, *Moving into the Future: National Standards for Physical Education* (2nd ed.); the *Seven Elements of High Quality Service Learning* (Service Learning 2000 Center); and the NYLC 2008 *K–12 Service Learning Standards and Indicators for Quality Practice*.

1. Form cooperative groups and create a course-embedded school-based or community-based service-learning project, or have different groups address each. Organize three groups to each address the project's alignment to the physical education content standards, the seven elements, and the K–12 service-learning standards. Each group will present their service-learning project to the class.
2. Given the virtual project just designed, describe the possible benefits to those being served as well as to those providing the service.
3. Using this project, identify ways in which you may become a more civically responsible (preservice) teacher candidate.

■ REFERENCES

Billig, S. H., & Weah, W. (2008). K–12 service learning standards and indicators for quality practice. *Growing to Greatness, 5,* 8–15. Retrieved December 18, 2008, from http://www.nylc.org/sites/nylc.org/files/files/G2G08.pdf

Duncan, D., & Kopperud, J. (2008). *Service learning companion.* Boston, MA: Houghton Mifflin.

Edward M. Kennedy Service America Act of 2009, Public Law No. 111-13, 123 Stat.1460 H.R. 1388 (2009).

Hazelbaker, C. B. (2011). Basics of service-learning. In M. P. Miller & J. D. Nendel (Eds.), *Service-learning in physical education and related professions: A global perspective* (pp. 45–59). Burlington, MA: Jones & Bartlett Learning.

Bartleby. (1989). *John F. Kennedy inaugural address, Friday, January 20, 1961.* Retrieved March 12, 2010, from http://www.bartleby.com/124/pres56.html

Kolb, D. A. (1984). *Experiential learning: Experience as the source of learning and development.* Englewood Cliffs, NJ: Prentice Hall.

Miller, J. (2011). Service versus service-learning. In M. P. Miller & J. D. Nendel (Eds.), *Service-learning in physical education and related professions: A global perspective* (pp. 101–111). Burlington, MA: Jones & Bartlett Learning.

Miller, M. P., & Nendel, J. D. (Eds.). (2011). *Service-learning in physical education and related professions: A global perspective.* Burlington, MA: Jones & Bartlett Learning.

National Association for Sport and Physical Education. (2004). *Moving into the future: National content standards for physical education.* Reston, VA: Author.

National Council for Accreditation of Teacher Education. (n.d.). *National blue ribbon*

panel initiates a mainstream move to more clinically based preparation of teachers. Retrieved January 17, 2010, from http://www.ncate.org/Public/Newsroom/NCATE-NewsPressReleases/tabid/669/EntryId/89/NCATE-Blue-Ribbon-Panel-Initiates-a-Mainstream-Move-to-More-Clinically-Based-Preparation-of-Teachers.aspx

National Youth Leadership Council. (2003). *Essential elements of effective service-learning practice.* Retrieved November 2, 2008, from http://www.nylc.org

Strength Assessment and Training in Adolescents

Disa Hatfield

Resistance exercise and youth have a controversial history. In the past, strength training was not recommended for prepubescents or adolescents primarily due to safety concerns. However, these concerns are now antiquated, and exercise physiologists and the American Academy of Pediatrics (AAP) both support the implementation of strength and resistance training programs for young children (American Academy of Pediatrics, 1990). Studies show that a moderate-intensity strength training program can help increase strength, decrease the risks of injury while playing sports, increase motor performance skills, increase bone density, and enhance growth and development in children (Fleck & Kraemer, 1993; Guy & Micheli, 2000; Payne, Morrow, Johnson, & Dalton, 1997; Tsuzuku, Ikegami, & Yabe, 1998).

The AAP position on strength training supports the implementation of strength and resistance training programs, even for prepubescent children, that are monitored by well-trained adults and take into account the child's maturation level. The only limitation the AAP suggests is to avoid repetitive maximal lifts (lifts that are one-repetition maximum lifts or are within two to three repetitions of a **one-repetition maximum lift (1RM)** until they have reached Tanner Stage 5 of developmental maturity. Tanner Stage 5 is the level in which visible secondary sex characteristics have been developed. Usually, in this stage adolescents will also have passed their period of maximal velocity of height growth. However, there is some evidence that 1RM testing can be safely administered if proper technique has been mastered (Faigenbaum et al., 2002).

The AAP's concern that children wait until this stage to perform maximal lifts is that the **epiphyseal plates**, commonly known as growth plates, are still vulnerable to injury before puberty. Repeated injury to these growth plates may hinder growth. Growth plate injury potential is actually decreased in preadolescents compared to adolescents, however, because growth cartilage may be less susceptible to shearing type forces (Faigenbaum et al., 2009). Further, several studies have been conducted that show that these types of injuries occur less frequently during weight training compared to other sports.

In published literature, all incidences of injury were attributed to either poor training design or lack of supervision; there is no evidence suggesting resistance training will affect the normal growth and maturation process (Faigenbaum, 2000). However, it is important to note that unsupervised resistance training can be dangerous. There have been reported cases of serious injury and even death in young people who attempt to perform resistance exercises without supervision. Heavy barbells and free weights can become loose and fall, resulting in injury, and it is possible to get a limb or finger stuck on a free weight machine. Any resistance exercise training should only be done under adult supervision, even if the youth has experience in resistance training.

■ PROGRAM DESIGN

Neither the AAP nor exercise physiologists have set a minimum age for a child to begin a resistance training program. Research has been conducted on moderate weight training programs with children as young as 4 years (Faigenbaum et al., 2002). Strength gains of 30–74% have been reported with short-term training (8 weeks) in both preadolescents and adolescents (Faigenbaum et al., 2009). Similar to adults, strength gains are dependent upon the intensity and the duration of the program.

The first objective of a training program is to introduce the body to the stresses of training and to teach basic technique and form, not the amount of weight lifted. Light weight training can be introduced in order to establish a foundation. Fleck and Kraemer (1993) recommend a training scheme of 10–15 repetitions and 1–3 sets per muscle group. The weight should be one that the child can lift for 10–15 repetitions without going to muscular failure. Once a base has been established, the amount of exercises and the weight lifted can be increased and a more advanced routine can be incorporated.

Before puberty and in the beginning 8 weeks of any strength training program, the majority of strength gains are neurological in nature, not from muscle hypertrophy or muscle growth. Higher repetitions allow children to build a physiological pathway for their technique. Neurological gains come from mastering a new motor pathway, increased muscle recruitment, and a decrease in mechanisms that normally inhibit force production (Behm, Faigenbaum, Falk, & Klentrou, 2008; Faigenbaum et al., 2009). These mechanisms usually exist to protect muscles, ligaments, and tendons from injury while producing force. Training for even a short period of time (1–2 weeks) can reduce these inhibitions, thus allowing more force production. It is important to note that these mechanisms never completely dissipate; they still exist for injury prevention.

Progression of intensity should be gradual. A normal resistance training progression includes an increase in the **volume** (amount of sets and repetitions) and/or the **intensity** (amount of weight lifted). Despite recent progress in the research of resistance training and children, there is still not enough information to make safe assumptions about program progressions. Children and adolescents should progress on an individual basis, and they should be able to maintain proper form while lifting when the volume or intensity of resistance exercise is increased.

Program Design Guidelines

The following are program design guidelines to which adolescents should adhere when engaging in a training program.

1. Incorporate a warm-up before training and a cool-down period after.
2. A beginning program should take place 2–3 days per week on nonconsecutive days.
3. The program should be a full-body program totaling about 8–12 exercises.
4. Slowly increase the intensity and volume over time. Begin with one set of each exercise, building to three sets over time. The repetition range should be 10–15 repetitions. Proper form should always be a guideline to increase the volume or intensity or stop the set. For instance, if form begins to decline at repetition 7, stop the set, take a break, and decrease the weight on the next set. If the youth can maintain proper form for 15 repetitions, then it is appropriate to increase the weight or increase the number of sets. In general, a weight increase of about 5–10% is a recommended starting point for increasing the intensity.
5. Always focus on correct form when lifting, not on the amount of weight lifted. Begin with exercises that don't require a great amount of coordination and balance first, then progress to movements that are multi-joint movements.

■ TRAINING MODALITIES

The most common form of strength training is using free weights or weight machines. However, using these methods requires a great amount of space to store the equipment and a large amount of money to buy the equipment. Most school systems have neither. Luckily, a resistance training modality can be anything that offers resistance. This includes water, rubber tubing or large rubber bands, handheld weights, partner-resistant movements, even water-filled bottles or cans. When beginning a program with preadolescents, it is advisable to start with body weight exercises. Sit-ups, push-ups, and weighted balls (also called medicine balls) can easily be incorporated into a program.

■ PLYOMETRIC TRAINING

Plyometric training, a form of training that involves powerful movements such as bounding, hopping, jumping, and throwing with and without resistance, is becoming a popular form of training with adolescents. Anecdotally, this form of training is similar to spontaneous playground activities and can be an enjoyable and low-cost form of training. Clinically, an appropriately prescribed and implemented program has been shown to be safe and effective in increasing power and overall conditioning (Faigenbaum et al., 2009).

■ ASSESSMENT

Strength assessment is not usually a focus in most physical education programs. However, anecdotal evidence suggests that strength testing can be a positive experience for some youth, especially those outside sociocultural body-type norms for different sports. Data from the Chambersburg's (Pennsylvania) school district reveal that hand grip strength was positively correlated with body mass index (BMI), suggesting that strength testing is an area in which overweight kids excel (Hatfield et al., 2004). Handgrip strength is highly correlated to overall body strength, and may be a better estimate of strength compared to the push-up test, which tests muscular endurance (Hatfield et al., 2004). Handgrip strength can be universally tested with a dynamometer, a device that is inexpensive and can easily be adapted to fit the hand. Normative data for this instrument exists across a wide range of ethnicities and ages. These factors make handgrip strength testing an attractive alternative to more expensive modalities.

Depending on the age and, most importantly, the experience of the youth being tested, 1RM testing on machines or free weights may be advisable. Although 1RM testing has been safely performed on children in multiple studies, care should be taken when performing one-repetition maximum testing (Faigenbaum et al., 2009). In one study that investigated maximal strength testing in children, the researchers needed 7 to 11 sets to determine a one-repetition maximum, as opposed to the normal 3 to 5 used in adult tests (Faigenbaum, Milliken, & Westcott, 2003). There are adult protocols that use a three- to five-repetition maximum testing scheme, but there is not currently any normative data for children. However, high volume testing through either increased sets or increased repetitions may lead to fatigue, which in turn can lead to a breakdown in form. Further, due to differences in protocols and equipment used, there is not enough data to produce norms for preadolescents and adolescents. In any situation, maximal strength testing should never be performed without proper adult supervision because of risk of injury.

Regardless of testing modality, it is important to take into account the experience of the children, program design, test specificity, equipment availability, and equipment type. The normal maturation and growth process of children also should be considered. Increases in strength will occur naturally as a child grows, making it difficult to assess whether strength increases are due to training or are occurring naturally. However, multiple studies utilizing age-matched controls compared to youth undertaking a well-designed strength training program report that preadolescents and adolescents can increase their strength above and beyond that of normal growth and maturation (Faigenbaum et al., 2009).

■ BENEFITS

Resistance exercise is highly adaptable to individuals of differing sizes and mental and physical capabilities, making it a viable modality to increase all aspects of health and fitness. Similar to other activities, participation in a regular strength and resistance training program has many benefits, including physical and sociological. Of importance, resistance exercise can enhance the mood and well-being of children. Further, a more positive attitude towards physical education and physical fitness has been reported in children who take part in both a multifaceted conditioning program and a resistance training program (Faigenbaum et al., 2009).

Physiological benefits include increases in strength, cardiovascular risk factor reductions, decreased risk for developing type 2 diabetes, and improvements in bone health (Faigenbaum et al., 2009). Although some of these improvements are obvious (strength increases), others are not well-publicized, such as cardiovascular benefits. Although aerobic activity still elicits the greatest improvements in cardiovascular health, resistance exercise training can decrease blood lipid levels and blood pressure (Faigenbaum et al., 2009). Like aerobic activity, participation in a regular resistance exercise program can also decrease body fat and improve body composition, which is also a risk factor for cardiovascular disease. Resistance exercise also has been shown to increase insulin sensitivity in overweight and obese young people, dramatically reducing their risk for type 2 diabetes (Faigenbaum et al., 2009). Bone health is also enhanced in all youth after a resistance training program when compared to age-matched controls, which is of particular importance to females, who have a greater risk of developing osteoporosis later in life. Approximately 50% of bone mass is acquired by the adolescent years, and implementation of a resistance training program at a young age is associated with decreased risk of osteoporosis later in life (Behm et al., 2008; Faigenbaum et al., 2009; Heinonen et al., 2000; Tsuzuku et al., 1998; Witzke & Snow, 2000).

In addition to these physiological factors, improvements in sports performance and motor skill development and decreased injury incidence are also benefits of regular resistance exercise training. Young female athletes in particular have a high incidence of knee-related injuries. Emerging research suggests that a variety of resistance exercise programs can significantly reduce the number of serious knee injuries in young female athletes (Faigenbaum et al., 2009).

■ TIPS FOR SUPERVISING A YOUTH STRENGTH AND RESISTANCE TRAINING PROGRAM

Safety should always come first when training a youth or child. It is helpful to prepare yourself for any and all possibilities. Preparation is also helpful in easing the minds of concerned parents. The following are some helpful tips that will help to ensure the safety of youth participating in resistance training:

- Make sure the equipment you will be using is free from defects and is adequate for young children, who may not be able to lift a normal 45-pound bar or may not be tall enough to use the squat racks or bench.
- It is important that young lifters are adequately hydrated and have had at least a small meal within a few hours of training.
- Athletes should be sufficiently warmed up before beginning a training session.
- Youth should always be under the direct supervision of a competent trainer, a coach, or an experienced physical education teacher when weight training.
- Employ a wide variety of exercises and training styles to keep interest levels high and encourage participation in a wide variety of sports and activities.
- Make sure that the environment is conducive to training. If you are training in a gym that doesn't have air conditioning in the summer months, take special precautions to ensure that adequate water is available and participants stay hydrated. If possible, train in the morning when it is cooler. Weather reporters sometimes use the term *wet bulb globe temperature*, especially in the summer. In hot weather, it is advantageous to pay attention to this number. The National Athletic Trainer's Association recommends that training or events be delayed if this temperature reaches 82 degrees. Keep in mind this is the wet bulb globe temperature, not what we normally consider the temperature to be. A wet bulb globe temperature of 73 degrees (which is a high-risk level) is approximately the same as a dry bulb temperature ("normal" temperature) of

73 degrees with 100% humidity and a dry bulb temperature of 93 degrees at 20% humidity.

- Be able to provide informational sources to parents of young lifters to erase any lingering doubts they have about their children lifting weights and to educate the parents about the importance of instilling healthy lifestyle choices at a young age. Coaches/teachers often have no control over the eating habits, sleeping patterns, and so on of their athletes, so communication with the parents is vital to enhance these very important ideals.
- Utilize workout logs to track progress and also make note of concerns or special considerations for each youth.

■ CONCLUSION

The research regarding resistance exercise in youth has consistently concluded that it can increase physical and mental health parameters, reduce the risk of injury, and is safe for youth when performed under trained adult supervision.

As a final reminder, because this cannot be stressed enough, at all times remember that youth should progress at in individual pace. Although this makes training difficult in a school or club setting because training programs will have to be individualized, it is incredibly important to ensure the health and safety of young participants. It is also important to stay abreast of the current research in this growing field.

■ KEY WORDS AND DEFINITIONS

epiphyseal plate   The growth plate of a long bone (femur, tibia, etc.). Epiphyseal plates are vulnerable to injury in youth

because they have not hardened into bone yet. It is the point of the long bone where growth is still occurring.

intensity   In resistance exercise terminology, this is expressed as a percentage of a person's one-repetition maximum. It can also simply be the amount of weight lifted if a maximal amount of weight lifted is not known.

one-repetition maximum (1RM)   The maximal amount of weight a person can lift once.

plyometric training   A type of power training that incorporates explosive movements such as jumping or throwing. It is often done using body weight, but also can incorporate small amounts of weights or medicine balls.

resistance exercise   Exercise that uses some form of resistance. Examples include elastic bands or rubber tubing, free weights (barbells, dumbbells), weight machine equipment, water, medicine balls, kettle bells, water- or sand-filled cans or bottles, partner resistance, or body-weight exercises.

volume   A measure of the total amount of work done in a period of time (e.g., a set, a workout, a month). In a single workout, it is defined as the number of repetitions performed multiplied by the number of sets.

■ DISCUSSION QUESTIONS

1. You have decided to begin a resistance training program in your school. A parent comes to you intending to pull their child out of class because they are afraid their child may injure themselves. What course of action do you take?
2. Describe the differences in a training program for a preadolescent who has

never lifted weights before and a program for an adolescent who has had weight training experience.

3. Describe the benefits of resistance training and give examples of different populations of people who may physically and mentally profit from it.

4. Design a 30-minute resistance training program for young preadolescents who do not have access to free weights or machines. What types of exercises would you include? What would the volume be like?

5. Describe the steps you would take to minimize the risk of injury to youth performing resistance exercise.

■ EXTENSION ACTIVITIES

1. List some body weight exercises, making sure you have at least one exercise for every major muscle group. Go through and perform these exercises by yourself or in a group. Once you have completed them, try to find ways to increase the intensity of each exercise *without* adding free weights that you have to purchase. For example, if you can do a set of push-ups or lunges easily, what can you do to increase the intensity to make it more difficult? Conversely, if there are certain exercises you struggled with, what can you do to modify the exercises to make them easier?

■ REFERENCES

American Academy of Pediatrics. (1990). Policy statement: Strength, weight and power lifting, and body building by children and adolescents. *Pediatrics, 5,* 801–803.

Behm, D. G., Faigenbaum, A. D., Falk, B., & Klentrou, P. (2008). Canadian Society for Exercise Physiology position paper: Resistance training in children and adolescents. *Applied Physiology, Nutrition, and Metabolism, 33*(3), 547–561.

Faigenbaum, A. D. (2000) Strength training for children and adolescents. *Clinical Sports Medicine, 4,* 593–619.

Faigenbaum, A. D., Kang, J., McFarland, J., Bloom, J., Magnatta, J., Ratamess, N., et al. (1996). *Youth resistance training: Position statement and literature review.* Retrieved September 12, 2010, from http://www.nsca-lift.org

Faigenbaum, A. D., Kraemer, W. J., Blimkie, C. J., Jeffreys, I., Micheli, L. J., Nitka, M., et al. (2009). Youth resistance training: Updated position statement paper from the National Strength and Conditioning Association. *Journal of Strength and Conditioning Research, 23*(5 Suppl), S60–S79.

Faigenbaum, A. D., Milliken, L. A., Loud, R. L., Burak, B. T., Doherty, C. L., & Westcott, W. L. (2002). Comparison of 1 and 2 days per week of strength training in children. *Research Quarterly for Exercise and Sport, 73*(4), 416–424.

Faigenbaum, A. D., Milliken, L. A., & Westcott, W. L. (2003.) Maximal strength testing in healthy children. *Journal of Strength and Conditioning Research, 17*(1), 162–166.

Fleck, S. J., & Kraemer, W. J. (1993). *Strength training for young athletes.* Champaign, IL: Human Kinetics.

Guy, J. A., & Micheli, L. J. (2000.) Strength training for children and adolescents. *Journal of the American Academy of Orthopedic Surgeons, 1,* 29–36.

Hatfield, D. L., Kraemer, W. J., Shoap, M., Gotwald, M., Trail, J., & Bowling, R. (2004). A gender comparison of physical fitness in 4th-graders. American College of Sports Medicine National Conference, Indianapolis, IN.

Heinonen, A., Sievanen, H., Kannus, P., Oja, P., Pasanen, M., & Vuori, I. (2000). High-impact exercise and bones of growing girls: A 9-month controlled trial. *Osteoporosis International, 12,* 1010–1017.

Payne, V. G., Morrow, J. R., Johnson, L., & Dalton, S. N. (1997). Resistance training in children and youth: A meta-analysis. *Research Quarterly for Exercise and Sport, 1*, 80–88.

Tsuzuku, S., Ikegami, Y., & Yabe, K. (1998). Effects of high-intensity resistance training on bone mineral density in young male powerlifters. *Calcified Tissue International, 4*, 283–286.

Witzke, K. A., & Snow, C. M. (2000). Effects of plyometric jump training on bone mass in adolescent girls. *Medical Science and Sports Exercise, 6*, 1051–1057.

Walking in Their Shoes: Empathy in Physical Education

Tony Monahan

Steve just shook his head when asked about his PE experience as a child.

> On certain days our PE teacher would spread all the balls and other equipment, you know, the fun stuff, on the gym floor. But he also had the door to the gym blocked with a vault box. Only the kids who could climb over the box and into the gym could play with all the stuff. The rest of us had to stand in the hallway and watch. It might as well have been 100 feet tall.

Unfortunately, Steve's story is not an isolated incident. Evidence suggests that generations of students have been "turned off" to lifelong physical activity because of a myriad of negative experiences in the "old PE." However, Steve's frustration did not necessarily stem from the PE curriculum, but from the attitude of the PE teacher himself. Specifically, Steve did not like (and never forgot) the way he was treated. The old PE has traditionally favored those students who were physically skilled while often alienating those who were not. This created an unequal educational situation where only the minority of elite students succeeded while lesser skilled students became disillusioned. Perpetuating the matter is the observance that PE teacher candidates tend to be attracted to the profession because of extensive involvement and achievement in K–12 PE and athletics (Dewar & Lawson, 1984). In other words, the majority of PE teacher candidates (as well as current teachers) are those elite students who were picked first and who dominated in PE classes. As a result, PE often is viewed as "a profession that talks and teaches to itself" (Gard, 2006, p. 2). In addition, studies on **empathy** and competition have shown that highly competitive children were found to have lower empathy scores than less competitive children (Barnet & Bryan, 1974; Kohn, 1986). This suggests that PE teacher candidates who come from rich and successful athletic backgrounds may not have the **empathic capacity** to fully understand those who are not as athletically skilled. So how do we convert them into teachers of *all* children?

■ THE CHANGE: A CALL FOR AFFECTIVE PRACTICE IN PHYSICAL EDUCATION

Although strides have been made to improve curriculum, accountability, and assessment in PE, the aspect of teaching practice still needs to be addressed. The current crisis in childhood obesity and other inactivity-related disorders speaks to the need for PE teachers to reach all students, not just those who exhibit athletic proficiency. If the definitive goal of PE is the realization of a physically fit society, then all levels of our profession should work on being more inclusive, more receptive, and more concerned.

With that said, there appears to be a need for teacher education programs to address the "human" aspect of our profession. Specifically, we need to start addressing the **affective** side of education in order to better prepare our future teachers to accommodate the needs of a diversity of ability in their classes. The effort to humanize PE should be directed toward making students feel more comfortable, confident, and supported in their PE experience. In order to do that, the PE teacher must have an empathetic understanding of his or her students.

Research on teaching practice demonstrates that multiple factors contribute to teaching excellence. In addition to specific teaching skills and subject-matter knowledge, affective characteristics such as enthusiasm, perseverance, and concern for children are essential for good teaching and lifelong learning (Darling-Hammond & Sykes, 2003). However, affective attributes are largely ignored in today's educational reform efforts (Noddings, 1992). Without specific attention devoted to the development of affective qualities, teachers may not have sufficient experience or training to properly recognize student needs, or display understanding and empathy for their students' unique situations. Teacher education programs should bring to light the reasons that students lose interest and stop participating in PE, and subsequently acquire a negative perception of physical activity and exercise throughout life. It is important for our future teachers to be aware of student perceptions (past and present) toward physical education and exercise.

■ CULTIVATING EMPATHY

Being able to put aside one's self-centered focus and impulses has social benefits: it opens the way to empathy, to real listening, to taking another person's perspective. Empathy . . . leads to caring, altruism, and compassion. Seeing things from another's perspective breaks down biased stereotypes, and so breeds tolerance and acceptance of differences. (Goleman, 1995, p. 285)

Empathy involves an affective mode of understanding, an ability to perceive and share the emotions of another—what it's like to be in someone else's shoes. Although there are many definitions of empathy, Hoffman's (1987) definition appears to be most applicable to the PE teacher/student situation. He describes empathy as "an affective response more appropriate to someone else's situation than one's own" (p. 48). In order to better engage those who have experienced difficulty or failure in PE, it will be necessary for PE teachers to put themselves into the shoes of students with physical abilities, experiences, and feelings quite different than their own.

Although research has shown empathy to be a naturally occurring human inclination, there is no guarantee that the capacity for higher-level empathy and **prosocial behavior** will naturally develop in all humans (Davis, 1996; Kohn, 1990). However, studies demonstrate that empathy can be enhanced by an educational program (Hatcher et al., 1994). With that in mind, improvements can be made in teaching future educators to better understand and accommodate student needs. PE should not limit itself solely to the practice of physical development. Attention must also be given to the social and psychological needs of our students. Participation in physical activity and play is extremely social and generates deep emotional feelings. Acknowledgement and appreciation of such emotions can add considerably to enjoyment and understanding of one's involvement in the activity. Interactive relationships between teacher and student play an important role in the formation of student attitudes, motivation, comfort level, and success in PE (Koka & Hein, 2006). Teachers who work on knowing and understanding students in order to gauge their perceptions and abilities will more likely have more success than teachers who do not (Noddings, 1992; Rogers, 1983).

■ UNDERSTANDING SOCIOMETRIC STATUS

It is conceivable that PE teachers can influence how students are accepted by peers in their classes. At the very least, PE teachers can influence how students perceive themselves. The views of lower-skilled students in PE should be of particular interest to PE educators because of developmental concerns related to the degree of social acceptance among peers. Lee et al. (1995) found that the criteria children use for judging ability changes with age and social development. Young children (kindergarten to grade one) tend to have an unrealistic and egotistical view of their ability and rarely engage in social comparison. However, as children grow older and more socially aware, they begin to judge ability in comparison to their peers. This social comparison among peers leads to a degree of acceptance, or **sociometric status**, ranging from popular (well liked by peers) to rejected (least liked by peers) (Dunn, Dunn, & Bayduza, 2007).

One can infer from this that PE class is ground zero for social comparison in school. Perceived athletic competence appears to be correlated to high sociometric status among children and may be an important factor that either increases or decreases student acceptance. An example of this is one of the most infamous "old" PE practices of selecting team captains to choose sides for a competition. Students who possess good sports skills (and high sociometric status) tend to be chosen as captains or picked first, whereas students with low skill levels tend to be either chosen last or excluded completely. Therefore, although the practice increases some students' social standing, it could be viewed as devastating to others. Negative experiences may lead to increased feelings of sadness, anxiety, depression, isolation, and withdrawal (Dunn et al., 2007; Fitzpatrick & Watkinson, 2003). Such withdrawal increases the social distance between these students and their peers and could increase the risk of negative social development (e.g., delinquency, school failure, and psychological maladjustment) (Gifford-Smith & Brownell, 2003).

Students who compare negatively to their peers and fear negative social comparison tend to be less optimistic, avoid participation, and develop negative attitudes towards PE. Because children beyond the early school grades begin to compare their ability with peers, low-skilled children tend to disassociate themselves from performance and actions that might attract negative attention. They also tend to become easily discouraged; appear indifferent, disinterested, or unmotivated; display difficulty concentrating; and give up quickly (Robinson, 1990).

■ UNDERSTANDING LEARNED HELPLESSNESS

As an athlete relishes the anticipation of an upcoming competition, and a champion savors a win, the player who is physically awkward is concerned about upcoming forced participation in a game or sport and the anticipated expectation of failure. (Fitzpatrick & Watkinson, 2003, p. 292)

The concept of **learned helplessness** may have additional application in understanding the experience of low-skilled students in PE. Learned helplessness is a perception of futility regardless of what one does, which could lead to a perceived lack of interest in performances and tasks and unwillingness to learn new skills (Martinek & Griffith, 1994). Portman (1995) suggested that "physical educators lack systematic information about low-skilled students' experiences in physical education and the long term consequences of being low skilled" (p. 445). Furthermore, student rejection by a teacher may be considered a "key factor" in school failure (Gifford-Smith & Brownell, 2003, p. 248).

In order to work toward success for all in PE, it is imperative for teachers to recognize student perceptions in order to establish a genuine, facilitative environment and enable students to maintain optimism and effort without having to compare themselves with others. Identification of social factors such as sociometric status and learned helplessness in PE could help the PE teacher to decrease situations that might expose students' weaknesses or portray them in a negative light. Adopting programs and activities that emphasize equal participation, enjoyment of movement, and foundations of lifetime activity could help to eliminate the negative social comparison associated with competitive activities.

■ EMPATHIC AWARENESS IN ACTION

In a PE methods class, preservice teacher Tammy taught "the hungry snake," a game involving groups of students racing around the gym and collecting items in mesh bags. When the bags were full, Tammy surprised everyone, including the instructor. She did not ask the groups to count the items to see who had the most. Instead, she had the students immediately redisperse the items and began another game. During a follow-up interview, Tammy stated that because of class discussions examining the negative effects of competition on children, she started to "think more strategically about making every game a win-win situation."

Tammy, an athlete herself, displayed a change in thinking away from the competitive urge to see who "won" and toward an empathetic approach where every student won through movement and enjoyment. The simple act of counting the items may have led to three-quarters of the class leaving the gymnasium as unhappy losers. Because empathy entails identifying and understanding the feelings of others in a helping capacity, it is considered a potential neutralizer of powerlessness (Pinderhughes, 1979). While teachers develop better ways to understand and help students through empathic practice, students also gain by being helped and supported, which could alleviate fears of failure and helplessness, increase motivation, and even help to advance their own empathy development.

■ CONCLUSION

Because PE teacher candidates tend to come from athletic backgrounds, their love for sport potentially blinds them to the feelings of those of lesser physical abilities. There appears to be a need for preservice PE teachers to develop and practice empathy and other affective qualities aimed at fostering a productive relationship with students. In order to address the "whole person" in physical education, development of skill proficiency must be balanced with both affective and cognitive development.

In the broadest sense, education, as practiced in a democracy, must make provisions so that all students have an opportunity to succeed (Dewey, 1966). With regards to PE, the challenge is to ensure that all students have an opportunity to lead a healthy, physical life. If the ultimate goal in PE is a physically fit society, then the PE challenge must be success for all. Empathic teachers walking in their students' shoes will be better able to understand a diversity of abilities and accommodate the needs of every student— from the physically elite to the physically challenged.

■ KEY WORDS AND DEFINITIONS

affective education   The domain of education that centers on the emotions, feelings, and relations of students. Affective objectives typically target attitudes, behavior, cooperation, emotion, motivation, and sportsmanship.

empathic capacity   The ability to express understanding and feeling toward another. Although most humans have the capacity for empathy, it must be developed through maturity, experience, and education.

empathy   An affective response more appropriate to someone else's situation than one's own. It involves putting oneself into another person's shoes in order to understand the feelings of that person.

learned helplessness   A perception of futility where a person believes that no matter how much a task is attempted or performed the result will be failure, which leads the person to avoid the task altogether.

prosocial behavior   The act of helping others in a positive way, including caring, rescuing, defending, cooperating, and sharing, as well as empathy.

sociometric status   The degree to which a person is liked or disliked by his or her peers.

■ DISCUSSION QUESTIONS

1. Consider the prevalence of people who have had negative PE experiences as students. Many of these people have children of their own. Some of them become professionals in positions of responsibility such as lawmakers, school board members, and principals. How will you convince the parents of your children that your PE class is different than the PE they had?

2. How will you convince the school board that your PE class is valuable to your students' education?

3. Consider the negative perception of PE in movies and media. Although this perception might be exaggerated, it exists. How can you help to change the perception of PE in the public eye?

4. Consider the following example: "Musical chairs" is a well-known competitive activity that typifies the old PE; a game that has only one winner while the rest of the class loses. It is also a game with little to no activity value because students are eliminated and spend much

of the game sitting and watching. How can the game be easily modified so that all students actively participate and contribute both physically and socially?

5. Think of an alternative version of a traditional PE activity. In what ways can you change a competitive game into one with a win-win outcome for all students?

■ REFERENCES

Barnett, M. A., & Bryan, J. H. (1974). Effects of competition with outcome feedback on children's helping behavior. *Developmental Psychology, 10*(6), 838–842.

Darling-Hammond, L., & Sykes, G. (2003). Wanted: A national teacher support policy for education: The right way to meet the "Highly Qualified Teacher" challenge? *Education Policy Analysis Archives, 11*(33). Retrieved July 12, 2011, from epaa.asu.edu/ojs/article/download/261/387

Davis, M. H. (1996). *Empathy: A social psychological approach*. Boulder, CO: Westview.

Dewar, A. M., & Lawson, H. A. (1984). The subjective warrant and recruitment into physical education. *Quest, 36*, 15–25.

Dewey, J. (1966). *Democracy and education: An introduction to the philosophy of education*. New York: Free Press. Originally published 1916/1944.

Dunn, J. C., Dunn, G. H., & Bayduza, A. (2007). Perceived athletic competence, sociometric status, and loneliness in elementary school children. *Journal of Sport Behavior, 30*, 249–269.

Fitzpatrick, D. A., & Watkinson, E. J. (2003). The lived experience of physical awkwardness: Adults' retrospective views. *Adapted Physical Activity Quarterly, 20*, 279–297.

Gard, M. (2006). Why understanding itself is physical education's greatest challenge: A response to Himberg. *Teachers College Record*. Retrieved March 5, 2008, from http://www.tcrecord.org

Gifford-Smith, M. E., & Brownell, C. A. (2003). Childhood peer relationships: Social acceptance, friendships, and peer networks. *Journal of School Psychology, 41*, 235–284.

Goleman, D. (1995). *Emotional intelligence*. New York: Bantam.

Hatcher, S. L., Nadeau, M. S., Walsh, L. K., Renyolds, M., Galea, J., & Marz, K. (1994). The teaching of empathy for high school and college students: Testing Rogerian methods with the interpersonal reactivity index. *Adolescence, 29*(116), 961–974.

Hoffman, M. L. (1987). The contribution of empathy to justice and moral judgment. In N. Eisenberg & J. Strayer (Eds.), *Empathy and its development* (pp. 47–80). Cambridge: Cambridge University Press.

Kohn, A. (1986). *No contest: The case against competition*. Boston, MA: Houghton Mifflin.

Koka, A., & Hein, V. (2006). Perceptions of teachers' positive feedback and threat to sense of self in physical education: A longitudinal study. *European Physical Education Review, 12*, 165–179.

Lee, A. M., Carter, J. A., & Xiang, P. (1995). Children's conceptions of ability in physical education. *Journal of Teaching in Physical Education, 14*(4), 384–393.

Martinek, T. J., & Griffith III, J. B. (1994). Learned helplessness in physical education: A developmental study of causal attributions and task persistence. *Journal of Teaching in Physical Education, 13*(2), 108–122.

Noddings, N. (1992). *The challenge to care in schools: An alternative approach to education*. New York: Teachers College Press.

Pinderhughes, E. B. (1979). Teaching empathy in cross-cultural social work. *Social Work, 24*(4), 312–316.

Portman, P. A. (1995). Who is having fun in physical education classes? Experiences of sixth-grade students in elementary and middle schools. *Journal of Teaching in Physical Education, 14*(4), 445–453.

Robinson, D. W. (1990). An attributional analysis of student demoralization in physical education settings. *Quest, 42*(1), 27–39.

Rogers, C. R. (1983). *Freedom to learn for the 80's*. Columbus, OH: Charles E. Merrill.

Research Review

Preventing Injuries in Physical Education and Physical Activity Programs: A Research Review of Pertinent Literature

Kevin E. Finn

Musculoskeletal injuries comprise the largest class of injuries sustained in sport and physical activity. They are classified as any injury to a structure that serves skeletal muscle, such as a tendon, ligament, joint, or blood vessel (Prentice, 2008). In the United States, musculoskeletal injuries make up some of the most common conditions affecting both children and adults. These injuries not only are the leading cause of physical and work-related disability but also place a dramatic financial burden on the healthcare system.

In children and teenagers, recreational activities account for a significant number of sport injuries. In recent years, high school sports participation has dramatically risen, and therefore, the frequency of muscular injuries has increased. It is estimated that 10% of children participating in organized sports will be injured each year. In addition to the large number of musculoskeletal injuries, a majority of adolescents do not meet the recommended requirement of 60 minutes of daily physical activity, as suggested by the Centers for Disease Control and Prevention (http://www.cdc.gov). As a result of these statistics, the education system has placed an emphasis on promoting physical activity

and preventing injuries in our schools. According to Healthy People 2010, one of the goals of the program is to promote physical activity through school physical education programs (U.S. Department of Health and Human Services, 2000).

Before children can become more physically active, they must be educated on how to prevent injuries. Three common factors associated with exercise-related musculoskeletal injury are muscle stiffness, lack of range of motion (Agre, 1985; Cornelius & Hinson, 1980), and poor balance (Verhagen et al., 2004). It has been widely accepted that a warm-up routine and stretching should be incorporated before and after participating in physical activity (Bishop, 2003; Shellock & Prentice, 1985). In recent years, there has been a debate over which stretching protocols are the most effective in the prevention of injuries. In addition, balance training has been identified as a factor in reducing the incidence of injury during physical activity (Caraffa et al., 1996).

In the field of physical activity, physical education, and even health education, teachers and coaches should be incorporating into their lessons injury prevention methods that have been shown to be effective and evidence based. The purpose of this article is to present and review the pertinent literature on preventing musculoskeletal injuries, focusing on warm-up routines, stretching, and balance.

■ WARM-UP ROUTINE

A **warm-up** routine is a widely accepted practice used by individuals prior to performing physical activity. Many coaches, athletes, and educators believe the warm-up is important for injury prevention, maximizing optimum performance, and preparing the body both psychologically and physiologically for exercise (Shrier, 2005). The literature shows there is a debate regarding the effectiveness of the warm-up in preventing injuries, but healthcare professionals empirically believe that it is an important precaution against unnecessary injury and muscle soreness (Cross & Worrell, 1999).

The goal of the warm-up is (1) to prepare the individual for physical activity and (2) to improve the physiological function (i.e., increase tissue temperature) of a muscle, thereby making it less likely to become injured (Woods, Phillip, & Jones, 2007). Traditionally, a warm-up entails several minutes of low- to moderate-intensity aerobic exercise followed by stretching. The purpose is to gradually stimulate the cardiorespiratory system to increase blood flow to skeletal muscle. In recent years, there has been a switch in focus to involve more dynamic activities that use low-, moderate-, and high-intensity movements aimed to increase body temperature and range of motion (Mann & Jones, 1999). A simple dynamic warm-up for students is the high knee walk, which entails walking forward while lifting each knee as high as possible (Yount, 2007).

Types of Warm-Ups

A warm-up routine can be either passive or active. The passive warm-up involves external factors leading to the increase in tissue temperature. In sports medicine, modalities such as moist heat packs, ultrasound, and warm whirlpools are examples of passive modes of heat. There are two types of active warm-ups, general and specific. The general active warm-up involves activities that are nonspecific to a sport or exercise but rather include whole body movements such as biking and jogging (Shellock & Prentice, 1985). The specific active warm-up targets certain muscles and movements that are pertinent for the particular activity. For example, a soccer player would focus on lower extremity stretching exercises because of the demands of the sport. The literature indicates that the specific warm-up is more effective at preparing the individual to perform a particular task (Faigenbaum, Bellucci, & Bernieri, 2005).

According to the American College of Sports Medicine (ACSM, 2000), the warm-up should be about 10 minutes in duration and focus on large muscle activity. It is recommended that the individual begin activity within 15 minutes of the warm-up in order to maximize the effects (Corbin, Corbin, Welk, & Welk, 2008). In a physical education classroom, teachers want to create a warm-up that involves both general and specific activities depending on the lessons for the day. The warm-up should be at a level of intensity and duration such that all students can perform the activities.

Effects on Injury Prevention

It has been accepted that people engaging in physical activity should participate in a warm-up routine (Prentice, 2008). A review of the literature indicates varying viewpoints around the effectiveness of warm-ups in reducing injury. Pope et al. (2000) reported that there was no reduction in the risk of injury as a result of a warm-up, but other studies have shown warm-up routines have had positive effects on decreasing the incidence of injuries (Bixler & Jones, 1992). In summary, the findings of many studies that have investigated the physiological responses to warm-up are difficult to interpret and apply to sport settings.

Regardless of the type of warm-up routine, physical educators and coaches should structure the warm-up to meet the needs and abilities of each individual. One of the positive physiological effects of warm-ups on injury prevention is to increase muscle temperature. To determine whether a person has warmed up properly, a physical educator should look for the individual to have light to mild sweating but without fatigue (Thomas, 2000). Educators should strive to teach students how to properly warm up in order to prevent injuries and to physiologically prepare their bodies for exercise. Students will know that they have reached a proper level of warm-up if they are sweating mildly.

■ IMPROVING FLEXIBILITY

Flexibility is defined as the ability to move a joint or series of joints through a full range of motion (Alter, 2004). The literature has indicated that an individual with good flexibility is more likely to be successful in sport and physical activity. For example, tight hamstrings lacking flexibility will directly affect the speed of a sprinter because the tight muscles will decrease the stride (Armiger, 2000). A lack of flexibility not only has been shown to have a negative effect on performance, but also can predispose a person to muscle strains (Blanke, 1999).

There are also factors that could limit an individual's flexibility. Bony structures can limit the range of motion. After a fracture, the body can deposit excess calcium in an attempt to heal the bone, but this could cause the joint space to be limited. Excessive fat can also limit flexibility. Due to the excess fat, an obese or overweight child has limited joint flexibility. Therefore, this child is more likely to sustain a musculoskeletal injury and be out of physical activity for a longer period of time. For example, a child with a large amount of fat on the abdomen will have restricted trunk flexion when asked to bend forward and touch the toes. This is a common hamstring stretching technique, and the child with excessive fat will not be able to fully stretch the muscle group due to the abdominal fat. As physical educators and coaches, we should be promoting and focusing on the improvement of flexibility in our children as a way to decrease the incidence of injury.

Types of Stretching

The goal of a flexibility program is to increase the range of motion at a joint by increasing the extensibility of the muscle (Gribble & Prentice, 1999). It is important to include stretching exercises that stretch the muscle over a period of time and therefore will increase the flexibility of a joint. Three main stretching techniques are used in physical activity.

1. **Static stretching** is the most widely used technique, and it has been shown to be a very effective method for increasing flexibility. It involves a passive stretch of the muscle by placing it in the maximal position and holding it for a period of time. Research has indicated a 30- to 60-second static stretch, repeated three

to four times, is the most effective procedure. It can be performed with a partner or solo. Using a hamstring stretching technique as an example, a partner static stretch would be done as follows: With the student lying supine with the knee extended and the ankle flexed to 90 degrees, the partner passively flexes the hip joint to the point at which there is slight discomfort in the muscle.

2. **Dynamic stretching** uses speed of movement, momentum, and muscle contractions to cause a stretch. Unlike static stretching, the end position is not held (Pearson, Faigenbaum, Conley, & Kraemer, 2000). Some examples of dynamic stretches are walking lunges (without weights), side bends, and trunk rotations. Recently, dynamic stretching exercises have become more popular because they are more closely related to the type of activity the person will engage in. A walking lunge dynamically stretches the hip flexors by emphasizing hip extension and can reduce muscle tightness around the hip joint necessary for competition. More recent scientific studies seem to suggest that dynamic stretches before competition are preferable to static stretches (Asselman et al., 2003; Curtis, 2006).

3. **Proprioceptive neuromuscular facilitation (PNF)** is a stretching technique that requires a partner. It uses a combination of contractions and relaxations followed by stretches in order to increase flexibility. The three types of PNF stretches are contract-relax, hold-relax, and slow reversal hold-relax. Using a hamstring stretching technique as an example, a PNF stretch would be done as follows:

   - With the student lying supine with the knee extended and the ankle flexed to 90 degrees, the partner passively flexes the hip joint to the point at which there is slight discomfort in the muscle.
   - At this point the student begins actively pushing against the partner's resistance by contracting the hamstring muscles.
   - After actively pushing for 10 seconds, the hamstring muscles are relaxed and the quadriceps (agonist) is actively contracted while the partner applies further pressure to stretch the hamstrings.
   - The relaxing phase lasts for 10 seconds, after which the student again actively pushes against the partner's resistance, beginning at this new position of increased hip flexion.

This sequence is repeated three times.

Effects on Injury Prevention

Several studies have examined the effects of stretching on injury prevention. All three of the techniques discussed have been demonstrated to effectively improve flexibility, but there is still debate over which technique demonstrates the greatest improvements in range of movement. There is no clear relationship between the type of stretching technique and injury prevention. Static stretching is the most widely used technique because it is simple and does not require a partner. Studies have indicated that PNF stretching techniques can produce significant increases in range of motion during one stretching session (Prentice, 2004). Dynamic stretching has seen a resurgence in popularity. Many professionals are arguing that dynamic stretching mimics the movements required of the activity, so it is considered a more functional form of stretching (Mann & Jones, 1999). There are positives and negatives to all of the stretching techniques. When considering what type of pre-exercise stretching protocol to use, the physical educator or coach should address the types of activities the students will be performing. The stretching protocol must be designed to address the specific muscle groups and movements that will be used in the physical activity of the day. In order to reduce injuries, stretching must be sport/activity specific.

■ BALANCE

Balance involves the integration of muscle forces, sensory information, and joint receptors.

In order to maintain **postural balance**, one must position the center of gravity within the base of support. When the center of gravity goes outside of the base of support, a person will stumble in order to prevent a fall (Cox, Lephart, & Irrgang, 1993). The lower extremity joints are primarily responsible for maintaining balance. The ability to balance and maintain stability is vital to a person acquiring complex motor skills (Tippett & Voight, 1995). Traditionally, balance training has been implemented into a rehabilitation program for an athlete returning from a lower extremity injury as a way to regain normal balance and proprioception. More recently, healthcare professionals have tried to incorporate balance training to prevent knee and ankle injuries (Verhagen et al., 2004). When examining pre-exercise protocols, many individuals will perform a warm-up routine involving a stretching protocol. As an educator, incorporating a balance program into the pre-exercise routine as an additional method to prevent ankle injuries can be an effective technique. Specific techniques are discussed in this section.

Balance Training Exercises

Of interest to physical educators and coaches, the literature has indicated that there is a decrease in the incidence of ankle sprains when athletes and students implement a preventative balance program (Verhagen et al., 2004). The balance ability could be determined by performing a balance assessment. One assessment is the timed, single leg balance on a stable surface with the eyes closed (Watson, 1999). A second type of assessment is the flamingo balance test, in which the individual attempts to balance on one foot a narrow beam for 1 minute, and the number of touches is counted. Another mode of balance assessment, which is more difficult, is on an unstable surface. Unstable and stable surfaces are two of the most common modes of balance exercises. In addition to stability of a surface, the student could remove the visual field to make the balancing more difficult.

In a classroom setting, educators would first have the students perform an exercise with their eyes open, while balancing on one leg for 30 seconds. Next, the progression exercise would be to perform a unilateral balance exercise with eyes closed. Removing the visual field will make the balance exercise more difficult for the students (Wester, Jespersen, & Nielsen, 1996). Incorporating balance exercises into the warm-up routine has been shown to decrease lower extremity injuries, and therefore educators and coaches are recommended to have students perform these during the warm-up routine (Verhagen et al., 2004).

■ CONCLUSION

Physical educators, coaches, and parents should be proactive to ensure the children they work with are physically active and injury free. In order to promote our youth being more physically active, educators must provide them with information and instruction on how to reduce their risk of injury while exercising. The goal of this article was to present and review the pertinent literature in preventing musculoskeletal injuries, focusing on warm-up routines, flexibility, and balance, and to present the methods that have been shown to be effective. Unfortunately, like many things in science and research, there are conflicting results around all three of the injury prevention routines. The examination of literature shows there are positive aspects and correct ways to design and implement warm-up routines, stretching protocols, and balance programs. Despite all the controversy around the types of warm-up routines and stretching protocols prior to physical activity, an individual should engage in some type of warm-up, stretching, and balance training as a method of reducing the chances of suffering from a musculoskeletal injury. In order to provide the most accurate exercises for students, coaches and educators must continue to examine current research because it continually changes.

■ **KEY WORDS AND DEFINITION**

dynamic stretch This type of stretch consists of functionally based exercises, which use sport-specific movements to prepare the body for movement. Some examples of dynamic stretches are walking lunges (without weights), side bends, and trunk rotations.

postural balance The optimal distribution of the body's mass relative to the force of gravity. In order to maintain postural balance, the center

of gravity must be within the base of support.

proprioceptive neuromuscular facilitation (PNF) A type of stretch most commonly characterized by a precontraction of the muscle to be stretched and a contraction of the antagonist muscle during the stretch. The PNF stretches must be done with a partner.

static stretch Entails a muscle being slowly stretched, then held in the stretched position for 30 to 60 seconds. It can be done solo or with a partner.

warm-up Light to moderate activity done prior to a workout. The purpose is to reduce the risk of injury and soreness and possibly improve performance in a physical activity.

■ **DISCUSSION QUESTIONS**

1. What are musculoskeletal injuries, and why are they on the rise?
2. Discuss the goals of a warm-up routine and describe the two types of warm-ups.
3. Compare ways to increase flexibility and describe how they may decrease the individual's susceptibility to injury.
4. What is balance? Describe how balance can reduce ankle sprains.
5. How can a physical educator or coach incorporate these injury prevention techniques into the classroom?

■ **REFERENCES**

Agre, J. (1985). Hamstring injuries: Proposed aetiological factors, prevention and treatment. *Journal of Sports Medicine, 2*, 21–33.

Alter, M. (2004). *The science of flexibility*. Champaign, IL: Human Kinetics

American College of Sports Medicine. (2000). *Guidelines for exercise testing and prescription.* Philadelphia: Williams and Wilkens.

Armiger, P. (2000) Preventing musculotendinous injuries: A focus on flexibility. *Athletic Therapy Today, 5*(4), 20.

Asselman, P., Witvrouw, E., Danneels, L., D'Have, T., & Cambier, D. (2003). Muscle flexibility as a risk factor for developing muscle injuries in male professional soccer players. *American Journal of Sports Medicine, 31*(1), 41–46.

Bishop, D. (2003). Performance changes following active warm-up and how to structure the warm-up. *Journal of Sports Medicine, 33*(7), 483–498.

Bixler, B., & Jones, R (1992). High-school football injuries: Effects of a post-halftime warm-up and stretching routine. *Family Practice Research Journal, 12*(2), 131–139.

Blanke, D. (1999). *Sports medicine secrets.* Philadelphia: Hanley and Belfus.

Caraffa, A., Cerulli, G., Projetti, M., et al. (1996). Prevention of anterior cruciate ligament injuries in soccer: A prospective controlled study of proprioceptive training. *Knee Surgical Sports Trauma Arthroscopy, 4*(1), 19–21.

Corbin, C., Corbin, W., Welk, G., & Welk, K. (2008). *Concepts of fitness and wellness: A comprehensive lifestyle approach.* New York: McGraw-Hill.

Cornelius, W., & Hinson, M. (1980). The relationship between isometric contractions of hip extensors and subsequent flexibility in males. *Journal of Sports Medicine and Physical Fitness, 20*, 75–80.

Cox, E., Lephart, S., & Irrgang, J. (1993). Unilateral balance training of noninjured individuals and the effect on postural sway. *Journal of Sports Rehabilitation, 2*(2), 87.

Cross, K., & Worrell, T. (1999). Effects of a static stretching program on the incidence of lower extremity musculotendonous strains. *Journal of Athletic Training, 34*(1), 11.

Curtis, N. (2006). Stretching and dynamic flexibility. *Athletic Therapy Today, 11*(3), 30

Faigenbaum, A., Bellucci, M., Bernieri, A., et al. (2005). Acute effects of different warm-up protocols on fitness performance in children. *Journal of Strength and Conditioning Research, 19*(2), 376–381.

Gribble, P., & Prentice, W. (1999). Effects of static and hold relax stretching on hamstring range of motion using the FlexAbility LE 1000. *Journal of Sport Rehabilitation, 8*(3), 195.

Mann, D., & Jones, M. (1999). Guidelines to the implementation of a dynamic stretching program. *Strength and Conditioning Journal, 21*(1), 53–55.

Pearson, D., Faigenbaum, A., Conley, M., & Kraemer, W. J. (2000). National Strength and Conditioning Association's basic guidelines for the resistance training of athletes. *Strength and Conditioning Journal, 22*(4), 14–27.

Pope, R., Herbert, R., Kirwan, J., et al. (2000). A randomized trial of preexercise stretching for prevention of lower-limb injury. *Medicine and Science in Sports and Exercise, 32*(2), 271–277.

Prentice, W. (2004). *Rehabilitation techniques in sports medicine and athletic training.* New York: McGraw-Hill.

Prentice, W. (2008). *Arnheim's principles of athletic training: A competency based approach.* New York: McGraw-Hill.

Shellock, F., & Prentice, W. (1985). Warming-up and stretching for improved physical performance and prevention of sports related injuries. *Journal of Sports Medicine, 2*(4), 267–279.

Shrier, I. (2005). When and whom to stretch? Gauging the benefits and drawbacks for individual patients. *The Physician and Sports Medicine, 33*(3), 22–26.

Thomas, M. (2000). The functional warm-up. *Journal of Strength and Conditioning, 22*(2), 51.

Tippett, S., & Voight, M. (1995). *Functional progressions for sports rehabilitation.* Champaign, IL: Human Kinetics.

U.S. Department of Health and Human Services. (2000). *Healthy people 2010: Understanding and improving health* (2nd ed.). Washington, DC: U.S. Government Printing Office.

Verhagen, E., van der Beek, A., Twisk, J., et al. (2004). The effect of a proprioceptive balance board training program for the prevention of ankle sprains: A prospective controlled trial. *American Journal of Sports Medicine, 32*(6), 1385–1393.

Watson, A. (1999). Ankle sprains in players of the field games Gaelic football and hurling. *Journal of Sports Medicine and Physical Fitness, 39*(1), 66–70.

Wester, J., Jespersen, S., & Nielsen, K. (1996). Wobble board training after partial sprains of lateral ligaments of the ankle: A prospective randomized study. *Journal of Orthopedic Sports Physical Therapy, 23*(5), 332–336.

Woods, K., Phillip, B., & Jones, E. (2007). Warm-up and stretching in the prevention of muscular injury. *Journal of Sports Medicine, 37*(12), 1089–1099.

Yount, K. (2007). *Ready to play: The dynamic warm-up.* Duke University. Retrieved August 27, 2010, from http://www.dukehealth.org

CHAPTER 9

Letters from the Field

■ CHAPTER OVERVIEW

This chapter presents an exciting theory into practice approach—we invited practitioners from the field to write about selected topics that are timely, meaningful, and relevant. The authors of the letters write to you, the reader, as if they are sending you a personal correspondence. With the letters written in first person, this personal connection with the author feels strong. The body of the letters, or the contents, provides practical information and advice about teaching, coaching, instructional methods, and some current issues with curriculum content.

The first of 10 letters in this chapter is written to health educators about how to deal with sensitive subjects in health education, but we could all benefit from reading about the need to provide accurate, age-appropriate instruction. The practical advice in the second letter about looking for a job, surviving the first year as a teacher, and helpful classroom management tips is provided by a first-year teacher and coach. Becoming an integral part of the school, sampling all-school physical activity programs, and role modeling are the topics in the third letter by a middle school physical education teacher. The similarities and differences between teaching and coaching are creatively discussed in the next letter. Then, a Teacher of

the Year shares her passion for teaching with a strong message to get involved with the school community. The title of the next letter, "Tips from the Top: What Directors Need to See from Teachers," defines the content; an experienced administrator outlines what teachers should be doing to teach well and to be a teacher leader in a school. A veteran physical education teacher then reminds us to make the most of all we do to teach others how to lead healthy and active lives, and she reminds us to take advantage of opportunities for professional development and networking in order to best serve our students and ourselves.

Another experienced teacher and administrator shares his thoughts about effective instructional strategies, including the use of instant activities, a proactive approach to discipline, lesson momentum, and the need for effective communication. The ninth letter will leave the reader with numerous ideas for outdoor winter activities for elementary school children; although the content in this letter describes snow activities, the overall message is to get students outside in nature. The tenth letter in this chapter is directed toward preservice teachers; the college professor, and past physical education teacher and coach, talks to the reader about his insights about teaching physical education. This final letter is a good ending for the chapter because the author challenges the reader to reflect on his or her own life experiences, to keep an open mind, but most importantly to learn how to become the most effective teacher and make a difference in our students' lives. We are confident these letters will help you bridge the gap from reading about pedagogical methods and theory to actually applying what you learn in the classroom, gymnasium, or sport field.

Addressing Sensitive Subjects in Health Education

Pat Degon

Dear Health Educator,

The goal of every health educator should be to partner with parents and share in the responsibility to provide insight, knowledge, experience, and support for students to understand and demonstrate the principles of maintaining health. We cannot do it by ourselves, and the best outcomes result from sharing the load. Comprehensive health education should include both content that is science based and topics that are personal and sensitive in nature. It is difficult to find another discipline that parallels the unique challenges of health education. One might easily argue that it is far less controversial to teach mathematical equations and geographical locations than it is to teach sexuality or substance abuse.

Curricula objectives for all health content should be developed and approved at the district level to ensure endorsement and approval. This is especially important as it applies to sensitive subjects. No health teacher, novice or veteran, should have to guess about district guidelines related to sexuality, substance abuse, mental health, suicide prevention, or any other topic that can connect to family values. Community dialogue is an important mechanism to develop support for essential content. Asking for parent input while developing or adopting new initiatives related to sensitive subjects is a key strategy to gain understanding and consensus. It is far better to uncover and understand any resistance or objections during the development and adoption phase than it is to be put on the spot to react to criticism or public assaults that could have been avoided.

Data are available to support the need for age-appropriate instruction that is sensitive in nature. The Youth Risk Behavior Surveillance System (YRBSS) data represent national, state, and in many school districts, individual community information about risk behaviors and perceptions. Sharing the self-reported responses of students related to tobacco, alcohol, and drug experimentation/use/abuse, sexual behavior, violence, and suicide can be compelling as well as alarming to many parents. We must publically affirm the capacity to reduce risk behaviors and promote healthy choices via comprehensive health education that teaches students why and how to maintain personal wellness. Demonstrating our professional knowledge and skill to deliver appropriate instruction can increase community support for skillful teaching and sensitive content.

Health educators must encourage parents to be the primary educators for their children and highlight their influence as a strong protective factor. Helping parents gain a clear understanding of the proactive and preventative messages and skills that are facilitated daily in our classrooms, as well as offering parent education that includes suggested dialogue and role plays, will increase the partnership between school and home. A good example of promoting parents as primary educators, and one that has worked very well in my district, is related to our elementary lessons on preventing sexual abuse. Obviously this is a topic that creates that "Oh no" feeling in our stomachs. By taking the initiative of being transparent with our content and promoting the skills of my professionally certified staff, we build partnerships with parents. For our safety units in grades 2 and 4 we activate parents' awareness with a parent letter describing the lesson and inviting parents to attend a viewing of the video the children will watch. Some parents have genuine questions and concerns about the information and the way it is presented. We should never be defensive with this level of parent responsibility and should, in my opinion, commend it. We ultimately share the same goal: to keep children healthy and safe. Routinely when we conduct this evening event parents leave reassured and thank us for tackling a tough topic in an age-appropriate manner. They also feel more comfortable and confident knowing the vocabulary and strategies that can be discussed at the dinner table and are more willing to partner with us to reinforce the lesson. Thus a win/win for all!

The most critical factor that must be adhered to in teaching sensitive subjects is accurate age-appropriate instruction. Whether our students are 6 or 16 there is a necessity to include all of the content, sensitive and not, in a manner that is matched to the cognitive ability of the class. It is as appropriate for first graders to learn HIV/AIDS prevention with basic understanding of germ transmission and universal precautions as it is for eleventh graders to know about sexually transmitted disease prevention.

It is my personal experience that sharing the objectives and classroom activities with parents who may call with questions or be concerned about sensitive subject instruction always leads to greater understanding, increased mutual respect, and decisions that are usually in the child's best interest. Adhering to the Parent Notification Laws (1996), enabling a parent to exempt a child from any portion of the curriculum that involves human sexuality education without penalty, is often seen by school personnel as a negative judgment against the teacher or the curriculum. I suggest you think of it differently. I have had many conversations with parents who have personal concerns related to sensitive subjects that are contained in our curriculum. I acknowledge their commitment to inquire and take an active role in the education of their child. Furthermore, I applaud their effort to be responsible as the primary educator and influence their child. I do offer the caution that conversations among peers on the bus or in the cafeteria are out of our management, and endorse dinner conversations to reinforce the family core values.

An excerpt of a conversation with parents who exercise their option to exempt a child from any lesson related to human sexuality would include the following:

Yours is not the child I worry about because you have demonstrated the commitment of discussing puberty with your child. You also have made the effort and taken the initiative to contact me. It is my job to worry and attend to the student that has have a parent that either does not know how or is uncomfortable bringing up the subject of sexuality. Your son/daughter is a lucky kiddo that has a parent that cares enough to be an advocate and primary educator!

In the vast majority of cases parents support the expertise and skill of professional health educators. Parents rely on schools and teachers to instill and nurture healthy lifestyles. Parents have also demonstrated their value for health education in schools as "definitely necessary." It is our job to plan effective age-appropriate instruction, matched to our individual community needs, that sequences through the grades and is comprehensive to include sensitive subjects and strategies to promote skill development. Partnering with parents will ensure reinforcement at home and increase community support, and is the most important factor to promote health and wellness.

My last tip to you would be to remember that many hands make the workload lighter. The more you can engage parents and increase awareness, assisting and partnering in the process, the greater the support and endorsement for your program from the community and the administration.

Sincerely,
Patricia Degon
Director of Health/PE/FCS
Shrewsbury Public Schools | Shrewsbury, Massachusetts

■ **DISCUSSION QUESTIONS**

1. In a comprehensive health curriculum, which of the content areas are commonly considered sensitive in nature and why?
2. Preview the Centers for Disease Control and Prevention's YRBSS instrument and list the categories that are clustered in the questionnaire.
3. What are the protective factors known today to keep children healthy, safe, and achieving in schools?
4. What responsibilities should parents attend to if they strive to be their child's primary sexuality educator?
5. What are three teacher strategies or initiatives that will create stronger collaboration with parents as partners?

My First Year as a Physical Education Teacher: Some Practical Advice

Aimee Doherty

Dear Prospective Teacher,

Graduating college and looking for a new job can be both exhilarating and nerve-wracking. As with many professions, becoming a good educator requires not only a knowledge base of the material, but also experience. I consider myself lucky in that I took part in a strong physical education program in undergraduate school at Salem State College in Massachusetts and an equally strong graduate program for health education at Boston University. As a current first-year physical education teacher, I would like to offer you some advice and guidance that I wish I had received prior to the start of my new position.

One of the first things that you need to decide when looking for a new job is whether you are willing to move to a new area. This decision must be made so that you know where to begin looking for open positions. Once you have an idea of the general area you would like to work or live in, then you can begin the search. There are a number of ways to do this; school websites can be used in the search for a job, in addition to newspapers, websites of professional organizations such as the Massachusetts Association for Health Physical Education Recreation and Dance (MAHPERD, which is my professional state organization), the American Alliance for Health, Physical Education, Recreation and Dance (AAHPERD), and other websites including monster.com and craigslist.com. Recently, one of the most popular and well-recognized job search websites—http://www.schoolspring.com—was being widely used by teacher applicants as well as employers. This website is a free electronic database to post, search for, and track jobs in education.

Once I decided what area I preferred to look in, I went to a map to see the nearby towns. I went to the school websites for approximately 15 towns within a 20-mile radius. Each school website had a list of open positions and briefly explained the application process. Most of this process can be done quickly via the Internet. If all goes well, the next step is the interview.

You can never be too prepared for a job interview. It is important to dress professionally and bring anything that may be of help, such as a portfolio in a hard copy or on a flash drive. Many interviewers will ask you what a typical lesson would look like in your class, or how you would handle a particular situation with a student. If you have a portfolio available with specific examples, this will help you to feel more comfortable answering the questions and show the prospective employer what you are capable of as an educator. It can be helpful to ask a current educator what types of questions to expect so that you can prepare possible answers before your interview. You can also find sample interview questions online, which will be helpful to practice.

If all goes well and you are offered a position, congratulations! That is when it's time for the work and fun to begin. The first thing you want to do is familiarize yourself with your new school and community. Spend some time in your school getting to know the building and introducing yourself to coworkers. It can be helpful to start off by making a positive and friendly impression. You want to be familiar with the school before the students arrive so that you can find the exits, fire escape routes, emergency procedures, classrooms, cafeteria, staff room, and restrooms. How can you help a student if you don't know the building yourself? Talk to coworkers and read the school handbook, if it's available, so that you can learn the rules and protocols for your building. If your school has a mentor program, take advantage of it by getting to know your mentor and asking him or her any questions that you may have. Once you're familiar with the building, you can move on to your office and storage room. For example, the first time I went into my gym I took pictures of all of my equipment, my office, and the gym so that I could plan lessons from home and remember what I had to work with. Take inventory of your supplies and equipment, and then make them your own! You may choose to rearrange equipment, decorate your bulletin boards, or begin hanging visual aids and posters on the walls. This is a great first step to feel comfortable in your new environment.

The beginning of the school year can be overwhelming. Prioritize the things that you would like to get accomplished and focus on one goal at a time. It is best to avoid taking on additional responsibilities until you are comfortable with your position and settled in to a routine. The first week of school will come around before you know it, and this time period is critical. You want to let students know what you expect from them, and what they can expect from you in return. For example, I spent the first day of school covering safety rules and protocols for my classes; I presently teach elementary physical education to grades K–4. I allowed students to suggest rules that they felt should be enforced throughout the year. Once each class had a chance to do this, I took the most popular ideas and created a set of rules from it. That way the students felt as though they had some control over the rules they would be responsible for following.

Classroom management is one of the most important things to consider during the first week of school. Have a specific entrance routine so the students will always come to the gymnasium and know where to go. My students know that when they enter class they go to their attendance squads first and then we begin an instant activity. At the end of class, we meet at the center circle in the middle of the gym to debrief. The best advice that I can give you to improve your classroom management is to choose a method and stick with it as long as it works. Students generally do well with set routines. If you try to change something each class period, it could lead to chaos.

When it is time to start planning your lessons, start by looking at the big picture. Use the curriculum and break it down into each unit that you will be covering over the course of the year. Then look at each unit individually and decide what your major goals will be for it, and how much time you plan to spend on each goal. From there it is easier to plan the individual lessons. Remember to always leave room for change because a lesson may take more or less time than you expected based on your students' abilities and prior knowledge of the subject. It is often beneficial to overplan so that your students do not become bored or restless with a lesson that they complete quickly. I have been typing all of my lessons and printing them out to make a binder of my unit plans. That way, in the future, I can simply make changes to the lessons that need them instead of planning every class from scratch. This will save you a lot of time in years to come!

If you plan on being a great teacher, then you are never done learning. In education, things are constantly changing. It is important to continue your own education by updating your knowledge and information using current research and trends. Join your professional or statewide organization (such as AAHPERD) in order to receive current information and to have the ability to join workshops specifically related to health and physical education. Remember, you are not expected to memorize every piece of information that you've learned throughout your schooling. Use the resources available to you to study and review information before teaching each unit. Once your first year of teaching winds down, as mine is doing now, and you have settled into a routine, you may want to look into professional development opportunities in order to continue your own education.

Keep in mind that there are no teacher "norms." Two of the best pieces of advice that I can give you are to be flexible and to learn from more experienced teachers. If you have the opportunity, observe other teachers within your district at the beginning of the year so you can see a variety of teaching and management styles. Your lessons and teaching style will depend on both your personality and the learning styles of your students. Keep in mind that your students will most likely have a variety of learning styles, so it is best if you are able to teach to them. I recommend reading about Howard Gardner's theory of multiple intelligences to help you better understand this concept. Chances are you will not learn everything that you need to know about the school and your students before the first day of classes. As with anything else in life, situations will arise that you will not have an immediate response for. Know that this is okay! Don't be afraid to go to your principal, mentor, or a fellow teacher with questions that you may have. Many things will simply come with experience.

There are several pros and cons about becoming a first-year teacher. Let's start with the cons. Your first year can be very overwhelming, especially in the beginning. This is the first time that you are truly putting your knowledge base to the test, and you're responsible for giving the students correct information. You need to figure out techniques that work best for your classroom management, your teaching style, and the needs of the students. The primary way to discover this is through trial and error; however, asking another teacher in your discipline can be very beneficial as well. You are essentially starting from scratch. You have a curriculum in place that needs to be followed, but you now have to plan enough lessons for every day of the school year! This is both a pro and a con. It's exciting to realize the freedom that you have when planning, but it can also be scary at first. This career can be discouraging once you realize the time and effort that must be put into it.

For most teachers, the school day does not end at 2:30 in the afternoon. You can generally expect to stay later at your school setting to complete student grades and lesson plans, and to become involved with the school community. Many schools today are experiencing budget cuts, especially in fields such as physical education, music, and art. This may affect the amount of equipment that you have to offer the students, the quality of the equipment, or the amount of time that you get to see the students each week. Teaching, especially in your first year, can lead to mental exhaustion on a daily basis, and that is not helped by the fact that class sizes seem to keep increasing with each year. Each of these factors can make it difficult to remain motivated.

However, there are many pros that go along with being a first-year teacher as well. There is the excitement of a new beginning! You are starting a new chapter in your life and it's what you've been working toward all these years. You now get paid to do something that you love. You finally have the chance to do things your own way (to an extent) and to put your creativity to the test. You have the opportunity to meet many new people including your coworkers, students, and families of your students. Educators have excellent hours, vacations several times a year, and summers and holidays off. As a first-year teacher, there is very little time for boredom. Time flies because there is so much going on in your life. In most cases (such as my own) you may have a very supportive administrative staff that is willing to help you in any way that they can. The most exciting part about being a first-year teacher is the rewarding feeling that you get when you first realize that you made a difference in someone's life, whether it's an individual or an entire class. If you truly have the personality and commitment to be an educator, then that is the greatest feeling there is, and it's the feeling that makes all of the cons worthwhile.

Some of the information in this letter was given to me prior to the start of my first year as a physical educator, some was given to me within the first few months of teaching, and some I learned on my own. Now I'm sharing these pieces of advice with you in the hope that you will be even more prepared for your first year than I was. Don't ever be bashful when it comes to asking your colleagues questions, because they were once in the same situation as you. For example, I still keep in contact with a few of my professors and advisors from both my undergraduate and graduate schools for advice. I hope that this letter will be helpful in giving you some guidance as you venture out into the world of education. Most importantly, remember why you love teaching and have confidence in yourself.

Sincerely,
Aimee Doherty
Physical Education Teacher and Field Hockey Coach
Burbank Elementary School | Belmont, Massachusetts

■ DISCUSSION QUESTIONS

1. What are some ways to prepare for a job interview? Try to list and then talk about five things you could do prior to the day of the interview.
2. What are the obstacles of starting a new job, as either a first-year teacher or a teacher at a new or different school, as a physical education or a health education teacher?
3. Why is it important to plan classroom management strategies and to implement them at the start of the school year?
4. If you feel overwhelmed as a first-year teacher, from whom could you seek advice?
5. Some school districts require induction teachers to become involved with a mentoring program. What are the positive aspects of having an assigned mentor? How could this person help you successfully teach during your first year?

The Role of the Physical Education Teacher in the School Community

Matt Freeman

Dear Prospective Physical Education Teacher,

It is a pleasure to have the opportunity to impart some words of wisdom to an up-and-coming physical education teacher. I am currently in my eleventh year teaching physical education at a middle school in the suburbs of Boston. Many people cannot understand why I decided to teach at the middle school level. Although working with young adolescents can at times be trying, I chose to teach at the middle school level because this is where I believe I can make the most impact on my students. To impact the students in a positive way, it is important to get rid of the stereotype of the "gym teacher." Your role is not only to teach physical education, but also to become involved in the school outside of the gym, support other curricula, and develop character in your classroom.

The new role of a physical education teacher is to be more than just a person who plays games in the gymnasium—we can no longer roll out a ball and read the paper like many of our predecessors may have done. We must disprove the stereotype that we are uneducated and our job is easy. No matter the grade level you teach, there are opportunities for you to get involved in the activities of the school. I try to do as much as possible to become a part of my school community and to support my students. I attend every concert, dance, and show—many of which are held at night. I chaperone ski trips, overnight trips, and field trips. I walk the halls of the school and talk with the students—a friendly "hello" or a simple conversation may be enough to change a student's day and make an impact. Communicate with the parents; let them know what their child is learning in physical education and how their child is doing in your class. When they see you at every function, they will remember you and appreciate what you do for their child.

Get involved with the teachers at your school. Spend time in the teachers' room sharing ideas or being a sounding board for a teacher who is having a tough day. Create opportunities for teachers to socialize after school. Organize a bocce tournament, or a pick-up softball or basketball game. Create a fun and safe environment where everyone feels welcome and comfortable playing at their own level—just like in your classroom. One of our biggest jobs is to repair the damage that may have occurred to teachers from a negative physical education experience as an adolescent. Let them know what the "new physical education" is all about.

In the past few years the Physical Education department at my school has also planned a number of athletic events, activities, and health contests with the staff. Last year my colleague and I had our own version of *The Biggest Loser*. Forty-five teachers competed in a healthy weight loss competition. We had the opportunity to share knowledge and ideas about eating right and exercising. We taught fitness classes and bonded with the staff while helping many people feel great about themselves. More importantly, we continued to build our relationship with the staff at our school and proved we are valuable members of the school community.

You have to support other curricula in the school. Cross-curriculum or interdisciplinary lessons are becoming more prevalent, and physical education is no exception. It is important to plan cross-curricular activities that tie physical education to the students' other classes. I often use vocabulary words from the students' English class in my lesson. To reinforce the mathematics curriculum, I devise point systems for a game that uses fractions, or students will graph their results from fitness tests. I try to bring the other curricula into my classroom as much as I can. You need to step out of the gymnasium and discover what is being taught in the other classrooms and subjects.

This does not have to work as a one-way street. In my building, my colleague and I started the Fit-Nut Program. Fit-Nut is a fitness and nutrition program that focuses on lifetime fitness and healthy eating habits. In math, the students discuss the rate at which calories are burned. In science they learn about the cardiovascular system and musculature. In social studies they study other cultures' sports and dietary habits. Exercise journals are written in English class. Art and chorus are also tied in through depicting their favorite sports activities on paper and putting movement to song. It is a team effort that could not happen without the full support of the teaching staff. Physical education should be a part of all the subjects' curriculum, just as all teachers should be a part of our physical education curriculum.

As a physical education teacher you have the ability to use your curriculum to teach character. Although you might not think of your gym as the ideal setting for character education, sport and play offer many opportunities for children to learn valuable life lessons that may otherwise have been lost. Family structure, unstructured play, and overall attitude are much different today, and it is up to you to help bring back certain values.

Over the past few years I have noticed a significant change in behavior in the athletic arena. My students arrived at middle school playing more physically, often disregarding rules and trying to win at all costs while disrespecting my authority and the self-esteem of their classmates. In addition, students are involved in more organized sports. I have a number of students who are booked every night of the week, including weekends, with different organized sporting events. On the surface it is great to be physically active, but the downfall is that students are no longer able to organize any sport for themselves. Pick-up sporting events are few and far between, and if it does happen it is riddled with cheating and arguing because students lack the core values that allow fair games to be played. This behavior has led to disruptions in my class.

I have most of my students for 3 years, so I decided that I needed to change their behavior or conflicts and inappropriate behavior would prevent me from teaching properly. I affirmed that I would assume roles in the students' development that once had been filled. In order to compensate for lessons that were formerly taught in the home or on the playground, I sought constructive and creative methods to convey values without infringing on the role of the parent. I had to teach character education.

The key to teaching character is being able to identify a teachable moment. Examples of good and bad character lead to these teachable moments, which happen in physical education on a regular basis. When you see examples of teamwork, respect, responsibility, fair play, or perseverance in your class, stop and make it known or make a note to yourself and discuss it later with the student. Teachable moments can be positive and negative, though I like to reinforce good behavior for the entire class while reserving negative behavior for a private conversation that can happen after class or more effectively immediately following the action.

When I was an athlete, some coaches and physical education teachers modeled admirable behavior on and off the field, whereas others modeled negative behaviors. Now being a teacher and coach, I appreciate the fact that my students watch and learn from my behavior. I believe that today's physical education teachers and coaches bear a responsibility to seize the opportunities unique to them and demonstrate moral and just behavior to the students. Once students see the benefits of just and fair play in the games, my hope is that they will start to behave morally outside of sport.

Although you are the teacher of most students' favorite class—some days you will walk into your gym and feel like a rock star—it is essential to remember the importance your job holds. Do not be a "gym teacher." Become an intricate member of the school community. Have the best class in the school not because it's "phys-ed" but because you, as the teacher, make a difference in the lives of your students

Sincerely,
Matt Freeman
Physical Education Teacher
Braintree, Massachusetts

■ DISCUSSION QUESTIONS

1. Why is it important for a physical education teacher or a health educator to make an effort to become part of the school community?

2. What are some examples in this letter that show exemplary school involvement?

3. Talk about other interdisciplinary programs, like the Fit-Nut Program, that combine or blend physical education with other subjects or disciplines.

4. Character education and teachable moments were mentioned. Cite a few examples of how physical or health educators can contribute to developing good character traits.

5. Is it important to be a good role model for your students? Why or why not? What does this role modeling include?

Teaching and Coaching: Similarities and Differences, and How to Succeed at Both

Laura Galopim

Dear Prospective Teacher,

As an advocate for teaching and coaching, it is my pleasure to share my love for working with and influencing young people. My 13-plus years as a physical education/health teacher and coach at the middle school level have taught me a great deal about what it takes to inspire and motivate those in my charge. It has taken more than a decade to absorb the reality that all students and athletes are different, and the need to tactically reach each is quite a challenge. As I reflect on what I consider to be an extremely rewarding endeavor, I find it difficult to separate what I do in the classroom from what I do on the field. At the end of the day I have more passion for the all-encompassing profession of educator as opposed to the slightly limiting ideas of what constitutes a coach or a teacher. When my long career in public school education ends, I hope my days of retirement are not spent reflecting on memories of student-athletes who could drive a field hockey ball or who have mastered the forehand pass in volleyball class. It is my wish that the thoughts of my career hover around remembrances of kids learning life skills through sports and activities.

It is amazing to think back to my undergraduate days where teaching was never a blip on my radar. It took a healthy dose of reality as a first-year high school coach to prompt me to pursue a graduate degree in education. I can remember thinking, "I can't believe I get paid for doing this; they actually pay me for coaching!" I had treasured my days as a high school and college student-athlete, so in my mind, what better decision to make than working with kids my livelihood?

Ignorance Is Not Bliss—Conscious Incompetence vs. Conscious Competence!

My Boston University teaching education afforded me the opportunity to learn and practice skills related to pedagogy and leadership. When I was hired as a middle school physical education teacher and high school coach, I was confident in my competence as an educator. My arrogance of knowing it all was quickly humbled when the students and athletes alike did not necessarily respond the way I envisioned. Although I was quick to point the finger at the unruly student or the so-called unappreciative athlete, my days at rejecting accountability were thankfully short-lived. The more I learned, the more I learned how much I did not know. Once this realization set in, I quickly worked hard to transform my "ignorance is bliss stage" into the realization that student and athlete success was not solely the responsibility of the student. If I have to attribute one event that put me on track to being a successful person in this field, it was the day I identified my conscious incompetence.

As was the case in my early years, I continue to spend my days planning and preparing in an attempt to evolve this conscious incompetence to a level of conscious competence. I found myself using success strategies in the classroom and employing them to assist with setbacks with my athletes. My jobs paralleled enough to be able to constantly use breakthroughs in both arenas. One of my favorite phrases to teach by came from noneducator Beth Sawi, the executive vice president of Charles Schwab, who suggested that, "The most creative breakthroughs happen when you break for reflection." When I stopped to reflect, I realized a glaring deficiency with my teaching and coaching. I attempted to create equal standards for all of my kids. I held all accountable for all expectations. If I assigned a task in physical education or health class, I was steadfast with my expectations. When I had my players in for preseason, I set the bar at the same height for all and did not waiver. I can remember asking the players to arrive to tryouts prepared to break a certain time on the mile run. It never occurred to me that the goalies should be held to a different standard than the cardiovascular-enduring midfielders. By the same token, in my heterogeneous class population, my students were also wrongfully held to one standard.

"Insanity Is Doing the Same Thing Over and Over and Expecting a Different Result"

Being attentive to my learning population was a goal I decided to set as both a teacher and a coach. With a new focus on getting to know my students and athletes alike, I believe I started connecting more and getting more out of them. It was important to know their academic, intellectual, and physical capabilities. It was also helpful to learn who they were as people and what limitations they possessed. Committed to unveiling how each person absorbed and learned lessons, I would often challenge myself to look through their lens. With this knowledge I was able to more appropriately modify goals and objectives. For those I was unsure of, I would utilize a myriad of strategies to teach. We understand from our teacher's education that learners learn in various ways, including watching, listening, seeing, and doing. When I employ a variety of teaching strategies it is amazing to see how students identify their own deficiencies and make necessary corrections. Being more cognizant and appreciative of student and athlete differences, I was able to clear paths for more success.

Ahaaa Moment

Oprah Winfrey coined it correctly when she spoke of those almost out of body experiences when work ethic and perseverance pay off to the tune of someone finally "getting it." This is the true reward of being an educator. It is even more amazing when frustration has nearly pushed the student or athlete to quit and something inspires them to move forward. It is that feeling of "Ahaaa, I knew you could do it!" If my steadily appearing crows' feet that now encase my eyes could talk, they'd speak volumes of how many Ahaaa moments I have had in my many years as an educator. The profession is truly as humbling as it is rewarding. Working for as long as I have, I often forget that there are a multitude of ways to arrive at the same conclusion. When a student or athlete takes a different route, as unorthodox as I may perceive it to be, and is successful, it is great to be proven wrong. A life lesson that shines through to the student is that nobody has all the answers. The lesson that I continue to experience is that it is okay to be wrong. It is okay to occasionally show your vulnerabilities. It is okay to keep learning. In fact, in my opinion, being a lifelong learner should be every educator's goal!

Leaderful Influence

I received a great deal of push-back when I gave one of my teams t-shirts with this slogan displayed boldly across the back. My players challenged whether "leaderful" was really a word. As I type this now, the computer-generated red has indicated that this word cannot be found in the dictionary. But still I adopted this powerful phrase from Joseph Ralein, a Northeastern University professor who is well-known for this leaderful leadership model. (Thank you, Stacy, for sharing Dr. Ralein's work, including his book *Creating Leaderful Organizations: How to Bring Out Leadership in Everyone*.) He explains that everyone should be given a voice. Whether I am in charge of my class or my team I work hard to afford everyone the opportunity to lead from any seat. The freshman on my varsity team, although quiet and shy, can still offer something to help our team improve. Similarly, the PE student not terribly blessed with athleticism and who traditionally struggles with team sports might have tremendous communication and problem-solving qualities that shine during our project adventure unit. Creating a culture that encourages everyone to contribute is essential. It also is a lesson they use throughout their lives. As a coach, I haven't been shy at pointing out how such lessons apply to life endeavors. I'll catch myself saying, "When you find yourself in a career where your business team must work towards a common goal, you will remember these all-important 'C' skills" (contribution, commitment, compromise, collaboration, and communication). Because these critical habits are formed as a result of many of these types of experiences, I believe it is the duty of the teacher and coach to connect with every student or athlete. It is important to provide every child the opportunity to experience all the great skills within a safe environment. If they practice enough, I am confident that many will retain the knowledge and will form lifelong habits.

Teaching/Coaching/Parenting = Educator

Establishing a learning environment, establishing rules of behavior, and establishing expectations of performance are all important tasks when you are a teacher and a coach. Setting process versus outcome goals and individual and team goals is also an important recipe for teaching and coaching success. Understanding student and athlete limitations and using different teaching strategies are critical for all teachers and coaches. Regardless of whether a student is in the classroom or on the playing field, creating a culture where everyone has an opportunity to lead from whichever seat they sit in is paramount. As I write of how the two jobs parallel each other, I am reminded that much of what I do in my job fits quite closely with what I do at home. As a lifelong learner, I continue to learn every day. As a parent of two small children, I use many of the same tools for coaching and teaching. As a parent of less than 5 years, I am not sure if I can claim success quite yet. As I continue to experience parenting, all I can do is hope that the efforts I use with my students and athletes are strong enough to educate my own children. Just like coaching and teaching, parenting falls under that large umbrella of educator! I have enjoyed my days as an educator and look forward to many more.

Sincerely,
Laura Galopim
Physical Education Teacher and Varsity Field Hockey Coach
Weston Middle School | Weston, Massachusetts
P.S. A very special thank you to Stacey Freda for her insight and assistance in writing this letter.

■ DISCUSSION QUESTIONS

1. What are some of the similarities and differences between teaching and coaching?
2. What specific examples did the author use to illustrate teaching and coaching situations?
3. Teaching and coaching to a specific population was mentioned here. Why is it important to know a great deal about your students and athletes to best meet their needs?
4. What does the author mean about "Ahaaa" moments? Have you had any "Ahaaa" moments? Share one with the group.
5. Why is it important for students and athletes on a team to feel they are contributing to the class? How is leadership defined in a PE class and a team?

I Am a Physical and Health Educator . . . and I Love My Job!

Linda M. Grossi

Dear Future Health and Physical Education Teacher,

I am excited to have this opportunity to share a bit of my experience as a health and physical education teacher with you. I have been teaching health and physical education for 14 years. Two and one-half of those years were spent in the suburbs, and the rest were in an urban setting. I spent 2 years as a substitute teacher before being hired permanently. One thing you will find out soon is that you do not always get the chance to choose the job or school in which you want to teach, because most of the time you are very lucky to have a teaching job no matter what level, school, or district. This might be particularly true in the current state of our economy!

I currently teach at the middle school level. I teach both health and physical education to boys and girls and I absolutely *love* my "job"! I never thought that I would ever want to teach at the middle school level because I have heard that it was a difficult level to teach, but now I would *never* want to leave! I am totally immersed in teaching and learning, as well as being part of the school community. It is extremely important that you become an integral part of the school community and advocate for health and physical education each and every chance that you find the opportunity.

Before I tell you about my program and the relationships I have within my school community, I want to extend a word of advice. I believe, even before graduation, as an undergraduate you must start to formulate your philosophy of health and physical education. In other words, you *must* decide what type of teacher you are going to become. It basically comes down to, are you going to be a health and physical education teacher or "just" a gym teacher who rolls out the ball, who comes to class unprepared, and who does not use standards-based lessons or best practices? We are in a profession that is sometimes thought of as not as important as other professions. Once you graduate you are a full professional, one of us, and it is up to you what part of us you are going to become. Make the decision now, are you going to be a "gym" teacher or a physical and health education teacher? It will be one of the most important decisions of your career.

I am a health and physical education teacher, and my gymnasium is my classroom. It is set up like every other classroom in the school with the exception of not having desks. My classroom/gymnasium has the National Association for Sport and Physical Education (NASPE) standards posted both in state language and in child-friendly terms, and there are criteria and rubrics, word walls, learning objects, school and district rules, character education posters, and students' work. It is very important to me that every administrator, teacher, and parent who steps into my classroom understands that health and physical education are an integral part of their child's education and not just an "elective."

My health and physical education programs are coeducational, as mandated by the state. My class sizes range from 32 to 56 students. I have what is called a half-gym, and there is a large field across the street from the school that we use during the warm weather. I consider myself very lucky to have these facilities and put them to great use . . . no complaints! I have my classes in groups and at stations much of the time, as well as in a large group. Since I have been teaching at this school (8 years, now), I have started programs in aerobics (step and regular) with DDR, dance, jump rope, Ultimate Frisbee, walking with pedometers, badminton, and speed stacking. There are the usual team sports of softball, flag football, volleyball, basketball, and soccer. We also offer wrestling and fitness.

Each year I try to add something new to my health and physical education programs, whether it be a whole new game or dance or just changing something up to keep the students on their toes and wondering. We did have a working fitness room, but currently we are writing a few grants to help renovate and repair the equipment and room. That is usually the route I have to take to get new programs and equipment. There is usually little to no budget available for health and physical education in my school, so I get innovative. As for my health and physical education programs, I am completely involved in my school community, which makes it easier to advocate for my program in my school. I am a member of the School Improvement Team (SIT), Positive-Based Inventions and Supports (PBIS, Behavior & Rewards Team), PTO (Parent-Teacher Organization), and Crisis Intervention Team. I work with other teachers and incorporate math, English, computers/technology, performing arts, science, and music into health and physical education. Each time I give an assignment in both health and physical education, I provide a copy of the criteria chart and rubric to the students and the other teachers with whom I am working. The teachers and I often collaborate and put a unit together following the standards for each subject. For example, the science teacher and I teamed up for an interdisciplinary lesson covering the systems of the human body, which enabled us to cover the needed material according to standards in less time and allowed the students extra hands-on time for their health and science fair projects with teacher assistance. Because I am so engaged in my school community, it makes it much easier to approach the administration when I want to start a new program or have an event in the school. One of the most important pieces of information I can give you is to keep your parents in the know because you will fulfill your part of parent engagement with your written and telephone logs, which is part of your duty, but the dialogue between you and the parents is priceless.

I know when the principal sees me coming down the hall he must think, "What does she want now?" That is exactly what I did—approach the principal for support—when I wanted to start the spirit team and jump rope team. But, before approaching the administration, I always write a proposal. I connect each team or event with academics and behavior rewards. I set criteria for how the program will run, how it will benefit the school community, and how to get parents involved; these are many of the key issues our school communities are facing today. As a result, I am getting the students and even the parents actively engaged and connected with their school community and giving them a chance of ownership.

The spirit team organizes school dances, spirit weeks, once a month homeroom spirit competitions, and teacher appreciation week; ushers for promotional exercises; and are the students the principal relies on when he needs student representation for special visits or events. The spirit team works on building school spirit in the school community. School spirit in our school community means having pride in your school, knowing the school colors and mascot (the Dragon), wearing the school colors and maybe the school uniform, and caring for the people within our school community. The students on the spirit team, because there are no funds, make all of the gifts the teachers will be receiving for their appreciation week. Just so you understand their dedication, that means 80 gifts each day for 5 days, 400 gifts total.

Another way of connecting with the community is through our school's jump rope team, formed out of the physical education jump rope unit. The more skilled students wanted more. They wanted to take their skills to another level, so that is what I did in class. I talked to the administration, and next thing you know tryouts were held. The jump rope team performed at the school and then at the Rhode Island chapter of Alliance for Health, Physical Education, Recreation and Dance (AAHPERD's) annual conference held at the Community College of Rhode Island (CCRI). There we were noticed by a representative from the American Heart Association (AHA), and the next thing we knew, the jump rope team was representing the AHA at other schools in Rhode Island, Massachusetts, and Connecticut. Our team would perform/demonstrate just before a school was to have a Jump Rope for Heart Event, and motivate the student body for their upcoming event. The jump rope team also performed and demonstrated at the Eastern District Association Conference when it was held in Newport, Rhode Island. We held a 90-minute session on jump rope skills and techniques, and then performed a 30-minute exhibition. It truly was an elite moment for the team to be performing for all the teachers and professionals. The jump rope team represented their school and themselves well! This year is a rebuild year, with only one eighth grade student returning, so tryouts were held with approximately 120 attending, and I chose a team of 20. The enthusiasm of these students is one reason why I am willing to invest my time, my expertise, my effort, my caring, my respect, and my heart along with them.

I have passion and enthusiasm for my health and physical education programs. I am always on the Internet and keeping my ears open for opportunities to obtain better equipment or cooperative learning activities. I attend many professional developments and conferences. Because I am involved at not only the school/district level but also the state level, I am awarded the opportunity to go to regional and national conferences such as AAHPERD. There are so many opportunities to network with the right people at these conferences. You will learn from these other professionals and they will certainly learn from you as you exchange ideas on what works in successfully engaging students to adopt a more physically active lifestyle. I never thought when I first started to teach that I would be up in front of my peers presenting sessions on dance and curriculum, or taking a place as one of four physical education lead team teachers leading the way for our profession. Imagine yourself at your state house in front of the legislative body promoting your profession and adding your support for a bill to strengthen the health and physical education programs in your state.

In closing, please remember that it does not matter in which school district, school, grade level, or area you teach; it just matters that you love what you teach. Make the best of the opportunity placed in your hands. All of our students deserve our best and our respect. In my teaching career, I have been in many types of situations, both with ample space and plenty of equipment and the reverse situation. You just need to make the best of any situation. Jump in there and see what you *can* do! Besides . . . is it not truly about your students? Remember, it does take the *whole* school community to educate a student, and someday you will have an opportunity to become an integral part of your school community!

Please make the best of each situation, enjoy being an educator, and if you need anything . . . just ask . . . we love sharing!

Sincerely,
Linda M. Grossi
Health and Physical Educator
Gilbert Stuart Middle School | Providence, Rhode Island
Providence PE Lead Team
Spirit Team Advisor and Jump Rope Team Coach
RIAHPERD Teacher of the Year 2009
"Keep a Smile!"

■ DISCUSSION QUESTIONS

1. Why is it important to connect with your school's community?
2. How important is school spirit? How would you cultivate school spirit at your school?
3. The author of this letter had to be creative with her curriculum because there was no budget at her school. Have you seen other teachers do the same in your school? Please explain why or why not.
4. What are the similarities and differences between urban and suburban school settings?
5. The author discusses the networking opportunities in which she participates. Why is it important to network with other professionals?

Tips from the Top: What Directors Need to See from Teachers

Teddi Jacobs

Dear Prospective Teacher,

Before becoming an administrator, I taught health, physical education, and adapted physical education and coached several sports. Acquiring those experiences, which included nearly all grade levels, allowed me to understand our students and learn what I now believe are the most important factors in the development of a highly qualified and highly effective teacher.

If I were to ask you what you believe to be the most important qualities of a skillful teacher, I wonder what your answer would be. In my frequent visits to the health and physical education class settings, I have observed a multitude of behaviors by both teachers and students. During my administrative years with the public schools of Brookline, Massachusetts, I learned through our work with the Tripod Project (http://www.tripodproject.org)—which has since morphed into Brookline's Educational Equity Project: Taking Action, Getting Results—that teachers need to master three areas: content, pedagogy, and relationships. If all three legs of this tripod are strong, achievement for all students will be raised and achievement gaps will be narrowed.

How do you strengthen content, pedagogy, and relationships? After graduating from an institution of higher education, move forward with wide open eyes and mind. Take risks and challenge yourself. Be inquisitive. Ask questions. *Listen* well. Don't let yourself become isolated, which may happen if your department is small or you are the only physical education or health teacher in your school. Visit other teachers' classes, both within your field and in other fields, at your school and in other communities. Attend workshops and conventions. Take courses. Join and get involved with your professional organization. Learn all that you can learn. Be creative. *Communicate* well. Ask for feedback from students, peers, parents, and supervisors and work to implement suggestions. Join or start a critical friends group (CFG), which is a small collaborative group that meets regularly to review student work and reflect on teacher practice. A CFG sustains focus on professional development to improve student learning. Be an integral part of your team (department and school community). Share your work and ask the same of others. Offer to do more than your contract states. Plan in advance and plan well. Be reflective. Be flexible. Be early and stay late; however, balance your life, allowing your family to remain a priority, and also allow yourself to remain fresh. Get to know your students well, maintaining professional boundaries. Show them you care about them and they will work hard. Have fun as you gain experience and learn. We all made mistakes along the way and we continue to do so. Learning from those mistakes and working so that we don't repeat them is the key.

As a teacher and a leader, your behavior will express your personal set of values and beliefs. We act within the context of our beliefs. Don't wait to be told what to do. Be eager and equip yourself to do a better job this year than you did last year as you continue through your career. This is hard, exciting, and good work. Look through a variety of lenses. Remember that the people with whom you work come to you from diverse backgrounds and experiences. Learn to appreciate and embrace your differences.

As a teacher, believe that all students are good people and all students can learn. Understand that behaviors are often their way of communicating. Think about what they are "saying" to you. For example, I recently had a high school student who appeared to refuse to comply with what I thought was a basic and simple expectation of wearing appropriate footwear to class. She clearly couldn't participate safely with her sandals or boots. Upon talking with her outside of class time and then checking in with her guidance counselor, I learned that her parents were divorcing and there were serious financial issues as well. I brought a pair of socks and sneakers for her to wear (in this case she wore my size), which allowed her to participate, learn, and most importantly to her, receive the necessary credit so that she could graduate. So I thought she was purposely unprepared for class due to disinterest in activity, but she was able to flourish once the problem was communicated and solved.

You will experience success if you consistently communicate your messages clearly, maintain high expectations, help students develop strategies for success, and continually reexamine your practice. Be determined, be clear, and be a continuous learner. Here are a few ways that the Brookline K–12 Physical Education and Health and Fitness staff has recently shown themselves to be continuous learners:

- Two physical education teachers applied for a local grant that allowed them to attend training in Yoga Education (http://www.yogaed.com). They returned to their schools ready to offer a new program to their students. One teacher also offered professional development to her colleagues, both within our district physical education department and within her school, where classroom teachers learned quick methods to shift students' energy level (up or down) to help focus on classwork.

- Our elementary physical education staff read and shared information at department meetings on the skill theme approach from *Children Moving* by George M. Graham. This approach guides teachers in the process of helping children develop their motor skills and physical fitness through developmentally appropriate activities. Two of our teachers led a department workshop that allowed everyone to gain an understanding of this approach by breaking down familiar games into the skill themes. Implementation then began with a focus on our K–2 classes.

- Our high school teachers recently read and discussed the book *Spark*, by Dr. John Ratey, and we are currently developing a project for our students' common grade-level assessment. This project will help students connect the importance of exercise to their overall physical and mental health.

- Two high school health and fitness teachers attended the Massachusetts Health Education, Physical Education, Recreation and Dance (MAHPERD) conference where they learned new, creative ideas on how to "grab" the students' attention for their lessons. They immediately took risks and put several ideas into action. For example, they purchased a wizard outfit and bubble machine and entered the class in full garb with bubbles flowing after students arrived. Needless to say they gained student attention and were able to maintain it as they taught a lesson about the teenage brain.

- I strongly recommend that you read *The Skillful Teacher* by Jon Saphier and Robert Gower and study their "map of pedagogical knowledge." This pyramid-shaped map groups teaching skills into functions, clarifying for us the importance of creating a strong base with classroom management and instructional strategies and working upward towards motivation and curriculum planning. Research for Better Teaching, Inc. offers courses to help you think through this map and practice your teaching behaviors and strategies.

Last, but not least, maintain your sense of humor. Working within an organization with a multitude of policies and personalities can occasionally become frustrating, but always stay focused on your mission and keep your sense of humor. Our students are most often our source for a good laugh. When teaching adapted physical education, I spent weeks teaching a young boy to hop. One morning, I went to pick him up from his classroom when he looked at me and began to shake his head negatively while pointing to his feet. I asked what was wrong and he said, "I have new sneakers and now you have to teach them to hop all over again." Needless to say, I had a good laugh and he was still able to hop that day!

In conclusion, if you remember anything from this letter, please remember to work hard and be a nice person. If you do this, your students and your school will benefit and good things will come your way. Best of luck as you enter this wonderful profession of teaching and leading!

Sincerely yours,
Teddi A. Jacobs, MEd
Coordinator of Physical Education K–12, Health Education 6–12
The Public Schools of Brookline | Brookline, Massachusetts

■ DISCUSSION QUESTIONS

1. What are the most important qualities of a skillful teacher?
2. Are there other areas of skill not mentioned in this letter?
3. What personality traits match well with the qualities of a skillful teacher?
4. If you felt "stuck" (e.g., developing your lessons, dealing with a behavior situation), where would you turn for help?
5. How would you develop positive relationships with your students while maintaining professional boundaries?

■ RESOURCES

DePree, M. (1992). *Leadership jazz.* New York: Dell.

Ferguson, R. F., & Ramsdell R. (2008). *The Tripod Project.* Westwood, MA: Cambridge Education.

Retrieved August 2, 2011, from http://www .tripodproject.org

Graham, G., Holt/Hale, S. A., & Parker, M. (2010). *Children moving: A reflective approach to teaching physical education.* Boston: McGraw-Hill Higher Education.

McEntree, G. H., Appleby, J., Grant, J., Dowd, J., Hole, S., & Silva, P. (2003). *At the heart of teaching.* New York: Teachers College.

Ratey, J. J., & Hagerman, E. (2008). *Spark: The revolutionary new science of exercise and the brain.* New York: Little, Brown.

Saphier, J., & Gower, R. (1997). *The skillful teacher.* Acton, MA: Research for Better Teaching.

Take Advantage of Each Opportunity That Comes Your Way

Catherine Moffitt

Dear Future Professional,

I have been teaching health and physical education for more than 20 years. I have had the pleasure of working in a school district in southern Rhode Island at the elementary level. The school I have been teaching in has very much been like being part of a family. I have been fortunate to work with incredibly supportive people. The school communities I have been a part of have allowed me the flexibility and encouragement to teach health and physical education in a way that teaches children the skills they need to be active throughout their lives while encouraging families to increase physical activity opportunities.

The hours that are spent at school are only a small part of our profession. The opportunities you create and take advantage of can make all the difference in your career. Early in my career I was invited to work with the Department of Education creating the Health Literacy Frame Work for Rhode Island. I was timid and unsure of what I would have to offer. I went to many meetings and listened to everything and eventually felt like I had information to contribute. Understanding what happens in an elementary classroom was important information that was useful in developing the frameworks. This experience was an instrumental point in my career; I realized the importance of what I was doing and the possibilities for the future. Other doors opened after that. I worked on creating health assessment items; when Rhode Island tested students in health education, I was trained in scoring the student responses to the items. I worked on creating physical education standards, and I have served in many roles in my state chapter of the Association of Health, Physical Education, Recreation, and Dance Executive Board.

These opportunities impacted my teaching in a positive way. I always am looking for some way to change what is happening. I also realized the importance of taking advantage of every opportunity presented. I am very grateful for the amazing people who saw potential in me and allowed me to become the professional I am today. My advice for all young professionals would be to take each opportunity presented and do as much with it as possible. There is always a lot going on, and there is very rarely the perfect time to take on extra responsibility. Do what you can with every challenge presented. Allow yourself the chance to investigate any opportunity presented to you.

One of the current challenges for physical education teachers is the issue of childhood obesity. Although the school cannot be entirely responsible for ensuring the health and fitness of students, as physical educators we are in a unique position to contribute to the health and wellness of families. There are federal and local laws that promote the health and wellness of children. There have been guidelines in place for many years concerning food and nutrition in schools. These guidelines have been updated to include regulations on nutrition and physical activity and apply to the entire school community, staff, faculty, and students. This issue presents a unique opportunity for health and physical educators to be leaders in their districts or schools, advocating for the wellness of the entire school population. We are in a position to promote quality programs and enhance the education experience for students and teachers.

The Child Nutrition and WIC Reauthorization Act of 2004 provides states and districts with criteria to help improve the health and wellness of students. The objectives of the Child Nutrition and WIC Reauthorization Act include setting goals for nutrition education and physical activities, and the implementation of activities to improve student wellness. The physical education departments within each school or district have the knowledge and expertise to develop and promote programs that follow these guidelines.

In Rhode Island, Kids First is one organization that is responsible for helping districts to meet the criteria necessary to comply with the laws and mandates. Its mission is to help communities improve students' nutritional and physical well-being. Kids First provides education and technical assistance to communities to create situations where all students have the opportunity to improve their health and wellness. It has been instrumental in the development of wellness committees around the state. Personnel from Kids First attend the wellness meetings and provide information about what is happening around the state. They also provide support for nutrition and physical education and physical activity. There is also a tool to evaluate the committee, policy, and the progress being made towards goals. The wellness committee is made up of community members, parents, teachers and faculty, students, and a school committee member who is required to be the chairperson. This is an ideal way for physical educators to become involved with their district and advocate for what they believe is important. Having a voice on a committee whose charge is to increase the amount of physical activity students are getting during the school day seems like a natural fit.

At this time in education we need to work smarter; we need to be sure what we do is valued. By being part of the development of policies we are better able to control some of our future. Joining the wellness committee, or a similar organization, for your school could provide you with many opportunities; some will be challenging, and some will be very rewarding. Networking with the people you meet and creating allies within the district will allow you professional growth in many ways. Being a champion for a cause can be very satisfying, and when you put yourself out there other opportunities will present themselves. Take every opportunity you can to surround yourself with excellence and enthusiasm.

Never underestimate what you have to offer; be confident even if you don't feel it. People will look to you for answers and solutions; it's okay to take the time you need to find the answers. You won't have them all at once, and the ones you do have may be wrong, but you need to start somewhere. Believe in yourself, and people will believe in you.

Sincerely,
Catherine Moffitt, EdD
Physical and Health Educator
Charlestown Elementary School | Charlestown, Rhode Island
RIAHPERD Past-President

■ DISCUSSION QUESTIONS

1. Compare wellness policies from different schools or districts. What are some ways that you as a health or physical education teacher can support the wellness policies?

2. What do you consider to be your role as a physical or health educator?

3. As a professional, how could you advocate for the wellness of your school community?

4. What benefits could you gain by joining committees?

5. Is there a connection between committee work and teaching?

Effective Instructional Strategies for Teaching Physical Education

Gary Nihan

Dear Prospective Teacher,

In my role as an administrator I have observed teachers in numerous disciplines including physical education, health education, fine arts, and technology education. Through these observations, I have come to realize that the foundation of effective teaching is classroom management. Without this skill, your students will be unlikely to process the content knowledge you plan to convey.

The teachers I observe that demonstrate strong classroom management skills not only are very effective teachers, but also thoroughly enjoy their profession. They love coming to work each day! Most importantly, student achievement and enthusiasm, as well as increased levels of moderate to vigorous physical activity, are all very apparent in their classes. These teachers tend to be great advocates for their profession and are more likely to be sought out by local colleges and universities for student teacher placements.

A key characteristic among teachers who have strong classroom management skills is the presence of clearly established routines. All of us tend to be creatures of habit and are more comfortable when we know what to expect. Your students will be no different. The use of routines is critical in effective teaching. Such routines include a distinct start and end to the lesson. Instant activity (IA) or ASAP activity is extremely useful because it allows students to start the lesson with immediate physical activity. This is typically the very reason they enjoy coming to physical education class. The IA can be structured with a connection to your prior or current lesson, or it can be strictly for fun. Engaging your students in a movement experience that encourages moderate to vigorous physical activity (MVPA) also gets their brain neurons firing, and will most likely help to better prepare them for listening and learning. I highly recommend posting your IA at the entrance of the gymnasium and expecting your students to stop and read the directions, then engage in the activity with little or no input from the teacher.

It is also a great strategy to finish your IA and start the main content of your lesson with an introduction that clearly states the intended performance outcome of the day. This agenda (which could also be posted inside the gymnasium) provides students with the intended lesson outcomes and, once again, what to expect; for example, "By the end of today's lesson you will be able to catch a ball while moving in open space better than when you came into the gym." When students know what to expect they are more likely to stay on task throughout the lesson. Of course, this agenda concept requires detailed lesson planning; that is a different topic for another letter.

Teachers with strong classroom management skills also use their allocated space well and provide lots of equipment. It is great to see all students working with their own manipulative in a station/center or personal space, because they are more likely to be on task and enjoying their time in class. Waiting in line for a turn is very likely to cause disruptive and/or off-task student behavior. Remember, you want the most number of students active throughout each lesson.

A proactive approach to discipline is also critical to effective classroom management skills. Setting clear and reasonable behavioral expectations for your students is essential to effective teaching and student achievement. Starting and stopping student activity works best with a consistent sound or gesture. I prefer a sound or a voice command, such as "and . . . stop" or "ready . . . begin!" Holding students accountable for following these directions is also important. Consistently using a tiered teacher response/student consequence to off-task behavior will make teaching more enjoyable and student success much more likely to occur. To modify student behavior, a simple three-strike system works well. First strike is a reminder, second is a quick timeout, and the third may be an extended timeout and a follow-up with the classroom teacher and/or communication home. Some physical educators shudder at the thought of denying activity as a consequence, and I can appreciate that perspective. However, the "three strikes and you're out" strategy has proved effective for me and for others I have observed. Of course, you need to consider the age and grade level when implementing behavior modification systems. What is effective at the elementary grade level may not work at the secondary level and vice versa. Through the implementation of such a strategy your students will begin to fully understand your expectations, and off-task behavior will rarely go beyond the student reminder. Of course, this strategy can only be successful if the students know you will follow through consistently (once again, a routine).

Maintaining lesson momentum is also a critical aspect of effective classroom management. Examples of maintaining momentum in physical education include having a distribution strategy to disperse equipment as opposed to one central spot where students will tend to create a logjam. It also means that you need to provide concise and accurate directions to your students. When you deliver these directions, you should also establish expected routines on whether your students are seated or standing, what type of student formation (full circle, half circle, straight line, squads), where they should meet (center circle, three-point line, sideline, basketball key area), and what they should do with their equipment as they listen for directions or instructions (nothing is more distracting than students dribbling a ball or playing catch with themselves). Once again, advanced planning is important.

Always communicate high expectations to your students. You should expect students to act appropriately by exhibiting proper behavior with a high level of participation. This will happen when you provide ongoing specific feedback when a student does well or needs improvement. Always maintain a calm and even disposition when providing this feedback, regardless of the circumstances. You should never appear unnerved or upset with what you observe. Students need to know that you like and respect them as individuals. Building a positive relationship with your students will go a long way towards changing or shaping expected behaviors. When you encourage your students by using positive reinforcement, they will be more likely to meet your high expectations.

My philosophy regarding classroom management stems from my personal experiences as a teacher in both the gymnasium and the classroom. I have also drawn from a course that I took as a teacher and administrator, entitled "Skillful Teacher," developed by John Saphier and Research for Better Teaching, Inc. Furthermore, Dr. George Graham of Penn State University has authored several books that provide great resources for classroom management strategies that are specific to physical education. I have also learned by attending state or national conferences where this topic was presented. For the importance it plays in effective teaching and learning, there can never be enough classroom management training!

In closing, I hope that by following this practical advice you will enjoy a productive and fulfilling career in physical education.

Sincerely yours,
Gary Nihan, MEd
K–12 Director of Health and Physical Education, Retired
Danvers Public Schools | Danvers, Massachusetts

DISCUSSION QUESTIONS

1. Why do you think that this topic is rarely a focus at professional conferences?
2. Are there other elements of classroom management not covered in this letter?
3. Why is it important to provide students with ongoing (specific) feedback?
4. How would you best position yourself in the gymnasium to observe student behaviors?
5. What are some strategies you could use to build a positive relationship with your students?

Creating Winter Outdoor Activities

Heather Perkins

Dear Prospective Physical Education Teacher,

I am currently in my twentieth year of teaching elementary physical education in southern Rhode Island, but when I was the "new kid on the block," the veteran teachers would comment that time flies. They were not kidding. Now I am that veteran teacher, advising you to make each lesson fun, creative, and exciting. Over the years I have had the opportunity to work with many age levels, K–12. The elementary level is where I feel that I have the most impact. Elementary students' enthusiasm for each class is contagious, and they are the clay that can be molded into physical learners.

If I could inspire or advise a future physical education major, it would be to put creativity into each lesson. Creativity is the magic that is needed to grab the attention of your students and keeps them enthusiastic about your lesson or unit. When I plan out my school year, I gear my lessons and units in a way that the students can practice fundamental skills that will lead into lifelong activities. At the elementary level, I try to avoid the typical competitive-style games. My goal as a physical educator is to create lessons of basic skill work, locomotion, and object control. This, in turn, leads to creative games that connect the social skills of cooperation, problem-solving, communication, and teamwork.

How many teachers or students do you know who love to have a snow day? (Please note that this applies to states and countries that have inclement winter snowy weather.) I most certainly do, but only if we are *in* school! I am an outdoor sports enthusiast. Seasonal games and activities are not necessarily always held in the gymnasium. I hold as many of my physical education classes outdoors as possible, even when the weather calls for snow. I feel that it is such a waste of beautiful snow to sit and watch it through the classroom or gym window. I want to have my classes out playing in it. My school's policy for outdoor recess allows the children to wear their snow gear to school for the opportunity to play in the snow. Realizing that the children were already prepared for outdoor play, I thought, why not have them go outside for their physical education classes as well? Of course, I needed to have permission and support from my principal, parents, and classroom teachers. Our school nurse also supplied donated outgrown snowsuits, gloves, and boots for those children who are in need of extra snow gear.

I am fortunate to have a small hill in front of my school where I am able to take my classes sledding. During the lessons, I not only stress sledding safety and the exercise benefits from climbing the hill, I also incorporate the science curriculum into the lessons. Our second grade students are taught the science of friction, force, gravity, incline planes, and simple machines. It is a perfect opportunity for the students to make these science connections. They become part of their very own experiment with this hands-on activity. Not leaving out the special population students, I incorporate them into this unit as well. One of my wheelchair-bound cerebral palsy students had the best time sliding down the hill with the wind in his face. He was able to enjoy this lesson with as much enthusiasm and excitement as his peers. As you could imagine, all of the physical education classes absolutely love this activity.

After several years of sledding, I decided to take on another winter unit. Behind our school, there is a quarter-mile walking trail that is ideal for our physical education classes to use during the spring and fall. How about using the trail in another season? Once again, putting my creativity to work, I thought if we can walk our trail with sneakers on how about with snowshoes? I applied for and received a physical education grant. I highly recommend for any physical education professional to seek grants. There are monies out there for your program. I was able to order 25 pairs of snowshoes at an end-of-the-season sale. The snowshoe unit mainly involves my older students—in this case, third graders. Their fine motor skills of putting their boots into the bindings and figuring out which strap tightens is even a bit tricky for this age level. However, after a few practices they can do it fairly quickly. It is recommended to teach the students in the late fall on the grass, when it is still warm, so they can figure the bindings out without their fingers getting cold, and so they have the opportunity to get used to the snowshoes on their feet.

Once out on the nature trail the children are in awe of the winter wonderland sights and sounds. They love to compare the path to the spring and how different the trail appears when it is covered with snow. I also incorporated classroom curriculum into these lessons with the emphasis in math, science, and even language arts. Here are a few websites that I found very helpful with starting my snowshoe program: http://www.winterfeelsgood.com and http://www.snowschool.org. They provided me with lesson plan ideas and valuable resources.

My hope is that by exposing and involving my students with these creative, "out of the box" physical education classes, it will keep them enthusiastic about winter snow sports. Entire families can benefit from these lifelong winter activities, too.

One of the best compliments that a student could give you about the uniqueness of your creative thinking and lesson planning is that they can't wait to see what you have planned next. You are the best part of their day! Being creative with modifying lessons is an important skill that is often never taught or learned from any textbook. It is a special gift that comes from within.

Sincerely,
Heather A. Perkins
Physical Education Teacher
Stony Lane Elementary School | North Kingstown, Rhode Island

■ DISCUSSION QUESTIONS

1. There are some great winter warm-up games or activities. Can you think of a creative lesson for outdoor play?
2. What resources could you use to start a winter program at your own school?
3. There are 25 students in your class, but you only have 15 pairs of snowshoes. How do you engage all of the students in the class?
4. Why, as the author points out, is enthusiasm contagious, particularly at the elementary level?
5. How can you include students with disabilities in an outdoor education curriculum?

Perceptions of Teaching Physical Education

Steven Wright

Dear Preservice Teacher,

The first thing I like to ask my freshmen physical education teacher education (PETE) students is why are they interested in being a physical education (PE) teacher? Typical answers include "I love kids," "I want to stay active," "I want to give back," and/or "I want to coach." Then I ask, who influenced you the most to want to teach PE? Answers range from parents, to siblings, to friends, to a PE teacher and/or coach. Then I ask, "What were your PE experiences like when you were in school?" Most say they were pretty enjoyable and that they experienced a lot of success in the "gym" environment. When I ask if at this point they want to teach PE or coach or do both, most say they want to do both. If I say that they can only select one, which would it be. Most say they want to coach.

All of these responses are typical for students who want to enter into our profession. Teacher socialization research examines the experiences and perceptions of people (recruits) who wish to enter into teaching. The results of these studies have found that PE recruits (students like yourselves and my students) typically were successful athletes who enjoyed their PE experiences. They liked team sports and games such as dodge ball that they remember dominating. When asked if they would like to someday teach physical education the way they were taught, or perhaps teach differently, the vast majority said they would teach similarly to how they were taught. This is known as the custodial approach, or in other words, desiring to maintain the status quo. Recruits also want to coach and, in fact, when honest about it often are much more enthusiastic about the idea of one day coaching than teaching.

As a former student, athlete, PE teacher, and coach I understand where recruits are coming from. Times have changed quite a bit though from when I took high school PE back in the 1970s. My memories are of a "militaristic" setting where my PE teachers resembled drill sergeants. Classes were either all male or all female, except of course when they were combined for everyone's favorite activity—square dancing. There was a lot of standing around in my classes back then and a lot of public performing, such as when the whole class would watch a classmate try to climb a rope to the top of the gym ceiling. Those that made it to the top felt good about themselves. Those that did not (the majority) felt humiliated and ashamed. I loved playing sports and did so whenever I could, whether on an interscholastic team or during my free time. I hated PE though, and I always thought it was crazy because it *should* have been my favorite class. Ironically, I decided to enter into our profession because I was so *uninspired* by my PE teachers. I was convinced that I could do a better job, and that it was important to have inspiring PE teachers in this world. When I studied PETE as an undergraduate, I was very receptive to new ideas related to teaching PE, but sadly none were being taught. I found my inspiration in "alternative" activities such as adventure-based learning, but perhaps that is a story for another time.

The point I am trying to make is that we are all products of our past. Our "biography"—the story of who we are, influences not only who we are, but also who we will become. Teacher socialization research tells us that someone's biography is potentially more influential than one's teacher education. If true, that means that you are more likely to teach PE the way you were taught when you were in school, rather than how you will be taught in your PETE program. I have to say, as a PETE professor, that is a depressing thought. If that is true, what the heck am I doing? Am I wasting my time?

I would like to think (although maybe I am in denial) that I do make a difference and that I do influence how my PETE students will eventually teach. How is that possible? Well first of all, we discuss my students' experiences, thoughts, and perceptions of PE, and then I implore them to have an open mind when it comes to teaching elementary, middle, or high school PE. I am happy that most of my students have rather fond memories of their PE experiences, but there is so much new happening in the world of PE. Higher education professors tend to want to be agents for change in the sense that they want their students to critically examine themselves and the world around them, with the hope that when they graduate they will go out into the world and help make it a better place. Well, I guess the question is, should PE be taught any differently—or is maintaining the status quo a good thing? My view, and that of many (most?) PETE professors, is that there is certainly room for improvement.

What do you think is the status of PE in the schools where you grew up? Is it considered as important as math, chemistry, or English? If you answer that question the same way my students do, then the answer is no. PE is marginalized in schools in so many ways that I do not have time or space to go into at the moment, but let's try to figure out why it is not so important. Many of the people in positions of power pertaining to the overall school curriculum are people of my generation. Many, if not most of them, hated PE! They didn't see any value in the subject and most likely were humiliated at times. Why do you think movies that depict scenes of PE do so in such derogatory ways? Perhaps it is because writers and directors hated PE and know that many viewers did as well. PE has a perception problem! Those in power (state education department officials, local school boards, superintendents, and principals) often have a poor opinion of it (based on their biographies), so why would they require it on a daily basis in grades K–12? The short answer is they do not. I tell my PETE students all the time—when you get a teaching job it will not be enough to educate your pupils about the importance of physical activity and a healthy lifestyle. You will also have to educate (at the very least) parents, administrators, and local school board members about the importance of quality physical education programs. You have to become an advocate for our subject. So, what does a quality PE program look like?

There has been a movement in education for some time now that preaches the importance of student standards, outcomes, and accountability. PE was a little late to the party when it came to developing standards and outcomes, but national standards for K–12 PE were developed in 1995. Accountability in PE classes has been even slower to arrive, but some states are requiring all teachers, including PE teachers, to show evidence of student learning. When I ask my students how they were graded in PE when they were in school, the answer typically is by showing up, being dressed out, and actively participating. I bet high school students would love to get a good grade by showing up to calculus class, having a sharpened pencil or two, and trying to solve the problems given to them in class. Of course their grade is not based on that, but rather on whether they learn the material covered. A quality PE program must be standards-based and show evidence of student learning.

As a former middle and high school PE teacher, I know that I did not relish the idea of giving my students pre- and post-unit skills tests and written tests (what are now referred to as traditional assessments). Those tests took up too much time and limited instruction and activity time, so I did not use them very often. Skills tests were also not very relevant to the game, in my view. A basketball skills test, for example, has students trying to hit a target on the wall with a chest pass as many times as they can in 30 seconds. Fortunately, today there is a new form of testing known as authentic assessment that does not take up much instruction/activity time, and assesses students in more appropriate settings, such as playing a 3 versus 3 basketball game. PE is often viewed very negatively, but when it is seen more positively it is often characterized as fun and games, not something that can be serious. Showing evidence of student learning makes it more than a frivolous experience. Let's talk about the concept of "fun" for a moment. When I ask my students what they think some of the goals of a PE program should be, they always at some point say for the students to have fun. I ask them if they think the calculus teacher has as one of her or his main goals that their students have fun? They laugh and say, well no. So I press them as to why they think students should have fun in PE. We eventually come to the conclusion that if students enjoy physical activity in their PE classes, they just may stay active for a lifetime, and if that were the outcome, then PE might be the most important subject that they ever take in school. So we talk about when they advocate for PE, they should talk about student enjoyment in PE that may captivate them enough to foster a lifetime of physical activity and wellness. It is semantics, but I suggest that the term *fun* greatly trivializes the objective of student enjoyment and subsequently motivation to move. So, quality PE programs should teach a range of activities that include lifetime sports.

I believe there is still a place for the inclusion of team sports/games in PE programs, but another example of how PE is changing is teaching these games via the tactical approach. We all have learned how to play games like basketball through the traditional, skill-based approach. Using this approach, skills such as dribbling and passing are taught as "closed" skills, in isolation, with no defense applied or much thought required. An example is having students dribble down the court using their right hand and then dribble back using their left. Once these skills are learned in this decontextualized environment, they are applied in more game-like settings. We wonder sometimes why students who are 5 years old absolutely *love* PE and many who are 14 years old are turned off to PE. One reason might be that many of these students have been asked to stand with a partner and complete chest passes for 5 minutes, with no movement or defense, *every year* for the past 10 years, and they are bored almost to tears. Often teachers hear their students say, "Why are we doing this stupid drill—when can we play a game?"

Well, the tactical approach to teaching basketball starts out the first class of the unit with a small-sided, modified game of basketball. The focus would be on possession of the ball (no dribbling or shooting at first) through passing. The game would be keep away, and the passing requirement is within the context of a game because there is defense and the option to throw different types of passes. Once the game is completed there would be a short question and answer period with the teacher asking the students why they were or were not successful completing passes. Students are required to think about what they did in the game and share their thoughts. The teacher and students quickly come to an understanding of what their strengths and weaknesses are and then there is a skill development phase that is based on what the students need to do to get better. I can assure you, it is not standing still sending chest passes back and forth to a partner. It might be working on L-cuts or V-cuts so that an offensive person without the ball does a better job of getting open and, yes, there is defense (perhaps more passive at first and then active) that simulates game activity. A typical lesson would finish with a second modified game, with students focusing on performing what they just worked on in the skill development phase, in the game. This approach still requires skill development, but only in the context of what pupils need to improve their game play. They do not ask the question, "Why are we doing this stupid drill" because they know why they are doing it and they work at it because they want to improve. Students will still want to play the regulation game of basketball and they will get to that point, but the activities leading up to it will make sense to them; they will be forced to think about offensive and defensive strategies and share these thoughts, they will be motivated to participate, and they will improve. Research has shown that PE teachers over the years have not done a very good job of explaining to students *why* they are asked to do things. One of the strengths of the tactical approach is that students understand why they are doing things, and this will help to motivate them.

Quality PE programs educate the *whole* child. When I go into local schools and read their mission or their motto they almost always talk about this concept. Educators often talk about developing the whole child by addressing issues related to the cognitive (intellectual), psychomotor (physical), and affective (social, emotional) domains. The muddy little secret is that schools mainly are concerned with the cognitive domain only—hence the importance of the "academic" subjects. The reality is that no subject area addresses all three domain areas better than physical education. I believe that schools do a terrible job of addressing the affective domain, for example. In most classes, most of the time, students get in trouble if they are "socializing," and the emotions students feel are often negative ones that surround the stress of assessments. I am hard pressed to think of an activity that stimulates all three domain areas more than having a student in a PE class climb a 40-foot indoor climbing wall. Cognitively the student needs to understand how to safely set up/prepare for the climb and she or he needs to pick one of a myriad of routes to get to the top—quite an intellectual challenge. The activity is very demanding physically, particularly if there are any overhangs on the wall. Affectively, the climber literally has her or his life in the hands of two classmates who are belaying and backup belaying them via a safety rope. The emotions a climber feels when beginning to climb can be very intense, and the sense of anxiety, trepidation, or even fear is replaced by satisfaction and often joy and exhilaration when she or he is successful. This experience can alter the self-concept of a student in very compelling and dramatic ways. Just talking about educating the whole child does not benefit them. PE provides a dynamic environment for doing it, and doing it better than in any other subject area taught in schools. Using the tactical approach to teaching games that was discussed earlier is another example of how we can educate the whole child very explicitly. Oh no, PE is much more than fun and games.

I urge you to go through your PETE program with an open mind. Listen to the many "new" ideas and approaches to teaching PE. Think about them critically, discuss them openly, experiment with them, and analyze them in relationship to your emerging philosophy about teaching PE and what it means to be an effective teacher. You have chosen a critically important major, and if you go out into the real world and teach PE, you will have a significant impact on the youth of America. Do it right, do it well, with enthusiasm and conviction, and you will be part of the generation of PE teachers that helps to transform PE from a marginalized subject to one that is as important as any in a school curriculum.

Best wishes,
Steven Wright
Kinesiology Pedagogy Coordinator
University of New Hampshire

■ DISCUSSION QUESTIONS

1. What are some ways that PE is marginalized in schools?
2. What can PE teachers do about these incidents of marginalization?
3. How were you graded in your high school PE classes?
4. Look at how you were graded objectively—what does that tell you about PE classes and your PE teachers?
5. How can PE teachers advocate for their program?

Glossary

A

abilities ". . . genetic traits that are a prerequisite for skilled performance" (Coker, C. (2009). *Motor learning and control for practitioners* (2nd ed.). Scottsdale, AZ: Holcomb Hathaway).

acceptable use policy (AUP) Provides acceptable guidelines for an individual using technology and will differ depending on the provider.

active gaming technology An interactive video game system such as a Wii or video game such as DDR that provides students with physical activity in a fun and challenging manner.

adapted physical education Physical education that has been modified to provide students with disabilities the opportunity to enhance gross motor and manipulative skill development in the least restrictive environment.

affective domain Pertains to the emotions, temperaments, and even the values of the learner.

affective education The domain of education that centers on the emotions, feelings, and relations of students. Affective objectives typically target attitudes, behavior, cooperation, emotion, motivation, and sportsmanship.

alternative assessment A less traditional form of a summative and/or formal measure of learning that can include creative ways to assess including the creation of a journal, public service announcement, or booklet (i.e., not a traditional test or quiz). Other examples include rubrics, peer assessments, checklists, and portfolios.

American College of Sports Medicine (ACSM) The primary, and most reputable, institution that governs exercise science–related research and creates exercise guidelines and recommendations for individuals based on the results of their studies.

amount of physical activity Measured by the number of steps each subject has taken. Steps are measured by the use of a pedometer. The average range of steps for fourth and fifth graders during a 45-minute physical education class is 1200–1600; 47.5 steps per minute.

assessment Consists of activities undertaken by teachers, students, and other entities (e.g., schools, districts, states) that provide information to be used as feedback to modify teaching and learning activities or to make a judgment about achievement.

assessment *for* learning Assessment that is formative in nature, but it goes beyond the traditional view of formative assessment as information that is used by teachers to track student progress on standards and plan instruction. Assessment for learning includes teachers providing descriptive (rather than evaluative) feedback to students and student actions such as self-assessment and goal setting, tracking learning, analyzing progress, and describing learning to others.

assessment literacy Includes understanding what assessment methods to use in order to gather dependable information about student achievement; communicating assessment results effectively, whether using report card grades, test scores, portfolios, or conferences; and understanding how to use assessment to maximize student motivation and learning by involving students as full partners in assessment, record keeping, and communication.

assessment *of* learning Also called summative assessment; it takes place at the end of instruction, to make a judgment about achievement and/or assign a score or grade. Examples are standardized tests used for accountability purposes, student assessments designed to determine mastery of standards, and classroom grades.

asynchronous communication Communication that does not take place in real-time. For example, one person writes an e-mail or online discussion post but the receiver reads it at a later time.

auditory learners Those who prefer to learn by hearing information presented.

authentic assessment Evaluates students' abilities in "real-world" contexts. In other words, students learn how to apply their skills to authentic tasks and projects. Authentic assessment does not encourage rote learning and passive test-taking. Instead, it focuses on students' analytical skills, ability to integrate what they learn, creativity, ability to work collaboratively, and written and oral expression skills. It values the learning process as much as the finished product (Pearson Product Education Group. (2011). Authentic assessment overview. Retrieved June 26, 2011, from http://www.teachervision.fen.com/teaching-methods-and-management/educational-testing/4911.html?page=2&detoured=1&for_printing=1). In physical education, authentic assessment measures include data when students are participating during physical education class activities, not simply skill tests. Heart rate monitors and pedometers are examples of motivational devices that are authentic assessment measures in physical education.

automaticity The ability of an expert to avoid unnecessary thinking while performing a routine task by depending on deep-rooted memory gained from repeated practice.

autonomy Feeling and having one's behaviors driven by self-authored motivations.

A/V port The input/output path on audio and video devices.

B

backward design Intentional planning in which the teacher begins with the exit goals and designs the curriculum toward those goals, from high school down to elementary school.

blended/hybrid instruction A substantial component (30–80%) of instructional time and learning activities take place online.

C

Call to Action to Prevent and Decrease Overweight and Obesity A report that encouraged schools to provide health education to students for the development of knowledge, attitudes, skills, and behaviors that they will carry with them throughout their life.

caring adult mentor An adult in the life of a youth who serves as an important other to a child or young adult: The caring adult mentor provides a sense of personal connection and value to the life of the given youth/young adult.

case study approach This style of research focuses on presenting a single institution or phenomenon for in-depth review.

Challenger Learning Centers Offer realistic mock-ups of Mission Control and an orbiting space station for students to learn about teamwork. They often partner with science centers, museums, universities, and schools.

character Moral or ethical quality/strength; instinctive qualities that make a person recognizable.

Child Nutrition and WIC Reauthorization Act of 2004 (CNR) Produced by the U.S. Congress, it mandates that local education agencies adopt and implement a local wellness policy.

civic responsibility An element of high quality service-learning. The service-learning project promotes students' responsibility to care for others and to contribute to the community. By participating in the service-learning project, students understand how they can impact their community.

cognitive domain Learning the rules of a game or sport, concepts about proper body mechanics, knowledge about content, or processing any factual information.

common health language Terminology and similar experiences introduced in health programs in order to foster increased communication among students and teachers. Social competency skills are reinforced that build a sense of community and promote positive relationships.

competence Being able to be successful and believing in one's abilities within a particular realm.

competitive foods "Foods that are available in schools but are not part of U.S. Department of Agriculture school meals. These include foods and beverages sold in schools through vending machines, a la carte purchases in cafeteria lines, school stores, and snack bars. Other sources include foods used in fundraising and other school activities, or provided by teachers" (Briefel, R. R. et al. (2009). School food environments and practices affect dietary behaviors of us public school children. *Journal of the American Dietetic Association, 109*(2 Suppl), S982).

comprehensive health education Coordinated school programs that are designed to deliver and evaluate planned and varied curricula with goals, objectives, and content sequence. Comprehensive health education takes into consideration different learning styles and individual uniqueness.

concepts-based fitness and wellness education A curriculum-based approach that focuses on one's knowledge and understanding of physical activity, physical fitness, and wellness.

cooperative learning A strategy for teaching and learning designed to foster cooperation based on the creation of small heterogeneous groups of students assigned learning tasks, that requires interdependence to enable completion, and that incorporates individual and group accountability.

course-embedded service-learning project A required or optional project used as a central theme of an academic course. Experiential learning is central to the knowledge development of academic course content and concepts. Service-learning is part of the course practice.

Creative Commons A nonprofit organization that releases licenses that allow the author of a product to specify the terms of use (which rights they reserve or waive).

criteria chart A learning tool used to clearly communicate to students what a particular task or assignment requires of them.

cross-training A term used to describe a teacher-made course that included 30 minutes of cardiovascular activity and 30 minutes of a team or individual sport.

curriculum Includes all knowledge, skills, and learning experiences that are provided to students within the school program.

curriculum and instructional models Blueprints for teaching and learning.

cyberbullying The use of email, instant messaging, websites, voting booths, and chat or bash rooms to deliberately antagonize and intimidate others.

D

design "The essence of design is helping to create an emotional connection to an intellectual problem or idea. It is the creation of an experience that engages us, moves us into action or new ideas, provokes a response, or helps to internalize ideas or methods in a way that we don't easily forget." (Napier, R. (1995). The art of design: The key to memory and learning. In C. Roland, R. Wagner, & R. Weigand (Eds.), *Do it and understand: The bottom line on corporate experiential learning* (p. 69). Dubuque, Iowa: Kendall/Hunt Publishing Company).

differentiated instruction The outcome of a planning process that results in the identification of instructional objectives, instructional approaches, and assessment methods that are appropriate to meet the needs of individual learners.

digital citizens People who "understand human, cultural, and societal issues related to technology and practice legal and ethical behavior" (ISTE. (2007). *National educational technology standards for students*. Retrieved July 22, 2009, from http://www.iste.org/Content/NavigationMenu/NETS/ForStudents/NETS_for_Students.htm).

disability An impairment that affects daily functioning, and in children, affects growth and development.

discourse The ways that meanings are made; these meanings are unique to times and places.

disposition An inclination or tendency; natural mental and emotional outlook, or mood; characteristic attitude.

diversity Individual differences along the dimensions of race, ethnicity, gender, sexual orientation, socioeconomic status, age, physical abilities, religious beliefs, political beliefs, or other ideologies.

diversity teaching mindset A personal philosophy or frame of mind regarding teaching a diverse group of students.

Doctrine of the Mean The doctrine of Aristotle (384–322 BC) that moral virtue is a disposition of choice lying in a mean between two extremes relative to our natural tendencies. The mean is the point we ought to pursue, and is determined by the moral insight of one with practical wisdom.

dynamic stretch This type of stretch consists of functional-based exercises, which use sport-specific movements to prepare the body for movement. Some examples of dynamic stretches are walking lunges (without weights), side bends, and trunk rotations.

E

educational technology The study and ethical practice of facilitating learning and improving performance by creating, using, and managing appropriate technological processes and resources.

effective teacher A teacher whose behaviors result in measurable gains in student achievement, usually gauged by standardized tests.

empathic capacity The ability to express understanding and feeling toward another. Although most humans have the capacity for empathy, it must be developed through maturity, experience, and education.

empathy An affective response more appropriate to someone else's situation than one's own. It involves putting oneself into another person's shoes in order to understand the feelings of this person.

epiphyseal plate The growth plate of a long bone (e.g., femur, tibia). Epiphyseal plates are vulnerable to injury in youth because they have not hardened into bone yet. It is the point of the long bone where growth is still occurring.

ethos The underlying sentiments that inform the beliefs, customs, or practices of a group or society; the dominant assumptions of a people.

evaluation The process of collecting and analyzing data that leads to a judgment.

exemplary/promising health programs The identification and designation of health programs that promote safe, disciplined, and drug-free schools. Programs that are proven effective when judged against rigorous criteria.

experiential learning Involves the student in his or her learning to a much greater degree than in traditional learning environments. Related terms/concepts include experience-based learning, active learning, hands-on learning, deep-level processing, and higher order thinking.

experiential learning cycle There are four steps in the experiential learning cycle: (1) concrete experience, (2) observation and reflection, (3) forming abstract concepts, and (4) testing the implication of concepts in new situations.

Experiential Learning Theory A theory developed by Kolb that describes a four-stage learning cycle—experience, reflection, abstract conceptualization, and active experimentation—to explain how knowledge is created

expert teacher A teacher whose knowledge, thinking, decision making, and reflection demonstrate a high level of expertise.

F

facilitation A process of leading individuals and/or groups through activities and reflection such that participants gain the most from the experience.

fitness assessment Assessment designed to provide individualized feedback regarding one's overall fitness status and/or physiological responses to physical effort.

formal assessment The practice of using a more standardized way to measure student learning.

formative assessment Assessment that takes place during the process of learning and teaching, yielding information that is used by teachers to track student progress on standards and plan instruction.

free and appropriate education Free means a child with a disability has the right to go to public school without an associated cost. An appropriate education encompasses a variety of scenarios depending on the individual needs of the child, including education in a regular education class, the use of aids and related services in a regular education class, a separate classroom for special education, and/or special services for all or portions of the school day.

frontloading A statement by the facilitator in advance of an activity to help students understand the intent of an activity. Frontloading can include the use of a story or scenario that sets the stage for the rationale of an activity.

G

gender expectations Beliefs about ability based on gender.

grading The act of assigning a symbol or number to denote student progress or decline.

gym class With the traditional or old PE, students and teachers used this term for the school class where sports and fitness were taught.

H

health education A comprehensive curriculum that includes a variety of health topics, that addresses various dimensions of wellness, and that provides students opportunities to gain knowledge, develop competence in skills, and develop attitudes that will allow them to become healthy individuals.

health literacy The goal of a comprehensive health education curriculum; defined as the ability of an individual to become healthy and maintain health through their lifetime by using a variety of health-enhancing skills.

health-related fitness An aspect of physical fitness that is known to positively impact overall health, such as cardiorespiratory fitness, muscular strength, muscular flexibility, muscular endurance, and body composition.

heart rate monitor (HRM) A device a person can wear that measures and displays heart rate information while participating in exercise. The device has a monitor strap held in place around the chest by an elastic band. The heart rate is displayed on a watch.

hierarchy An actual or assumed ranking of individuals or groups that indicates who has power.

high-energy, low-nutrient foods Foods high in sugar and/or fat content, which contribute to their high energy content. These foods are usually low in other nutrients, and are often referred to as empty-calorie foods or junk food. Examples of high-energy, low-nutrient foods include cookies, potato chips, and sugared soda drinks (Wardlaw, G. M., & Hampl, J. S. (2007). *Perspectives in nutrition* (7th ed., p. 41). Boston: McGraw-Hill Higher Education).

home-grown health programs Health education programs and activities devised by local teachers and administrators that are designed to provide positive learning experiences. Favorite lessons often govern the selection of instruction.

hypothesis A specific, testable prediction about what one expects to happen in a scientific study.

I

individualized education program (IEP) The written articulation (which serves as a legal contract) of an individualized designed plan that specifies annual goals and objectives, along with a description of services and supports, that will be used to meet the unique needs of students with disabilities receiving special education services and supports as required by IDEA.

Individuals with Disabilities Education Act (IDEA) One of the key components of IDEA is that it removes a child from "regular" class only when supplementary aides and services are not adequate for the child to succeed.

indoor/outdoor experiential activities Engaging activities and simulations that allow students to get out of their seats and on their feet, creating a link between the actual activity and "real world" behaviors and practices. Many activities can be facilitated indoors or outdoors, depending on time, equipment needed, and weather conditions.

induction physical educators Those educators at the beginning of their career.

informal assessment The practice of using less methodical ways to measure student learning.

instructional media Media that is used to deliver instruction, for example, CDs or videos.

intellectual empathy The capacity to understand quickly and thoroughly what others know and how they think and to imagine how to help them learn better.

intensity   In resistance exercise terminology, expressed as a percentage of a person's one-repetition maximum. It can also simply be the amount of weight lifted if a maximal amount of weight lifted is not known.

intentional activities   Behaviors, thinking, or goals that we choose to engage with and that we purposefully put effort toward.

interactive class technologies   A broad range of technologies in the classroom that facilitate interaction between the students and the technology.

interdisciplinary lessons   Academic subjects (classroom curriculum) that are included in the physical education curriculum. Research suggests that students learn best when movement is involved. Using activities and games collaboratively supports learning in the classroom and movement setting (Kovar, S., Combs, C., Campbell, K., Napper-Owen, G., & Worrell, V. (2007). *Elementary classroom teachers as movement educators*. New York: McGraw-Hill).

intersectionality   An approach to understanding society and individuals that demands that multiple aspects of one's identity be considered in analysis.

intrinsic motivation   The incentive to engage in a task for the sheer enjoyment of the activity itself rather than the external benefits one might gain.

J

journal   A type of written assessment in which students record, respond to, and reflect on various class materials and topics.

K

kinesthetic learners   Those who prefer active engagement during learning.

L

laboratory experiences   Activities designed to provide an arena for cognitive concepts to be applied and understood within a fitness education approach; the experience usually involves some sort of personal awareness or application.

learned helplessness   A perception of futility where a person believes that no matter how much a task is attempted or performed the result will be failure, which leads the person to avoid the task altogether.

learning environment   The overall environment that the teacher and the students create together.

learning goals   Determined and developed in an effort to guide professional growth. Learning goals should be consistent with desired personal and professional benchmarks.

learning management system (LMS)   Software that enables users to deliver, track, and manage instruction.

learning style preference   The preferred method of taking information from the environment into the senses for further processing.

least restrictive environment (LRE)   A provision in IDEA that requires students with disabilities to be educated, to the extent appropriate, with their nondisabled peers with the use of necessary services and supports.

leave no trace   A program designed to help people take responsibility for the wilderness areas in which they travel, such that their impact is minimized.

level of physical activity   Measured by each subject's heart rate information. Heart rate is measured in beats per minute using a heart rate monitor.

lifestyle chronic health conditions   A chronic disease lasting at least several months or more; typically related to lifestyle behaviors such as lack of regular physical activity, poor nutrition, cigarette smoking, or other personal health habits. Chronic diseases generally cannot be prevented by vaccines or cured by medication, nor do they just disappear.

M

mentee   A less experienced professional that participates in a mentoring relationship (synonymous with protégé).

mentor   A person who is a more experienced professional that participates in a mentoring relationship.

mentoring   A process in which a more experienced professional offers support and guidance to a less experienced professional.

model-based instruction A way of creating and then delivering a coherent physical education program.

moderate-intensity physical activity A level of effort in which a person should experience some increase in breathing or heart rate, a "perceived exertion" of 11 to 14 on the Borg scale—the effort a healthy individual might expend while walking briskly, mowing the lawn, dancing, swimming, or bicycling on level terrain, or performing any activity that burns 3.5 to 7 calories per minute (kcal/min).

moral relativism The view that ethical standards, morality, and positions of right or wrong are culturally based and therefore, "we can all decide what is right for ourselves." The concept that there are no moral absolutes, that "anything goes," and that life is ultimately without meaning.

N

National Association of Sport and Physical Education (NASPE) Part of the American Alliance for Health, Physical Education, Recreation, and Dance; a professional membership association that sets the standard for best practices in quality physical education and sport.

National School Lunch Program (NSLP) A program that provides lunch and snacks to low-income children that was permanently instituted into public and nonprofit schools in 1946.

Net generation or digital natives Students who were born after 1980 and have grown up with digital technologies.

New physical education (new PE) The following are characteristics of a new PE class: class is called *physical education* because physical education teachers educate student in the three domains of learning, the psychomotor (physical), affective, and cognitive; everyone is active, all-inclusive; small groups; no humiliation and intimidation; cooperative focus; fitness is blended with other PE content; motivational devices are used to personalize and monitor physical activity; enjoyment levels are raised; individuals work at their own physical level and challenge themselves by establishing personal goals; a wellness or health-related focus; each child has their own piece of equipment (most of the time, or all are active in some way); each child is working towards their own personal fitness goals throughout the lesson; assessment is more authentic; technology supports the pedagogy (pedometers, heart rate monitors, computers, and other fitness devices such as personal digital assistants [PDAs]); and national, state, and district standards are addressed (Sullivan, E., & Clapham, E. (2008). Teaching an old dog new tricks: Traditional or the old PE versus the new PE. A teacher script about the old and the new PE).

norms Societal expectations of how one is supposed to be or to act; that which is considered to be normal.

nutrient-dense foods Foods that provide relatively high quantities of nutrients for a small amount of energy (compared with other food sources). The more nutrient-dense the food is, the better it is as a nutrient source. Examples of nutrient-dense foods include low-fat milk, beans, berries, dark-green leafy vegetables, and whole-grain bread

O

obesity A condition of excess body fat; because methods to determine body fat directly are difficult, the diagnosis of obesity is often based on body mass index (BMI), a measure of the ratio of weight and height. Obesity at any age negatively affects health and well-being.

one-hit wonders Resource speakers, plays, and demonstrations designed to have a positive impact on a student audience so as to change behavior and enrich health instruction.

one-repetition maximum (1RM) The maximal amount of weight a person can lift once.

online education Instruction that takes place completely or at least 80% online (i.e., via the Internet).

outcome-based education This includes three basic ideas: all students can learn and succeed (but not on the same day and/or in the same way), success breeds success, and schools control the conditions of success (Spady, W. G. (1991). Beyond traditional outcome-based education. *Education Leadership, 2*(49), 67–72).

P

participatory learning A style of learning/instruction that uses modeling, observation, and practice to teach skills and that encourages and facilitates student involvement in the learning and teaching process.

pedagogy A teaching method or teaching style; the study of teaching; the practice of teaching.

pedometer (PED) A noninvasive tool that allows for instant feedback regarding a person's activity level. It measures vertical accelerations of the body (steps) and captures a variety of activities that enhance the concept of "lifestyle activity."

peer assessment The assessment of one student completed by a classmate. Peer assessments may be completed in rubric or checklist form and assess class material and development.

physical activity Bodily movement produced by skeletal muscles; requires expenditure of energy and produces progressive health benefits.

physical education The proper title for the new PE class that is taught in schools and aligned with district, state, and national standards.

physical education–specific mentoring program A specific curriculum designed to address the professional needs of new teachers in the field of physical education.

plyometric training A type of power training that incorporates explosive movements such as jumping or throwing. It is often done using body weight, but can also incorporate small amounts of weights or medicine balls.

podcasts A multimedia file that can be played on computers, MP3 players, or advanced cell phones (derived from the words *iPod* and *broadcast*).

portfolio A collection of student work that is compiled over a period of time, such as an academic quarter, a semester, or a year, and is reviewed against predetermined criteria.

positive psychology A new branch of psychology concerned with happiness and thriving of individuals and communities.

postural balance The optimal distribution of the body's mass relative to the force of gravity. In order to maintain postural balance, the center of gravity must be within the base of support.

processing Also referred to as debriefing; encourages individuals to plan, reflect, describe, analyze, and communicate about experiences before, during, or after an activity.

process–product research Research on effective teaching that follows a pattern of pretest-intervention-posttest to change teaching behaviors and measure student outcomes.

professional development A comprehensive, sustained, and intensive approach to improving teachers' and principals' effectiveness in raising student achievement.

professional development event A structured learning opportunity that has measurable learning outcomes for the participant.

professional development plan A well-thought-out proposal for professional growth that is built on personal strengths, areas in need of improvement, and interests of the educator.

professional learning community A group of educators and/or administrators who work collaboratively to address an identified educational concern. Often, it is developed to meet a specific need within a school or content area and results in shared professional growth.

professional learning opportunities Include events or activities that are combined to provide an opportunity for professional growth. Professional learning opportunities may come in many forms and are not necessarily a specific event or single opportunity. Examples may include self-study, research, study groups, or an advanced degree course.

professional model of sport leadership The goal of coaching is to win, regardless of the process or method. Typically, such methods rely on coercion, intimidation, and control for success.

proprioceptive neuromuscular facilitation (PNF) A type of stretch most commonly characterized by a precontraction of the muscle to be stretched and a contraction of the antagonist muscle during the stretch. The PNF stretches must be done with a partner.

prosocial behavior The act of helping others in a positive way including, caring, rescuing, defending, cooperating, and sharing as well as empathy.

protégé One who is a less experienced professional that participates in a mentoring relationship.

psychomotor domain Teaching to the physical content, such as how to run, jump, throw, or leap; the physical skills needed to play a sport, physical fitness activities, and any skill that involves "doing" or an action.

R

reflection An element of high-quality service-learning in which students think, share, and produce reflective products individually or as group members. Examples may include but are not limited to discussion, journal writing, and surveys.

reflective teachers Teachers who use a variety of formal and informal assessments to critique their lessons and examine their teaching behaviors.

reflective teaching The process of a teacher critically examining his or her instruction through a formal or informal means of thoughtful questions and assessment in order to improve instruction based on the feedback and to enhance student learning.

relatedness Feeling in harmony and connected with valued others.

resistance exercise Exercise that uses some form of resistance. Examples include elastic bands or rubber tubing, free weights (barbells, dumbbells), weight machine equipment, water, medicine balls, kettle bells, water- or sand-filled cans or bottles, partner resistance, or body-weight exercises.

risk behavior spectrum Behavioral, environmental, and inherited influences that provoke action toward behavior that promotes ill health.

rituals and routines Used by teachers to create structure and/or a pattern that students understand that they will follow before, during, and/or after a lesson

rubric An assessment instrument that describes the standards being taught and the techniques needed to attain proficiency at each level of scoring. Rubrics help teachers to objectively determine scores and grades.

S

School Breakfast Program (SBP) A program providing breakfast to low-income children that was permanently instituted into public and nonprofit private schools up to and including high school in 1975.

screen time Includes time spent watching television, playing video games, using computers, and surfing the Internet. Among children and adolescents, screen time is positively associated with obesity and inversely related to time spent being physically active.

self-assessment A teacher who dissects his or her lesson, thinks about what happened during the teaching process, and analyzes student performance is using self-assessment. Self-assessment should also include the step of asking good questions about the teaching and making plans to improve practices.

self-efficacy A person's belief that they can do something.

service-learning A teaching method that combines academic instruction, meaningful service, and critical reflective thinking to enhance student learning and civic responsibility.

skill theme curriculum "Skill themes are fundamental movements that are later modified into the more specialized patterns on which activities of increasing complexity are built." Once the basic skill themes are learned to a certain degree of proficiency, they can be combined with other skills and used in more complex settings, such as those found in dance, games, and gymnastics. The intent is to help children learn a variety of locomotor, nonmanipulative, and manipulative skills that they can use to enjoyably and confidently play a sport or perform a dance consisting of an intricate set of movements. The intention of this model is to help physical educators think about and design curricula that will "guide youngsters in the process of becoming physically active for a lifetime" (Graham, G., Holt/Hale, S. A., & Parker, M. (2004). *Children moving: A reflective approach to teaching* *physical education* (4th ed., p. 12). Mountain View, CA: Mayfield).

skills   Something students need to be able to do and have competence in to lead a healthy lifestyles by avoiding risky behaviors and engaging in health-enhancing behaviors (i.e., goal-setting).

skills-based health education   A curriculum designed around teaching students skills in the context of health. This includes teaching specific sets of skills, establishing beliefs and attitudes towards health that are health enhancing, and providing students with the knowledge they need to apply the skills and be healthy. This is similar to the definition of health education, but the key point to remember is *the focus is on skills*. The planning should start with expected behavioral outcomes based on health-related skills and then specific content should be included.

Social Cognitive Theory (SCT)   A theory that proposes that health behavior is determined by knowledge, perceived self-efficacy that one has control over their health habits, outcome expectations, health goals, and perceived facilitators and impediments to action (Bandura, A. (2004). Health promotion by social cognitive means. *Health Education & Behavior, 31*(2), 143–164).

social norming   Rather than scare students out of participating in risky behaviors, this strategy uses survey data of actual student behavior to accentuate the fact that many students do the right thing. The intent of the approach is that if students knew the truth they would feel less pressure to engage in dangerous activities.

sociometric status   The degree to which a person is liked or disliked by his or her peers.

Stages of Change model   A model for behavior change that includes five stages: precontemplation, contemplation, preparation, action, and maintenance.

standards   Curriculum goals established at the national, state, or district level that identify the skills, knowledge, and dispositions that students should demonstrate.

standards-based curriculum   A program that is developed by looking at the standards or criterions or statements of intent (district, state, or national); identifying the skills, knowledge, and dispositions that students should demonstrate to meet these standards; and identifying activities that will allow students to reach the goals stated in the standards.

standards-based education   Defines what it is students should know and be able to do; instructors then create curriculum, and design instructional processes and assessment tools that reflect those outcomes.

static stretch   Entails a muscle being slowly stretched, then held in the stretched position for 30 to 60 seconds. It can be done solo or with a partner.

stations   In physical education, used to structure the participation of students in a lesson where they will go from one activity to another, in separate groups, usually for a specific amount of time (e.g., stations in a basketball lesson could include passing, shooting, 3v3 game, and free throws).

stereotypes   A belief that has been "normalized" in society, usually about a person or a group of people that embody a certain image.

student centered   When a curriculum, unit, and/or lessons are developed and implemented with the focus on students and their learning instead of teachers.

summative assessment   Assessment that takes place at the end of instruction, to make a judgment about achievement and/or assign a score or grade. Summative assessment is also known as assessment of learning.

supervisor assessment   Teacher evaluation when a principal, administrator, colleague, or a person of higher authority evaluates the teaching.

supportive curricula   The instruction provided by the teacher to participant groups receiving special pedagogy designed to provide the student a conceptual framework for using the technological devices. The instruction provided by the teacher will aim to get the student excited and motivated about using heart rate monitors (HRMs) and pedometers (PEDs) and also supply the student with background information on using the HRMs and

PEDs during PE class. The teacher will use interdisciplinary lessons for this purpose.

synchronous communication Two or more persons communicate in real-time and there is no delay in communication. For example, two people are online at the same time, are logged into the same chat software, and chat with each other.

T

tactile learners Those who prefer to be able to touch, feel, and engage with materials used in their learning.

teacher expectations Assumptions about student performance and behaviors based on the teacher's value and belief system. Negative teacher expectations are typically grounded in bias and prejudicial ideas.

teacher portals Large websites that provide lesson plans, ideas, and solutions to learner problems, which teachers can adapt to their individual contexts.

teaches for transfer When a coach, who values teaching transferrable life skills, prioritizes helping his or her athletes take lessons learned in sport and apply them to other important areas of their lives—particularly that of academic pursuits.

team building A process that builds and develops shared goals, interdependence, trust, commitment, and accountability among team members and that seeks to improve team members' problem-solving skills.

team building activities for schools and communities Engaging activities and simulations that allow students to "get out of their seats and on their feet," creating a link between the actual activity and real-world behaviors and practices. Many activities can be facilitated indoors or outdoors depending on time, equipment needed, and weather conditions.

teamwork Two or more people organized to work together interdependently, collaboratively, and cooperatively to reach a common goal.

technological device A device that assists with measuring the level and amount of physical activity; for example, pedometers, and heart rate monitors.

telos The end of a goal-oriented process; ultimate end.

Third School Nutrition Dietary Assessment Study This study was conducted in 2004–2005 and the researchers collected data from 2300 students in 287 schools that participated in the National School Lunch Program. The researchers reviewed menu data, observed competitive food options, collected 24-hour dietary records, and interviewed parents. The researchers also measured heights and weights of students. SNDA III therefore provides the most widespread and recent information about the food provided by the schools, competitive foods, and the general school food environment in elementary, middle, and high schools (Story, M. (2009). The Third School Nutrition Dietary Assessment Study: Findings and policy implications for improving the health of US children. *Journal of the American Dietetic Association*, *109* (2 Suppl.), S7–S13).

Title IX An educational reform act passed in 1972 that requires all programs and schools receiving federal monies to ensure that all persons regardless of race or gender have equitable access and resources in educational settings.

traditional assessment Type of assessment previously used in physical education, including tests on game rules, skills performances, and teacher observations.

traditional (or old) Physical Education (PE) The class or program in schools that taught elimination games, competitive team-based sports, and isolated fitness activities through teacher-directed lessons that often humiliated the non-athlete. It turned off most of the students from exercising and being active outside the school day.

traditional physical education class Also commonly referred to as the "old" physical education class. The following are characteristics of a traditional PE class: class is called *gym*, teacher-directed lessons, long lines, squads for exercises, structured classes, intimidating procedures, competition stressed, skills taught but games usually played at end of units, fitness often presented as a separate unit and not integrated into the other units, students often do not have fun as they practice skills, and students do not know how hard they are working or their level of physical activity (Sullivan, E., & Clapham, E. (2008). Teaching an old dog new tricks: Traditional or the old PE versus the new PE. A teacher script about the old and the new PE).

transferable life skills   From the high school sport perspective, skills the athlete learns in sport that can be used in other aspects of his or her life. Some examples include respect and being on time.

transformative teacher   A teacher who has earned a reputation for teaching in a way that produces dramatic and long-lasting improvements in students' lives.

triangulation assessment   Three evaluators or coders record a teacher's behaviors.

U

uniform resource locator (URL)   The address of a website that includes information such as when the website was last updated, the website author's qualifications, the purpose of the website, and at least one method of contacting the website author.

universal design for learning (UDL)   A conceptual model used to guide instructional planning in a manner that recognizes the learning differences among students by universally incorporating multiple means of presentation, responding, and assessment.

V

value-added research   Educational research that measures, usually by comparing test scores, the value that individual teachers, schools, and/or districts add to the achievement of students.

virtual classroom   The mental image of a teacher's learning setting, including the physical, emotional, moral, and intellectual environments, where she or he practices teaching moves in preparation for instruction in the real setting.

virtual school   A K–12 learning activity or program that uses the Internet or other technologies.

virtue   Moral excellence, goodness, uprightness; force, potency.

visual learners   Those who prefer to learn with a visual representation of concepts.

volume   A measure of the total amount of work done in a period of time (e.g., a set, a workout, a month). In a single workout, it is defined as the number of repetitions performed multiplied by the number of sets.

W

warm-up   Light to moderate activity done prior to a workout. The purpose is to reduce the risk of injury and soreness and possibly improve performance in a physical activity.

Web-enhanced instruction   Classroom instruction that is supplemented with online resources, a website, or online activities.

WebQuests   Interactive online lessons where students navigate through different tasks either individually or in groups in order to learn about a specific topic.

wellness   An active process of becoming aware of and making choices toward a more successful life through balancing the social, physical, and emotional dimensions of life.

wiki   A collection of web pages that is very similar to a traditional website, but that can be created, edited, and managed by multiple users at the same time.

Y

youth development approach   A coaching philosophy that emphasizes the holistic development, well-being, and success promotion of their athletes.

Index